Krause - Minkus

STANDARD CATALOG OF
U.S. STAMPS

1998 EDITION • LISTINGS 1845 - DATE

Fred Bauman & George Cuhaj
Editors

Wayne Youngblood
Publisher, Philatelics Division, Krause Publications

Special Contributors
Denis J. Norrington • Albert Curulli • Joann Perry
Robert L. Markovits • Robert A. Lacey • David S. Macdonald • Michael Jaffee

A fully illustrated catalog for the postage stamps of the United States with stories of the men, women, places and events that have made America's history.

Published by

**krause
publications**

700 E. State Street • Iola, WI 54990-0001
Telephone: 715/445-2214

www.krause.com

Please call or write for our free catalog.
Our toll-free number to place an order or obtain a free catalog is 800-258-0929
or please use our regular business telephone 715-445-2214
for editorial comment and further information.

ISBN: 0-87341-590-6

Printed in the United States of America

Traditionally, numbers are used by stamp catalogs for the purpose of identifying particular stamps. Collectors, when buying, selling, trading or organizing their collection of stamps, use reference numbers to assist in the identification of specific stamps. The MINKUS™ stamp catalogs have historically used one set of reference numbers to identify the stamps illustrated or listed, and other similar catalogs, including the SCOTT® catalogs, have used a different set of reference numbers which has created confusion or, at the least, inconvenience in attempting to compare or relate different reference number for the same stamps. For the convenience of our readers, this catalog includes the MINKUS™ reference number associated with each stamp and, for cross-reference purposes only, the corresponding SCOTT® number appears in parenthesis.

MINKUS is a trademark of Krause Publications, Inc. SCOTT is a registered trademark of Amos Press, Inc. which is in no way related to Krause Publications. Cross-references from MINKUS™ numbers to SCOTT® numbers contained herein are solely for the convenience of our readers and/or stamp collectors.

Table of Contents

Introduction I

Regular Issues
Postmaster's Provisionals. 1
Regular Issues 4
Plate Number Coil Strips 148

Commemoratives 157

Air Mail Stamps. 368

Special Delivery 384

Air Mail Special Delivery. 386

Special Handling. 386

Parcel Post. 388

Parcel Post Postage Due 389

Registration 389

Certified Mail 389

Official Carriers 390

Newspaper 391

Official Stamps 396

Envelopes & Wrappers 404

Airmail Envelopes & Air Letter Sheets 459

Official Envelopes 467

Postal Cards 472

Message/Reply Cards 498

Air Mail Postal Cards. 504

Postal Savings 508

Federal Boating Stamps 512

Federal Hunting Permit (Duck) Stamps 513

Post Offices in China 522

Confederate States 523

Catalog Introduction

While such factors as age, quantity issued, scarcity and especially demand all have a bearing on the value of a given stamp or cover, the fundamental determinants of value for any given stamp are its grade and its condition. In general, the scarcer and more valuable the basic stamp, the greater the importance of grade or centering in determining its market value.

Grade is a rough measure of the relationship between the printed design of the stamp and its edges or margins, a characteristic that also is often referred to as a stamp's *centering*.

Generally speaking, the more nearly equal in width all margins of a stamp are and the farther those equal margins are from the printed design, the more desirable the stamp will be to collectors. A stamp with unusually broad margins of identical width on all sides may sell for as much as 100 times the price of an otherwise identical stamp with unbalanced margins and perforations or, in the case of imperforate stamps, a copy with a straightedge cutting the printed design.

Condition refers to the overall appearance and quality of the stamp -- the state of its health, so to speak -- which can enhance or detract from the desirability (and hence the demand and value) of a stamp.

Stamp Grade

Values shown in this catalog reflect the prices that you may expect to pay for a listed stamp in a grade between **fine** (visibly off-center on two sides, with margins or perforations either just touching or barely clear of the printed design on one side) and **very fine** (barely off-center on one side, with all margins or perforations almost equally distant and well clear of the printed stamp design).

This intermediate grade, which has been the predominant grade in which stamps have been collected for more than a century, is referred to as **fine-to-very-fine**, often abbreviated as "**f-vf**." To define the term more explicitly, fine-to-very-fine stamps may be perceptibly off-center to one side, or very slightly off-center on two sides, with the stamp design printed clear of all sides and untouched by any of the margins. (Imperforate stamps graded f-vf will have at least two and usually three margins clear of the printed design.)

Stamps of grades lower than fine-to-very-fine (such as **very good** and **fine**) will usually sell for less than the f-vf copies that are priced here, whereas stamps of grades higher than fine-to-very fine (including **very fine** and the elusive **extremely fine** or **superb**) will sell for more than the stamps that are priced here.

Unused United States stamps in a grade of fine-to-very-fine

Stamp Condition

Values shown in this catalog reflect the prices that you may expect to pay for a listed stamp in fault-free condition, clear of any detectable defects.

Defects of condition on stamps include (but are not necessarily limited to) tears, scrapes, thins (places where some of the paper is missing from the back of a stamp, often due to inept removal of a hinge), stains, foxing and so-called tropical toning (brown spots on the gum or perforation tips), absence of original gum, the presence of substantial hinge remnantsinclusions (pieces of foreign matter accidentally embedded in the stamp paper during manufacture), heavy, smeared or otherwise disfiguring cancellations or postal markings, pulled, torn or clipped perforations, creases, pinholes, missing corners, and faded, bleached or oxidated pigments and other color changelings (wherein the color of the stamp has changed after it was produced). Extremely defective stamps, with pieces missing , the design unrecognizable due to strains or postmarks and other serious shortcomings, may be virtually uncollectible and unsalable at any price, even if sound, well-centered examples of the same stamp have a high catalog value. The actual, nominal value of stamps in such poor condition has no relationship whatsoever to the values listed in this or any other catalog.

Stamps that have been repaired or altered (with filled thins, regumming, reperforation, repaired tears, bleaching to remove soiling or lighten a cancel, hand-printed notes on the back of the stamp) also are generally regarded as defective and valued accordingly. Repaired stamps may be quite presentable and collectible, but they will generally have only a fraction of the value of a comparable, sound example of the same stamp. Knowingly attempting to represent and sell a repaired copy of a damaged stamp as a sound copy in original condition is fraud.

Just as defects and other undesirable traits detract from a stamp's condition, thereby diminishing its value, exceptionally desirable aspects of a stamp's condition can enhance that value, sometimes substantially.

Positive attributes to a stamp's condition can include unusually wide margins on all sides, exceptionally fresh-looking paper and ink color and sharpness of the printing, unusually crisp, sharp and regular perforations (especially on older stamps), the presence of margin selvage (especially with a plate number or other marginal printing of significance) and, on 19th-century stamps, most or all of the original gum.

Minkus Catalog Values

Values in the left column adjacent to each stamp listing are for unused, original-gum f-vf stamps. Values in the right column are for canceled f-vf stamps. Most unused stamps of the last 60 years are collected in mint, never-hinged condition, with full, undisturbed and unblemished original gum on the back.

Where a stamp or other catalog-listed item is seldom sold publicly or frequently, values appear in italics. Where adequate pricing information for a specific item has proven to be currently unobtainable (as in the case of a recently discovered error or, more prosaically, a common plate block in used condition) in the place of a value a line appears (—).

Every reasonable effort has been made to make the values in this catalog as accurate, realistic and up-to-date as possible. Sources for pricing information may include (but are not necessarily limited to) dealers' published retail price lists and advertisements, auction catalogs with published prices realized, and prices solicited from selected dealers, individuals and collector organizations. This information may have been reviewed for accuracy and consistency by individual specialist-collectors and specialist-dealers.

The minimum stamp value in this catalog (20c) represents the cost to a retail stamp dealer to maintain in inventory and supply to a collector on demand a single copy of even the most common stamp in fault-free condition and a grade of fine-to-very-fine. The comparable minimum for a first day cover is $1. These figures more accurately reflect a dealer's cost of doing business than the scarcity of a given stamp or FDC.

Values in this catalog do not reflect the generally much lower cost of stamps acquired in mixtures, collections, bulk lots or other large-quantity purchases, nor stamps sold at unusually advantageous prices to attact additional business or offered as approvals premiums, and so forth. In addition, some stamps can be acquired at lower prices through public auctions and mail-bid sales in which the collector may sometimes secure a lot at an uncontested minimum bid or reserve price.

The publishers of this catalog neither buy nor sell stamps.

Minkus Catalog Listings

Shown nearby is a typical listing from the catalog , displaying most of the kinds of information that this catalog can provide.

1988. New Hampshire Statehood Issue is the ninth stamp in the Constitution Ratification Bicentennial series. (See also CM380.) *Gravure, American Bank Note Co., perforated 11.*

CM1312 *Old Man of the Mountain*

CM1312 *(2344)*		
25c multicolored, tagged	.40	.20
Plate block of four	3.95	
FDC *(June 21, 1988)*		1.00

A. Year of Issue

B. Title of Issue often as assigned by the U.S. Post Office Department or the U.S. Postal Service.

C. Description of Issue a brief synopsis of the person, place or thing depicted on or commemorated by the issue, with information on any special characteristics or significance and any series of which it is a part.

D. Printing details of the type of printing, printer(s) and gauge of the perforations or rouletting.

E. Minkus Catalog Number appears adjacent to the image of the stamp and also at the beginning of the corresponding priced listing for stamps in a grade of fine-to-very-fine. Collectors can use the Minkus catalog numbers to organize their collections, and to identify stamps when buying, selling or exchanging stamps for their collections. Minkus catalog numbers also are used in Minkus stamp albums and supplements.

Each Minkus catalog number refers to a specific stamp. Varieties of that stamp are identified by suffixes appended to the basic catalog number (see item N). Where stamps that are similar in appearance are regarded as distinct issues, collectors are referred to the other issue or issues in a footnote (see item O).

With but few exceptions, and unlike other catalogs, Minkus catalog numbers are assigned in strict chronological sequence, and definitive issues (stamps that may go back to press for additional printings at any time to furnish new stocks) are listed separately from commemorative issues (typically printed in a single, much smaller run than their definitive counterparts). Definitive series that extend over many years are identified by series name, but are listed in the order and at the intervals at which they were released by the U.S. Postal Service. This avoids the confusing situation clumps of stamps from an ongoing series being listed at random and arbitrary intervals throughout the catalog, and the necessity of introducing additional subnumbers (e.g., 123B, 123C, 123D) due to a miscalculation of the number of stamps in a given set or series. The stamps are organized into their natural sets in Minkus stamp albums and supplements.

Minkus catalog numbers consist of numerals only for regular definitive issues (e.g., Minkus 123, which refers to the Continental Bank Note Co. 5c Prussian blue Zachary Taylor definitive released in 1875). Other types of postage and revenue stamps listed in this catalog are indicated by a suffix. "CM" indicates commemorative stamps (e.g. Minkus CM123, which refers to the 3c blue Byrd Antarctic Expedition II commemorative of 1933), "A" indicates airmail stamps (e.g. Minkus A123, which refers to the 45c multicolored Hypersonic Airliner stamp in the se-tenant block of four from the Future Mail Transportation issue of 1989), and so on.

F. Scott Catalog Number, which appears in italics in parentheses immediately following the Minkus catalog number, refers to the numeration system of a popular United States stamp catalog that values stamps exclusively in a grade of very fine. This number is provided for the convenience of collectors, dealers and organizations to facilitate the buying, selling and trading stamps between parties using either the Minkus catalog or the Scott catalog systems. Not every minor variety of every U.S. stamp is cross-referenced, although many are, and cross-reference numbers usually can be easily deduced for most of those that are not.

G. Description of Image sometimes but not invariably the same as item B, this is intended to represent the design title by which collectors refer to the individual stamp. In practice, many stamps are readily recognized both ways. For example, Minkus CM24 is well-known to stamp collectors both as the $1 denomination from the Trans-Mississippi commemoratives of 1898 (the title of the issue) and as the $1 black Cattle in a Storm commemorative (the description of the image).

H. Denomination is the numeric value of the stamp (or in the case of a lettered value issue or an un-valued issue, the equated value at time of issue.

I. Color(s) when a single color or up to three distinct colors are used they are listed, else the term multicolor is used.

J. Tagging where relevant, on selected U.S. stamps beginning in the 1960s, refers to the presence of a special ink on the face of the stamp visible only under ultraviolet light, used to position the envelope on which the stamp is affixed correctly so that the cancellation will be applied in automated facing-canceling equipment.

K. Quantity Printed is recorded, where available, typically for U.S. commemorative and airmail issues. For U.S. definitives, which may go back to press many times in the course of their working life, accurate figures are rarely available. Quantities include accurate counts and approximate estimates made by the U.S. Post Office Department and Postal Service, counts of quantities shipped but not including stamps returned, unused or destroyed when the issue was taken off sale and, in some cases, accurate counts of copies sold.

L. Catalog Values are expressed in U.S. dollars for unused stamps (left) and used stamps (right) in a grade of **fine-to-very-fine.** Unused stamps refer to those that have not been canceled with most of their original gum (for 19th-century issues) or full original gum, lightly hinged (for 20th-century stamps). Stamps issued without gum are identified in the listings. Used stamps refer to those that have been canceled correctly in the course of performing their intended function.

M. Date of Issue is displayed, in most cases on the same line as that used for the basic first day cover listing.

N. Additional Varieties includes (where relevant) plate blocks, se-tenant configurations, paper type, gum type, tagging presence and type, perforation varieties, major errors, plate flaws and varieties.

O. Footnotes convey additional important information about the stamp and related varieties or issues.

Introduction to Stamps

The ability to accurately identify a stamp is indispensible to your full enjoyment of and participation in the stamp hobby. Differences in printing, gum, paper, watermark, ink, perforation, luminescence and design — variations that may be slight, but which are readily apparent to the trained eye — can be the key to getting the most out of the time you spend with your collection. They also can be the difference between a common stamp that is worth a handful of pennies and a rarity that is valued at thousands of dollars.

There is no substitute for the knowledge that you can gain from the experience of closely examining and working with stamps, not only those in your own collection, but also those that you can read about in philatelic literature, and see on display at stamp shows and, if you are fortunate, in the albums of friends at the local stamp club.

The following text is intended to familiarize you with the basic considerations of collecting stamps and the terminology and jargon of the stamp hobby. Inquiries, suggestions and requests for additional clariffications may be addressed to Editor, Krause-Minkus Stamp Catalog, Krause Publications, 700 East State Street, Iola, WI 54990-0001. (www.krause.com)

Stamp Printing

All stamps may be characterized by the technique or techniques by which they are printed. Although others exist, five primary printing technologies have been used, alone or in combination, on virtually all United States postal paper: intaglio; lithography; gravure; letterpress; and embossing. (Since 1989, holography also has been used to print the special foil patches that have served as stamped images on several U.S. stamped envelopes.)

Intaglio (also known as Line-Engraving, Engraving, Etching)

The first step in the intaglio process is creating a **master die**, a small, flat block of soft steel upon which the stamp design is recessed engraved in reverse. The original art intended for use on the stamp is photographically reduced to the appropriate size, and will serve as a tracing guide for the initial outline of the design on steel.

The highly skilled and detailed work of creating the master die is done by an engraver, who lightly traces the design on the steel, then slowly develops the fully detailed engraving, using gravers, burins and other small chisel-like tools to carve a fine pattern of precisely positioned grooves that collectively form the finished image.

At various points during the engraving process, the engraver hand-inks the dies and makes an impression to check his progress, thereby creating incomplete images what will become the finished design, known as **progressive die proofs**.

After the engraving is complete, the soft steel of the master die is hardened greatly through various processes so that it will be able to withstand the stress and pressure of the subsequent operations that are needed to convert it into an intaglio printing plate.

Next, a **transfer roll** is prepared, consaisting of a roll of soft steel mounted on a mandrel which, as the name implies, is used to transfer the engraved subject from the master die to the intaglio printing plate. A blank roll of soft steel, mounted at the center of a mandrel, which is a metal axle of lesser diameter. The mandrel is placed in a transfer press, in which it rotates freely, and the highly polished soft steel of the transfer roll is brought into contact with the hardened master die in the bed of the press.

The bed of the transfer press is slowly rocked back and forth under increasing pressure, forcing or "rocking in" the soft steel of the transfer roll in every finely engraved line of the hard master die, and eventually transferring the complete engraved image. The resulting design on the transfer roll, now positive in appearances (with its design components as they are intended to appear on the printed stamp), is referred to as a **relief transfer**, because the lines of engraving that were carved into the master die stand out on the completed roll. The soft steel of the transfer roll is hardened, as was the master die before it, after the number of relief transfers that are required have been created.

Because the relief is what is used to create the intaglio printing plate, any imperfections during the creation of the relief transfer may result in flaws that will appear on the finished stamps. A small fleck of foreign material present during the rocking-in process may leave a mark on the relief transfer. Similarly, imperfections in the steel of the transfer roll may cause the loss of part of the design from the master die. These flaws are known as **relief breaks**, which appear as small, uninked areas on the finished stamp. Reliefs also may be deliberately modified to minimize or rectify such flaws, resulting in what is referred to as an **altered relief**, the characteristics of which again will be expressed on the finished stamp.

When the transfer roll has been completed and hardened, it is used to rock in the design to a large plate of polished, soft steel, where it again appears in reversed form as on the original master die. Layout lines or position dots are placed to precisely locate the transfer roll over the plate, and may sometimes later appear on stamps if they are not burnished away during final plate preparation.

It is during this process that double transfers, shifted transfers and dropped transfers occur.

A **shifted transfer** on a plate is one that shows doubling of part ot or all the design (typically one edge or corner of the design), usually because the relief transfer shifted slightly while the design was being rocked into the printing plate.

A similar effect also can be achieved on the plate when a defective transfer is incompletely removed, and a second transfer is rocked in over it. Any place where the engraving of the original transfer remains and is not covered by the second transfer is likely to appear on the printed stamp as a **double transfer** (or, in cases where traces of two previous transfers exist, a **triple transfer**). Sometimes the printers need to delete the original transfer from a plate and enter it from scratch again. Should this completed transfer show some traces of the original, impression, it is referred to as a **partial double transfer**.

A **dropped transfer** is one that is made normally but is misaligned with respect to the other designs on the plate. A stamp printed from such a dropped transfer will be noticably out of alignment with the stamps around it in the final sheet.

Failure to center the transfer roll correctly on the plate will result in the failure of the relief transfer to completely record all portions of the master die, resulting in the loss of the edge of the engraved design on the finished stamp. This is known as a **short transfer**,

The impressions of the transfer roll on the plate often are referred to as **subjects**, and as many of these subjects are transferred as are required for the final plate (typically 200 or 400 subjects on most plates up to the 1950s and 1960s).

When all the subjects have been put in place, all position dots, layout lines and any other minor scratches, burrs or imperfections are removed from the printing surface. With the addition of marginal and other sheet markings including guide lines, arrows and plate numbers, a **plate proof** is printed to confirm that the plate is rerady to produce stamps. (**Trial color proofs** may also be printed in a variety of colors other than those eventually selected for the finished stamps, to test the clarity and appearance of the finished print in different hues.) When these impressions are approved, the **printing plate** is machined for fitting onto a press, hardened and sent off to the plate vault, ready to be used.

On the press, the intaglio plate is inked and its smooth surface is wiped clean, leaving ink only in the lines created by the relief transfer. Paper is then forced under pressure into the engraved recessed lines, the ink of which is transferred to the surface of the stamp paper. When dry, the lines of raised ink on the intaglio stamp are slightly raised, giving such stamps their characteristic crisply ridged feel, and slight depressions (known as debossing) on the back of the stamp show where therse inked lines appear on the front.

For the first century or so of U.S. intaglio stamp production, prior to the advent of modern, high-speed presses, paper used in intaglio stamp production often was moistened to facilitate the transfer of the ink, known as a **wet printing**. However, this sometimes led to uneven shrinkage by the time the stamps were perforated, resulting in improperly perforated stamps, or misperfs. More modern presses that supplantred early models do not require the use of moistened paper, thus giving rise to stamps that exist in both **wet print** and **dry print** versions.

Dry Printing

Wet Printing

Until 1915, only **flat press plates** were used to print engraved United States stamps. **Rotary press** printing was introduced in that year and slowly spread to account for an ever larger share of U.S. stamp production. Older **rotary press plates** require additional machining , and are curved under pressure to fit the press cylinder. The stretching of the plate during the curving process distorts the subjects on it, with the result that stamps printed from rotary press plates usually are longer or wider than the same stamps printed from flat plate presses. The two basic versions of the Harding Memorial Issue (Minkus CM60 and CM62) provide a good example of this frequently encountered phenomenon. With the exception of the 1919 coil waste issues (Minkus 410-12), all rotary press issues up to 1953 have between one and four **gum breaker ridges** per stamp, impressed on the gum to break its even surface across theback of the stamp during manufacture to inhibit the natural tendency of rotary press-printed stamps to curl.

In the early days of intaglio flat-plate printing, heavily worn plates were sometimes spruced up to give additional service by re-entering their designs, reapplying the transfer roll to the old plate to sharpen worn-down designs. However, if the registration between the transfer roll and the engraving on the worn plate is not exact, or if the original transfer is not completely burnished flat before the design is rocked in again, the result is often a **re-entry**. In a **re-entry**, another sort of **double transfer** can be created, which will appear on stamps printed from such a subject as a design with portions of the previous, worn design still visible.

If the alignment is exact and the placement of the transfer roll is true, a skillful re-entry may be all but undetectable.

Other, slightly less radical techniques of rendering a worn plate fit for continued use usually require that the plate be softened by having its temper drawn (generally by the precise application of heat and cooling) for retooliong by hand. Among the techniques involved are **retouching** (the deepening or modification of lines by etching), and **recutting** (the deepening or alteration of lines with an engraving tool). If the resulting inked impression varies slightly from the original, it is referred to as a **re-engraved** stamp.

The intricate line patterns of intaglio printing are an excellent safeguard against would-be counterfeiters, but additional techniques also have been used to make intaglio stamps even more difficult to forge. One of these that was especially popular in the early days of U.S. stamp production was the incorporation of **lathework** and other **engine-turned designs** into the backgrounds and frames of various issues -- complicated and precisely repeated designs produced on a mechanical device called an engraving engine. Examples of such patters can clearly be seen in the frame and spandrels of the 1851 3c Washington stamps (Minkus 10-11) and the complex frame of the 1860 24c Washington (40).

Bicolored engraved stamps, such as the high values of the 1869 Pictorial issue (92-96), the 1901 Pan-American commemoratives (CM26-31) and the 24c Jenny airmail stamp of 1918 (A3), are created by passing the printing sheet through a flat-bed press two times, once with a plate to print the frame, and a second time, with a second plate inked in a different color, to print the vignette at the center of the design. Performing either of these operations with the sheet incorrectly oriented would result in one part of the stamp beiung printed upside-down in relation to the resto of the design, creeating the category of major error referred to as inverted-center (or inverted-frame) errors, or **inverts**, in common parlance.

Except for such bicolored issues, all other engraved U.S. stamps for more than a century were single-color designs until the advent of the **Giori Press** at the Bureau of Engraving and Printing in 1957. The Giori Press, capable of intaglio printing in two or three colors simultaneously, made its philatelic debut with the 4c 48-Star Flag commemorative (CM406) on July 4, 1957, and soon made a distictive mark on U.S. postage stamps, including the multicolored high values of the Champions of Liberty series, the Conservation series and the American Credo series.

Another innovation in intaglio printing was the **Huck Multicolor Press**, first used in 1969 to print the first multicolored U.S. coil stamp, the 6c Flag and White House coil (650), followed by the 6c Angel Gabriel stamp from the 1969 Christmas issue (649). The Huck Press not only printed in as many as nine colors and applied phosphorescent taggant to stamps, but also gummed and perforated them all at the same time.

Lithography (also Photolithography, Offset Lithography, Stone Lithography, Dilitho, Planography, Collotype)

Lithography uses the principle that oil and water do not mix to produce a printed design. The design is produced from original artwork and transferred in an oily or greasy ink onto the printing surface, originally a prepared surface of stone (from which lithography takes its name) but now more frequently a metal surface. This greasy design can attract and hold the ink for transfer onto the surface to be printed, while the rest of the plate is moistened with an acidic fluid that repels such ink, corresponding to the uninked portions of the design. To create a plate, special transfer paper is used to make duplicates of the desired design from the original lithographic stone or plate, which are in turn assembled to create the final lithographic printing plate.

In a well-crafted lithographic stamp, the design may have fine and sharply printed lines as in an intaglio stamp, but its design also will have distinct, solidly inked areas that are not to be seen either on intaglio or on gravure issues. Also, unlike either intaglio printing (where lines of ink are raised on the surface of the stamp) or letterpress printing (where the inked areas are impressed into the paper, leaving a debossed surface on the back of the stamp), both sides of a stamp printed by lithography are completely flat.

Offset Lithography, also known as offset printing refers to a refinement of the basic lithographic technique, whereby a greasy ink impression on a rubber blanket transfers the lithographic image from the printing surface to the paper. The first use of offset lithography on regular United States postage stamps took place with the Washington-Franklin definitives of 1918-20 (Minkus 403-09), when the technique was introduced due to manpower and material restrictions on intaglio printing caused by World War I. Offset lithography and intaglio were used together in printing the 5c Homemakers commemorative of 1964 (CM538) and the 1976 Bicentennial souvenir sheets (CM839-42), which showcased the ability of lithography to convey subtle textures, tints and tones.

Because of its greater ease of use and range of applications, offset lithography has largely replaced lithography today, and is now frequently (but actually erroneously) referred to simply as "offset."

Gravure (including such variants as Photogravure, Rotogravure, Heliogravure)

The preparation of stamps for printing by gravure begins with the photographing of the intended design through a fine mesh, referred to as a dot-matrix screen, which renders it onto a metal plate as a pattern of tiny dots. A chemical process etches this fine dot or halftone pattern onto the plate, where it is converted into a multitude of shallow pits or depressions, known as cells, which hold the ink during the printing process.

In the gravure printing process, the paper pressed against the gravure plate lifts the ink out of the **cells** to produce the intended design. Deeper, larger cells produce the more heavily inked and frequently darker portions of the printed design, with shallow, small cells producing more lightly inking and often lightly colored areas on the stamp.

The chief use of gravure is in producing multi-colored stamps. Using only the primary colors red, yellow and cyan (blue), along with black, gravure's dot pattern can be combined and recombined tro furnish almost any color that might be required. These overlapping patterns of dots, clearly visible under magnification, are they key characteristic by which gravure stamps may be easily identified.

The first gravure U.S. stamps were printed by private firms: the 1967 5c Thomas Eakins commemorative (Minkus CM585), printed by Photogravure & Color Co. of Moonachie, N.J.; and the 1968 6c Walt Disney issue (CM602), printed by the Achrovure Division of Union-Camp Corp. in Englewood, N.J. In 1970, Guilford Gravure Inc. of Guilford, Conn., produced both the se-tenant Anti-Pollution issue (CM643-46) and all the Christmas stamps (655-59) for the Bureau of Engraving and Printing.

The following year, the BEP acquired the multicolor Andreotti Press, and began printing its own gravure stamps, the first of these being the 8c Missouri Statehood issue (CM654).

Letterpress (also known as Typography, Surface Printing, Flexography, Dry Offset, High Etch)

Essentially the oppositeof intaglio printing, in letterpress printing it is the raised rather than the incised areas of the printing plate that are inked to print the finished design. In fact, the process of creating the printing plate is an inversion of the intaglio process as well, with an additional step in which the design is transferred to another surface before the creation of the transfer roll. This results in the transfer roll having a recessed rather than a relief design, which means that the final plate will have the areas that are to be inked raised above rather than carved into the surface, similar to a rubber handstamp.

Reproducing a letterpress transfer electrome-chanically is referred to as **electrotype** or **stereotype** production, and these are then gathered together in the desired configuration to form the plate from which stamps are produced. A plate for letterpress printing made using the assembled electrotypes is referred to as an **electroplate**.

The first postage stamps for nationwide use to make use of letterpress printing were the first newspaper and periodical issues of 1865 (Minkus N1-4), which was printed by the National Bank Note Co. in combination with embossing and an engine-turned engraved design to create an almost forgery-proof set. The American Bank Note Co. also combined offset vignettes showing the flags with engraved frames in 1943-44 to produce the Overrun Countries series (CM251-63). More typically (and less dramatically), letterpress was used to create the Molly Pitcher and Hawaii Sesquicentennial over-prints of 1928 (CM79-81), the Kansas-Nebraska over-prints of 1929 (495-516) and the many different Bureau precancels used over the years.

As with a piece of paper printed using a handstamp or a typewriter, paper printed by letterpress will show a slight depression (debossing) in the printed portion of the printed side of the paper, and a slight elevation (embossing) on the reverse side of the paper. This is characteristic of this printing method.

Embossing (also Colorless Embossing, Blind Embossing, Relief Printing)

Not truly a printing technique (since, technically, ink need not be involved), embossing is, however, an important security technique used on U.S. postal paper (chiefly stamped envelopes). In embossing, a design is carved into a die, which is reproduced to yield a shallow, three-dimensional sculpture from which additional embossing dies are made. A similar back plate, or platen, mirroring the design is created, and the two sides are pressed together to create the embossed image (often with ink on the inside of the die in front, producing the inscribed, denominated printed collar around the embossed portrait or image).

Embossing also has been used on some U.S. stamps, including the first issue newspaper and periodical stamps of 1865.

Stamp Components and Characteristics

If a stamp's image is derived in large measure from its printing (and the techniques used), the rest of the characteristics that define it have to do with the materials used in the stamp's creation -- ink, gum, paper and separation technique -- and some of the key obserevable characteristics of these materials, including the watermark, the method of stamp separation and the gauge of its perforations or rouletting,, as well as the presence or absence of luminscence.

Examples may be found of otherwise identical stamps that differ in only one or two subtle respects, creating, at the least, two interesting varieties to seek out for your album and, at the most, an opportunity for the obwservant stamp collector to pick out a gem amid a pile of perfectly common postage. Few of us may ever have such an experience, to be sure, but fortune favors those who have prepared. Contrarily, collectors who are unaware that a rarity exists will never find it.

Ink and Color

Ink is the basic stuff of printing, typically consisting of a finely powdered admixture or suspension of mineral, natural organic or synthetic organic pigment in a liquid solvent or base.

Ink is directly related to color. Many of the inks used in printing 19th-century stamps were mixed by hand to the closely guarded specifications of the private printing firms that did the work, and often varied perceptibly from batch to batch. This gave rise to at least some of the many collectible shades and hues found on a number of classic U.S. issues, such as the 24c Washington definitives (Minkus 54-56) of 1861-63.

This wealth of color varieties continued briefly even after the Bureau of Engraving and Printing assumed responsibility for printing virtually all U.S. stamps in 1894, best reflected in the manmy shades of the 2c issues of 1894 (170-74) and 1895-988 (189-92). Thereafter, inks became coinsiderably more standardized and the number and variety of color varieties decreased consierably. Still, there are some highly collectible exceptions to this rule, such as the 1922 11c Hayes definitive (430).

One consequence of the arrival of single-press-run multicolor printing in the 1950s and 1960s was that minor variations in the individual colors on a stamp became harder to clearly discern, and in time came to be largely ignored, except on monochrome engraved stamps where such varieties remained easy to see. At the same time, however, there slowly developed a considerable increase in the number of color-omitted errors -- errors that could never have taken place on monochrome intaglio stamps.

An important transition in inks took place in the 1970s under federal health regulations, when solvent-based inks used at the BEP were screened for potential toxicity and adverse health and environmental effects, and replaced with new, safer water-based inks of similar color. As a result, different shades can be seen on the versions of some values of the Prominent Americans and Americana definitives printed both before and after this period.

In fact, ink is not the only variable that determines the color of a stamp. The quantity of ink, the pressure with which it is applied, the type of paper and its moisture content at the time that the printing takes place and the type of base that carries the pigment in the ink all can affect the apparent color.

Of special concern to collectors are stamps printed in **fugitive ink**, which is soluble and tends to run or dissolve when the stamp is immersed in such otherwise innocuous liquids as water or watermark fluid. Fugitive inks include synthetic organic pigments produced as derivatives of nitrobenzene (aniline inks) and some photogravure stamps as well. Some modern U.S. commeoratives printed in purple can suffer ink damage when immersed in watermark fluid, including the 1963 5c Eleanor Roosevelt (CM522), 1964 5c Amateur Radio (CM541) and the 1980 15c Edith Wharton (CM953).

Stamps that have had their color altered after they were printed, intentionally or accidentally, are referred to as **color changelings**.

Generally such changelings occur as the result of a photochemical reaction (such as prolonged exposure to sunlight or artificial light) or chemical activity (such as the useof a cleaning agent or solvent to remove soiling or lighten a heavy cancel).

One especially notorious kind of accidental color changeling is often seen on 19th-century and early 20th-century yellow, orange and red U.S. stamps in which the oxidation of sulfur compounds in the pigment turns the image a deep brown shade,occasionally approaching black. The immersion of one of these affected stamps in a mild solution of hydrogen peroxide frequently will reverse the effects of such oxidation, though it may not return the stamp precisely tro its original color.

While many collectors retain color changelings as curios, they are in fact nothing more than stamps in which the ink has been irreversibly damaged (much as the paper or perforations might be damaged). Color changelings have no place in an authentic collection of the production varieties of U.S. stamps.

Gum

Stamp gum is known in a wide range of textures, shades and degrees of reflectivity. In addition, the gum arabic usedon many 19th-century and early 20th-century U.S. stamps was applied to the stamps in two formulations -- a harder mixture intended to remain dry in storage even during months of relatively high seasonal heat and humidity (summer gum), and a softer gum that was used on stamps produced for use in the drier, cooler months (winter gum). Most stamp gums today use dextrine or polyvinyl alcohol as a base.

Shiny and matt gum varieties are cataloged separately in those instances where both are known to be found on the same U.S. definitive stamps, even though such stamps may not be distinguishable in used condition or used on cover.

The gum on unused stamps encountered by collectors exists in a variety of conditions, which are listed, abbreviated and defined here in decreasing order of desirability:

Mint Never Hinged (MNH) stamps have pristine gum just as originally acquired from the post office, without a blemish, fingerprint or mark of any kind. Mint prices in this catalog for stamps issued since 1945 refer to stamps in this condition.

Lightly Hinged (LH) stamps have 50 percent to 100 percent of their original gum, but show a minor disturbance on the back, such as traces where a stamp hinge was previously located, so-called disturbed gum or a fingerprint. Mint prices in this catalog for stamps issued prior to 1945 are for stamps in this condition, although in practice many earlier 19th-century stamps are less likely to have much of their original gum still intact.

Heavily Hinged (HH) stamps have less than 50 percent of their original gum and/or remnants of older non-peelable paper hinges still affixed to the back of the stamp.

All three of the preceding types of unused stamps are sometimes referred to as **original gum** stamps, their desirability and value increasing according to the the quantity and quality of the gum. However, not all unused stamps have original gum.

No Gum (NG) stamps are stamps from which the original gum has been removed. For purposes of saving the stamp, it may sometimes be advisable to soak off an especially heavy hinge remnant, which may otherwise cause a stamp to warp, buckle or even tear internally. Stamps issued without gum, such as the Farley issues (CM142-61) and the Continental Bank

Note Co. special printing of the 1875 newspaper and periodical stamps (SPN5-28), are for all practical purposes regarded as mint, never-hinged in that state.

Regummed (R, RG or RE) stamps are stamp from which the original gum has been removed and other gum has been added later. When it is clearly identified as such, there is nothing objectionable about a regummed stamp, and auction catalog realizations often seem to suggest that collectors are willing to pay a bit more for an expertly regummed stamp than for its NG counterpart.

However, it is fraud to knowingly represent and sell regummed stamps as original-gum copies, which is often attempted to obtain the considerably higher price that such OG stamps typically command Similarly, it is fraudulent to chemically or otherwise remove a light cancellation from a stamp and offer it as unused. Both regumming and removal of cancellations have some skilled practioners, which is why expertization is recommended for valuable mint stamps.

Paper

Paper, the medium for all printing, consists of dried sheets of processed vegetable fiber laid down on a fine screen from a water suspension. The two basic broad classifications of paper are **laid paper** in which the lines left by the screen during the papermaking process are still visible in transmittefd light, and **wove paper**, which has no such visible grain or lines. Papers also may be categorized as thin or thick, soft or hard, and according to its naturally occurring color (as in the listings for some U.S. stamped envelopes).

A very thin, hard translucent paper known as **pelure** also has occasionally been used for U.S. stamps, including the 1847 5c and 10c St. Louis postmaster provisionals (Minkus PM28-29). **India paper**, refers both to a softer, thin translucent paper used for pulling intaglio die and plate proofs and to a tougher, opaque thin paper, rarely but occasionally used in U.S. stamp printing, including varieties of the 1851 3c and 12c Washington (10p, 17p).

In addition, **colored paper** has been deliberately selected for use in specific issues, as in the orange paper of the 1956 3c Nassau Hall issue (CM395), the light Venetian red paper used for the 1965 5c Dante issue (CM549) and the tan paper of the 1976 Telephone Centennial commemorative (CM836).

Ribbed paper, which has actual ridges on the front or back side of the stamp, or both, was used for some of the Continental Bank Note Co. issues of 1873 (119-30). The ribs are parallel and typically run horizontally across the stamp, although vertical ribbed paper is known as well on stamps including the CBNC 15c Daniel Webster (128).

Double paper has two very different meanings. On the previously mentioned 1873 CBNC issues (119-30), it refers to a security paper patented by Charles F. Steel, in which a thin, weak surface paper and a thicker, stronger backing paper were bonded before printing. This produced a two-layer stamp, the printed design of which would be ruined if any attempt were made to clean a cancel after the stamp had been used.

The second meaning of double paper is in reference to the rotary presses that began producing U.S. stamps in 1915. Rotary presses print stamps on a continuous roll of paper, and when one roll of paper ends, the beginning of a new roll is spliced to the end of it so that production will not be interrupted. Stamps printed on the splice, where paper of the old and new rolls overlaps, is typically marked, cut out and discarded when the stamps are separated into sheets and panes. However, stamps printed across the splice do occasionally escape detection and survive to reach collectors, and these are known as **rotary press double paper** varieties.

Paper with silk fibers also was used in printing 1873 CNBC issues (119-30). As the name implies, this is paper with one or several long colored silk threads embedded in it. In this it differs from some early U.S. revenue stamps printed on so-called "silk paper," in which more numerous short, colored fibers are impressed during the papermaking process. Although it has rarely been used on U.S. stamps, a third silk-related paper is **granite paper** of the sort found on the 1967 5c Lions International issue (CM576), in which the grayish paper is shot through with short red and blue silk fibers, mimicing the veins in the rock for which it is named.

In an effort to better control uneven paper shrinkage during stamp manufacturing, in 1909 the Bureau of Engraving and Printing tried using high rag-content paper in place of the wood fiber paper then chiefly used to print stamps. This experimental stock, used for some 1c to 15c definitives and a small part of the printing of the 1909 2c Lincoln Memorial commemorative (CM42), is referred to as **bluish paper**, although many people describe it as actually more gray in color, best seem in comparing the back of the stamp to others of the same period. See the note preceding Minkus 263-72. Unscrupulous fakers have sometime attempted to simulate these pricey varieties of otherwise relatively inexpensive stamps by tinting them, so competent expertizing is recommended.

A very small number of the definitives of this same periofd were printed on a grayish, thick, hard stock known as **China Clay paper**, said to have mineral content of 5 percent to 20 percent rather than the 2 percent that was the standard at the time (although recent research conducted on paper from long-authenticated copies of these stamps failed to confirmed the presence of such clay). These China Clay paper varieties, which appear even darker than the bluish paper varieties and also are known on the 1c to 15c definitives, are cataloged here as subvarieties of the 1908-09 definitives (237p-46p).

For information about Hi-Brite paper, fluorescent papers, phosphor-tagged and pre-phosphored papers, and other papers characterized by their response to ultraviolet light, please refer to the section of this introduction on luminescence.

Watermarks

A watermark is a pattern laid down on paper during manufacturing. Shallow designs in metal, called bits, are woven into the screen on which the pulp is formed and drained. When the paper is dry and light is transmitted through it, the impression of the designs of these bits shows as a bright pattern in the paper, which is slightly thinner where the bits were positioned.

On most stamps, watermarks also may best be seen by immersing them in **watermark fluid**, a non-aqueous fluid that will not moisten gum on mint stamps. The fluid increases the transparency of the paper, to make watermarks show more clearly as dark patterns when the stamp is placed face-down in the fluid. (Look under Ink for fugitive inks, which notes U.S. stamps printed with inks that are soluble in watermark fluid.)

The widest range of U.S. watermarks on postal paper consists of those on U.S. postal stationery, including 1873-75 postal cards (PC1-3), Official Mail envelopes of 1991 (PDEN82-83) and a wide range of watermarks on stamped envelopes of 1853-1968 (EN1-855).

Single line USPS watermark

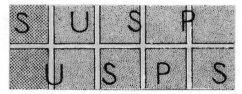

Double line USPS watermark

U.S. postage stamps are known with three watermarks: the double-line watermark "USPS" (for "U.S. Postage Stamp") used on the definitives of 1895-98 (187-210) and the single-line "USPS" watermark used on paper for the 1910-15 Washington-Franklin definitives (273-347); and the watermark "USIR" (for "U.S. Internal Revenue") intended for use on U.S. revenue stamps but used in error in a 1951 printing of the $1 Woodrow Wilson stamp from the 1938 Presidential definitive series (553w).

Perforation Errors

In addition to plate manufacturing errors, which include double impressions in the engraving, and printing errors, which include missing or inverted colors, and folding of the paper in the press, the widest variety of errors occur in the perforation process. To aid with the explaination of these errors, we have the following illustrations. However, none of these errors occur on the stamp illustrated.

Horizontal Pair, Imperforate-between

Horizontal Pair, Imperforate Vertically

Horizontal Pair, Imperforate

Vertically Pair, Imperforate-between

Vertical Pair, Imperforate Horizontally

Vertical Pair, Imperforate

Postmasters' Provisionals

Although the first government-issued adhesive stamps did not appear until 1847, the postmaster at New York City began using his own adhesives in July 1845, immediately after the Congressional act establishing the new postal rates. He was followed by a number of postmasters in other cities, who used either handstamps or adhesives of their own design.

ALEXANDRIA, VA

1846. Postmaster Daniel Bryan issued *typeset and imperforate* stamps without gum. Known copies of stamps are cut to shape. The circle of the 5c black-on-buff is found with 39 (Type I) or 40 asterisks (Type II).

PM1-PM2

PM1
5c black on buff paper, Type I   — —
     v. Type II   — 78,000.
PM2
5c blue on buff paper, Type I, on cover — —

ANNAPOLIS, MD

1846. Postmaster Martin E. Revell issued red stamps printed onto the upper right corner of white envelopes. Envelopes with circular design and figure "2" handstamped are known and believed to be locals. Blue circular designs without numeral or "PAID" were used as postmarks.

PM3

PM3
5c carmine red   — 225,000.

BALTIMORE, MD

1845. Envelopes in various shades of paper with the signature of the postmaster, James M. Buchanan, printed in black, blue or red. Colors listed below are those of the "PAID," numeral, and oval.

PM4-PM5

PM4
5c blue   — 5,000.
PM5
5c red   — 8,500.
PM6
5c blue + 5c red   — 18,000.
PM7
5c blue + 5c blue   — —
PM8
10c red   — 20,000.
PM9
10c blue   — 18,000.
PM10
10c black   — —

1846. Adhesive stamps *printed by intaglio on white or bluish papers, and imperforate,*. Eleven varieties of the 5c and five varieties of the 10c stamps are known.

PM11

PM11
5c black, on white paper   — 5,000.
     p. Bluish paper   25,000.   5,000.
PM12
10c black, on white paper   — 55,000.
     p. Bluish paper   — 60,000.

BOSCAWEN, NH

1846. Postmaster Worcester Webster issued a *typeset, imperforate* stamp of which only one copy is known.

PM13

PM13
5c dull blue   — 180,000.

BRATTLEBORO, VT

1846. Postmaster Frederick N. Palmer issued *intaglio, imperforate* stamps printed from plates of 10 separately engraved subjects. The imprint "Eng'd by Thos. Chubbuck, Bratto." appears below the middle stamp of the bottom row. Eleven varieties are known.

PM14

PM14
5c black on buff paper   — 6,000.
     On cover   — 15,000.

LOCKPORT, NY

1846. Postmaster Hezekiah W. Scovell issued adhesive labels with double-lined oval handstamped in red, "PAID" in black, and a handwritten "5."

PM15

PM15
5c red on buff paper, on cover   — 150,000.

MILLBURY, MA

1846. Postmaster Asa H. Waters issued imperforate stamps printed singly from a *woodcut on a hand press.*

PM16 *George Washington*

PM16
5c black on bluish paper   135,000.   25,000.
On cover   —   85,000.

NEW HAVEN, CT

1845. Postmaster Edward A. Mitchell used a brass handstamp to impress envelopes with his provisional stamp as the envelopes were brought to the post office. The postmaster's signature was added to prevent forgery. Reprints are known having been made at various times between 1871 and 1932.

PM17-PM18

PM17
5c red   —   75,000.
PM18
5c blue, on buff paper   —   75,000.

NEW YORK, NY

1845. Robert H. Morris was the first postmaster to issue adhesive stamps in July 1845, and featured George Washington's portrait, adapted from the then-current banknotes. The New York provisionals were also used by postmasters at Albany, Boston, Philadelphia, Washington, and probably other cities with a view of testing the practical usage of adhesive stamps. Reprints in black, blue, green, red, and brown were struck from a new plate.

The original stamps were *printed by intaglio* from plates of 40 by Rawdon, Wright & Hatch. They were *imperforate* and usually initialed "A.C.M." (Alonzo Castle Monson, a clerk in the post office) before sale.

PM19 *George Washington*

PM19
5c black on bluish paper   625.   350.
On cover   —   500.
Pair   1,600.   850.
a. Signed "R.H.M."   12,500. 2,500.
b. without signature   1,200.   550.
p. Blue paper   6,000. 1,400.
p1. Gray paper   5,000. 1,400.

PROVIDENCE, RI

1846. Postmaster Welcome B. Sayles issued *intaglio-printed, imperforate* stamps produced from copper plates containing 12 subjects. The stamps were engraved directly onto the plate.

PM20   PM21

PM20
5c black   200.   1,250.
PM21
10c black   1,000.   —
Pair, one each 5c and 10c   1,400.   —
Reprints with initials on the back were made in 1898.

ST. LOUIS, MO

1845-46. Postmaster John M. Wimer issued *imperforate* stamps printed from copper plates of six subjects. Varieties of each stamp are known. *Wove paper.*

            PM22-PM29 *Missouri coat of arms*

PM22
5c black on greenish paper   5,000.   2,500.
PM23
10c black on greenish paper   4,500.   2,500.
PM24
20c black on greenish paper   —   20,000.

1846. Previous stamps in new paper color. Varieties exist.

PM25
  5c black on gray lilac paper   —   4,500.
PM26
  10c black on gray lilac paper   4,500.   2,250.
PM27
  20c black on gray lilac paper   —   11,000.

1847. Previous stamp designs on pelure paper.

PM28
  5c black on bluish paper   —   6,500.
PM29
  10c black on bluish paper   —   5,500.

Regular Postal Issues [2] (2)

1847. The First Government Stamps were put into use early in July 1847. They superseded Postmasters' Provisionals and other stamps which were thereafter not tolerated by the Postmaster General. The 5c stamp paid for carrying an ordinary letter up to 300 miles, and the 10c value was used for letters requiring higher postage.

Rawdon, Wright, Hatch & Edson of New York engraved the stamps and printed them in sheets of 200 that were cut into panes of 100 before distribution to the post offices. *The stamps were printed on thin, bluish wove paper. They were unwatermarked and imperforate, Intaglio.*

1 *Benjamin Franklin, after painting by James R. Longacre*

1 *(1)*

5c red brown *July 1, 1847*	4,500.	450.
orange brown	4,500.	550.
black brown	4,500.	475.
bright orange brown	5,000.	550.
bright reddish brown	—	—
brown orange	—	1,100.
dark brown	4,500.	475.
dark brown orange	—	—
dark olive brown	—	—
gray brown	4,500.	450.
orange	—	—
reddish brown	—	—
On cover		525.
Mark in "S" at upper right	5,000.	550.
Double impression	—	—
Double transfer, top frame line	—	550.
Double transfer, top and bottom frame lines	—	550.
Double transfer, bottom and lower part of left frame line	—	550.
Double transfer, top, bottom, left frame lines	—	1,000.
Double transfer, "U," "POST OFFICE," and left numeral	—	—
Double transfer, top and upper part of side frame lines, "U," "POST OFFICE"	—	—

2 *George Washington, after painting by Gilbert Stuart, Boston Museum of Fine Arts*

10c black *(July 1, 1847)*	17,500.	1,250.
gray black	17,500.	1,150.
greenish black	—	1,150.
On cover		1,500.
Mark across lips	—	1,800.
Mark in necktie	—	1,800.
Short transfer at top	18,000.	1,250.
Vertical line through second "F" of "OFFICE"	—	1,400.
Double transfer, left and bottom frame line	—	1,800.
Double transfer, "POST OFFICE"	—	1,800.
Double transfer, "X" at lower right	—	1,800.
v. Diagonal bisect on cover		10,000.
v1. Horizontal bisect on cover		—
v2. Vertical bisect on cover		—

Government imitations of the 5c (in blue) and 10c (in Venetian red) were printed in 1947 and are listed as CM290 in the commemorative stamp section.

SPECIAL PRINTING

1875. Official Reproductions of the 1847 Issue. New dies were engraved and the stamps were printed by the Bureau of Engraving and Printing on *gray-blue paper. They are imperforate, without gum, and both shorter and wider than the originals. Intaglio.* Reproductions on laid paper are known. Not valid for postage.

1 *Original (1847): The top edge of Franklin's shirt touches the frame on a level with the top of the "F" of "FIVE"*

SP1 *Reproduction (1875): The top of the shirt is on a level with the top of the figure "5"*

2 *Original (1847): The left and right vertical outlines of the coat point at the "T" of "TEN" and between the "T" and "S" of "CENTS," respectively*

SP2 *Reproduction (1875): Above lines point to the right edge of "X" and to the center of the "S" of "CENTS"*

SP1 *(3)*

5c red brown (4,779 copies sold)	800.
brown	800.
dark brown	800.

SP2 *(4)*

10c black (3,883 copies sold)	950.
gray black	950.

1851-57. The 1851-57 Series consisted of 1c, 3c, 5c, 10c, and 12c denominations, issued to cover the needs of a rapidly expanding postal service.

While the production methods of the day were excellent, they did not equal present-day uniformity. As a result, more than one type of some of the stamps are recognized by collectors. It will add to your pleasure and profit to determine the correct types of your stamps through the use of illustrations in this catalog.

Toppan, Carpenter, Casilear & Co. printed the stamps on *unwatermarked* paper. *Intaglio, imperforate.*

3, 18 Benjamin Franklin, after bust by Jean Antoine Houdon. For detailed descriptions of Types I-V, see Nos. 3-9 and 18-24.

3 Type I is the most complete design of the various types of this stamp. It shows the full scroll work at the top and bottom of the design. The ornaments in the upper right corner are "doubled."

3 *(5)*

1c blue, Type I *(July 1, 1851)*	175,000.	15,000.
dark blue	—	—
pale blue	—	—
On cover		20,000.
Pair, one each Type I and Type II	—	25,000.

4, 19 Type Ia has the design complete at the bottom but incomplete at the top

4 *(6)*

1c blue, Type Ia	25,000.	6,500.
On cover		7,000.
Curl on "C"	26,000.	7,000.
Curl on shoulder	26,000.	6,500.

Earliest documented cover: Apr. 19, 1857

5. Type Ib has the design at the top complete and the design at the bottom nearly complete. Type Ib is often mistaken for Type I

5 *(5A)*

1c blue, Type Ib *(July 1, 1851)*	9,000.	3,500.
dark blue	9,000.	3,000.
pale blue	9,000.	3,000.
On cover		3,500.

Catalog prices for the above stamp are for nice examples of the type. Stamps with a slightly less complete design at the bottom are worth less, perhaps

6, 20 Type II has the top line always complete, the top ornaments complete or may be partially cut away. The bottom line is always complete, while the little balls of the bottom scrolls and the bottom of the lower plume ornaments are missing.
1/3 to 1/2 of the listed value.

6 *(7)*

1c blue, (Plate 1) Type II *(July 1, 1851)*	500.	95.
dark blue	500.	95.
pale blue	500.	95.
On cover		100.
Double transfer	500.	100.
Plate 2 *(Dec. 5, 1855)*	500.	95.
Cracked plate	675.	225.
Double transfer	500.	95.
Triple transfer	800.	250.
Plate 3 *(May 6, 1856)*	—	325.
Double transfer	—	350.
Plate 4 *(Apr. 19, 1857)*	2,000.	500.
Curl in hair	—	650.

7, 21 Type III has both the top and bottom lines broken. It should be noted particularly that the side ornaments are complete. If they are not, the stamp has been cut out of a perforated stamp of Type V (No. 24). The finest examples of No. 7 are found in position 99R2, which is why that item is listed separately.

7 *(8)*

1c blue, Type III	7,500.	1,600.
On cover		1,800.
Position 99R2	12,000.	3,250.

8, 22 *Type IIIa has the outer line broken at the top or bottom of the stamp but both lines are not broken on the same stamp*

8 *(8A)*

1c blue (Plate 1E), Type IIIa	2,400.	550.
dark blue	2,400.	550.
pale blue	2,400.	550.
On cover		750.
Double transfer, one inverted (blue)	2,800.	700.
Double transfer, one inverted (dark blue)	2,800.	700.
Double transfer, one inverted (pale blue)	2,800.	700.
Plate 2	—	—
Plate 4	—	800.

9, 23

9t5,

23t5

9, 23 *Type IV, similar to Type II, but with the outer lines recut in several different ways*

9 *(9)*

1c blue, Type IV (recut once at top and once at bottom)	400.	85.
On cover		95.
Plate block of eight, with imprint	—	
Bottom frame line broken	—	200.
Cracked plate	475.	125.
Double transfer	425.	90.
Triple transfer, one inverted	475.	125.
t. Recut once at top	425.	85.
t1. Recut once at top and twice at bottom	425.	90.
t2. Recut twice at bottom	450.	95.
t3. Recut once at bottom	475.	110.
t4. Recut once at bottom and twice at top	475.	110.
t5. Recut twice at top and twice at bottom	550.	150.
t6. Printed both sides	—	—
t7. Double impression	—	—
v. Perforated 12 1/2 (unofficial)	—	3,000.
v1. Diagonal bisect on cover	—	
v2. Vertical bisect on cover	—	

Earliest documented cover: June 18, 1852

10, 11, 25 *George Washington, after bust by J.W. Houdon, Mount Vernon, Pennsylvania. Type I with outer frame lines at top and bottom. For descriptions of Types II and III, see Nos. 26 and 27*

10 *(10)*

3c orange brown, Type I *(July 1, 1851)*	1,700.	50.
deep orange brown	1,700.	50.
copper brown	1,850.	75.
On cover		—
Mark on lower right diamond	—	80.
Nick on shoulder	—	50.
Double transfer	—	60.
Triple transfer	—	200.
p. Thin, India-like paper	—	250.
t. Printed both sides	—	—

11 *(11)*

3c Venetian red, Type I	120.	7.
claret	150.	10.
bright brown carmine	135.	8.50
brown carmine	135.	8.50
dark brown carmine	135.	8.50
dark violet	135.	8.50
dull brown carmine	135.	8.50
dull carmine red	175.	13.50
dull orange red	120.	7.
dull rose carmine	120.	7.
Plate block of eight	—	
Mark on lower right diamond	165.	20.
Nick on shoulder	135.	7.50
Cracked plate	375.	55.
Worn plate	125.	7.
Double transfer in "GENTS"	190.	25.
Double transfer in "THREE CENTS"	150.	8.
Double transfer in "THREE CENTS" and rosettes double)	215.	35.
Triple transfer	190.	25.
t. Double impression	—	—
v. Perforated 12 1/2 (unofficial)	1,500.	—

Earliest documented cover: Oct. 4, 1851

12, 28-30 *Thomas Jefferson, after painting by Gilbert Stuart. Type I, with full projections at top and bottom as well as the sides. Copies that do not have these complete projections at top and bottom are trimmed from perforated varieties issued at a later date. For a description of Type II see Nos. 31 and 32*

12 *(12)*

5c red brown, Type I	8,500.	900.
dark red brown	8,500.	900.
Double transfer	—	1,150.

Earliest documented cover: Mar. 24, 1956

13, 33 *George Washington, after painting by Gilbert Stuart. Type I. For description of Types II-IV, see Nos. 14-16 and 34-37*

13, 33 *Type I has the "shells" at the lower corners almost complete. The line below "TEN CENTS" is very nearly complete. The outer lines above the middle of the stamp and over the "X" in each upper corner are broken. There are three small circles on each side opposite the words "TEN CENTS"*

13 *(13)*

10c green, Type I *(May 1855)*	*11,000.*	585.
dark green	*11,000.*	585.
yellow green	*11,000.*	585.
On cover		645.
Curl in left "X"	*11,500.*	660.
Double transfer	*11,500.*	660.

14, 34 *Type II has the outer line at the bottom broken in the middle, the "shells" are partially cut away, and the design is complete at the top. There are three small circles on each side.*

14 *(14)*

10c green, Type II	1,900.	200.
dark green	1,900.	200.
yellow green	1,900.	200.
On cover		260.
Curl opposite left "X"	1,950.	290.
Double transfer	1,950.	270.
Earliest documented cover: May 12, 1855		

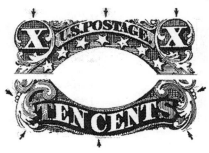

15, 35 *Type III has outer lines broken above the top label that contains words "U.S. POSTAGE" and the lines are broken above the "X" numerals. The shells and outer line at the bottom are partially cut away. There are three small circles on each side.*

15 *(15)*

10c green, Type III	1,900.	200.
dark green	1,900.	200.
yellow green	1,900.	200.
On cover		260.
Curl on forehead	2,000.	265.
Curl to right of left "X"	2,000.	265.
Double transfer at top and bottom	—	—
Earliest documented cover: May 23, 1855		

16, 36 *Type IV has had the outer lines at the top or bottom of the stamp, or at both places, recut. There are three small circles on each side.*

16 *(16)*

10c green, Type IV (outer line recut at top only)	*12,500.*	1,200.
dark green	*12,500.*	1,200.
yellow green	*12,500.*	1,200.
On cover		1,450.
t. Outer line recut at bottom only	*12,500.*	1,200.
t1. Outer line recut at top and bottom	14,000.	1,300.

All four types of the 10c stamp occur on the same sheet, so that pairs and blocks showing combination of these types exist.

17, 38 *George Washington. Type I, with complete frame lines. For Type II see No. 39*

17 *(17)*

12c black, Type I *(July 1, 1851)*	2,600.	225.
deep black	2,600.	225.
gray black	2,600.	225.
On cover		1,250.
Double transfer	2,700.	250.
Recut in lower left corner	2,800.	275.
Triple transfer	2,900.	300.
p. Thin, India-like paper	—	550.
t. Printed on both sides	—	5,500.
y. Diagonal bisect on cover		2,500.
On "Via Nicaragua" cover		5,500.
y2. Vertical bisect on cover		8,500.
y1. Quarter on cover		—

1857-61. This series of stamps, printed by Toppan, Carpenter & Co., had the same designs and types as the preceding issue, with some further types being noted. Three new values, the 24c, 30c, and 90c stamps, were added to this issue.

This issue marked a great milestone in postal service progress. Due to a pressing need for a faster stamp dispensing method, the stamps were machine perforated and were now easily and quickly separated, instead of being cut apart by scissors. *Intaglio, perforated 15.*

While No. 18 has the complete design like the imperforate stamp No. 3, it does not have the "doubled" ornaments in the upper right corners.

18 *(18)*

1c blue, Type I	725.	325.
On cover		450.
Cracked plate	—	500.
Double transfer	775.	400.

Earliest documented cover: Jan. 15, 1861

The normal setting of the perforating machine was such that perforations cut the design on almost every stamp. Prices quoted are for such copies. Where the perforations do not cut the design No.18 stamps command very high premiums.

19 *(19)*

1c blue, Type Ia	12,000.	3,250.
On cover		4,000.
Curl on shoulder	12,500.	3,500.

Earliest documented cover: Nov. 2, 1857

20 *(20)*

1c blue (Plate 2), Type II	475.	135.
On cover		160.
Cracked plate	700.	325.
Double transfer	525.	150.
Plate 4	—	750.
Curl in hair	—	*650.*
Double transfer	—	*1,000.*
Plate 11	600.	175.
Double transfer	—	—
Plate 12	475.	135.

Earliest documented cover: July 26, 1857

21 *(21)*

1c blue, Type III	*5,000.*	*1,150.*
On cover		*1,500.*
Position 99R2	—	*7,500.*

Earliest documented cover: Nov. 20, 1857

The finest examples of No. 21 are found in position 99R2, which is why that item is listed separately.

22 *(22)*

1c blue (Plate 4), Type IIIa	800.	260.
On cover		290.
Double transfer	850.	290.
v. Horizontal pair, imperforate between	—	*5,000.*

Plate 11	900.	
Double transfer	950.	320.
Triple transfer	—	—
Plate 12	900.	290.
Double transfer	950.	320.

Earliest documented cover: July 26, 1857

23 *(23)*

1c blue, Type IV, recut once at top and once at bottom	3,000.	325.
Cracked plate	3,500.	425.
On cover	—	340.
Double transfer	3,250.	350.
Triple transfer, one inverted		
t. Recut once at top		
t1. Recut once at top and twice at bottom	3,250.	350.
t2. Recut twice at bottom	3,500.	375.
t3. Recut once at bottom	3,250.	360.
t4. Recut once at bottom and twice at top	3,250.	375.
t5. Recut twice at top and twice at bottom	3,250.	410.

Earliest documented cover: July 25, 1857

24. *Type V occurs only on the perforated stamps. The top and bottom lines are broken and the sides of the design have been partially cut away. Trimmed copies of this stamp often are offered as Type III imperforate. They easily can be detected since Type III, and all other types that come imperforate, have the complete design at the sides.*

24 *(24)*

1c blue, Type V	120.	24.
On cover		30.
Plate block of eight, with imprint	3,250.	
Curl in hair	160.	33.
Curl on shoulder	160.	33.
Curl over "C" of "CENT"	170.	38.
Curl over "E" of "CENT"	180.	47.
Horizontal dash in hair	200.	48.
"Ring" below ear	210.	55.
Double curl in hair	190.	45.
Double transfer, at bottom	195.	55.
Double transfer, at top	160.	50.

Plate 5 — 315. 75.
   Curl in "O" of "ONE" — —
   Curl on shoulder — —
   p. Laid paper — —
   v. Vertical strip of five,
      imperforate horizontally — —
   Earliest documented cover: *Nov. 17, 1857*

25 *(25)*

3c rose, Type I 900. 30.
   brownish carmine 900. 30.
   dull red 900. 30.
   On cover 35.
   Gash on shoulder 925. 35.
   Cracked plate 1,200. 100.
   Double transfer 975. 45.
   Double transfer, "GENTS" — 250.
   Triple transfer — 300.
   Worn plate 850. 30.
   v. Horizontal pair, imperforate
      vertically — —
   v1. Vertical pair, imperforate
      horizontally — 10,000.
   Earliest documented cover: Feb. 28, 1857

Fakes are known of the Horizontal pair, imperforate vertically.

26. *Type II has the outer frame removed at the top and bottom of the design. The side frame lines were recut to form continuous lines from the top to the bottom of the plate so they extend beyond the design of the stamp*

26 *(26)*

3c Venetian red, Type II 45. 3.50
   bright carmine — —
   brown carmine 52. 4.
   dull red 45. 3.50
   dull rose brown 45. 3.50
   orange brown — —
   On cover 4.
   Cracked plate 425. 130.
   Double transfer 65. 11.
   Double transfer in rosettes, line
      through "POSTAGE" — 65.
   Left frame line double 65. 9.
   Right frame line double 65. 9.
   Transfer damage above lower
      left rosette 50. 4.50
   Transfer damage, retouched 55. 5.
   Transfer damage, retouched with
      two vertical lines 65. 6.
   Worn plate 50. 3.50
   t. Double impression — —
   v. Horizontal pair, imperforate
      between — —

   v1. Horizontal pair, imperforate
      vertically — —
   v2. Vertical pair, imperforate
      horizontally — —
   Earliest documented cover: *Sept. 15, 1857*

27 *Type III has the outer frame lines removed at the top and bottom of the design. The side frame lines extend only to the top and bottom of the stamp design.*

27 *(26a)*

3c Venetian red, Type III 110. 20.
   brownish carmine 110. 20.
   dull red 110. 20.
   claret 120. 24.
   On cover 75.
   Damaged transfer, above lower
      left rosette 120. 21.
   Damaged transfer, retouched 125. 23.
   Double transfer 175. 32.
   Double transfer, bottom part of
      stamp and rosettes — 75.
   Triple transfer — 100.
   Worn plate 110. 20.
   Earliest documented cover: July 11, 1857

28 *(28)*

5c red brown, Type I 1,350. 260.
   bright red brown 1,350. 260.
   pale red brown 1,350. 260.
   henna brown (Indian red) 1,900. 400.
   On cover 400.
   Earliest documented cover: Aug. 22, 1857

29 *(27)*

5c brick red, Type I 9,000. 600.
   On cover — 1,000.
   Earliest documented cover: Oct. 6, 1858

30 *(29)*

5c brown, Type I 950. 250.
   dark brown 950. 250.
   pale brown 950. 250.
   yellow brown 950. 250.
   On cover — 300.
   Earliest documented cover: Apr. 4, 1859

Partially cut   *Completely cut*

31, 32 Type II does not have full projections at the top and bottom. These projections have been partially or completely cut away.

31 *(30A)*

5c brown, Type II	500.	175.
dark brown	500.	175.
yellow brown	500.	175.
On cover		230.
Cracked plate	—	—
t. Printed on both sides	3,800.	4,000.

Earliest documented cover: May 14, 1860

32 *(30)*

5c orange brown, Type II	800.	1,100.
dark orange brown	800.	1,100.
On cover		2,300.

Earliest documented cover: May 8, 1861

33 *(31)*

10c green, Type I	8,250.	500.
bluish green	8,250.	500.
dark green	8,250.	500.
yellowish green	8,250.	500.
On cover		825.
Curl in left "X"	8,750.	600.
Double transfer	8,750.	600.

Earliest documented cover: Oct. 29, 1857

34 *(32)*

10c green, Type II	2,500.	200.
bluish green	2,500.	200.
dark green	2,500.	200.
yellowish green	2,500.	200.
On cover		225.
Curl opposite left "X"	—	240.
Double transfer	2,600.	210.

Earliest documented cover: July 27, 1857

35 *(33)*

10c green, Type III	2,600.	200.
bluish green	2,600.	200.
dark green	2,600.	200.
yellowish green	2,600.	200.
On cover		225.
Curl in left "X"	—	260.
Curl on forehead	—	260.
Double transfer	—	—

36 *(34)*

10c green, Type IV, recut at top	17,500.	1,500.
bluish green	17,500.	1,500.
dark green	17,500.	1,500.
yellowish green	17,500.	1,500.
On cover		1,900.
t. Recut once at bottom	18,000.	1,500.
t1. Recut at top and bottom	18,500.	1,600.

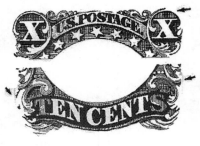

37 Type V had the side ornaments partially cut away. In no case do three small circles remain on each side of the stamp. There usually is one small circle at each side, but some copies show two or three small circles on the right side. The outer lines at the top are complete except over the right "X." Trimmed copies of this stamp are offered as imperforates. If an imperforate does not have three small circles at each side it is a trimmed fake.

37 *(35)*

10c green, Type V	200.	60.
bluish green	200.	60.
dark green	200.	60.
yellowish green	200.	60.
On cover		70.
Plate block of eight, with imprint	—	9,000.
Curl in "E" of "CENTS"	250.	80.
Curl in "T" of "CENT	250.	80.
Curl (small) on forehead	240.	70.
Double transfer at bottom	250.	80.
Cracked plate	—	—

Earliest documented cover: Apr. 29, 1859

38 *(36)*

12c black, Type I	380.	100.
gray black	380.	100.
On cover		485.
Double transfer	430.	110.
Triple transfer	525.	—
v. Diagonal bisect on cover		17,500.
v1. Horizontal pair, imperforate between	—	—

Earliest documented cover: July 30, 1857

39 Type II has the frame line broken or missing on one or both sides

39 *(36b)*

12c black, Type II	360.	115.
deep black	360.	115.
On cover		575.
Double transfer, frame line at left	390.	125.
Double transfer, frame line at right	390.	125.
Vertical line through rosette	460.	160.

Earliest documented cover: Dec. 9, 1859

40 *George Washington*

40 *(37)*

24c gray lilac	725.	210.
gray	725.	210.
lilac	725.	210.
On cover		750.
Plate block of 12, with imprint	32,000.	
v. Pair, imperforate	—	—

Earliest documented cover: July 7, 1860

41 *Benjamin Franklin*

41 *(38)*

30c orange	850.	300.
reddish orange	850.	300.
yellow orange	850.	300.
On cover		1,250.
Cracked plate	—	—
Double transfer	950.	350.
Recut at bottom	1,000.	450.
v. Pair, imperforate	—	—

Earliest documented cover: Aug. 8, 1860

42 *Gen. George Washington, after a painting by John Trumbull, Yale University*

42 *(39)*

90c deep blue	1,300.	5,500.
blue	1,300.	5,500.
On cover		4,500.
Double transfer at bottom	1,400.	—
Double transfer at top	1,400.	—
Short transfer at bottom, left, and right	1,350.	—
v. Pair, imperforate	—	—

Earliest documented cover: Sept. 11
Many fake cancellations exist on this stamp.

SPECIAL PRINTING

1875. Reprints of the 1857-61 Issue. The original dies were intact, but new plates were made of the 1c, 3c, 10c, and 12c values. Since these were perforated 12, while the originals were 15, they are quite easy to distinguish from the originals. The issue is very bright in color, *printed on white paper, issued without gum.* Printed by the Continental Bank Note Co. Not valid for postal use. *Intaglio.*

SP3 *(40)*

1c brilliant blue (3,846 copies sold)	500.	
Cracked plate	600.	
Double transfer	600.	

SP4 *(41)*

3c bright vermilion (479 copies)	2,000.

SP5 *(42)*

5c bright orange brown (878 copies)	950.
Margin strip of four, with plate number	10,000.

SP6 *(43)*

10c bluish green (516 copies	1,750.

SP7 *(44)*

12c greenish black (489 copies)	2,000.

SP8 *(45)*

24c dark violet black (479 copies)	2,000.

SP9 *(46)*

30c yellow orange (480 copies)	2,000.

SP10 *(47)*

90c indigo (454 copies)	3,300.

This set is known imperforate.

1861-66. Upon the outbreak of the War Between the States in 1861, the postal authorities in Washington found it advisable to demonetize all U.S. postage stamps issued up to that time in order to prevent possible use in the Confederate States. It is interesting to note that due to the scarcity of metal coins during this period, stamps — encased in small containers — often were pressed into use as small change.

The National Bank Note Co. obtained the engraving and printing contract and prepared a set of eight essay designs in the form of finished 1c, 3c, 5c, 10c, 12c, 24c, 30c, and 90c stamps, and evidently submitted them for approval prior to August 1. As least six of these mis-called "August" designs were not approved. Beginning August 17, postage stamps were issued from new plates of 1c, 3c, 5c, 10c, 12c, and 90c made from altered designs. The set was completed by regular printings from the 24c and 90c essay plates after possible alterations on them. A second printing from the 10c essay plate was issued and is known used in September 1861.

The second set of designs, regularly issued, are listed here, as well as two denominations, 2c and 15c, added in 1863 and 1866 respectively. The essays as well as the issued stamps are on *unwatermarked* paper and are *Intaglio and perforated 12.*

43 *Benjamin Franklin, after bust by Jean Cafferi, Pennsylvania Academy of Fine Arts*

Unissued design: There is no dash under the tip of the ornaments at the right of the numeral in the upper left corner.

43 *Benjamin Franklin. A dash has been added under the tip of the ornament at the right of the numeral in the upper left corner.*

43 *(63)*

1c blue *(Aug. 17, 1861)*	150.	16.
bright blue	150.	16.
pale blue	150.	16.
ultramarine	360.	45.
dark blue	300.	25.
indigo	300.	25.
On cover		21.
Plate block of eight, with imprint	2,450.	
Dot on "U"	160.	18.
Double transfer	—	24.
t. Printed both sides	—	2,500.
p. Laid paper	—	—
v. Vertical pair, imperforate horizontally	—	—

44 *Andrew Jackson, after miniature by John Wood Dodge*

44 *(73)*

2c black	175.	24.
deep black	175.	24.
gray black	175.	24.
On cover		42.
Plate block of eight, with imprint	8,000.	
Cracked plate	—	—
Double transfer	200.	27.
Double transfer of top left corner and "POSTAGE" ("Atherton shift")	6,000.	—
Double transfer of right side ("Preston shift")	—	—
Short transfer	190.	25.
Triple transfer	—	—
p. Laid paper	—	—
t. Printed on both sides	—	5,000.
y. Diagonal bisect on cover	—	1,250.

y1. Horizontal bisect on cover	—	—
y2. Vertical bisect on cover	—	1,250.

Earliest documented cover: July 6, 1863

45 *George Washington, after bust by J.A. Houdon*

Unissued Design: The ornaments forming the corners of the design are plain

45 *George Washington. A ball has been added to each corner of the design and the ornaments have been enlarged.*

45 *(64)*

3c pink *(Aug. 17, 1861)*	4,500.	450.
On cover		500.
a. rose pink	70.	1.75
On cover		2.00
av. Vertical pair, imperforate horizontally	1,200.	750.
b. pigeon blood pink	2,700.	—
On cover		4,000.

It is almost impossible to describe a "pink" in words, but it should be kept in mind that the inking on a "pink" is rather heavy, and the lines of the design do not stand out as sharply as on the other shades. The color, while not as outstanding as a dull pink ribbon, is nevertheless on that order. It is not any of the shades of brown, dull red, rose red, or brown red so often mistaken for the real pink.

46 *(65)*

3c brown carmine	625.	—
dull brown red	625.	—
dull red	625.	—
pale carmine red	625.	—
dark brown red	625.	—
On cover		—
Plate block of eight, with imprint	19,000.	
Cracked plate	—	—
Double impression	2,900.	—
Double transfer	—	—
p. Laid paper	—	—
t. Printed on both sides	—	—
v. Vertical pair, imperforate horizontally	—	—

47 *Thomas Jefferson*
Unissued Design (left): No leaflets project from the corner ornaments
Issued design right): A leaflet projects from each corner ornament

47 *(67)*
5c buff	9,000.	425.
brown yellow	9,000.	425.
olive yellow	9,000.	425.
On cover		725.

Earliest documented cover: Aug. 19, 1861

48 *(75)*
5c red brown	2,000.	225.
dark red brown	2,000.	225.
On cover	—	475.
Double transfer	2,300.	250.

Earliest documented cover: Jan. 2, 1862

49 *(76)*
5c brown	—	—
dark brown	—	—
pale brown	—	—
black brown	—	—
On cover		—
Double transfer, bottom frame line	—	—
Double transfer, bottom and top frame lines	—	—
Double transfer, top frame line	—	—
p. Laid paper	—	—

Earliest documented cover: Feb. 3, 1863

50, 51 *George Washington*

50 *Type I does not have a heavy curved line cut below the stars, and the ornament directly over the center star at the top has only one outer line. This stamp is found only on thin, semi-transparent paper*

50 *(68)*
10c green, Type I *(Sept. 17, 1861)*	4,500.	550.
dark yellow green	4,500.	550.
On cover		900.
Double transfer	—	—

51 *Type II has a heavy curved line cut below the stars. The ornament directly over the center star at the top has a double outer line.*

51 *(68)*
10c green, Type II *(Aug. 17, 1861)*	325.	30.
dark green	350.	32.
yellow green	325.	30.
blue green	325.	35.
On cover		45.
Plate block of eight, with imprint	5,000.	
Double transfer	375.	40.
v. Vertical pair, imperforate horizontally	—	3,500.

52 *George Washington*   Unissued *Design. The four corners of the design are rounded.*   52 *The four corners of the design have had ovals and scrolls added to form "square corners"*

52 *(69)*
12c black *(Aug. 17, 1861)*	625.	55.
gray black	625.	55.
On cover		85.
Double transfer of bottom frame line	650.	65.
Double transfer of top frame line	650.	65.
Double transfer of top and bottom frame lines	675.	75.

53 *Abraham Lincoln*

53 *(77)*
15c black *(Apr. 14, 1866)*	650.	72.
On cover		125.
Plate block of eight, with imprint	—	
Cracked plate	—	—
Double transfer	600.	80.

54-56 *George Washington*

54 *(70c)*
24c violet	6,500.	575.
gray violet	1,400.	350.

No. 54 is found only on thin, semi-transparent paper, while Nos. 55 and 56 are on a thicker and more opaque paper.

55 *(70)*

24c red lilac	800.	80.
brown lilac	750.	80.
steel blue	5,000.	325.
blackish violet	800.	80.
violet, on thin paper *(Aug. 17, 1861)*	—	—
grayish lilac, on thin paper	—	—
On cover		135.
Scratch under "A" of "POSTAGE"	—	—

Earliest documented cover: Oct. 4, 1861

56 *(78)*

24c lilac	400.	55.
gray lilac	400.	55.
gray	400.	55.
dark lilac	12,500.	1,200.
On cover	—	125.
Scratch under "A" of "POSTAGE"	—	—
p. Printed on both sides	—	3,500.
v. Pair, imperforate	—	—

Earliest documented cover: Oct. 29, 1862

57 *Benjamin Franklin*

57 *(71)*

30c orange *(Aug. 17, 1861)*	650.	75.
deep orange	650.	75.
On cover		350.
p. Printed on both sides	—	—

58 *George Washington*

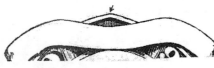

Unissued design. There is no spot of color in the apex of the lower line of the angle at the top of the design. No row of dashes appear between the lines of the angle, and the lines in the leaf at the left of the "U" at the lower left of the design run at an angle.

58 *There is a spot of color in the apex of the lower line of the angle at the top of the design. A row of small dashes appear between the lines of the angle, and the lines in the leaf at the lower left corner of the stamp are nearly vertical*

58 *(72)*

90c blue *(Aug. 17, 1861)*	1,500.	250.
dark blue	1,650.	300.
pale blue	1,500.	250.
dull blue	1,500.	250.
On cover		13,500.

SPECIAL PRINTING

1875. Re-Issues of the 1861-66 Stamps, again the dies were available, and new plates were made of the 1c, 2c, 5c, 10c, and 12c values. Printed on hard, extremely white paper, absolutely white gum, and without grill. They can be distinguished by their color shades, which are very deep and clear, and the white paper (compared to the slightly yellowish of the originals). *Intaglio* by the National Bank Note Co. and *perforated 12.* Used copies are seldom found.

SP11 *(102)*		
1c dark ultramarine (3,195 copies)	500.	800.
SP12 *(103)*		
2c jet black (979 copies)	2,300.	4,000.
SP13 *(104)*		
3c brown red (465 copies)	2,500.	4,300.
SP14 *(105)*		
5c light yellow brown (672 copies)	1,850.	2,300.
SP15 *(108)*		
10c bluish green (451 copies)	2,000.	3,750.
SP16 *(107)*		
12c deep black (389 copies)	2,800.	4,500.
SP17 *(108)*		
15c deep black (397 copies)	2,250.	4,800.
SP18 *(109)*		
24c deep brown violet (346 copies)	3,250.	6,000.
SP19 *(110)*		
30c brown orange (346 copies)	3,500.	6,000.
SP20 *(111)*		
90c dark blue (317 copies)	4,800.	20,000.

1867-68. Stamps of 1861-66, impressed with grills of various sizes. The grills were adopted in order to prevent the removal of cancellations from used stamps. They were impressed into the stamps in the form of small pyramids arranged in parallel rows as noted for each type of grill listed.

Grills with points projecting upward from the face of the stamp

Grill A. *Grill covers the entire stamp and appears as small mounds that have small breaks in their tops. An essay grill is similar, but paper breaks appear on only a few, if any, of each of the individual mounds that make up the entire grill.*

59 *(79)*
3c rose, grill A	2,200.	475.	
On cover		675.	
a. Printed on both sides	11,000.	—	

Earliest documented cover: Aug. 13, 1867

60 *(80)*
5c brown, grill A	42,000.	—	
dark brown	—	45,000.	

61 *(82)*
30c orange, grill A	—	32,500.	

Grill B. *This grill, about 18 x 15 mm in size, containing 22 x 18 rows of points projecting upward from the face of the stamp, exists on one copy of the 3c rose. The grill points differ from any other issued grill. A variety of Grill C, No. 62, often is mistaken for this item.*

61A *(82)*
3c rose, grill B	—	45,000.	

Earliest documented cover: Feb. 1868

Grill C. *The grill was produced by the same grill roller as Grill A, after the roller had been machined to "erase" portions of the grill so that it now formed groups of grill points on each stamp rather than grilling all over the stamps. This grill is about 13 x 16 mm, with 16 to 17 by 18 to 21 points projecting upward from the face of the stamp.*

62 *(83)*
3c rose, grill C	3,000.	650.	
On cover		575.	
Double grill	4,200.	1,500.	
Grill with points down	3,750.	650.	

Earliest documented cover: Nov. 26, 1867

No. 62 shows rows of grill points, not as heavily impressed as the normal grill, forming a grill whose total area is about 18 x 15 mm. Caused by a failure to cut deep enough into the grill roller when it was bring machined, which left a few areas on the roller only "partially erased."

Grills with points projecting downward

Grill D. *The tips of the grill points form vertical ridges. This grill is about 12 x 14 mm, always has 15 points in each horizontal row, with 17 to 18 points in each vertical row.*

 Detail of Grill D

63 *(84)*
2c black, grill D	9,500.	1,500.	
On cover		1,750.	
Double transfer	—	—	
Split grill	—	1,600.	

Earliest documented cover: Feb. 15, 1868

64 *(85)*
3c rose, grill D	3,000.	475.	
On cover		600.	
Double grill	—	—	
Split grill	—	525.	

Earliest documented cover: Feb. 2, 1868

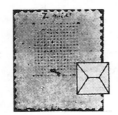
Detail of Grill Z

Grill Z

Grill Z. *When originally discovered by William L. Stevenson, this then unknown grill was given the algebraic "unknown" symbol of "Z" and it has thus been called from the beginning. It is very easy to tell from the other pyramid grills because the tip of the pyramids are horizontal ridges, all through the entire area of the grill, while on the D, E, and F grills these ridges are vertical. The grill is about 11 x 14 mm, with 13 to 14 by 17 to 18 points.*

65 *(85A)*
1c blue, grill Z	—	—	

66 *(85B)*
2c black, grill Z	3,000.	400.	
On cover		550.	
Double grill	—	—	
Double transfer	3,100.	450.	

Earliest documented cover: Mar. 13, 1868

67 *(85C)*
3c rose, grill Z	5,000.	1,200.	
On cover		1,600.	
Double grill	6,000.	—	

Earliest documented cover: Feb. 1868

68 *(86D)*
10c green, grill Z	47,500.	—	

69 *(85E)*
12c black, grill Z	4,000.	600.	
Double transfer of top frame line	—	675.	
On cover	—	1,000.	

Earliest documented cover: Feb. 19, 1868

69A *(85F)*
15c black, grill Z	100,000.	—	

Grill E. *This grill is about 11 x 13 mm. and has 14 by 15 to 17 points*

70 *(86)*
1c blue, grill E	1,100.	275.	
dull blue	1,000.	250.	
On cover		325.	
Split grill	1,100.	275.	
Double grill	—	375.	

Earliest documented cover: Mar. 9, 1868

71 *(87)*

2c black, grill E	525.	75.
gray black	525.	75.
intense black	560.	80.
On cover	—	110.
Grill with points up	—	—
Split grill	575.	85.
Double grill	560.	80.
Double transfer	550.	80.
Triple grill	—	—
v. Diagonal or Vertical Bisect on cover		2,000.

Earliest documented cover: Mar. 11, 1868

72 *(88)*

3c rose, grill E	375.	10.
pale red	375.	10.
pale rose	375.	10.
lake red	475.	13.
On cover		14.
Split grill	450.	12.
Double grill	—	—
Triple grill	—	—
p. Very thin paper	500.	12.

Earliest documented cover: May 23, 1868

73 *(89)*

10c green, grill E	2,000.	175.
blue green	2,000.	175.
dark green	2,000.	175.
On cover		275.
Double transfer	—	225.
Split grill	2,100.	190.
Double grill	2,900.	300.
p. Very thin paper	2,100.	190.

Earliest documented cover: May 6, 1868

74 *(90)*

12c black, grill E	2,250.	210.
gray black	2,250.	210.
On cover	—	340.
Double transfer of bottom frame line	2,350.	225.
Double transfer of top frame line	2,350.	225.
Double transfer of top and bottom frame line	2,500.	260.
Split grill	2,400.	225.

Earliest documented cover: Mar. 3, 1868

75 *(91)*

15c black, grill E	4,750.	460.
gray black	4,750.	460.
On cover		750.
Split grill	—	550.
Double grill	—	750.

Earliest documented cover: June 25, 1868

Grill F. *This grill is about 9 x 13 mm, and has 11 to 12 by 15 to 17 points*

76 *(92)*

1c blue, grill F	500.	100.
dark blue	500.	100.
pale blue	500.	100.
On cover		130.
Split grill	525.	120.
Double grill	—	200.
Double transfer	525.	125.
p. Very thin paper	525.	110.

Earliest documented cover: Mar. 19, 1868

77 *(93)*

2c black, grill F	200.	35.
Gray black	200.	35.
On cover		45.
Plate block of eight, with imprint	—	
Split grill	220.	40.
Double grill	—	125.
Double transfer	220.	40.
v. Bisect (any) on cover		1,300.

Earliest documented cover: Mar. 27, 1868

78 *(94a)*

3c rose, grill F	175.	3.50
a. rose red	175.	3.50
On cover		3.75
Plate block of eight, with imprint	2,500.	
Double transfer	200.	5.50
Grill with points up	—	—
Split grill	185.	4.00
Quadruple split grill	325.	85.
Double grill	—	—
Triple grill	—	100.
p. Very thin paper	185.	4.00
t. Printed on both sides	1,100.	—
v. Vertical pair, imperforate horizontally	1,000.	—

Earliest documented cover: May 28, 1868

79 *(95)*

5c brown, grill F	1,500.	225.
black brown	1,600.	250.
On cover		350.
Double transfer of top frame line	—	—
Split grill	1,600.	250.
Double grill	—	—
p. Very thin paper	1,600.	250.

Earliest documented cover: Dec. 2, 1868

80 *(96)*

10c yellow green, grill F	1,200.	120.
blue green	1,200.	120.
dark green	1,200.	120.
green	1,200.	120.
Double transfer	—	—
Split grill	1,300.	125.
Quadruple split grill	—	350.
Double grill	—	210.
p. Very thin paper	1,250.	130.

Earliest documented cover: Oct. 1, 1868

81 *(97)*

12c black, grill F	1,500.	125.
gray black	1,500.	135.

On cover		150.
Split grill	1,600.	145.
Double grill	—	270.
Double transfer of bottom frame line	1,600.	135.
Double transfer of top frame line	1,600.	135.
Double transfer of top and bottom frame lines	—	165.
Triple grill	—	—
p. Very thin paper	1,550.	130.

Earliest documented cover: May 27, 1868

82 *(98)*

15c black, grill F	1,500.	140.
gray black	1,500.	135.
On cover		150.
Plate block of eight, with imprint	25,000.	
Double transfer of upper right corner	—	—
Split grill	1,600.	150.
Quadruple split grill	2,250.	350.
Double grill	—	250.
p. Very thin paper	1,500.	140.

Earliest documented cover: May 4, 1868

83 *(99)*

24c gray lilac, grill F	2,100.	450.
gray	2,100.	450.
On cover		900.
Plate block of eight, with imprint	30,000.	
Scratch under "A" in "POSTAGE"	—	—
Split grill	2,200.	475.
Double grill	2,700.	800.

Earliest documented cover: Jan. 5, 1869

84 *(100)*

30c orange, grill F	2,750.	400.
deep orange	2,750.	400.
On cover		1,200.
Split grill	2,750.	450.
Double grill	3,250.	750.
Double grill, one split	—	—

Earliest documented cover: Nov. 21, 1868

85 *(101)*

90c blue, grill F	5,000.	850.
dark blue	5,000.	850.
On cover		—
Split grill	5,250.	950.
Double grill	7,000.	—

Earliest documented cover: May 8, 1869

Note: *Most of the stamps that bear grills can be found with double grills, triple grills, split grills, and quadruple split grills. Double grills are two impressions of the grill on the same stamp, triple grills are three impressions of the grill on the same stamp, split grills are those with about half of a normal grill on each end or on each side of the stamp, and quadruple split grills are those that show just a small portion of the grill on each corner of the stamp. The split grill varieties were caused by misplacing the stamps under the grill roller so that the grills were not properly placed on the stamps. Faked grills exist.*

1869. Pictorial Issue. This series of stamps was printed by the National Bank Note Co. The stamps are square in design. For some reason now difficult for us to understand, this series was not popular and was replaced with a new series in about a year. The stamps were grilled with a new size of grill, Grill G, 9 1/2 x 9 1/2 mm in size. The stamps were *printed in intaglio on hard wove paper, unwatermarked, and were perforated 12.*

Three denominations of these stamps are known with inverted centers and are extremely scarce. This was the first time an error of this type was issued, and was due to carelessness when printing the bi-colored stamps.

86 *Benjamin Franklin*

86 *(112)*

1c buff	275.	65.
brown orange	275.	65.
dark brown orange	275.	65.
On cover		135.
Plate block of 10, with imprint	—	
Margin block of four, with arrow	1,400.	
Double transfer	—	—
Split grill	300.	75.
Double grill	450.	150.
Double grill, one split	—	—
Grill omitted, original gum	775.	—

Earliest documented cover: May 2, 1869

87 *Pony Express*

87 *(113)*

2c brown	225.	28.
dark brown	225.	28.
pale brown	225.	28.
yellow brown	225.	28.
On cover		70.
Plate block of 10, with imprint	—	
Margin block of four, with arrow	975.	
Double transfer	—	40.
Split grill	250.	40.
Quadruple split grill	—	225.
Double grill	—	150.
Grill omitted, original gum	600.	—
p. Printed on both sides	—	—
v. Bisect (any) on cover	—	—

Earliest documented cover: Mar. 26, 1869

88 *Early Locomotive*

88 *(114)*

3c ultramarine	175.	8.00
blue	175.	8.00
dark blue	175.	8.00
dark ultramarine	175.	8.00
pale ultramarine	175.	8.00
On cover		14.
Plate block of 10, with imprint	7,000.	
Margin block of four, with arrow	900.	
Double transfer	190.	9.00
Split grill	185.	9.00
Quadruple split grill	400.	65.
Double grill	350.	45.
Triple grill	—	—
Grill omitted	600.	—
t. Double impression	—	—

Earliest documented cover: Mar. 27, 1869

89 *George Washington*

89 *(115)*

6c ultramarine	950.	100.
pale ultramarine	950.	100.
On cover		300.
Margin block of four, with arrow	5,000.	
Double transfer	—	120.
Split grill	1,025.	120.
Quadruple split grill	—	400.
Double grill	—	300.
v. Vertical bisect on cover		—

Earliest documented cover: Apr. 26, 1869

90 *Shield and Eagle*

90 *(116)*

10c yellow	1,000.	90.
yellowish orange	1,000.	90.
On cover		335.
Margin block of four, with arrow	5,300.	
Split grill	1,050.	110.
Double grill	—	275.

Earliest documented cover: Apr. 1, 1869

91 *Steamship* Adriatic

91 *(117)*

12c green	975.	100.
bluish green	975.	100.
dark green	975.	100.
yellowish green	975.	100.
On cover		375.
Margin block of four, with arrow	5,000.	
Split grill	1,025.	125.
Double grill	—	300.

Earliest documented cover: Apr. 1, 1869

92 *Landing of Columbus. Type I has a white area coming to an apex under the "T" of "POSTAGE." It is also known as the "unframed picture."*

92 *(118)*

15c brown and blue, Type I	2,500.	350.
dark brown and blue	2,800.	350.
pale brown and blue	2,800.	350.
On cover		1,000.
Split grill	3,000.	380.
Double grill	—	550.
Grill omitted	4,000.	—

Earliest documented cover: Apr. 2, 1869

93 *Landing of Columbus. Type II has a diamond ornament under the "T" of* "POSTAGE," *a line has been drawn around the circumference of the central design so that picture appears to be framed. Some diagonal shading lines have been drawn around the base of the picture.*

93t *Inverted center*

93 *(119)*

15c brown and blue, Type II	1,200.	160.
dark brown and blue	1,200.	160.
On cover		800.
Plate block of eight, with imprint	20,000.	
Double transfer	—	—
Split grill	1,300.	180.
Double grill	2,100.	295.
v. Center inverted	180,000.	14,500.
v1. Center doubled, one inverted	—	—

Earliest documented cover: May 23, 1869

94 *Declaration of Independence*

94t *Inverted Center*

94 (120)

24c green and violet	3,100.	550.
bluish green and violet	3,100.	550.
On cover		10,000.
Split grill	3,100.	550.
Double grill	—	1,000.
Grill omitted	5,600.	—
v. Center inverted	160,000.	16,000.
On cover		110,000.

Earliest documented cover: Apr. 7, 1869

95 *Shield, Eagle, and Flags*

95 (121)

30c blue and carmine	3,100.	350.
dull blue and dark carmine	3,100.	350.
On cover		16,000.
Split grill	3,200.	300.
Double grill	—	650.
Grill omitted	4,500.	—
Double paper, grill omitted	3,800.	—
v. Flags inverted	170,000.	57,000.

Earliest documented cover: May 22, 1869

96 *Abraham Lincoln*

96 (122)

90c carmine and black	6,000.	1,250.
carmine rose and black	6,000.	1,250.
On cover		—
Split grill	—	—
Grill omitted	11,000.	—

SPECIAL PRINTINGS

1875. Re-Issues of the 1869 Issue. Again the dies were available, and a new plate was made for the 1c and for the frame of the 15c. The frame is similar to the Type I of the 1869 issue except that it is without the fringe of brown shading lines around the central vignette. *Printed by the National Bank Note Co., without grill, printed in intaglio on hard white paper, with white crackly gum and perforated 12.*

SP21 (123)

1c buff (approx. 2,750 copies sold)	335.	230.

SP22 (124)

2c brown (4,755 copies)	385.	330.

SP23 (125)

3c ultramarine (1,406 copies)	3,000.	*10,000.*

SP24 (126)

6c ultramarine (2,226 copies)	900.	600.

SP25 (127)

10c yellow (1,947 copies)	1,400.	1,200.

SP26 (128)

12c bright green (1,584 copies)	1,500.	1,250.

SP27 (129)

15c brown and blue, Type III (1,981 copies)	1,400.	600.
a. Imperforate horizontally (single stamp)	1,650.	

SP28 (130)

24c deep green and violet (2,091)	1,300.	600.

SP29 (131)

30c bright blue and carmine (1,356)	1,750.	1,000.

SP30 (132)

90c carmine and black (1,356)	3,800.	*4,300.*

1880. Re-Issue of 1889 Issue *on soft porus paper, without grill. Perforated 12. Printed by the American Bank Note Co.*

SP31 (133)

1c buff, without gum (approx. 2,500)	210.	190.
Plate block of 10, with imprint	18,000.	
brown orange, without gum (approx. 3,000 copies)	180.	125.

1870-71. National Bank Note Company Printing. The short-lived pictorial issue of 1869 was replaced by a series of new portraits, produced by the National Bank Note Company. The new stamps were issued both with and without grills. The grilled stamps are listed as Nos. 97-107 and the ungrilled stamps are Nos. 108-118. The grills are of two sizes, *Grill H,* about 10 x 12 mm with sharp tips on the grill points, and *Grill I,* about 8 1/2 x 10 mm having rather blunt tips on the grill points. Grill H was used on all values while Grill I was used only on the 1c through 7c values. *Intaglio on thin to medium thick white wove paper, unwatermarked, and perforated 12.*

Nos. 97-107 are with grill

97, 108 *Benjamin Franklin after bust by Rubricht.*
The pearl at the left of the numeral "1" is clear

97 *(134)*

1c ultramarine, grill H		850.	65.
dark ultramarine		850.	65.
dull ultramarine		850.	65.
On cover			90.
Double transfer		900.	70.
Split grill		925.	75.
Quadruple split grill		—	225.
Double grill		—	130.
v. Grill I		—	—

Earliest documented cover: Apr. 9, 1870

98, 109 *Andrew Jackson after bust by Hiram Powers.*

In the notch formed underneath the semi-circular ornament to the left of the "S" of "U.S." the lines forming the notch do not quite join at the apex of the notch. This stamp is always of a red brown shade.

98 *(135)*

2c red brown, grill H		480.	38.
dark red brown		480.	38.
dull red brown		480.	38.
On cover			57.
Split grill		525.	50.
Quadruple split grill		1,200.	125.
Double grill		650.	80.
v. Diagonal bisect on cover			—
v1. Grill I		—	—

Earliest documented cover: Sept. 1, 1870

99, 110 *George Washington. Under the word "THREE," the long tail of the ribbon is lightly shaded along its lower edge*

99 *(136)*

3c green, grill H		370.	10.
deep green		370.	10.
pale green		370.	10.
yellow green		370.	10.
On cover			15.
Plate block of ten, with imprint	5,500.		
Plate block of twelve, with imprint	6,500.		
Cracked plate		—	50.
Double transfer		—	12.
Split grill		400.	12.
Quadruple split grill		—	75.

Double grill		550.	40.
v. Grill I		—	—
v1. Printed on both sides		—	—

Earliest documented cover: Mar. 25, 1870

100, 111 *Abraham Lincoln after bust by Leonard Volk. The first four vertical lines of the shading in the lower part of the left ribbon, to the left and downward from the "S" of "SIX," are of normal strength*

100 *(137)*

6c carmine, grill H		2,000.	300.
carmine rose		2,000.	300.
dull carmine		2,000.	300.
On cover			500.
Split grill		2,200.	375.
Quadruple split grill		—	570.
Double grill		—	500.
v. Grill I		—	—

Earliest documented cover: Aug. 1870

101, 112 *Edwin Stanton. Edwin M. Stanton, Attorney General under Buchanan and Secretary of War under Lincoln and Johnson, actively opposed the latter's Reconstruction policies. An attempt to dismiss him served as the pretext for Johnson's impeachment in 1868. Appointed to the Supreme Court in 1869, Stanton died before he could take office.*

There are no semi-circles around the ends of the lines forming the ball in the lower right corner

101 *(138)*

7c vermilion, grill H		1,325.	275.
On cover			450.
Split grill		1,400.	300.
Quadruple split grill		—	500.
Double grill		—	450.
v. Grill I		—	—

102, 113, 138 *Thomas Jefferson after bust by Hiram Powers. The scroll ornament at the right end of the upper label, below the letter "E" of "POSTAGE," is clear*

Earliest documented cover: Feb. 12, 1871

102 *(139)*

10c brown	1,800.	450.
dark brown	1,800.	450.
yellow brown	1,800.	450.
On cover		750.
Split grill	1,900.	500.
Double grill	—	800.

Earliest documented cover: June 11, 187

103, 114 *Henry Clay after bust by Joel T. Hart. Clay was the first prominent Speaker of the House and "The Great Pacificator" of the Senate, where he effected compromises between slavery and anti-slavery forces. Twice a candidate for President, in 1824 he threw his electoral votes to John Quincy Adams, defeating Jackson, and served as Adams' Secretary of State.*

The "2" in the figure "12" has balls nearly round in shape at the upper and lower portion of the figure

103 *(140)*

12c pale violet	14,000.	1,750.
On cover		4,700.
Split grill	—	1,850.

Earliest documented cover: Feb. 9, 1872

104, 115 *Daniel Webster after bust by S.V. Clevenger. (For Webster's biography, see CM115) The thin lines shading the triangles, and below the letters "U.S. POSTAGE" are fine but of normal color and strength*

104 *(141)*

15c orange	2,600.	750.
bright orange	2,600.	750.
dark orange	2,600.	750.
On cover		1,350.
Split grill	2,500.	820.
Double grill	—	—

Earliest documented cover: Oct. 29, 1870

105, 116, 129 *Gen. Winfield Scott after bust by Coffee (For Scott biography, see CM173)*

105 *(142)*

24c purple	—	*10,000.*
dull purple	—	*10,000.*
On cover	—	—
Split grill	—	—

106, 117 *Alexander Hamilton was Washington's aide and secretary during the Revolution and commanded troops at Yorktown. One of the drafters of the Constitution, he advocated extremely strong central government. As first Secretary of the Treasury, "the Hamiltonian system" established the fiscal policy, strengthened federal government and the public credit, promoted industrialization as opposed to Jefferson's concept of an agricultural economy, and aroused factionalism which led to the development of political parties in America. Thwarting Aaron Burr's election as President in 1800 and as governor of New York in 1804, he was killed by the latter in a pistol duel.*

106 *(143)*

30c black	3,750.	550.
Deep black	3,750.	550.
On cover		2,100.
Double grill		—

Earliest documented cover: Aug. 1870

107 *(144)*

90c carmine	4,250.	550.
Dark carmine	4,250.	550.
On cover		—
Double grill		—
Split grill		1,100.

National Bank Note Company Printing

1870-71. Same as Nos. 97-07, but without grill

108 *(145)*

1c ultramarine	120.	5.00
dark ultramarine	120.	5.00
gray blue	120.	5.00
pale ultramarine	120.	5.00
On cover		—
Double transfer	—	15.
Worn plate	300.	10.

Earliest documented cover: July 18, 1870

109 *(146)*

2c red brown	90.	3.50
dark red brown	90.	3.50
orange brown	90.	3.50
pale red brown	90.	3.50
On cover		7.50
Bisect (any) on cover		—
Double transfer	—	8.00
v. Double impression	—	

Earliest documented cover: June 11, 1870

110 *(147)*

3c green	90.	.50
dark green	90.	.50
pale green	90.	.50
yellow green	90.	.50
On cover		1.50
Plate block of ten, with imprint	1,750.	
Double transfer	—	8.00
Cracked plate	—	4.50
Worn plate	225.	1.00
v. Double impression	—	1,000.
v1. Printed both sides	—	1,500.

Earliest documented cover: March 13, 1870

111 *(148)*

6c carmine	175.	7.50
brown carmine	175.	7.50
dark carmine	175.	7.50
rose	175.	7.50
violet carmine	175.	7.50
On cover		135.
Vertical bisect on cover		—
Double paper	—	—
Double transfer	—	—
v. Double impression	—	1,250.

Earliest documented cover: March 28, 1870

112 *(149)*

7c vermilion	200.	30.
deep vermilion	200.	30.
On cover		140.
Cracked plate	—	—
Double transfer	—	

Earliest documented cover: May 11, 1871

113 *(150)*

10c brown	185.	9.00
dark brown	185.	9.00
yellow brown	185.	9.00
On cover		30.
Double transfer	—	60.

Earliest documented cover: May 1870

114 *(151)*

12c pale violet	400.	40.
dark violet	400.	40.
violet	400.	40.
On cover		350.

Earliest documented cover: July 9, 1870

115 *(152)*

15c orange	400.	50.
deep orange	400.	50.
On cover		225.
v. Double impression	—	

Earliest documented cover: Sept. 24, 1870

116 *(153)*

24c purple	400.	50.
bright purple	400.	50.
dark purple	400.	50.
dull purple	400.	50.
On cover		1,250.
Double paper	—	—

Earliest documented cover: Nov. 18, 1870

117 *(154)*

30c black	950.	75.
On cover		675.

Earliest documented cover: Jan. 31, 1871

118 *(155)*

90c carmine	950.	100.
dark carmine	950.	100.
On cover		—

Earliest documented cover: Sept. 1, 1872

1873. The Continental Bank Note Company Printing.
The Continental Bank Note Company was awarded the printing contract for the period of May 1, 1873, through April 30, 1877. This contract later was extended until this company was consolidated with the American Bank Note Company on February 4, 1879. When Continental took over the printing contract, it took over some of the plates and the dies used by National in the production of the stamps of 1870-71. While the designs of the stamps printed by Continental are similar or identical to those printed by National, the 1c through 12c easily may be identified because the Continental stamps had so-called "secret marks." The 15c can be distinguished by plate wear and some shade variation, and the 30c and 90c can be distinguished by slight shade differences. The stamps were printed on hard, white wove paper, varying from thin to thick, that generally is difficult or impossible to differentiate from the paper used by National. *The paper is unwatermarked and the stamps are printed by intaglio and perforated 12.*

119, 132 *Benjamin Franklin. In the pearl at the left of the numeral "1" there is a small dash of color*

119 *(156)*

1c ultramarine	70.	1.25
blue	70.	1.25
dark ultramarine	70.	1.25
dull ultramarine	70.	1.25
gray blue	70.	1.25
On cover		3.25
Plate block of 12, with imprint	2,500.	
"Cogwheel" punch cut in paper	275.	
Cracked plate	—	—
Double paper	—	
Double transfer	2.00	5.00
p. Paper with silk fibers	—	17.50
p1. Ribbed paper	175.	3.25
v. With grill	1,500.	
v1. Pair, imperforate	—	500.

Earliest documented cover: Aug. 22, 1873

120, 121, 133 *Andrew Jackson.*
In the notch formed underneath the semi-circular ornament immediately to the left of the "S" of "U.S." the lines forming the apex of the notch join in a small point of color

120 *(157)*

2c brown	115.	7.00
dark brown	115.	7.00
dark red brown	115.	7.00
yellow brown	115.	7.00
On cover		17.50
Vertical bisect on cover		—
Cracked plate	—	—
Double paper	400.	25.
Double transfer	—	17.50
With secret mark	325.	14.
p. Ribbed paper	300.	14.
v. Double impression	—	
v1. With grill	1,300.	550.

Earliest documented cover: July 12, 1873

121 *(178)*

2c vermilion	115.	3.50
On cover		8.50
Plate block of 12, with imprint	—	
Double paper	—	—
Double transfer	—	—
p. Paper with silk fibers	325.	9.00
p1. Ribbed paper	—	—
p2. With grill	350.	

Earliest documented cover: July 15, 1875

122, 134 *George Washington.*
Under the word "THREE," the long tail of the ribbon is heavily shaded along its lower edge

122 *(158)*

3c green	40.	.20
bluish green	40.	.20
dark green	40.	.20
yellow green	40.	.20
dark yellow green	40.	.20
olive green	40.	.20
On cover		40.
Plate block of ten, with imprint	1,500.	
Plate block of 12, with imprint	2,250.	
Plate strip of five, with imprint	600.	
Plate strip of six, with imprint	675.	
"Cogwheel" punch cut in paper	200.	150.
Cracked plate	—	30.
Double transfer	—	4.50
Double paper	150.	5.00

Short transfer	—	12.50
p. Ribbed paper	75.	1.50
p1. Paper with silk fibers	—	4.50
p2. With grill	200.	
v. Double impression	—	1,100.
v1. Printed on both sides	—	
v2. Horizontal pair, imperforate between	—	1,200.
v3. Horizontal pair, imperforate vertically	—	

Earliest documented cover: July 9, 1873

123, 136 *Zachary Taylor. This is an historically interesting stamp for it marked the inauguration of the Universal Postal Union, setting a 5c rate for mail abroad and the blue color which was generally adhered to after 1898. Also standing almost unique in a changing world is the fact the 5c rate for a letter to Europe stood for 78 years, until November 1, 1953, when the rate was changed to 8c*

123 *(179)*

5c Prussian blue	145.	5.50
bright blue	145.	5.50
dark blue	145.	5.50
greenish blue	145.	5.50
pale blue	145.	5.50
On cover		22.50
Cracked plate	—	125.
Double paper	450.	—
Double transfer	—	20.
p. Paper with silk fibers	—	20.
p1. Ribbed paper	—	—
p2. With grill	700.	

Earliest documented cover: July 12, 1875

124, 137 *Abraham Lincoln.*
The first four vertical lines of the shading in the lower part of the left ribbon, to the left and downward from the "S" in "SIX" have been made heavier

124 *(159)*

6c dull Venetian red	140.	7.00
brown rose	140.	7.00
rose	140.	7.00
On cover		37.50
Plate block of 12, with imprint	11,000.	
Double paper	—	
p. Paper with silk fibers	—	32.50
p1. Ribbed paper	—	14.
p2. With grill	1,250.	

Earliest documented cover: July 24, 1873

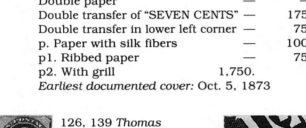

*125 Edwin Stanton.
A small semi-circle has
been drawn around each
end of the two lines that
outline the ball in the
lower right corner*

125 *(160)*

7c vermilion		300.	30.
dark vermilion		300.	30.
On cover			150.
Plate block of 12, with imprint		—	
Double paper		—	—
Double transfer of "SEVEN CENTS"	—		175.
Double transfer in lower left corner	—		75.
p. Paper with silk fibers		—	100.
p1. Ribbed paper		—	75.
p2. With grill		1,750.	

Earliest documented cover: Oct. 5, 1873

*126, 139 Thomas
Jefferson.
The scroll ornament at
the right end of the upper
label, below the letter "E"
of "POSTAGE," has a
small crescent of color within it*

126 *(161)*

10c brown		200.	8.00
dark brown		200.	8.00
yellow brown		200.	8.00
On cover			25.
Plate block of ten, with imprint		8,750.	
Plate block of 12, with imprint		9,250.	
Double paper		550.	
Double transfer		—	
p. Paper with silk fibers		—	25.
p1. Ribbed paper		—	22.50
p2. With grill		2,250.	
v. Horizontal pair, imperforate between		—	2,250.

Earliest documented cover: Aug. 2, 1873

*127 Henry Clay.
The balls of the figure
"2" are crescent shaped
instead of nearly round*

127 *(162)*

12c blackish violet		500.	40.
On cover			300.
p. Ribbed paper		—	75.
p1. With grill		3,500.	

Earliest documented cover: Jan. 3, 1874

*128, 140 Daniel Webster.
The thin lines shading the
triangles and below the
letter "U.S. POSTAGE" are
worn. These areas show
less color and therefore
appear more white than the 15c National Printing*

128 *(163)*

15c yellow orange		475.	37.50
dull orange		475.	37.50
red orange		475.	37.50
On cover			250.
Double paper		—	
p. Paper with silk fibers		1,250.	80.
p1. Paper with vertical ribs		1,100.	75.
p2. With grill		3,500.	

Earliest documented cover: July 22, 1873

*The 24c Continental has been the subject of much
controversy. It is known that 365,000 copies of this stamp
were printed and delivered to the Stamp Agent, but there is
no proof that any of them were issued to post offices. In
1885, 364,950 copies of the 24c stamps were destroyed,
for they were no longer needed to make up the then-existing
postage rates. It is not known whether or not these were all
Continentals. Some experts think that unused examples can
be distinguished by their gum, with the Continentals
bearing a thinner and lighter colored gum than the
Nationals. Another possible means of identification lies in
the paper. The Continental 24c was printed from the same
plate as the National 24c, so they are identical in design.
The Philatelic Foundation issued a certificate of
genuineness to a 24c on vertically ribbed paper; experts
believe that only Continental used such paper. The listing
below is based on that single item.*

129 *(164)*

24c light purple		—	—

*The 30c Continental and 30c National are identical except
in shade.*

130 *(165)*

30c gray black		600.	37.50
greenish black		600.	37.50
On cover			625.
Double paper		—	85.
Double transfer		—	625.
p. Paper with silk fibers		—	
p1. Ribbed paper		1,250.	75.
p2. With grill		3,500.	

Earliest documented cover: Oct. 30, 1874

*The 90c Continental and the 90c National are identical
except in shade.*

131 *(166)*

90c rose carmine		1,100.	105.
dull rose carmine		1,100.	105.
On cover			5,500.

SPECIAL PRINTING

1875. Special Printings of the 1873 Issue, which was still in use. Printed by the Continental Bank Note Co. by intaglio on hard white wove paper, perforated 12, and issued without gum. For some reason, these stamps usually were cut apart with scissors so that the perforations generally are mutilated. The special printing can be identified by the color shades and by the very white paper (instead of the yellowish of the original issue). Numbers sold are not known. Some estimate can be made by studying the table that follows SP57.

SP32 *(167)*
  1c bright ultramarine   7,250.
SP33 *(168)*
  2c blackish brown   3,000.
SP34 *(180)*
  2c carmine vermilion   20,000.
SP35 *(169)*
  3c bluish green   9,250.
SP36 *(181)*
  5c bright blue   27,500.
SP37 *(170)*
  6c pale rose   8,000.
SP38 *(171)*
  7c scarlet vermilion   1,500.
SP39 *(172)*
  10c yellow brown   8,000.
SP40 *(173)*
  12c black violet   2,750.
SP41 *(174)*
  15c bright orange   8,000.
SP42 *(175)*
  24c dull purple   1,750.
SP43 *(176)*
  30c greenish black   5,750.
SP44 *(177)*
  90c violet carmine   7,500.

1879-88. American Bank Note Company absorbed the Continental Bank Note Company on February 4, 1879, and continued to print postage, department, and newspaper stamps. American used many of the plates bearing the Continental imprints, so the imprint does not always accurately indicate the producing firm. The American Bank Note Company printed on unwatermarked soft, porous paper instead of the hard paper used by National and Continental. With the exception of one type of the 10c, all the stamps from 1c through the 12c carry the same "secret marks" as the Continentals. With the exception of the color changes on the 3c, 30c, and 90c that were issued later, these stamps were issued in 1879. *All were printed by intaglio and perforated 12.*

132 *(182)*
  1c dark ultramarine   75.   1.00
    blue   75.   1.00
    gray blue   75.   1.00
    On cover   2.25

Plate block of ten, with imprint 3,000.
Double transfer   —   6.00
Earliest documented cover: April 25, 1879

133 *(183)*
  2c vermilion   45.   1.00
    orange vermilion   45.   1.00
    On cover   2.25
Plate block of ten, with imprint 1,250.
Plate block of 12, with imprint 1,750.
Double transfer   —
Double impression   —   400.
Earliest documented cover: Feb. 4, 1879

134 *(184)*
  3c green   35.   .25
    dark green   35.   .25
    dull green   35.   .25
    On cover   .50
Plate block of ten, with imprint 800.
Plate block of 12, with imprint 1,000.
Plate block of 14, with imprint 1,300.
Double transfer   —   4.00
Short transfer   —   5.00
Double impression   —   —
Earliest documented cover: Feb. 7, 1879

135 *(214)*
  3c vermilion   45.   20.
    On cover   75.
Plate block of ten, with imprint 900.
Plate block of 12, with imprint 1,100.
Plate strip of five, with imprint 350.
Plate strip of six, with imprint 400.
Earliest documented cover: Oct. 18, 1887

136 *(185)*
  5c blue   145.   6.00
    bright blue   145.   6.00
    dark blue   145.   6.00
    dull blue   145.   6.00
    On cover   17.50
Plate block of 12, with imprint 7,000.
Earliest documented cover: May 12, 1879

137 *(186)*
  6c dull pink   257.   8.50
    brown pink   257.   8.50
    pink   257.   8.50
    On cover   32.50
Earliest documented cover: July 1, 1879

138 *(187)*
  10c brown, like No. 102, but no
      secret mark   550.   12.50
    yellow brown   550.   12.50
    On cover   35.
    Double transfer   —   30.
Earliest documented cover: Sept. 5, 1879

139 *(188)*
10c brown, like No. 126, with

secret mark	425.	12.50
black brown	425.	12.50
yellow brown	425.	12.50
On cover		32.50
Cracked plate	—	—
Double transfer	—	35.
Pair, one each Nos. 138,139	—	200.
v. Vertical pair, imperforate		
between	—	

Earliest documented cover: Feb. 21, 1879

140 *(189)*
15c orange

	100.	11.
red orange	100.	11.
yellow orange	100.	11.
On cover		75.
Plate block of 12, with imprint 5,750.		

Earliest documented cover: Jan. 20, 1879

141 *(190)*
30c black

	300.	22.50
greenish black	300.	22.50
On cover		375.
Plate block of ten, with		
imprint	8,500.	

Earliest documented cover: Nov. 13, 1882

142 *(217)*
30c orange brown

	325.	40.
dark orange brown	325.	40.
On cover		1,200.
Plate block of ten, with imprint 6,000.		
Plate block of 12, with imprint	—	
Plate strip of five, with imprint 2,200.		

Earliest documented cover: Sept. 22, 1888

143 *(191)*
90c carmine

	725.	95.
carmine rose	725.	95.
rose	725.	95.
On cover		4,000.
Double paper	—	—

Earliest documented cover: June 17, 1880

SPECIAL PRINTING

1880. Special Printings of the 1879 Issue by the
American Bank Note Co.. Previous designs on *soft
porous paper, printed by intaglio, perforated 12.*

SP45 *(192)*
  1c deep ultramarine   9,000.
SP46 *(193)*
  2c blackish brown   5,750.
SP47 *(203)*
  2c scarlet vermilion   13,500.
SP48 *(194)*
  3c bluish green   11,000.

SP49 *(204)*
  5c deep blue   2,000.
SP50 *(195)*
  6c pale rose   9,500.
SP51 *(196)*
  7c scarlet vermilion   3,500.
SP52 *(197)*
  10c deep brown   11,250.
SP53 *(198)*
  12c black purple   3,500.
SP54 *(199)*
  15c orange   7,500.
SP55 *(200)*
  24c blackish violet   8,750.
SP56 *(201)*
  30c greenish black   18,500.
SP57 *(202)*
  90c pale carmine   30,000.

The Post Office Department kept no separate records of
the sales of the 1875 and 1880 Special Printings, but did
list the combined sales. The 1880 printing is the scarcer
of the two.

	Cat. Nos.	Combined Total Printed
1c	SP32, SP45	388
2c	SP33, SP46	416
2c	SP34, SP47	917
3c	SP35, SP48	267
5c	SP36, SP49	317
6c	SP37, SP50	185
7c	SP38, SP51	473
10c	SP39, SP52	180
12c	SP40, SP53	282
15c	SP41, SP54	169
24c	SP42, SP55	286
30c	SP43, SP56	179
90c	SP44, SP57	170

144 *(218)*
90c dark red violet

	750.	85.
bright purple	750.	85.
On cover		6,500.
Plate block of ten, with imprint 18,500.		
Plate block of 12, with imprint	—	
Plate strip of five, with imprint 5,000.		

1881-82. Re-Engraved Designs of 1873 for the 1c, 3c,
6c, and 10c denominations. They were printed by the
American Bank Note Company by *intaglio on soft porous,
unwatermarked paper and were perforated 12.*

145 *The vertical lines forming the background in the
upper part of the stamp have been made much heavier
and the background now appears to be almost solid.
Lines of shading also have been added to the curving
ornaments in the upper corners of the stamp*

Preceding design   Re-engraved

145 (206)

1c ultramarine		
	22.50	.35
bright ultramarine	22.50	.35
dull blue	22.50	.35
gray blue	22.50	.35
On cover		1.00
Plate block of ten, with imprint	900.	
Plate block of 12, with imprint	1,000.	
Plate strip of five, with imprint	300.	
Plate strip of six, with imprint	350.	
"Cogwheel" punch cut in paper	125.	
Double transfer	65.	3.50

Earliest documented cover: Dec. 5, 1881

Preceding design   Re-engraved

146 *The shading at the sides of the large central oval is only about half the previous thickness. A short horizontal dash has been added just below the "TS" of "CENTS"*

146 (207)

3c blue green		
	27.50	.20
green	27.50	.20
yellow green	27.50	.20
On cover		.75
Plate block of ten, with imprint	1,100.	
Plate strip of five, with imprint	350.	
Cracked plate	—	
Double transfer	—	7.00
v. Punched with eight small holes in a circle	150.	
v1. Plate block of ten, with imprint	2,000.	
v2. Double impression	—	—

Earliest documented cover: Oct. 24, 1881

147 *There are only three vertical lines from the outside of the panel to the outside of the stamps. The preceding issue had four lines*

147 (208)

6c rose		
	150.	27.50
dull rose	150.	27.50
brown red	125.	30.
On cover		125.
Double transfer	450.	65.
Block of four	1,600.	

Earliest documented cover: Sept. 27, 1882

148 *There are only four vertical lines between the left side of the oval and the edge of the shield while the preceding issues had five lines. The lines of the background have been made heavier so that these stamps appear much more heavily inked than their predecessors*

148 (209)

10c brown		
	50.	1.50
olive brown	50.	1.50
orange brown	50.	1.50
purple brown	50.	1.50
yellow brown	50.	1.50
black brown	100.	9.00
On cover		7.00
Plate block of ten, with imprint	1,500.	
Plate block of 12, with imprint	1,800.	
Plate strip of five, with imprint	650.	
Plate strip of six, with imprint	750.	
v. Double impression	—	

Earliest documented cover: May 11, 1882

1882-88. New designs. American Bank Note Company. *Intaglio by American Bank Note Company. Unwatermarked soft porous paper, perforated 12.*

149 *Benjamin Franklin*

149 (209)

1c ultramarine		
	32.50	.65
bright ultramarine	32.50	.65
On cover		1.50
Plate block of ten, with imprint	1,000.	
Plate block of 12, with imprint	1,250.	
Plate strip of five, with imprint	450.	
Plate strip of six, with imprint	550.	
Double transfer	—	

Earliest documented cover: July 28, 1887

150, 151 *George Washington. This stamp was issued to pay the reduced rate for first class letters as provided by an Act of Congress approved March 3, 1883, and effective October 1, 1883*

150 *(210)*

2c red brown *(Oct. 1, 1883)*	20.	.20
dark red brown	20.	.20
orange brown	20.	.20
On cover		.50
Plate block of ten, with imprint	750.	
Plate block of 12, with imprint	1,000.	
Plate strip of five, with imprint	225.	
Plate strip of six, with imprint	375.	
Double transfer	40.	1.25

151 *(213)*

2c green	15.	.20
bright green	15.	.20
dark green	15.	.20
On cover		.75
Plate block of ten, with imprint	650.	
Plate block of 12, with imprint	750.	
Plate strip of five, with imprint	175.	
Plate strip of six, with imprint	240.	
Double transfer	—	2.50
v. Printed on both sides	—	—

Earliest documented cover: Sept. 21, 1887

152, 153 *Andrew Jackson. This denomination was issued to take care of the rate on first class letters of double weight*

152 *(211)*

4c deep bluish green *(Oct. 1, 1883)*	80.	4.00
blue green	80.	4.00
On cover		32.50
Plate block of 12, with imprint	3,500.	
Plate strip of six, with imprint	1,200.	
Cracked plate	—	
Double transfer	—	
v. Horizontal pair, imperforate between	—	

SPECIAL PRINTING

1883. Special Printings of the 2c and 4c Stamps of 1883. Printed by the American Bank Note Co. *by intaglio on soft porous paper, the 2c with gum and the 4c without gum, both perforated 12.* Quantities are not known.

SP59 *(211B)*

2c red brown	600.
v. Horizontal pair, imperforate between	1,800.

SP60 *(211D)*

4c blue green	14,500.

153 *(215)*

4c carmine	75.	7.50
dull rose	75.	7.50
rose carmine	75.	7.50
On cover		35.
Plate block of ten, with imprint	3,000.	
Plate block of 12, with imprint	3,850.	
Plate strip of five, with imprint	1,000.	
Plate strip of six, with imprint	1,100.	
Double transfer	—	

Earliest documented cover: July 11, 1889

154 *James Garfield. This design was issued to honor the late President, assassinated while in office*

154 *(205)*

5c olive brown *(April 10, 1882)*	80.	3.00
brown	80.	3.00
gray brown	80.	3.00
On cover		12.50
Plate block of 12, with imprint	3,500.	
Plate strip of five, with imprint	900.	
Plate strip of six, with imprint	1,100.	

SPECIAL PRINTING

1882. Special Printing of the 5c Garfield stamp of 1882 is very difficult to distinguish from the regular printing of the same year. The special printing was produced by the American Bank Note Co. *Intaglio on soft porous paper, without gum, perforated 12.*

SP58 *(205C)*

5c light brownish gray	—
(2,463 sold)	

155 *(216)*

5c indigo	75.	4.00
dark blue	75.	4.00
blue	75.	4.00
On cover		20.
Plate block of ten, with imprint	3,000.	
Plate block of 12, with imprint	3,750.	
Plate strip of five, with imprint	900.	
Plate strip of six, with imprint	1,100.	

Earliest documented cover: April 7, 1888

1890. The American Bank Note Company produced this issue in a smaller size than had been used previously. All these stamps are *intaglio on unwatermarked soft porous paper, perforated 12.*

156 *Benjamin Franklin*

156 *(219)*
1c dull blue *(Feb. 22, 1890)*	17.50	.20
blue	17.50	.20
dark blue	17.50	.20
ultramarine	17.50	.20
On cover		.50
Plate block of ten, with imprint	450.	
Plate block of 12, with imprint	600.	
Plate block of 14, with imprint	750.	
Plate strip of five, with imprint	125.	
Plate strip of six, with imprint	150.	
Plate strip of seven, with imprint	175.	
Double transfer	—	—

159 *Andrew Jackson* 160 *Abraham Lincoln*

159 *(221)*
3c dark lilac *(Feb. 22, 1890)*	47.50	5.00
bright lilac	47.50	5.00
lilac	47.50	5.00
On cover		12.50
Plate block of ten, with imprint	1,750.	
Plate strip of five, with imprint	350.	

160 *(222)*
4c dark brown	47.50	2.00
black brown	47.50	2.00
On cover		11.
Plate block of ten, with imprint	1,800.	
Plate strip of five, with imprint	350.	
Double transfer	70.	

Earliest documented cover: Oct. 22, 1890

158t *Cap on left "2"*   158t1 *Cap on right "2"*

157, 158 *George Washington*

157 *(219D)*
2c lake *(Feb. 22, 1890)*	125.	.60
bright lilac carmine	125.	.60
lilac carmine	125.	.60
On cover		1.25
Plate block of ten, with imprint	2,750.	
Plate strip of five, with imprint	800.	
Double transfer	—	—

158 *(220)*
2c carmine	14.	.20
carmine rose	14.	.20
dark carmine	14.	.20
On cover		.50
Plate block of ten, with imprint	400.	
Plate block of 12, with imprint	500.	
Plate block of 14, with imprint	650.	
Plate strip of five, with imprint	100.	
Plate strip of six, with imprint	130.	
Plate strip of seven, with imprint	150.	
Double transfer	—	2.50
v. Cap on left "2"	60.	1.50
Plate block of 12, with imprint	1,250.	
v1. Pair, one with cap, one without		—
v2. Cap on both "2"'s	150.	12.50
v3. Pair, one with cap on one "2," one with cap on both "2"'s	—	—

Earliest documented cover: May 31, 1890

161 *Ulysses Grant*   162 *James Garfield*

161 *(223)*
5c chocolate	47.50	2.00
yellow brown	47.50	2.00
On cover		9.00
Plate block of ten, with imprint	1,750.	
Plate strip of five, with imprint	300.	
Double transfer	70.	2.00

Earliest documented cover: June 14, 1890

162 *(224)*
6c brown red *(Feb. 22, 1890)*	50.	15.
dark brown red	50.	15.
On cover		30.
Plate block of ten, with imprint	1,800.	
Plate strip of five, with imprint	350.	

163 *W.T. Sherman*   164 *Daniel Webster*

163 *(225)*
8c purple brown	37.50	9.00
gray lilac	37.50	9.00
magenta	37.50	9.00
On cover		25.
Plate block of ten, with imprint	1,250.	
Plate strip of five, with imprint	300.	

Earliest documented cover: May 21, 1893

164 *(226)*

10c deep bluish green *(Feb. 22, 1890)*	95.	2.25
dark green	95.	2.25
green	95.	2.25
On cover		7.00
Plate block of ten, with imprint 3,000.		
Plate strip of five, with imprint 800.		
Double transfer	—	—

165 *Henry Clay*   166 *Thomas Jefferson*

165 *(227)*

15c indigo *(Feb. 22, 1890)*	145.	16.
dark indigo	145.	16.
On cover		55.
Plate block of ten, with imprint 5,500.		
Plate strip of five, with imprint 750.		
Double transfer	—	—
Triple transfer	—	—

166 *(228)*

30c black *(Feb. 22, 1890)*	225.	19.
gray black	225.	19.
full black	225.	19.
On cover		500.
Plate block of ten, with imprint 1,450.		
Plate strip of five, with imprint 1,000.		
Double transfer	—	—

167 *Oliver Hazard Perry*

167 *(229)*

90c orange *(Feb. 22, 1890)*	325.	90.
red orange	325.	90.
yellow orange	325.	90.
On cover		—
Plate block of ten, with imprint 19,500.		
Plate strip of five, with imprint 2,250.		
Short transfer at bottom	—	—

Stamps of all values of the 1890 issue exist imperforate, which are considered finished proofs.

Issues of the Bureau of Engraving and Printing at Washington, D.C.

Issues from this point through the present have been printed by the Bureau of Engraving and Printing, except where otherwise noted.

1894. The first issue of stamps by the Bureau was very similar in design to the issue of 1890 but triangles were added to the upper corners of the stamps and there were some differences in the denominations issued. The stamps were *printed by intaglio on unwatermarked paper, and perforated 12.*

All of the perforation varieties listed here are believed to have been issued legitimately. Other perforation and imperforate varieties exist on some values, but they were not released through regular postal methods.

170-174, 189-192   168, 169, 187, 188
George Washington   *Benjamin Franklin*

I   II   III

170-172, 189 *Type I. The horizontal lines of background are of same thickness*

173, 190 *Type II. The horizontal lines are thin within the triangle*

174, 191, 192 *Type III. The horizontal lines are interrupted by the frame of the triangle and thin within the triangle*

168 *(246)*

1c ultramarine	20.	3.50
bright ultramarine	20.	3.50
dark ultramarine	20.	3.50
On cover		10.
Plate block of six, with imprint 250.		
Plate strip of three, with imprint 90.		
Double transfer	30.	4.00
Earliest documented cover: Oct. 24, 1894		

169 *(247)*

1c blue	47.50	2.00
bright blue	47.50	2.00
dark blue	47.50	2.00
On cover		14.
Plate block of six, with imprint 475.		
Plate strip of three, with imprint 225.		
Double transfer	—	3.00
Earliest documented cover: Nov. 11, 1894		

170 *(248)*

2c pink, triangle I		15.	3.00
dull pink		15.	3.00
On cover			10.
Plate block of six, with imprint	175.		
Plate strip of three, with imprint	75.		
Double transfer		—	—
v. Vertical pair, imperforate horizontally		2,250.	

Earliest documented cover: Oct. 20, 1894

171 *(249)*

2c carmine lake, triangle I		95.	2.00
dark carmine lake		95.	2.00
On cover			7.50
Plate block of six, with imprint	1,000.		
Plate strip of three, with imprint	400.		
Double transfer		—	2.50

Earliest documented cover: Oct. 11, 1894

172 *(250)*

2c carmine, triangle I		17.50	.35
dark carmine		17.50	.35
dull scarlet		17.50	.35
scarlet		17.50	.35
On cover			1.50
Plate block of six, with imprint	250.		
Plate strip of three, with imprint	100.		
Double transfer		—	1.25
v. Vertical pair, imperforate horizontally		1,750.	
v1. Horizontal pair, imperforate between		—	

Earliest documented cover: Oct. 19, 1894

173 *(251)*

2c carmine, triangle II		150.	3.25
dark carmine		150.	3.25
On cover			10.
Plate block of six, with imprint	1,900.		
Plate strip of three, with imprint	700.		

Earliest documented cover: Feb 18, 1895

174 *(252)*

2c carmine, triangle III		85.	3.50
dull carmine		85.	3.50
On cover			10.
Plate block of six, with imprint	1,100.		
Plate strip of three, with imprint	400.		
v. Horizontal pair, imperforate between		—	
v1. Horizontal pair, imperforate vertically		—	

Earliest documented cover: Oct. 11, 1894

175, 193
Andrew Jackson

176, 194, 195
Abraham Lincoln

175 *(253)*

3c dark lilac		60.	6.50
lilac		60.	6.50
On cover			20.
Plate block of six, with imprint	800.		
Plate strip of three, with imprint	350.		
Margin block of four, with arrow	375.		

Earliest documented cover: Jan. 5, 1895

176 *(254)*

4c dark brown		75.	3.50
brown		75.	3.50
On cover			15.
Plate block of six, with imprint	900.		
Plate strip of three, with imprint	425.		
Margin block of four, with arrow	500.		

Earliest documented cover: Jan. 5, 1895

177, 196, 197
Ulysses S. Grant

178, 198, 199
James Garfield

177 *(255)*

5c chocolate		65.	4.00
dark chocolate		65.	4.00
yellow brown		65.	4.00
On cover			15.
Plate block of six, with imprint	700.		
Plate strip of three, with imprint	300.		
Margin block of four, with arrow	325.		
Diagonal lines omitted in oval background (worn plate)		80.	5.00
Double transfer		85.	5.00
v. Vertical pair, imperforate horizontally		1,250.	

Earliest documented cover: Nov. 22, 1894

178 *(256)*

6c red brown		115.	17.50
On cover			37.50
Plate block of six, with imprint	1,800.		
Plate strip of three, with imprint	525.		
Margin block of four, with arrow	500.		
v. Vertical pair, imperforate horizontally		900.	

Earliest documented cover: Aug. 11, 1894

179, 200
W.T. Sherman

180, 201-203
Daniel Webster

179 *(257)*

8c purple brown	95.	12.50
dark purple brown	95.	12.50
On cover		37.50
Plate block of six, with imprint	900.	
Plate strip of three, with imprint	475.	
Margin block of four, with arrow	525.	
Earliest documented cover: Sept. 15, 1895		

180 *(258)*

10c blue green	150.	8.50
dark green	150.	8.50
dull green	150.	8.50
On cover		30.
Plate block of six, with imprint	1,800.	
Plate strip of three, with imprint	700.	
Double transfer	200.	9.00
Earliest documented cover: Nov. 19, 1894		

181, 204, 205
Henry Clay

182, 206
Thomas Jefferson

181 *(259)*

15c indigo	185.	40.
dark blue	185.	40.
On cover		80.
Plate block of six, with imprint	3,000.	
Plate strip of three, with imprint	875.	
Margin block of four, with arrow	900.	
Earliest documented cover: Feb. 20, 1895		

182 *(260)*

50c orange	275.	75.
dark orange	275.	75.
On cover		850.
Plate block of six, with imprint	4,250.	
Plate strip of three, with imprint	1,300.	
Margin block of four, with arrow	1,500.	
Earliest documented cover: Jan. 15, 1895		

183, 184, 207, 208
Oliver Hazard Perry

185, 209
James Madison

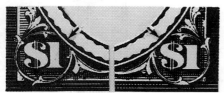

183, 207 *Type I.
Circles enclosing
"$1" are broken*

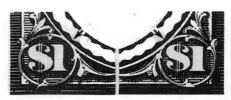

184, 208 *Type II.
Circles are
complete*

183 *(261)*

$1 black, Type I		
gray black	575.	225.
On cover		1,950.
Plate block of six, with imprint	12,500.	
Plate strip of three, with imprint	2,850.	
Margin block of four, with arrow	3,250.	
Earliest documented cover: Aug. 1895		

184 *(261A)*

$1 black, Type II		
gray black	1,500.	450.
On cover		3,400.
Plate block of six, with imprint (including 2 of No. 183)	22,000.	
Plate strip of three, with imprint (including 1 of No. 183)	4,800.	
Block of four, two each No.183,184	6,000.	
Pair, one each Type I and II	2,850.	
Margin block of four, with arrow	7,250.	
Earliest documented cover: March 22, 1895		

185 *(262)*

$2 dark blue	1,900.	650.
bright blue	1,900.	650.
On cover		3,400.
Plate block of six, with imprint	28,000.	
Plate strip of three, with imprint	9,750.	
Margin block of four, with arrow	10,500.	
Earliest documented cover: July 18, 1895		

 186, 210 John Marshall, after painting by Henry Inman, the first great Chief Justice of the United States, was appointed to the office by John Adams in 1801. In 34 brilliant and forceful years' service, he firmly established the Constitution as the supreme law of the land, and the Court as its final arbiter. In the case of Marbury vs. Madison in 1803, he created a precedent in setting aside an act of Congress as unconstitutional.186, 210 John Marshall, after painting by Henry Inman, the first great Chief Justice of the United States, was appointed to the office by John Adams in 1801. In 34 brilliant and forceful years' service, he firmly established the Constitution as the supreme law of the land, and the Court as its final arbiter. In the case of Marbury vs. Madison in 1803, he created a precedent in setting aside an act of Congress as unconstitutional.

186 *(263)*

$5 dark green	2,900.	1,250.
On cover		—
Plate strip of three, with imprint	—	
Margin block of four, with arrow	—	

1895-1898. Designs of 1894 on Watermarked Paper.
Although in the planning stages for some time, the
issuance of U.S. postage stamps on watermarked paper
coincided with the discovery of a counterfeit of the 2c
denomination. It was believed that the new paper would
add a measure of protection. The paper is watermarked
with the letters "USPS" in double-lined capital letters, each
letter 16 mm high and so arranged that on each pane of
100 stamps they appear 90 times. The watermarks appear
both horizontally and vertically on the stamps.

The color changes of 1898 are integrated with
this sequence of stamps. *Intaglio and perforated 12.*

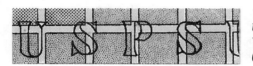

187 *Double-line
USPS
Watermark
(187)*

187 *(264)*

1c deep blue	5.00	.20
dark blue	5.00	.20
indigo	5.00	.20
pale blue	5.00	.20
On cover		1.00
Plate block of six, with imprint	150.	
Plate strip of three, with imprint	20.	
Double transfer	—	.75

Earliest documented cover: July 7, 1895

188 *(279)*

1c deep green *(Jan. 25, 1898)*	7.50	.20
dark green	7.50	.20
dark yellow green	7.50	.20
yellow green	7.50	.20
On cover		.50
Plate block of six, with imprint	150.	
Plate strip of three, with imprint	32.	
Double transfer	10.	

189 *(265)*

2c carmine, Type I	22.50	.90
dark carmine	22.50	.90
dull carmine	22.50	.90
On cover		2.00
Plate block of six, with imprint	300.	
Plate strip of three, with imprint	90.	
Double transfer	35.	3.00

Earliest documented cover: July 7, 1895

190 *(266)*

2c carmine, Type II	20.	3.00
dark carmine	20.	3.00
dull carmine	20.	3.00
On cover		6.00
Plate block of six, with imprint	300.	
Plate strip of three, with imprint	90.	
Horizontal pair, No. 189,190	60.	

Earliest documented cover: Oct. 25, 1895

191 *(267)*

2c carmine, Type III	4.00	.20
dark carmine	4.00	.20
dull carmine	4.00	.20
On cover		.50
Plate block of six, with imprint	100.	
Plate strip of three, with imprint	15.	
Double transfer	12.50	1.00
Triple transfer	—	
Shading omitted in right upper triangle (worn plate)	—	

Earliest documented cover: July 7, 1895

192 *(279B)*

2c red, type III	7.50	.20
deep red	7.50	.20
orange red	8.00	.30
rose carmine	150.	100.
On cover		.50
Plate block of six, with imprint	150.	
Plate strip of three, with imprint	32.	
Double transfer	15.	
n. Booklet pane of six	325.	

Earliest documented cover: Dec. 19, 1897

193 *(268)*

3c dark red violet	27.50	1.00
dark purple	27.50	1.00
dull purple	27.50	1.00
On cover		5.00
Plate block of six, with imprint	425.	
Plate strip of three, with imprint	120.	
Margin block of four, with arrow	140.	
Double transfer	35.	2.25

Earliest documented cover: Feb. 18, 1896

194 *(269)*

4c dark brown	27.50	1.50
black brown	27.50	1.50
dark yellow brown	27.50	1.50
On cover		7.50
Plate block of six, with imprint	450.	
Plate strip of three, with imprint	125.	
Margin block of four, with arrow	150.	
Double transfer	35.	2.50

Earliest documented cover: Oct. 12, 1895

195 *(280)*

4c chocolate *(Oct. 7, 1898)*	22.50	.90
brownish claret	22.50	.90
dark orange brown	22.50	.90
lilac brown	22.50	.90
orange brown	22.50	.90
rose brown	22.50	.90
On cover		8.00
Plate block of six, with imprint	450.	
Plate strip of three, with imprint	100.	
Margin block of four, with arrow	120.	
Double transfer	30.	1.25
Extra frame line at top	45.	3.50

196 *(270)*

5c dark orange brown	27.50	1.65
brown	27.50	1.65
dark red brown	27.50	1.65
reddish brown	27.50	1.65
On cover		6.00
Plate block of six, with imprint	400.	
Plate strip of three, with imprint	120.	
Diagonal lines omitted in oval		
background (worn plate)	32.50	2.25
Double transfer	35.	3.00
Margin block of four, with		
arrow	130.	

Earliest documented cover: Sept. 14, 1895

197 *(281)*

5c dark blue *(March 8, 1898)*	25.	.75
blue	25.	.75
bright blue	25.	.75
dull blue	25.	.75
On cover		8.00
Plate block of six, with imprint	450.	
Plate strip of three, with imprint	120.	
Diagonal lines omitted in oval		
background (worn plate)	35.	.75
Double transfer	40.	1.50
Margin block of four, with arrow	140.	

198 *(271)*

6c red brown	55.	4.00
dull brown	55.	4.00
On cover		22.50
Plate block of six, with imprint	1,100.	
Plate strip of three, with imprint	250.	
Margin block of four, with arrow	395.	
p. Thin paper	80.	4.00
w. Watermarked "USIR"	2,000.	325.

Earliest documented cover: Sept. 14, 1895

199 *(282)*

6c lake *(Dec. 31, 1898)*	35.	2.25
claret	35.	2.25
lilac carmine	35.	2.25
purple lake	42.50	3.00
On cover		14.
Plate block of six, with imprint	700.	
Plate strip of three, with imprint	150.	
Double transfer	52.50	3.00
Margin block of four, with arrow	150.	

200 *(272)*

8c purple brown	40.	1.25
dark lilac brown	40.	1.25
lilac brown	40.	1.25
On cover		11.
Plate block of six, with imprint	450.	
Plate strip of three, with imprint	200.	
Double transfer	62.50	2.25
Margin block of four, with arrow	220.	
w. Watermarked "USIR"	1,450.	85.

Earliest documented cover: Dec. 24, 1895

201, 202 *Type I. Oval below "TEN CENTS" is intact*

203 *Type II. Oval below "TEN CENTS" is broken by lines*

201 *(273)*

10c dark green, Type I	50.	1.25
green	50.	1.25
On cover		12.50
Plate block of six, with imprint	750.	
Plate strip of three, with imprint	275.	
Double transfer	80.	3.25

Earliest documented cover: Feb. 16, 1896

202 *(282C)*

10c brown, Type I *(Nov. 11, 1898)*	135.	2.50
dark brown	135.	2.50
On cover		12.50
Plate block of six, with imprint	700.	
Plate strip of three, with imprint	650.	
Double transfer	150.	4.00
Pair, one each (202, 203)	13,000.	

203 *(283)*

10c orange brown, Type II		
(Nov. 11, 1898)	75.	2.00
brown	75.	2.00
yellow brown	75.	2.00
On cover		14.
Plate block of six, with imprint	950.	
Plate strip of three, with imprint	400.	
Margin block of four, with arrow	425.	

204 *(274)*

15c indigo	150.	9.00
blackish blue	150.	9.00
On cover		50.
Plate block of six, with imprint	2,100.	
Plate strip of three, with imprint	700.	
Margin block of four, with arrow	725.	

Earliest documented cover: Feb. 27, 1897

205 *(284)*

15c olive green *(Nov. 30, 1898)*	115.	7.50
dark olive green	115.	7.50
On cover		27.50
Plate block of six, with imprint	1,500.	
Plate strip of three, with imprint	500.	
Margin block of four, with arrow	625.	

206 *(275)*

50c orange	200.	20.
dark red orange	200.	20.
dull red orange	200.	20.
red orange	200.	200.
On cover		325.
Plate block of six, with imprint 3,750.		
Plate strip of three, with imprint 850.		
Margin block of four, with arrow 900.		
Earliest documented cover: Feb. 27, 1897		

207 *(276)*

$1 black, Type I	450.	55.
greenish black	450.	55.
On cover		2,000.
Plate block of six, with imprint 3,000.		
Plate strip of three, with imprint 2,100.		
Margin block of four, witharrow 2,200.		
Earliest documented cover: Sept. 5, 1898		

208 *(276A)*

$1 black, Type II	900.	125.
greenish black	900.	125.
On cover		3,350.
Plate block of six, with imprint (four Type II, two Type I) 19,500.		
Plate strip of three, with imprint (two Type II, one Type I) 3,750.		
Margin block of four, with arrow 4,750.		
Pair, one each Nos. 207, 208 1,950.		
Earliest documented cover: April 6, 1896		

209 *(277)*

$2 dark blue	775.	250.
bright blue	775.	250.
On cover		3,200.
Plate block of six, with imprint 14,000.		
Plate strip of three, with imprint 3,500.		
Margin block of four, with arrow 4,000.		

210 *(278)*

$5 dark green	1,600.	375.
On cover		10,000.
Plate block of six, with imprint 60,000.		
Plate strip of three, with imprint 7,250.		
Margin block of four, with arrow 8,500.		
Earliest documented cover: Nov. 3, 1896		

1902-03. Regular Issues of 1902, had only two of its 14 values actually released in 1902, the balance being issued during 1903. All of these stamps were *perforated*, with the *1c, 4c, and 5c being issued imperforate as well*, although the 4c imperforate now exists only with the large slots of the Schermack coil cut into the sides. The 1c and 5c also were issued in coil form. Finally the 1c and 2c stamps were issued as booklet panes, six stamps to a pane. *Intaglio, watermarked double line USPS (187) and perforated 12.*

211, 225, 228, 230
Benjamin Franklin

212
George Washington

211 *(300)*

1c deep bluish green *(Feb. 4, 1903)*	6.50	.20
dark green	6.50	.20
gray green	6.50	.20
green	6.50	.20
yellow green	6.50	.20
On cover		.50
Plate block of six, with imprint 145.		
Plate strip of three, with imprint 27.50		
Cracked plate	8.00	.60
Double transfer	11.	.75
Worn plate	8.00	.60
n. Booklet pane of six (March 6, 1907)	425.	
n1. Pane with plate number on the left	—	
v. Arrow block with "color ball"	—	

212 *(301)*

2c carmine *(Jan. 19, 1903)*	8.50	.20
bright carmine	8.50	.20
dark carmine	8.50	.20
carmine rose	8.50	.20
On cover		.50
Plate block of six, with imprint 150.		
Plate strip of three, with imprint 40.		
Cracked plate	—	.75
Double transfer	17.50	.75
n. Booklet pane of six (Jan. 24, 1903)	400.	

213 *Andrew Jackson after engraving by A. Sealey*

214, 226
U.S. Grant

213 *(302)*

3c dark red violet *(Feb. 12, 1903)*	37.50	2.50
bright violet	37.50	2.50
violet	37.50	2.50
Plate block of six, with imprint 600.		
Plate strip of three, with imprint 175.		
Cracked plate	—	
Double transfer	65.	3.50
On cover		8.00
v. Arrow block with "color ball"	—	

214 *(303)*

4c brown *(Feb. 11, 1903)*		40.	1.25
dark brown		40.	1.25
dark yellow brown		40.	1.25
orange brown		40.	1.25
reddish brown		40.	1.25
yellow brown		40.	1.25
On cover			10.
Plate block of six, with imprint	600.		
Plate strip of three, with imprint	175.		
Double transfer		60.	2.25

215, 227, 229   216 *James Garfield*
Abraham Lincoln

215 *(304)*

5c deep blue *(Jan. 21, 1903)*		40.	1.25
blue		40.	1.25
dark blue		40.	1.25
dull blue		40.	1.25
On cover			7.00
Plate block of six, with imprint	600.		
Plate strip of three, with imprint	175.		
Cracked plate		55.	4.00
Double transfer		65.	3.00

216 *(305)*

6c brown red *(Feb. 21, 1903)*		50.	2.25
claret		50.	2.25
deep claret		50.	2.25
dull brown red		50.	2.25
On cover			10.
Plate block of six, with imprint	700.		
Plate strip of three, with imprint	200.		
Double transfer		62.50	3.00

217   218
Martha Washington   *Daniel Webster*

217 *(306)*

8c violet black *(Dec. 8, 1902)*		30.	1.75
black		30.	1.75
blue black		30.	1.75
blue lilac		30.	1.75
blue violet		30.	1.75
On cover			7.50
Plate block of six, with imprint	550.		
Plate strip of three, with imprint	120.		
Double transfer		37.50	2.00

218 *(307)*

10c pale red brown *(Feb. 6, 1903)*		45.	1.25
dark red brown		45.	1.25
red brown		45.	1.25
On cover			7.00
Plate block of six, with imprint	750.		
Plate strip of three, with imprint	150.		
Double transfer		60.	8.00

219   220 *Henry Clay*
Benjamin Harrison

219 *(308)*

13c black brown *(Nov. 19, 1902)*		30.	7.00
purple black		30.	7.00
On cover			32.50
Plate block of six, with imprint	500.		
Plate strip of three, with imprint	125.		

220 *(309)*

15c olive green *(May 28, 1903)*		120.	6.00
dark olive green		120.	6.00
On cover			70.
Plate block of six, with imprint	1,950.		
Plate strip of three, with imprint	500.		
Double transfer		160.	8.00
Margin block of four, with arrow		550.	

221 *Thomas Jefferson*   222 *David Farragut*

221 *(310)*

50c orange *(March 24, 1903)*		300.	25.
deep orange		300.	25.
On cover			600.
Plate block of six, with imprint	5,250.		
Plate strip of three, with imprint	1,250.		
Margin block of four, with arrow	1,500.		

222 *(311)*

$1 black *(June 2, 1903)*		550.	50.
gray black		550.	50.
On cover			1,250.
Plate block of six, with imprint	10,500.		
Plate strip of three, with imprint	1,950.		
Margin block of four, with arrow	2,250.		

223, 365
James Madison

224, 366
John Marshall

223 *(312)*

$2 dark blue *(June 2, 1903)*	700.	150.
blue	700.	150.
On cover		2,100.
Plate block of six, with imprint	22,000.	
Plate strip of three, with imprint	3,200.	
Margin block of four, with arrow	4,000.	

224 *(313)*

$5 dark green *(June 2, 1903)*	2,000.	550.
On cover		4,250.
Plate block of six, with imprint	42,000.	
Plate strip of three, with imprint	8,000.	
Margin block of four, with arrow	10,000.	

1906-08. Stamps of 1902-03, *imperforate*

225 *(314)*

1c deep bluish green *(Oct. 2, 1906)*	20.	17.50
dark green	20.	17.50
green	20.	17.50
On cover		17.50
Plate block of six, with imprint	165.	
Margin block of four, with arrow	80.	60.
Center line block	120.	80.
Double transfer	30.	15.

226 *Four Cent, imperforate, with Schermack slots at sides. These slots, made by a private company, turned imperforate stamps into coils to be vended by the machines of the Schermack Company*

226 *(314A)*

4c brown *(May 15, 1908)*	22,500.	15,000.
On cover		57,500.
Pair	52,500.	
Line pair	135,000.	

227 *(315)*

5c blue *(March 30, 1908)*	375.	475.
On cover		—
Plate block of six, with imprint	2,800.	
Center line block	2,800.	
Margin block of four, with arrow	1,800.	

Please exercise caution in buying singles of this stamp, particularly used copies.

1908. The coil stamps of the 1902-03 series were the first coils issued. They have been faked extensively by fraudulently perforating the imperforates in the case of the 1c stamps and also by trimming off perforations on both the 1c and 5c stamps. It is recommended that these stamps be collected in pairs.

Perforated 12 horizontally

228 *(316)*

1c blue green, pair *(Feb. 18, 1908)*	68,500.	
Line pair	110,000.	

229 *(317)*

5c blue, pair *(Feb. 24, 1908)*	9,000.	
Line pair	19,500.	

Perforated 12 vertically

230 *(318)*

1c blue green, pair *(July 31, 1908)*	6,000.	
Line pair	11,000.	
Double transfer	—	

1903. The Two-Cent Shield Stamp was issued because of public dislike for the 2c "Flag" design of the 1902-03 series. The "Shield" stamp comes in a wide range of shades. It was issued perforated, imperforate, in booklet panes, and also in coil form, so that a considerable display can be made of this single denomination. *The stamps were flat-plate printed and watermarked double-line USPS (wmk 187).*

231-236 *George Washington*

Type I: The leaf next to the "2" at left penetrates the border.

Type II: Border to the left of the leaf is formed by a strong line.

Perforated 12
Type I

231 *(319)*

2c carmine *(Nov. 12, 1903)*	4.00	.20
bright carmine	4.00	.20
red	4.00	.20
carmine rose	4.50	.20
scarlet	4.00	.20
On cover		.50
Plate block of six, with imprint	75.	
Plate strip of three, with imprint	16.	
Double transfer	8.00	1.50
n. Booklet pane of six	100.	
v. Vertical pair, rouletted between	800.	
v1. Vertical pair, imperforate horizontally	2,500.	
v2. Vertical pair, imperforate between	1,000.	

Earliest documented cover: Oct. 29, 1908.

232 *(319f)*
2c lake, Type II	7.50	.50
carmine	7.50	.50
carmine lake	7.50	.50
scarlet	7.50	.50
Plate block of six	150.	
n. Booklet pane of six	150.	

Earliest documented cover: June 11, 1908.

Imperforate
233 *(320)*
2c carmine, Type I *(Oct. 2, 1906)*	20.	15.
scarlet	20.	15.
carmine rose	20.	15.
scarlet	20.	15.
On cover		15.
Plate block of six, with imprint	200.	
Center line block	140.	175.
Double transfer	22.50	12.50
Margin block of four, with arrow	80.	85.

234 *(320a)*
2c lake, Type II	50.	40.
scarlet	50.	40.
On cover		70.
Plate block of six, with imprint	700.	
Center line block	400.	
Margin block of four, with arrow	180.	

Coil Stamp, perforated 12 horizontally
235 *(321)*
2c carmine, Type I, pair *(Feb. 18, 1908)*	95,000.	100,000.
Line pair	—	

Coil Stamp, perforated 12 vertically

236

236 *(322)*
2c scarlet, Type II, pair *(July 31, 1908)*	7,000.	4,250.
Double transfer	7,750.	
Line pair	—	

1908-09 Series, consists of 12 stamps, ranging from 1c to $1. The 1c stamp has a portrait of Franklin in the central medallion with the words "ONE CENT" at the base of the stamp. The 2c stamp, with Washington in the medallion, is inscribed "TWO CENTS." The 3c stamp to $1 stamps have Washington in the medallion with numerals of value in each of the lower corners.

As an experiment to counteract the shrinking caused by printing on wet paper, some rows of stamps were separated by 3 mm spacing instead of the usual 2 mm. Intermediate-size spacings exist and command the lower of the two prices listed for different spacings. *Flat plate printing, watermarked double-line USPS (187), and perforated 12.*

A very few of this series, up through the 15c value, were printed on a grayish, hard, thick paper known as *China Clay.* The paper had up to 10 times the mineral content of normal stamp paper of the time.

237
Benjamin Franklin

237 *(331)*
1c green *(Dec. 14, 1908)*	6.00	20.
bright green	6.00	20.
dark green	6.00	20.
yellow green	6.00	20.
On cover		.50
Plate block of six, with imprint	45.	
Plate block of six, with imprint and open star	50.	
Plate block of six, with small solid star	75.	
Block of four, 2 mm spacing	25.	1.25
Block of four, 3 mm spacing	27.50	1.50
Cracked plate	—	
Double transfer	8.00	.60
n. Booklet pane of six *(Dec. 2, 1908)*	140.	120.
p. China Clay paper	800.	

238 *George Washington, value in words*

239 *George Washington, value in numerals.*

238 *(332)*
2c carmine *(Dec. 1, 1908)*	6.00	.20
dark carmine	6.00	.20
pale carmine	6.00	.20
On cover		.50
Plate block of six, with imprint	45.	
Plate block of six, with imprint and open star	50.	
Plate block of six, with small solid star	70.	
Block of four, 2 mm spacing	22.50	.60
Block of four, 3 mm spacing	25.	.75
Cracked plate	—	
Double transfer	10.	
Double transfer (1c design of No. 237)	1,250.	
n. Booklet pane of six *(Nov. 16, 1908)*	125.	110.
p. China Clay paper	1,000.	

248 *(342)*
$1 violet brown

	(Jan. 29, 1909)	375.	75.
	dull violet brown	375.	75.
	On cover		5,250.
	Plate block of six, with imprint	11,500.	
	Margin block of four, with arrow	1,900.	
	Double transfer	—	

Imperforate

249 *(343)*
1c green *(Dec. 23, 1908)*

	(Dec. 23, 1908)	6.00	4.00
	bright green	6.00	4.00
	dark green	6.00	4.00
	yellow green	6.00	4.00
	On cover		8.00
	Plate block of six, with imprint	55.	
	Plate block of six, with imprint and open star	60.	
	Plate block of six, with small solid star	600.	
	Block of four, 2 mm spacing	25.	
	Block of four, 3 mm spacing	25.	
	Center line block	35.	
	Margin block of four, 2 or 3 mm spacing, with arrow	30.	
	Double transfer	—	

250 *(344)*
2c carmine *(Dec. 14, 1908)*

	(Dec. 14, 1908)	7.50	3.00
	dark carmine	7.50	3.00
	pale carmine	7.50	3.00
	On cover		4.50
	Plate block of six, with imprint	75.	
	Plate block of six, with imprint and star	80.	
	Block of four, 2 or 3 mm spacing	30.	
	Center line block	40.	
	Double transfer	12.50	3.50
	Double transfer (1c design of No. 237)	1,000.	
	Margin block of four, 2 or 3mm spacing, with arrow	35.	

251 *(345)*
3c violet, Type I *(March 3, 1909)*

	(March 3, 1909)	17.50	20.
	On cover		40.
	Plate block of six, with imprint	175.	
	Center line block	75.	80.
	Double transfer	20.	
	Margin block of four, with arrow	60.	80.

252 *(346)*
4c brown *(Feb. 25, 1909)*

	(Feb. 25, 1909)	27.50	22.50
	orange brown	27.50	22.50
	dark orange brown	27.50	22.50
	dull orange brown	27.50	22.50
	On cover		70.
	Plate block of six, with imprint	200.	

	Plate block of six, with imprint and star	225.	
	Block of four, 2 or 3 mm spacing	95.	
	Center line block	125.	
	Double transfer	40.	
	Margin block of four, 2 or 3 mm spacing, with arrow	100.	

253 *(347)*
5c blue *(Feb. 27, 1909)*

	(Feb. 27, 1909)	42.50	30.
	On cover		90.
	Plate block of six, with imprint	350.	
	Center line block	220.	200.
	Cracked plate	—	
	Margin block of four, with arrow	200.	160.

1908-10. *Coil stamps. Flat plate printing, double-line USPS watermark (wmk 187), and perforated 12 either on the sides or at the top and bottom of the stamp.*

Perforated 12 horizontally

254 *(348)*
1c green *(Dec. 29, 1908)*

	(Dec. 29, 1908)	22.50	12.50
	dark green	22.50	12.50
	On cover		35.
	Pair	60.	65.
	Line pair	150.	275.

255 *(349)*
2c carmine *(Jan 2, 1909)*

	(Jan 2, 1909)	37.50	8.00
	dark carmine	37.50	8.00
	On cover		25.
	Pair	65.	30.
	Line pair	275.	135.
	Double transfer (1c design of No. 237)	—	1,350.

256 *(350)*
4c brown *(Aug. 15, 1910)*

	(Aug. 15, 1910)	85.	70.
	On cover		150.
	Pair	225.	300.
	Line pair	650.	550.

257 *(351)*
5c blue *(Jan. 2, 1909)*

	(Jan. 2, 1909)	100.	85.
	dark blue	100.	85.
	On cover		165.
	Pair	275.	300.
	Line pair	750.	550.

Perforated 12 vertically

258 *(352)*
1c green *(Jan. 2, 1909)*

	(Jan. 2, 1909)	50.	30.
	On cover		60.
	Pair, 2 mm spacing	135.	105.
	Pair, 3 mm spacing	120.	95.
	Line pair	350.	200.
	Double transfer	—	

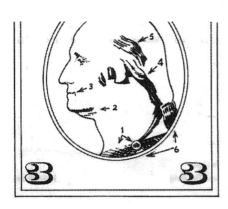

239. George Washington. Type I: All stamps of this design and perforated 12 are Type I. While the description of the type is given here in detail, the areas noted by the small figures "1" and "3" in the drawing will almost always prove sufficient as checking areas

Details of Type I:

1. The top line of the toga from the front of the neck to the top of the button is very weak, as are the upper parts of the fine lines of shading that join this top line. The top part of the fifth of these shading lines is missing.
2. Two shading lines under the point of the chin are heavy.
3. The line between the lips is thin. This usually is an easy checking point for this type.
4. The lock of hair behind the ear is formed at the bottom by two lines of shading, the lower line being considerably shorter than the upper.
5. The hair lines above and a little to the right of the ear form an "arrowhead."
6. The outline of the inner oval forms a solid line at the bottom.

239 *(333)*

3c violet, Type I *(Dec. 26, 1908)*	27.50	2.50
dark violet	27.50	2.50
pale violet	27.50	2.50
On cover		7.50
Plate block of six, with imprint	200.	
Plate block of six, with imprint and star	300.	
Block of four, 2 mm spacing	110.	15.
Block of four, 3 mm spacing	120.	17.50
Double transfer	37.50	4.00
p. China Clay paper	800.	

240 *(334)*

4c orange brown *(Dec. 26, 1908)*	30.	1.00
brown	30.	1.00
dark orange brown	30.	1.00
dull orange brown	30.	1.00
On cover		5.00
Plate block of six, with imprint	300.	
Plate block of six, with imprint and star	475.	
Block of four, 2 mm spacing	140.	7.50
Block of four, 3 mm spacing	150.	9.00
Double transfer	45.	
p. China Clay paper	1,000.	

241 *(335)*

5c blue *(Dec. 21, 1908)*	40.	2.00
bright blue	40.	2.00
dark blue	40.	2.00
On cover		8.00
Plate block of six, with imprint	400.	
Plate block of six, with imprint and star	600.	
Block of four, 2 mm spacing	175.	12.50
Block of four, 3 mm spacing	185.	10.
Double transfer	45.	
p. China Clay paper	800.	

242 *(336)*

6c red orange *(Dec. 31, 1908)*	47.50	5.00
dull orange	47.50	5.00
orange	47.50	5.00
On cover		17.50
Plate block of six, with imprint	600.	
p. China Clay paper	625.	

243 *(337)*

8c olive green *(Dec. 18, 1908)*	37.50	2.50
dark olive green	37.50	2.50
On cover		16.
Plate block of six, with imprint	400.	
Double transfer	47.50	
p. China Clay paper	800.	

244 *(338)*

10c yellow *(Jan. 7, 1909)*	55.	1.50
On cover		8.00
Plate block of six, with imprint	650.	
Double transfer	—	
p. China Clay paper	800.	
p1. Very thin paper	—	

245 *(339)*

13c blue green *(Jan. 11, 1909)*	37.50	20.
dark blue green	37.50	20.
On cover		90.
Plate block of six, with imprint	400.	
p. China Clay paper	800.	

246 *(340)*

15c gray blue *(Jan. 18, 1909)*	50.	6.00
dull gray blue	50.	6.00
On cover		110.
Plate block of six, with imprint	525.	
p. China Clay paper	800.	

247 *(341)*

50c gray lilac *(Jan. 13, 1909)*	250.	17.50
dull gray lilac	250.	17.50
On cover		4,500.
Plate block of six, with imprint	6,000.	
Margin block of four, with arrow	1,100.	

Washington-Franklin Identifier

PERF.	WMK.	1c Text	2c Text	1c Numeral	2c Numeral	Wash. Numeral	Frank. Numeral
12	Double	237, 263	238, 264			239-248, 265-272	313-314
	Single	273	274	297	298	275-282	305-312
Coil 12	Double	254-258	255,259			256, 257, 260-262	
	Single	285, 287	286, 288			289	
Imperforate	Double	249	250			251-253	
	Single	283	284	299	300, *342*		
	Unwmk.			367, 406	368, **407-407D**	369-370, **408**	
Coil 8 1/2	Single	290, 292	291, 293	301, 303	302, 304	294-296	
10	Double						331
	Single			315	316	317-321	322-330
	Unwmk			348, **414**	349	350-355	356-364
Coil 10	Double			333, 335	334, 336	337-339	
	Single			*340, 343*	*341, 344*	*345-347*	
	Unwmk			371, 374	372, 375	373, 376-378	379
11	Double		399				
	Single				332		
	Unwmk			380, **403**, *415, 416*	381, **404-404D**, *417*	382-387, **405-405A**	388-398
12x10, 10x12	Single			315	316	319	
12 1/2	Unwmk			**409**			
11x10, 10x11	Unwmk.			*410, 413*	*411-411A*	*412*	

237 -- Numbers in normal type designate stamps printed by intaglio on a flat-bed press.
340 -- Numbers in italic designate stamps printed by intaglio on a rotary press.

407 -- Numbers in bold designate stamps printed by offset. These stamps are characterized by the smoothness of printed surface and by the blurred appearance of the image.

259 *(353)*

2c carmine *(Jan. 12, 1909)*	47.50	7.50
On cover		20.
Pair, 2 mm spacing	125.	30.
Pair, 3 mm spacing	115.	25.
Line pair	350.	125.

260 *(354)*

4c brown *(Feb. 23, 1909)*	115.	55.
On cover		90.
Pair, 2 mm spacing	325.	250.
Pair, 3 mm spacing	340.	270.
Line pair	850.	400.

261 *(355)*

5c blue *(Feb. 23, 1909)*	125.	75.
dark blue	125.	75.
On cover		150.
Pair	350.	325.
Line pair	900.	550.

262 *(356)*

10c yellow *(Feb. 23, 1909)*	1,750.	850.
On cover		8,500.
Pair	4,200.	3,800.
Line pair	7,500.	6,850.

1909. Stamps of 1908-09 on Bluish Gray paper. The paper used in this experimental printing was made with a 30% rag stock instead of all wood pulp. Here is a quote from the Report of the Third Assistant Postmaster General for the fiscal year ending June 30, 1909: "The intaglio process by which our postage stamps are printed necessitates a preliminary wetting down of the paper, which is bleached chemical wood stock. This wetting down causes a varying shrinkage, which has resulted in heavy waste from the cutting of the perforations into the stamp design. The Bureau of Engraving and Printing experimented with a paper made of about 30% rag stock, in the hope that it would show less shrinkage, but this paper did not overcome the difficulty as it was found to shrink very unevenly. Some of the stamps printed on this paper, which was of a slightly bluish tinge, were issued to the Postmaster of Washington, D.C., and to others." Actually, the paper is of a distinctly different color than the normal paper, but this shows up better by comparison than it does by the examination of just a single copy of either the normal or the bluish gray paper. We have noted the presence of tiny black specks on much of the blue paper, sometimes only a few to a stamp and best seen with the aid of a glass. These stamps were *Flat Plate printing, watermarked double-line USPS (187), and perforated 12.*

263 *(357)*

1c green *(Feb. 16, 1909)*	85.	85.
On cover		185.
Plate block of six, with imprint	900.	
Plate block of six, with imprint and star	2,500.	
Block of four, 2 mm spacing	350.	375.
Block of four, 3 mm spacing	675.	

264 *(358)*

2c carmine *(Feb. 16, 1909)*	75.	70.
On cover		150.
Plate block of six, with imprint	900.	
Plate block of six, with imprint and star	1,150.	
Block of four, 2 mm spacing	340.	400.
Block of four, 3 mm spacing	380.	
Double transfer	—	

265 *(359)*

3c deep violet, Type I	1,600.	1,600.
On cover		—
Plate block of six, with imprint	15,000.	

266 *(360)*

4c orange brown	15,000.	—
Plate block of six, with imprint	115,000.	

267 *(361)*

5c blue	3,500.	3,750.
On cover		5,250.
Plate block of six, with imprint	30,000.	

268 *(362)*

6c red orange	1,150.	1,000.
On cover		11,000.
Plate block of six, with imprint	12,500.	
Earliest documented cover: Sept. 14, 1911		

269 *(363)*

8c olive green	16,000.	—
Plate block of six, with imprint	120,000.	

270 *(364)*

10c yellow	1,400.	1,150.
On cover		—
Plate block of six, with imprint	15,000.	
Earliest documented cover: Feb. 3, 1910		

271 *(365)*

13c blue green	2,350.	1,450.
On cover		—
Plate block of six, with imprint	17,500.	

272 *(366)*

15c pale ultramarine	1,150.	1,000.
On cover		—
Plate block of six, with imprint	7,500.	

1910-14. This issue was identical with the 1908-09 series in design, but a 7c stamp was added while the 50c and $1 stamps were discontinued. The stamps were *printed on paper with a new watermark, single-line USPS. Flat plate printing. Perforated 12.*

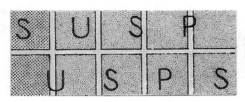

273 *Single-line USPS watermark*

273 *Benjamin Franklin*

274 *George Washington*

273 *(374)*

1c green *(Nov. 23, 1910)*	6.00	.20
dark green	6.00	.20
pale green	6.00	.20
yellowish green	6.00	.20
On cover		.50
Plate block of six, with imprint and "A"	60.	
Plate block of six, with imprint and star	70.	
Block of four, 2 mm spacing	22.50	2.75
Block of four, 3 mm spacing	25.	2.75
Cracked plate	—	
Double transfer	10.	
n. Booklet pane of six	125.	100.
Earliest documented cover: July 31, 1911		

274 *(375)*

2c carmine *(Nov. 23, 1910)*	5.75	.20
dull carmine	5.75	.20
lake	200.	—
On cover		.50
Plate block of six, with imprint and "A"	60.	
Plate block of six, with imprint and star	65.	
Block of four, 2 mm spacing	22.50	1.00
Block of four, 3 mm spacing	21.	.80
Cracked plate	—	
Double transfer	9.00	—
Double transfer (1c design of No. 273)	—	850.
n. Booklet pane of six	100.	
Earliest documented cover: June 1, 1911		

275-282 *George Washington*

275 *(376)*

3c violet, Type I *(Jan. 16, 1911)*	15.	1.50
deep violet	15.	1.50
lilac	17.50	1.50
On cover		7.00
Plate block of six	125.	
Plate block of six, with imprint and star	165.	
Block of four, 2 mm spacing	65.	8.00
Block of four, 3 mm spacing	67.50	8.00

276 *(377)*

4c brown *(Jan. 20, 1911)*	22.50	.75
dark brown	22.50	.75
orange brown	22.50	.75
On cover		7.00
Plate block of six	240.	
Plate block of six, with imprint and star	200.	
Block of four, 2 mm spacing	100.	
Block of four, 3 mm spacing	95.	

277 *(378)*

5c blue	22.50	.75
Dark blue	22.50	.75
Pale blue	22.50	.75
On cover		4.50
Plate block of six	200.	
Plate block of six, with imprint	180.	
Plate block of six, with imprint and "A"	200.	
Plate block of six, with imprint and star	175.	
Block of four, 2 mm spacing	100.	5.00
Block of four, 3 mm spacing	95.	4.50
Double transfer	—	
Earliest documented cover: Mar. 28, 1911		

278 *(379)*

6c red orange *(Jan. 25, 1911)*	30.	.85
dull red orange	30.	.85
On cover		40.
Plate block of six, with imprint	300.	
Plate block of six, with imprint and star	275.	
Block of four, 2 mm spacing	125.	8.00
Block of four, 3 mm spacing	120.	7.50

279 *(407)*

7c black *(April 1914)*	70.	8.50
deep black	70.	8.50
gray black	70.	8.50
On cover		50.
Plate block of six	850.	
Earliest documented cover: May 1, 1914		

280 *(380)*

8c light olive green *(Feb. 8, 1911)*	95.	12.50
dark olive green	95.	12.50
On cover		50.
Plate block of six, with imprint	900.	
Plate block of six, with imprint and star	1,100.	
Block of four, 2 or 3 mm spacing	400.	65.

281 *(381)*

10c yellow *(Jan. 24, 1911)*	85.	4.00
On cover		15.
Plate block of six, with imprint	900.	

Plate block of six, with imprint
and star   850.
Block of four, 2 or 3 mm spacing 375.   25.

Earliest documented cover: Feb. 17, 1911

282 *(382)*
15c pale ultramarine *(March 1, 1911)* 225.   15.
On cover   85.
Plate block of six   2,000.

Imperforate

283 *(383)*
1c green *(Dec. 1910)*   3.00   2.75
dark green   3.00   2.75
pale green   3.00   2.75
yellowish green   3.00   2.75
On cover   4.00
Plate block of six, with imprint
and "A"   40.
Plate block of six, with imprint
and star   65.
Block of four, 2 or 3 mm spacing 9.50   11.
Center line block   20.   15.
Double transfer   6.00
Margin block of four, with arrow 10.   11.
Earliest documented cover: March 1, 1911

284 *(384)*
2c carmine *(Dec. 1910)*   5.50   3.00
On cover   3.00
Plate block of six, with imprint
and "A"   115.
Plate block of six, with imprint
and star   150.
Block of four, 2 or 3 mm spacing 20.   12.50
Margin block of four, with arrow 25.   17.50
Center line block   42.50   40.
Cracked plate   —
Double transfer   7.50
Double transfer (1c design
of No. 283)   1,200.
Earliest documented cover: April 23, 1911

This stamp is relatively common in singles and vertical
pairs and very scarce in horizontal pairs and blocks.

Coil Stamps. Perforated 12 horizontally

285 *(385)*
1c green *(Nov. 1, 1910)*   22.50   12.50
dark green   22.50   12.50
On cover   35.
Pair   50.   35.
Line pair   250.   225.

286 *(386)*
2c carmine *(Nov. 1, 1910)*   37.50   17.50
dark carmine   37.50   17.50
pale carmine   37.50   17.50

On cover   40.
Pair   135.   75.
Line pair   425.

Coil Stamps. Perforated 12 vertically

287 *(387)*
1c green *(Nov. 1, 1910)*   85.   37.50
dark green   85.   37.50
On cover   60.
Pair, 2 mm spacing   200.   90.
Pair, 3 mm spacing   220.   100.
Line pair   325.   260.

288 *(388)*
2c carmine *(Nov. 1, 1910)*   575.   250.
dark carmine   575.   250.
pale carmine   575.   250.
On cover   600.
Pair, 2 or 3 mm spacing   1,950.
Line pair   4,000.   3,150.

289 *(389)*
3c deep violet, Type I
(Jan. 24, 1911)   28,500.   7,000.
red violet   28,500.   7,000.
violet   28,500.   7,000.
On cover   15,500.
Pair   78,500.

Known as the "Orangeburg Coil" (because it is only
known used from Orangeburg, New York) No. 289 is the
rarest of all U.S. coil stamps. One coil of 500 stamps was
made and only about a dozen unused copies are known.
The stamps were used by the Bell Chemical Company of
Orangeburg to mail samples of products.

Coil Stamps. Perforated 8 1/2 horizontally

290 *(390)*
1c green *(Dec. 12, 1910)*   450.   5.00
dark green   450.   5.00
On cover   7.50
Pair   8.00   16.50
Line pair   25.   40.

291 *(391)*
2c carmine *(Dec. 23, 1910)*   30.   12.50
dark carmine   30.   12.50
pale carmine   30.   12.50
On cover   20.
Pair   75.   32.50
Line pair   150.   125.

Coil Stamps. Perforated 8 1/2 vertically

292 *(392)*
1c green *(Dec. 12, 1910)*   20.   20.
dark green   20.   20.
On cover   50.
Double transfer   20.   20.

Pair	55.	65.
Line pair	115.	135.

293 *(393)*

2c carmine *(Dec. 16, 1910)*

	40.	10.
dark carmine	40.	10.
pale carmine	40.	10.
On cover		20.
Pair	85.	22.50
Line pair	165.	80.

294 *(394)*

3c violet, *(Sept. 18, 1911)* Type I

	50.	50.
deep violet	50.	50.
red violet	50.	50.
On cover		100.
Pair, 2 or 3 mm spacing	110.	125.
Line pair	250.	275.

295 *(395)*

4c brown *(April 15, 1912)*

	50.	50.
dark brown	50.	50.
On cover		100.
Pair, 2 or 3 mm spacing	110.	125.
Line pair	250.	250.

296 *(396)*

5c blue *(March 1913)*

	50.	50.
dark blue	50.	50.
On cover		100.
Pair	110.	105.
Line pair	250.	300.

1912. Modified Designs. 1c and 2c stamps with numerals instead of words for denomination. *Flat Press printing, single-line USPS watermark (wmk 273), perforated 12.*

297, 298 *George Washington*

297 *(405)*

1c green *(Feb. 14, 1912)*

	5.00	.20
dark green	5.00	.20
pale green	5.00	.20
yellow green	5.00	.20
On cover		.25
Plate block of six	55.	
Plate block of six, with "A"	60.	
Plate block of six, with "A" and imprint	65.	
Cracked plate	11.	
Double transfer	5.00	
n. Booklet pane of six (Feb. 10, 1912)	65.	
v. Vertical pair, imperforate horizontally	700.	

298 *George Washington, Type I. The following detailed description is provided, although any 2c that fits Point 1 is a Type I.*

1. The line from the front of the neck to and over the top of the button is very weak. The shading linesthat run into this line (top of toga) are thin in the area above the cross hatching lines.
2. One shading line in the first (upper) curve of the ribbon above the left numeral and one line in the second (middle) curve above the right numeral.
3. There is a white dash below the ear.
4. The shading lines of the face terminate in front of the ear and are not joined with each other.
5. The lock of hair behind the ear is formed at the bottom by two lines of shading, the lower one being considerably shorter than the other.
6. The hair lines above the ear and slightly to the right form an arrowhead.
7. The shading lines just to the left of the ear form a fairly solid color.

298 *(406)*

2c carmine, Type I *(Feb. 14, 1912)*

	4.50	.20
dark carmine	4.50	.20
lilac carmine	4.50	.20
On cover		.25
Plate block of six	70.	
Plate block of six, with "A"	85.	
Double transfer	6.25	
n. Booklet pane of six	65.	
v. Double impression	—	

Earliest documented cover: June 6, 1912

Imperforate

299 *(408)*

1c green *(March 9, 1912)*

	1.25	.60
dark green	1.25	.60
pale green	1.25	.60
yellow green	1.25	.60
On cover		1.00
Plate block of six	17.50	
Plate block of six, with "A"	25.	
Plate block of six, with "A" and imprint	42.50	
Center line block	8.00	8.00
Cracked plate	—	
Double transfer	2.25	.75
Margin block of 4, with arrow	4.50	2.75

300 *(409)*
2c carmine, Type I

(Feb. 23, 1912)	1.30	.60
dark carmine	1.30	.60
scarlet red	1.30	.60
On cover		1.00
Plate block of six	30.	
Plate block of six, with "A"	40.	
Plate block of six, with "A" and imprint	45.	
Center line block	9.00	8.00
Cracked plate	—	
Margin block of four, with arrow	5.50	

Coil Stamps. Perforated 8 1/2 horizontally

301 *(410)*
1c green *(March 18, 1912)*

	5.50	4.50
dark green	5.50	4.50
On cover		7.25
Pair	12.50	8.00
Line pair	27.50	20.
Double transfer	—	

302 *(411)*
2c carmine, Type I *(March 18, 1912)*

	7.50	4.50
dark carmine	7.50	4.50
On cover		10.
Pair	20.	9.00
Line pair	35.	25.
Double transfer	10.	

Coil Stamps. Perforated 8 1/2 vertically

303 *(412)*
1c green *(May 18, 1912)*

	22.50	6.25
On cover		12.50
Pair	45.	12.50
Line pair	75.	40.

304 *(413)*
2c carmine, Type I *(March 21, 1912)*

	35.	1.25
dark carmine	35.	1.25
On cover		7.00
Pair	75.	7.00
Line pair	150.	20.
Double transfer	35.	

1912-14. Redesigned values from 8c through 50c stamps. *Flat plate printing, single-line USPS watermark (273), perforated 12.*

305-314 *Benjamin Franklin*

305 *(414)*
8c pale olive green *(Feb. 14, 1912)*

	30.	1.25
olive green	30.	1.25
On cover		12.50

Plate block of six, with imprint and "A"	400.	

306 *(415)*
9c salmon pink *(April 1914)*

	45.	12.50
rose red	45.	12.50
On cover		40.
Plate block of six	550.	

Earliest documented cover: May 1, 1914

307 *(416)*
10c orange yellow *(Jan. 20, 1912)*

	32.50	.50
brown yellow	300.	5.00
yellow	32.50	.50
On cover		2.25
Plate block of six, with "A"	370.	
Plate block of six, with "A" and imprint	420.	
Double transfer	—	

308 *(417)*
12c chocolate *(April 1914)*

	40.	4.25
deep chocolate	40.	4.25
On cover		22.50
Plate block of six	450.	
Double transfer	47.50	
Triple transfer	65.	

Earliest documented cover: June 2, 1914

309 *(418)*
15c gray black *(Feb. 14, 1912)*

	65.	4.00
gray	65.	4.00
On cover		15.
Plate block of six	650.	
Plate block of six, with "A"	625.	
Plate block of six, with "A" and imprint	600.	
Double transfer	—	

310 *(419)*
20c gray blue *(April 1914)*

	150.	17.50
ultramarine	150.	17.50
On cover		125.
Plate block of six	1,650.	

Earliest documented cover: May 1, 1914

311 *(420)*
30c orange red *(April 1914)*

	115.	17.50
dark orange red	115.	17.50
On cover		225.
Plate block of six	1,250.	

Earliest documented cover: May 1, 1914

312 *(421)*
50c violet *(April 1914)*

	350.	20.
pale violet	350.	20.
On cover		1,750.
Plate block of six	8,250.	

Earliest documented cover: May 1, 1914

Double-line USPS watermark (wmk 187)

313 *(422)*

50c violet *(Feb. 14, 1912)*	225.	20.
On cover		1,750.
Plate block of six, with "A" and imprint	4,000.	
Margin block of four, with arrow	950.	

314 *(423)*

$1 violet brown *(Feb. 14, 1912)*	425.	65.
On cover		6,250.
Plate block of six, with "A" and imprint	9,100.	
Double transfer	475.	
Margin block of four, with arrow	1,950.	

1914-15 Issue with new *perforation 10. Flat plate printing, single-line USPS watermark (wmk 273).*

322-331	315-321
Benjamin Franklin	*George Washington*

315 *(424)*

1c green *(Sept. 5, 1914)*	2.75	.20
bright green	2.75	.20
dark green	2.75	.20
yellow green	2.75	.20
On cover		.25
Plate block of six	35.	
Plate block of ten, with "COIL STAMPS"	120.	
Cracked plate	—	
Double transfer	4.00	
n. Booklet pane of six	3.75	1.25
n1v. Booklet pane of six, ungummed, imperforate	1,000.	
v. Perforated 12 x 10	750.	650.
v1. Perforated 10 x 12	—	300.
v2. Vertical pair, imperforate horizontally	425.	—
v3. Vertical pair, imperforate between	8,000.	

Earliest documented cover: Dec. 20, 1913.

316 *(425)*

2c rose red, Type I *(Sept. 5, 1914)*	225.	.20
dark carmine	225.	.20
dark rose	225.	.20
scarlet	225.	.20
red	225.	.20
rose	225.	.20
On cover		.25
Plate block of six	25.	
Plate block of ten, with "COIL STAMPS"	125.	

Cracked plate	8.00	
Double transfer	—	
n. Booklet pane of six	22.50	4.50
v. Perforated 12 x 10	—	750.

Earliest documented cover: Jan. 6, 1914

317 *(426)*

3c violet, Type I *(Sept. 18, 1914)*	12.50	2.00
bright violet	12.50	2.00
dark violet	12.50	2.00
reddish violet	12.50	2.00
On cover		3.00
Plate block of six	160.	

318 *(427)*

4c brown *(Sept. 7, 1914)*	30.	.75
dark brown	30.	.75
orange brown	30.	.75
yellow brown	30.	.75
On cover		475.
Plate block of six	450.	

319 *(428)*

5c blue *(Sept. 14, 1914)*	27.50	.70
bright blue	27.50	.70
dark blue	27.50	.70
indigo blue	27.50	.70
On cover		2.50
Plate block of six	375.	
v. Perforated 12 x 10	—	2,000.

Earliest documented cover: April 14, 1915

320 *(429)*

6c red orange *(Sept. 28, 1914)*	45.	2.00
dark red orange	45.	2.00
pale red orange	45.	2.00
On cover		7.50
Plate block of six	475.	
Plate block of six, with imprint and star	375.	
Block of four, 2 or 3mm spacing	170.	12.50

321 *(430)*

7c black *(Sept. 10, 1914)*	75.	5.00
deep black	75.	5.00
gray black	75.	5.00
On cover		32.50
Plate block of six	800.	

322 *(431)*

8c yellow olive *(Sept. 26, 1914)*	30.	1.25
dull yellow olive	30.	1.25
On cover		7.00
Plate block of six, with "A"	475.	
Plate block of six, with "A" and imprint	425.	
Double transfer	—	
v. Double impression	—	

323 *(432)*

9c salmon *(Oct. 6, 1914)*	35.	2.00
dark salmon	35.	2.00
On cover		22.50
Plate block of six	550.	

324 *(433)*

10c orange yellow *(Sept. 9, 1914)*	40.	.40
golden yellow	40.	.40
yellow	40.	.40
On cover		6.50
Plate block of six	775.	
Plate block of six, with "A"	850.	
Plate block of six, with "A" and imprint	600.	

325 *(434)*

11c deep bluish green *(Aug. 12, 1915)*	20.	9.00
dark green	20.	9.00
green	20.	9.00
On cover		22.50
Plate block of six	225.	

326 *(435)*

12c maroon *(Sept. 10, 1914)*	23.	4.25
dark maroon	23.	4.25
copper red	25.	4.50
On cover		17.50
Plate block of six	275.	
Double transfer	25.	
Triple transfer	30.	

So-called vertical pair, imperforate between, really have at least one perforation hole between the stamps.

327 *(437)*

15c gray black *(Sept. 16, 1914)*	110.	8.50
gray	110.	8.50
On cover		47.50
Plate block of six	900.	
Plate block of six, with "A"	925.	
Plate block of six, with "A" and imprint	900.	

328 *(438)*

20c pale ultramarine *(Sept. 19, 1914)*	175.	4.50
ultramarine	175.	4.50
On cover		130.
Plate block of six	2,850.	

329 *(439)*

30c orange red *(Sept. 19, 1914)*	225.	20.
dark orange red	225.	20.
On cover		225.
Plate block of six	3,250.	

330 *(440)*

50c violet *(Dec. 13, 1915)*	525.	22.50
On cover		1,500.
Plate block of six	11,500.	

Double-line watermark USPS (wmk 187)

331 *(460)*

$1 violet black *(Feb. 8, 1915)*	725.	85.
On cover		9,500.
Plate block of six, with "A" and imprint	10,500.	
Margin block of four, with arrow	3,000.	
Double transfer	750.	

Single-line watermark USPS (wmk 273). Perforated 11

332 *(461)*

2c rose red, Type I	100.	225.
On cover		900.
Plate block of six	950.	
Earliest documented cover: July 19, 1915		

As an experiment toward finding a more satisfactory perforation, 190,000 Type I 2c stamps were perforated 11 and sold through the Washington post offices, mostly to large users who were asked to report concerning the perforations.

Coil Stamps. Perforated 10 horizontally

333 *(441)*

1c green *(Nov. 14, 1914)*	1.25	1.25
dark green	1.25	1.25
On cover		2.00
Pair	2.75	3.50
Line pair	6.50	6.00

334 *(442)*

2c carmine, Type I *(July 22, 1914)*	8.50	8.00
dark carmine	8.50	8.00
On cover		12.50
Pair	17.50	17.50
Line pair	45.	60.

Coil Stamps. Perforated 10 vertically

335 *(443)*

1c green *(May 29, 1914)*	22.50	7.50
dark green	22.50	7.50
On cover		12.50
Pair	60.	15.
Line pair	125.	55.

336 *(444)*

2c carmine, Type I *(April 25, 1914)*	32.50	1.75
dark carmine	32.50	1.75
red	32.50	1.75
On cover		10.
Pair	80.	5.00
Line pair	175.	17.50

337 *(445)*

3c violet, Type I *(Dec. 18, 1914)*	225.	125.
dark violet	225.	125.
On cover		200.
Pair	475.	280.
Line pair	900.	775.

338 *(446)*

4c brown *(Oct. 2, 1914)*	120.	47.50
On cover		100.
Pair	275.	220.
Line pair	600.	550.

339 *(447)*

5c blue *(July 30, 1914)*	47.50	32.50
On cover		52.50
Pair	90.	175.
Line pair	200.	425.

The Rotary Press, was first used in production of the following coil stamps. The Press plates are curved into a half circle. Two plates are fitted around a cylinder and when the cylinder is rotated it prints on the paper being passed beneath it. An increase in printing speed and efficency is attained as the paper is a continuous roll.

When plates are curved to fit the cylinder, there is a slight increase in the size of each stamp design in the direction the plate is curved. Designs on the flat-plate presses run about 18 1/2 to 19 mm wide by 22 mm high. They stretch to 19 1/2 to 20 mm wide on the rotary plates that are curved sidewise to the design, and to 22 1/2 to 23 mm high when the plates are curved lengthwise to the design. A line of ink is deposited on the paper between stamp designs, where the two plates are joined.

1914-16 Rotary Press Coil Stamps. Designs 18 1/2 to 19 mm wide by 22 1/2 mm high, *single-line USPS watermark (wmk 273), perforated 10 horizontally.*

The designs of rotary press stamps are larger in one dimension than those of flat press stamps. Above illustration shows to the left the rotary press coil No. 340 being taller than the flat press No. 333

The designs of rotary press stamps are larger in one dimension than those of flat press stamps. Above illustration shows to the left the rotary press coil No. 340 being taller than the flat press No. 333

340 *(448)*

1c green *(Dec. 12, 1915)*	6.50	4.25
pale green	6.50	4.25
On cover		8.00
Pair	15.	9.00
Line pair	40.	27.50

341 *Type III. Same as Type II except two lines of shading in the curves of the ribbons*

341 *(450)*

2c carmine, Type III	10.	4.25
carmine rose	10.	4.25
red	10.	4.25
On cover		9.00
Pair	25.	10.
Line pair	55.	22.50
(449) v. carmine, Type I	2,000.	325.

Earliest documented cover: Dec. 21, 1915

Imperforate, Sidewise Coil. Design 19 1/2 to 20 mm wide by 22 mm high

342 *(459)*

2c carmine, Type I *(June 30, 1914)*	375.	750.
On cover		—
Pair	675.	2,250.
Line pair	1,250.	8,500.

Perforated 10 vertically. Designs 19 1/2 to 20 mm wide by 22 mm high

343 *(452)*

1c green *(Nov. 11, 1914)*	10.	2.50
On cover		4.00
Pair	25.	2,250.
Line pair	65.	12.50

Earliest documented cover: Mar. 22, 1915

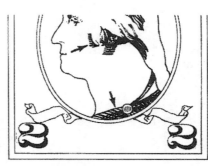

344t *Type II. Shading lines in ribbons same as Type I. The top line of toga rope is heavy and the rope is heavily shaded. The shading lines on the face, in front of the ear, are joined by a heavy vertical curved line.*

344 *(455)*

2c carmine, Type III *(Dec. 1915)*	10.	1.15
carmine rose	10.	1.15
On cover		2.25
Pair	22.50	2.75
Line pair	55.	7.25

(454)	v. carmine, Type II *(June 1915)*	85.	10.50
(453)	v1. carmine, Type I		
	(June 30, 1914)	110.	4.25

345 *(456)*

3c violet, Type I *(Feb. 2, 1916)*	225.	115.
dark violet	225.	115.
red violet	225.	115.
On cover		180.
Pair	550.	300.
Line pair	1,100.	700.

346 *(457)*

4c yellow brown *(Nov. 5, 1915)*	27.50	20.
brown	27.50	20.
On cover		45.
Cracked plate	35.	
Pair	60.	50.
Line pair	150.	100.

347 *(458)*

5c blue *(March 9, 1916)*	32.50	17.50
On cover		42.50
Pair	75.	50.
Line pair	180.	100.
Double transfer	—	

1916-17 Issue. *Flat plate printing, unwatermarked, perforated 10.*

348 *(462)*

1c green *(Sept. 27, 1916)*	6.00	.50
blue green	6.00	.50
dark green	6.00	.50
dull green	6.00	.50
On cover		.50
Plate block of six	150.	
a. Booklet pane of six		
(Oct. 15, 1916)	10.	

349 *(463)*

2c carmine, Type I *(Sept. 25, 1916)*	4.00	35.
dark carmine	4.00	35.
rose red	4.00	35.
On cover		.50
Double transfer	6.00	
Plate block of six	130.	
a. Booklet pane of six		
(Oct. 8, 1916)	85.	

350 *(464)*

3c violet, Type I *(Nov. 11, 1916)*	65.	15.
dark violet	65.	15.
On cover		40.
Plate block of six	1,400.	
Double transfer in "CENTS"	90.	

351 *(465)*

4c yellow brown *(Oct. 7, 1916)*	42.50	2.25
dark brown	42.50	2.25
On cover		12.50

Double transfer	—	
Plate block of six	675.	

352 *(466)*

5c blue *(Oct. 17, 1916)*	65.	2.25
dark blue	65.	2.25
dull blue	65.	2.25
On cover		12.50
Plate block of six	900.	

353 *The "Five Cent Red Error' was caused by mistakenly using a 5c transfer roll in reentering three positions on plate 7942, a plate of the 2c stamps. Of the 400 positions on the plate, 397 copies were 2c and three copies were 5c. The error was not discovered until a considerable number of sheets were in the post offices and many of them were picked up by collectors. The error exists perforated 10, perforated 11, and imperforate. The shade actually is carmine, but the stamp commonly is called the "Red Error."*

353 *(467)*

5c carmine	550.	700.
On cover		1,950.
Block of nine, one 5c error in		
middle of block of 2c stamps	750.	
Block of twelve, two 5c errors		
(two middle stamps) with ten		
2c stamps	1,500.	

Earliest documented cover: May 25, 1917

354 *(468)*

6c red orange *(Oct. 10, 1916)*	80.	7.50
orange	80.	7.50
On cover		40.
Double transfer	—	
Plate block of six	1,400.	

355 *(469)*

7c black *(Nov. 10, 1916)*	100.	12.50
deep black	100.	12.50
gray black	100.	12.50
On cover		45.
Plate block of six	1,400.	

356 *(470)*

8c yellow olive *(Nov. 13, 1916)*	55.	6.50
dark yellow olive	55.	6.50
On cover		30.
Plate block of six, with "A"	625.	
Plate block of six, with "A"		
and imprint	575.	

357 *(471)*

9c salmon *(Nov. 16, 1916)*	50.	15.
On cover		40.
Plate block of six	775.	

358 *(472)*

10c orange yellow *(Oct. 17, 1916)*	95.	1.25
On cover		8.00
Plate block of six	1,400.	

359 *(473)*

11c deep bluish green *(Nov. 16, 1916)*	35.	22.50
On cover		45.
Plate block of six	375.	

360 *(474)*

12c chocolate *(Oct. 10, 1916)*	45.	5.50
On cover		22.50
Plate block of six	650.	
Double transfer	60.	6.00
Triple transfer	70.	9.00

361 *(475)*

15c gray black *(Nov. 16, 1916)*	165.	12.50
gray	165.	12.50
On cover		85.
Plate block of six	2,900.	
Plate block of six, with "A" and imprint	—	

362 *(476)*

20c pale blue *(Dec. 5, 1916)*	225.	12.50
blue	225.	12.50
On cover		725.
Plate block of six	3,750.	

362A *A full sheet of 100 stamps of the 30c denomination was discovered without any trace of watermark. This fact was authenticated by The Philatelic Foundation's expert committee.*

362A *(467A)*

30c orange red	4,500.	—
Plate block of six	—	

363 *(477)*

50c light violet *(March 2, 1917)*	950.	65.
On cover		2,250.
Plate block of six	42,500.	

364 *(478)*

$1 violet black *(Dec. 22, 1916)*	625.	20.
On cover		3,000.
Plate block of six, with "A" and imprint	14,000.	
Margin block of four, with arrow	3,250.	
Double transfer	850.	22.50

365 *James Madison*   366 *John Marshall*

365 *(479)*

$2 dark blue *(March 22, 1917)*	325.	45.
On cover		1,250.
Plate block of six	4,500.	
Margin block of four, with arrow	1,450.	
Double transfer	—	

366 *(480)*

$5 light green *(March 22, 1917)*	250.	50.
On cover		1,250.
Plate block of six	3,250.	
Margin block of four, with arrow	1,150.	

Imperforate

367 *(481)*

1c green *(Dec. 8, 1916)*	1.15	1.00
bluish green	1.15	1.00
dark green	1.15	1.00
On cover		1.50
Plate block of six	12.50	
Center line block	8.50	6.25
Margin block of 4, with arrow	4.50	3.25
Double transfer	2.50	1.25

368 *(482)*

2c carmine, Type I *(Dec. 8, 1916)*	1.40	1.30
carmine rose	1.40	1.30
dark carmine	1.40	1.30
dark rose	1.40	1.30
On cover		2.50
Plate block of six	22.50	
Plate block of six, from plate No. 7942	140.	
Center line block	8.50	7.00
Cracked plate	—	
Margin block of four, with arrow	6.50	5.75

369 3c. On Type II the top line of the toga rope is heavy and the rope shading lines are also heavy and complete. The line between the lips is heavy.

369 *(483)*

	3c violet, Type I *(Oct. 13, 1917)*	15.	8.50
	dull violet	15.	8.50
	On cover		17.50
	Plate block of six	125.	
	Center line block	70.	70.
	Double transfer	17.50	
	Margin block of four, with arrow	60.	35.
	Triple transfer	—	
(484)	v. violet, Type II	12.50	5.50
	dark violet	12.50	5.50
	On cover		11.50
	Plate block of six	100.	
	Center line block	60.	60.
	Margin block of four, with arrow	47.50	30.
	Double transfer	12.50	

Earliest documented cover: April 30, 1918

370 *(485)*

5c carmine *(March 1917)*	12,500.	
On cover	—	
Block of nine, one 5c error in middle		
of block of 2c stamps	15,000.	
Block of twelve, two 5c errors		
(two middle stamps)		
with ten 2c stamps	27,500.	

This stamp commonly is called the "Red Error," but really is carmine.

1916-22. Rotary Press Coil Stamps, *unwatermarked*

Perforated 10 horizontally. Stamp designs 18 1/2 to 19 mm wide by 22 1/2 high

371 *(486)*

1c green *(Jan 10, 1918)*	.75	.20
yellowish green	.75	.20
On cover		.50
Pair	2.00	.65
Line pair	4.00	.75
Cracked plate	—	
Double transfer	2.25	

372 *(488)*

	2c carmine, Type III *(1919)*	3.00	1.75
	On cover		3.50
	Pair	5.75	4.00
	Line pair	20.	
	Cracked plate	12.	7.50
(487)	v. carmine, Type II		
	(Nov. 15, 1916)	14.50	4.75
	On cover		10.
	Pair	32.50	7.50
	Line pair	125.	
	Cracked plate	—	

373 *(489)*

3c violet, Type I *(Oct. 10, 1917)*	4.50	1.50
bluish violet	4.50	1.50
dull violet	4.50	1.50
On cover		2.50
Pair	11.	4.00
Line pair	27.50	10.

Perforated 10 vertically. Stamp designs 19 1/2 to 20 mm wide by 22 mm high

374 *(490)*

1c green *(Nov. 17, 1916)*	.60	.20
yellowish green	.60	.20
On cover		.50
Pair	1.25	.65
Line pair	4.00	1.25
Cracked plate	7.50	
Double transfer	—	
Rosette crack on head	50.	

375 *(492)*

2c carmine, Type III *(Nov. 17, 1916)*	8.50	.20
carmine rose	8.50	.20
On cover		.50

	Pair	21.	.65
	Line pair	50.	3.50
	Cracked plate	—	
	Double transfer	—	
(491)	v. carmine, Type II		
	(Nov. 17, 1916)	1,650.	800.
	On cover		850.
	Pair	4,000.	17.50
	Line pair	9,000.	5,000.

376 *(494)*

	3c violet, Type II *(Feb. 4, 1918)*	11.50	1.25
	dull violet	11.50	1.25
	gray violet	11.50	1.25
	On cover		1.00
	Pair	24.	2.25
	Line pair	60.	2.75
(493)	v1. violet, Type I *(July 23, 1917)*	17.50	3.25
	reddish violet	17.50	3.25
	On cover		7.00
	Pair	35.	8.00
	Line pair	125.	45.

377 *(495)*

4c yellow brown *(Oct. 19, 1917)*	10.50	4.00
On cover		8.50
Pair	24.	10.
Line pair	65.	17.50
Cracked plate	—	

378 *(496)*

5c blue *(Jan. 15, 1919)*	3.50	1.25
On cover		1.75
Pair	8.00	2.25
Line pair	25.	7.00

379 *(497)*

10c orange yellow *(Jan. 31, 1922)*	19.	12.50
On cover		17.50
Pair	47.50	27.50
Line pair	125.	50.

1917-19 Issue. *Flat press printing, unwatermarked paper, and perforated 11.*

380 *(498)*

1c green *(March 23, 1917)*	.55	.20
dark green	.55	.20
pale green	.55	.20
yellowish green	.55	.20
On cover		.35
Plate block of six	17.50	
Cracked plate	7.50	
Double transfer	5.50	2.00
n. Booklet pane of six		
(Apr. 6, 1917)	2.75	.35
n1. Booklet pane of thirty	1,100.	
v. Double impression	175.	
v1. Horizontal pair, imperforate		
between	75.	

v2. Perforated 10 at top   675.
v3. Perforated 10 at bottom   675.
v4. Vertical pair, imperforate
    between   400.
v5. Vertical pair, imperforate
    horizontally   200.
Earliest documented cover: Sept. 10, 1917

381 *(499)*

2c rose red, Type I *(March 23, 1917)*   .50   .20
    dark rose   .50   .20
    rose carmine   .50   .20
    On cover   .35
    Plate block of six   18.
    Cracked plate   —
    Double transfer   6.00
    Retouch in hair   —
    Double impression   160.
    n. Booklet pane of six
       (Mar. 31, 1917)   4.50
    n1. Booklet pane of 30   27,500.
    v. Horizontal pair, imperforate
       vertically   200.   125.
    v1. Vertical pair, imperforate
       between   500.   250.
    v2. Vertical pair, imperforate
       horizontally   150.
(500)   a. deep rose, Type Ia   225.   175.
       dark rose   225.   175.
       On cover   325.
       Plate block of six   1,800.
       Plate block of six, two
          stamps Type I   7,500.
    Pair, one each Type I and Ia   1,000.
Earliest documented cover: Aug. 12,1917

Type Ia is similar to Type I, but lines of the design are stronger. This is particularly noticeable on the toga button, toga rope and rope shading lines, which are heavy. Lines in the ribbons are similar to Type I.

382 *(501)*

3c violet, Type I *(March 23, 1917)*   12.50   .20
    dark violet   12.50   .20
    dull violet   12.50   .20
    reddish violet   12.50   .20
    On cover   .35
    Plate block of six   100.
    n. Booklet pane of six
       (Oct. 17, 1917)   60.   17.50
    v. Double impression   200.
    v1. Vertical pair, imperforate
       horizontally   400.

382A *(502)*

3c violet, Type II *(Feb. 25, 1918)*   15.   .40
    dark violet   15.   .40
    On cover   .65
    Plate block of six   150.
    n. Booklet pane of six   50.
    v. Double impression   200.

v1. Perforated 10 at top   625.
v2. Perforated 10 at bottom   625.
v3. Vertical pair, imperforate
    horizontally   250.   150.
Earliest documented cover: June 18, 1918

383 *(503)*

4c yellow brown *(March 23, 1917)*   11.50   .30
    brown   11.50   .30
    dark brown   11.50   .30
    orange brown   11.50   .30
    On cover   2.00
    Plate block of six   140.
    Double transfer   15.
    v. Double impression   —

384 *(504)*

5c blue *(March 23, 1917)*   8.50   .25
    dark blue   8.50   .25
    dull blue   8.50   .25
    On cover   .35
    Plate block of six   125.
    Double transfer   10.50
    v. Horizontal pair, imperforate
       between   2,250.

385 *(505)*

5c rose   400.   500.
    On cover   1,500.
    Strip of three
       (Nos. 381-385-381)   500.
    Block of nine, one 5c error in
       middle of 2c block   600.
    Block of twelve, two 5c errors
       (two middle stamps) within
       ten 2c stamps   1,000.
Earliest documented cover: Mar. 27, 1917

386 *(506)*

6c red orange *(March 23, 1917)*   12.50   .40
    orange   12.50   .40
    On cover   2.50
    Plate block of six   145.
    Double transfer   —
    v. Perforated 10 at bottom   650.
    v1. Perforated 10 at top   650.

387 *(507)*

7c black *(March 24, 1917)*   25.   1.25
    deep black   25.   1.25
    gray black   25.   1.25
    On cover   8.00
    Plate block of six   220.
    Double transfer   —

388 *(508)*

8c yellow olive *(March 24, 1917)*   12.50   1.00
    dark olive green   12.50   1.00
    olive green   12.50   1.00
    On cover   300.
    Plate block of six   125.

Plate block of six, with "A"	150.	
Plate block of six, with "A" and imprint	200.	
v. Perforated 10 at bottom	12.50	
v1. Perforated 10 at top	12.50	
v2. Vertical pair, imperforate between	—	

389 *(509)*

9c salmon *(March 12, 1917)*	14.	2.50
On cover		15.
Plate block of six	125.	
Double transfer	20.	5.00
v. Perforated 10 at bottom	1,000.	
v1. Perforated 10 at top	1,000.	

390 *(510)*

10c orange yellow *(March 24, 1917)*	17.50	.25
On cover		2.00
Plate block of six	165.	
Plate block of six, with "A"	300.	

391 *(511)*

11c deep bluish green *(May 19, 1917)*	9.00	3.00
dull green	9.00	3.00
green	9.00	3.00
On cover		8.50
Plate block of six	115.	
Double transfer	12.50	3.25
v. Perforated 10 at bottom	1,000.	375.
v1. Perforated 10 at top	1,000.	375.

392 *(512)*

12c brown purple *(May 12, 1917)*	9.00	.65
brown carmine	9.00	.65
On cover		4.00
Plate block of six	115.	
Double transfer	12.50	
Triple transfer	20.	
v. Perforated 10 at bottom	14.	6.00
v1. Perforated 10 at top	14.	6.00

393 *(513)*

13c apple green *(Jan. 11, 1919)*	10.50	6.50
dark apple green	10.50	6.50
pale apple green	10.50	6.50
On cover		20.
Plate block of six	125.	

394 *(514)*

15c gray black *(May 21, 1917)*	37.50	1.25
gray	37.50	1.25
On cover		22.50
Plate block of six	450.	
Double transfer	—	

395 *(515)*

20c pale blue *(May 12, 1917)*	47.50	.50
dark blue	47.50	.50
gray blue	47.50	.50

On cover		75.
Plate block of six	500.	
Double transfer	—	
v. Double impression	1,250.	
v1. Perforated 10 at bottom	1,600.	
v2. Perforated 10 at top	1,600.	
v3. Vertical pair, imperforate between	425.	

396 *(516)*

30c orange red *(May 12, 1917)*	37.50	1.25
dark orange red	37.50	1.25
On cover		150.
Plate block of six	500.	
Double transfer	—	
v. Double impression	—	
v1. Perforated 10 at bottom	1,100.	
v2. Perforated 10 at top	1,100.	

397 *(517)*

50c reddish violet *(May 19, 1917)*	65.	.90
pale violet	65.	.90
red violet	65.	.90
On cover		400.
Plate block of six	1,650.	
Double transfer	100.	1.50
v. Perforated 10 at bottom	—	950.
v1. Perforated 10 at top	—	950.
v2. Vertical pair, imperforate between	1,800.	1,000.

398 *(518)*

$1 black purple *(May 19, 1917)*	55.	1.75
brown purple	55.	1.75
blackish brown	1,100.	750.
On cover		550.
Plate block of six, with "A" and imprint	1,350.	
Double transfer	75.	2.00
Margin block of four, with arrow	250.	

1917. The 2c carmine stamp of 1908-09 issues existed in 1917 in the imperforate form at the New York Post Office. The old stock was returned to the Bureau of Engraving and Printing and was perforated with the then-current perforation 11. We list this stamp under the year in which it came into use. It is identical with No. 238, except for the perforation. *Flat plate printing, double-line USPS watermark (187), perforated 11.*

399 *(519)*

2c carmine	275.	450.
On cover		2,000.
Plate block of six, with imprint	2,250.	

Earliest documented cover: Oct. 10, 1917

1918-20. New Designs. *Flat plate printing, unwatermarked, perforated 11.*

400-402 *Benjamin Franklin*

400 *(523)*

   $2 orange and black *(Aug. 23, 1918)* 650.   225.
     On cover   1,850.
     Center line block   3,000.
     Margin block of four, with arrow 2,800.
     Plate block of eight, with
         arrow   13,500.

401 *(547)*

   $2 carmine and black

         (Nov. 1, 1920)   190.   40.
     lilac carmine and black   190.   40.
     Plate block of eight, with arrow   —
     Center line block   —
     Margin block of four, with arrow   —
     On cover   —

402 *(524)*

   $5 deep green and black

         (Aug. 23, 1918)   225.   35.
     On cover   1,500.
     Center line block   1,050.
     Margin block of four, with arrow 1,000.
     Plate block of eight, with arrow 3,850.

1918-20. Offset Printing. This is the first time the Post Office Department did not use engraved plates. It was a direct result of World War I. During this period the Bureau of Engraving and Printing was hard pressed by the demands for stamps and government printing of all types. Printing inks for postage stamps used barites as a base, and as the war went on this basic material grew inferior in quality and contained a gritty substance which wore out the engraved plates quicker; high quality steel was difficult to obtain, so all conditions combined resulted in the unsatisfactory experiment of offset printing. These stamps can easily be identified by the smoothness of the printed surface when contrasted with any of the earlier stamps, all of which were engraved. This can be told apart by actual touch, as the engraved stamps have a "rough" feeling, and the offsets a "soapy" feeling. If you hold an engraved stamp at a flat angle against a light and observe it through a magnifying glass, the actual ridges of the ink may be observed, while on the offsets there is no fine detail, and the stamps have a blurred appearance. The offsets are smaller than the engraved, usually about 1/2 mm narrower in width (with the exception of the Type IV 3c) and from 1/2 mm to 1 mm less in length. The offsets run from 21 to 21 1/2 mm high. Three denominations were made in this style of printing, 1c, 2c, and 3c, each value being *perforated 11* and *imperforate*, and the 1c also came *perforated 12 1/2*.

Unwatermarked, perforated 11

403 *George Washington*

403 *(525)*

   1c dull green *(Dec. 24, 1918)*   2.00   .75
     dark green   2.25   .75
     emerald   2.00   .75
     On cover   1.50
     Plate block of six   16.50
     "Flat nose" (nose appears so)   —
     v. Double impression   25.
     v1. Horizontal pair, imperforate
         between   95.

There are five types of the 2c offset stamps, with each of these types appearing only on the offset stamps.

Type IV: *Top line of toga rope is broken. Lines inside toga button read "D (reversed) ID." The line of color in the left "2" is very thin and is usually broken.*

from bottom.

Type V: *Top line of the toga is complete. Five vertical shading lines in toga button. Line of color in left "2" is very thin and usually broken. Shading dots on nose form a triangle with six dots in third row*

Type Va: *Same as Type V except on the shading dots on the nose, in which the third row from the bottom has only four dots instead of six.*

Type VI: *Same as Type V but there is a heavy line of color in the left "2."*

Type VII: *The line of color in the left "2" is clear and unbroken, heavier than on Type V or Va but not as heavy as on Type VI. An extra vertical row of dots has been added on the lip, making four rows of three dots instead of two dots. Additional dots have been added to the hair on top of the head.*

404-404D

404 *(528B)*

2c rose red, Type VII	17.50	.35
On cover		.40
Plate block of six	135.	
Retouch on cheek	375.	
v. Double impression	65.	

Earliest documented cover: Nov. 10, 1920

404A *(527)*

2c rose red, Type V	15.	1.00
bright carmine	15.	1.00
rose carmine	15.	1.00
On cover		2.50
Plate block of six	125.	
Line through "2" and "EN"	30.	
v. Double impression	55.	8.50
v1. Horizontal pair, imperforate vertically	1,000.	
v2. Vertical pair, imperforate horizontally	600.	

Earliest documented cover: April 20,1920

404B *(528)*

2c rose red, Type Va	8.00	.35
On cover		.65
Plate block of six	75.	
Plate block of six, with monogram over number "CRNTS" rather than "CENTS"	90.	
Retouch of "P" in "POSTAGE"	50.	
Retouch on toga	—	
v. Double impression	25.	
v1. Vertical pair, imperforate between	1,000.	

Earliest documented cover: July 16, 1920

404C *(528A)*

2c rose red, Type VI	45.	1.50

bright carmine	45.	1.50
On cover		3.75
Plate block of six	350.	
Plate block of six, with monogram over number	450.	
v. Double impression	150.	
v1. Vertical pair, imperforate between	1,000.	
v2. Vertical pair, imperforate horizontally	—	

Earliest documented cover: July 30, 1920

404D *(526)*

2c rose red, Type IV	25.	4.25
carmine	25.	4.25
On cover		10.
Plate block of six	185.	
Misformed "2" at left	35.	
Scar on forehead	45.	

Earliest documented cover: March 15, 1920

405 *George Washington. There are two types of the 3c offset stamps, each of which appears only on the offset printing.*

Type III: *Top line of toga is strong but the fifth shading line is missing. The center shading line of the toga button consists of two vertical dashes with a dot between them. The "P" and "O" of "POSTAGE" have a line of color between them.*

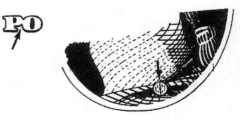

Type IV: *The "P" and "O" of "POSTAGE" are joined with no line of color between them. The center shading line runs right through the dot in the toga button.*

405 *(529)*

3c purple, Type III *(March 23, 1918)*	3.00	.40
dark purple	3.00	.40
dull purple	3.00	.40
On cover		.50
Plate block of six	40.	
v. Double impression	35.	
v1. Printed on both sides	425.	

405A (530)
3c purple, Type IV | 1.25 | .20
dull purple | 1.25 | .20
violet | 1.25 | .20
On cover | | .25
Plate block of six | 15.
"Blister" under "U.S." | 4.25
Retouch under "U.S." | 4.25
v. Double impression | 17.50 | 6.00
v1. Printed on both sides | 225.
Earliest documented cover: June 30, 1918

Imperforate Offset Stamps

406 (531)
1c dull green (Jan. 21, 1919) | 10. | 8.50
green | 10. | 8.50
On cover | | 15.
Plate block of six | 75.
Center line block | 55. | 45.
Margin block of four, with arrow | 40. | 36.

407 (532)
2c rose red, Type IV | 35. | 30.
On cover | | 65.
Plate block of six | 285.
Center line block | 200.
Margin block of four, with arrow | 175.
Earliest documented cover: April 30, 1920

407A (533)
2c rose red, Type V | 190. | 85.
On cover | | 200.
Plate block of six | 1,750.
Center line block | 900. | 450.
Margin block of four, with arrow | 800.
Earliest documented cover: June 30, 1920

407B (534)
2c rose red, Type Va | 12.50 | 8.50
carmine | 12.50 | 8.50
On cover | | 14.
Plate block of six | 85.
Plate block of six, with
  monograph over number | 200.
Center line block | 50. | 60.
Margin block of four, with arrow | 50. | 40.
Earliest documented cover: July 3, 1920

407C (534A)
2c rose red, Type VI | 35. | 22.50
On cover | | 35.
Plate block of six | 300.
Center line block | 190. | 175.
Margin block of four, with arrow | 165.
Earliest documented cover: Sept. 7, 1920

407D (534B)
2c rose red, Type VII | 1,500. | 575.
On cover | | 1,050.
Plate block of six | 12,500.

Center line block | 7,700.
Margin block of four, with arrow 5,500.
Earliest documented cover: Nov. 3, 1920

408 (535)
3c violet, Type IV | 8.75 | 6.00
On cover | | 11.
Plate block of six | 50.
Center line block | 45. | 45.
Margin block of four, with arrow | 40. | 30.
v. Double impression | 100.
Earliest documented cover: Oct. 5, 1918

Perforated 12 1/2

The 1c offset was issued with a trial perforation 12 1/2 made by the Rossbach perforating machine, a two-way rotary perforator that perforated a single sheet one direction, and then the other. The machine was proved unsatisfactory as nearly half of the sheets that were perforated had to be destroyed. Of the 6,641 sheets of 400 images that were perforated by this machine, only 3,466 were good enough to send to the post offices. These were cut into panes of 100 before they were issued. Even the sheets that were released consisted, for the most part, of very badly centered stamps.

409 (536)
1c dull green (Aug. 15, 1919) | 14. | 16.50
On cover | | 50.
Plate block of six | 140.
v. Horizontal pair, imperforate
  vertically | 450.

The Rotary Press Issues that follow form the final group of issues that bear the Washington design of 1914-15. Here is how Rotary Press intaglio stamps can be distinguished from stamps of similar designs printed by flat press intaglio or offset.

1. Rotary press stamps are always wider or taller than flat press or offset stamps. This measurement concerns the printed design only.
2. The back of a rotary press stamp is almost always free of color, while flat press stamps very often have small bits of color on the back.
3. With the exception of stamps printed from coil waste, the perforated rotary press stamps will show one or more ridges extending across the back of the stamp. These ridges were forced into the paper in an effort to keep the stamps from curling. This easily is apparent on unused stamps, but much more difficult to detect on used stamps. Most flat press stamps do not have these ridges.

1919. Rotary Press Printing. Designs 19 1/2 to 20 mm wide by 22 mm high. Printed from coil waste sheets, no "breaker bar" ridges on back of stamps, *unwatermarked, perforated 11 x 10.*

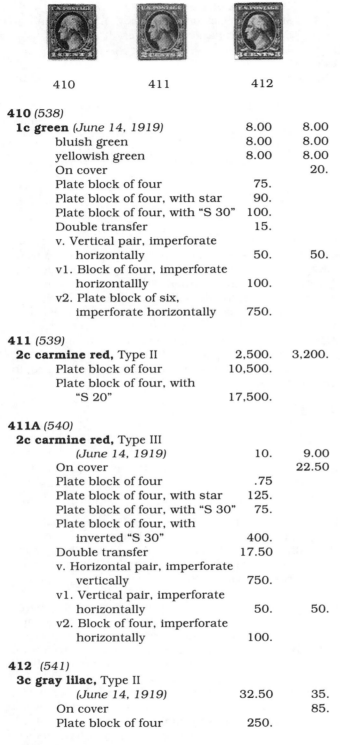

410   411   412

410 *(538)*

1c green *(June 14, 1919)*	8.00	8.00
bluish green	8.00	8.00
yellowish green	8.00	8.00
On cover		20.
Plate block of four	75.	
Plate block of four, with star	90.	
Plate block of four, with "S 30"	100.	
Double transfer	15.	
v. Vertical pair, imperforate horizontally	50.	50.
v1. Block of four, imperforate horizontallly	100.	
v2. Plate block of six, imperforate horizontally	750.	

411 *(539)*

2c carmine red, Type II	2,500.	3,200.
Plate block of four	10,500.	
Plate block of four, with "S 20"	17,500.	

411A *(540)*

2c carmine red, Type III *(June 14, 1919)*	10.	9.00
On cover		22.50
Plate block of four	.75	
Plate block of four, with star	125.	
Plate block of four, with "S 30"	75.	
Plate block of four, with inverted "S 30"	400.	
Double transfer	17.50	
v. Horizontal pair, imperforate vertically	750.	
v1. Vertical pair, imperforate horizontally	50.	50.
v2. Block of four, imperforate horizontally	100.	

412 *(541)*

3c gray lilac, Type II *(June 14, 1919)*	32.50	35.
On cover		85.
Plate block of four	250.	

1920. Rotary press, stamp designs 18 1/2 to 19 mm wide by 22 1/2 mm high, *unwatermarked, perforated 10 x 11.* Breaker bar ridges on stamps.

413 *(542)*

1c green, *(May 26, 1920)*	10.	1.00
bluish green	10.	1.00
On cover		5.50
Plate block of six (vertical), with		

plate number opposite center
horizontal row   135.

1921. Rotary press, stamp designs 18 1/2 to 19 mm wide by 22 1/2 mm high, *unwatermarked, perforated 10,* breaker bar ridges on stamps.

414 *(543)*

1c green *(May 26, 1921)*	.55	.20
dark green	.55	.20
On cover		.35
Plate block of six (vertical), number opposite center horizontal row	27.50	
Plate block of four	12.50	
Double transfer	—	
Triple transfer	—	
v. Horizontal pair, imperforate between	1,000.	

1922. Rotary press, stamp design 19 mm wide by 22 1/2 mm high, *unwatermarked, perforated 11,* breaker bar ridges on stamps.

415 *(544)*

1c green *(1922)*	12,000.	2,400.
On cover		3,500.
Earliest documented cover: Dec. 21, 1922		

1921. Rotary press, stamp design 19 1/2 to 20 mm wide by 22 mm high, *unwatermarked, perforated 11,* no breaker bar ridges on stamps.

416   417

416 *(545)*

1c green	120.	130.
On cover		1,800.
Plate block of four	900.	
Plate block of four, with star	950.	
Plate block of four, with "S 30"	850.	
Earliest documented cover: June 25, 1921		

417 *(546)*

2c carmine, Type III	85.	115.
On cover		700.
Plate block of four	700.	
Plate block of four, with star	725.	
Plate block of four, with "S 30"	675.	
Recut in hair	120.	
v. Perforated 10 on left side	—	
Earliest documented cover: May 5, 1921		

1922-26. New Designs. Some of the denominations were produced, in part, with what are known as "Star Plates." On these particular plates the vertical rows are spaced 3 mm apart instead of 2 3/4 mm in an effort to improve the perforating. The plates are identified with a large 5-

point or 6-point star placed with the plate number. *Flat plate printing, unwatermarked, perforated 11.*

418 *Nathan Hale from a statue by Bela Lyon Pratt, Yale Campus. Hale, a 21-year-old captain in the Continental Army, in 1776 volunteered for spy duty behind the British lines on Long Island. Captured by the British on September 21, he was hanged the next morning. His last words were: "I only regret that I have but one life to lose for my country."*

418 (551)

1/2c olive brown *(April 4, 1925)*	.25	.20
dark olive brown	.25	.20
dull olive brown	.25	.20
Plate block of six	4.50	
Plate flaw on fraction bar	.75	.20

419 *Benjamin Franklin*   420 *Warren Harding*

419 (552)

1c green *(Jan. 17, 1923)*	1.45	.20
dark green	1.45	.20
dull green	1.45	.20
Plate block of six	17.50	
Double transfer	3.50	
n. Booklet pane of six	7.00	
Earliest documented cover: Jan. 10, 1924		

420 (553)

1 1/2c yellow brown *(March 19, 1925)*	2.75	.25
brown	2.75	.25
dull yellow brown	2.75	.25
Plate block of six	25.	
Double transfer	—	

421 *George Washington. Type I has thin hair lines at top center of head*

421 (554)

2c carmine, Type I *(Jan. 15, 1923)*	1.75	.20
Plate block of six	17.50	
Plate block of six, with small 5-point star (top only)	450.	
Plate block of six, with large 5-point star (top only)	550.	
Plate block of six, with large 5-point star (side only)	60.	

Plate block of six, with large 6-point star (top only)	700.	
Plate block of six, with large 6-point star (side only)	850.	
Double transfer	2.50	.75
n. Booklet pane of six	8.50	1.00
v. Horizontal pair, imperforate vertically	250.	
v1. Vertical pair, imperforate horizontally	500.	
v2. Perforated 10 at bottom	—	
v3. Perforated 10 at top	—	
Earliest documented cover: Feb. 10, 1923		

422 *Abraham Lincoln*   423 *Martha Washington*

422 (555)

3c reddish violet *(Feb. 12, 1923)*	17.50	1.25
bright violet	17.50	1.25
dark violet	17.50	1.25
violet	17.50	1.25
Plate block of six	125.	

423 (556)

4c yellow brown *(Jan. 15, 1923)*	17.50	.20
brown	17.50	.20
Plate block of six	130.	
Double transfer	—	
v. Perforated 10 at bottom	420.	
v1. Perforated 10 at top	420.	
v2. Horizontal pair, imperforate between	—	
v3. Vertical pair, imperforate horizontally	—	

424 *Theodore Roosevelt*   425 *James Garfield*

424 (557)

5c Prussian blue *(Oct. 27, 1922)*	17.50	.20
Plate block of six	145.	
Double transfer	—	
v. Horizontal pair, imperforate vertically	1,500.	
v1. Pair, imperforate	1,600.	
v2. Perforated 10 at bottom	—	450.
v3. Perforated 10 at top	—	450.

425 (558)

6c red orange *(Nov. 20, 1922)*	32.50	.85
dull red orange	32.50	.85
Plate block of six	300.	
Double transfer	50.	1.75
Double transfer, recut	50.	1.75

426 *William McKinley*   427 *Ulysses S. Grant*

426 (559)
7c black *(May 1, 1923)*	8.00	.75
gray black	8.00	.75
Plate block of six	55.	
Double transfer	—	

427 (560)
8c yellow olive *(May 1, 1923)*	42.50	.85
dull yellow olive	42.50	.85
Plate block of six	550.	
Double transfer	—	

428 *Thomas Jefferson*   429 *James Monroe*

428 (561)
9c carmine rose *(Jan. 15, 1923)*	16.50	1.25
dull carmine rose	16.50	1.25
Plate block of six	150.	
Double transfer	—	

429 (562)
10c orange yellow		
(Jan. 15, 1923)	22.50	.25
dull orange yellow	22.50	.25
Plate block of six	150.	
v. Pair, imperforate	1,250.	
v1. Vertical pair, imperforate		
horizontally	750.	
v2. Perforated 10 at bottom	—	750.
v3. Perforated 10 at top	—	750.

430 *Rutherford B. Hayes*   431 *Grover Cleveland*

430 (563)
11c turquoise blue *(Oct. 4, 1922)*	1.50	.50
dull bluish green	1.50	.50
dull yellowish green	1.50	.50
greenish blue	1.50	.50
Plate block of six	24.	
v. Pair, imperforate	—	

No. 430 is known in a wide range of color shades, between yellow, green, and light blue.

431 (564)
12c maroon *(March 20, 1923)*	7.50	.25
deep maroon	7.50	.25
Plate block of six	80.	
Plate block of six, with large		
5-point star (side only)	125.	
Plate block of six, with large		
6-point star (side only)	250.	
Double transfer	12.50	1.00
v. Horizontal pair, imperforate		
vertically	1,000.	
v1. Pair, imperforate	—	

432 *Benjamin Harrison*

432 (622)
13c green *(Jan. 11, 1926)*	14.	.65
dull green	14.	.65
Plate block of six	130.	
Plate block of six, with large		
5-point star	1,950.	

433 *American Indian from a photograph of Chief Hollowhorn Bear of the Brule Sioux tribe, taken on his visit to Washington for the inauguration of Theodore Roosevelt*

433 (565)
14c blue *(May 1, 1923)*	4.75	.80
Plate block of six	130.	
Double transfer	—	

434 *Statue of Liberty*

434 (566)
15c gray black *(Nov. 11, 1922)*	22.50	.20
light gray black	22.50	.20
Plate block of six	225.	
Plate block of six, with large		
5-point star (side only)	450.	

435 *Woodrow Wilson*

436 *Golden Gate*

435 (623)
17c black *(Dec. 28, 1925)*	17.50	.35
gray black	17.50	.35
Plate block of six	170.	

Identifier of the 1922-32 Regular Issues

Frame	Perf. 11	Perf. 11 x 10	Perf . 10	Coil 10	Perf. 11 x 10 1/2 or 10 1/2 x 11	Imperf.
	418-434, 448-449	446, 447	450-460	461-471, 520, 522	473-489, 517, 519	443-445 472
	435-442				490-494	

436 *(567)*

20c carmine red *(May 1, 1923)*	22.50	.20
dark carmine red	22.50	.20
Plate block of six	220.	
Plate block of six, with large 5-point star (side only)	425.	
v. Horizontal pair, imperforate vertically	2,000.	

438 *Bison*   437 *Niagara Falls*

437 *(568)*

25c green *(Nov. 11, 1922)*	17.50	.75
yellow green	17.50	.75
Plate block of six	175.	
Double transfer	—	
v. Perforated 10 at bottom	—	
v1. Perforated 10 at top	—	
v2. Vertical pair, imperforate horizontally	1,000.	

438 *(569)*

30c olive brown *(March 20, 1923)*	32.50	.50
Plate block of six	220.	
Double transfer	50.	2.00

439 *Niagra Falls*   440 *Lincoln Memorial*

439 *(570)*

50c gray lilac *(Nov. 11, 1922)*	55.	.20
dull gray lilac	55.	.20
Plate block of six	625.	

440 *(571)*

$1 purple brown *(Feb. 12, 1923)*	45.	.50
purple black	45.	.50
Plate block of six	350.	
Double transfer	85.	1.00
Margin block of four, with arrow	175.	

441 *U.S. Capitol*   442 *"America"*

441 *(572)*

$2 blue *(March 20, 1923)*	100.	10.
Plate block of six	800.	
Margin block of four, with arrow	400.	

442 *(573)*

$5 carmine and blue *(March 20, 1923)*	200.	13.50
lilac carmine and dark blue	200.	13.50
Plate block of eight, with arrow and two plate numbers	2,150.	
Center line block	850.	
Margin block of four, with arrow	825.	

Imperforate

443 *(575)*

1c green *(March 16, 1923)*	7.50	4.50
dark green	7.50	4.50
dull green	7.50	4.50
Plate block of six	70.	
Center line block	40.	
Margin block of four, with arrow	35.	

444 *(576)*

1 1/2c yellow brown *(April 4, 1925)*	1.50	1.45
brown	1.50	1.45
Plate block of six	17.50	
Center line block	10.50	
Margin block of four, with arrow	7.00	
Double transfer	—	

No. 444 exists in a rotary press printing, No. 472.

445 *(577)*

2c carmine *(March 20, 1923)*	1.50	1.45
dark carmine	1.50	1.45
dull carmine	1.50	1.45
Plate block of six	25.	
Plate block of six, with large 5-point star	70.	
Center line block	12.50	
Margin block of four, with arrow	7.50	

1923-24. Rotary Press Printings from coil waste, no breaker bar ridges on back of stamps, designs 19 1/2 to 20 mm wide by 22 mm high, *unwatermarked.*

Perforated 11 x 10

446 *(578)*

1c green	70.	110.
Plate block of four, with star	700.	
Earliest documented cover: March 26, 1924		

447 *(579)*

2c carmine	55.	100.
dark carmine	55.	100.
Plate block of four, with star	375.	
Recut in eye	90.	125.
Earliest documented cover: Feb. 20, 1923		

Perforated 11

448 *(594)*

1c green	15,000.	4,000.
dark green	15,000.	4,000.
dull green	15,000.	4,000.
Earliest documented cover: March 25, 1924		

449 *(595)*

2c carmine	185.	235.
Plate block of four, with star	1,750.	
Recut in eye	—	
Earliest documented cover: Nov. 17, 1923		

Nos. 448 and 449 were made from coil waste. Design 18 1/2 to 19 mm wide by 22 1/2 mm high.

449A *(596)*

1c green	—	42,500.

1923-26. Rotary Press Printing, breaker bar ridges on backs of stamps, designs 18 1/2 mm to 19 mm wide by 22 1/2 mm high, *unwatermarked, perforated 10.*

450 *(581)*

1c green *(Oct. 17, 1923)*	7.50	1.00
light green	7.50	1.00
yellow green	7.50	1.00
Plate block of four	75.	

451 *(582)*

1 1/2c yellow brown *(March 19, 1925)*	3.75	1.00
dark brown	3.75	1.00
Plate block of four	30.	
Gutter pair, Horizontal or vertical	150.	

452 *(583)*

2c carmine *(April 1924)*	2.00	.35
Plate block of four	17.50	
n. Booklet pane of six (Aug. 27, 1926)	75.	

453 *(584)*

3c reddish violet *(Aug. 1, 1925)*	20.	2.50
Plate block of four	170.	

454 *(585)*

4c yellow brown *(April 4, 1925)*	14.	.80
dark yellow brown	14.	.80
Plate block of four	125.	

455 *(586)*

5c blue *(April 4, 1925)*	14.	.80
deep blue	14.	.80
Plate block of four	120.	
Double transfer	—	
v. Horizontal pair, imperforate vertically	—	

456 *(587)*

6c orange *(April 4, 1925)*	6.25	.75
dull orange	6.25	.75
Plate block of four	60.	

457 *(588)*

7c black *(May 29, 1926)*	9.00	6.50
Plate block of four	65.	

458 *(589)*

8c yellow olive *(May 29, 1926)*	20.	4.00
pale yellow olive	20.	4.00
Plate block of four	150.	

459 *(590)*

9c red *(May 29, 1926)*	4.25	2.50
Plate block of four	32.50	

460 *(591)*
10c orange yellow *(June 8, 1925)*	50.	.45
Plate block of four	325.	

Coil Stamps

Designs 19 1/2 to 20 mm wide by 22 1/4 mm high, *perforated 10 vertically.*

461 *(597)*
1c yellow green *(July 18, 1923)*	.35	.20
green	.35	.20
Pair	.75	.20
Line pair	2.00	.25
Double transfer	2.50	.75
Gripper cracks	2.50	.75

462 *(598)*
1 1/2c yellow brown *(March 19, 1925)*	.75	.20
dark brown	.75	.20
Pair	2.00	.25
Line pair	6.00	.50

 463

Type II. There are three heavy hair lines at the top center of the head

463 *(599)*
2c carmine, Type I	.45	.20
dark carmine	.45	.20
Pair	.75	.20
Line pair	2.00	.25
Line pair, one each Type I and Type II	625.	
Double transfer	1.75	.50
Gripper cracks	2.00	1.75
(599A) v. carmine, Type II	115.	12.50
dark carmine	115.	12.50
Pair	—	
Line pair	525.	

Earliest documented cover: Jan. 10,1923

464 *(600)*
3c reddish violet *(May 10, 1924)*	5.50	.30
dark violet	5.50	.30
Pair	12.50	.50
Line pair	30.	1.00
Cracked plate	—	

465 *(601)*
4c yellow brown	3.75	.50
brown	3.75	.50
Pair	9.00	1.00
Line pair	35.	2.75

466 *(602)*
5c blue *(March 5, 1924)*	1.75	.20
Pair	3.50	.40
Line pair	12.50	.60

467 *(723)*
6c orange *(Aug. 18, 1932)*	9.50	.35
Pair	22.50	.50
Line pair	50.	2.50

468 *(603)*
10c orange yellow *(Dec. 1, 1924)*	3.50	.20
Pair	7.50	.25
Line pair	22.50	1.00

Coil Stamps

Designs 18 1/2 to 19 mm wide by 22 1/2 mm high, *perforated 10 horizontally*

469 *(604)*
1c yellow green *(July 19, 1924)*	.35	.20
green	.35	.20
Pair	.75	.25
Line pair	3.00	.50

470 *(605)*
1 1/2c yellow brown *(May 9, 1925)*	.35	.20
brown	.35	.20
Pair	.75	.25
Line pair	3.00	.50

471 *(606)*
2c carmine *(Dec. 31, 1923)*	.35	.20
Pair	.75	.25
Line pair	2.00	
Cracked plate	5.00	2.00

Imperforate

Design 18 1/2 to 19 mm wide by 22 1/2 mm high. Most of these stamps show the breaker bars on the back, but there was a printing of this stamp that did not have them. The stamp was issued in sheets of 400, with both vertical and horizontal gutters.

472 *(631)*
1 1/2c yellow brown *(Aug. 27, 1926)*	2.25	2.00
brown	2.25	2.00
Plate block of four	55.	
Center block with crossed gutters and dashes	20.	22.50
Gutter block of four	8.50	9.50
Margin block, with dash	9.50	13.50
Without gum breaker ridges	2.50	
Gutter pair, vertical or horizontal	—	

1926-34. Rotary Press Printing. Designs 18 1/2 to 19 mm wide by 22 1/2 mm high, breaker bar ridges on back of stamps, *unwatermarked, perforated 11 x 10 1/2*

473 *(653)*
1/2c olive brown *(May 25, 1929)* .25 .20
    Plate block of four 1.50
    Damaged plate 1.35
    Gutter pair 125.
    Retouched plate 1.35

474 *(632)*
1c green *(June 10, 1927)* .25 .20
    yellow green .25 .20
    Plate block of four 2.00
    Cracked plate —
    Gutter pair 135.
    n. Booklet pane of six
      (Nov. 2, 1927) 5.50
    v. Horizontal pair, imperforate
      between —
    v1. Vertical pair, imperforate
      between 750. —
    Earliest documented cover: May 24,1927

475 *(633)*
1 1/2c yellow brown *(May 17, 1927)* 2.00 .20
    dark brown 2.00 .20
    Plate block of four 70.

476 *(634)*
2c carmine red, Type I *(Dec. 10, 1926)* .25 .20
    lilac carmine .25 .20
    Plate (corner) block of four 2.00
    Plate block (vertical) of ten,
      with number opposite third
      horizontal row, (experimental
      electric eye plates) 4.50
    Margin block of four, with
      electric eye marking .35 .25
    Gutter pair 180.
    n. Booklet pane of six 2.00
    p. Thin (experimental) paper —
    v. Horizontal pair, imperforate
      between 2,250.
    v1. Vertical pair, imperforate
      between —
476A *(634A)*
2c carmine red, Type II 220. 15.
    Plate block of four 1,800.
    Gutter pair, vertical or
      horizontal 1,000.
    Earliest documented cover: Dec. 19, 1928

477 *(635)*
3c reddish violet *(Feb. 3, 1927)* .55 .20
    Plate block of four 8.00
(635a) v. red violet (re-issue)
      (Feb. 7, 1934) .25 .20
      Plate block of four 4.75
      Gripper cracks 3.00

478 *(636)*
4c yellow brown *(May 17, 1927)* 2.75 .20
    dark brown 2.75 .20

    Plate block of four 70.
    Gutter pair 200.
479 *(637)*
5c blue *(March 24, 1927)* 2.25 .20
    Plate block of four 15.
    Gutter pair 275.
    Double transfer —

480 *(638)*
6c orange *(July 27, 1927)* 2.25 .20
    dull orange 2.25 .20
    Plate block of four 15.
    Gutter pair, horizontal or
      vertical 200.

481 *(639)*
7c black *(March 24, 1927)* 2.25 .20
    Plate block of four 15.
    v. Vertical pair, imperforate
      between 125. 75.
    v1. Block of four, imperforate
      between 250.

482 *(640)*
8c yellow olive *(June 10, 1927)* 2.25 .20
    pale yellow olive 2.25 .20
    Plate block of four 15.

483 *(641)*
9c red *(1931)* 2.00 .20
    orange red 2.00 .20
    salmon 2.00 .20
    Plate block of four 15.
    Gutter pair —
    v. rose *(May 17, 1927)* 2.00 .20

484 *(642)*
10c orange yellow *(Feb. 3, 1927)* 4.00 .20
    Plate block of four 25.
    Double transfer —

485 *(692)*
11c turquoise green *(Sept. 4, 1931)* 2.75 .20
    Plate block of four 12.50
    Retouch on forehead 6.50 .75

486 *(693)*
12c brown purple *(Aug. 25, 1931)* 6.00 .20
    purple brown 6.00 .20
    Plate block of four 27.50

487 *(694)*
13c yellow green *(Sept. 4, 1931)* 2.25 .20
    blue green 2.25 .20
    pale yellow green 2.25 .20
    Plate block of four 14.
    Gutter pair 1.50

488 *(695)*
14c blue *(Sept. 8, 1931)* 4.00 .50
    Plate block of four 20.

489 *(696)*
15c gray black *(Aug. 27, 1931)*	8.00	.20
gray	8.00	.20
Plate block of four	35.	

The designs of the following stamps are horizontal rather than vertical, so perforation measurements are 10 1/2 x 11.

490 *(697)*
17c black *(July 25, 1931)*	5.50	.20
Plate block of four	25.	

491 *(698)*
20c carmine rose *(Sept. 8, 1931)*	9.50	.20
Plate block of four	50.	
Double transfer	20.	

492 *(699)*
25c green *(July 25, 1931)*	11.	.20
Plate block of four	50.	

493 *(700)*
30c olive brown *(Sept. 8, 1931)*	17.50	.20
Plate block of four	85.	
Cracked plate	27.50	.75
Retouch in head	27.50	.75

494 *(701)*
50c lilac *(Sept. 4, 1931)*	42.50	.20
red lilac	42.50	.20
Plate block of four	200.	

1929. The Kansas and Nebraska Overprints were issued to help prevent loss by post office burglaries. It was thought that stolen stamps could be traced more easily if they were overprinted. Approximately one year's supply was printed and delivered to the post offices in Kansas and Nebraska, but no further printings were made. The overprinting was done on the regular 1c to 10c stamps of the 1926-27 designs, *rotary press printing, unwatermarked, perforated 11 x 10 1/2.* All denominations were issued May 1, 1929.

    "Wide spacing pairs" noted below designate vertical pairs where the overprints are 32 mm apart rather than 22 mm.

 Kans.

495-505 *Kansas overprint*

495 *(658)*
1c green	2.00	1.50
Plate block of four	30.	
Wide spacing pair	30.	
v. Vertical pair, one without overprint	300.	

496 *(659)*
1 1/2c yellow brown	3.00	2.25
Plate block of four	40.	

Wide spacing pair	60.	
v. Vertical pair, one without overprint	325.	

497 *(660)*
2c carmine red	3.00	1.00
Plate block of four	35.	
Wide spacing pair	45.	

498 *(661)*
3c reddish violet	15.	11.
Plate block of four	145.	
v. Vertical pair, one without overprint	400.	

499 *(662)*
4c yellow brown	15.	8.50
Plate block of four	145.	
v. Vertical pair, one without overprint	400.	

500 *(663)*
5c blue	12.50	9.00
Plate block of four	120.	

501 *(664)*
6c orange	25.	15.
Plate block of four	325.	

502 *(665)*
7c black	25.	20.
Plate block of four	375.	
v. Vertical pair, one without overprint	400.	

503 *(666)*
8c yellow olive	70.	60.
Plate block of four	675.	

504 *(667)*
9c salmon	12.50	10.
Plate block of four	150.	

505 *(668)*
10c orange yellow	20.	12.50
Plate block of four	275.	
Gutter pair	—	

 Nebr.

506-516 *Nebraska overprint*

506 *(669)*
1c green	2.25	2.00
Plate block of four	30.	
Period omitted after "Nebr"	40.	
Wide spacing pair	35.	
v. Vertical pair, one without overprint	275.	

507 *(670)*

1 1/2c yellow brown	2.25	2.00
Plate block of four	40.	
Wide spacing pair	35.	

508 *(671)*

2c carmine red	2.25	1.00
Plate block of four	25.	
Wide spacing pair	50.	

509 *(672)*

3c reddish violet	11.	8.00
Plate block of four	120.	
Wide spacing pair	70.	
v. Vertical pair, one without overprint	400.	

510 *(673)*

4c yellow brown	15.	10.
Plate block of four	175.	
Wide spacing pair	110.	

511 *(674)*

5c blue	12.50	11.50
Plate block of four	175.	

512 *(675)*

6c orange	35.	17.50
Plate block of four	350.	

513 *(676)*

7c black	18.50	12.50
Plate block of four	225.	

514 *(677)*

8c yellow olive	25.	17.50
Plate block of four	325.	
Wide spacing pair	160.	

515 *(678)*

9c salmon	30.	22.50
Plate block of four	350.	
Wide spacing pair	140.	
v. Vertical pair, one without overprint	600.	

516 *(679)*

10c orange yellow	85.	17.50
Plate block of four	775.	

1930-32. New Designs. Rotary press printing, *unwatermarked, perforated 11 x 10 1/2.*

517, 520 *Warren G. Harding*

517 *(684)*

1 1/2c yellow brown *(Dec. 1, 1930)*	.25	.20
dull brown	.25	.20
Plate block of four	2.25	

Gutter pair, horizontal or vertical	175.	

518, 521, 523 *George Washington*

518 *(720)*

3c reddish violet *(June 16, 1932)*	.25	.20
pale reddish violet	.25	.20
Plate block of four	1.25	
Double transfer	1.00	.25
Gripper cracks	1.10	.30
Recut on nose	1.75	.60
Gutter pair	2.00	
n. Booklet pane of six *(July 25, 1932)*	37.50	
v. Vertical pair, imperforate between	300.	

519, 522 *William H. Taft*

519 *(685)*

4c yellow brown *(June 4, 1930)*	.90	.20
dark brown	.90	.20
Plate block of four	11.50	
Gouge on right "4"	2.00	.60
Recut on right "4"	2.00	.60
Gutter pair	—	

Coil Stamps. Perforated 10 vertically

520 *Line pair*

520 *(686)*

1 1/2c yellow brown *(Dec. 1, 1930)*	1.50	.20
Pair	3.50	.20
Line pair	7.50	.50

521 *(721)*

3c reddish violet *(June 24, 1932)*	1.75	.20
pale violet	1.75	.20
Pair	4.25	.50
Line pair	5.50	.60
Gripper cracks	—	
Recut on nose	—	
Recut around eyes	—	

522 *(687)*

4c yellow brown *(Sept. 18, 1930)*	2.75	.75
Pair	6.00	.85
Line pair	17.50	1.50

Coil Stamps. Perforated 10 horizontally

523 *(722)*

3c reddish violet *(Oct. 12, 1932)*	1.00	.75
pale violet	1.00	.75
Pair	3.00	.80
Line pair	4.00	1.50

1938-43. Presidential Issue. This issue is known as the Presidential Issue because all but three of its 32 values feature the portraits of former Presidents of the United States. *The values from 1/2c through 50c are printed by rotary press intaglio and are perforated 11 x 10 1/2. The $1, $2, and $5 values are printed by flat press intaglio, perforated 11.*

 524. *Benjamin Franklin (1706-1790), first Postmater General appointed by the Continental Congress, began his career as a printer and editor in Philadelphia, where he founded the first circulating library in America, the American Philosophical Society, and the nucleus for the University of Pennsylvania; he invented the Franklin stove, and made important experiments identifying lightning with electricity. He was deputy postmaster at Philadelphia 1737-53 and then (with William Hunter) postmaster general for the colonies until 1774, greatly expanding and improving postal service. An active patriot, both here and in England, for 20 years before the Revolution, he served in the 2nd Continental Congress, was appointed postmaster general, and aided in drafting the Declaration of Independence, of which he was a signer. Sent to France as a diplomat in 1776, he was enormously popular and successful there. With John Jay and John Adams, he negotiated the peace treaty with Great Britain in 1783. An important member of the Constitutional Convention in 1787, he signed the Constitution without entirely approving it. His last public act was in signing a petition to Congress for the abolition of slavery.*

524 *(803)*

1/2c red orange *(May 19, 1938)*	.25	.20
Plate block of four	.50	

 525 *George Washington, unanimously elected first President, mainly supported the federalist and industrialist policies of Alexander Hamilton (see No. 106) against the states' rights and agrarian theories of Thomas Jefferson (see No. 47). He was criticized for "aristocratic tendencies," for the 1794 Jay's Treaty with Great Britain, and for the excise tax that led to the Whiskey Rebellion of 1794; he brought the nation power and prestige, put down severe Indian troubles, and effected treaties opening the Mississippi to navigation.*

525 *(804)*

1c green *(April 25, 1938)*	.25	.20
pale green	.25	.20
Plate block of four	.50	
Gutter pair	—	
n. Booklet pane of six	2.00	

 526 *Martha Washington, wife of the first President, was known as "the prettiest and richest widow in Virginia" when Washington met her in 1758. Married to him in January 1759, she managed his plantations during the Revolution, visited him at Valley Forge and Newburgh, and was a gracious and popular First Lady.*

526 *(805)*

1 1/2c yellow brown *(May 5, 1938)*	.25	.20
ocher	.25	.20
Plate block of four	.50	
Gutter pair, horizontal or vertical	175.	
v. Horizontal pair, imperforate between	175.	
z. Tagged	—	

No. 526z was produced circa 1955 as a result of experiments conducted by Pitney-Bowes for the Post Office Department. A single copy is known in collector's hands.

 527 *John Adams, second President (1797-1801), attacked the Stamp Act in 1765, served in the 1st and 2nd Continental Congress, nominated George Washington to command the American forces, helped to draft the Declaration of Independence, and (according to Jefferson) was "the pillar of its support on the floor of Congress." He served as commissioner to France 1777-79, went with John Jay and Benjamin Franklin to England to negotiate the peace treaty, and was first American envoy to the Court of St. James. Serving as Vice President in both of Washington's terms, he was elected President in 1796. He was opposed by the Jefferson faction for the Alien and Sedition Acts, for which he was directly responsible, and by the Hamilton faction for his conciliatory policy toward France, which averted war. Defeated by Jefferson in the election of 1800, he retired to private life in Massachusetts.*

527 *(806)*

2c rose *(June 3, 1938)*	.25	.20
rose pink	.25	.20
Plate block of four	.50	
Plate block of ten (vertical), with number opposite third horizontal row	7.50	
Gutter pair, horizontal or vertical	—	
Recut at top of head	2.50	1.25
n. Booklet pane of six	6.00	
p. Thin, translucent paper	—	

528 *Thomas Jefferson, third President (1801-09), was the chief author of the Declaration of Independence and one of its signers. As a wartime legislator and governor in Virginia, he worked to abolish a landed aristocracy, separate church from state, and establish public schools. Returning to Congress in 1783, he headed the committee debating the peace treaty, devised the American monetary system, and laid the basis for later organization of western territories. He was minister to France 1785-89, became first Secretary of State, and was elected Vice President under John Adams. Strongly opposed to Alexander Hamilton, whose policies he felt led toward monarchy, he championed individual liberties, states' rights and an agrarian economy. Tied with Burr for electoral votes in 1800, he was supported by Hamilton and chosen President by the House of Representatives. In his two terms he authorized the Louisiana Purchase (CM32-CM36), warred against the Tripolitan pirates (CM178), dispatched the Lewis-and-Clark and Pike expeditions, and obtained a Congressional act abolishing the importation of slaves. A distinguished scholar, philosopher and patron of the arts, he founded the University of Virginia and greatly influenced the revival of classical architecture in America.*

528 *(807)*

3c violet *(June 16, 1938)*	.25	.20
Plate block of four	.50	
Plate block of ten (vertical), with number opposite third horizontal row	25.	
Gutter pair, horizontal or vertical	175.	
n. Booklet pane of six	8.50	
v. Horizontal pair, imperforate between	800.	
v1. Pair, imperforate	2,250.	

529 *James Madison, fourth President (1809-17), is known as "the father of the Constitution." A Virginian identified with Jefferson's liberal reforms there, he joined with Hamilton in proposing the Constitutional Convention, acted as recorder of the procedings, took a large part in framing the Constitution, greatly aided its ratification, and proposed the first 10 amendments: The Bill of Rights. Criticized as inept in his leadership in the War of 1812, he successfully advocated a protective tariff, a strong military organization, and a national system of roads and canals.*

529 *(808)*

4c bright purple *(July 1, 1938)*	1.15	.20
rose lilac	1.15	.20
Plate block of four	4.50	

530 *The White House*

530 *(809)*

4 1/2c gray *(July 11, 1938)*	.25	.20
dark gray	.25	.20
Plate block of four	1.25	

531 *James Monroe, fifth President (1817-25), fought in the 3rd Virginia Regiment at Harlem Heights, White Plains, Trenton (where he was wounded), Brandywine, Germantown, and Monmouth. He studied law under Jefferson, served in the Continental Congress, 1783-86, and fought the Constitution because he believed it made the federal government too powerful. As a senator, he biterly opposed Washington and Hamilton. As minister to France, he was recalled for over-sympathizing with the French Revolution and failing to follow Washington's instructions. Four times governor of Virginia, he was sent back to France in 1803 to aid in negotiating the Louisiana Purchase (CM34). Secretary of State and of War under Madison, he was elected President in 1816, ushering in the "Era of Good Feeling," and re-elected in 1820 with all but one vote, which was given to John Quincy Adams so that only Washington might have the honor of unanimous election. Monroe acquired Florida from Spain, supported the Missouri Compromise, settled the Canadian border and eliminated its forts, and proclaimed the Monroe Doctrine prohibiting further European colonization or interference in the Americas.*

531 *(810)*

5c light blue *(July 21, 1938)*	.25	.20
pale blue	.25	.20
Plate block of four	1.25	
Gutter pair	—	

532 *John Quincy Adams, sixth President (1825-29), was the son of John Adams (No. 527). When appointed Secretary of State by Monroe, he already had seen diplomatic service in France, the Netherlands, Prussia, Russia, and England; spent five years in the Senate; taught rhetoric at Harvard; and headed the peace commission that negotiated the Treaty of Ghent in 1814. He obtained the cession of Florida from Spain and shared credit with Monroe in formulating the Monroe Doctrine. Running second to Andrew Jackson in the popular vote in 1824, he was elected President by the House of Representatives through the support of Henry Clay (No. 103). As President, he expanded the executive powers, favored internal improvements and refused to build a personal politcal machine. Defeated by Jackson in 1828, he was elected to the House of Representatives in 1831 and served there until his death 17 years later.*

532 *(811)*

6c orange *(July 28, 1938)*	.35	.20
Plate block of four	1.50	

533 *Andrew Jackson, seventh President (1829-37), symbolized the common people's rise in power. A frontiersman, military hero (CM173), and senator from Tennessee, he received the largest popular vote in 1824, but* was defeated in the House of Representatives when Henry Clay threw his own electoral votes to John Quincy Adams. Elected by a landslide in 1828, Jackson instituted national politcal conventions and the "spoils system," expanded the President's power, checked federal spending on internal improvements, paid off the national debt, and destroyed the privileged Bank of the United States. Opposed to the states'-rights theories of John Calhoun, he countered South Carolina's refusal to collect protective-tariff duties by sending troops and naval forces to Charleston.

533 (812)

7c sepia (Aug. 4, 1938)	.45	.20
lilac brown	.45	.20
Plate block of four	2.00	

534 *Martin Van Buren, eighth President (1837-41), was a senator, governor of New York, and Secretary of State and Vice President under Jackson, whose policies he attempted to follow as President. He inaugurated the independent* treasury, opposed federal spending for internal improvements, and advocated tariffs for revenue only. Alienating the North by his appeasement of the British in a Canadian border incident, and the South by his opposition to the annexation of Texas, he was defeated by William Henry Harrison in the 1840 election, failed to win the Democratic nomination in 1844, and was defeated by Zachary Taylor in 1848.

534 (813)

8c olive green (Aug. 11, 1938)	.45	.20
light olive green	.45	.20
olive	.45	.20
Plate block of four	2.20	

535 *William Henry Harrison, ninth President (1841), fought in the Battle of Fallen Timbers, served as secretary of the Northwest Territory and as its delegate to Congress, was first governor of the Indiana Territory (CM338),* defeated the Indians under Tecumseh at Tippecanoe, defeated the British and Indians in the Battle of the Thames, was a member of both houses of Congress, and served briefly as minister to Colombia. After his overwhelming victory in the 1840 election, he died of pneumonia a month after taking office.

535 (814)

9c rose pink (Aug. 18, 1938)	.50	.20
pink	.50	.20
Plate block of four	2.25	
Gutter pair	—	

536 *John Tyler, 10th President (1841-45), had served as governor of Virginia and as a member of both houses of Congress before his election as Vice President in 1840. As President after Harrison's death, he differed* with the Whig Party on constitutional principles and lost his party's support. He signed the Preemption Act enabling settlers to get government land, reorganized the Navy, annexed Texas and settled the boundary between Maine and Canada. Later, in 1861, he was chairman of the unsuccessful peace conference at Washington, and remained loyal to Virginia when it seceded.

536 (815)

10c Venetian red (Sept. 2, 1938)	.45	.20
dull Venetian red	.45	.20
Plate block of four	2.00	

537 *James Knox Polk, 11th President (1845-49), served as Speaker of the House and as governor of Tennessee before his highly successful term as President. He fought the spoils system, settled the Oregon boundary* dispute by accepting the 49th parallel and giving Vancouver to the Bitish, reduced the tariff, restored the independent treasury system abolished under Tyler, and won a war with Mexico. An expansionist but not an imperialist, he approved the acquistion of Texas, New Mexico, and California, but opposed retaining Mexico by force.

537 (816)

11c cobalt (Sept. 8, 1938)	.75	.15
Plate block of four	4.25	

538 *Zachary Taylor, 12th President (1849-50), came to the White House after a distinguished 40-year Army career in which he gained the nickname "Old Rough and Ready." He fought in the War of 1812, the Black Hawk and* Seminole Wars, and the Mexican War, which he ended by defeating Santa Anna at Buena Vista in 1847. In his 16 months as President, he resumed the spoils system. A former slave-holder, he worked for California's admission as a free state. He died of typhus in 1850.

538 (817)

12c light reddish violet (Sept. 14, 1938)	1.40	.20
Plate block of four	6.00	

539 *Millard Fillmore, 13th President (1850-53), spent four terms in the House of Representatives before his election as Vice President under Taylor. As President he favored the compromise policy in the slavery* issue, signed the Fugitive Slave Act, approved the negotiations leading to the opening of Japan (CM363), and maintained neutrality in foreign wars.

539 (818)

13c blue green (Sept. 22, 1938)	2.25	.20
dark blue green	2.25	.20
Plate block of four	9.50	

540 *Franklin Pierce, 14th President (1853-57), Congressman, Senator, and brigadier general in the Mexican War, won the Democratic nomination in 1852 on the 49th ballot. As President, he effected the Gadsden Purchase, sent Matthew Perry to open trade with Japan (CM363), attempted to secure a base in Santo Domingo and annex Cuba, Hawaii, and Alaska, and signed the Kansas-Nebraska Bill leaving slavery in those territories to popular vote. Attempting impartiality in domestic policy and imperialism in foreign policy, he generally failed at both and retired to obscurity.*

540 *(819)*
  14c blue *(Oct. 6, 1938)*   1.15   .20
      Plate block of four   6.00

541 *James Buchanan, 15th President (1857-61), had served successively as Congressman, minister to Russia, senator, Secretary of State under Polk, and minister to Great Britain. A conservative and ineffective President, he expressed moral opposition to slavery and secession, but furthered one and condoned the other. His administration saw the growth of the new Republican Party, the Lincoln-Douglas debates, and the abolitionist John Brown's raid on the federal armory at Harper's Ferry, Virginia, for which Brown was hanged. Failing to meet the challenge of South Carolina's secession and her firing on Fort Sumter, Buchanan left the office on the brink of the Civil War.*

541 *(820)*
  15c slate *(Oct. 13, 1938)*   .65   .20
      Plate block of four   3.00

542 *Abraham Lincoln, 16th President (1861-65), worked as a rail-splitter, surveyor, and postmaster of Salem, Illinois; served a term in Congress; and became an outstanding jury lawyer before attaining national prominence through a series of debates with Stephen A. Douglas, against whom he was running for the Senate in 1858. Nominated as the Republican Presidential candidate in 1860 because of his conservative views on slavery, his election signaled the secession of seven Southern states. Given almost dictatorial powers in the Civil War, he followed a middle course between the radicals and defeatists, ably commanding the Union war effort and diplomatically handling his cabinet and his generals. Although he had hoped for a gradual, compensated abolition of slavery, in 1863 he issued the Emancipation Proclamation freeing all slaves in rebel territory. The same year marked his Gettysburg Address (CM320). Re-elected in the dark days of 1864, he made his great Second Inaugural Address: "With malice toward none, with charity for all ... let us strive on to finish the work we are in; to bind up the nation's wounds ... to do all which may achieve a just and lasting peace." His compassionate program for conciliation and reconstruction was never achieved. Ten days later, five days after Lee's surrender at Appomattox, he was assassinated by a Southern fanatic while attending the theater.*

542 *(821)*
  16c black *(Oct. 20, 1938)*   1.25   .60
      Plate block of four   6.00

543 *Andrew Johnson, 17th President (1865-69), a self-educated tailor, was a Congressman, governor of Tennessee, and the only Southern senator to support the Union in the Civil War. His success as military governor of Tennessee led to his election as Vice President. As President after Lincoln's death, he attempted to carry out Lincoln's conciliatory policies of Reconstruction, but was thwarted by the Radical Republicans in Congress. His removal of War Secretary Edwin M. Stanton (No. 101) for conspiracy led to his impeachment, which fell one vote short of the two-thirds majority needed to remove him from the White House. Elected to the Senate again in 1875, he died the same year.*

543 *(822)*
  17c rose red *(Oct. 27, 1938)*   1.25   .20
      Plate block of four   6.00

544 *Ulysses S. Grant, 18th President (1869-77), led the Union forces to victory in the Civil War (see CM174). As President, he authorized harsh Reconstruction policies that kept sectional hatreds alive, and, although he was personally honest, his administration was involved in grave scandals. His achievements included civil service reform and the funding of the national debt. Left penniless by the collapse of a banking house in 1884, he was persuaded by Mark Twain (CM0205) to write his "Personal Memoirs," which he finished four days before his death in 1885. They realized almost $450,000.*

544 *(823)*
  18c brown carmine *(Nov. 3, 1938)*   2.25   .25
      rose brown   2.25   .25
      Plate block of four   10.

545 *Rutherford B. Hayes, 19th President (1877-81), former Congressman and governor of Ohio, ran second to Samuel J. Tilden in the 1876 election, but was chosen President by a partisan electoral commission by a vote of 185-184. His administration returned local government to the South, ending the Reconstruction, and made ineffective attempts at civil service reform.*

545 *(824)*
  19c light reddish violet *(Nov. 10, 1938)* 2.00   .60
      Plate block of four   9.50

546 *James A. Garfield, 20th President (1881), Republican leader of the House, was a Senator-elect when chosen President in 1880. Four months after his inauguration, he was fatally shot by a disappointed office-seeker.*

546 *(825)*
  20c blue green *(Nov. 10, 1938)*   1.25   .20
      bright blue green   1.25   .20
      Plate block of four   5.00

547 *Chester A. Arthur, 21st President (1881-85), who succeeded to the office after Garfield's assassination, was an able and honest administrator. He supported civil service reform, arranged a canal treaty (unratified) with Nicaragua, vetoed a Chinese-exclusion bill, and began the rebuilding of the Navy.*

547 *(826)*
21c slate blue *(Nov. 22, 1938)*   2.25   .20
   Plate block of four   10.

 548 *Grover Cleveland, 22nd and 24th President (1885-89 and 1893-97), reform governor of New York, was an honest and independent President. In his first term he enlarged the civil service, followed a conciliatory policy toward the South, avoided the spoils system, opposed pork-barrel pension bills, and vetoed more than two-thirds of the Congressional acts presented to him. Defeated by Benjamin Harrison in 1888, he ran again and was re-elected in 1892. His second term was marked by a severe depression, a fight against inflation, an income tax law (declared unconstitutional), the use of troops to end the mail stoppage in the Pullman strike, and a firm stand against the British use of force in a boundary dispute with Venezuela.*

548 *(827)*
22c vermilion *(Nov. 22, 1938)*   1.50   .75
   Plate block of four   12.50

 549 *Benjamin Harrison, 23rd President (1889-93), was a grandson of William Henry Harrison, ninth President. A Union regimental commander in the Civil War, and senator for one term, as President he greatly expanded the pension list, signed the McKinley high-tariff bill and the Sherman silver purchase act, followed imperialistic policies in the Pacific, convened the first Pan-American Conference in 1889 and aided the admission to the Union of the Dakotas, Montana, and Washington in 1889, and Idaho and Wyoming in 1900.*

549 *(828)*
24c gray green *(Dec. 2, 1938)*   4.25   .35
   Plate block of four   20.

 550 *William McKinley, 25th President (1897-1901), former Congressman and governor of Ohio, was elected on a platform of high tariff and maintenance of the gold standard; raised the tariff to the highest level in American history and signed the Gold Standard Act of 1900. After the sinking of the Maine at Havana, public opinion forced his intervention in the Cuban rebellion; the resulting Spanish-American War ended in a temporary American protectorate over Cuba, the purchase of the Philippine Islands, the annexation of Puerto Rico and Guam, and the establishment of the United States as a world power. His administration also marked the annexation of Hawaii, intervention in China, and agitation for a Panama Canal.*

Re-elected on the "full dinner pail" platform, he was fatally shot by an anarchist the following September while visiting the Pan-American Exposition (CM26-31).

550 *(829)*
25c claret *(Dec. 2, 1938)*   1.20   .20
   rose lilac   1.20   .20
   Plate block of four   5.00

 551 *Theodore Roosevelt, 26th President (1901-09), achieved early fame as Assistant Secretary of the Navy under McKinley, as organizer of the Rough Riders (CM315) in the Spanish-American War, and as a crusading governor of New York. Given the Republican vice presidential nomination "to get him out of the way," upon McKinley's death he became at 43 America's youngest President. He fought government corruption by big business, recognized Panama when it revolted from Colombia, began the construction of the Panama Canal (CM48 and CM198), won the Nobel Peace Prize for his successful mediation of the Russo-Japanese War, organized conservation of national resources, and instituted the Pure Food and Drugs Act. Virtually bequeathing the Presidency to William Howard Taft, he became dissatisfied with Taft's conservative policies and ran against him in 1912, splitting the Republican ticket so that both lost to Woodrow Wilson. He also was noted as a naturalist, explorer, and writer.*

551 *(830)*
30c deep ultramarine *(Dec. 8, 1938)*   5.00   .20
   ultramarine   5.00   .20
   blue   15.00   —
   deep blue   110.00   —
   Plate block of four   22.50

 552 *William Howard Taft, 27th President (1909-13), had distinguished careers before and after his Presidency. He was a federal judge, Solicitor General under Benjamin Harrison, dean of the University of Cincinnati Law School, president of the Philippines Commission, first civil governor of the Philippines, Secretary of War and provisional governor of Cuba. His administration dissolved the Standard Oil and American Tobacco Company trusts, set up the Department of Labor, and drafted the 16th and 17th Amendments (authorizing the income tax and the direct election of Senators). Defeated in 1912, he became a lecturer and Yale law professor. Appointed Chief Justice of the United States in 1919, he served until his death in 1930.*

552 *(831)*
50c light red violet *(Dec. 8, 1938)*   8.50   .20
   Plate block of four   40.

Flat plate printing, perforated 11.

553 *Woodrow Wilson, 28th President (1913-21), was president of Princeton University and a reform governor of New Jersey before his election in 1912. His first administration instituted the Federal Reserve Act, Farm Loan Act, Federal Trade Commission, Clayton Anti-Trust Act and Adamson Eight-House Law. (His entire tenure saw three Constitutional Amendments: direct election of Senators, prohibition, and women's suffrage.) In foreign affairs, in his first term he had difficulties with some Latin American countries, sent the Pershing Expedition into Mexico, established partial protectorates in Santo Domingo, Haiti and Nicaragua; and maintained neutrality in World War I despite foreign pressures and the infringement of American rights. Re-elected with the slogan, "He kept us out of war," within a month of his inauguration he was forced by German sinking of American ships to ask for a declaration of war. An apostle of international cooperation, he went to Paris to negotiate the peace treaty, in which he said the League of Nations was the "most essential part." When the Senate rejected both the treaty and the League, he toured the country for public support, suffered a stroke, and became an invalid. He won the Nobel Peace Prize in 1919, and died in 1924.*

553 *(832)*
$1 dark purple and black

(Aug. 19, 1938)	10.	.20
Plate block of four	45.	
Center line block	30.	
Margin block of four, with arrow	27.50	
w. Watermarked "USIR"	300.	70.
w. Plate block of four	1,800.	
v. Vertical pair, imperforate between	1,500.	
v1. Vertical pair, imperforate horizontally	1,500.	
a. red violet and black (Aug. 31, 1954)	9.00	.20
Plate block of four	40.	
av. Vertical pair, imperforate between	1,250.	
av1. Vertical pair, imperforate horizontally	1,250.	

553a *is printed on pre-gummed, whiter and thicker paper. It was printed on "dry" paper; No. 553 was printed on pre-dampened paper.*

554 *Warren G. Harding, 29th President (1921-23), was an Ohio newspaperman and senator who supported prohibition, anti-strike legislation, women's suffrage, and high tariffs; opposed the League of Nations as a threat to national sovereignty. Overwhelmingly elected in 1920 on a "return to normalcy" platform, he worked to repeal excess profits and high income taxes and to revise the tariff. In 1921 he called the Washington Conference to limit naval armaments. Returning from a visit to Alaska in 1923, he died unexpectedly at San Francisco.*

554 *(833)*

$2 green and black *(Sept. 29, 1938)*	27.50	4.75
yellow green and black	27.50	4.75
Plate block of four	135.	
Center line block	—	
Margin block of four, with arrow	—	

555 *Calvin Coolidge, 30th President (1923-29), attained prominence in 1919, when, as governor of Massachusetts, he suppressed the Boston police strike on the grounds that "there is no right to strike against the public safety." Elected Vice President, he succeeded to the Presidency upon Harding's death. In a period of prosperity, his administration was cautious and passive in domestic affairs and isolationist toward Europe. He opposed the League of Nations, approved the World Court, vetoed the Soldiers' Bonus Act, twice vetoed the Farm Relief Bill, refused to intervene in the coal strike of 1927, and reduced the national debt by $2 billion in three years. He declined to run for a third term.*

555 *(834)*

$5 carmine and black *(Nov. 17, 1938)*	115.	4.50
red brown and black	115.	4.50
Plate block of four	500.	
Center line block	—	
Margin block of four, with arrow	—	

Rotary press coil stamps, perforated 10 vertically.

556 *(839)*

1c green *(Jan. 10, 1939)*	.25	.20
light green	.25	.20
Pair	.50	
Line pair	1.50	

557 *(840)*

1 1/2c yellow brown *(Jan. 20, 1939)*	.25	.20
ocher	.25	.20
Pair	.50	
Line pair	1.50	

558 *(841)*

2c rose *(Jan. 20, 1939)*	.25	.20
Pair	.50	
Line pair	1.50	

559 *(842)*

3c violet *(Jan. 20, 1939)*	.25	.20
Pair	.50	
Line pair	1.50	
Gripper cracks	—	
p. Thin, translucent paper	—	

560 *(843)*

4c bright purple *(Jan. 20, 1939)*	7.50	.75
Pair	17.50	
Line pair	32.50	

561 *(844)*
4 1/2c gray *(Jan. 20, 1939)*	.75	.50
Pair	1.50	
Line pair	5.50	

562 *(845)*
5c bright blue *(Jan. 20, 1939)*	6.00	.50
Pair	12.50	
Line pair	27.50	

563 *(846)*
6c orange *(Jan. 20, 1939)*	1.25	.50
Pair	2.00	
Line pair	7.50	

564 *(847)*
10c Venetian red *(Jan. 20, 1939)*	12.50	1.25
Pair	22.50	
Line pair	50.	

Rotary press coil stamps, perforated 10 horizontally.

565 *(848)*
1c green *(Jan. 27, 1939)*	.75	.25
Pair	1.25	
Line pair	2.25	

566 *(849)*
1 1/2c yellow brown *(Jan. 27, 1939)*	1.50	.75
Pair	4.50	
Line pair	2.75	

567 *(850)*
2c rose *(Jan. 27, 1939)*	2.50	.75
Pair	6.00	
Line pair	4.00	

568 *(851)*
3c violet *(Jan. 27, 1939)*	2.25	.75
Pair	6.00	
Line pair	4.00	

1954-59 Liberty Series, issued to replace the Presidential issue (1938-43). This new set utilized contemporary paintings rather than formal busts as the basis for the portrait stamps. Details of the printing method for some stamps of this issue are given although each stamp was only printed via one method. For example, No. 571 notes a "dry paper" printing, although there is no known "wet paper" variety. *Printed by intaglio: rotary press, perforated 11 x 10 1/2 or 10 1/2 x 11 (horizontal), 8c flat press or rotary press, perforated 11. $5 flat plate press, perforated 11 x 11.*

1954-66 Sheet stamps and booklets

569 *Benjamin Franklin*   570, 587 *George Washington*

569 *(1030)*
1/2c vermilion, wet paper *(Oct. 20, 1955)*	.25	.20
Plate block of four	.50	
p. Dry paper *(May 1958)* (1030a)	.25	
Plate block of four	.50	

570 *(1031b)*
1c dull green, wet paper *(Aug. 26, 1954)*	.25	.20
Plate block of four	.50	
Gutter pair		
p. Dry paper *(March 1956)*	.25	
Plate block of four	.50	
p. Hi-Brite paper	—	

 571 *Mount Vernon, home of George Washington, on the south bank of the Potomac, 16 miles below Washington, D.C. Land was part of the Royal Grant to Lord Culpepper, who in 1674 granted 5,000 ares to Nicolas Spencer and John Washington, great-grandfather of George. Since 1858 preserved and restored by Mount Vernon Ladies Association.*

571 *(1032)*
1 1/2c brown carmine, dry paper *(Feb. 22, 1956)*	.25	.20
Plate block of four	.50	

572, 588   573, 578, 589
Thomas Jefferson   *Statue of Liberty*

572 *(1033)*
2c rose, dry paper *(Sept. 15, 1954)*	.25	.20
Plate block of four	.50	
Gutter pair	—	
(1033a)p. Silkote paper *(Dec. 1954)*	1,100.	
Plate block of four	—	

573 *(1035e)*
3c violet, wet paper *(June 24, 1954)*	.25	.20
Plate block of four	.50	
Gutter pair	—	
n. Booklet pane of six *(June 30, 1954)*	4.50	
nv. Booklet pane of six, imperforate between vertically	—	
(1035) p1. Dry paper *(Sept. 1956)*	.25	.20
Plate block of four	.50	
p1n. Booklet pane of six	4.50	
(1035b)p1z. Tagged, Type II *(July 6, 1966)*	.25	.20
Plate block of four	5.00	
p1z1. Tagged, Type III		
Plate block of four	—	
p2. Hi-Brite paper	—	
Plate block of four	—	

> v. Horizontal pair, imperforate
>   between   1,500.
> v1. Imperforate pair
>   (18 3/4 x 22 1/2 mm)   2,000.

Type II tagging: roll tagging. When continuously surfaced rolls replaced the previously used tagging mats. Only the plate number selvage margin is partially tagged and the plate number blocks have one untagged margin.

Type III tagging: curved metal plate tagging. Sheet margins are almost fully tagged but a "hot line" of intense phosphor-tagging or untagged narrow gap, 1 mm or less in width, appears on stamps from any position in the pane.

574, 590 *Abraham Lincoln*   575 *James Monroe*

574 *(1036c)*

4c bright purple, wet paper		
(*Nov. 19, 1954*)	.25	.20
Plate block of four	.50	
Gutter pair	—	
n. Booklet pane of six		
(*July 31, 1958*)	2.75	
nv. Booklet pane of six,		
imperforate between		
horizontally	—	
(1036) p. Dry paper (*July 1956*)	.25	.20
Plate block of four	.50	
Gutter pair	—	
n. Booklet pane of six	2.75	
(1036b)pz. Tagged, Type I (*Nov. 2, 1963*)	.50	.45
Plate block of four	.50	
pz1. Tagged, Type II	.50	
Plate block of four	.50	
p1. Hi-Brite paper	—	
Plate block of four	—	
v. Horizontal pair,		
imperforate between	3,600.	

Type I tagging: mat tagging. The four separate mats used did not cover the entire sheet of 400 stamps and certain untagged areas help to identify this variety. See expanded definition in the Catalog Introduction.

575 *(1038)*

5c blue (*Dec. 2, 1954*)	.25	.20
Plate block of four	.65	
Gutter pair	—	

576 *Theodore Roosevelt*   577 *Woodrow Wilson*

576 *(1039a)*

6c rose red, wet paper (*Nov. 18, 1955*)	.25	.20
Plate block of four	1.75	
(1039) p. Dry paper (*March 1957*)	.40	
Plate block of four	1.70	

577 *(1040)*

7c carmine red, dry paper (*Jan. 10, 1956*)	.25	.20
Plate block of four	1.25	
p. Hi-Brite paper	—	
Plate block of four	—	

578 *(1041)*

8c deep blue and carmine (*April 9, 1954*)	.25	.20
Plate block of four, both		
red and blue numbers	2.00	
Plate block (corner) of four,		
blue number only	—	
Plate block (corner) of four,		
red number only	—	
v. Double impression,		
carmine	—	

This stamp was produced on both flat-bed and rotary presses.

 579 *The Alamo, called the "Cradle of Texas Liberty," founded in 1718 as Mission de San Antonio de Valero, beseiged in 1836 by Gen. Santa Anna and 1,000 Mexicans; the 184 Texan defenders under Col. William Barrett Travis, including Davy Crockett and James Bowie, fought to the last man. Site is now a historic shrine and museum*

579 *(1043)*

9c rose lilac (*June 14, 1956*)	.25	.20
Plate block of four	1.25	
a. deep rose lilac	—	
Plate block of four	—	

 580 *Independence Hall, where the Declaration of Independence was adopted and which for many years housed the Liberty Bell.*

580 *(1044)*

10c brown purple, dry paper		
(*July 4, 1956*)	.25	.20
Plate block of four	1.00	
a. deep brown purple	—	
Plate block of four	—	
p. Hi-Brite paper	—	
Plate block of four	—	
z. Tagged, Type II (*July 6, 1966*)	2.50	1.50
Plate block of four	25.00	
z1. Tagged, Type III	—	
Plate block of four	—	

 581 *Monticello, Thomas Jefferson's estate in Virginia.*

581 (1047)
20c bright blue (April 13, 1956)	.50	.20
Plate block of four	1.75	
a. deep blue	—	
Plate block of four	—	
p. Hi-Brite paper	—	
Plate block of four	—	

582 Robert E. Lee

583 John Marshall

582 (1049a)
30c black, wet paper (Sept. 21, 1955)	1.50	.25
Plate block of four	6.00	
(1049) p. dry paper (June 1957)	1.00	.20
Plate block of four	5.50	

583 (1050a)
40c brown carmine, wet paper (Sept. 24, 1955)	2.75	.25
Plate block of four	13.00	
(1050) p. Dry paper (April 1958)	2.00	.20
Plate block of four	8.00	

584 Susan Anthony

585 Patrick Henry

584 (1051a)
50c red violet, wet paper (Aug. 25, 1955)	2.00	.20
Plate block of four	13.00	
Cracked plate (No. 25231, top left)	—	
(1051) p. Dry paper (April 1958)	1.50	.20
Plate block of four	7.00	

585 (1052a)
$1 dark lilac, wet paper (Oct. 7, 1955)	7.00	.20
Plate block of four	25.	
(1052) p. Dry paper (Oct. 1958)	5.00	.20
Plate block of four	22.50	

586 Alexander Hamilton

586 (1053)
$5 black, (March 19, 1956)	70.	6.50
Plate block of four	300.	

1954-68 Coil Stamps
Intaglio and perforated 10 vertically.

587 (1054c)
1c dull green, wet paper (Oct. 8, 1954)	.45	.25
Pair	.75	
Line pair	1.50	
(1054) p. Dry paper, large holes (Aug. 1957)	.50	.20
Pair	.35	
Line pair	.75	
(1054a)pv. Dry paper, small holes (Feb. 1960)	.50	.20
Pair	.75	
Line pair	1.00	
v. Imperforate pair	2,250.	

588 (1055d)
2c rose, wet paper (Oct. 22, 1954)	.25	.20
Pair	.35	
Line pair	.75	
(1055) p1. Dry paper, large holes (May 1957)	.25	.20
Pair	.35	
Line pair	.75	
(1055a)p1ss. Dry paper, small holes, shiny gum (Aug. 1961)	.25	.20
Pair	.35	
Line pair	.75	
p1ssz. Tagged, Type II (May 6, 1968)	—	
Pair	—	
Line pair	—	
(1055c)p1sszv. Imperforate pair	600.	
Imperforate Line pair	900.	
p1smz. Dry paper, small holes, matt gum, tagged	.25	.20
Pair	.70	
Line pair	2.00	
(1055b)p1smv. Imperforate pair, dry paper, small holes, matt gum,untagged	575.	
Line pair	—	

The imperforate pair, untagged, listed above (588p1smv) is known with a Bureau precancel of Riverdale, MD.

589
3c purple, wet paper (July 20, 1954)	.25	.20
Pair	.50	
(1057a)Line pair	1.00	
(1057) p. Dry paper, large holes shiny gum (May 1957)	.75	.20
Pair	1.00	
Line pair	1.50	
Gripper cracks	—	
p1m. Matt gum (dull finish)	—	
p1s. Dry paper, small holes (July 31, 1958)	.30	
Pair		
Line pair	.50	
p1v. Imperforate pair, (19 1/2 x 22 mm)	1,650.	
Imperforate Line pair	—	

(1057b)z. Tagged (*Look* Magazine
          printing, *Oct. 1966)*   6.   3.
          Pair   12.
          Line pair   150.
       ps1z1. Tagged, Type II
          philatelic printing,
          (June 26, 1967)   2.50   .75
          Pair   5.00
          Line pair   25.00

No. 589p1sz., the "Look Coil," is so-called because the stamps were prepared for Look magazine in coil rolls of 3,000 subjects. All but 99,000 of this issue were affixed to outgoing mail and return addressed envelopes on an automatic labeling machine at Des Moines, Iowa. The common usage was in combination with a 2c Jefferson coil (No. 588). The paper on which the stamps were printed is plain, without fluorescent content and tagging is uniform and brilliant. A special printing was issued, in coils of 500 subjects, to satisfy collector demands (No. 589p1sz1). The stamps can be distinguished from the original printing by a sharper, more well-defined design, a more intense shade of purple ink and the slightly fluorescent paper on which they were printed. The tagging is less intense and, on some coils across-the-web tagging marks known as "hot lines" repeat every 24th stamp.

590 *(1058b)*
4c bright purple, wet paper
          (Bureau precancel)   25.   1.00
          (July 31, 1958)
       Pair   50.
       Line pair   350.
(1058) p1. Dry paper, large holes
          (June 1958)   .75   .20
       Pair   1.00
       Line pair   2.00
(1058s)p1s. Dry paper, small holes
          (July 31, 1958)   .75   .20
       Pair   1.00
       Line pair   2.00
       p1sv. Imperforate pair   100.   75.
          Imperforate line pair   200.
       p2. Hi-Brite paper   —
          Pair   —
          Line pair   —

1958.

Giori press printing, perforated 11.

578   591

Giori press printing differs from No. 578 in that the torch and flame do not break through the wording "U.S. POSTAGE," the Statue of Liberty is enlarged, the word "LIBERTY" is smaller and lower.

591 *(1042)*
8c deep blue and carmine
          (March 22, 1958)   .25   .20
       Plate block of four   1.00

Intaglio, perforated 11 x 10 1/2.

592 *John Jay (1745-1829), stateman, first Chief Justice of the Supreme Court, (1789-94), governor of New York (1795-1801). He was a delegate and, in 1778, president of the Continental Congress. Aided Franklin in negotiating peace with Great Britain.*

592 *(1046)*
15c brown purple *(Dec. 12, 1958)*   .75   .20
       Plate block of four   2.75
       p1. Hi-Brite paper   —
          Plate block of four   —
(1046a)p1z. Tagged, type II   1.25   .50
          (July 6, 1966)
          Plate block of four   9.00
       p1z1. Tagged, type III   —
          Plate block of four   —

593, 614 *Paul Revere 91735-1818), silversmith, copper engraver, one of three patriots made famous by Longfellow for his ride from Charleston to Lexington, April 18, 1775, to warn of British march. He designed and printed first issue of continental currency; and designed and engraved first official seal for colonies.*

593 *(1048)*
25c deep blue green *(April 18, 1958)*   1.50   .20
       Plate block of four   5.00
       p1. Hi-Brite paper   —
          Plate block of four   —

1959-60.

Intaglio, 2 1/2c, 12c (perforated 11 x 10 1/2), 4 1/2c (perforated 10 1/2 x 11).

594 *Bunker Hill Monument (220 feet high) erected in 1843 on the site (then called Breed's Hill) of the first major battle of the Revolutionary War (June 17, 1775). Gen. Joseph Warren, commander of U.S. forces at this battle issued the now-famous order,* "Don't shoot until you see the whites of their eyes." *Outnumbered four-to-one, the colonists lost the battle but inflicted very heavy casualties on the British troops. This moral victory gave the colonists new inspiration. Background of the stamp shows the Pine Tree flag adopted by the Commonwealth of Massachusetts at the beginning of the Revolutionary War.*

594 *(1034)*
2 1/2c slate blue *(June 17, 1959)*   .25   .20
       Plate block of four   .65

595, 597 *Hermitage, home of Andrew Jackson*

595 *(1037)*
4 1/2c blue green *(March 16, 1959)*   .25   .20
    Plate block of four   .75

596 *Benjamin Harrison (see No. 549)*

596 *(1045)*
12c carmine red *(June 6, 1959)*   .30   .20
    Plate block of four   1.50
*(1045a)*z. Tagged, type IIa (May 6, 1968)   35   .20
    Plate block of four   4.00

Type IIa tagging: wide roll tagging. All margins are fully tagged.

Coil, intaglio, perf.10 horizontally

597 *(1059)*
4 1/2c blue green, large holes
    (May 1, 1959)   2.00   .50
    Pair   3.00
    Line pair   15.00
    s. Small holes *(April 1961)*   20.00   2.00
    Pair   30.00
    Line pair   425.

Coil, intaglio perf. 10 vertically

598 *(1056)*
2 1/2c slate blue, large holes
    (Sept. 9, 1959)   .25   .20
    Pair   .50
    Line pair
    s. Small holes (Bureau
      precancel) *(Jan. 1961)*   —   .35
    Pair   —
    Line pair   —

Iintaglio and perforated 10 1/2 x 11

599 *Palace of the Governors, Santa Fe, New Mexico, was built in 1610. It is now an historical shrine and memorial to early Spanish life and culture in this country, and reflects the contributions made to the progress and development of the Southwestern United States.*

599 *(1031A)*
1 1/4c turquoise blue
    (June 17, 1960)   .25   .20
    Plate block of four   .50

Coil, intaglio, perf. 10 horizontally

600 *(1054A)*
1 1/4c turquoise blue, large holes
    (June 17, 1960)   .25   .20
    Pair   2.00
    Line pair   .30
    p. Small holes *(May 1960)*   .50
    Pair   250.
    Line   25.

1961.

601 *Statue of Liberty*

Giori Press Printing, perforated 11

601 *(1044a)*
11c carmine red and blue
    (June 15, 1961)   .30   .20
    Plate block of four   1.25
*(1044A)*z. Tagged, type OP *(Jan. 11, 1967)*   2.00   1.00
    Plate block of four   33.00

Type OP tagging: Used on multicolor stamps previously designated to be printed on Giori presses.

Rotary press printing, perforated 11 x 10 1/2

602 *John J. Pershing (1860-1948) commanded the American Expeditionary Forces in Europe during World War I. A leader of vision and courage, Pershing was honored by Congress in 1917 with the title "General of the Armies."*

602 *(1042)*
8c brown *(Nov. 17, 1961)*   .25   .20
    Plate block of four   1.00

There is disagreement concerning whether No. 602 is actually part of the Liberty series. Although printed within the same period,, it does not match the design characteristics of others stamps in the series.

1962. This first Christmas stamp issued by the United States was intended for use on season's greeting cards and also to remind the public to shop and mail early. *Giori press printing, perforated 11.*

603 *Evergreen wreath and burning candles*

603 *(1205)*
4c green and red *(Nov. 1, 1962)*   .25   .20
    Plate block of four   .75

Intaglio, perforated 11 x 10 1/2

Issued to meet the increased postal rates effective Jan. 7, 1963.

604 *George Washington from bust by Houdon*

604 (1213)

5c gray blue *(Nov. 23, 1962)*	.25	.20
Plate block of four	.45	
Gutter pair	—	
v. Horizontal pair, imperforate between	12.50	
p1. Hi-Brite paper	—	
Plate block of four	—	
z. Tagged, type I *(Oct. 28, 1963)*	—	
Plate block of four	—	
zn. Tagged booklet pane of five, with label (2 different)	6.50	2.25
z1. Tagged, type II *(April 1964)*	—	
Plate block of four	—	
z1n. Booklet pane of five, with label	15.00	9.50
z2. Tagged, type IIa	—	
Plate block of four	—	
z3. Tagged, type III	—	
z3n. Booklet pane of five, with label	2.75	2.25

Coil, intaglio perforated 10 vertically

605 (1229)

5c gray blue *(Nov. 23, 1962)*	.25	.20
Pair	2.00	
Line pair	4.00	
p1. Hi-Brite paper		
Pair		
Line pair		
p1v. Imperforate pair	350.	
Imperforate line pair	750.	
z. Tagged, type I *(Oct. 28, 1963)*	.25	.20
Pair	2.50	
Line pair	5.00	
z1. Tagged, type II	—	
Pair	—	
Line Pair	—	

1963. This stamp is the first regular issue that does not contain any text other than the denomination. *Giori Press Printing, perforated 11.*

 606 *U.S. flag and White House*

606 (1208)

5c blue and red *(Jan. 9, 1963)*	.25	.20
Plate block of four	.75	
Gutter Pair	—	
(1208a)z. Tagged, type OP *(Aug. 25, 1966)*	.25	.20
Plate block of four	5.00	
zv. Imperforate horizontal pair	1,750.	

 607 *Andrew Jackson*

Intaglio, perforated 11 x 10 1/2

607 (1209)

1c green *(March 22, 1963)*	.25	.20
Plate block of four	.75	
Gutter Pair	—	
p1. Hi-Brite paper	—	
Plate block of four	—	
(1209a)z. Tagged, type II or III *(July 6, 1966)*	.25	.20
Plate block of four	.25	

Coil, intaglio perforated 10 vertically

608 (1225)

1c green *(May 31, 1963)*	.25	.20
Pair	.25	
Line pair	2.00	
(1225a)z. Tagged, type II *(July 6, 1966)*	.25	.20
Pair	.25	
Line pair	.75	

1963. This second Christmas stamp was based on an on-the-spot painting made by artist Lily Spandorf of President Kennedy lighting the National Christmas tree. *Giori press printing, perforated 11.*

 609 *Christmas Tree and White House*

609 (1240)

5c dark blue, indigo and red *(Nov. 1, 1963)*	.25	.20
Plate block of four	.50	
Gutter Pair	—	
(1240a)z. Tagged, type OP *(Nov. 2, 1963)*	.65	.50
Plate block of four	4.50	

1964. The third Christmas issue also was a U.S. postal first, featuring four different stamp designs in a regular size pane of 100 stamps. *Giori Press Printing, perforated 11.*

 610 *Holly*

 611 *Mistletoe*

 612 *Poinsettia*

 613 *Pine cone*

610 *(1254)*
5c carmine, green and black
    (Nov. 9, 1964) .25 .20
611 *(1255)*
5c carmine, green and black .25 .20
612 *(1256)*
5c carmine, green and black .25 .20
613 *(1257)*
5c carmine,green and black .25 .20
  Se-tenant block of four 1.00 1.00
  Plate block of four 1.25
  z. Tagged, Type OP (any single)
    (Nov. 10, 1964) 1.75 .50
    Se-tenant block of four 3.50
    Plate block of four 5.00

Coil, Intaglio and perforated 10 vertically
614 *(1059A)*
25c deep blue green, large holes
    (Feb. 25, 1965) .45 .25
  Pair 1.00
  Line pair 2.25
  Imperforate pair .35
  Imperforate line pair 75.
(1059Ab) zss. Tagged, small holes,
    shiny gum *(April 3, 1973)* .45 .25
    Pair 1.25
    Line Pair 3.00
(1059Ad) zsm. Tagged, small holes,
    matt gum (1980) .45 .25
    Pair 1.50
    Line pair 3.50

1965. Christmas Stamp. The design is based on a watercolor by Lucille Gloria Chabot. *Giori press printing, perforated 11.*

615 *Angel Gabriel blowing his horn*

615 *(1276)*
5c red, green, and yellow
    (Nov. 2, 1965) .25 .20
  Plate block of four .55
  Gutter pair
  z. Tagged, type OP*(Nov. 15, 1965)* .75 .20
    Plate block of four 5.50

1965-68. Prominent Americans Series, issued to replace the Liberty series. These new regular issues honor Americans whose contributions have enriched the culture and welfare of all people. Thirteen of the Americans selected never had appeared on U.S. postage stamps before. *Intaglio, perforated 11 x 10 1/2 or 10 1/2 x 11.*

616 *Thomas Jefferson*   617 *Albert Gallatin, statesman*

616 *(1278)*
1c green, tagged type II or III
    (Jan. 12, 1968) .25 .20
  Plate block of four .25
  n. Booklet pane of eight
(1278a) nm. Booklet pane of eight,
    matt gum
(1278b) n1. Booklet pane of four 1.00
    plus two labels .75
  zo.Tagging omitted (error)
    Plate block of four —
    Plate block of four,
    half untagged. —
(1278ae) zn. Booklet pane of eight —
    znm. Booklet pane of eight,
    matt gum 1.25
  zx.Untagged (Bureau precancel) —

617 *(1279)*
1 1/4c light green *(Jan. 30, 1967)* .25 .20
  Plate block of four 7.50

618 *Frank Lloyd Wright,architect*   619 *Francis Parkman, historian*

618 *(1280)*
2c blue, tagged type II or III
    (June 8, 1966) .25 .20
  Plate block of four .25
  Gutter pair —
*(1280a)*n. Booklet pane of five, plus label
    (Jan. 8, 1968) 1.25
*(1280c)*n1. Booklet pane of six
    (May 7, 1971) 1.00
  zo. Tagging omitted (error)
    Plate block of four —
  zn. Booklet pane of five,
    plus label —
  zn1. Booklet pane of six —
  zx. Untagged (Bureau precancel) —
  zxo. Tagged with Bureau
    precancel (error) —

619 *(1281)*
3c purple, tagged type II
    (Sept. 16, 1967) .25 .20
  Plate block of four .30
  zo. Tagging omitted (error)
    Plate block of four —
  zx. Untagged (Bureau precancel) —

620 *Abraham Lincoln*   621 *George Washington*

620 *(1282)*

4c black *(Nov. 19, 1965)*	.25	.20
Plate block of four	.40	
Gutter pair	—	
(1282a)z. Tagged, type II or III		
(Dec. 1, 1965)	.25	.20
Plate block of four	.55	

621 *(1283)*

5c deep blue *(Feb. 22, 1966)*	.25	.20
Plate block of four	.60	
Gutter pair	—	
(1283a)z. Tagged, type II or III		
(Feb. 23, 1966)	.25	.20
Plate block of four	.60	

622 *Franklin D. Roosevelt*   623 *Albert Einstein, physicist*

622 *(1284)*

6c black brown *(Jan. 29, 1966)*	.25	.20
Plate block of four	.65	
Gutter pair	—	
(1284a)z. Tagged, type II or III		
(Dec. 29, 1966)	.25	.20
Plate block of four	.75	
(1284b)zn. Booklet pane of five		
plus label *(Jan. 9, 1968)*	1.50	
(1284c)zn1. Booklet pane		
of eight *(Dec. 28, 1967)*	1.50	
zo. Tagging omitted (error)	—	

623 *(1285)*

8c violet *(March 14, 1966)*	.25	.20
Plate block of four	1.00	
z. Tagged, Type II or III		
(July 6, 1966)	.25	.20
Plate block of four	1.00	

624 *Andrew Jackson*   624A *Henry Ford auto manufacturer*

624 *(1286)*

10c lavender, tagged Type II or III		
(March 15, 1967)	.25	.20
Plate block of four	1.00	

zo. Tagging omitted (error)	—	
Plate block of four	—	
zx. Untagged (Bureau precancel)	—	

624A *(1286A)*

12c black, tagged type II *(July 30, 1968)*	.25	.20
Plate block of four	1.20	
zo. Tagging omitted (error)	—	
Plate block of four	—	
zx. Untagged (Bureau precancel)	—	

625 *John F. Kennedy*   626 *Oliver Wendell Holmes, Supreme Court justice*

625 *(1287)*

13c brown, tagged type II or III		
(May 29, 1967)	.25	.20
Plate block of four	1.35	
zo. Tagging omitted (error)	—	
zx. Untagged (Bureau precancel)	—	

626 *(1288)*

15c maroon, design type I, tagged Type II		
(March 8,1968)	.40	.20
Plate block of four	1.50	
Gutter pair	—	
zx. Untagged (Bureau precancel)	—	
(1288d)i.Type II (design)	.50	.20
Plate block of four	8.50	
iizo. Tagging omitted (error)	—	
Plate block of four	—	
(1288Bc)iin. Booklet pane of eight,		
type III *(July 14, 1978)*	2.50	2.50
iinv. Imperforate between	—	

Type I: crosshatching on tie complete and strong; bottom of necktie just touches coat. Type II: crosshatching on tie (lines running upper left to lower right) very faint; necktie does not touch coat. Type III (only known on booklet pane) overall design smaller and "15c" closer to head.

627 *George C. Marshall, dip;omat and general*   628 *Frederick Douglass, abolitionist and statesman*

627 *(1289)*

20c olive brown *(Oct. 24, 1967)*	.35	.20
Plate block of four	1.75	
(1289a)z. Tagged *(April 3, 1973)*	.40	.20
Plate block of four	2.00	

628 *(1290)*

25c maroon *(Feb. 14, 1967)*	.50	.25
Plate block	1.75	
a. lilac carmine	—	
Plate block of four	—	
(1290a)z. Tagged *(April 3, 1973)*	.40	.20
Plate block of four	2.00	

629 *John Dewey, philosopher and educator*

630 *Thomas Paine, essayist*

629 *(1291)*

30c purple *(Oct. 21, 1968)*	.55	.25
Plate block of four	2.75	
(1291a)z. Tagged *(April 3, 1973)*	.45	.25
Plate block of four	2.25	

630 *(1292)*

40c dark blue *(Jan. 29, 1968)*	.75	.25
Plate block of four	3.30	
(1292a)z. Tagged *(April 3, 1973)*	.75	.25
Plate block of four	2.25	
(1292ad)zm. Matt gum	.75	
Plate block of four	3.00	.25

631 *Lucy Stone, suffrogist and reformer*

632 *Eugene O'Neil, playwright*

631 *(1293)*

50c maroon *(Aug. 13, 1968)*	1.00	.25
Plate block of four	4.50	
Gutter pair	—	
(1293a)z. Tagged *(April 3, 1973)*	1.00	.25
Plate block of four	3.00	

632 *(1294)*

$1 dark purple *(Oct. 16, 1967)*	2.25	.50
Plate block of four	10.00	
(1294A)z. Tagged *(April 3, 1973)*	1.75	.50
Plate block of four	7.00	

633 *John Bassett Moore, jurist*

633 *(1295)*

$5 dark gray *(Dec. 3, 1966)*	10.00	3.00
Plate block of four	40.00	
(1295a)z. Tagged *(April 3, 1973)*	8.00	3.00
Plate block of four	30.00	

High values of this series were tagged for use with automated equipment for postmarking large envelopes.

Coil, intaglio, perforated 10 vertically

634 *(1299)*

1c green, tagged *(June 12, 1968)*	.25	.20
Pair	.25	
Line pair	.25	
v. Imperforate pair	27.50	
Imperforate line pair	600.	
zo. Tagging omitted (error)	—	
Pair	—	
Line pair	—	
(1299a)zx. Untagged (Bureau precancel)	.20	
Pair	.25	
Line pair	.60	

635 *(1303)*

4c black, tagged type II *(May 28, 1966)*	.25	.20
Pair	.25	
Line pair	.75	
v. Imperforate pair	850.	
Imperforate line pair	1,500.	
v1. Imperforate-between pair	—	
zo. Tagging omitted (error)	—	
Pair	—	
Line pair	—	
zx. Untagged (Bureau precancel)	1.00	
Pair	10.00	
Line pair	125.00	

636 *(1304)*

5c deep blue, tagged type II *(Sept. 8, 1966)*	.25	.25
Pair	.25	
Line pair	.40	
v. Imperforate pair	200.	
Imperforate line pair	350.	
zo. Tagging omitted (error)	—	
Pair	—	
Line pair	—	
(1304a)zx. Untagged (Bureau precancel)	1.00	
Pair	10.00	
Line pair	100.00	
zxv. Imperforate untagged (precanceled) pair	400.	
Imperforate untagged (precanceled) line pair	1,000.	
(1304b)m. Matt gum	.25	.20
Pair	1.25	
Line pair	6.00	

Coil, intaglio, perforated 10 vertically

637, 638 *Franklin D. Roosevelt*

637 *(1305)*

6c black brown, tagged *(Feb. 28, 1968)*	.25	.20
Pair	.20	

Line pair	.55	
v. Imperforate pair	—	
Imperforate line pair	—	
zo. Tagging omitted	—	
Pair	—	
Line pair	—	
(1305b) zx. Untagged (Bureau precancel)	2.00	
Pair	17.50	
Line pair	250.00	

Coil, intaglio, perforated 10 horizontally
638 *(1298)*

6c black brown, tagged *(Dec. 28, 1967)*	.25	.20
Pair	.25	
Line pair	1.25	
v. Imperforate pair	2,500.	
Imperforate line pair	—	
zo. Tagging omitted (error)	—	
Pair	—	
Line pair	—	

The 1966 Christmas Stamp, the fifth in the series, features a design showing a portion of Hans Memling's 15th century painting *Madonnna and Child with Angels. Giori press printing and offset, perforated 11.*

644 Madonna and Child

644 *(132)*

5c multicolored *(Nov. 1, 1966)*	.25	.20
Plate block of four	.75	
z. Tagged, type OP *(Nov. 2, 1966)*	.30	.20
Plate block of four	1.75	

The 1967 Christmas Stamp design was the same as the 1966 issue, but printed in much larger size. *Giori press printing and offset, perforated 11.*

645

645 *(1336)*

5c multicolored *(Nov. 6, 1967)*	.25	.20
Plate block of four	.65	
zo. Tagging omitted (error)	—	
Plate block of four	—	

1967. The 5c George Washington stamp (No. 621) issued February 22, 1966, was criticized severely by the American public. The Post Office Department prepared a redesigned version of the stamp (No. 646) with a so-called 'clean shaven' portrait. *Giori press printing and offset, perforated 11.*

621 *Original*   646 *Redesigned*

646 *(1283B)*

5c deep blue, tagged, shiny gum *(Nov. 17, 1967)*	.25	.20
Plate block of four	.75	
zo. Tagging omitted, shiny gum (error)	—	
Plate block of four	—	
(1283Bd) m. matt gum	.25	.20
Plate block of four	1.50	
mzo. Tagging omitted, matt gum (error)	—	
Plate block of four	—	
zx. Untagged (Bureau precancel)	—	

Giori press printing, perforated 11

647, 650, 654 *Flag towering over the White House*

647 *(1338)*

6c dark blue, green, and red, tagging type OP *(Jan. 24, 1968)*	.25	.20
Plate block of four	.50	
v. Imperforate-between vertical pair	500.	
v1. Vertical pair, imperforate horizontally	500.	
zo. Tagging omitted (error)	—	
Plate block of four	—	

1968. The Serviceman's Airlift Stamp, issued for use on parcels to and from servicemen based overseas, chiefly in Vietnam. Upon payment of $1. plus parcel post charges from point of mailing, parcels weighing up to 30 pounds and not exceeding 60 inches in width and girth, were mailed to military post offices. This stamp also was valid for paying regular rates for other types of mail. *Giori press printing and offset, perforated 11.*

648 *Flying eagle*

648 *(1341)*

$1 multicolored *(April 4, 1968)*	3.00	2.00
Plate block of four	12.75	
Gutter pair	—	

1968. The Christmas Stamp features a design showing a portion of *The Annunciation* by the 15th century Flemish artist Jan van Eyck. This was the first stamp printed on the multicolor Huck press. *Intaglio, perforated 11.*

649 *Angel Gabriel*

649 *(1363)*

6c multicolored, tagged type B		
(Nov. 1, 1968)	.25	.20
Plate block of 10	2.00	
v. Light yellow omitted	—	
v1. Imperforate pair	250.	
zx. Untagged *(Nov. 2, 1968)*	.30	.20
Plate block of 10	.30	.20
zxv. Imperforate pair	300.	

Type B tagging: Billet or bar-like shapes designed to register within the limits of a single stamp. Untagged areas surround the design and were intended to register with the perforations.

Coil, intaglio and perforated 10 vertically
This was the first multicolored postage stamp to be produced in coil form. Same design as No. 647.

650 *(1338A)*

6c dark blue, green, and red,		
tagged *(May 30, 1969)*	.25	.20
Pair-Line pair	2.00	
v. Pair, imperforate	—	
zo. Tagging omitted (error)	—	

1969. The Christmas Stamp features the 19th century painting by an unknown artist. From the collection of the New York State Historical Association, Cooperstown, NY. *Intaglio, perforated 11 x 10 1/2.*

651

651 *(1384)*

6c multicolored, tagged *(Nov. 3, 1969)*	.25	.20
Plate block of 10	1.95	
Experimental precancel		.25
all 4 cities singles		2.75
Plate block of 10		85.
v. Light green omitted	25.	
v1. Light green, red,		
and yellow omitted	950.	
v2. Yellow omitted	2,500.	
v3. Yellow and red omitted	—	
v4. Imperforate pair	1,100.	
zo. Tagging omitted (error)	—	
Plate strip of 10	—	

Intaglio and perforated 11 x 10 1/2

  652, 653 *Dwight D. Eisenhower*

652 *(1393)*

6c blue, tagged Type II *(Aug. 6, 1970)*	.25	.20
Plate block of four	.50	
(1393v) m. Matt gum	.25	
Plate block of four	1.00	
(1393a) n. Booklet pane of eight	1.50	
(1393e) nm. Booklet pane of eight,		
matt gum	2.00	
(1393b) n1. Booklet pane of five		
plus label	1.50	
zo. Tagging omitted (error)	—	
zx. Untagged (Bureau precancel)	—	

Coil, intaglio, perforated 10 vertically

653 *(1401)*

6c blue, tagged *(Aug. 6, 1970)*	.25	.20
Pair	.25	
Line pair	.50	
(1401d) m. Matt gum	.25	.20
Pair	.60	
Line pair	1.50	
v. Imperforate pair	—	
Imperforate line pair	—	
zo. Tagging omitted (error)	8.50	
(1401a) zx. Untagged (Bureau precancel)	1.00	

Intaglio, perforated 11 x 10 1/2

Same design as No. 647 (Giori Press) and No. 650 (Huck Press). Huck Press printings are 0.05 inches smaller than Giori Printings.

654 *(1338D)*

6c dark blue, green, and red,		
tagged type B *(Aug.7, 1970)*	.25	.20
Margin block of 20	3.25	
v. Imperforate-between		
horizontal pair	—	
zo. Tagging omitted (error)	—	
Margin block of 20	—	

1970. Christmas Issue consists of four different designs printed se-tenant, and a single design which appears separately. *Gravure at Guilford Gravure, Inc., Guilford, Connecticut. Horizontal stamps are perforated 11 x 10 1/2; vertical stamp 10 1/2 by 11.*

655 *Antique toy locomotive*
656 *Toy wheeled horse*
657 *Mechanical tricycle toy*
658 *Doll carriage toy*

655 *(1415)*
  6c multicolored, tagged *(Nov. 5, 1970)* .25   .20
656 *(1416)*
  6c multicolored, tagged   .25   .20
    v. Black omitted   —
    v1. Imperforate pair (Nos. 656, 658)—
657 *(1417)*
  6c multicolored, tagged   .25   .20
658 *(1418)*
  6c multicolored, tagged   .25   .20
    w. Se-tenant block of four   1.50
       Plate block of eight   3.50
    v. Black omitted, any single   2,500.
       Black omitted, block of 4   —
    x. Precanceled, any single   .25   .20
       Precanceled Se-tenant block
       of four   1.25
    xw. Se-tenant block of four,
       precanceled   1.50
    zo. Tagging omitted (error),
       any single   —
    zow. Se-tenant block of four,
       tagging omitted (error)   —

659 The Nativity *by Lorenzo Lotto*

659 *(1414)*
  6c multicolored, tagged *(Nov. 5, 1970)* .25   .20
     Plate block of eight   1.50
    v.   Black omitted   .25   .20
*(1414a)*x.   Precanceled
       Plate block of eight   2.50
    xv. Precanceled, blue omitted   1,650.
*(1414d)*ii   Type II   .85   .35
       Plate block of eight   8.50
(1414e) iix. Type II, precanceled   1.00   .35
       Plate block of eight   12.50

Type I has a slightly blurry impression and no gum breaker ridges. Type II has a shiny surfaced paper, sharper impression, and both horizontal and vertical gum breaker ridges. Type I precancel is gray black; Type II precancel is intense black.

1971. The Ernie Pyle Issue honors the World War II correspondent and newsman who died by enemy gunfire on April 18, 1945. He won the Pulitzer Prize in 1943. *Cottrell press printing, perforated 11 x 10 1/2.*

660 *Ernie Pyle*

660 *(1398)*
  16c brown, tagged *(May 7, 1971)*   .30   .20
     Plate block of four   1.30
    zo. Tagging omitted (error)   —
       Plate block of four   —
    zx. Untagged (Bureau precancel)   —

661, 662 *Flag towering over White House*
Printed by intaglio, perforated 11 x 10 1/2

661 *(1338F)*
  8c dark blue, red, and slate green, tagged
     Type B *(May 10, 1971)*   .25   .20
     Plate block of 20   3.75
    v.   Green omitted   500.
    v1. Imperforate-bewteen
       horizontal pair   55.
    v2. Imperforate vertical pair   55.

Coil, intaglio, perforated 10 vertically
662 *(1338G)*
  8c dark blue, red, and slate green, tagged
     Type B *(May 10, 1971)*   .20   .20
     Pair   1.75
    v. Imperforate pair   50.
    zo Tagging omitted (error)   —
       Pair   —
Giori press printing, perforated 11

663, 664 *Dwight D. Eisenhower*

663 *(1394)*
  8c black, blue gray, and red, tagged
     Type OP *(May 10, 1971)*   .25   .20
     Plate block of four   .75
     Gutter pair   —
    p. Hi-Brite paper   —
       Plate block of four   —
    zo. Tagging omitted (error)   —
       Plate block of four   —

Intaglio and perforated 11 x 10 1/2

663A *(1395)*
  8c reddish brown, tagged type II in booklet form only,
     or III, in booklet form only *(May 10, 1971)*
*(1395b)*n. Booklet pane of six   1.00
    nzo. Booklet pane of six,
       tagging omitted (error)   —
    n1. Booklet pane of eight   2.00
*(1395a)*n1zo. Booklet pane of eight,
       tagging omitted (error)   —
*(1395d)*n2. Booklet pane of seven
       plus label. taged type II
       (Jan. 28,1972)   2.00

n2zo. Booklet pane of seven
plus label, tagging
omitted (error) —
n2z1. Booklet pane of seven
plus label, tagged type III 2.00
n2v. Booklet pane of seven
plus label, imperforate
between horizontally 2.00
(1395c) n3. Booklet pane of four,
plus two labels, tagged
type II *(Jan. 28, 1972)* 1.50
n3z1. Booklet pane of four,
plus two labels,
tagged type III 2.00
n3zo. Tagging omitted (error),
single stamp —

All these booklet stamps have 1 or 2 straight edges.

Coil, intaglio and perforated 10 vertically
664 *(1402)*
  8c reddish brown, tagged *(May 10, 1971)* .25 .20
  Pair .60
  Line pair —
  v. Imperforate pair —
    Imperforate line pair —
  v1. Imperforate-between pair —
  zx. Untagged (Bureau precancel) 6.50 1.00

1971. The U.S. Postal Service Issue marks the
transition from the U.S. Post Office Department to the
U.S. Postal System under the direction of Postmater
General Winton M. Blount.
Gravure, perforated 11 x 10 1/2.

  665 *Postal service emblem*

665 *(1396)*
  8c multicolored, tagged *(July 1, 1971)* .25 .20
  Plate block of twelve 2.00

1971. The 1971 Christmas Issue consists of two
separate stamps.

  666 A Partridge in   667 Nativity *by Giorgione*
  a pear tree

Gravure, perforated 10 1/2 x 11.
666 *(1444)*
  8c multicolored, tagged *(Nov. 10, 1971)* .25 .20
  Plate block of twelve 3.00
  zo. Tagging omitted (error) —

667 *(1445)*
  8c multicolored, tagged *(Nov. 10, 1971)* .25 .20
  Plate block of twelve 3.00
  v. gold omitted —

1972. The Fiorello H. LaGuardia Issue pays tribute to
a prominent American who served his country as a
congressman and as mayor of New York City. *Intaglio,
perforated 11 x 10 1/2.*

  668 *Fiorello H. LaGuardia*

668 *(1397)*
  14c dark brown, tagged *(April 24, 1972)* .25 .20
  Plate block of four 1.25
  zx. Untagged (Bureau precancel) —

1972. The Benjamin Franklin Issue honors the
printer, writer, postmaster general, and statesman with
a stamp intended primarily to pay postage for
educational materials. *Intaglio, perforated 10 1/2 x 11.*

  669 *Benjamin Franklin*

669 *(1393D)*
  7c light blue, shinny gum tagged
    (Oct. 20, 1972) .25 .20
  Plate block of four .75
(1393Dv)   m. matt gum .25 .20
  Plate block of four 1.35
  zo. Tagging omitted (error) — —
  Plate block of four —
  zx. Untagged —
    (Bureau precancel)

1972. The Christmas Issue. *Photogravure, perforated
11 x 10 1/2.*

  670 *Santa Claus*

670 *(1472)*
  8c multicolored, tagged *(Nov. 9, 1972)* .25 .20
  Plate block of twelve 3.00

  671 *Angels from painting* Mary, Queen of
  Heaven, *in the National Gallery of Art*

671 *(1471)*
 8c multicolored, tagged *(Nov. 9, 1972)* .25 .20
  Plate block of twelve 3.00
  v. black omitted 4,500.
  v1. pink omitted 175.

1973. Eugene O'Neill Coil Issue, see design for No. 632. *Intaglio and perforated 10 vertically. This was the first high-value stamp issued in tagged form.*

672 *(1305C)*
 $1 dark purple, tagged *(Jan. 12, 1973)*2.00 .75
  Pair 3.50
  Line pair 5.00
 (1305cd) m. Matt gum 2.00 .75
  Pair 4.00
  Line pair 10.
  v. Imperforate pair 2,250.
  Imperforate line pair 4,250.

1973. Amadeo P. Giannini Issue honors the great American banker who rose from humble origins to develop the world's largest private bank. *Intaglio and perforated 11 x 10 1/2*

673 *Amadeo P. Giannini*

673 *(1400)*
 21c banknote green, tagged *(June 27, 1973*.40 .25
  Plate block of four 1.60

1973. The Christmas Issue consists of two stamps, one with the traditional religious motif, the other with a secular theme. *Gravure, Andreotti press.*

664 Madonna and 675 *Christmas Tree needlepoint*
Child *by Raphael* *by Dolli Tingle*

674 *(1507)*
 8c multicolored, tagged *(Nov. 7, 1973)* .25 .20
  Plate block of twelve 3.00
  Gutter Pair —

675 *(1508)*
 8c multicolored, tagged *(Nov. 7, 1973)* .25 .20
  Plate block of twelve 3.00
  Vertical gutter pair —
  v. Imperforate-between
   vertical pair 325.

1973. Crossed Flags Issue was made available in anticipation of higher postal rates. Use of the 13-star flag in the design was in tribute to the American Revolution Bicentennial. *Intaglio, perforated 11 x 10 1/2*

676, 677 *50-star and 13-star flags*

676 *(1509)*
 10c red and blue, tagged *(Dec. 8, 1973)* .25 .20
  Plate block of 20 4.00
  v. Blue omitted 175.
  v1. Imperforate-between
   horizontal pair —
  v2. Horizontal pair,
   imperforate vertically —
  v3. Imperforate-between
   horizontally vertical pair —
  v4. Vertical pair, imperforate 950.
  zo. Tagging omitted (error) —
  Plate strip of 20 —

Coil, intaglio, perforated 10 vertically
677 *(1519)*
 10c red and blue, tagged *(Dec. 8, 1973)* .40 .25
  Pair 2.00
  Line pair 4.75
  v. Imperforate pair 37.50
  Imperforate line pair 50.
  zo. Tagging omitted (error) —
  Pair —

1973. Jefferson Memorial Issue met the new postal rates. *Intaglio, perforated 11 x 10 1/2*

678, 679 *Jefferson Memorial*

678 *(1510)*
 10c blue, tagged, type II or III
  (Dec. 14, 1973) .25 .20
  Plate block of four .85
 *(1510b)*n. Booklet pane of five
  plus label 1.50
 *(1510d)*n1. Booklet pane of six
  (Aug. 5, 1974) 5.75
 *(1510e)*n2. Booklet pane of eight 1.75
  n2zo. Booklet pane of eight,
   tagging omitted (error) —
  v. Imperforate-between
   vertical pair 800.
  v1. Vertical pair,
   imperforate horizontally 500.
  zo. Tagging omitted (error) —
  zx. Untagged (Bureau precancel) —

679 *(1520)*
10c blue, tagged *(Dec. 14, 1973)*	.25	.20
Pair	.40	
Line pair	.75	
v. Imperforate pair		
Line pair	40.	
*(1520a)*zx. Untagged (Bureau precancel)	65.	

1974. ZIP Code Issue, another in the series of new 10c stamps, underlined the importance of moving mail rapidly. *Gravure, perforated 11 x 10 1/2.*

 680 *Zip moves mail rapidly*

680 *(1511)*
10c multicolored, tagged with small rectangle in center of stamp *(Jan. 4, 1974)*	.25	.20
Plate block of eight	1.75	
Gutter pair	—	
v. Yellow omitted	55.	
zv. Overall tagging (error)	—	

1974. Elizabeth Blackwell Issue honors the first woman medical doctor of modern times. *Intaglio and perforated 11 x 10 1/2.*

 681 *Dr. Elizabeth Blackwell*

681 *(1399)*
18c purple, tagged *(Jan. 23, 1974)*	.30	.25
Plate block of four	1.25	

1974. Bulk Rate Coil. *Intaglio and perforated 10 vertically.*

 682 *Swinging Liberty Bell*

682 *(1518)*
6.3c brick red, tagged *(Oct. 1, 1974)*	.25	.20
Pair	.40	
Line pair	.75	
v. Imperforate pair	175.	
Imperforate line pair	—	
*(1518a)*zx. Untagged (Bureau precancel)	.25	.20
Pair	.90	
Line pair	1.50	
zxv. Imperforate pair	95.	
Imperforate line pair	250.	

1974. Christmas Issue consists of three stamps, two of which were traditional and the third which was a pressure-sensitive self-adhesive, precanceled with a die-cut cross in the design to deter reuse. *Gravure, perforated 11 x 10 1/2*

 683 The Road — Winter, *by Currier and Ives*

683 *(1551)*
10c multicolored, tagged *(Oct. 23, 1974)*	.25	.20
Plate block of twelve	2.25	
v. buff omitted, pane of 50	600.	

Imperforate, die cut, self-adhesive with backing

 684 *Dove of Peace weather vane atop Mount Vernon*

684 *(1552)*
10c multicolored, self-adhesive *(Nov. 15, 1974)*	.25	.20
Plate block of 20	2.25	

Perforated 10 1/2 x 11

 685 The Perussis Altarpiece, *artist unknown, Metropolitan Museum of Art, New York City*

685 *(1550)*
10c multicolored, tagged *(Oct. 23, 1974)*	.25	.20
Plate block of ten	2.25	

1975. Christmas Issue features two stamps that for the first time in U.S. postal history were issued without a printed denomination. The stamps were valid for the first-class rate at the time of issue. *Gravure.*

 686 *Louis Prang Christmas card*

686 *(1580)*
(10c) multicolored, perforated 11 1/4 tagged (Oct.14, 1975)	.30	.20
Plate block of 12	3.75	
v. Imperforate pair	—	

686A
(10c) multicolored, perforated 11,
    tagged   .30   .20
    Plate block of 12   3.75

686B *(1580b)*
(10c) multicolored, perforated 10 1/2 x 11
    tagged   .30   .20
    Plate block of 12   3.75

687 *Ghirlandaio* Madonna and Child

687 *(1579)*
(10c) multicolored, tagged *(Oct. 14, 1975)*.30   .20
    Plate block of 12   3.75
    Damaged "d" (plate flaw)   —
    v. Imperforate pair   —

1975-81 Americana Series.

Intaglio, perforated 11

688 *Capitol Dome*   689 *Early printing press*

688 *(1591)*
9c green on gray paper, tagged
    (Nov. 24, 1975)   .25   .20
    Plate block of four   .75
(1591v)m. Matt gum   1.00   .20
    Plate block of four   5.25
    zo. Tagging omitted (error) —
    zx. Untagged (Bureau precancel) —

689 *(1593)*
11c orange on gray paper, tagged
    (Nov. 13, 1975)   .25   .20
    Plate block of four   1.00
    Gutter pair   —
    zo. Tagging omitted (error) —

690, 694 *Flag over Independence Hall*

690 *(1622)*
13c dark blue and red, perforated
    11 x 10 1/2, tagged Huck Press
    (Nov. 15, 1975)   .25   .20

    Plate block of 20   5.50
    v. Imperforate-between
        horizontal pair   50.
    v1. Imperforate vertical pair 1,000.

690A *(1622c)*
13c dark blue and red, perforated 11, tagged
    Combination press (1981) .75   1.00
    Plate block of 20   70.
    v. Horizontal pair,
        imperforate vertically —
    v1. Imperforate vertical pair 150.
    zo. Tagging omitted (error) —

691 *Eagle and shield*   692 *Old North Church,Boston*

691 *(1596)*
13c multicolored, perforated 11 1/4,
    tagged with eagle-shape untagged
        area *(Dec. 1, 1975)*   .25   .20
    Plate block of 12   3.50
    Gutter pair   —
    v. Yellow omitted   175.
    v1. Imperforate pair   —

691A *(1596d)*
13c multicolored, perforated 10
    (line perforation)   30.   15.
    Plate block of 12   400.

692 *(1603)*
24c red on blue paper,
    tagged *(Nov. 14, 1975)* .50   .25
    Plate block of four   2.00
    zo. Tagging omitted (error) —
    Plate block of four   —

693 *Francis Parkman*   694 *Flag over Independence Hall*

Coil, intaglio, perforated 10 horizontally

693 *(1297)*
3c purple, tagged *(Nov. 4, 1975)* .25   .20
    Pair   .30
    Line pair   .35
    m. Matt gum   .25
        Pair   .30
        Line pair   .35
    v. Imperforate pair   27.50
        Imperforate line pair 45.

zx. Untagged (Bureau precancel) .25
    Pair .30
    Line pair .35
zxv. Imperforate pair 6.50
    Imperforate line pair 20.

Intaglio, perforated 10 vertically
694 *(1625)*
  13c dark blue and red, tagged
      (Nov. 15, 1975) .25 .20
  Pair .30
  Line pair .45
  v. Imperforate pair —
  zo. Tagging omitted (error) —

695, 696 *Liberty Bell*

Booklet panes, intaglio, perforated 11 x 10 1/2, matt gum
695 *(1595)*
  13c brown, from booklet panes only,
      tagged *(Oct.. 31, 1975)* .25 .20
  v. Imperforate-between
    vertical pair 325.
(1595d) n. Booklet pane of five
    plus label *(April 2, 1976)* 1.50 2.00
(1595a) n1. Booklet pane of six 2.00 2.00
(1595b) n2. Booklet pane of seven
    plus label 1.75 2.50
  n2zo. Booklet pane of seven
    plus label, tagging omitted (error) —
(1595c) n3. Booklet pane of eight 2.00 2.75
  n3zo. Booklet pane of eight,
    tagging omitted (error) —

Coil, intaglio, perforated 10 vertically
696 *(1618)*
  13c brown, shinny gum, tagged
      (Nov. 25, 1975) .25 .20
  Pair .50
  Line pair .80
  m. Matt gum —
    Pair —
    Line pair —
  v. Imperforate pair 25.
    Imperforate line pair 60.
  v1. Imperforate-between pair 1,400.
(1618a) zx. Untagged (Bureau precancel) .50 .50
  Pair 1.00
  Line pair 6.50
  zx. Untagged (Bureau precancel)
    matt gum —
  zo. Tagging omitted (error) —

697 *Capitol Dome*   698 *American eagle and drum*

697 *(1616)*
  9c green on gray paper, shinny gum,
      tagged *(March 5, 1976)* .25 .20
  Pair .40
  Line pair 1.00
  m. Matt gum —
    Pair —
    Line pair —
  v. Imperforate pair 165.
  v1. Imperforate line pair 375.
  z.x Untagged (Bureau precancel) —
  zxv. Imperforate pair 800.
    Imperforate line pair 2,000.

698 *(1615)*
  7.9c red on canary paper, shinny gum
      tagged *(April 23, 1976)* .25 .20
  Pair .50
  Line pair 3.75
  m. Matt gum —
    Pair —
    Line pair —
(1615cd) zx. Untagged (Bureau precancel) 2.00
  v. Imperforate pair 575.
  v1. Imperforate line pair —

1976. Christmas Issue consists of two designs. The religious theme features John Singleton Copley's *Nativity*, and the contemporary stamp shows Currier's *Winter Pastime*. The gravure press was used for the religious stamp while the contemporary stamp was printed for the most part (about 70 percent) on a new multicolor press. The gravure-press printing has all-over tagging and the lettering at the base is black; the multicolor-press printing has block tagging and the letter at the base is gray black.

699, 699A *Winter Pastime*

699 *(1702)*
  13c multicolored, overall tagging
      (Oct. 27, 1976) .40 .25
  Plate block of 10 4.00
  v. Imperforate pair 95.

699A *(1703)*
  13c multicolored, block tagging .40 .25
  Plate block of 20 7.75
  v. Imperforate pair 100.
  v1. Imperforate-between
    vertical pair —
  v2. red omitted —
  v3. yellow omitted —
  zo. Tagging omitted (error) —

700 *Nativity*

700 *(1701)*
13c multicolored,
tagged *(Oct. 27, 1976)*	.40	.25
Plate block of 12	4.75	
v. Imperforate pair	120.	

1977. Americana Series.

701 *Saxhorns*

Coil, Intaglio, perforated 10 vertically.
701 *(1614)*
7.7c brown on canary paper, tagged
(Nov. 20, 1976)	.25	.20
Pair	.50	
Line pair	1.00	
*(1614a)*zx. Untagged (Bureau precancel)	4.00	
zxv. Imperforate pair	1,750.	
Imperforate line pair	—	

1977. Vending Machine Booklet consists of seven 13c stamps and one 9c stamp in a single pane. *Intaglio, produced with two different perforations.*

702, 703 *Capitol dome and flag over Independence Hall*

Perforated 11 x 10 1/2
702 *(1590)*
9c green, tagged *(March 11, 1977)*	50.	.75

703 *(1623)*
13c red and blue, tagged *(March 11, 1977)*	.25	.20
n. Booklet pane of eight (seven No. 703, and one No.702)	2.75	
y. Se-tenant pair, No 703,702	1.00	1.00

Perforated 10
702A *(1590a)*
9c green *(March 11, 1977)*	20.	22.50

703A *(1623c)*
13c red and blue *(March 11, 1977)*	.75	.50
n. Booklet pane of eight (seven No. 703A, and one No. 702A)	30.	18.50
y. Se-tenant pair, No. 703A , 702A	25.	

1977. Christmas Issue consists of two different stamps: one showing Washington kneeling in prayer at Valley Forge, based on a paining by J.C. Letendecker; the other features holiday mail in a rural mail box. *Gravure.*

704 *Rural mail box*

705 *Gen. Washington kneeling at prayer*

704 *(1730)*
13c multicolored *(Oct. 21, 1977)*	.40	.20
Plate block of ten	4.00	
v. Imperforate pair	300.	
zv. Overall tagging (error)	—	

705 *(1729)*
13c multicolored, tagged *(Oct. 21, 1977)*	.40	.20
Plate strip of 20	8.00	
v. Imperforate pair	70.	
zv. Overall tagging (error)	—	

The multicolor combination press issue (No. 705) has "floating" plate numbers: a set of five numbers sandwiched between two or three blanks, so that on a plate strip of 20 there are five numbers and five blanks, six numbers and four blanks, seven numbers and three blanks, or eight numbers and two blanks. There are no Zip or Mail Early slogans.

The Engergy and Conservation issue formerly listed as 706 and 707 have been moved to the commemorative section, and can now be found as CM876A and CM876B.

706 *Conservation*

707 *Development (Se-tenant pair: the sun's rays, light bulb, and building heated by solar energy.)*

1977. Americana Series.

Intaglio and perforated 11 x 10 1/2

708, 709 *Contemplation of Justice*

708 *(1592)*
  10c purple on gray paper, shiny gum
              tagged *(Nov. 17, 1977)*   .25   .20
      Plate block of four   .70
(1592v) m. Matt gum   .25   .20
         Plate block of four   1.00
      zo. Tagging omitted (error)   —
      zx. Untagged (Bureau precancel) —

Coil, intaglio and perforated 10 vertically
709 *(1617)*
  10c purple on gray paper,
            tagged *(Nov. 4, 1977)*   .25   .20
      Pair   .40
      Line pair   1.00
      v. Imperforate pair   —
         Imperforate line pair   —
(1617v) m. Matt gum   .50   .20
         Pair   .75
         Line pair   2.50
      mv. Imperforate pair   —
         Imperforate line pair —
(1617a) zx. Untagged (Bureau precancel) 2.00

Intaglio.

710 *Quill pen and inkwell*   711 *Symbols of speech*

710 *(1581)*
  1c blue on green paper, tagged
            (Dec. 8, 1977)   .25   .20
      Plate block of four   .25
      Gutter pair   —
(1581v) m. Matt gum   .25   .20
         Plate block of four   .25
      z. Untagged (Bureau precancel) —
      zo. Tagging omitted (error)   —
(1581c) p. White paper

711 *(1582)*
  2c brown on green paper *(Dec. 8, 1977)* .50   .20
      Plate block of four   2.00
(1582v) m. Matt gum   .25   .20
         Plate block of four   .25
      xo. Tagging omitted (error)   —
      zx. Untagged (Bureau precancel) —

711A *(1582b)*
  2c brown on white paper, matt gum,
            tagged *(1981)*   .25   .20
      Plate block of four   .25

712 *Ballot box*   713 *Reading and learning*

712 *(1584)*
  3c olive on green paper, shiny gum,
            tagged *(Dec. 8, 1977)* .25   .20
      Plate block of four   .30
      Gutter pair   —
(1584v) m. Matt gum   .25   .20
         Plate block of four   .50
      zo. Tagging omitted (error)   —
      zx. Untagged (Bureau precancel) —

713 *(1585)*
  4c maroon on green paper, tagged
            (Dec. 8, 1977)   .25   .20
      Plate block of four   .50
(1585v) m. Matt gum   .25   .20
         Plate block of four   1.25
      zo. Tagging omitted (error)   —
      zx. Untagged (Bureau precancel) —

1978. Experimental Stamp Issue.

1978. Experimental Stamp Issue. For the first time, a U.S. difinitive was specially designed in a smaller size so that 150 stamps could be produced in place of the usual 100 stamp pane. *Intaglio, perforated 11.*

 714 *Indian Head penny*

714 *(1734)*
  13c brown and blue on tan paper, tagged
            (Jan. 11, 1978)   .25   .20
      Plate block of four   1.75
      Gutter pair   —
      v. Horizontal pair,
         imperforate vertically 275.
      zo. Tagging omitted (error)   —

1978. Americana Series.

Intaglio and perforated 11 x 10 1/2

 715, 716 *Statue of Liberty*

715 *(1599)*
  16c blue, tagged *(March 31, 1978)* .30   .20
      Plate block of four   1.50

Coil, intaglio, perforated 10 vertically
716 *(1619)*
  16c blue, overall tagging *(March 31, 1978)* .35   .20
    Pair   .70
    Line pair   1.50
    z. Block tagging   —
        Pair   —

717 *Sandy Hook Lighthouse*

Intaglio and perforated 11 x 10 1/2
717 *(1605)*
  29c blue on blue paper, shiny gum
        tagged *(April 14, 1978)*   .50   .65
    Plate block of four   2.75
  (1605v) m. Matt gum   2.00   .25
    Plate block of four   15.25

1978. Non-Denominated "A" Stamp Issue marks the
new first class postage rate (15 cents) which went into
effect May 29. The stamps were printed in 1975 and
1976 and had been stored for use in this contingency.

Gravure

718-720 *"A" design to left of stylized eagle*

718 *(1735)*
  15c orange, perforated 11, tagged
        (May 22, 1978)   .30   .25
    Plate block of four   1.50
    v. Imperforate pair   95.
    v1. Vertical pair, imperforate
        horizontally   750.
718A *(1735c)*
  15c orange, perforated 11 1/4, tagged .30   .25
    Plate block of four   1.50

Booklet stamps, intaglio, perforated 11 x 10 1/2
719 *(1736)*
  15c orange, tagged *(May 22, 1978)*   .25   .20
    n. Booklet pane of eight   2.25   2.75
    v. Vertical pair, imperforate
        between   1,750.

Coil, intaglio, perforated 10 vertically
720 *(1743)*
  15c orange, tagged *(May 22, 1978)*   .25   .15
    Pair   .50
    Line pair   .75
    v. Imperforate pair   95.
    Imperforate line pair   195.

1978. Prominent Americans Series. Oliver W. Holmes
(same design as No. 626) issued to meet the new postal
rates. *Intaglio, coil, perforated 10 vertically.*

721 *(1305E)*
  15c maroon, Type I, tagged *(June 14, 1978)* 25   .20
    Pair   .50
    Line pair   1.25
  (1305d) m. Matt gum, type I   .25   .20
    Pair   1.25
    Line pair   2.00
  (1305ef) zx. Untagged (Bureau
        precancel)   42.50   4.00
    v. Imperforate pair, shinny gum —
    Imperforate line pair,
    shinny gum   —
    mv. Imperforate pair, matt gum —
    v1. Imperforate-between pair —
    Imperforate-between line pair —

721A *(1305Ei)*
  15c maroon, type II shiny gum,
        tagged   .25   .20
    Pair   .50
    Line pair   2.50
    m. Matt gum   —
    Pair   —
    Line pair   —
    mv. Imperforate pair, matt gum —
    Imperforate line pair, matt
    gum   —

For booklet pane issued the same date see No. 626.

1978. Americana Series: Fort McHenry flag which, in
1814, inspired Francis Scott Key to compose *The Star
Spangled Banner. Intaglio.*

722, 722A, 723 *American flag*

722 *(1597)*
  15c red, blue, and gray, perforated 10,
        tagged *(June 30, 1978)*   .30   .20
    Plate block of 20   7.00
    v. Gray omitted   600.
    v1. Imperforate vertical pair —
    zo. Tagging omitted (error) —

722A *(1598)*
  15c red, blue and gray, booklet stamp ,
    perforated 11 x 10 1/2,
    tagged *(June 30, 1978)*   .35   .20
    n. Booklet pane of eight   3.50   2.50

Coil, intaglio, perforated 10 vertically
723 *(1618C)*
  15c red, blue and gray (June 30, 1978) .25   .20
    Pair   1.00
    v. Imperforate pair   20.
    v1. Imperforate-between pair   165.
    v2. Gray omitted   35.
    zo. Tagging omitted (error) —

1978. American Roses Issue. Booklet, *Intaglio, perforated 10.*

724 *Two roses: Red Masterpiece (1974 Rose of the Year) and Medallion (winner of two high honors)*

724 *(1737)*
15c orange, red, and green, booklet stamp, tagged *(July 11, 1978)*   .25   .20
   n. Booklet pane of eight   2.25   3.00
   nv. Imperforate pane of eight   —
   nv1. Imperforate pair   400.
   nzo. Pane of eight, tagging omitted (error)   —

1978. Americana Series, bulk rate coil. *Intaglio, perforated 10 vertically.*

725 *Steinway grand piano*

725 *(1615c)*
8.4c blue on canary paper, shiny gum, tagged *(July 13, 1978)*   .25   .20
   Pair   .40
   Line pair   3.75
*(1615cd)*zx. Untagged (Bureau precancel) 40.   25.
   zxv.Imperforate pair   15.
   Imperforate line pair   25.
   zxv1.Imperforate-between pair   50.
   Imperforate-between line pair 135.
   m. Matt gum   —
   Pair   —
   Line pair   —

Intaglio, perforated 11 x 10 1/2

726 *Reconstructed blockhouse at Fort Nisqually, Washington*

726 *(1604)*
28c brown on blue paper, tagged, shiny gum *(Aug. 11, 1978)*   .50   .20
   Plate block of four   2.40
(1604v) m. Matt gum   1.25   .25
   Plate block of four   10.

1978. Christmas Issue consisted of two stamps. *Gravure, perforated 11.*

727 *Child astride a hobby horse, by Dolli Tingle*

727 *(1769)*
15c multicolored, tagged *(Oct. 18, 1978)* .40   .20
   Plate block of 12   5.50
   Gutter pair   —
   v. Imperforate pair   95.
   v1. Vertical pair, imperforate horizontally   2,250.

728 Madonna and Child with Cherubim, *Sculpture by Andrea della Robbia*

728 *(1768)*
15c multicolored, tagged *(Oct. 18, 1978)* .40   .20
   Plate block of 12   5.50
   v. Imperforate pair   90.

1978. Americana Series. *Intaglio and offset.*

729 *Kerosene table lamp*

729 *(1611)*
$2 multicolored, tagged *(Nov. 16, 1978)* 3.50   1.00
   Plate block of four   14.50

1979. Americana Series: *Intaglio and offset, perforated 11.*

730 *Rush lamp and candle holder*   731 *Railroad conductor's lantern*

730 *(1610)*
$1 multicolored, tagged *(July 2, 1979)* 2.00   1.25
   Plate block of four   9.50
   v. Brown inverted   —
   v1. Brown omitted   275.
   v2. Orange, tan, and yellow omitted   350.
   zo. Tagging omitted (error)   —

731 *(1612)*
$5 multicolored, tagged *(Aug. 23, 1979)* 8.50   2.25
   Plate block of four   33.

732 *Country schoolhouse, Morris Township School No. 2*   733 *Iron "Betty" lamp*

Intaglio, perforated 11 x 10 1/2
732 *(1606)*
> **30c green on blue paper,** tagged
> > *(Aug. 27, 1979)*   1.00   .30
> Plate block of four   2.50
> zo. Tagging omitted (error)   —

733 *(1608)*
> **50c black, orange, and tan,** tagged
> > *(Sept. 11, 1979)*   1.00   .30
> Plate block of four   3.50
> v. Black omitted   300.
> v1. Vertical pair, imperforate
> > horizontally   —
> zo. Tagging omitted (error)   —

1979. Christmas Issue features two different designs. One depicts Madonna and Child from the Gerard David painting *The Rest on the Flight into Egypt*, which hangs in the National Gallery of Art in Washington, D.C. The other design shows a Santa Claus Christmas tree ornament. *Gravure press, perforated 11.*

734 Santa Claus Christmas tree ornament

734 *(1800)*
> **15c multicolored,** tagged *(Oct. 18, 1979)* .45   .20
> Plate block of 12   5.50
> v. Green and yellow omitted   650.
> v1. Green, yellow, and tan
> > omitted   675.

735 Madonna and Child from the Gerard David painting The Rest on the Flight into Egypt

735 *(1799)*
> **15c multicolored,** tagged *(Oct. 18, 1979)* .45   .20
> Plate block of 12   5.50
> v. Imperforate pair   90.
> v1. Imperforate-between vertical
> > pair   2,250.
> v2. Vertical pair, imperforate
> > horizontally   750.

1979. Americana Series: Non-profit coil. *Intaglio, perforated 10 vertically.*

736 Standard six-string guitar

736 *(1613)*
> **3.1c brown on canary paper,** tagged
> > *(Oct. 25, 1979)*   .25   .20
> Pair   .35
> Line pair   1.50

v. Imperforate pair
> Imperforate line pair   1,375.
> zx. Untagged (Bureau precancel) 4.00   .25

1980. Historic Windmills Issue. *Intaglio, perforated 10 1/2*

737 *Robertson Windmill, Williamsburg, Virginia;*
738 *Replica of The Old Windmill, Portsmouth, Rhode Island;* 739 *Cape Cod Windmill, Eastham, Massachusetts;* 740 *Dutch Mill at Fabyan Park Forest Preserve, near Batavia, Illinois;* 741 *A Southwestern windmill*

737 *(1738)*
> **15c brown on yellow paper,** tagged
> > *(Feb. 7, 1980)*   .30   .20
738 *(1739)*
> **15c brown on yellow paper**, tagged   .30   .20
739 *(1740)*
> **15c brown on yellow paper**, tagged   .30   .20
740 *(1741)*
> **15c brown on yellow paper**, tagged   .30   .20
741 *(1742)*
> **15c brown on yellow paper**, tagged   .30   .20
> a. Se-tenant strip of five   1.50   .75
> n. Booklet pane of 10
> > (two of each design)   3.50   4.50

1980. Americana Series: "The Ability to Write — A Root of Democracy — same design as No. 710. *Intaglio, perforated 10 vertically.*

742 *(1811)*
> **1c blue on green paper,** shiny gum,
> > tagged *(March 6, 1980)*   .25   .20
> Pair   .25
> Line pair   .50
> m. Matt gum   .25   .20
> > Pair   .25
> > Line pair   .50
> mv. Imperforate pair   175.
> > Imperforate line pair   275.
> zo. Tagging omitted (error)   —

1980. Dolley Madison Issue honors the wife of James Madison on the anniversary of her death. The stamp was produced in the mini-stamp format identical in size to the 1978 Indian Head Cent stamp (No. 714). *Intaglio, perforated 11.*

743 Dolley Madison, pencil sketch from Gilbert Stuart painting

743 *(1822)*
> **15c red brown and sepia,** tagged
> > *(May 20, 1980)*   .40   .20
> Plate block of four   2.00

1980. Americana Series: Coil stamp to meet non-profit organization rate. *Intaglio, perforated 10 vertically.*

744 *Weaver manufactured violins*

744 (1813)
3.5c purple on yellow paper, tagged

(June 12, 1980)	.25	.20
Pair	.25	
Line pair	1.00	
v. Imperforate pair	225.	
Imperforate line pair	325.	
(1813a)zx. Untagged (Bureau precancel)	.25	.20
Pair	.50	
Line pair	2.00	

1980. Christmas Issue consists of two different designs. The contemporary design shows antique toys on a window sill. The other stamp depicts a detail, in the vignette of a Madonna and Child, from the stained glass Epiphany Window in the Bethlehem Chapel of the Washington Cathedral. *Gravure, perforated 11.*

745 *Season's Greetings, toys on a window sill*

745 (1842)
15c multicolored, tagged (Oct. 31, 1980)

	.50	.20
Plate block of 20	10.	
v. Light brown omitted	25.	
v1. Imperforate pair	85.	
v2. Vertical pair, imperforate horizontally	—	
v3. Plate block of 20, imperforate	850.	
v4. Horizontal pair, imperforate vertically	3,400.	
zo. Tagging omitted (error)	—	

746 *Vignette of Madonna and Child from the Epiphany Window*

746 (1843)
15c multicolored, tagged (Oct. 31, 1980)

	.50	.20
Plate block of 12	5.50	
Gutter pair	—	
v. Imperforate pair	85.	
v1. Plate block of 12, imperforate	650.	

1980. Sequoyah Issue honored the Cherokee Indian scholar who devised a written alphabet for his tribe. This was the first issue of a new series, the Great American Series. *Intaglio, perforated 11 x 10 1/2.*

747 *Sketch from portrait of Sequoyah by Charles Banks Wilson*

747 (1859)
19c brown, tagged (Dec. 27, 1980) .30 .20
Plate block of four

747A *"Shaved" Washington coil*

747A (1304)
5c deep blue, tagged (April 1981)

	.25	.20
Pair	.30	
Line pair	1.25	
v. Imperforate pair	—	

U.S. Postal Service Plate-Numbering Change

In response to collector complaints that its plate-numbering system resulted in many inconvenient and costly plate blocks of 10, 12 and 20 stamps, the USPS in January 1981 instituted a new plate number arrangement. Under the new system, most sheets were to contain a single plate number consisting of one (for monocolor stamps) to six digits, each digit representing a given printing plate and color. Thus, under this system most plate blocks returned to blocks of four.

Booklet panes hereafter also contain a plate number in the selvage.

In coils, a plate number was incorporated into some copies of a roll, at various intervals between stamps.

1981. Non-Denominated "B" Stamp Issue marks the change of the first class domestic postage rate to 18c, which went into effect March 22, 1981. The design was identical to the "A" stamp except for the background color and the letter. *Gravure, perforated 11 x 10 1/2.*

748-750 *"B" to left of stylized eagle*

748 (1818)
18c purple, tagged (March 15, 1981) .30 .20
Plate block of four 1.40
Gutter pair —

Booklet pane, intaglio, perforated 10
749 (1819a)
18c purple, tagged (March 15, 1981)
n. Booklet pane of eight 3.50 3.50

Coil, intaglio, perforated 10 vertically

750 *(1820)*
18c purple, tagged *(March 15, 1981)*	.60	.25
Pair	.80	
Line pair	1.65	
v. Imperforate pair	110.	
Imperforate line pair	185.	

1981. Americana Series, Freedom of Conscience — an American right. *Intaglio, perforated 11 x 10 1/2.*

751, 752 *Torch in the upraised right hand of the Statue of Liberty.*

751 *(1594)*
12c brown on gray paper, tagged *(April 8, 1981)*	.25	.20
Plate block of four	1.15	
zo. Tagging omitted (error)	—	

Coil, intaglio, perforated 10 vertically
752 *(1816)*
12c brown on gray paper, tagged *(April 8, 1981)*	.50	.25
Pair	.75	
Line pair	1.50	
v. Imperforate pair	150.	
Imperforate line pair	275.	
zx. Untagged (Bureau precancel)	—	

1981. American Flag Issues featured the same American flag across the top and a scene beneath the flag which depicted a phrase from *America the Beautiful*, written by Katherine Lee Bates in 1893. *Intaglio, perforated 11.*

753 *"... for amber waves of grain"*

753 *(1890)*
18c multicolored, tagged *(April 24, 1981)*	.30	.20
Plate block of 20	8.50	
v. Imperforate pair	100.	
v1. Vertical pair, imperforate horizontally	1,000.	

Coil, perforated 10 vertically

754 *"... from sea to shining sea"*

754 *(1891)*
18c multicolored, tagged *(April 24, 1981)*	.30	.20
Pair	.50	
v. Imperforate pair	18.	
v1. Imperforate-between pair	—	
zo. Tagging omitted (error)	—	

Listings and prices for plate number coil strips and singles appear at the end of this difinitive section of the Krause-Minkus catalog.

1981. Vending Machine Booklet Pane consisting of two 6c and six 18c stamps. *Intaglio, perforated 11 x 10 1/2.*

755 *Circle of stars*

756 *"... for purple mountain majesties"*

755 *(1892)*
6c blue, tagged *(April 24, 1981)*	.55	.20

756 *(1893)*
18c multicolored, tagged	.30	.20
x. Se-tenant pair, No. 756, 755.	.90	
n. Booklet pane of eight (two No. 755, six No. 756)	3.00	
nv. Booklet pane, vertically imperforate between	75.	

1981. George Mason Issue honored an early leader of pre-Revolutionary Virginia patriots. This was the second issue in the Great Americans' series. *Intaglio, perforated 11 x 10 1/2.*

757 *George Mason*

757 *(1858)*
18c blue, tagged *(May 7, 1981)*	.30	.20
Plate block of four	2.50	
zo. Tagging omitted (error)	—	

Great Americans Series Identifier

Entries are by denomination, in order of issue of that denomination. All stamps listed provide basic data: denomination, person honored, and catalog number. There is information in the columns for perforation, gum and tagging **only** when such information better identifies the different varieties of the stamp.

This series is still being issued, and as such, this listing will be updated and modified in future editions.

Denomination/Name	Cat.	Perf.	Gum	Tagging	Without Tagging
1c Dorothea Dix	807	11 1/4 H			
1c Dorothea Dix	807A	11 L			
1c Margaret Mitchell	857				Error (857zo)
2c Igor Stravinsky	798				Error (798zo)
2c Mary Lyon	872				Error (872zo)
2c Mary Lyon	872zx				Intentional
3c Henry Clay	804				Error (804zo)
3c Paul Dudley White	861				Error (861zo)
3c Paul Dudley White	861zx				Intentional
4c Carl Schurz	801				Error (801zo)
4c Father E.J. Flanagan	858				
4c Father E.J. Flanagan	858zx				Intentional (light gray violet)
4c Father E.J. Flanagan	858z1				Intentional (slate violet)
5c Pearl Buck	803				
5c Hugo Black	854				Error (854zo)
5c Luis Muñoz Marin	927				Error (927zo)
5c Luis Muñoz Marin	927z				Intentional
6c Walter Lippmann	848				
7c Abraham Baldwin	819				
8c Henry Knox	847				
9c Sylvanus Thayer	842				
10c Richard Russell	815				
10c Red Cloud	877			Block	Error (877zo)
10c Red Cloud	877pz			Pre-phosphored	
10c Red Cloud	877z1			Overall	
10c Red Cloud	877zx				Intentional
11c Alden Partridge	823				Error (823zo)
13c Crazy Horse	785				Error (785zo)
14c Sinclair Lewis	826				
14c Julia Ward Howe	871				
15c Buffalo Bill Cody	894			Block	
15c Buffalo Bill Cody	894z			Overall	
15c Buffalo Bill Cody	894z2			Pre-phosphored	Error (894zo)
17c Rachel Carson	769				Error (769zo)
17c Belva Ann Lockwood	856				Error (856zo)
18c George Mason	757				Error (757zo)
19c Sequoyah	747				
20c Ralph J. Bunch	784				Error (784zo)
20c Thomas H. Gallaudet	802				Error (802zo)
20c Harry S Truman	811	11 L		Block	
20c Harry S Truman	904	11 1/2 H		Block	Error (904zo)*
20c Harry S Truman	904z1	11 1/2 H		Overall	Error (904zo)*
20c Harry S Truman	904pz			Pre-phosphored	
20c Virginia Apgar	1052				
21c Chester Carlson	911				
22c John J. Audubon	839	11 L			Error (839zo)
22c John J. Audubon	839A	11 1/2 H			
23c Mary Cassatt	915			Block	
23c Mary Cassatt	915z1			Pre-phosphored	
23c Mary Cassatt	915z			Overall	Error (915zo)

Denomination/Name	Cat.	Perf.	Gum	Tagging	Without Tagging
25c Jack London (sheet)	853	11 L			
25c Jack London (booklet)	888	11 L			Error (888zo)
25c Jack London (booklet)	889	10			Error (889zo)
28c Sitting Bull	919				
29c Earl Warren	983				
29c Thomas Jefferson	1009				
30c Frank C. Laubach	816	11 L		Block (small)	
30c Frank C. Laubach	816A	11 1/2 H		Block (large)	
30c Frank C. Laubach	816Az1	11 1/2 H		Overall	
32c Milton S. Hershey	1096				
32c Cal Farley	1124				
35c Charles Drew	770				Error (770zo)
35c Dennis Chavez	946				
37c Robert A. Millikan	786				Error (786zo)
39c Grenville Clark	825	11 L			
39c Grenville Clark	825A	11 1/2 H			
40c Lillian Gilbreth	813	11 L			
40c Lillian Gilbreth	813A	11 1/2 H			
40c Claire Lee Channault	932			Overall	
40c Claire Lee Channault	932z1			Pre-phosphored	
45c Harvey W. Cushing	895			Block	Error (895zo)
45c Harvey W. Cushing	895z			Overall	
46c Ruth Benedict	1114				
50c Chester W. Nimitz	824	11 L	Shiny	Overall	Error (824zo)
50c Chester W. Nimitz	824A	11 1/2 H	Matt	Block	Error (824Azo)
50c Chester W. Nimitz	824Apz	11 1/2 H	Shiny	Pre-phosphored	
50c Chester W. Nimitz	824zo	11 1/2 H	Matt	Overall	
50c Chester W. Nimitz	824pzm	11 1/2 H	Matt	Pre-phosphored	
52c Hubert H. Humphrey	957				
52c Hubert H. Humphrey	957z1			Pre-phosphored	
55c Alice Hamilton	1093				
56c John Harvard	860				
65c H.H. "Hap" Arnold	916				Error (916zo)
75c Wendell Wilkie	981		Matt	Pre-phosphored	
75c Wendell Wilkie	981z1		Shiny	Pre-phosphored	
78c Alice Paul	1095				
$1 Bernard Revel	862				
$1 Johns Hopkins	918		Matt	Block	
$1 Johns Hopkins	918z1		Matt	Pre-phosphored	
$1 Johns Hopkins	918z2		Shiny	Pre-phosphored	
$1 Johns Hopkins	918z		Matt	Overall	Error (918zo)
$2 William Jennings Bryan	855				Error (855zo)
$5 Bret Harte	878			Block	Error (878zo)
$5 Bret Harte	878pz			Pre-phosphored	

Symbols: (in *Perf.* column) H = Harrow (perfect corners); L = L perforator

Footnotes

* Impossible to tell if "tagging omitted" version is from block- or overall-tagged version.

1981. Wildlife Booklet Issue featured 10 wild animals native to the United States. *Intaglio, perforated 11 x 10 1/2.*

758 *Bighorned sheep*
759 *Puma*

760 *Harbor seal*
761 *Bison*

762 *Brown bear*
763 *Polar bear*

764 *Elk (wapiti)*
765 *Moose*

766 *White-tailed deer*
767 *Pronghorned antelope*

758 *(1880)*
  18c brown, tagged *(May 14, 1981)*   .50   .20
759 *(1881)*
  18c brown, tagged   .50   .20
760 *(1882)*
  18c brown, tagged   .50   .20
761 *(1883)*
  18c brown, tagged   .50   .20
762 *(1884)*
  18c brown, tagged   .50   .20
763 *(1885)*
  18c brown, tagged   .50   .20
764 *(1886)*
  18c brown, tagged   .50   .20
765 *(1887)*
  18c brown, tagged   .50   .20
766 *(1888)*
  18c brown, tagged   .50   .20
767 *(1889)*
  18c brown, tagged   .50   .20
    n. Booklet pane of ten   8.50   4.00
    nv. Booklet pane of ten,
      imperforate-between
      vertically   1,500.

1981 Transportation Series, "Surrey" first in a new series. *Coil, intaglio, perforated 10 vertically.*

768 *"Surrey with the Fringe on Top"*

768 *(1907)*
  18c brown, tagged *(May 18, 1981)*   .35   .35
    Pair   .50
    v. Imperforate pair   125.

Listings and prices for plate number coil strips and singles appear at the end of this definitive section of the Krause-Minkus catalog.

1981. Rachel Carson Issue honors the scientist and author of *Silent Spring.* When published the book touched off an international controversy over pesticides. *Intaglio, perforated 11 x 10 1/2.*

769 *Rachel Carson*

769 *(1857)*
  17c green, tagged *(May 28, 1981)*   .30   .20
    Plate block of four   1.50
    zo. Tagging omitted (error)   —

1981. Charles Drew Issue honors the scientist and surgeon who discovered and developed methods to preserve blood plasma in large quantities. He was the first black surgeon selected for membership on the American Board of Surgery. Great Americans series. *Intaglio, perforated 11 x 10 1/2.*

770 *Dr. Charles R. Drew*

770 *(1865)*
  35c gray, tagged *(June 3, 1981)*   .50   .25
    Plate block of four   3.50
    zo. Tagging omitted (error)   —

1981. Transportation Series, Electric auto. *Coil, intaglio, perforated 10 vertically.*

771 *1917 electric auto*

771 *(1906)*
  17c blue, tagged *(June 25, 1981)*   .35   .35
    Pair   .50
    v. Imperforate pair   —
  *(1906a)*zx1. Untagged Bureau precancel, type I:
      "PRESORTED / FIRST CLASS"
      11 1/2mm   .35   .35
  *(1906ab)*zx2. Untagged Bureau precancel type II:
      "PRESORTED / FIRST CLASS"
      12 1/2mm   .75   .60
  *(1906ae)*zx3. Untagged Bureau precancel type III:
      "PRESORTED / FIRST CLASS"
      13 1/2mm   1.00   .50
    zv. Imperforate pair   650.
    z1. Tagging omitted (error)   —

Listings and prices for plate number coil strips and singles appear at the end of this difinitive section of the Krause-Minkus catalog.

1981. Non-Denominated "C" Issue marked the new first-class postage rate of 20c, which went into effect Nov. 1, 1981. The stamp was intended for domestic use only. Design same as the "A" and "B" issues, except for letter and background color.

Gravure, perforated 11 x 10 1/2, design size 19 x 22 mm

772-774 *"C" to left of stylized eagle*

772 *(1946)*
    (20c) brown, tagged *(Oct. 11, 1981)*   .35   .20
      Plate block of four   1.00
      zo. Tagging omitted (error)   —

Booklet panes, intaglio, perforated 11 x 10 1/2, design size 15 x 18 mm

773 *(1948)*
    (20c) brown, from booklet pane, tagged
        (Oct. 11, 1981)   .50   .20
      n. Booklet pane of ten   5.00   5.00

Coil, intaglio, perforated 10 vertically, design size 19 x 22mm

774 *(1947)*
    (20c) brown, tagged *(Oct. 11, 1981)*   .60   .20
      Pair   1.00
      Line pair   1.50
      v. Imperforate pair   1,000.
      Imperforate line pair   —

1981. Christmas Issue consisted of two stamps. Neither stamp bears a denomination, but had a face value at the first class postage rate that went into effect November 1, 1981. The stamps were intended only for domestic use. The contemporary stamp featured a Teddy Bear seated on a sleigh. The vignette of the traditional design featured a detail from *Madonna and Child*, a 15th century painting by Sandro Botticelli. *Gravure, perforated 11.*

375 *Teddy Bear on a sleigh*

775 *(1940)*
    (20c) multicolored, tagged *(Oct. 28, 1981)* .50   .20
      Plate block of four   2.50
      v. Imperforate pair   250.
      v1. Vertical pair, imperforate
        horizontally   —

776 Madonna and Child, *by Botticelli, Art Institute of Chicago*

776 *(1939)*
    (20c) multicolored, tagged *(Oct. 28, 1981)* .50   .20
      Plate block of four   2.50
      v. Imperforate pair   110.
      v1. Vertical pair, imperforate
        horizontally   1,550.

1981. Transportation Series, Fire pumper. *Coil, intaglio, perforated 10 vertically.*

777 Fire pumper, *1860's*

777 *(1908)*
    20c fire engine red, tagged
        (Dec. 10, 1981)   .40   .40
      Pair   .60
      v. Imperforate pair   1,000.

Listings and prices for plate number coil strips and singles appear at the end of this definitive section of the Krause-Minkus catalog.

1981. Transportation Series, mail wagon, bulk rate. *Coil, printed by intaglio, perforated 10 vertically.*

778 Mail wagon, *1880's*

778 *(1903)*
    9.3c dark red, tagged *(Dec. 15, 1981)*   .25   .20
      Pair   .25
      zv. Imperforate pair   115.
      zx. Untagged (Bureau precancel)   —

Listings and prices for plate number coil strips and singles appear at the end of this definitive section of the Krause-Minkus catalog.

1981. Flag over Supreme Court, issued in sheet, coil and booklet formats. *Intaglio.*

779-782 *Flag over Supreme Court Building; in the foreground is statue* Contemplation of Justice *by noted American sculptor James Earle Fraser.*

779 *(1894)*
    20c black, dark blue and red, perforated 11,
        tagged *(Dec. 17, 1981)*   .35   .20
      Plate block of 20   15.00
      v. Vertical pair, imperforate   35.

v1. Vertical pair, imperforate
horizontally 500.
v2. Block of four, imperforate 75.
v3. Black omitted 300.
v4. Blue omitted 85.
v5. Dark blue omitted —

779A *(1894e)*
20c black, dark blue and red, perforated 11 1/4,
tagged .35 .20
Plate block of 20 9.00

Coil, perforated 10 vertically
780 *(1895)*
20c black, dark blue and red, tagged
(Dec. 17, 1981) .50 .20
Pair .60
a. slate blue, dark blue and red —
b. black, dark blueand brick red —
v. Black omitted 50.
v1. Dark blue omitted —
v2. Imperforate pair 8.00
v3. Imperforate pair between —
zx. Untagged (Bureau precancel) .50 .20
z1. Tagging omitted (error) —

Listings and prices for plate number coil strips and
singles appear at the end of this definitive section of the
Krause-Minkus catalog.

Booklet pane, perforated 11 x 10 1/2
781 *(1896)*
20c black, dark red and blue, tagged
(Dec. 17, 1981) .35 .20
n. Booklet pane of six 2.50 3.00
n1. Booklet pane of ten
(July 1, 1982) 4.50 4.75

Intaglio, perforated 11

782 *Flag over Independence Hall*

782 *(1622c)*
13c dark blue and red, tagged *(1981)* .60 .25
Plate block of 20 70.
v. Imperforate vertical pair —
zo. Tagging omitted (error) —

1982. Bighorn Sheep Issue features a design of
bighorned sheep depicted in 1981 Wildlife booklet.
Booklet pane, intaglio, perforated 11.

Type I: is 18 3/4 mm wide, Type II: is 18 1/2 mm wide.

783 *Bighorn sheep*

783 *(1949)*
20c blue, type I, overall tagged
(Jan. 8, 1982) .45 .20
n. Booklet pane of ten 5.00 5.00
nv. Booklet pane, imperforate-
between vertically 110.
zo. Tagging omitted (error) —
Booklet pane of ten —
783A *(1949)*
20c blue, type II, block tagged
n Booklet pane of ten —
zo. Tagging omitted (error)
Booklet pane of ten —

1982. Ralph J. Bunche Issue honors the first black
Nobel Peace Prize winner. Dr. Bunche was awarded the
Nobel Prize in 1950 for his successful efforts in
negotiating an armistice between the Palestinian Arabs
and the Israelis in 1949 and for other efforts on behalf of
the United Nations. Great Americans series. *Intaglio.*

784 *Dr. Ralph J. Bunche*

784 *(1860)*
20c maroon, tagged *(Jan. 12, 1982)* .35 .20
Plate block of four 2.75
zo. Tagging omitted (error) —

1982. Crazy Horse Issue honors the Oglala Sioux
Indian leader who, joining Sitting Bull and other Sioux
on the Little Big Horn River, was prominent in the defeat
of Gen. George A. Custer and the Seventh Cavalry there
on June 25, 1876. Great Americans series. *Intaglio,
perforated 11 x 10 1/2*

785 *Crazy Horse*

785 *(1855)*
13c light maroon, tagged *(Jan. 15, 1982)*.35 .20
Plate block of four 1.50
zo. Tagging omitted (error) —

1982. Robert A. Millikan Issue honors the Nobel prize-
winning physicist, educator, humanitarian, and key
figure in the development of the California Institute of
Technology. Great Americans series. *Intaglio.*

786 *Robert Millikan*

786 *(1866)*
37c blue, tagged *(Jan. 26, 1982)* .60 .20
Plate block of four 3.50
zo. Tagging omitted (error) —

Transportation Series Identifier

As with the Great Americans Identifier, entries here are by denomination, in order of issue of that denomination. All stamps listed provide basic data: denomination, form of transportation depicted, and catalog number. There is information in the gum, tagging and without tagging columns **only** when such information will assist in properly identifying a stamp.

This table is as up -to date as possible.

Denomination/Name	Cat.	Gum	Tagging	Without Tagging
1c Omnibus (USA 1)	806			
1c Omnibus (1 USA)	867pz		Prephosphored	
1c Omnibus	867zxm	Matt		
1c Omnibus	867zxs	Shiny		
2c Locomotive (USA 2c)	790			
2c Locomotive (2c USA)	873			
3c Handcar	800			
3c Conestoga Wagon	883			
3c Conestoga Wagon	883zxm	Matt		Intentional
3c Conestoga Wagon	883zxs	Shiny		Intentional
3.4c School Bus	843			
3.4c School Bus	843z			Bureau precancel
4c Stagecoach (19 1/2mm long)	791			Error (791zo)
4c Stagecoach	791z			Bureau precancel
4c Stagecoach (17mm long)	868	Block		
4c Stagecoach	868z1	Overall		
4c Steam Carriage	943			
4c Steam Carriage	943z			Intentional
4.9c Buckboard	846			
4.9c Buckboard	846z			Bureau precancel
5c Motorcycle	808			
5c Milk Wagon	879			
5c Circus Wagon (05 USA,intaglio)	931			
5c Circus Wagon	931z			Intentional
5c Circus Wagon (05 USA, gravure)	1007	No		Intentional
5c Circus Wagon (USA 5c)	1077	No		Intentional
5c Canoe (brown)	955	No		Bureau service indicator
5c Canoe (red)	979	No		Bureau service indicator
5.2c Sleigh	799			Error (799zo)
5.2c Sleigh	799zx			Bureau precancel
5.3c Elevator	906			Bureau service indicator
5.5c Star Route Truck	865			
5.5c Star Route Truck	865zx			Bureau service indicator
5.9c Bicycle	787			
5.9c Bicycle	787z			Bureau precancel
6c Tricycle	841			
6c Tricycle	841z			Bureau precancel
7.1c Tractor	870			
7.1c Tractor	871z			Bureau service indicator ("Nonprofit Org.")
7.1c Tractor	871zt			Bureau service indicator ("Nonprofit 5-Digit Zip+4")
7.4c Baby buggy	814			
7.4c Baby buggy	814z			Bureau precancel
7.6c Carreta	903	No		Bureau service indicator
8.3c Ambulance (18 1/2 mm long)	845			
8.3c Ambulance	845z			Bureau precancel
8.3c Ambulance (18mm long)	846A	No		Bureau precancel
8.4c Wheel Chair	901	No		Bureau service indicator
8.5c Tow Truck	869			
8.5c Tow Truck	869z			Bureau service indicator

Denomination/Name	Cat.	Gum	Tagging	Without Tagging
9.3c Mail Wagon	778			
9.3c Mail Wagon	778zx			Bureau precancel
10c Canal Boat	874	Matt	Block	
10c Canal Boat	874pz	Shiny	Pre-phosphored	
10c Canal Boat	874zx1	Matt	Overall	
10c Tractor Trailer	954		No	Bureau service indicator, gray
10c Tractor Trailer	1042			Bureau service indicator, black
10.1c Oil Wagon	837			
10.1c Oil Wagon	837zx			Bureau precancel, red
10.1c Oil Wagon	837zx1			Bureau precancel, black
10.9c Hansom Cab	788			
10.9c Hansom Cab	788z			Bureau precancel
11c Caboose	812			
11c Caboose	812zx			Bureau precancel
11c Caboose	812zx1			Intentional
11c Stutz Bearcat	844			
12c Stanley Steamer (18mm long)	831		Block	Error (831zo)
12c Stanley Steamer	831p		Hi-Brite Paper	
12c Stanley Steamer	831zx		No	Bureau precancel
12c Stanley Steamer (17.5mm long)	831A		No	Bureau precancel
12.5c Pushcart	838			
12.5c Pushcart	838zx		No	Bureau precancel
13c Police Patrol Wagon	914		No	Bureau service indicator
13.2c Coal Car	900		No	Bureau service indicator
14c Iceboat (17 1/2mm long)	827		Overall	Error (827zo)
14c Iceboat (17 1/4mm long)	827A		Block	
15c Tugboat	899		Block	
15c Tugboat	899z1		Overall	
16.7c Popcorn Wagon	898		No	Bureau service indicator
17c Electric Auto	771			Error (771zo)
17c Electric Auto	771zx1			Bureau precancel 11 1/2mm
17c Electric Auto	771zx2			Bureau precancel 12 1/2mm
17c Electric Auto	771zx3			Bureau precancel 13 1/2mm
17c Dog Sled	859			
17.5c Racing Car	880			
17.5c Racing Car	880zx			Bureau service indicator
18c Surrey	768			
20c Fire Pumper	777			
20c Cable Car	913		Block	
20c Cable Car	913zx		Overall	
20c Cog Railway	1086			
20.5c Fire Engine	907		No	Bureau service indicator
21c Railroad Mail Car	902		No	Bureau service indicator
23c Lunch Wagon	949	Matt	Overall*	
23c Lunch Wagon	949zs	Shiny	Prephosphored*	
23c Lunch Wagon	949zm	Dull	Prephosphored**	
24.1c Tandem Bicycle	912		No	Bureau service indicator
25c Bread Wagon	866			Error (866zo)
32c Ferryboat	1085			
$1 Seaplane	928			

Footnotes

* Tagging is solid, smooth-appearing
** Tagging is mottled

1982. Transportation Series, High Wheel Bicycle, for bulk mailings by non-profit organizations. *Coil, intaglio, perforated 10 vertically.*

787 *High wheeler bicycle, 1870's*

787 *(1901)*

   5.9c blue, tagged *(Feb. 17, 1982)*   .25   .20
     Pair   .30
     z. Untagged (Bureau precancel)   —

     zv. Imperforate pair   200.
        Imperforate line pair   —

Listings and prices for plate number coil strips and singles appear at the end of this definitives section of the Krause-Minkus catalog.

1982. Transportation Series, Hansom Cab, bulk rate. *Coil, intaglio, perforated 10 vertically.*

788 *Hansom cab, 1890's*

788 *(1904)*
    10.9c purple, tagged *(March 26, 1982)* .25   .20
      Pair   .30
      z. Untagged (Bureau precancel)   —
      zv. Imperforate pair   160.
        Imperforate line pair   —
Listings and prices for plate number coil strips and singles appear at the end of this definitives section of the Minkus catalog.

1982. Consumer Education Issue served to bring attention to consumer education issues by educators, government agencies, consumer organizations, business, labor organizations, and media. *Coil, intaglio, perforated 10 vertically.*

789 *Consumer education, wise shoppers stretch dollars*

789 *(2005)*
    20c blue, tagged *(April 27, 1982)*   .50   .20
      Pair   .75
      v. Imperforate pair   95.
        Imperforate line pair   —
      zo. Tagging omitted (error)   —
Listings and prices for plate number coil strips and singles appear at the end of this definitives sections of the Krause-Minkus catalog.

1982. Transportation Series, Steam Locomotive. *Coil, intaglio, perforated 10 vertically.*

790 *Locomotive, 1870's*

790 *(1897A)*
    2c black, tagged *(May 20, 1982)*   .25   .20
      Pair   .30
      v. Imperforate pair   50.
        Imperforate line pair   —
(For similar design with "2 USA" see No. 873.)
Listings and prices for plate number coil strips and singles appear at the end of this definitives sections of the Krause-Minkus catalog.

1982. Transportation Series, Stagecoach with title "STAGE COACH 1890s" at 19 1/2mm long. *Coil, intaglio, perforated 10 vertically.*

791 *Stagecoach, 1890's*

791 *(1898A)*
    4c brown, tagged *(Aug. 19, 1982)*   .25   .20
      Pair   .30
      z. Untagged (Bureau precancel: "Nonprofit Org")

      zxv. Imperforate pair, untagged (precanceled)   750.
      zo. Tagging omitted (error)   —
(See also No. 868.)
Listings and prices for plate number coil strips and singles appear at the end of this definitive section of the Kruase-Minkus catalog.

1982. Christmas Issue consists of a single traditional design and a block of four contemporary designs. The single stamp depictes a Madonna and Child by Giovanni Battista Tiepolo, 18th-century painter. The contemporary design features a block of four of children and snow scenes designed by Dolli Tingle. *Gravure, perforated 11.*

792 *Children sledding*
793 *Children building a snowman*
794 *Children skating*
795 *Children decorating a Christmas tree*

792 *(2027)*
    20c multicolored, tagged *(Oct. 28, 1982)* .35   .20
793 *(2028)*
    20c multicolored, tagged   .35   .20
794 *(2029)*
    20c multicolored, tagged   .35   .20
795 *(2930)*
    20c multicolored, tagged   .35   .20
      a. Se-tenant block of four   1.50
        Plate block of four   3.50
      v. Imperforate block of four   4.00
      v1. Block of four, imperforate horizontally   —

796 *Madonna and Child, Tiepolo, National Gallery of Art*

796 *(2026)*
    20c multicolored, tagged *(Oct. 28, 1982)* .35   .20
      Plate block of 20   13.75
      v. Horizontal pair, imperforate vertically   —
      v1. Vertical pair, imperforate horizontally   —
      v2. Imperforate pair   —

1982. Kitten and Puppy Issue was a postcard-rate stamp issued to satisify demand for those who sent a holiday postcard. *Gravure, perforated 11.*

797 *Kitten and puppy playing in snow*

797 *(2025)*
13c multicolored, tagged *(Nov. 3, 1982)* .35   .20
    Plate block of four   2.00
    v. Imperforate pair   —

1982. Igor Stravinsky Issue markes the 100th anniversary of the birth of the Russian born Stravinsky. He became a U.S. citizen in 1945. Great Americans series. *Intaglio.*

798 *Igor Stravinsky*

798 *(1845)*
2c brown, tagged *(Nov. 18, 1982)*   .25   .20
    Plate block of four   .30
    Gutter pair   —
    zo. Tagging omitted (error)   —

1983. Transportation Series, Sleigh, for use by authorized non-profit organizations. *Coil, intaglio, perforated 10 vertically.*

799 *Sleigh, 1880's*

799 *(1900)*
5.2c red, tagged *(March 21, 1983)*   .25   .20
    Pair   .30
    zx. Untagged (Bureau precancel)   —
Listings and prices for plate number coil strips and singles appear at the end of this definitives section of the Krause-Minkus catalog.

1983. Transportation Series, Handcar. *Coil, intaglio, perforated 10 vertically.*

800 *Handcar, 1880*

800 *(1898)*
3c green, tagged *(March 25, 1983)*   .25   .20
    Pair   .30
Listings and prices for plate number coil stgrips and singles appear the at the end of this definitive section of the Krause-Minkus catalog.

1983. Carl Schurz Issue honors the German-born American reformer, public official, and journalist. Great American series. *Intaglio, perforated 11 x 10 1/2.*

801 *Carl Schurz*

801 *(1874)*
4c purple, tagged *(June 3, 1983)*   .25   .20
    Plate block of four   .30
    zo. Tagging omitted (error)   —

1983. Thomas H. Gallaudet Issue honors the pioneer educator who devoted his life to the education of the speaking- and hearing-impaired. Great Americans series. *Intaglio, perforated 11 x 10 1/2.*

802 *Thomas H. Gallaudet*

802 *(1861)*
20c green, tagged *(June 10,1983)*   .35   .20
    Plate block of four   1.00
    zo. Tagging omitted (error)   —

1983. Pearl Buck Issue honors the author, humanitarian, and winner of both the Pulitzer and Nobel Prizes. Great Americans Series. *Intaglio, perforated 11 x 10 1/2.*

803 *Pearl Buck*

803 *(1848)*
5c red brown, tagged *(June 25, 1983)*   .25   .20
    Plate block of four   .30

1983. Henry Clay Issue honors the American statesman. Great Americans series. *Intaglio, perforated 11 x 10 1/2.*

804 *Henry Clay*

804 *(1846)*
3c olive, tagged *(July 13, 1983)*   .25   .20
    Plate block of four   .30
    zo. Tagging omitted (error)   —

1983. Express Mail Issue, although not labeled as such nor restricted to that class of mail, was released principally for Express Mail Next Day Service use. *Booklet pane, gravure, perforated 10 vertically.*

805 *Eagle and moon*

805 *(1909)*
$9.35 multicolored, tagged *(Aug. 12, 1983)* .25   .20
  n. Booklet pane of three   .60

1983. Transportation Series, Omnibus. *Coil, intaglio, perforated 10 vertically.*

806 *Omnibus, 1880's*

806 *(1897)*
1c purple, tagged *(Aug. 19, 1983)*   .25   .20
  Pair   .30
  v. Imperforate pair   675.
(For similar design with "1 USA" see No. 867.)
Listings and prices for plate number coil strips and singles appear at the end of this definitives section of the Krause-Minkus catalog.

1983. Dorothea Dix Issue honors the 19th century crusader for the poor and mentally impaired. Great Americans series. *Intaglio.*

Perforated 11 1/4

807 *Dorothea Dix*

807 *(1844)*
1c black, tagged *(Dec. 1983)*   .25   .20
  Plate block of 20   .30
  v. Imperforate pair   450.
  v1. Imperforate-between
    vertical pair   —

Perforated 11 1/4
807A *(1844C)*
1c black, tagged *(Sept. 23, 1983)*   .25   .20
  Plate block of 20   .30
  v. Vertical pair, imperforate
    horizontally   2,750.

1983. Transportation Series, Pope Motorcycle. *Coil, intaglio, perforated 10 vertically.*

808 *Motorcycle, 1913*

808 *(1899)*
5c dark green, tagged *(Oct. 10, 1983)*   .25   .20
  Pair   .30
  v. Imperforate pair   2,750.
Listings and prices for plate number coil strips and singles appear at the end of this definitives section of the Krause-Minkus catalog.

1983. Christmas Issue consists of two single stamps. The traditional stamp depicts *Madonna and Child* by Raphael, an Italian Renaissance painter. The contemporary stamp design features a jovial Santa Claus. *Gravure, perforated 11.*

809 *Santa Claus*

809 *(2064)*
20c multicolored, tagged *(Oct. 28, 1983)*   .35   .20
  Plate block of 20   12.50
  v. Imperforate pair   —

810 Madonna and Child, *by Raphael, National Gallery of Art*

810 *(2063)*
20c multicolored, tagged *(Oct. 28, 1983)*   .35   .20
  Plate block of four   2.50

1984. Harry S Truman Issue honors the former president on the centennial of his birth. Great Americans Series. *Intaglio, perforated 11.*

811, *Harry S Truman*

811 *(1862)*
20c black, perforated 11, overall tagged
    (Jan. 26, 1984)   .35   .20
  Plate block of 20   12.
(See also No. 904.)

1984. Transportation Series, Railroad Caboose, bulk rate. *Coil, intaglio, perforated 10 vertically.*

812 *Railroad caboose, 1890's*

812 *(1905)*
11c red, tagged *(Feb. 3, 1984)*   .25   .20
  Pair   .35
  zx. Untagged (Bureau precancel)   —

zx1. Untagged unprecancelled,
(Sept. 25, 1991)   —

Listings and prices for plate number coil strips and singles appear at the end of this definitive section of the Krause-Minkus catalog.

1984. Lillian Gilbreth Issue honors the pioneering American engineer who searched for efficient working methods in industry and the home. Together with her husband, she laid the foundation for the field of industrial engineering. Great Americans series. *Intaglio, perforated 11 or 11 1/4.*

Perforated 11

813, 813A *Lillian Gilbreth*

813 *(1868)*
   40c green, tagged *(Feb. 24, 1984)*   .60   .20
     Plate block of 20   10.

Perforated 11 1/4
813A *(1868A)*
   40c green, tagged *(1987)*   .60   .20
     Plate block of four   2.00

1984. Transportation Series, Baby Buggy, issued to meet rate for carrier-route presorted bulk mailings. *Coil, intaglio, perforated 10 vertically.*

814 *Baby Buggy, 1880's*

814 *(1902)*
   7.4c brown, tagged *(April 7, 1984)*   .25   .20
     Pair   .35
     zx. Untagged (Bureau precancel:
       "Blk. Rt. CAR-RT SORT")   .25   .20

Listings and prices for plate number coil strips and singles appear at the end of this definitive section of the Krause-Minkus catalog.

1984. Richard Russell Issue honors the former U.S. Senator and his 50 years of public service. Two years after becoming, at age 33, the youngest governor in Georgia's history, Russell was elected to fill the unexpired term of one of the state's U.S senators. He was subsequently re-elected six times to the U.S. Senate. Great Americans series. *Intaglio.*

815 *Richard Russell*

815 *(1853)*
   10c blue, tagged *(May 31, 1984)*   .25   .20
     Plate block of 20   7.00

v. Horizontal pair, imperforate
   between   2,000.
v1. Imperforate-between
   vertical pair   1,100.
v2. Vertical pair, imperforate
   horizontally   —
v3. Imperforate pair   1,250.

Imperforate printer's waste is known to exist, and in one case was used as postage.

1984. Frank C. Laubach Issue honors the literacy advocate and educator. Who developed methods to educate the illiterate and created alphabets and written languages where none previously existed. Great Americans series. *Intaglio.*

Perforated 11

816, 816A *Frank C. Laubach*

816 *(1864)*
   30c green, tagged *(Sept. 2, 1984)*   .75   .20
     Plate block of 20   18.

Perforated 11 1/4
816A *(1864A)*
   30c green, block tagging *(June 25, 1988)* .75   .20
     Plate block of four   2.25
     z1. Overall tagging *(1990)*   .75
       Plate block of four   2.25

1984. Christmas Issue consists of two single stamps. The traditional stamp features a Madonna and Child by 15th-century painter Fra Filippo Lippi. The contemporary stamp depicts a Santa Claus designed by Danny La Boccetta, winner of a students' stamp design project. *Gravure, perforated 11.*

817 *Santa Claus, by Danny La Boccetta*

817 *(2108)*
   20c multicolored, tagged *(Oct. 30, 1984)* 25   .20
     Plate block of four   1.50
     v. Horizontal pair,
       imperforate vertically   975.

818 *Madonna and Child, by Fra Filippo Lippi, National Gallery of Art*

818 *(2107)*
   20c multicolored, tagged *(Oct. 30, 1984)*25   .20
     Plate block of four   1.50

1985. Abraham Baldwin Issue honors the man who wrote the charter for Franklin College, the first to establish a state university in the United States. Great Americans Series. *Intaglio, perforated 11.*

 819 *Abraham Baldwin*

819 *(1850)*
   7c red, tagged *(Jan. 25, 1985)*   .25   .20
     Plate block of 20   4.00

1985. The Non-Denominated "D" Issue marks the new first class post rate of 22c, which went into effect February 17, 1985. The issue was for domestic use only. Issued in sheet, coil, and booklet form. *Gravure.*

Perforated 11

 820-822 *"D" and stylized eagle*

820 *(2111)*
   (22c) green, tagged *(Feb. 1, 1985)*   .45   .20
     Plate block of 20   25.
     v. Imperforate vertical pair   50.
     v1. Vertical pair,
       imperforate horizontally   1,300.

Coil, perforated 10 vertically
821 *(2112)*
   (22c) green, tagged *(Feb. 1, 1985)*   .80   .20
     Pair   1.00
     v. Imperforate pair   45.
     vzo. Imperforate pair,
       Tagging omitted (error)   —
Listings and prices forf plate number coil strips and singles appear at the end of this definitive section of the Krause-Minkus catalog.

Booklet stamps, perforated 11
822 *(2113)*
   (22c) green, tagged *(Feb. 1, 1985)*   .40   .20
     n. Booklet pane of ten   8.50
     nv. Booklet pane of ten,
       imperforate between
       horizontally   —

1985. Alden Partridge Issue honors the military educator on his 200th birthday. Great Americans series. *Intaglio, perforated 11.*

 823 *Alden Partridge*

823 *(1854)*
   11c blue, tagged *(Feb. 12, 1985)*   .25   .20
     Plate block of four   1.20
     zo. Tagging omitted (error)   —

1985. Chester W. Nimitz Issue honors the fleet admiral, whose leadership during World War II brought about key naval victories. He was acknowledged as one of the Navy's foremost administrators and strategists. Great Americans series. *Gravure.*

 824, 824A *Chester W. Nimitz*

824 *(1869)*
   50c brown, overall tagging, perforated 11,
      shiny gum *(Feb. 22, 1985)*   .90   .20
     Plate block of four   8.00
     zo. Tagging omitted (error)   —
824A *(1869a)*
   50c brown, block tagging, perforated 11 1/4
      matt gum *(Aug. 28, 1986)*   .90   .20
     Plate block of four   6.50
     zo. Tagging omitted (error)   —
     z1. Overall tagging   —
       Plate block of four   —
     pz. Pre-phosphored paper,
       shiny gum   —
     pzm. Matt gum   —

1985. Grenville Clark Issue honors a leading advocate of civil liberties and peace through world federalism. Great Americans series. *Intaglio.*

Perforated 11

 825, 825A *Grenville Clark*

825 *(1867)*
   39c purple, tagged (small block)
      (March 20, 1985)   .75   .20
     Plate block of 20   24.
     v. Imperforate-between
       vertical pair   —
     v1. Vertical pair, imperforate
       horizontally   575.

Perforated 11 1/4
825A *(1867C)*
   39c purple, tagged (large block)
      (Aug. 25, 1986)   .75   .20
     Plate block of four   4.00

1985. Sinclair Lewis issue honors the novelist and short story writer on the centennial of his birth. In 1930, Lewis became the first American to win a Nobel Prize for Literature. Great Americans series. *Intaglio, perforated 11.*

826 *Sinclair Lewis*

826 *(1856)*
14c gray, tagged *(March 21, 1985)* .25 .20
  Plate block of twenty 9.00
  v. Horizontal pair, imperforate
    between 8.00
  v1. Vertical pair, imperforate
    between 1,900.
  v2. Vertical Imperforate pair
    horizontally 125.

1985. Transportation Series, Iceboat, to meet new first-class rate for postcards. *Coil, intaglio, perforated 10 vertically.*

827, 827A *Iceboat 1880's*

827 *(2134)*
14c blue, type I, overall tagged
    (March 23, 1985) .25 .20
  Pair .35
  v. Imperforate pair 100.
  zo. Tagging omitted (error) —
827A *(2134B)*
14c blue, type II, block tagged
    (Sept. 30, 1986) .25 .20
  Pair .35
Type I is 17 1/2 mm wide with overall tagging; Type II is 17 1/4 mm wide with block tagging.
Listings and prices for plate number coil strips and singles appear at the end of this definitives section of this Krause-Minkus catalog.

1985. American Flag over the Capitol Issues consists of sheet and coil versions, and a booklet stamp the width of two normal definitive stamps. This was the first U.S. booklet pane in the format of a single row of five stamps. *Intaglio, perforated 11.*

828, 829, 876 *Flag over the U.S. Capitol*

828 *(2114)*
22c black, blue, and red, tagged
    (March 29, 1985) .35 .20
  Plate block of four 3.00
  Gutter pair —

Coil, Intaglio
829 *(2115)*
22c black, blue, and red, tagged
    (March 29, 1985) .40 .20
  Pair 1.00
  a. Black stars in flag (rather
    than blue) 1.00
  b. slate blue, blue, and red —
  v. Imperforate pair 12.50
  zo. Tagging omitted (error) —
For similar design with "T" at bottom, see No. 876. Listings and prices for plate number coil strips and singles appear at the end of this definitive section of the Krause-Minkus catalog.

Booklet pane, intaglio, perforated 10 horizontally

830 *Flag over the U.S. Capitol*

830 *(2116)*
22c black, blue, and red, tagged
    (March 29, 1985) .40 .20
  n. Booklet pane of five 3.00 2.50
Issued for use in vending machines, and was available with one and two panes.

1985. Transportation Series, 1909 Stanley Steamer, first successfully operated steam automobile in New England. *Coil, Intaglio, perforated 10 vertically.*

831, 831A *Stanley Steamer*

831 *(2132)*
12c blue, type I, tagged *(April 2, 1985)* .25 .20
  Pair .30
  p. Hi-Brite paper —
  zx. Untagged, Bureau precancel:
    PRESORTED FIRST-CLASS .25 .20
    Pair —
  zo. Tagging omitted (error) —

831A *(2132lc)*
12c blue, type II, untagged, Bureau
    precancel: PRESORTED
    FIRST-CLASS *(Sept. 3, 1987)* .25 .20
  Pair .30
Type I: "Stanley Steamer 1909" is 18 mm long;
Type II: "Stanley Steamer 1909" is 17 1/2 mm long.
Listings and prices for plate number coil strips and singles appear at the end of this definitive section of the Krause-Minkus catalog.

1985. Seashell Booklet

832 *Frilled dogwinkle*

833 *Reticulated helmet*

834 *New England neptune*

835 *Calico scallop*

836 *Lightning whelk*

832 *(2117)*
  22c black and brown, tagged *(April 4, 1985)* .35 .20
833 *(2118)*
  22c black and multicolored, tagged .35 .20
834 *(2119)*
  22c black and brown, tagged .35 .20
835 *(2120)*
  22c black and purple, tagged .35 .20
836 *(2121)*
  22c multicolored, tagged .35 .20
    a. Se-tenant strip of five 3.00
    n. Booklet pane of ten (two
      of each design) 4.00
    nv. Purple omitted, horizontal
      pair of 835, pane 700.
    nv. Booklet pane, imperforate
      -between vertically 650.
    nv1. Imperforate booklet pane —
    zo. Tagging omitted (error) —
Mis-registered tagging is common on this issue.

1985. Transportation Series,

1890's Oil Wagon and 1880's Pushcart. The 10.1c denomination first was issued to meet the rate for bulk third class mail presorted to the five-digit ZIP code; the later version met the carrier-route presort rate. The 12.5c denomination was issued as the basic rate for bulk third class mail. *Coils, intaglio, perforated 10 vertically.*

837 *Oil Wagon 1890's*

837 *(2130)*
  10.1c blue, tagged *(April 18, 1985)* .25 .20
    Pair .35
    zx. Untagged, Bureau precancel:
      in black: "Bulk Rate" .25 .20
    zxv. Imperforate pair 85.
    zx1. Untagged,Bureau precancel:
      in red: "Bulk Rate / Carrier
      Route Sort" .25 .20
    zx1v. Imperforate pair —

838 *Pushcart 1880's*

838 *(2133)*
  12.5c olive, tagged *(April 18, 1985)* .25 .20
    Pair .35
    zx. Untagged, Bureau precancel:
      "Bulk Rate" .25 .20
    zxv. Imperforate pair 50.
Listings and prices for plate number coil strips and singles appear at the end of this definitive sections of the Krause-Minkus catalog.

1985. John James Audubon Issue honors the 200th birthday of the artist-naturalist. Great Americans Series. *Intaglio, perforated 11.*

Perforated 11

839, 839A *John J. Audubon*

839 *(1863)*
  22c blue, tagged *(April 23, 1985)* .40 .20
    Plate block of 20 16.
    v. Horizontal pair, imperforate
      between 2,850.
    v1. Vertical pair, imperforate
      between —
    v2. Vertical pair, imperforate
      horizontally 2.500.

Perforated 11 1/4
839A *(1863D)*
  22c blue, tagged *(June 1,1987)* .40 .20
    Plate block of four 1.50

1985. Express Mail Issue, although valid for use on other classes of mail, was intended for use in four types of Express Mail Service: 1) Same Day Airport Service, 2) Custom Designed Service, 3) Next Day Service, and 4) International Service. *Booklet pane, gravure, perforated 10 vertically.*

840 *Eagle and Moon*

840 *(2122)*
$10.75 multicolored, type I, tagged
(April 29, 1985)   15.   9.00
n. Booklet pane of three   52.
a. type II *(June 19, 1989)*   17.   12.
an. Booklet pane of three   52.

Type I: overall dull appearance, "$10.75" appears grainy; type II: more intense colors, "$10.75" smoother, much less grainy.

1985. Transportation Series, Tricycle, issued for basic rate for third class bulk mailings by non-profit organizations. *Coil, intaglio, perforated 10 vertically.*

841 *Tricycle, 1880's*

841 *(2126)*
6c brown, tagged *(May 6, 1985)*   .25   .20
Pair   .30
z. Untagged, Bureau precancel:
  "Nonprofit Org."   .25   .20
Pair   .30
zxv. Imperforate pair   225.

Listings and prices for plate number coil strips and singles appear at the end of this definitives sections of the Krause-Minkus catalog.

1985. Sylvanus Thayer Issue honors the former commandant of the U.S. Military Academy at West Point, NY. Great Americans Series. *Intaglio, perforated 11.*

842 *Sylvanus Thayer*

842 *(1852)*
9c green, tagged *(June 7, 1985)*   .25   .20
Plate block of 20   4.25

1985. Transportation Series, School Bus, issued for basis rate for carrier-route presort third class bulk mailings by non-profit organizations. *Coil, intaglio, perforated 10 vertically.*

843 *School bus, 1920's*

843 *(2123)*
3.4c green, tagged *(June 8, 1985)*   .25   .20
Pair   .30
z. Untagged, Bureau precancel:
  "Nonprofit Org. CAR-RT SORT" .25   .20
Listings and prices for plate number coil strips and singles appear at the end of this definitive section of the Krause-Minkus catalog.

1985. Transportation Series, Stutz Bearcat Automobile. *Coil, intaglio, perforated 10 vertically.*

844 *Stutz Bearcat, 1933*

844 *(2131)*
11c green, tagged *(June 11, 1985)*   .25   .20
Pair   .30
Listings and prices for plate number coil strips and singles appear at the end of this definitive section of the Krause-Minkus catalog.

1985. Transportation Series, 1860's Ambulance and 1890's Buckboard. The 8.3c denomination was issued for third class mail presorted by carrier route. The 4.9c denomination was issued for non-profit third class mail presorted to the five-digit ZIP code. *Coil, intaglio, perforated 10 vertically.*

845, 845A *Ambulance, 1860's*

845 *(2128)*
8.3c green, type I, tagged
(June 21, 1985)   .25   .20
Pair   .30
z. Untagged, Bureau precancel:
  "Blk. Rt. CAR-RT SORT"
Pair   .30

845A *(2231)*
8.3c green, type II, Untagged, Bureau
  precancel:"Blk. Rt. / CAR-RT /
  SORT" *(Aug. 29, 1986)*   .25   .20
Pair   .30
Type I: "Ambulance 1860s" is 18 1/2 mm long; type II: "Ambulance 1860s" is 18 mm long

846 *Buckboard, 1880's*

846 *(2124)*
4.9c brown, tagged *(June 21, 1985)*   .25   .20
Pair   .30
z. Untagged, Bureau precancel:
  "Nonprofit Org."   .35   .20

Listings and prices for plate number coil strips and singles appear at the end of this definitives section of the Krause-Minkus catalog.

1985. Henry Knox Issue honors the first U.S. Secretary of War during the 200th anniversary year of his appointment. Great Americans series. *Intaglio, perforated 11.*

 847 *Henry Knox*

847 *(1851)*
8c olive, tagged *(July 26, 1985)*   .25   .20
   Plate block of four   .40

1985. Walter Lippmann Issue honors the newsman, political analyst, and author. Among many other awards and prizes Lippmann earned, two Pulitzer Prizes and a Peabody award. Great Americans series. *Intaglio, perforated 11.*

 848 *Walter Lippmann*

848 *(1849)*
6c orange, tagged *(Sept. 9, 1985)*   .25   .20
   Plate block of 20   2.90
   v. Vertical pair,
     imperforate-between   2,450.

1985. Envelope Stamp prepaid first-class rate for mailers using ZIP + 4. *Coil, gravure, perforated 10 vertically.*

 849 *Letters*

849 *(2150)*
21.1c multicolored, tagged
     (Oct. 22, 1985)   .35   .20
   Pair   .50
   z. Untagged, Bureau-printed
     service indicator: "ZIP+4"   .35   .20
   Pair   .50
Some precanceled stamps are known with light tagging.

1985. Christmas Issues consists of two stamps. The contemporary stamp is a painting of poinsettias by James Dean of Annandale, VA. The traditional stamp depicts one of the four versions of *The Genoa Madonna*, an enameled terra-cotta Madonna and Child by Luca della Robbia. *Gravure, perforated 11.*

 850 *Poinsettia plants*

850 *(2165)*
22c multicolored, tagged *(Oct. 30, 1985)*35   .20
   Plate block of four   1.00
   v. Imperforate pair   125.

 851 *Sculpture by Luca della Robbia, Detroit Institute of Arts*

851 *(2166)*
22c multicolored, tagged *(Oct. 30, 1985)*35   .20
   Plate block of four   1.00
   v. Imperforate pair   100.

1985. The Washington Monument - George Washington Issue met the basic presort rate for first-class letter mail. *Coil, gravure, perforated 10 vertically.*

852 *(2149)*
18c multicolored, tagged *(Nov. 6, 1985)*.35   .20
   Pair   .50
   v. Imperforate pair   975.
   z. Untagged (Bureau-printed service
     indicator: "PRESORTED
     FIRST-CLASS"   .35   .20
   zo. Tagging omitted (error)   —
   zm. Matt gum   .35
   Pair   .50
   zxv. Imperforate pair,
     Precancelled   800.
Some precanceled stamps are known with light tagging. Listings and prices for plate number coil strips and singles appear at the end of this definitive section of the Krause-Minkus catalog.

1986. Jack London Issue honors the author of fifty books including *The Call of the Wild, White Fang,* and *The Sea-Wolf.* Great Americans series. *Intaglio, perforated 11.*

 853, 888, 889 *Jack London*

853 *(2182)*
25c blue, perforated 11, block tagging
     (Jan.11,1986)   .45   .20
   Plate block of four   1.50
   zo. Tagging omitted (error)   →
For booklet panes of ten, see Nos. 888-889.

1986. Hugo L. Black Issue honors the Supreme Court justice on the 100th birthday. Great Americans series. *Intaglio, perforated 11.*

 854 *Hugo L. Black*

854 *(2172)*
  5c deep olive green, tagged

(Feb. 27, 1986)	.25	.20
Plate block of four	.90	
zo. Tagging omitted (error)	—	

1986. William Jennings Bryan Issue honors the famed orator and legislator. Great Americans series. *Intaglio, perforated 11.*

 855 *William Jennings Bryan*

855 *(2195)*
  $2 purple, tagged *(March 19, 1986)* 3.25   .75

Plate block of four	20.	
zo. Tagging omitted (error)	—	

1986. Belva Ann Lockwood Issue honors the first woman candidate for president and the first woman admitted to practice before the U.S. Supreme Court. Great Americans Series. *Intaglio, perforated 11.*

 856 *Belva Ann Lockwood*

856 *(2178)*
  17c blue green, tagged *(June 18, 1986)* .35   .20

Plate block of four	1.75	
zo. Tagging omitted (error)	—	

1986. Margaret Mitchell Issue honors the famed author of the novel *Gone With the Wind.* Great Americans Issue. *Intaglio, perforated 11.*

 857 *Margaret Mitchell*

857 *(2168)*
  1c brown, tagged *(June 30, 1986)* .25   .20

Plate block of four	.30	
zo. Tagging omitted (error)	—	

1986. Edward J. Flanagan Issue, released on the centennial of his birth, honors the founder of Boys Town. The center protects and educates abused and underprivileged youth.Great Americans series. *Intaglio, perforated 11.*

 858 *Father Edward Joseph Flanagan*

858 *(2171)*

4c purple, tagged *(July 14, 1986)*	.25	.20
Plate block of four	.40	
zx. Untagged, light gray violet *(1991)*	.25	.20
Plate block of four	.40	
z1. Untagged, slate violet *(1993)*	.25	.20
Plate block of four	.40	

1986. Transportation Series, Dog sled. The 17c denomination represents the rate for the second ounce of first class mail. *Coil, intaglio, perforated 10 vertically.*

 859 *Dog sled, 1920's*

859 *(2135)*

17c blue, tagged *(Aug. 20, 1986)*	.30	.20
Pair	.50	
v. Imperforate pair	475.	

Listings and prices for plate number coil strips and singles appear at the end of this definitive section of the Krause-Minkus catalog.

1986. John Harvard Issue honors the 17th century American colonist and philanthropist, coinciding with the 350th anniversary of Harvard University, the oldest institution of higher learning in the United States. Great Americans series. *Intaglio, perforated 11.*

 860 *John Harvard*

860 *(2190)*

56c crimson, tagged *(Sept. 3, 1986)*	1.10	.20
Plate block of four	5.25	

1986. Paul Dudley White Issue honors the authority on cardiovascular disease and a pioneer in its diagnosis, treatment, and prevention. Great Americans Series. *Intaglio, perforated 11.*

 861 *Dr. Paul Dudley White*

861 *(2170)*

3c blue, tagged *(Sept. 15, 1986)*	.25	.20
Plate block of four	.35	
zo. Tagging omitted (error)	—	
zx. Untagged (intentional)	—	

1986. Bernard Revel Issue honors the scholar and educator in conjunction with the centennial of Yeshiva University, the nation's oldest and largest Jewish institution of higher learning. Great Americans series. *Intaglio, perforated 11.*

 862 *Dr. Bernard Revel*

862 *(2193)*

$1.00 blue, tagged *(Sept. 23, 1986)*	2.00	.25
Plate block of four	13.	

1986. Christmas Issue. The contemporary stamp featurs a winter village scene, which was designed by Dolli Tingle of Westport, CT. The traditional stamp depicts the oil-on-wood painting *Perugino Madonna*, by Il Perugino. *Gravure, perforated 11.*

 863 *Village scene*

863 *(2245)*

22c multicolored, tagged		
(Oct. 24, 1986)	.50	.20
Plate block of four	2.75	

 864 Perugino Madonna

864 *(2244)*

22c multicolored, tagged		
(Oct. 24, 1986)	.50	.20
Plate block of four	2.75	

1986. Transportation Series, Star Route Truck used for mail transportation following horse-drawn vehicles. The 5.5c rate was for nonprofit third class mail presorted to the carrier route. *Coil, intaglio, perforated 10 vertically.*

 865 *Star Route truck, 1910's*

865 *(2125)*

5.5c maroon, tagged *(Nov. 1, 1986)*	.25	.20
Pair	.35	
zx. Untagged, Bureau-printed service indicator: "Nonprofit Org. CAR-RT SORT"	.25	.20

Listings and prices for palte number coils strips and singles appear at the end of this definitives section of the Krause-Minkus catalog.

1986. Transportation Series, Bread Wagon. *Coil, intaglio, perforated 10 vertically.*

 866 *Bread wagon, 1880's*

866 *(2136)*

25c orange brown, tagged		
(Nov. 22, 1986)	.40	.20
Pair	1.00	
v. Pair, imperforate	10.	
v1. Imperforate-between pair	500.	
zo. Tagging omitted (error)	—	

Listings and prices for plate number coil strips and singles appear at the end of this definitives section of the Krause-Minkus catalog.

1986. Transportation Series, Omnibus, type of No. 806, redesigned, ("1 USA" instead of "USA 1"). *Coil, intaglio, perforated 10 vertically.*

 867 *Omnibus, 1880's*

867 *(2225)*

1c violet, tagged *(Nov. 26, 1986)*	.25	.20
Pair	.30	
v. Imperforate pair	2,400.	
pz. Prephosphored paper	.25	.20
Pair	.30	
(2225a)zxm. Untagged, matt gum	.25	.20
Pair	.30	
(2225sv)zxs. Untagged, shinny gum	.25	.20
Pair	.30	

(For similar desing with "USA 1c" see No. 806)
Listings and prices for palte number coil strips and singleas appear at the end of this definitives section of the Krause-Minkus catalog.

1986. Transportation Series, Stagecoach, type of No. 791, re-engraved. "Stagecoach 1890's" is 17 mm long. *Coil, intaglio, perforated 11.*

 868 *Stagecoach 1890's*

868 *(2228)*

4c red brown, block tagging *(Aug. 1986)*	.25	.20
Pair	.30	
v. Imperforate pair	300.	
(2228a)z1. Overall tagging *(1990)*	.50	.20
Pair	.75	

(See also No. 791.)
Listings and prices for palte number coil strips and singles appear at the end of this definitives section of the Krause-Minkus catalog.

1987. Transportation Series, Tow truck. The 8.5c rate was for nonprofit, third class mail. *Coil, intaglio, perforated 11.*

869 *Tow Truck, 1920's*

869 *(2129)*
  8.5c dark gray, tagged *(Jan. 24, 1987)*
    Pair   .50   .20
    z. Untagged, Bureau-printed red
      service indicator:"Nonprofit Org.".25   .20
      Pair
Listings and prices for plate number coil strips and singles appear at the end of this definitives section of the Krause-Minkus catalog.

1987. Transportation Series, Tractor, shows an early model with steel tires and projected grips around the wheels. The 7.1c value was issued for third-class non-profit mail presorted by Zip code. *Coil., intaglio, perforated 11.*

870 *Tractor, 1920's*

870 *(2127)*
  7.1c dark red, tagged *(Feb. 6, 1987)* .25   .20
    Pair   .50
    z. Untagged, Bureau-printed service
      indicator: "Nonprofit Org."
      (Feb. 6, 1987)   .25   .20
    z. Pair   .50
    zt. Untagged, Bureau-printed service indicator:
      "Nonprofit 5-Digit Zip+4"
      (May 26, 1989)   .25   .20
      Pair   .50

1987. Julia Ward Howe Issue honors the social reformer and author of *The Battle Hymn of the Republic.* Well-known for her abolitionist sentiment, she also was a champion of the rights of women and the less fortunate. Great Americans series. *Intaglio, perforated 11.*

871 *Julia Ward Howe*

871 *(2176)*
  14c red, tagged *(Feb. 12, 1987)*   .25   .20
    Plate block of four   .75

1987. Mary Lyon Issue honors a pioneer of higher education for women. Lyon organized Wheaton College in 1834 and founded Mount Holyoke College in 1837. Great Americans series. *Intaglio, perforated 11.*

872 *Mary Lyon*

872 *(2169)*
  2c blue, tagged *(Feb. 28, 1987)*   .25   .20
    Plate block of four   .30
    zo. Tagging omitted (error)   —
    zx. Untagged (intentional)   —

1987. Transportation Series, Steam locomotive, type of No. 790, redesigned. *Coil, intaglio. perforated 11.*

873 *Locomotive, 1870's*

873 *(1897A)*
  2c black, tagged *(March 6, 1987)*   .25   .20
    Pair   .30
For similar design with "USA 2c" see No. 790.)
Listings and prices for plate number coil strips and singles appear at the end of this definitives section of the Krause-Minkus catalog.

1987. Transportation Series, Canal Boat. *Coil, intaglio, perforated 11.*

874 *Canal boat, 1880's*

874 *(2257)*
  10c sky blue, block tagging, matt gum
        (April 11, 1987)   .25   .20
    Pair   .35
    z1. Overall tagging, matt
      gum (1993)   .25   .20
    pz. Prephosphored paper,
      shiny gum   .25   .20
    z. Overall tagging, matt gum   .25   .20
Listings and prices for plate number coil strips and singles appear at the end of this definitives section of the Krause-Minkus catalog.

1987. Flag with Fireworks. This stamp was released to replace the Flag over Historic Buildings issues. *Gravure, perforated 11.*

875 *Flag with Fireworks*

875 *(2276)*
  22c multicolored, tagged *(May 9, 1987)*.35   .20
    Plate block of four   1.75
    n. Booklet pane of 20
      (Nov. 30, 1987)   8.50

1987. Flag over Capitol Test Coil. This stamp was issued to test prephosphored paper, which is tagged before printing. Every stamp has an imprinted "T" in the lower margin. *Coil, intaglio, perforated 10 vertically.*

876 *(2115B)*
22c black, blue, and red, with "T" at
    bottom *(May 23, 1987)*   .40   .20
    Pair   .75

*Listings and prices for plate number coil strips and
singles appear at the end of this definitives section of the
Krause-Minkus catalog.*

1987. Red Cloud Issue honors the Chief of the Oglala
Sioux. Great Americans series. *Intaglio, perforated 11.*

877 *Red Cloud*

877 *(2175)*
10c carmine red, block tagging
    (Aug. 15, 1987)   .25   .20
    Plate block of four   .75
    z. Tagging omitted (error)   —
    pz. Pre-phosphored paper   .25   .20
    Plate block of four   .75
    z1. Overall tagging *(1991)*   .25   .20
    Plate block of four   .75
    zx. Untagged (intentional)   .25   .20

1987. Bret Harte Issue honors the author and poet.
Famous for stories and poems of the American West.
Great Americans series. *Intaglio, perfored 11.*

878 *Bret Harte*

878 *(2196)*
$5 Venetian red, block tagging
    (Aug. 25, 1987)   8.00   2.00
    Plate block of four   40.
    zo. Tagging omitted (error)
    pz. Pre-phosphored paper
    (March 1992)   8.00   2.00
    Plate block of four   35.

1987. Transportation Series, Milk Wagon. *Coil,
intaglio, perforated 10 vertically.*

879 *Milk wagon, 1900's*

879 *(2253)*
5c charcoal, tagged *(Sept. 25, 1987)*   .25   .20
    Pair   .30

*Listings and prices for plate number coil strips and
singles appear at the end of this definitives section of the
Krause-Minkus catalog.*

1987. Transportation Series, Marmon Wasp, a 1911
racing car. Denomination covers rate for ZIP+4 presorted
mail. *Coil, intaglio, perforated 10 vertically.*

880 *Racing car, 1911*

880 *(2262)*
17.5c blue violet, tagged *(Sept. 25, 1987)* .30   .20
    Pair   .50
    v. Imperforate pair   2,250.
    zx. Untagged, Bureau-printed red service
    indicator: "ZIP + 4 Presort"   .30   .20
    Pair   .50

*Listings and prices for plate number coil strips and
singles appear at the end of this definitives section of the
Krause-Minkus catalog.*

1987. Christmas Issue. The contemporary design
consists of tree ornaments; the traditional design
displays a portion of Giovanni Battista Moroni's painting
*A Gentleman in Adoration before the Madonna. Gravure,
perforated 11.*

881 *Madonna and Child*

881 *(2367)*
22c multicolored, tagged *(Oct. 23, 1987)* 50   .20
    Plate block of four   2.75

882 *Tree ornament*

882 *(2368)*
22c multicolored, tagged *(Oct. 23, 1987)* 50   .20
    Plate block of four   2.75
    Gutter pair   —

1988. Transportation Series. Conestoga Wagon. Coil,
intaglio, perforated 10 vertically.

883 *Conestoga wagon, 1800's*

883 *(2252)*
3c dark lilac purple, tagged
    (Feb. 29, 1988)   .25   .20
    Pair   .30
(2252a)zxm. Untagged, matt gum *(1992)* .25   .20
(2252b)zxs. Untagged, shinny gum   .30

*Listings and prices for plate number coil strips and
singles appear at the end of this definitves section of the
Krause-Minkus catalog.*

1988. Non-Denominated "E" Issue consists of three versions: sheet, coil, and booklet. The stamps were released to meet the new 25-cent first class rate. *Gravure.*

884-886 *"E" and Earth*

Perforated 11
884 (2277)
  25c multicolored, tagged
        (March 22, 1988)   .50   .20
    Plate block of four   1.50
    zo. Tagging omitted (error)   —

Coil, perforated 10 vertically
885 (2279)
  25c multicolored, tagged
        (March 22, 1988)   .50   .20
    Pair   .75
    v. Imperforate pair   —

Listings and prices for plate number coil strips and singles appear at the end of this definitives section of the Krause-Minkus catalog.

Booklet, perforated 10
886 (2282)
  25c multicolored, tagged
        (March 22, 1988)   .50   .20
    n. Booklet pane of ten   6.50

1988. Pheasant Booklet Issue. Designed for sale in vending machines as well as over the counter, this booklet is the first produced for the U.S. Postal Service by the American Bank Note Co. *Gravure.*

887 *Pheasant*

887 (2283)
  25c multicolored, tagged (April 29, 1988) .50   .20
    Booklet pane of ten   6.00
    a. Red removed from background
       sky   6.00   .50
    an. Booklet pane of ten   75.
    nv. Horizontally imperforate-between
       booklet pane of ten   —

Fully imperforate panes were cut from printer's waste

1988. Jack London Booklet Issue are of the same design as No. 853. *Intaglio.*

888 (2182a)
  25c blue, perforated 11, tagged
        (May 3, 1988)
    n. Booklet pane of ten   4.50   5.00

889
  25c blue, perforated 10, booklet stamps only,
        tagged (May 3, 1988)

  n. Booklet pane of six
  zo. Tagging omitted (error)
  zon. Tagging omitted, booklet pane of six

1988. Flags with Clouds Issue in sheet and booklet versions. *Gravure.*

890, 890A *Flag with clouds*

Sheet version, perforated 11
890 (2278)
  25c multicolored, tagged (May 6, 1988) .35   .20
    Plate block of four   3.25
    Gutter pair   —

Booklet version, perforated 10
890A (2285A)
  25c multicolored, tagged (May 6, 1988) .50   .20
    n. Booklet pane of six   2.75   3.00

1988. Flag over Yosemite Issue shows the U.S. flag billowing over Half Dome, Yosemite's most striking example of glacier-carved granite. *Coil, intaglio, perforated 10 vertically.*

891 *Flag over Yosemite*

891 (2280)
  25c multicolored, tagged
        (May 20, 1988)   .40   .20
    Pair   .75
    v. Imperforate pair   25.
    pz. Pre-phosphored paper
       (Feb. 14, 1989)   .40   .20
       Pair   .75
    pzv. Imperforate pair,
       prephosphored-paper   10.
    v1. Imperforate-between pair   450.
    a. Black trees   —
    zo. Tagging omitted (error)   —

Listings and prices for palte number coil strips and singles appear at the end of this definitives section of the Krause-Minkus catalog.

1988. Owl and Grosbeak Issue depicts two colorful birds in a booklet format. *Gravure, perforated 10.*

892 *Saw-whet owl*   893 *Rose-breasted grosbeak*

892 (2284)
  25c multicolored, tagged (May 28, 1988) .40   .20

893 *(2285)*
  25c multicolored, tagged   .40   .20
     y. Se-tenant pair, Nos 892-93 1.00   .50
     n. Booklet pane of ten   4.50   6.00
     yzo. Tagging omitted (error),
       se-tenant pair   —

1988. Buffalo Bill Cody Issue honors the military scout, showman, and raconteur of the Wild West. Great Americans series. *Intaglio, perforated 11.*

   894 *Buffalo Bill Cody*

894 *(2177)*
  15c maroon, block tagging *(June 6, 1988)*.30   .20
    Plate block of four   3.50
    z1. Overall tagging (1990)   .30   .20
     Plate block of four   2.00
    z2. Phosphored paper
     (surface tagged)   .30   .20
     Plate block of four   2.00
    zo. Tagging omitted (error)   —

1988. Harvey W. Cushing Issue honors the "father of neurosurgery." He is credited with laying the foundation for the field of brain surgery. Great Americans series. *Intaglio, perforated 11.*

   895 *Harvey W. Cushing, M.D.*

895 *(2188)*
  45c blue, block tagging *(June 17, 1988)* 1.00   .20
    Plate block of four   4.00
    z1. Overall tagging *(1990)*   1.50   .50
     Plate block of four   11.
    zo. Tagging omitted (error)   —

Nos. 896, 897 are not assigned

1988. Transportation Series, Popcorn Wagon. This value represented the prepaid base bulk mail rate. *Coil, intaglio, perforated 10 vertically.*

   898 *Popcorn wagon, 1902*

898 *(2261)*
  16.7c dark rose, Bureau-printed service
    indicator: "Bulk Rate."
      (July 7, 1988)   .35   .20
    Pair   .50
    v. Imperforate pair   175.

Listings and prices for plate number coil strips and single as appear at the end of this definitives section of the Krause-Minkus catalog.

1988. Transportation Series, Tugboat. *Coil, intaglio, perforated 10 vertically.*

   899 *Tugboat, 1900's*

899 *(2260)*
  15c purple, block tagging *(July 12, 1988)*.30   .20
    Pair   .50
    z1. Overall tagging *(July 1990)*   .30   .20
    Pair   .50
Listings and prices for plate number coil strips and singles appear at the end of this definitives section of the Krause-Minkus catalog.

1988. Transportation Series, Railroad Coal Car. Issued to pay a single third-class bulk mail item presorted to five-digit ZIP codes. *Coil, intaglio, perforated 10 vertically.*

   900 *Coal car, 1870's*

900 *(2259)*
  13.2c dark green, Bureau-printed red service
    indicator "Bulk Rate"
      (July 19, 1988)   .30   .20
    Pair   .50
    v. Imperforate pair   100.
Listings and prices for palte number coil strips and dingles appear at the end of this definitives section of the Krause-Minkus catalog.

1988. Transportation Series, Wheel Chair. Issued to pay postage for nonprofit bulk rate mail. *Coil, intaglio, perforated 10 vertically.*

   901 *Wheel chair, 1920's*

901 *(2256)*
  8.4c dark violet, Bureau-printed red service
    indicator: "Nonprofit" *(Aug. 12, 1988)*.30   .20
    Pair   .50
    v. Imperforate pair   650.
Listings and prices for plate number coil strips and singles appear at the end of this definitives section of the Krause-Minkus catalog.

1988. Transportation Series, Railway Mail Car. Issued to meet the single-piece rate for presorted first-class mail to either the three- or five-digit ZIP code. *Coil, intaglio, perforated 10 vertically.*

902 *Railroad mail car, 1920's*

902 *(2265)*
21c green, Bureau-printed red service
indicator "Presorted First-Class"
(*Aug. 16, 1988*) .35 .20
Pair .75
v. Imperforate pair 65.

1988. Transportation Series, Caretta, a cart used by
settlers in Spanish California. Issued to pay the rate for
non-profit bulk mailers. *Coil, gravure, perforated 10
vertically.*

903 *Carreta, 1770's*

903 *(2255)*
7.6c brown, Bureau-printed red service
indicator: "Nonprofit" *(Aug. 30, 1988)*.25 .20
Pair .30
*Listings and prices for plate number coil strips and
singles appear at the end of this definitives section of the
Krause-Minkus catalog.*

1988. New version of the **Harry S. Truman** stamp in the
Great Americans series, perforated 11 1/4.

904 *(1862A)*
20c black, perforated 11 1/4, block tagging
(*Sept. 1, 1988*) .35 .20
Plate block of four 3.50
z1. Overall tagging *(1990)* .35 .20
Plate block of four 4.00
pz. Phosphored paper (embeded) —
Plate block of four —
zo. Tagging omitted (error) —
(See also No. 811)

1988. Honeybee Issue. *Coil, offset and intaglio,
perforated 11.*

905 *Honeybee*

905 *(2281)*
25c multicolored, tagged *(Sept. 2, 1988)*40 .20
Pair .75
v. Black (intaglio) omitted 65.
v1. Black (offset) omitted 550.
v2. Yellow (offset) omitted —
v3. Imperforate pair 55.
v4. Imperforate-between
pair —
zo. Tagging omitted (error) —

*Listings and prices for palte number coil strips and
singles appear at the end of this definitives section of the
Krause-Minkus catalog.*

1988. Transportation Series, Elevator. Issued to pay
the nonprofit third-class rate for mail presorted to the
carrier route. *Coil, intaglio, perforated 10 vertically.*

906 *Elevator, 1900's*

906 *(2254)*
5.3c black, Bureau-printed red service indicator:
"Nonprofit / Carrier Route Sort"
(*Sept. 16, 1988*) .25 .20
Pair .30
*Listings and prices for plate number coil strips and
singles appear at the end of this definitives section of the
Kruase-Minkus catalog.*

1988. Transportation Series, Fire Engine. Issued to
prepay the first-class mail rate presorted by ZIP+4. *Coil,
intaglio, perforated 10 vertically.*

907 *Fire engine, 1900's*

907 *(2264)*
20.5c red, Bureau-printed black
service indicator: "ZIP + 4
Presort" *(Sept. 28, 1988)* .35 .20
Pair .30
*Listings and prices for plate number coil strips and
singles appear at the end of this definitives section of the
Krause-Minkus catalog.*

1988. Eagle and Moon Issue was designed to meet the
increased rate for Express Mail. Although intended for
that use, it also was valid for postage classes where a
high value was needed. *Intaglio and offset, perforated 11.*

908 *Eagle and Moon*

908 *(2394)*
$8.75 multicolored, tagged *(Oct. 4, 1988)*25. 8.00
Plate block of four 110.

1988. Christmas Issue. The contemporary issue depicts
a snowy scene and was released at Berlin, NH, to honor
Irving Berlin and his song *White Christmas*. The
traditional issue is based on the painting *Madonna and
Child* by Italian master Sandro Botticelli.

909 *Snowy village scene*

Gravure, perforated 11 1/2
909 *(2400)*
    25c multicolored, tagged *(Oct. 20, 1988)*40   .20
        Plate block of four   1.25
        Gutter pair   —

910 *Madonna and Child by Botticelli*

Intaglio and offset, perforated 11 1/2
910 *(2399)*
    25c multicolored, tagged *(Oct. 20, 1988)*40   .20
        Plate block of four   1.25
        v. Gold omitted   30.

1988. Chester Carlson Issue honors the man who invented xerography and began an office copying revolution. Great Americans series. *Intaglio, perforated 11.*

911 *Chester Carlson*

911 *(2180)*
    21c blue violet, tagged *(Oct. 21, 1988)* .35   .20
        Plate block of four   1.25

1988. Transportation Series, Tandem Bicycle. Issued to meet the rate for unpresorted ZIP+4 mail, of particular use to mid-size businesses. *Coil, intaglio, perforated 10 vertically.*

912 *Tandem bicycle, 1890's*

912 *(2266)*
    24.1c deep blue violet, Bureau-printed
        red service indicator: "ZIP+4"
            (Oct. 26, 1988)   .40   .20
        Pair   .75
Listings and prices for plate number coil strips and singles appear at the end of this definitives section of the Krause-Minkus catalog.

1988. Transportation Series, Cable Car. Issued to prepay the rate for the second ounce of first-class mail. *Coil, intaglio, perforated 10 vertically.*

913 *Cable car, 1880's*

913 *(2263)*
    20c dark violet, block tagged
          (Oct. 28, 1988)   .35   .20
        Pair   .75
        v. Imperforate pair   75.
        z1. Overall tagging *(1990)*   .35   .20
            Pair   .75
Listings and prices for palte number coil strips and singles appear at the end of this definitives section of the Krause-Minkus catalog.

1988. Transportation Series, Police Patrol Wagon. Issued to meet the single-piece rate for presorted first class mailings of postcards. *Coil, intaglio, perforated 10 vertically.*

914 *Police patrol wagon, 1880's*

914 *(2258)*
    13c black, Bureau-printed red service
        indicator:"Presorted First-Class"
            (Oct. 29, 1988)   .30   .20
        Pair   .50
Listings and prices for plate number coil strips and singles appear at the end of this definitives section of the Krause-Minkus catalog.

1988. Mary Cassatt Issue honors the famed painter. Great Americans series. *Intaglio, perforated 11.*

915 *Mary Cassatt*

915 *(2181)*
    23c purple, block tagging *(Nov. 4, 1988)*.45   .20
        Plate block of four   2.25
        z. Overall tagging *(1990)*   .60   .20
            Plate block of four   3.00
        z1. Phosphored paper (surface
            tagged)   .60   .20
            Plate block of four   3.00
        zo. Tagging omitted (error)   —

1988. H.H. "Hap" Arnold Issue honors the "father of the modern air force." The stamp met the rate for a three-ounce first-class letter. Great Americans series. *Intaglio, perforated 11.*

916 *Gen. Hap Arnold*

916 *(2191)*

> **65c dark blue,** tagged *(Nov. 5, 1988)*   1.25   .20
>> Plate block of four   5.00
>> zo. Tagging omitted (error)   —

1989. Johns Hopkins Issue honors the founder of the hospital and university that bears his name. Hopkins dedicated his fortune to the relief of suffering and advancement of knowledge. Great Americans series. *Intaglio, perforted 11.*

No. 917 not assigned.

918 *Johns Hopkins*

918 *(2194)*

> **$1 blackish blue,** block tagged, matt gum
>> *(June 7, 1989)*   1.75   .20
>> Plate block of four   7.00
>> z. Overall tagged (1990)   1.75   .20
>> Plate block of four   7.00
>> z1. Phosphored paper (taggant
>> on surface)   1.75   .20
>> Plate block of four   7.50
>> z2. Phosphored paper (taggant
>> embedded)   1.75   .20
>> Plate block of four   8.00
>> zo. Tagging omitted   —

1989. Sitting Bull Issue honors the chief, spiritual and political leader of the Hunkpapa Sioux. Issued to meet the rate for postcards sent via surface mail from the United States to all foreign destinations other than Canada and Mexico. Great Americans series. *Intaglio, perforated 11.*

919 *Sitting Bull*

919 *(2183)*

> **28c dark green,** tagged *(Sept. 14, 1989)* .50   .20
>> Plate block of four   3.00

1989. Christmas Issue. Both the traditional and contemporary stamps were available in both sheet and booklet versions. The two versions of the sleigh contemprary design are noticeably different. The booklet version is printed in five colors, the sheet stamp in four. Sleigh runners of the booklet version are decidedly thicker than on the sheet version. The package to the rear of the sleigh has a bow the same color as the package on the booklet stamp, where the bow is of a

different color on the sheet version. Finally, the board running under the sleigh is pink on the booklet version and the same color as the sleigh on the sheet version. The two versions of the traditional are identical, other than the booklet stamp having perforations on only two or three sides

920, 921 *Sleigh with gifts*

Gravure, perforated 11

920 *(2428)*

> **25c multicolored,** tagged *(Oct. 19, 1989)*40   .20
>> Plate block of four   1.25
>> v. Vertical pair, imperforate
>> horizontally   650.

921 *(2429)*

> **25c multicolored,** booklet stamp, tagged
>> *(Oct. 19, 1989)*   .40   .20
>> n. Booklet pane of ten   3.00
>> nv. Booklet pane of ten, Red
>> omitted   7,150.
>> nv1. Booklet pane of ten, horizontally
>> imperforate between   —

922 The Dream of St. Alexandria *by Ludovico Carracci*

Intaglio, perforated 11 1/2

922 *(2427)*

> **25c multicolored,** tagged
>> *(Oct. 19, 1989)*   .40   .20
>> Plate block of four   1.25
>> n. Booklet pane of ten   3.00
>> nv. Booklet pane of ten, offset
>> red omitted   750.
>> nv1. Imperforate booklet
>> pane of ten   —

No. 923 is not assigned.

1989. Eagle and Shield Self-Adhesive Issue was available in a do-it-yourself booklet format that permitted the purchaser to fold the pane of 18 die-cut stamps into a more convenient pocket-sized package. The stamps also were available in strips of 18 with the stamps spaced apart for use in affixing machines. *Gravure, imperforate and die-cut between.*

924 *Eagle and Shield*

924 (2431)
25c multicolored, tagged (Nov. 10, 1989)40   .20
    n. Booklet pane of 18   16.
    v. Vertical pair, no die cutting
       between   —
    v1. Pair, no die cutting   —

No. 925 is not assigned.

1990. Beach Umbrella Issue equates the idea of
vacations and a stamp meeting for the postcard rate.
Booklet stamp, gravure, perforated 11 1/2.

 926 *Beach umbrella*

926 (2443)
15c multicolored, booklet stamp, tagged
    (Feb. 3, 1990)   .30   .20
    n. Booklet pane of ten   4.25
    nv. Booklet pane of ten,
      blue omitted   1,650.
    nv1. Single stamp, blue omitted 175.

1990. Luis Muñoz Marin Issue honors the first
popularly elected governor of Puerto Rico. This is a
major design change for the Great Americans series in
which a zero precedes denominations of less than 10
cents, and information about the subject ("Governor,
Puerto Rico") appears in the selvage. *Intaglio.*

 927 *Luis Muñoz Marin*

927 (2173)
5c dark rose, tagged (Feb. 18, 1990) .25   .20
    Plate block of four   .30
    z. Untagged   .25   .20
    Plate block of four   .65
    (plate No. 2)
    zo. Tagging omitted, plate   —
    block of four (Plate No. 1)

1990. Transportation Series, Seaplane. *Coil, intaglio.*

 928 *Seaplane, 1914*

928 (2468)
$1 dark blue and red, tagged
    (April 20, 1990)   2.00   .50
    Pair
    v. Imperforate pair   —   —
*Listings and prices for palte number coil strips and
singles appear at the end of this definitives section of the
Krause-Minkus catalog.*

1990. Flag Issue for Automatic Teller Machines,
tested dispensing of stamps through bank ATM
equipment. This stamp was *self-adhesive, die cut,
imperforate.* Available in panes of 12-the same size as a
dollar bill- and *printed on polyester film by gravure.* This
issue was available as a test through 22 machines in the
Seattle, WA, area.

 929 *U.S. flag*

929 (2475)
25c red and dark blue, tagged
    (May 18, 1990)   .50   .50
    n. Pane of twelve   6.00

1990. Bobcat Issue was the first high-value stamp in
the Wildlife Series. Printed in pane of 20, with four plate
numbers, copyright notice and descriptive information
on the selvage. *Intaglio and offset, perforated 11.*

 930 *Bobcat*

930 (2482)
$2 multicolored, tagged (June 1, 1990)4.00   1.25
    Plate block of four   18.
    t. Intaglio black omitted   300.
    zo. Tagging omitted (error)   —

1990. Transportation Series, Circus Wagon. *Coil,
intaglio, perforated 10 vertically.*

 931 *Circus wagon, 1900's*

931 (2452)
5c carmine red, tagged (Aug. 31, 1990) .25   .20
    Pair   .30
    z. Untagged   .25   .20
    Pair   .30
    v. Imperforate pair   875.
*For stamps of this design inscribed "USA 5c" see No. 1007
(gravure) or No. 1077 (intaglio).*

*Listings and prices for plate number coil strips and
singles appear at the end of this definitives section of the
Krause-Minkus catalog.*

1990. Claire Lee Chennault Issue honors the pioneer
air power tactician who led the Flying Tigers in China in
World War II. Great Americans series. *Intaglio, perforated
11.*

932 *Clair Chennault*

932 *(2187)*
40c dark blue, overall tagging
    (Sept. 6, 1990) .75 .20
    Plate block of four 3.75
    z1. Phosphored paper
        (taggant on surface) .75 .20
        Plate block of four 4.00

1990. Christmas Issues. The contemporary stamp features a cut-paper Christmas tree. The traditional stamp incorporates a portion of Sicilian painter Antonello da Messina's *Madonna and Child.*

933, 934 *Christmas tree*

Gravure, perforated 11 1/2
933 *(2515)*
25c multicolored, tagged *(Oct. 18, 1990)* .40 .20
    Plate block of four 1.50
    v. Vertical pair, imperforate
        horizontally 1,100.

934 *(2516)*
25c multicolored, booklet stamp, tagged
    (Oct. 18, 1990) .40 .20
    n. Booklet pane of ten 8.00
There are noticeable design and color differences between the sheet and booklet versions of this stamp.

935, 936 Madonna and Child *by Antonello da Messina*

Intaglio and offset, perforated 11 1/2
935 *(2514)*
25c multicolored, tagged
    (Oct. 18, 1990) .40 .20
    Plate block of four 1.50
936 *(2514A)*
25c multicolored, booklet stamp, tagged
    (Oct. 18, 1990) .40 .20
    n. Booklet pane of ten 8.00
The booklet version has a much heavier shading in the Madonna's veil where it meets the right frame line.

1991. "F" (Flower) Non-Denominated Issue came in sheet, coil, and two different booklet types. Its face value was 29c, the new first-class mail rate. *Gravure.*

937-940 *"F" and tulip*

Perforated 13
937 *(2517)*
(29c) multicolored, tagged
    (Jan. 22, 1991) .50 .20
    Plate block of four 2.25
    v. Vertical pair, imperforate 750.
    v1. Horizontal pair,
        imperforate vertically —

Perforated 11 1/4
938 *(2519)*
(29c) multicolored, booklet stamp, printed by
    Bureau of Engraving and Printing
    (BEP), tagged *(Jan. 22, 1991)* .50 .20
    n. Booklet pane of ten 6.00
939 *(2520)*
(29c) multicolored, booklet stamp, printed by
    KCS Industries, tagged
    (Jan. 22, 1991) .50 .20
    n. Booklet pane of ten 25.
    z. Phosphored paper *(1993)* .50 .20
    z1. Booklet pane of 10 25.
BEP version has dark green leaf, KCS version bright green leaf; yellow background of KCS version paler than BEP version; KCS version has much less pronounced black lines in leaf. BEP version is perforated nearly 11 1/4; KCS version is perforated 11.

Coil, perforated 10 vertically
940 *(2518)*
(29c) multicolored, tagged *(Jan. 22, 1991)* .60 .20
    Pair .75
    v. Imperforate pair 35.

1991. Non-Denominated Make-Up Issue has a value of 4c, to be used with a 25c stamp to meet the new 29c first-class rate. *Offset, perforated 11.*

941 *Text explaining how to use stamp*

941 *(2521)*
(4c) bister and carmine *(Jan. 22, 1991)* .25 .20
    Plate block of four .30
    v. Vertical pair, imperforate
        horizontally 100.

1991. "F" Non-Denominated ATM Flag Issue was identical in design and material to No. 929, with the denomination replaced by an "F" and the inclusion of "For U.S. Addresses Only." *Gravure, die cut, imperforate.*

942 "F" and U.S. flag

942 (2522)
(29c) black, dark blue and red, tagged
    (Jan. 22, 1991)   .50   .20
    n. Pane of 12   7.00

1991. Transportation Series, Steam Carriage, the
"Richard Dudgeon," which is now in the Museum of
American History of the Smithsonian Institution. *Coil,
intaglio, perforated 10 vertically.*

943 *Steam carriage, 1866*

943 (2451)
4c maroon, tagged (Jan. 25, 1991)   .25   .20
    Pair   .30
    v. Imperforate pair   625.
    zx. Untagged (intentional)   —
        Pair   —
*Listings and prices for plate number coil strips and
singles appear at the end of this definitives section of the
Krause-Minkus catalog.*

1991. Fawn Issue, part of the Wildlife series and meets
the rate for postcards. *Gravure, perforated 11 1/4.*

944 *Fawn*

944 (2479)
19c multicolored, tagged (March 11, 1991) .40   .20
    Plate block of four   1.50
    v. Red omitted   850.
    zo. Tagging omitted (error)   —

1991. Flag over Mount Rushmore Issue markes the
50th anniversary of the South Dakota monument. *Coil,
intaglio, perforated 10 vertically.*

945 *Flag, Mt. Rushmore*

945 (2523)
29c red, blue, and maroon, tagged
    (March 29, 1991)   .50   .20
    Pair   .75
    v. Imperforate pair   20.

945A (2523C)
29c red, blue and brown color error,
        tagged   .50   .20
    Pair   3.00

*For gravure version of this design, see No. 963.
Listings and prices for palte number coil strips and
singles appear at the end of this definitives section of the
Krause-Minkus catalog.*

1991. Dennis Chavez Issue honors the first U.S.-born
Hispanic elected to the U.S. Senate. Great Americans
series. *Intaglio, by Stamp Venturers, perforated 11.*

946 *Dennis Chavez*

946 (2186)
35c black, tagged (April 3, 1991)   .75   .20
    Plate block of four   3.50

1991. Flower Issue is a "denominated" version of the
"F" stamp, initially released in sheet and booklet types.
Gravure.

947, 947A, 948 *Tulip*

Perforated 11
947 (2524)
29c multicolored, tagged (April 5, 1991) .45   .20
    Plate block of four   1.75

Perforated 12 1/2 x 13
947A (2524a)
29c multicolored, tagged   .45   .20
    Plate block of four   1.75

Perforated 11
948 (2527)
29c multicolored, booklet stamp, tagged
        (April 5, 1991)   .45   .20
    n. Booklet pane of ten   8.00
    nv. Pane of ten, vertically
        imperforate between   1,900.
    nv1. Pane of ten, imperforate
        horizontally   —
    nv2. Horizontal pair, imperforate
        vertically   375.
For coil version of the Flower Issue, see Nos. 966 and 982.

1991. Transportation Series, Lunch Wagon, met the
new second-ounce first-class mail rate. *Coil, intaglio,
perforated 10 vertically.*

949 *Lunch wagon, 1890's*

949 *(2464)*
  23c dark blue, tagged, matt gum
     (April 12, 1991)   .50   .20
    Pair   .75
    zs. Prephosphored paper, (mottled
        tagging), shiny gum (1993)   .50   .20
        Pair   .75
    zm. Prephosphored paper (mottled
        tagging) matt gum (1993)   .50   .20
        Pair   .75
    v. Imperforate pair   150.
Listings and prices for palte number coil and singles appear at the end of this definitives section of the Krause-Minkus catalog.

1991. Wood Duck Issue was a booklet stamp in the Wildlife series. Version produced by the Bureau of Engraving and Printing with lettering and numbers in black and by KCS Industries with the lettering and numbers in red. *Gravure.*

    950, 951 *Wood duck*

Perforated 10
950 *(2484)*
  29c multicolored, booklet stamp, black
      inscription (BEP), tagged
        (April 12, 1991)   .75   .20
    n. Booklet pane of ten   8.00
    nv. Pane of ten, horizontaly
        imperforate-between   1,200.
    nv1. Vertical pair, imperforate
        horizontally   275.

Perforated 11
951 *(2485)*
  29c multicolored, booklet stamp, red inscription
      (KCS Industries), tagged
        (April 12, 1991)   1.00   .20
    n. Booklet pane of 10   8.75

1991. U.S. Flag with Olympic Rings Issue was a booklet version with a flag motif. *Gravure, perforated 11.*

    952 *U.S. flag, Olympic rings*

952 *(2528)*
  29c multicolored, booklet stamp, tagged
        (April 21, 1991)   .75   .20
    n. Booklet pane of ten   8.00
    nv. Pane of ten, horizontally
        imperforate-between   —
    nv1. Vertical pair, imperforate
        between   —

1991. Hot Air Balloon Issue met the postcard rate for first-class mail and was available in booklet form. *Gravure, perforated 10.*

    953 *Hot air balloon*

953 *(2530)*
  19c multicolored, booklet stamp, tagged
        (May 17, 1991)   .30   .20
    n. Booklet pane of ten   4.50

1991. Transportation Series, Tractor Trailer and Canoe. Both stamps were issued for use by permit mailers, the canoe stamp by nonprofit mailers and the tractor trailer by bulk business mailers. *Coil, intaglio, perforated 10 vertically.*

    954 *Tractor trailer, 1930's*

954 *(2457)*
  10c green, Bureau-printed gray service indicator:
      "Additional Presort Postage Paid"
        (May 25, 1991)   .25   .20
    Pair   .30
    v. Imperforate pair   400.
For version with service indicator in black, see No. 1042.

    955 *Canoe, 1800's*

955 *(2453)*
  5c brown, printed gray service indicator:
      "Additional Nonprofit Postage Paid"
        (May 25, 1991)   .25   .20
    Pair   .30
    v. Imperforate pair   —
For gravure version of No. 955 in red, see No. 979. Listings and prices for plate number coil strips and singles appear at the end of this definitives section of the Krause-Minkus catalog.

1991. Flags on Parade Issue celebrates the 125th anniversary of Memorial Day. *Gravure, perforated 11.*

    956 *Flags on Parade*

956 *(2531)*
  29c multicolored, tagged *(May 30, 1990)* .50   .20
    Plate block of four   2.00

1991. Hubert H. Humphrey Issue honors the former vice president, Minnesota senator, and mayor of Minneapolis. A date error in the selvage inscription, showing the wrong beginning date of his tenure as vice president, was corrected with a re-release of the stamp in 1993. Great Americans series. *Intaglio, perforated 11.*

 957 *Hubert H. Humphrey*

957 *(2189)*
   52c purple, tagged *(June 3, 1991)*   1.50   .20
     Plate block of four   6.00
     z1. Phosphored paper (taggant
       on surface)   1.50   .20
     Plate block of four   5.00

1991. Eagle and Olympic Rings Issue met eight-ounce Express Mail rate. The stamp was valid for other mail as well. *Intaglio and offset, perforated 11.*

 958 *Eagle and Olympic rings*

958 *(2541)*
   $9.95 multicolored, tagged
         (June16, 1991)   25.   11.
     Plate block of four   100.

1991. Wildlife Series, 1c American Kestrel, 3c Bluebird, and 30c Cardinal. The 30c value met the postcard rate to Canada and Mexico.

 959 *Kestrel*

Offset, perforated 11
959 *(2476)*
   1c multicolored *(June 22, 1991)*   .25   .20
     Plate block of four   .30
For versions inscribed "USA 1c", see No. 1079 (sheet) and No.1115 (Coil).

 960 *Blue bird*

960 *(2478)*
   3c bluebird *(June 22, 1991)*   .25   .20
     Plate block of four   .30

 961 *Cardinal*

Gravure, perforated 11 1/2 x 11
961 *(2480)*
   30c multicolored, on phosphored paper
         (June 22, 1991)   .45   .20
     Plate block of four   2.00

1991. Liberty Torch Self-Adhesive Issue was designed for sale through ATM machines. This issue provided 18 stamps on a backing sheet the same size as a dollar bill. Unlike its predecessor, this issue was printed on paper. *Gravure, die cut, imperforate.*

 962 *Liberty torch*

962 *(2531A)*
   29c black, gold and green, tagged
         (June 25, 1991)   .60   .30
     n. Pane of 18, plain
       paper back   14.50
     nv. Pane of 18, printed
       backing paper   15.
     nv1. Pair, die cut omitted   3,750.

1991. Flag over Mt. Rushmore Issue, type of No. 945 re-issued with essentially the same colors. *Coil, gravure,American Bank Note Co., perforated 10 vertically.*

 963 *Flag over Mt. Rushmore*

963 *(2523a)*
   29c blue, red and brown, tagged
         (July 4, 1991)   .50   .25
     Pair   1.00
     v. Phosphor-coated "Lenz" paper 2.00   .50

For intaglio version of the same design, see No. 945. Listings and prices for plate number coil strips and singles appear at the end of this definitives section of the Krause-Minkus catalog.

1991. Bald Eagle and Olympic Rings Issue met the Priority Mail rate for second-day delivery of up to two pounds. *Intaglio and offset, perforated 11.*

 964 *Eagle and Olympic rings*

964 (2540)

$2.90 multicolored, tagged

(July 7, 1991)   5.00   2.75

Plate block of four   25.

1991. Fishing Boat Issue met the first class rate for domestic postcards. *Coil, gravure, American Bank Note Co., perforated 11.*

965 *Fishing boat*

965 (2529)

19c multicolored, type I, tagged

(Aug. 8, 1991)   .40   .20

Pair   .75

a. type II (lighter colors, sharper

printing) (1992)   .40   .20

Pair   .75

zo. Tagging omitted (error,

wrong paper used)   —

Pair   —

z. Untagged (1993)   .75   .20

Imperforates in this design came from printer's waste. For version with one loop of rope tying boat to piling, see No. 1044.

1991. Flower Issue coil version. The separations are "roulettes" rather than "perforations." With rouletting, only a series of slits are made to facilitate separation, rather than drilling holes to create perforations. *Coil, gravure, Stamp Venturers, rouletted 10 vertically.*

966 *Tulip*

966 (2525)

29c multicolored, tagged (Aug. 16, 1991) .75   .20

Pair   1.25

1991. Eagle over Coastline with Olympic Rings Issue met the rate for international Express Mail pieces weighing up to eight ounces to 109 countries. *Intaglio and offset, perforated 11.*

967 *Eagle over Coastline, Olympic rings*

967 (2542)

$14 multicolored, tagged (Aug. 31, 1991) 30.   17.50

Plate block of four   130.

No. 968 is not assigned.

1991. U.S. Flag Issue includes a service indicator and met the first class presort rate. *Coil, gravure, American Bank Note Co., perforated 10 vertically.*

  969 *U.S. flag*

969 (2605)

23c red and blue, printed service

indicator: "Presorted First-Class,"

tagged (Sept. 27, 1991)   .65   .20

Pair   1.00

1991. USPS Olympic Sponsor Issue was released to promote the USPS sponsorship of the olympic games in Barcelona, Spain. *Gravure, perforated 11.*

970 *Eagle and Olympic rings*

970 (2539)

$1 multicolored, tagged (Sept. 29, 1991) 2.75   .75

Plate block of four   12.

1991. Christmas Issues. Non-denominated in anticipation of a rate increase that did not materialize. A traditional and a contemporary design were produced in sheet form, and six additional contemporary designs in booklet form. Of the additional contemporary designs, four are totally different and two are modifications of the sheet stamp design. *All perforated 11.*

971, 972, 972A *Santa descending a chimney*

Gravure

971 (2579)

29c multicolored, tagged (Oct. 17, 1991) .45   .20

Plate block of four   1.50

v. Vertical pair, imperforate

horizontally   500.

v1. Horizontal pair imperforate

vertically   325.

972 (2580)

29c multicolored, booklet stamp, type I, tagged

(Oct. 17, 1991)   .45   .20

972A (2581)

29c multicolored, booklet stamp, type II,

tagged   .45   .20

y. Se-tenant pair, Nos. 972, 972A. —

n. Booklet pane of four —

Type I has an extra vertical line of brick in the top row of bricks at left; type II is missing that vertical line of brick.

973 *Santa checking his list*

973 (2582)
29c multicolored, booklet stamp, tagged
(Oct. 17, 1991) .45 .20
n. Booklet pane of four 1.50

974 *Santa leaving gifts*

974 (2583)
29c multicolored, booklet stamp,
tagged .45 .20
n. Booklet pane of four 1.50

975 *Santa ascending chimney*

975 (2584)
29c multicolored, booklet stamp,
tagged .45 .20
n. Booklet pane of four 1.50

976 *Santa departing in sleigh*

976 (2585)
29c multicolored, booklet stamp,
tagged .45 .20
n. Booklet pane of four 1.50

977 *From* Madonna and Child with Donor *by Antoniazzo Romano*

Intaglio and offset
977 (2578)
29c multicolored, tagged (Oct. 17, 1991) .45 .20
Plate block of four 1.50
n. Booklet pane of ten 8.00
v. Booklet single, red and black
(intaglio) omitted 3,750.

No. 978 is not assigned.

1991. Transportation Series, Canoe. *Coil, gravure, Stamp Venturers, perforated 10 vertically.*

979 *Canoe, 1800's*

979 (2454)
5c red, printed service indicator: "Additional
Nonprofit Postage Paid"
(Oct. 22, 1991) .25 .20
Pair .30
For intaglio version in brown, see No. 955.
Listings and prices for plate number coil strips and singles appear at the end of this definitives section of the Krause-Minkus catalog.

1991. Eagle and Shield Non-Denominated Issue met the needs of permit mailers on presorted bulk mail pieces. The value of the stamp is 10c, with additional postage paid by mailers at the time of mailing. *Coil, gravure, American Bank Note Co. (plate numbers beginning with "A"), perforated 10 vertically.*

980 *Eagle and Shield*

980 (2602)
(10c) multicolored, printed service indicator:
"Bulk Rate" *(Dec. 13, 1991)* .25 .20
Pair .30
v. Imperforate pair —
See Nos. 1011 and 1012 for similar stamps printed by the Bureau of Engraving and Printing and Stamp Venturers.

1992. The Wendell Willkie Issue honors the man who lost in the 1940 presidential election and then served the Roosevelt administration on a diplomatic mission. Great Americans series. *Intaglio, perforated 11.*

981 *Wendell Wilkie*

981 (2192)
75c maroon, phosphored paper (taggant on
surface), matt gum, tagged
(Feb. 16, 1992) 1.25 .50
Plate block of four 5.50
z1. Pre-phosphored (taggant
embedded) paper, shiny gum 1.25 .50
Plate block of four 5.50
Listings and prices for plate number coil strips and singles appear at the end of this definitives section of the Krause-Minkus catalog.

1992. Flower Perforated Coil Issue. *Gravure, perforated 10 vertically.*

982 *Tulip*

982 (2526)
29c multicolored, tagged *(March 3, 1992)* .75 .20
Pair 1.25

Listings and prices for palte number coil strips and singles appear at the end of this deinitives section of the Krause-Minkus catalog.

1992. Earl Warren Issue honors the former Chief Justice of the United States. Great Americans series. *Intaglio, perforated 11.*

 983 *Earl Warren*

983 *(2184)*
29c blue, tagged *(March 9, 1992)* .50 .20
    Plate block of four   2.75

1992. Flag over White House Issue honors the 200th anniversary of the home and office of the President of the United States. *Intaglio, perforated 10 vertically.*

 984 *U.S. flag, White House*

984 *(2609)*
29c blue and red, tagged *(April 23, 1992)* .50 .20
    Pair   2.00
    a. indigo and red   —
        Pair   —
    v. Imperforate pair   —

1992. USA Issue was for presorted first class mailings. The background is a graduated blue. *Coil, gravure, American Bank Note Company, perforated 10 vertically.*

 985 *"USA"*

985 *(2606)*
23c multicolored, printed service indicator:
    "Presorted First-Class"
        (July 21, 1992)   .50 .20
    Pair   .75
See Nos. 994 and 1010 for similar stamps printed by the Bureau of Engraving and Printing and by Stamp Venturers.
Listings and prices for plate number coil strips and singles appear at the end of this deinitives section of the Krause-Minkuse catalog.

1992. ECA GARD Variable Denomination Issue was released as a test of new postage and mail center equipment that weighed items for mailing, determined the postage necessary for the desired level of service, and printed stamps with the appropriate amount of postage. *Coil, intaglio, perforated 11 horizontally.*

 986 *Shield, bunting*

986 *(cv31)*
(-) red and blue, tagged on surface
    denomination (.02 to 9.99) printed in black,
    matt gum *(Aug. 20, 1992)*   1.50 .50
    a. Embedded taggant,
        shiny gum   1.50 .50
For narrow, tall format, see No. 1040.

1992. Pledge of Allegiance Issue honors the centennial of the pledge, first recited by school children for the 400th anniversary of Columbus' voyage of discovery. *Gravure, perforated 10.*

 987, 1008 *Flag, "I pledge allegiance ..."*

987 *(2593)*
29c multicolored, black inscription, booklet
    stamp, tagged *(Sept. 8, 1992)* .75 .20
    n. Booklet pane of 10   7.50
    a. Perforated 10x11 on two or three
        sides   1.25 .50
    an. Booklet pane of 10   12.
For version with red inscription see No. 1008.

1992. Eagle and Shield Self-Adhesive Issue was produced by three different contractors, each is identifiable through the color of the inscription ("USA 29"): red for Stamp Venturers of Fairfax, VA; green for Dittler Brothers, Inc., of Oakwood, GA; and, brown for Banknote Corporation of America, Inc., of Suffern, NY. These stamps were issued in panes of 17 plus a label on flexible backing paper, suitable for folding into a booklet. The stamps also were available in strips of 17 with the stamps spaced apart for use in affixing machines. *Imperforate (die cut).*

 988, 990, 992 *Eagle and shield*

Gravure
988 *(2597)*
29c multicolored, red inscription, tagged
    (Sept. 25, 1992)   .45 .30
    n. pane of 17, plus label   12.

No. 989 is not assigned.

990 *(2596)*
29c multicolored, green inscription,
    tagged *(Sept. 25, 1992)*   .45 .30
    n. Pane of 17, plus label   12.

No. 991 is not assigned

Intaglio and offset
992 *(2595)*
  29c multicolored, brown inscription,
        tagged *(Sept. 25, 1992)*   .45   .30
    n. Pane of 17, plus label   12.
    v. Imperforate pair   —
    v1. Brown omitted   450.

No. 993 is not assigned.

1992. "USA" Issue for presorted first class mailings was reformatted in larger coils. The background is solid blue. *Coil, gravure, Bureau of Printing and Engraving (plate number beginning with a numeral rather than a letter), perforated 10 vertically.*

 994 *"USA"*

994 *(2607)*
  23c multicolored, printed service indicator:
    "Presorted First-Class," shiny gum
       (Oct. 9, 1992)   .50   .20
    Pair   .75
    m. Matt gum   .50   .20
      pair   .75
    v. Imperforate pair   —
In this version, "23" is 7 mm long. See Nos. 985 and 1010 for versions printed by the American Bank Note Company or by Stamp Venturers.
Listings and prices for palte number coil strips and singles appear at the end of this definities section of the Krause-Minkus catalog.

1992. Christmas Issues consist of a traditional stamp in sheet and booklet formats, a se-tenant block of four contemporary stamps in both sheet and booklet formats (with design differences between the two formats) and a contemporary self-adhesive stamp with essentially the same basic design as one of the sheet and booklet designs.

995, 999, 1005 *Locomotive*

996, 1000 *Pony and rider*

997, 1001 *Steam engine*

998, 1002 *Steamship*

Offset, perforated 11 1/2 x 11
995 *(2711)*
  29c multicolored, tagged *(Oct. 22, 1992)*45   .20
996 *(2412)*
  29c multicolored, tagged   .45   .20
997 *(2713)*
  29c multicolored, tagged   .45   .20

998 *(2714)*
  29c multicolored, tagged   .45   .20
    y. Se-tenant block of four   3.50
    Plate block of four   4.50

Gravure, Multi-Color Corporation, perforated 11
999 *(2715)*
  29c multicolored, booklet single
      (Oct. 22, 1992)   .45   .20
1000 *(2716)*
  29c multicolored, booklet single   .45   .20
1001 *(2717)*
  29c multicolored, booklet single   .45   .20
1002 *(2718)*
  29c multicolored, booklet single   .45   .20
    n. Booklet pane of four   3.50
    nv. Imperforate pane of four   —
    nv1. Pane of four, imperforate
      horizontally   —

 1003 Madonna and Child *by Bellini*

Intaglio and offset, perforated 11 1/2 x 11
1003 *(2710)*
  29c multicolored, tagged *(Oct. 22, 1992)* .45   .20
    Plate block of four   3.00
    a. Booklet pane of ten   8.00

No. 1004 is not assigned.

Gravure, die cut, self-adhesive.
1005 *(2719)*
  29c multicolored, tagged *(Oct. 22, 1992)* .75   .20
    n. Pane of 18   12.

1992. Pumpkinseed Sunfish Issue. This Wildlife series stamp meets the second half-ounce rate for international mail and the one-ounce rate to Mexico. *Intaglio and offset, perforated 11 1/2 x 11.*

 1006 *Pumpkinseed sunfish*

1006 *(2481)*
  45c multicolored, tagged *(Dec. 2, 1992)* 1.00   .20
    Plate block of four   5.50
    v. Intaglio black omitted   600.   —

1992. Transportation Series, Circus Wagon. This is a redesigned version of the stamp of 1990 (No. 931). *Coil, gravure, perforated 10 vertically.*

1007 *(2454)*
  5c red *(Dec. 8, 1992)*   .25   .20
    Pair   .30

For intaglio stamps of this design see No. 931 ("05 USA") and No. 1077 ("USA 5c).
Listings and prices for plate number coil strips and singles appear at the end of this definitives section of the Krause-Minkus catalog.

1993. Pledge of Allegiance. New version with red, "USA" and denomination, printed by Stamp Venturers. The booklets in which the stamps are found were assembled by KCS, a division of Banta Corp.

1008 *(2594)*
29c multicolored, red inscription, tagged
     (March 1993)   .75   .20
    n. Booklet pane of 10   7.50
    v. Imperforate pair   —
For similar stamp with black inscription see No. 987.

1993. Thomas Jefferson Issue honors the third president of the United States on the 250th anniversary of his birth. Great Americans series. *Intaglio, Stamp Venturers, perforated 11 1/2 x 11.*

1009 *Thomas Jefferson*

1009 *(2185)*
29c indigo *(April 13, 1993)*   .50   .30
    Plate block of four   2.50
    Plate block of eight, with
        position diagram   5.50

1993. USA Issue for presorted first-class mailings. The background is violet blue. *Coil, gravure Stamp Venturers (plate number beginning with an "S"), perforated 10 vertically.*

1010 *(2608)*
23c multicolored, printed service indicator:
    "Presorted First-Class"
      (Oct. 9, 1992)   .75   .20
    Pair   1.00
    v. Imperforate pair   —
In this version, "23" is 8 1/2 mm long. See No. 985 and No. 994 for versions printed by the American Bank Note Co. and by the Bureau of Engraving and Printing.

1993. Eagle and Shield Non-Denominated Issue met the needs of permit mailers on presorted bulk mail pieces. Similar to earlier version, No. 980. Design differences include reversal of "USA" and "BULK RATE" and colors reversed to "USA" in blue and "BULK RATE" in red. The stamp's face value is 10 cents, with additional postage paid by mailers at the time of mailing. *Coil, printed by gravure by the Bureau of Engraving and Printing (plate number beginning with numeral rather than letter) and Stamp Venturers (plate numbers*

beginning with "S"), *perforated 10 vertically. The Stamp Venturers version has the eagle in metallic gold, the BEP version in orange yellow.*

 1011, 1012 *"USA" before "Bulk Rate"*

1011 *(2602)*
(10c) multicolored, (BEP)*(May 29, 1993)* .30   .20
    Pair   .40
    v. Imperforate pair   27.50

1012 *(2604)*
(10c) multicolored, (Stamp Venturers)
    (May 29, 1993)   .30   .20
    Pair   .40
See No. 980 for similar design printed by the American Bank Note Co.

1993. Futuristic Space Shuttle Issue. Prepaid the Priority Mail rate. *Offset and intaglio, perforated 11.*

 1013

1013 *(2543)*
$2.90 multicolored *(June 23, 1993)*   6.50   2.50
    Plate block of four   27.50

1993. Red Squirrel. Self-adhesive first-class letter-rate stamp in the Wildlife Series. *Gravure, Dittler Brothers, Inc., imperforate (die cut.)*

 1014 *Squirrel*

1014 *(2489)*
29c multicolored, from booklet,
    tagged *(June 25, 1993)*   .50   .20
    n. Pane of 18   15.

No. 1015 is not assigned

1993. Rose. Self-adhesive stamp with design characteristics of the Wildlife Series. *Gravure by Stamp Venturers, imperforate and die cut.*

 1016 *Rose*

1016 *(2490)*
29c multicolored, from booklet,
    tagged *(Aug. 1994).*   .50   .20
    n. Pane of 18   15.

No. 1017 is not assigned

1993. African Violet. Booklet stamp, part of the wildlife Series. *Gravure by KCS Industries, perforated 10 x 11.*

1017 *African Violet*

1018 *(2486)*
29c multicolored, from booklet ,
　　　tagged *(Oct. 8, 1993)*　　　.75　　.20
　　n. Pane of 10　　　　　　8.50

1993. Christmas Issues consisted of four contemporary designs and a single Traditional design. The Contemporary designs were available in sheets, booklets, and self-adhesive panes. The Snowman design of the Contemporary issues is available self-adhesive both with the other three design and by itself in panes available through ATM machines. The Traditional design was available in sheets and booklets. Contemporary stamps were printed by gravure by the Bureau of Engraving and Printing (sheets and booklets), and Avery Dennison (self-adhesive); perforated 11 (Contemporary booklet), 11 1/2 x 11 (Traditional booklet); and imperforate and die-cut (self-adhesive).

1019 Jack-in-the-box
1020 *Reindeer*
1021 *Snowman*
1022 *Toy soldier*

1019 *(2791)*
29c Jack-in-the-box, tagged
　　　(Oct. 21, 1993)　　　.50　　　.20
1020 *(2792)*
29c Reindeer, tagged　　　.50　　　.20
1021 *(2793)*
29c Snowman, tagged　　　.50　　　.20
1022 *(2794)*
29c Toy Soldier, tagged　　　.50　　　.20

Booklet Pane

1023 *(2795)*
29c Jack-in-the-box, single, tagged　.50　　.20
1024 *(2796)*
29c Reindeer, single, tagged　　.50　　.20
1025 *(2797)*
29c Snowman, single, tagged　　.50　　.20
1026 *(2798)*
29c Toy Soldier, tagged　　.50　　.20
　　n. Booklet pane of 10 (three

each Nos. 1023, 1024; two
each Nos. 1025, 1026)　　9.50
　　n1. Booklet pane of 10 (two each
　　　Nos. 1023, 1024; three each
　　　Nos. 1025, 1026)　　9.50

Traditional, from sheet of fifty

1027

1027 *(2789)*
29c multicolored, tagged *(Oct. 21, 1993)*.50　　.20
　　Plate block of four　　3.50

Traditional , from booklet pane

1028 *(2790)*
29c multicolored, booklet single, tagged
　　　(Oct. 21, 1993)　　.50　　.20
　　n. Booklet pane of four　3.75

The booklet version of this design is larger than the sheet version (booklet overall stamp 28.95 x 22.09mm; sheet overall stamp 23.1 x 30.2mm). There are design differences between the two items, also.

Contemporary, from self-adhesive panes

1029 *(2799)*
29c Jack-in-the-box, single, tagged
　　　(Oct. 28, 1993)　　.50　　.20
1030 *(2800)*
29c Reindeer, single, tagged　.50　　.20
1031 *(2801)*
29c Snowman, single, tagged　.50　　.20
1032 *(2802)*
29c Toy Soldier, single, tagged　.50　　.20
　　n. Pane of 12 (three inch design) 9.50

Nos. 1033-1036 are not assigned

Contemporary, from ATM pane

1037 *Snowman*

1037 *(2803)*
29c Snowman, single, tagged
　　　(Oct. 28, 1993)　　.75　　.25
　　n. Pane of 18　　15.

Although the placement is different, the Snowmen depicted on Nos. 1021 and 1031 have three buttons and seven snowflakes beneath the nose. No. 1025 has two buttons and five snowflakes beneath the nose.

1993. Pine Cone. Self-adhesive stamp with design characteristics of the Wildlife Series. *Gravure by the Banknote Corporation of America, imperforate and die cut.*

 1038 *Pine cone*

1038
   29c multicolored, from booklet,
        tagged *(Nov. 5, 1993)*   .50   .20
      n. Pane of 18   15.

 1039 *Eagle*

1039 *(2491a)*
   29c red, cream and blue, single,
        tagged *(Feb. 4, 1994)*   .50   .20
      n. Pane of 18   15.

1994. Postage and Mail Center (PMC) Issue. Similar to No. 986, issued in 1992, this issue is perforated horizontally. *Gravure by Guilford Gravure for American Bank Note Co., perforated 10 vertically.*

 1040 *Shield and bunting*

1040 *(CV31a)*
   (variable rate) red and blue, denomination
      printed in black. *(Feb. 19, 1994)* 1.50   .50

1994. Surrender at Saratoga. Design of this stamp was taken from an engraving originally prepared to be part of the 1869 definitive series, the first U.S. pictorial postage stamps. John Trumbull's painting *The Surrender of Gen. Burgoyne at Saratoga* is the basis for the stamp design. *Intaglio by Stamp Venturers in panes of 20, perforated 11 1/2.*

 1041 *Virctory at Saratoga*

1041 *(2590)*
   $1 dark blue, tagged *(May 5, 1994)* 2.00   .75
      Plate block of four   9.00

1994. Tractor Trailer. Reprint of No. 954, showing a 1930's tractor trailer, issued for use by permit mailers. *Gravure, perforated 10 vertically.*

 1042 *Tractor Trailer*

1042 *(2458)*
   10c green. Bureau-printed gray service
      indicator (in gray): "Additional
      Presort Postage Paid"
        (May 25, 1994)   .25   .20
      Pair   .30
      v. Pair, imperforate   —

1994. Statue of Liberty. Self adhesive pane. Imperforate and die cut.

 1043 *Statue of Liberty*

1043 *(2599)*
   29c multicolored, single, tagged
        (June 24, 1994)   .50   .20
      a. Pane of 18   9.50

1994. Fishing Boat Issue reprint. Originally issued in 1991, No. 965, this design was reprinted in 1992 in lighter colors (No. 965zl). This reprinting easily is identifiable by counting the "loops" of rope on the mooring. The original and initial two reprintings had two loops, this reprinting has a single loop. *Gravure by Stamp and Venturers, perforated 10 vertically.*

 1044 *Boat*

1044 *(2529a)*
   19c multicolored, untagged
        (June 25, 1994)   .50   .20
      Pair   .60

1994. Moon Landing. Celebrated the 25th Anniversary of the Moon Landing with an Express Mail denomination.

 1045 *Moon Landing, 25th Anniversary*

1045 *(2541)*
   $9.95 multicolored, tagged
        (July 20, 1994)   25.   10.
      Plate block of four   100.

1994. Washignton and Jackson. A design submitted by a firm seeking to win the contract for the 1869 issue. *Intaglio by Stamp Veturers in panes of 20, perforated 11 1/2.*

1046 *Washington and Jackson*

1046 *(2592)*
$5 dark green, tagged *(Aug. 19, 1994)* 10. 3.75
Plate block of four 50.

1994. Christmas Issues this year consist of two Contemporary designs and Traditional design. The Santa Claus stamp was issued only as a self-adhesive. The Holiday Stocking design was issued both in sheet form and in booklets of 20 stamps. The Traditional stamp was issue both as sheet and in booklet form, with the total size of the booklet version 0.05 mm more horizontally and 0.03 mm less vertically than the sheet version. Printed by gravure by Avery Dennison (Santa self-adhesive), by Ashton-Potter USA Ltd. (Holiday Stocking), and by offset and intaglio by the Bureau of Printing and Engraving (Traditional). Perforated 11 (Nos. 1047 and 1048),10 x 11 (Nos. 1049), and imperforate and die cut (No. 1050).

1047 *Christmas Stocking*

1047 *(2871)*
29c multicolored, tagged
(Oct. 20, 1994) .50 .20
Plate block of four 3.50

1048 *Madonna and Child*

1048 *(2872)*
29c multicolored, tagged .50 .20
Plate block of four 3.50

1049 *Madonna and Child*

1049 *(2892v)*
29c multicolored, single, tagged .50 .20
n. Pane of 20 17.50

1050 *Santa Claus*

1050 *(2873)*
29c multicolored, tagged .50 .20
n. Pane of 12 10.50

1994. Cardinal. This is a self-adhesive stamp in panes of 18 for automated teller machines (ATM). The stamp was issued at the same time and as the Christmas issues, with the design having a decidedly winter motif. *Gravure by Avery. Imperforate and die cut.*

1051 *Cardinal in snow*

1051 *(2874)*
29c multicolored, tagged
(Oct. 20, 1994) .50 .20
n. Pane of 18 14.50

1994. Virginia Apgar Issue, Great Americans Series, honored medical researcher whose simple assessment method allows doctors and nurses in the delivery room to make an immeidate evaluation of a newborn baby's general condition. This process aids in the identification of those infants who need immediate medical attention. *Intaglio by the Banknote Corporation of America, perforated 11.*

1052 *Virginia Apgar*

1052
29c brown, tagged *(Oct. 24, 1994)* .50 .20
Plate block of four 2.50

1994. The Postage and Mail Center (PMC) Issue, with variable denomination, similar to No. 1040, with different type font. Initial release was in Detroit.

1053 *Shield and bunting*

1053
(variable rate) red and blue, denomination
rinted in black, *(Nov. 9, 1994)* .75 .50

1994. The "G" (Old Glory) Non-Denominated Issue is the most prolific of the rate-change issues. A total of 16 items were released, including specific items for first class letter rate, first class presort, postal card rate, coils and booklets, and two types of self-adhesives.

Sheet stamps, overall dimensions 0.84 x 0.99 inches, *gravure*

Printed by Bureau of Engraving and Printing, black "G"

 1054 *Old Glory*

1054 *(2881)*
   (32c) red, blue, gray & black, tagged .50   .20
     Plate block of four   3.50

 1055

Printed by Stamp Venturers, red "G"
1055 *(2882)*
   (32c) red,blue, gray & black, tagged .50   .20
     Plate block of four   3.50

Booklet stamps, overall dimensions 0.87 x 0.96 inches, *gravure.*

 1056

Printed by Bureau of Engraving and Printing, black "G"
1056 *(2883)*
   (32c) red, blue, gray & black, tagged .50   .20
     n. Booklet pane of ten   9.00

 1057

Printed by American Bank Note Co., blue "G"
1057 *(2884)*
   (32c) red, blue, gray & black, tagged .50   .20
     n. Booklet pane of ten   9.00

 1058

Printed by KCS, red "G"
1058 *(2885)*
   (32c) red, blue, gray & black, tagged .50   .20
     n. Booklet pane of ten   9.00

Coil stamps, *printed by gravure.*

 1059

Printed by Bureau of Engraving and Printing, black "G"
1059 *(2889)*
   (32c) red, blue, gray & black, tagged .50   .20
     Pair   1.25

 1060

Printed by American Bank Note Co., blue "G"
1060 *(2890)*
   (32c) red, blue, gray & black, tagged .50   .20
     Pair   1.25

 1061

Printed by Stamp Venturers, red "G"

Perforated 10 vertically
1061 *(2891)*
   (32c) red, blue, gray & black, tagged .50   .20
     Pair   '1.00

 1061A

Rouletted vertically
1061A
   (32c) red, blue gray & black, tagged .50   .20
     Pair   1.00

Self-adhesives, *printed by gravure by Avery Denison, imperforate and die cut.*

 1062

1062 *(2886)*
   (32c) red, dark blue, light blue,
          gray and black, tagged   1.00   .35
     n. Pane of eighteen   17.50

ATM-dispensed sheetlet, self-adhesive, *printed by gravure by Avery Denison, imperforate and die cut.*

 1063

1063 *(2887)*
(32c) red, blue and black, tagged   1.00   .35
    n. Pane of 18   17.50

First Class presort rate. *Gravure by Stamp Venturers.*
Coil stamp, perforated 10 vertically.

First Class presort rate

1064

1064 *(2888)*
(25c) red, dark blue, gray, black
      and light blue   .75   .20
    Pair   1.50

Postcard rate. *Gravure, perforated 11.*

1065

Printed by Bureau of Engraving and Printing, black "G"
1065 *(2879)*
(20c) red, blue, gray, yellow and
      black, tagged   .50   .20
    Plate block of four   3.00

1066

Printed by Stamp Venturers, red "G"
1066 *(2880)*
(20c) red, blue, gray, yellow and
      black, tagged   .50   .20
    Plate block of four   3.00

1994. Non-Denominated "Make-Up" Rate Issue had a
value of three cents, to be used with a 29-cent stamp to
meet the new first class rate. *Offset, perforated 11.*

Make up rate

1067 *Dove*

Printed by American Bank Note Co., *bright blue with thin
lettering.*
1067 *(2877)*
(3c) red, bright blue and tan   .25   .20
    Plate block of four   .50

1068 *Dove*

Printed by Stamp Venturers, *darker blue with thick
lettering.*
1068 *(2878)*
(3c) red, dark blue and tan   .25   .20
    Plate block of four   .50

Non-profit presort rate. *Coil, gravure by American Bank
Note Co., perforated 10 vertically*

1069 *Old Glory and 'Nonprofit Presort'*

1069 *(2893)*
(5c) green and multicolored, untagged
      (Jan. 12, 1995)   .25   .20
    Pair   .30   .25
First-day covers received a Dec. 13, 1994, cancellation
although these stamps were not yet available on that
date.

1995. Non-denominated Service-Inscribed Coils.
Beginning early in 1995, the USPS introduced several
series of coils for use by various mass mailers that
showed the service but no denomination. The additional
cost of the mail service was prepaid directly by the
mailer at the time and post office where the mailing took
place. *Gravure.*

*Printed by J.W. Fergusson & Sons for Stamp Venturers,
perforated 10 vertically.*

1070 *Butte and 'Nonprofit Org.'*

1070 *(2902)*
(5c) yellow, blue and red, untagged
      (March 10, 1995)   .25   .20
    Pair   .30   .25
    v. Imperforate pair   —

*J.W. Fergusson & Sons for Stamp Venturers, serpentine
die cut 11 1/4 vertically.*

1071 *Car Hood and 'Bulk Rate'*

1071 *(2905)*
(10c) black, brown and red brown,
      untagged *(March 17, 1995)*   .30   .20
    Pair   .35   .25

Printed by BEP, serpentine die cut 11 1/2 vertically.

1072 *Tail Fin and 'Presorted First-Class Card'*

1072 *(2908)*
(15c) yellow orange and multicolored,
  untagged *(March 17, 1995)*   .40   .30
  Pair   .50   .35

J.W. Fergusson & Sons for Stamp Venturers, serpentine die cut 11 1/2 vertically

1073 *Tail Fin and 'Presorted First-Class Card'*

1073 *(2909)*
(15c) buff and multicolored, untagged
  (March 17, 1995)   .40   .30
  Pair   .50   .35

1074-75, 1134, 1153 *Juke Box and 'Presorted First-Class'*

Printed by BEP, serpentine die cut 11 1/2 vertically.

1074 *Juke Box and 'Presorted First-Class'*

1074 *(2911)*
(25c) dark red, yellow green and multicolored,
  untagged *(March 17, 1995)*   .65   .40
  Pair   .75   .50

J.W. Fergusson & Sons for Stamp Venturers

1075 *Juke Box and 'Presorted First-Class'*

1075 *(2912)*
**(25c) orange red, bright yellow green and
  multicolored,** untagged
  (March 17, 1995)   .65   .40
  Pair   .75   .50

Avery Dennison, self-adhesive, imperforate (die cut).

1076 *Flag over Field*

1076 *(2919)*
32c multicolored, tagged
  (March 17, 1995)   1.00   .30
  n. Pane of 18   14.50

1995 Transportation Series, Circus Wagon. This was a redesigned gravure version of the earlier coil issued in intaglio (No. 931) and gravure (No. 1007). Coil, intaglio by Stamp Venturers, perforated 9 3/4 vertically.

1077 *Circus Wagon, 1900s*

1077 *(2452D)*
5c red, untagged *(March 20, 1995)*   .25   .20
  Pair   .30
For intaglio and gravure versions of this design inscribed '05 USA' see Nos. 931 and 1007.

1995 Flag over Porch. Self-adhesive booklets. *Gravure by Avery Dennison, serpentine die cut 8 3/4.*

1078, 1080-83 *Flag Over Porch*

1078 *Flag over Porch*

1078 *(2920)*
32c multicolored, phosphred paper,
  large '1995'   1.00   .30
  n. Pane of 20 plus label   17.50
  n1. Pane of 15 plus label
    (various layouts)   —
*(2920b)*a. Small '1995'   2.00   .60
  an. Pane of 20 plus label   38.

1995. Wildlife Series. Redesigned denomination. *Offset by BEP, perforated 11 1/4 x 11.*

1079, 1115 *American Kestrel*

1079 *American Kestrel*

1079 *(2477)*
1c multicolored, untagged
  (May 10, 1995)   .25   .20
  Plate block of four   .30
For version inscribed 'USA 01' see No. 959. For coil see No. 1115.

1995. Flag over Porch. *Gravure by J.W. Fergusson & Sons for Stamp Venturers, perforated 10 1/4 x 10 1/2.*

1080 *Flag over Porch*

1080 *(2897)*
32c multicolored, tagged
  (May 19, 1995)   .70   .20
  Plate block of four   1.75
  v. Imperforate pair   —

1081 *Flag over Porch*

Booklet, gravure by BEP, perforated 11 x 9 3/4.
1081 *(2916)*
32c multicolored, tagged
    (May 19, 1995) .80 .20
  n. Booklet pane of ten 8.00
  nv. Imperforate booklet pane of ten —

1082 *Flag over Porch*

Coil, gravure by BEP, perforated 9 3/4 vertically.
1082 *(2913)*
32c multicolored, tagged, red '1995'
    (May 19, 1995) .50 .20
  Pair 1.00
  v. Imperforate pair —

1083 *Flag over Porch*

Coil, gravure by J.W. Fergusson & Sons for Stamp
Venturers, perforated 9 3/4 vertically.
1083 *(2914)*
32c multicolored, tagged, blue '1995'
    (May 19, 1995) .75 .20
  Pair 1.00
Listings and prices for plate number coil strips and
singles appear at the end of this definitive section of the
Krause-Minkus catalog.

1995. Rose. A new color, denomination and die-cut
format to simulate perforations undated this self-
adhesive booket for use in the 32c rate period. *Gravure*
by J.W. Fergusson & Sons for Stamp Venturers,
serpentine die cut.

1084 *Pink Rose*

1084 *(2492)*
32c pink, green and black, phosphored
    paper *(June 2, 1995)* .80 .30
  n. Booklet pane of 20 plus label 16.
  n1. Booklet pane of 15 plus label 11.
  n2. Booklet pane of 14 11.
  n3. Booklet pane of 16 13.
  v. Imperforate-between
    horizontal pair (no die cut) —

1995. Transportation Series, Ferryboat and Cog
Railroad. Coil, *intaglio, perforated 9 3/4 vertically.*

1085 *Ferryboat 1900s*

1085 *(2466)*
32c deep blue, phosphored paper
    (June 2, 1995) .75 .20
  Pair 1.25
  v. Imperforate pair —

1086 *Cog Railway 1870s*

1086 *(2463)*
20c green, phosphored paper
    (June 9, 1995) .40 .20
  Pair .75
  v. Imperforate pair

1995. Wildlife Issue. Produced in booklet form to pay
the first-class domestic postcard rate. *Gravure by Stamp*
Venturers, perforated 11 x 10 on two or three margins.

1087, 1135-36 Blue Jay

1087 *(2483)*
20c multicolored, phosphored paper
    (June 15, 1995) .45 .20
  n. Booklet pane of ten 6.00

1995. Space Shuttle Challenger Issue. Prepaid the
Priority Mail rate. *Offset and intaglio (panes of 20) by*
Ashton-Potter (USA) Ltd., perforated 11.

1088 *Space Shuttle*
Challenger

1088 *(2544)*
$3.00 multicolored, phosphored paper
    (June 22, 1995) 6.00 3.00
  Plate block of four 25.

1995. Peaches and Pair Issues. Conventional and self-
adhesive booklets.

Gravure by BEP, perforated 11 x 9 3/4.

1089-90 *Peaches*
and Pear

1089 *(2487)*
32c multicolored, phosphored paper
    (July 8, 1995)   .75   .20
1090 *(2488)*
32c multicolored, phosphored paper
    (July 8, 1995)   .75   .20
    y. Se-tenat pair, No. 1089-90 1.50   1.20
    n. Booklet pane of 10 (five each
        Nos. 1089-90)   8.50

Gravure by Avery Dennison, self-adhesive, serpentine die cut.

1091 *Peaches*

1091 *(2493)*
32c multicolored, phosphored paper
    (July 8, 1995)   .85   .30

1092 *Pear*

1092 *(2494)*
32c multicolored, phosphored paper
    (July 8, 1995)   .85   .30
    n. Booklet pane of 20 (10
        each Nos. 1091-92 plus label) 16.

1995. Alice Hamilton Issue paid tribute to a pioneer in industrial medicine, the first woman on the faculty of Harvard University and a socially committed physician who played a key role in documenting and taking steps to prevent lead poisoning in the workplace. Issued to pay two-ounce first-class letter rate. Great Americans series. *Intaglio by Banknote Corporation of America, perforated 11 1/4 x 11.*

1093 *Alice Hamilton*

1093 *(2940)*
55c green, phosphored paper
    (July 11, 1995)   1.10   .20
    Plate block of four   2.50

1995. Space Shuttle Endeavor Issue. Prepaid the basic Express Mail rate. *Offset and intaglio (panes of 20) by Ashton-Potter (USA) Ltd., perforated 11.*

1094 *Space Shuttle
Endeavor*

1094 *(2544A)*
$10.75 multicolored, phosphored paper
    (Aug. 4,1995)   21.   8.00
    Plate block of four   92.50

1995. Alice Paul Issue recognizes a leader in the U.S. movement to extend the right to vote to women (honored at about the same time on a commemorative, CM 1745) and one of the earliest proponents of the Equal Rights Amendment. Issues to pay three-ounce first-class letter rate. Great Americans series. *Intaglio by Banknote Corporation of America, perforated 11 1/4 x 11.*

1095 *Alice Paul*

1095 *(2943)*
78c purple, phosphored paper
    (Aug. 18, 1995)   1.75   .25
    Plate block of four   8.00
    a. Dark violet, shiny gum
        (April, 1996)   1.75   —
        Plate block of four   8.00

1995. Milton S. Hershey Issue celebrates the chocolate manufacturer and philanthropist whose orphans' home, established in 1909, has provided a home and education for generations of disadvantaged boys and girls. Issued to pay basic first-class letter rate. Great Americans series. *Intaglio by Banknote Corporation of America, perforated 11 1/4 x 11.*

1096 *Milton S. Hershey*

1096 *(2933)*
32c chocolate brown, phosphored paper
    (Sept. 13, 1995)   .65   .20
    Plate block of four   3.75

1995. Eddie Rickenbacker Issue honors the racing car driver and automotive and aviation manufacturer who earned his greatest recognition as a flying ace during World War I, in which he shot down 22 enemy aircraft and four observation balloons. Issued to pay the half-ounce rate for letters to foreign nations other than Canada and Mexico - mail typically carried by air, in keeping with the subject of the stamp, but without the 'airmail' designation - no longer needed on such mail, all of which is now typically carried by air. Pioneers of Aviation series. *Gravure by BEP, perforated 11 1/4.*

1097 *Eddie Rickenbacker*

1097 *(2998)*
  60c multicolored, phosphored paper
        (Sept. 25, 1995)   .75   .20
        Plate block of four   6.00

1995. Christmas Issues. The traditional stamp, adapted from an altar panel titled Enthroned Madonna and Child by 14th century Florentine artist Giotto di Bodone, was offered in conventional sheet form and booklet form, supplemented by a striking self-adhesive Midnight Angel design. Contemporary stamps included four Victorian-era designs - two depicting Santa Claus and two portraying children with toys - produced in sheet, booklet and self-adhesive booklet and coil form and a single Children Sledding design in self-adhesive booklet and coil form only.

Offset by Sterling Sommer for Ashton-Potter (USA) Ltd., perforated 11 1/2.

1098 *Santa on Rooftop*
1099 *Child and Jumpingjack*
1100 *Child and tree*
1101 *Santa in workshop*

1098 *(3004)*
  32c multicolored, phosphored paper
        (Sept. 30, 1995)   .60   .20
1099 *(3005)*
  32c multicolored, phosphored paper   .60   .20
1100 *(3006)*
  32c multicolored, phosphored paper   .60   .20
1101 *(3007)*
  32c multicolored, phosphored paper   .60   .20
      y. Se-tenant block or strip of four 3.00
         Plate block of four   3.50
      v. Imperforate block or strip of four
      n. Booklet pane of ten (three
         of Nos 1098-99 and two
         of Nos. 1100-01)   7.50
      n1. Booklet pane of ten (two
         of Nos 1098-99 and three
         of Nos. 1100-01)   7.50

Nos. 1102-05 not assigned.

Gravure for Avery Dennison, serpentine die cut (booklet) and vertical derpentine die cut (coil).

1106 *Santa in Workshop*

1106 *(3010)*
  32c multicolored, phosphored paper
        (Sept. 30, 1995)   .60   .20

1107 *Child and Jumping Jack*

1107 *(3009)*
  32c multicolored, phosphored paper   .60   .20

1108 *Santa on Rooftop*

1108 *(3011)*
  32c multicolored, phosphored paper   .60   .20

1109 *Child and Tree*

1109 *(3008)*
  32c multicolored, phosphored paper   .60   .20
      n. Booklet pane of 20 (Five each of 1106-09
         plus label)
1106A *(3016)*
  32c multicolored, phosphored paper   .60   .20
1107A *(3015)*
  32c multicolored, phosphored paper   .60   .20
1108A *(3017)*
  32c multicolored, phosphored paper   .60   .20
1109A *(3014)*
  32c multicolored, phosphored paper   .60   .20
      y. Coil strip of four (one each of
         Nos. 1106A-09A)   3.00

Offset by Banknote Corporation of America, serpentine die cut (booklet) and vertical serpentine die cut (coil)

1110, 1110A *Midnight Angel*

1110 *(3012)*
  32c multicolored, phosphored paper
        (Oct. 19, 1995)   1.75   .45
      v. Imperforate vertical pair
         (no die cutting between)   —
      n. Booklet pane of 20 plus label   15.

Coil
1110A *(3018)*
  32c multicolored, phosphored paper
        (Oct. 19, 1995)   .75   .45

Listing and prices for plate number coil strips and singles appear at the end of this definitive section of the Krause-Minkus catalog.

Gravure by Avery Dennison, serpentine die cut.

1111 *Children Sledding*

1111 *(3013)*
    32c multicolored, phosphored lacquer on
        surface of stamps
        (Oct. 19, 1995)   .75   .45
      n. Booklet pane of 18   14.

Offset and intaglio by BEP.

1112 *Enthroned Madonna and Child by Giotto*

1112 *(3003)*
    32c multicolored, phosphored paper,
        perforated 11 1/4
        (Oct. 19, 1995)   .75   .20
      Plate block of four   3.50

1113 *Enthroned Madonna and Child by Giotto*

1113 *(3004)*
    32c multicolored, phosphored paper,
        perforated 9 3/4 by 11
        (Oct. 19, 1995)   .75   .20
      n. Booklet pane of ten   7.50

1995. Ruth Benedict Issue celebrates a social anthropologist whose 1934 text, Patterns of Culture, was influential throughtout the world and who fought racism and intolerance through numerous other publications. Issued to pay the half-ounce letter rate to Canada and the ounce letter rate to Mexico. Great American series. *Intaglio by Beep, perforated 11 1/4 x 11.*

1114 *Ruth Benedict*

1114 *(2938)*
    45c carmine, phosphored paper
        (Oct. 20, 1995)   1.00   .25
      Plate block of four   4.75

1996. Wildlife Series. Coil, *offset by BEP, perforated 9 3/4 vertically.*

1115 *American Kestrel*

1115 *(3044)*
    1c multicolored, untagged
        (Jan. 20, 1996)   .25   .20
      Pair   .30
For sheet version see No. 1079. For version inscribed 'USA 01' see No. 959.

1996. Flag over Porch. Self-adhesive booklet with stamps showing '1996' in blue. *Gravure by Avery Dennison, serpentine die cut 11 1/4.*

1116 *Flag over Porch*

1116 *(2920d)*
    32c multicolored, phosphored paper
        (Jan 20, 1996)   .75   .30
      n. Booklet pane of ten   7.50

1996. Unisys Variable Denomination Issue. Vended through Postage and Mail Centers. Coil showing '1996' in red at bottom-left corner of design. *Gravure by BEP, perforated 9 3/4.*

1117 *Shield and Bunting*

1117 *(CVP33)*
    ( ) red and blue, denomination (.20 to $20.00)
        printed in black *(Jan. 26, 1996)* .95   .50

1996. Wildlife Series. *Offset by BEP, perforated 11 1/4 x 11.*

1118 *Red-headed Woodpecker*

1118 *(3032)*
    2c multicolor, untagged *(Feb. 2, 1996)* .25   .20
      Plate block of four   .50

1996. Space Shuttle Challenger Issue. Stamps show '1996' in bottom-left corner. *Offset and intaglio (panes of 20) by Ashton-Potter (USA) Ltd., perforated 11.* No first day.

1119 *Space Shuttle*

1119 *(2544v)*
$3.00 multicolored, phosphored paper
      (March 1996)   6.00   3.00
      Plate block of four   25.

1996. Jacquline Cochran Issue memoralizes the first woman ever to break the sound barrier, a highly skilled pilot who won the Bendix Transcontinental air race in 1938, and founded the Woman's Air Force Serivce Pilots program during World War II. Issued to pay the international postcard rate. Pioneers of Aviation series. *Offset and intaglio by BEP, perforated 11 1/4.*

1120 *Jacquline Cochran*

1120 *(3066)*
50c multicolored, phosphored paper
      (March 9, 1996)   1.20   .40
      Plate block of four   5.00
      v. Intaglio black (inscriptions)
         omitted   —

1996. Non-denominated service-inscribed coils. Coil stamp with small '1996' in purple in bottom-left corner. *Gravure by BEP, perforated 9 3/4.*

1121-22, 1131, 1152. *Mountains*

1121 *Mountains*

1121 *(2903)*
(5c) purple and multicolored, untagged
      (March 16, 1996)   .25   .20

Coil stamp with large '1996' in blue in bottom-left corner. *Gravure by J.W. Fergusson & Sons for Stamp Venturers, perforated 9 3/4.*

1122 *Mountains*

1122 *(2904)*
(5c) blue and multicolored, untagged
      (March 16, 1996)   .25   .20

1996. Wildlife Series. Redesigned denomination. *Offset by BEP, perforated 11 1/4 x 11.*

1123 *Eastern Bluebird*

1123 *(3033)*
3c multicolored, untagged
      (April 3, 1996)   .25   .20
      Plate block of four   .65

1996. Cal Farley Issue recalls the founder of the Cal Farley's Boys Ranch foster home near Amarillo, TX. Issued to pay standard first-class letter rate. Great American series. *Intaglio by Banknote Corporation of America, perforated 11 1/4 x 11.*

1124 *Cal Farley, Humanitarian*

1124 *(2934)*
32c green, phosphored paper
      (April 26, 1996)   .65   .20
      Plate block of four   3.75

1996 Flag over porch. Self-adhesive booklet stamps with small red '1996'. *Gravure by BEP, serpentine dine cut 9 3/4 on two or three sides.*

1125 *(2921)*
32c multicolored, phosphored paper
      (May 21, 1996)   .75   .30
      n. Booklet pane of ten   7.50

Self-adhesive coil stamps with small red '1996'. *Gravure by BEP, serpentine die cut 9 3/4 vertically.*

1126 *Flag over Porch*

1126 *(2915A)*
32c multicolored, phosphored paper
      (May 21, 1996)   1.00   .30

Self-adhesive coil stamps with small red '1996'. *Gravure by BEP, serpentine die cut 11 vertically.*

1127 *Flag over Porch*

1127 *(2915C)*
32c multicolored, phosphored paper
      (May 21, 1996)   1.50   .50

Self-adhesive coil stamps with large blue '1996'. *Gravure by J.W. Fergusson & Sons for Stamp Venturers, serpentine die cut.*

1128 *Eagle and Shield*

1128 *(2915B)*
32c multicolored, phosphored paper
          (June 15, 1996)   .75   .30
     Pair

On this issue, stamps are spaced apart on the 10,000 stamp coil roll.

1996. Eagle and Shield Non-Denominated Issue. Self-adhesive coil with blue '1996'. *Gravure by J.W. Fergusson & Sons for Stamp Venturers, serpentine die cut perforations.*

1129 *Flag over Porch*

1129 *(2907)*
(10c) multicolored, untagged
          (May 21, 1996)   .25   .25

On this issue, stamps are spaced apart on the 10,000 stamp coil roll.

1996. Non-denominated Service-Inscribed Coils. Self-adhesive coils with '1996'. *Gravure by J.W. Fergusson & Sons for Stamp Venturers, serpenting die cut vertically.*

On following issues, stamps are spaced apart on a 10,000 stamp coil roll.

1130 *Butte*

1130 *(2902B)*
(5c) yellow, blue and red, untagged
          (June 15, 1996)   .25   .20

1131 *Mountains*

1131 *(2904A)*
(5c) purple and multicolored, untagged .25   .20

1132 *Auto*

1132 *(2906)*
(10c) black, brown and red brown,
          untagged   .25   .20

1133 *Car Tail Fin*

1133 *(2910)*
(15c) buff and multicolored, untagged .35   .30

1134 *Juke Box*

1134 *(2912A)*
**(25c) orange red, bright yellow green and
          multicolored,** untagged   .60   .30

Listings and prices for plate number coil strips and singles appear at the end of this definitive section of the Krause-Minkus catalog.

1996. Wildlife Issue. Self-adhesive Blue Jay booklets and coils with '1996'. *Gravure by J.W. Fergusson & Sons for Stamp Venturers, serpentine die-cut perforations.*

1135 *Bluebird*

1135 *(3048)*
20c multicolored, phosphored paper
          (Aug. 2, 1996)   .45   .25
     n. Booklet pane of ten   4.50

1136 *Bluebird*

1136 *(3053)*
20c multicolored, phosphored paper
          (Aug. 2, 1996)   .40   .20

1996. Christmas Issues. The traditional stamp, taken from a detail of Adoration of the Shepherds by the 18th century Italian artist Paolo de Matteis, was offered in convential sheets and self-adhesive booklets, supplemented by new stocks of the Midnight Angel stamps that had proven popular the previous year. Contemporary Christmas stamps included se-tenant sheets and self-adhesive booklets of four Christmas Family scenes and a generic Holiday Skater design for sale in ATMs offered in self-adhesive booklets only.

Offset by Ashton-Potter (USA) Ltd., perforated 11 1/4

1137, 1141 *Family at Yule Hearth*

1138, 1142 *Family Trimming Tree*

1139, 1143 *Dreaming of Santa*

1140, 1144 *Christmas Shopping*

1137 *(3108)*
   32c multicolored, phosphored paper
      (Oct. 8, 1996)   .60   .20
1138 *(3109)*
   32c multicolored, phosphored paper .60   .20
1139 *(3110)*
   32c multicolored, phosphored paper .60   .20
1140 *(3111)*
   32c multicolored, phosphored paper .60   .20
     y. Se-tenant block strip of four 3.00
     Plate block of four   3.50

Offset by Banknote Corporation of America, serpentine die cut.

1141 *Family at Yule Hearth*

1141 *(3113)*
   32c multicolored, phosphored paper
      (Oct. 8, 1996)   .60   .20

1142 *Family Trimming Tree*

1142 *(3114)*
   32c multicolored, phosphored paper .60   .20

1143 *Dreaming of Santa*

1143 *(3115)*
   32c multicolored, phosphored paper .60   .20

1144 *Christmas Shopping*

1144 *(3116)*
   32c multicolored, phosphored paper .60   .20
     n. Booklet pane of 20 (five each
       of Nos. 1141-44 plus label) 15.

Gravure by Avery Dennison, imperforate (die cut)

1145 *Holiday Skaters*

1145 *(3117)*
   32c multicolored, phosphored lacquer on
      surface of stamps
      (Oct. 8, 1996)   .75   .30
     n. Booklet pane of 18   14.

Offset and intaglio by BEP, perforated 11 1/4.

1146 *Detail from Adoration of the Shepherds by Matteis*

1146 *(3107)*
   32c multicolored, phosphored paper
      (Nov. 1, 1996)   .70   .20
     Plate block of four   3.50

1147 *Detail from Adoration of the Shepherds by Matteis*

1147 *(3112)*
   32c multicolored, tagged
      (Nov. 1, 1996)   .95   .30
     n. Booklet pane of 20 plus label 15.

1996. Hannukah Issue. For the first time, the USPS released a stamp honoring the Jewish Festival of Lights, a joint issue of the United States and Israel. *Gravure (self-adhesive booklets of 20) by Avery Dennison, serpentine die cut.*

1148 *Hannukah Menorah*

1148 *(3118)*
   32c multicolored, phosphored paper
      (Oct. 22, 1996)   .70   .25
     Plate block of four   3.25
     n1. Booklet of 15   12.
     n2. Pane of 20   14.

1996. Rose. This hardy perennial gained a new lease on life in a new color, issued in self-adhesive form in booklets of three sizes. *Gravure by J.W. Fergusson & Sons for Stamp Venturers, serpentine die cut.*

1149, 1163 *Yellow rose.*

1149 *(3049)*
32c yellow and multicolored, phosphored
    paper *(Oct. 24, 1996)*   .75   .25
  n. Booklet pane of 20 plus label   14.
  n1. Booklet pane of 15 plus label   12.
    (Dec. 1996)
  pn1. Plate number single (bottom-left
    corner of pane)   —
  n2. Booklet pane of 30
    (December 1996)   17.50
  pn2. Plate number single (bottom-right
    corner of pane)   —

1997. Flag over Porch. Self adhesive booklet stamps with red '1997'. G*ravure by BEP, serpentine die cut on two or three sides.*

1150 *Flag over Porch*

1150 *(2921)*
32c multicolored, phosphored paper
    (Jan. 24, 1997)   .75   .30
  n. Booklet pane of five   4.00
  n1. Booklet pane of ten   7.50

Self-adhesive coil stamps with red '1997'. *Gravure by BEP, serpentine die cut vertically.*

1151 *(2915D)*
32c multicolored, phosphored paper
    (Jan. 24, 1997)   .75   .30

1997. Non-denominated Service-Inscribed Coils. Self-adhesive, 3,000 stamp coils of Mountains and Juke Box designs with '1997'. *Gravure by BEP, serpentine die cut vertically.*

1152 *Mountains*

1152 *(2904B)*
(5c) purple and multicolored, untagged
    (Jan. 24, 1997)   .25   .20

1153 *Juke Box*

1153 *(2912B)*
(25c) multicolored, untagged   .60   .20

1997. Statue of Liberty. LRevised denomination version of the 1994 design for use at the 32c first-class domestic letter rate. Self-adhesive booklets. *Gravure by Avery Dennison, serpentine die cut on two or three sides.*

1154 *Statue of Liberty*

1154 *(2902)*
32c multicolored, phosphored paper
    (Feb.1, 1997)   .75   .20
  pn. Plate number single (bottom-left
    corner of booklet pane)   —
  n. Booklet pane of four   275.
  n1. Booklet pane of five plus
    label   350.
  n2. Booklet pane of six   4.00
  n3. Booklet pane of 20   13.

1997. Merian Botanical Prints. Self-adhesive booklet stamps in two distinct sizes and die-cutting guages, based upon two botanical prints made by Anna Maria Sibylla Merian during her 1699-1701 travels in Surinam. *Gravure by Stamp Venturers.*

Design 20x27mm, serpentine die cut 10 3/4 x 10 1/4 on two, three or four sides.

1155 *Citron*   1156 *Flowering*
and insects   *Pineapple*

1155 *(3126)*
32c multicolored, tagged
    (March 3, 1997)   .75   .20
1156 *(3127)*
32c multicolored, tagged   .75   .20
  n. Booklet pane of 20 (10 each Nos.
    1155-56 plus label)   13.

Design 18 1/2 x 24mm, serpentine die cut 11 1/4 x 10 3/4 on two or three sides (Nos. 1157-58) or 11 1/4 x 11 1/4 x 11 1/4 x 10 3/4 (Nos. 1159-60)

1157, 1159.   1158, 1160.
Citron and Insects   *Flowering Pineapple*

1157 *(3128)*
32c multicolored, tagged
    (March 3, 1997)   .75   .20
1158 *(3129)*
32c multicolored, tagged   .75   .20

1159 *(3128a)*
32c multicolored, tagged   1.25   .50
    n. Booklet pane of five (one No.1159
      sideways, two each of
      No. 1157-58)   3.50
1160 *(3129a)*
32c multicolored, tagged *(March 3, 1997)* 1.25   .50
    n. Booklet pane of five (one
      No.1160 sideways, two each
      of No. 1157-58)   3.75

Nos. 1159-60, which are die cut on all four sides, have a single irregular large serration near the middle of the right side created by die cutting.

1997. Non-denomination Service-Inscribed Coils. Self-adhesive 10,000- and 30,000-stamp experimental linerless (no backing paper) coils, *manufactured by 3M Corp. and finished by Stamp Venturers, gravure, imperforate with simulated perforations (black circles) and black bars at top and bottom.*

          1161 *Juke Box with*
              simulated perforations

1161 *(3132)*
(25c) multicolored, untagged
    (March 14, 1997)   .60   .20

1997. Flag over Porch. Self-adhesive 100-stamp experimental linerless (no backing paper) coils, *manufactured by 3M Corp. and finished by Stamp Venturers, gravure, serpentine die cut 10 vertically.*

          1162 *Flag over porch*

1162
32c multicolored, tagged
    (March 14, 1997)   .75   .20

Listings and prices for plate number coil strips and singles appear at the end of this definitive section of the Krause-Minkus catalog.

1997. Rose. Self-adhesive coil. *Gravure by BEP, serpentine die cut vertically.*

        1163 *Rose*

1163
32c yellow and multicolored, tagged
    (Aug. 1, 1997)   .65   .20
    Imperforate coil of 100   —

1997. Christmas Issues. For the first time in several years the Traditional and Contemporary Christmas stamps were issued in moderation. Only one design of each, and in a total of four formats. The Traditional design depicts Sano di Pietro's Madonna and child with saints from the collection of the National Gallery of Art. *Offset by the Bureau of Engraving and Printing,* in self-adhesive panes of 20. The Contemporary design depicts American Holly. *Offset by Banknote Corporation of America* in self-adhesive panes of 20, and self-adhesive booklets of 15 and 30. All with serpentine die-cut perforations.

1164 Sano di Pietro's *Madonna and child with saints*

1164
32c multicolored, tagged, single   .50   .20
    Booklet of 20   8.50
    FDC *(Oct. 27, 1997)*   1.00

        1165 *American Holly*

1165
32c multicolored, tagged, single   .50   .20
    Booklet of 15   6.00
    Booklet of 20   8.50
    Booklet of 30   12.50
    FDC *(Oct. 30, 1997)*   1.00

1997. Mars Pathfinder Issue. This Priority Mail stamp commemorated the Pathfinder's Mission to Mars and the successful landing of July 4, 1997, and the subsequent deployment of the Sojourner rover. The view on the sheetlet is based on one of the first views sent back showing the rover and the Ares Vallis region of Mars. The stamp design incorporates hidden images. *Gravure, Stamp Ventures.*

        1166 *Sojourner rover on*
          Mars surface

1166
$3.00 multicolored, tagged *(15,000,000)* 4.50   2.50
    FDC *(Dec. 10, 1997)*   4.50

Coil Strips

	Strip of 5	3	Single Used
806 *(1897)*			
1c Omnibus (USA 1c)			
Pl# 1,2,5,6	.60	.50	.25
Pl# 3,4	.60	.50	.30
867 *(2225)*			
1c Omnibus (1c USA)			
Pl#1,2	.50	.45	.25
867zxm *(2225a)*			
1c Omnibus, (1c USA) untagged			
Pl# 2,3	.65	.55	.30
867zxs *(2225s)*			
1c Omnibus, (1c USA) shiny gum, tagged			
Pl# 3	6.50	5.00	3.50
(2225sv)			
1c Omnibus, untagged			
Pl# 3	.65	.55	.30
1115 *(3044)*			
1c Kestrel			
Pl# 1111	.55	.50	.25
790 *(1897a)*			
2c Locomotive, (USA 2c)			
Pl# 2,6	.55	.50	.25
Pl# 3,4,8,10	.60	.55	.30
873 *(2226)*			
2c Locomotive, (2c USA)			
Pl# 1	.75	.60	.35
(2226a)			
2c Locomotive, untagged			
Pl# 2	.75	.60	.35
800 *(1898)*			
3c Handcar			
Pl# 1,2,3,4	.70	.60	.35
883 *(2252)*			
3c Conestoga Wagon			
Pl# 1	.85	.75	.40
883zxm *(2252a)*			
3c Conestoga Wagon, untagged, matt gum			
Pl# 2,3	1.00	.90	.50
883zxs *(2252b)*			
3c Conestoga Wagon, shiny gum			
Pl# 3	1.25	1.00	.65
Pl# 6	2.00	1.50	1.00
843 *(2123)*			
3.4c School Bus			
Pl# 1,2	.85	.75	.45
843z *(2123a)*			
3.4c School Bus, Nonprofit Org.			
Pl# 1,2	4.75	4.50	2.50
791 *(1898A)*			
4c Stagecoach, title 19 1/5mm long			
Pl# 1,2,3,4	1.00	.95	.50
Pl# 5,6	1.80	1.70	.80
791z *(1898Ab)*			
4c Stagecoach, Nonprofit Org.			
Pl# 3,4,5,6	5.00	4.75	2.25
868 *(2228)*			
4c Stagecoach, title 17mm long			
Pl# 1	1.50	1.40	.75
868z1 *(2228a)*			
4c Stagecoach, overall tagging			
Pl# 1	11.	10.	5.00
943 *(2451)*			
4c Steam Carriage			
Pl# 1	.95	.80	.55
943zx *(2451b)*			
4c Steam Carriage, untagged			
Pl# 1 untagged	1.00	.80	.50
846 *(2124)*			
4.9c Buckboard			
Pl# 3,4	.90	.70	.45
846z *(2124a)*			
4.9c Buckboard, Nonprofit Org.			
Pl# 1,2,3,4,5,6	1.30	1.20	.60
808 *(1899)*			
5c Motorcycle			
Pl# 1,2,3,4	.95	.80	.45
879 *(2253)*			
5c Milk Wagon			
Pl# 1	1.00	.80	.50
931 *(2452)*			
5c Circus Wagon, Intaglio			
Pl# 1	1.25	1.00	.65
931z *(2452a)*			
5c Circus Wagon, untagged			
Pl# 1	1.25	1.00	.65
1007 *(2452B)*			
5c Circus Wagon, Gravure			
Pl# A1,A2	1.50	1.25	.75
Pl# A3, Hi-Brite paper	1.50	1.25	.75
1077 *(2452D)*			
5c Circus Wagon (c sign)			
Pl# S1,S2	1.50	1.25	.75
955 *(2453)*			
5c Canoe, Brown, Intaglio			
Pl# 1,2,3	1.50	1.25	.75
979 *(2454)*			
5c Canoe, Red, Gravure			
Pl# S11	1.50	1.25	.75
1030 *(2893)*			
(5c) "G" Butte, Non-Profit			
Pl# A11111,A21111	1.50	2.00	.75
1170 *(2902)*			
(5c) Butte (1995)			
Pl# S111	1.75	1.50	.90

1121 *(2903)*
(5c) Mountain, BEP
Pl# 11111 ..... 2.25 2.00 1.00
1122 *(2904)*
(5c) Mountain, SVS
Pl# S111 ..... 2.25 2.00 1.00
799 *(1900)*
5.2c Sleigh
Pl# 1,2 ..... 10.75 5.50 5.00
Pl# 3,5 ..... 225. 175. 100.
799zx *(1900a)*
5.2c Sleigh, precancel
Pl# 1,2,3,4,5,6 ..... 15. 14. 7.50
906 *(2254)*
5.3c Elevator
Pl#1 ..... 12.50 2.00 6.00
865 *(2125)*
5.5c Star Route Truck
Pl# 1 ..... 2.00 1.50 1.00
865zx *(2125a)*
5.5c Star Route Truck, Nonprofit Org.
Pl# 1,2 ..... 2.00 1.50 1.00
787 *(1901)*
5.9c Bicycle
Pl# 3,4 ..... 20. 7.50 10.
787z *(1901a)*
5.9c Bicycle, precancel
Pl# 3,4 ..... 40. 39. 20.
Pl# 5,6 ..... 90. 85. 45.
841 *(2126)*
6c Tricycle
Pl# 1 ..... 2.00 1.50 1.00
841z *(2126a)*
6c Tricycle, Nonprofit Org.
Pl# 1 ..... 2.25 1.75 2.25
Pl# 2 ..... 8.75 8.00 4.50
870 *(2127)*
7.1c Tractor
Pl# 1 ..... 3.00 2.50 1.50
870z *(2127a)*
7.1c Tractor, Nonprofit Org.
Pl# 1 ..... 4.00 3.50 2.00
870zt *(2127av)*
7.1c Tractor, Zip + 4
Pl# 1 ..... 2.75 2.25 2.75
814 *(1902)*
7.4c Baby Buggy
Pl# 2 ..... 13. 7.50 7.00
814zx *(1902a)*
7.4c Baby Buggy, Blk. Rt. Car. Rt. Sort
Pl# 2 ..... 6.50 6.00 3.25
903 *(2255)*
7.6c Carreta
Pl# 1,2 ..... 3.00 2.50 3.00
Pl# 3 ..... 6.50 6.00 3.00
845 *(2128)*
8.3c Ambulance, title 18 1/2mm long
Pl# 1,2 ..... 2.00 1.50 1.00
845z *(2128a)*
8.3c Ambulance, Blk. Rt.
Pl# 1,2 ..... 2.00 1.50 1.00

Pl# 3,4 ..... 6.50 5.50 6.50
845A *(2231)*
8.3c Ambulance, title 18mm long
Pl# 1 ..... 7.50 6.50 7.50
Pl# 2 ..... 10. 8.00 5.00
901 *(2256)*
8.4c Wheel Chair
Pl# 1,2 ..... 2.50 2.00 1.25
Pl# 3 ..... 15. 14. 7.50
869 *(2129)*
8.5c Tow Truck
Pl# 1 ..... 4.00 3.50 2.00
869z *(2129a)*
8.5c Tow Truck, Nonprofit Org.
Pl# 1 ..... 3.75 3.25 1.50
Pl# 2 ..... 14. 13. 7.00
778 *(1903)*
9.3c Mail Truck
Pl# 1,2 ..... 18. 6.75 9.00
Pl# 3,4 ..... 45. 38. 22.50
Pl# 5,6 ..... 260. 335. 120.
778zx *(1903a)*
9.3c Mail Truck
Pl#1,2 ..... 17. 15. 8.50
Pl# 3 ..... 40. 35. 20.
Pl# 4 ..... 25. 23. 10.
Pl# 5,6 ..... 4.50 3.75 2.50
Pl# 8 ..... 185. 200. 100.
874 *(2257)*
10c Canal Boat
Pl# 1 ..... 2.25 2.00 1.00
874z1*(2257a)*
10c Canal Boat, overall tagging
Pl# 1,2 ..... 4.00 3.50 2.00
874pz *(2257ad)*
10c Canal Boat, overall tagging, matt gum
Pl# 1, ... 6.25 5.75 3.00
954 *(2457)*
10c Tractor Trailer, Intaglio
Pl# 1 ..... 3.00 2.50 1.50
1042 *(2458)*
10c Tractor Trailer, Gravure
Pl# 11 ..... 8.00 7.50 4.00
Pl# 22 ..... 2.75 2.25 1.50
980 *(2602)*
(10c) Eagle & Shield
A11111,A11112,A21112,A22112,
 A22113,A33333,A43334
 A43335,A53335 ..... 2.75 2.25 1.50
A12213 ..... 28. 25. 14.
A21113,A33335,A43324,A43325,
 A43326,A43426,A54444,
 A54445 ..... 3.25 2.75 1.50
A34424,A34426 ..... 6.50 5.75 3.00
A32333 ..... 240. - 125.
A33334 ..... 85. - 45.
A77777,A88888,A88889,A89999
 A99998,A99999 ..... 3.00 2.50 1.50
A1010101010,A1110101010,
 A1011101011,etc. 4.00 3.00 2.00
A111010101011 ..... 14. 13. 7.00

1011 *(2603)*
(10c) Eagle & Shield, BEP
  Pl# 11111,22221,22222   2.75   2.50   1.50
(2603v)
(10c) Eagle & Shield, matt gum
  Pl# 22222,33333   4.25   3.50   2.50
(2603b)
(10c) Eagle & Shield, tagged
  Pl# 11111,22221   17.   16.   8.50
1012 *(2604)*
(10c) Eagle & Shield, SVS
  Pl# S11111,S22222   3.75   3.25   2.00
1071 *(2905)*
(10c) Automobile Hood, Bulk rate
  Pl# S111,S222,S333   3.00   2.50   1.50
837 *(2130)*
10.1c Oil Wagon
  Pl# 1   3.25   2.50   1.50
837zx *(2130av)*
10.1c Oil Wagon, Black precancel
  Pl# 1,2   3.25   2.75   1.50
837zx1 *(2130av)*
10.1c Oil Wagon, Red precancel
  Pl# 2,3   4.75   4.25   2.50
788 *(1904)*
10.9c Hansom Cab
  Pl# 1,2   43.   11.   20.
  (1904a) Pl# 1,2   40.   38.   20.
  Pl# 3,4   365.   325.   150.
812 *(1905)*
11c Caboose
  Pl# 1   5.25   3.50   2.50
812x1 *(1905a)*
11c Caboose, untagged
  Pl# 1   4.75   4.25   2.00
812zx *(1905a)*
11c Caboose, untagged, precancel
  Pl# 2   3.25   2.75   1.50
844 *(2131)*
11c Stutz Bearcat
  Pl# 1,2,3,4   2.00   1.50   1.00
831 *(2132)*
12c Stanley Steamer, title 18mm long, tagged
  Pl# 1,2   3.00   2.50   1.50
831zx *(2132a)*
12c Stanley Steamer, untagged
  Pl# 1,2   3.00   2.50   1.50
831A *(2132b)*
12c Stanley Steamer, title 17 1/2mm long
  Pl# 1   30.   28.   15.
838 *(2133)*
12.5c Pushcart
  Pl# 1,2   3.50   2.75   1.50
  (2133a) Pl# 1,2   3.50   3.00   1.50
914 *(2258)*
13c Patrol Wagon
  Pl# 1   5.00   4.25   2.50
900 *(2259)*
13.2c Coal Car
  Pl# 1,2,3,4   3.75   3.00   1.50
827 *(2134)*

14c Iceboat, overall tagged
  Pl# 1,2,3,4   2.75   2.25   1.50
827A *(2134b)*
14c Iceboat, block tagged
  Pl# 2   5.00   4.25   2.50
899 *(2260)*
15c Tugboat, block tagged
  Pl# 1,2   3.25   2.50   1.50
899zl *(2260a)*
15c Tugboat, overall tagged
  Pl# 2   5.00   4.25   2.50
1072 *(2908)*
(15c) Auto Tail Fin, BEP
  Pl# S11111   4.50   3.75   2.00
1073 *(2909)*
(15c) Auto Tail Fin, SVS
  Pl# S11111   3.75   3.00   1.50
898 *(2261)*
16.7c Popcorn Wagon
  Pl# 1,2   3.75   3.25   1.50
771 *(1906)*
17c Electric Car
  Pl# 1,2,3,4,5   2.75   1.75   1.25
  Pl# 6   19.   18.   6.50
  Pl# 7   7.50   6.25   3.50
771zx1 *(1906a)*
17c Electric Car, precancel 11 1/2mm long
  Pl# 3A,4A,5A   4.75   8.75   2.25
  Pl# 6A,7A   20.   17.   10.
771zx2 *(1906ab)*
17c Electric Car, precancel 12 1/2mm long
  Pl# 3B,4B   32.   30.   16.
  Pl# 5B,6B   36.   34.   18.
771zx3 *(1906ac)*
17c Electric Car, precancel 13 1/2mm long
  Pl#1C,2C,3C,4C   15.   13.   7.50
  Pl# 5C,7C   38.   35.   15.
859 *(2135)*
17c Dog Sled
  Pl# 2   4.25   3.00   2.00
880 *(2262)*
17.5c Racing Car
  Pl# 1   5.00   4.25   2.50
880zx *(2262a)*
17.5c Racing Car, Zip+4 Presort
  Pl# 1   5.50   4.75   2.50
(1891)
18c Flag
  Pl#1   345.   85.   150.
  Pl# 2   50.   25.   25.
  Pl# 3   840.   225.   100.
  Pl# 4   10.   6.00   5.00
  Pl# 5   6.75   6.00   3.50
  Pl# 6   3,500.   -   -
  Pl# 7   38.   33.   20.
768 *(1907)*
18c Surrey
  Pl# 1   85.   100.   40.
  Pl# 2,5,6,8   3.50   2.25   1.75
  Pl# 3,4   70.   65.   35.
  Pl# 7   40.   35.   20.

Pl# 9,10,15	14.	10.	7.50
Pl# 11,12,15,16	16.	15.	8.00
Pl# 13,14,17,18	8.75	6.50	4.00

852 *(2149)*
18c George Washington & Monument

Pl# 1112,3333	3.75	2.75	1.75
(2149a) Pl# 11121,33333	4.25	3.50	2.25

852zm *(2149b)*
18c George Washington & Monument, dry gum

Pl# 33333	5.50	4.75	2.50
Pl# 43444	12.	10.	6.00

965 *(2529)*
19c Fishing Boat, Type I

Pl# A1111,A1212,A2424	4.50	3.75	2.25
Pl# A1112	15.	14.	7.50

965a *(2529a)*
19c Fishing Boat, Type II, Gravure

Pl# A5555,A5556,A6667,A7667			
A7679,A7766,A7779	4.50	4.75	2.25

965z *(2529b)*
19c Fishing Boat, Type II, untagged

Pl# A5555	13.	10.	7.50

1044 *(2529C)*
19c Fishing Boat, Type III

Pl# S111	6.00	5.00	3.00

780 *(1895)*
20c Flag over Supreme Court

Pl# 1	100.	8.50	4.00
Pl# 2,11,12	10.	7.50	3.50
Pl# 3,5,9,10,13,14	5.25	2.75	1.75
Pl# 4	600.	35.	10.
Pl# 6	185.	90.	45
Pl# 8	15.	7.50	7.50

780zx *(1895e)*
20c Flag over Supreme Court, precancel

Pl# 14	8.00	5.00	4.00

777 *(1908)*
20c Fire Pumper

Pl# 1	175.	33.	17.50
Pl# 2	950.	160.	80.
Pl# 3,4,13,15,16	5.25	3.00	3.00
Pl# 5,9,10	3.50	2.25	1.75
Pl# 6	43.	35.	20.
Pl# 7,8	165.	110.	85.
Pl# 11	80.	40.	40.
Pl# 12,14	8.00	5.00	4.00

789 *(2005)*
20c Consumer Education

Pl# 1,2	175.	30.	85.
Pl# 3,4	135.	25.	65.

913 *(2263)*
20c Cable Car, block tagged

Pl# 1,2	4.25	3.50	2.50

913zl *(2263b)*
20c Cable Car, overall tagged

Pl# 2	7.50	6.00	3.50

1086 *(2463)*
20c Cog Railway

Pl# 1,2	5.50	4.75	3.00

907 *(2264)*
20.5c Fire Engine

Pl# 1	4.75	4.00	2.50

902 *(2265)*
21c Railroad Mail Car

Pl# 1,2	5.00	4.00	2.50

849 *(2150)*
21.1c Envelopes

Pl# 111111	4.75	3.50	2.50
Pl# 111121	5.75	4.25	2.75

849z *(2150a)*
21.1c Envelopes, Zip+4

Pl# 111111	5.50	4.50	2.75
Pl# 111121	6.25	5.00	3.00

821 *(2112)*
(22c) "D" Series, Eagle

Pl# 1,2	10.	6.50	5.00

829 *(2115)*
22c Flag over Capitol

Pl# 1	14.	10.	7.50
Pl# 2,8,10,12	4.00	3.00	2.00
Pl# 3	55.	15.	25.
Pl# 4,5,6,11	7.50	6.00	3.50
Pl# 7,13	15.	13.	7.50
Pl# 14	35.	30.	16.
Pl# 15,19,22	4.00	3.00	2.00
Pl# 16,17,18,20,21	8.75	7.50	4.00

876 *(2115b)*
22c Flag over Capitol Test Coil

Pl# T1	5.50	4.25	2.50

949 *(2464)*
23c Lunch Wagon, tagged, matt gum

Pl# 2,3	4.50	3.75	2.00

949zm *(2474p)*
23c Lunch Wagon, prephosphored, matt gum

Pl# 3	6.75	5.75	3.00

949zs *(2464ps)*
23c Lunch Wagon, prephosphored, shiny gum

Pl# 3	6.75	5.75	3.00

969 *(2605)*
23c Flag, Pre-sorted First Class

Pl# A111,A212,A222 (Thick)	4.75	3.75	2.25
Pl# A112,A122,A333,			
A222(Thin)	5.25	4.25	2.50

985 *(2606)*
23c USA, Pre-sorted First Class, ABNCo.

Pl# A1111,A2222,A2232,A2233,			
A3333,A4443,A4444,			
A4453,A4364	4.75	3.75	2.50

994 *(2607)*
23c USA, Pre-sorted First Class, BEP

Pl# 1111	6.00	5.00	3.00

994m *(2697v)*
23c USA, Pre-sorted First Class, matt gum

#1111	6.25	5.25	3.00

1010 *(2608)*
23c USA, Pre-sorted First Class, SVS

Pl# S1111	6.50	5.50	3.00

912 *(2266)*
24.1c Tandem Bicycle

Pl# 1	5.75	4.75	2.75

866 *(2136)*
25c Bread Wagon

Pl# 1,2,3,4,5	4.75	3.25	2.50

885 *(2279)*
(25c) "E" Series, Earth

Pl# 1111,1222	4.50	3.50	2.00
Pl# 1211	6.00	5.00	3.00
Pl# 2222	7.50	6.50	3.00

891 *(2280)*
25c Flag over Yosemite, block tagged

Pl# 1,7	8.50	7.50	4.00
Pl# 2,3,4,5,8	4.25	3.50	2.00
Pl# 9	14.	13.	7.00

891pzv *(2280v)*
25c Flag over Yosemite, phosphored tagged

Pl# 1	55.	53.	20.
Pl# 2,3,7,8,9,10,11,13,14	4.25	3.50	2.00
Pl# 5,15	8.50	7.50	4.00
Pl# 6	16.	14.	8.00

905 *(2281)*
25c Honeybee

Pl# 1,2	4.50	3.25	2.00

1064 *(2888)*
(25c) "G" Series, Old Glory

Pl# S11111	7.00	6.00	3.50

1075 *(2911)*
(25c) Juke Box, BEP

Pl# 111111,212222,222222, 332222	6.25	5.25	3.00

1075 *(2912)*
(25c) Juke Box, SVS

Pl# S11111,S22222	5.25	4.25	2.50

940 *(2518)*
(29c) "F" Series, Tulip flower

Pl# 1111,1222,2222	4.75	3.50	2.50
Pl# 1211	25.	23.	11.
Pl# 2211	7.50	6.25	3.50

945 *(2523)*
29c Flag over Mt. Rushmore, Intaglio

Pl# 1,2,3,4,5,6,7	4.75	3.50	2.50
Pl# 8	7.50	6.25	3.50
Pl# 9	15.	14.	7.50

963 *(2523A)*
29c Flag over Mt. Rushmore, Gravure

Pl# A11111,A22211	5.75	4.50	3.00

966 *(2525)*
29c Tulip flower, rouletted

Pl# S1111,S2222	5.50	4.25	2.50

982 *(2526)*
29c Tulip flower, perforated

Pl# S2222	5.50	4.25	2.50

984 *(2609)*
29c Flag over White House

Pl# 1,2,3,4,5,6,7,8	5.50	4.25	2.50
Pl# 9,10,11,12,13,14,15,16,18	6.75	5.50	3.50

1059 *(2889)*
(32c) Black "G" Series, Old Glory

Pl# 1111,2222	8.75	7.50	4.50

1060 *(2890)*
(32c) Blue "G" Series, Old Glory

Pl# A1111,A1112,A1113,A1211,A1212
A1211,A1313,A1314,A1324,
A1417,A1344,A2211,A2212,
A2213,A2214,A2223,A3113,

A3314,A3315,A3323,A3324,
A3423,A3433,A3435,A3436,
A4426,A4427,A5327,A5417,

A5427,A5437	6.50	5.25	3.25
Pl# A1222,A3114,A3426	9.00	7.75	4.50
Pl# A4435	170.	165.	85.

1061 *(2891)*
(32c) Red "G" Series, Old Glory

Pl# S1111	6.50	5.25	3.00

1061A *(2892)*
(32c) "G" Series, Old Glory, rouletted

Pl# S1111,S2222	8.00	6.50	4.00

1085 *(2466)*
32c Ferry Boat, shiny gum

Pl# 2,3,4,5	8.00	6.75	4.00

(2466v)
32c Ferry Boat, low gloss gum

Pl# 3,5	8.00	6.75	4.00
Pl# 4	22.	20.	11.

1082 *(2913)*
32c Flag over Porch, BEP

Pl# 11111,22222,33333,44444,45444, 66646, 66666,77767,78767, 99999	6.25	5.25	3.00
Pl# 22322	50.	48.	25.

(2913a)
32c Flag over Porch, matt gum

Pl# 11111,22221,22222	6.25	5.25	3.00

1083 *(2914)*
32c Flag over Porch, SVS

Pl# S11111	5.75	4.75	2.50

928 *(2468)*
$1 Seaplane, dull gum

Pl# 1	14.	10.	7.50

(2468s)
$1 Seaplane, shiny gum

Pl# 3	14.	10.	7.00

(O135)
20c Official

Pl# 3	85.	15.	10.

(O139)
(22c) "D" Official

Pl# 1	90.	48.	15.

Variable-Denomination Coils

986 *(CV31)*
29c Shield, horizontal, matt gum

Pl# 1	11.	10.	5.00

986a *(CV31a)*
29c Shield, horizontal, shiny gum

Pl# 1	11.	10.	5.00

(CV31b)
32c Shield, horizontal, matt gum

Pl# 1	15.	13.	7.50

(CV31c)

32c Shield, horizontal, shiny gum
Pl# 1   14.   12.   7.00
1040 *(CV32)*
29c Shield, vertical design
Pl# A11   10.   8.75   5.00
1117 *(CV33)*
32c Shield, vertical design
Pl# 11   10.   8.75   5.00

Self-Adhesive Plate Number Strips

1130 *(2902B)*
(5c) Butte
Pl# S111   2.00   1.75   1.00
1131 *(2904A)*
(5c) Mountain, perforated 11 1/2
Pl# V222222,V333323,V333333,
     V333342,V333343   2.00   1.75   1.00
(2904B)
(5c) Mountain, perforated 10
Pl# 1111   2.00   1.75   1.00
(2906)
(10c) Eagle & Shield
Pl# S111   3.00   2.75   1.50
1132 *(2907)*
(10c) Automobile
Pl# S11111   3.00   2.75   1.50
1133 *(2910)*
(15c) Auto Tail Fin
Pl# S11111   3.50   3.00   1.75
1134 *(2912A)*
(25c) Juke Box, perforated 11 1/2
Pl# S11111   5.00   4.50   2.50
(2912B)
(25c) Juke Box, perforated 10
Pl# 111111   5.00   4.50   2.50
(2915)
32c Flag over Porch, perforated 9
Pl# V11111   8.00   6.75   4.00
(2491v)
29c Pine Cone
Pl# B1   8.00   6.75   4.00
(2492v)
32c Pink Rose
Pl# 5111   7.50   6.00   3.50
(2495-96v)
32c Peach & Pear
Pl# V11111   7.50   6.00   3.50
(2598v)
29c Eagle & Shield
Pl# 111   8.00   6.75   4.00
(2599v)

29c Statue of Liberty
Pl# D1111   8.00   6.75   4.00
(2799-2802v)
29c Christmas
Pl# V1111111   11.   10.   5.00
(2813v)
29c Love
Pl# B1   8.00   6.75   4.00
1050 *(2873v)*
29c Santa Claus
Pl# V1111   8.25   7.50   4.00
(2886v)
(32c) "G" Series
Pl# V11111   8.25   7.50   4.00
1126 *(2915A)*
32c Flag over Porch, perforated 9 3/4
Pl# 66666,78777,87888,87898,
     88888,89878,89888,
     97898,99899,99999   9.00   7.50   4.50
1128 *(2915B)*
32c Flag over Porch, perforated 11 1/2
Pl# S11111   8.00   6.75   4.00
(2915C)
32c Flag over Porch, perforated 11
Pl# 55555,66666   8.00   6.75   2.00
(2915D)
32c Flag over Porch, perforated 10,
     stamps seperate
Pl# 1111   8.00   6.75   2.00
(3014-17)
32c Santa & Children
Pl# V1111   8.00   7.50   2.00
1110A *(3018)*
32c Midnight Angel
Pl# B1111   7.50   5.75   2.00
(3053)
20c Blue Jay
Pl# S1111   4.75   4.00   2.50
1161 *(3132)*
(25c) Juke Box, Linerless
Pl# M11111   5.00   4.00   2.50
1162 *(3133)*
32c Flags over Porch, Linerless
Pl# M11111   5.50   4.25   2.75

Self-Adhesive Panes and Booklets

924 *(2431a)*
25c Eagle & Shield (18)
Pl# A1111   11.
929 *(2475a)*
25c Flag, Plastic (12)   6.00
1014 *(2489a)* **29c Red Squirrel** (18)
Pl# D11111,D22211,D22221,
     D22222,D23133   10.
1016 *(2490a)*
29c Rose (18)
Pl# S111   10.
1038 *(2491A)*
29c Pine Cone (18)

Pl# B1   18.
Pl# B2,3,4,5,6,7,8,9,10,11,13,14,15,16   11.
Pl# B12   14.
(2492a)

32c Pink Rose (20)
Pl# S111,S112,S333   12.
(2492r)

32c Pink Rose, Die-Cut "Time to Reorder"
Pl# S444   12.

1091-92 *(2429a)*

32c Peach & Pear (20)
PL# V11111,V11122,V11132,V12131,
   V12132,V12211,V12221,V22212,
   V22221,V22222,V33142,V33143,
   V33243,V33333,V33353,V33343,
   V33353,V33363,V44424,V44434,
   V44454,V45434,V45464,V54365,
   V54565,V55365,V55565   12.
V11131,V12131,V12232   18.
V11232   250.
V33323   20.

942 *(2522a)*

(29c) "F" Flag (12)   6.50

962n *(2531Ab)*

29c Statue of Liberty Torch (18)   11.

962nv *(2531Av)*

29c Statue of Liberty Torch,
   revised back   11.

992 *(2595a)*

29c Eagle, Brown text (17)
Pl# B1111-1,B1111-2,B3434-1,B4344-1,
   B4444-1,B4444-3   13.
Pl# B2222-1,B2222-2,B3333-1,
   B3333-3,B3434-3   13.
Pl#4344-3   225.

990 *(2596a)*

29c Eagle, Green text (17)
Pl# D11111,D21221,D22322,D32322,
   D54573,D65784   10.
PL#D54561,D54563   14.
Pl#D43352,D43452,D43453,
   D54571,D32342,D61384   18.

988 *(2597a)*

29c Eagle, Red text (17)
Pl# S1111   10.

1039 *(2598a)*

29c Eagle (18)
Pl# M1111,M1112   10.50

1043 *(2599a)*

29c Statue of Liberty (18)
Pl# D1111,D1212   10.50
(2719a)

29c Locomotive (18)
Pl# V11111   10.

1029-32 *(2802a)*

29c Christmas (12)
Pl# V111-1111,V222-1222,V222-2112,
   V222-2122,V222-2221,V222-2222   7.50
V333-3333   8.50

1037 *(2803a)*

29c Snowman (18)

Pl# V11111   10.
Pl# V22222   12.
(2813a)

29c Love & Sunrise (18)
Pl# B111-1, B111-2,B111-3,B111-4,
   B222-4,B222-5,B222-6,B333-9,
   B333-10,B333-11,B333-12,
   B333-17,B344-12,B344-13,
   B444-7,B444-8,B444-9,B444-10,
   B444-13, B444-14,B444-15,
   B444-17,B444-18,B444-19,
   B555-20, B555-21   11.
Pl#B111-5   115.
Pl#B121-5,B221-5   12.
Pl#B333-5,B333-7,B333-8   18.
Pl#B333-14   90.
Pl#B334-11   750.
Pl#B344-11   50.
Pl#B434-10   120.
Pl# B444-16   13.

1050 *(2873a)*

29c Santa Claus (12)
Pl# V1111   6.50

1051 *(2874a)*

29c Cardinal in Snow (18)
Pl# V1111,V2222   11.

1062 *(2886a)*

(32c) "G" Surface (18)
Pl# V11111,V22222   11.

1063 *(2887a)*

(32c) "G" Overall (18)
No Plate Number   11.

1076 *(2919a)*

32c Flag over Field (18)
Pl#V1111   11.

1078 *(2920a)*

32c Flag over Porch, large 1995 (20)
Pl#V12211,V12212,V12312,V12321,
   V12322,V12331,V13322,V13831,
   V13834,V13836,V22211,V23322,
   V23422,V23432,V34743,V34745,
   V36745,V42556,V45554,V56663,
   V56665,V56763,V65976,V78989   12.

1078 *(2920c)*

32c Flag over Porch, small 1995 (20)
Pl# V11111

1078 *(2920e)*

32c Flag over Porch, perforated 11 1/4 (10)
Pl#V11111,V12111,V23222,V31121,
   V32111,V32121,V44444,V55555,
   V66666,V66886,V67886,V76989,
   V77666,V77668,V77776,V78698,
   V78898   7.00
Pl#44322   10.

1078 *(2920f)*

32c Flag over Porch, (15)
BK226A $4.80 (1 Pane)   10.
BK227 $9.60 (2 Panes)   11.
(2921a)

32c Flag over Porch, perforated 10 (10)
Pl# P21221   9.00

BK228A $6.40 (2 Panes)   22.
(2921b)

32c Flag over Porch (5) No#   4.00
BK227A $4.80,#2921a(1),
2921b(1) Pl# 11111   12.
BK228A $9.60,#2921a(2),
2921b(2) Pl# 11111   22.

CM1695 *(2949a)*
(32c) Love & Cherub (20)
Pl# B1111-1,B2222-1,B2222-2,B3333-2   11.50

CM1706 *(2960a)*
55c Love Cherub (20)
Pl# B1111-1, B2222-1   17.

1101n *(3011a)*
32c Santa & Children (20)
Pl# V1111,V1211,V3233,V3333,V4444   11.
Pl#V1212   20.

1110n *(3012a)*
32c Midnight Angel (20)
Pl# B1111,B2222   11.
(3012c)
32c Midnight Angel (15)
BK233A $4.80 (1)   11.
BK233B $9.60 (2 Panes)   22.

1111 *(3013a)*
32c Children Sledding (20)
Pl# V1111   11.

CM1798n *(3030a)*
32c Love Cherub (20)
Pl# B1111-1,B1111-2,B2222-1,B2222-2   12.

CM1798n1 *(3030b)*
32c Love Cherub (15)
BK235 $4.80 (1 Pane)   12.
BK236 $9.60 (2 Panes)   22.

1135 *(3048a)*
20c Blue Jay (10)
Pl#S11111,S22222   5.00

1149n *(3049a)*
32c Yellow Rose (20)
Pl# S1111,S2222   12.
(3049b)
32c Yellow Rose (4) No #   3.00
(3049c)
32c Yellow Rose (5)
Pl# S1111   3.50
(3049d)
32c Yellow Rose (6) No #   4.50
BK241 $4.80
(1 ea. #3049b,c,d)   11.
BK242 $9.60 (5 #3049d)   21.

CM1830 *(3071a)*
32c Tennessee (20)
Pl# S11111   11.
(3089a)
32c Iowa (20)   11.

1147 *(3112a)*
32c Madonna (20)
Pl#1111-1,1211-1,2212-1,2222-1,2323-1,
3333-1,3334-1,4444-1,5556-2,
5656-2,6666-2,6766-1,7887-1,
7887-2,7888-2,7988-2,   12.

Pl#5544-1   60.
Pl#5555-1,5556-1,6656-2   25.
Pl#3323-1,6666-1   20.

1144n *(3116a)*
32c Family Scenes (20)
Pl# B1111,B2222,B3333   12.

1145 *(3117a)*
32c Skaters (18)
Pl# V1111   12.

1154 *(3122a)*
32c Liberty & Torch (20)
Pl# V1111,V1211,V2122,V2222   3.00

1154n *(3122b)*
32c Liberty (4) No #   3.50

1154n1 *(3122c)*
32c Liberty (5)
Pl# V1111   4.00

1154n2 *(3122d)*
32c Liberty (6) No #
BK259 $4.80 (1 ea. #3122b,c,d)   10.
BK260 $9.60 (5 #3122d)   20.

CM1884 *(3123a)*
32c Love & Swans (20)
Pl# B1111,B2222,B3333,B4444,
B5555   12.

CM1885 *(3124a)*
55c Love & Swans (20)
Pl# B1111,B2222,B3333,B4444   17.

1156n *(3127c)*
32c Merian Botanical Prints (20)
Pl# S11111,S22222   17.
Pl#S33333   12.

1159-60 *(3128b)*
32c Merian Botanical Prints (5)
(2 ea. 3128-29, 1-3129a)
Pl# S11111   3.50
BK261 $4.80
#3128b (2), 3129b (1)
Pl# S11111   10.50

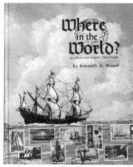

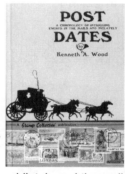

Commemorative Issues

1893. Columbian Issues, released in connection with the World's Columbian Exposition held in Chicago, IL, commemorated the 400th anniversary of the first voyage to America by Christopher Columbus. They are considered to be the First True Commemoratives. All the stamps except the 8c were issued Jan. 2nd. The 8c value, not originally planned with the others, appeared on March 3rd, 1893.

Christoforo Colombo was born in Genoa, Italy, ca.1451. He went to sea at an early age and settled in Portugal. His wife was Felipa Perestrello, daughter of a distinguished navigator who left many charts that Columbus studied with care. He conceived the idea of reaching Asia by sailing due west and vainly sought support in Portugal, Spain, Italy and England for such an expedition.

In 1491, Columbus was on his way to France when he paused to stay with old friends at the monastery of La Rabida (CM10) in Spain. Juan Perez, former confessor to Queen Isabella, obtained for him an audience with the queen, who listened to his theories (CM5) and brought him before King Ferdinand.

Columbus was turned down by the sovereigns, whose treasury had been depleted by war with the Moors. Setting out overland for France, he had gone only six miles when a royal courier overtook him (CM11) to summon him back to court. Isabella had decided to raise the needed money, tradition says, by pledging her jewels (CM12). An agreement was signed giving Columbus three caravels: the *Santa Maria* (CM3), a 100-ton ship with a crew of 52; the 50-ton *Pinta*; and the 40-ton *Niña*. The latter two each had a crew of 18. The little fleet sailed from Palos on August 2.

After rebellious outbursts among the crews, on the night of Oct. 11, 1492, Columbus thought he saw a light. The next morning Rodrigo de Triana sighted land (CM1): Guanahani, now believed to be Watling's Island in the Bahamas. Naming the place San Salvador (Holy Savior), Columbus kissed the soil and gave thanks to God (CM2).

Excited by the native tales of gold, the fleet sailed south, finding Cuba on Oct. 28 and Hispaniola on Dec.6. Leaving a colony of 40 men to build a fort at Hispaniola, where the *Santa Maria* had run aground, Columbus returned to Spain. At court, in Barcelona, he was given a great welcome (CM6), reported his discoveries (CM9) and displayed the natives he brought back with him (CM8).

He sailed again Sept. 25 with three galleons, 14 caravels, and 1,500 men. He reached Dominica, Guadaloupe, and Puerto Rico, found his Haitian colony destroyed by natives, and returned to Spain in March with 225 men and 30 natives.

Charged by enemies in court with mistreating the natives, he successfully defended himself, but his third voyage was delayed until May 1498. Given six vessels, he sent three to Hispaniola and took the others south to explore.

Returning to Hispaniola, he was put in chains (CM13) by Francisco de Bobadilla, sent from Spain in investigate new rumors of mistreatment of natives. Stripped of his honors and returned to Spain, he was released by the queen (CM7). Telling of the discoveries of his third expedition (CM14), he obtained four vessels and set out again in May 1502, discovering Honduras and Panama. The queen's death after his return in 1504 marked the end of his fortunes. He died at Valladolid in 1504, convinced that he had discovered the coast of Asia.

Intaglio, American Bank Note Company, unwatermarked paper, perforated 12.

CM1 *Columbus in Sight of Land. From a painting by William H. Powell.*

CM1 *(230)*

1c deep blue *(449,195,550)*	17.50	.35
pale blue	17.50	.35
Plate strip of three, with imprint	95.	
Plate stripof four, with imprint and letter	100.	
Plate block of six, with imprint	325.	
Plate block of eight, with imprint and letter	500.	
Double transfer	25.	1.00
Cracked plate	90.	5.00
On cover		.75
FDC *(Jan. 2, 1893)*		5,000.

CM2 *Columbus Landing on Guanahani. From a painting by Vanderlyn in the Rotunda of the Capitol in Washington, D.C.*

CM2c The Broken Hat variety is found in the hat of the knight to the left of Columbus.

CM2 *(231)*

2c dull purple *(1,464,588,750)*	17.50	.20
brown violet	20.	.20
gray violet	20.	.20
Plate strip of three, with imprint	75.	
Plate strip of four, with imprint and letter	125.	
Plate block of six, with imprint	225.	
Plate block of eight, with imprint and letter	450.	
Double transfer	25.	.30
Triple transfer	75.	
Quadruple transfer	90.	

Broken frame line	25.	.20
Recut frame lines	25.	.20
Cracked plate	90.	
On cover		.50
FDC (Jan. 2, 1893)	3,750.	
v. Broken Hat variety	65.	.50

Imperforate 2c Columbians are from printer's waste.

CM3 *Columbus' flagship*, Santa Maria. *From a Spanish engraving*

CM3 (232)

3c deep bluish green (11,501,250)	40.	11.
dull green	40.	11.
Plate stripof three, with imprint	200.	
Plate stripof four, with imprint and letter	275.	
Plate block of six, with imprint	650.	
Plate block of eight, with imprint and letter	1,200.	
Double transfer	75.	
On cover		35.
FDC (Jan. 2, 1893)	10,000.	

CM4 Santa Maria, Pinta *and* Niña. *From a Spanish engraving.*

CM4 (234)

4c gray blue (19,181,550)	60.	5.50
dull ultramarine	60.	
Plate stripof three, with imprint	275.	
Plate stripof four, with imprint and letter	3.50	
Plate block of six, with imprint	1,100.	
Plate block of eight, with imprint and letter	2,000.	
Double transfer	125.	25.
On cover		
FDC (Jan. 2, 1893)	10,500.	
v. blue (error)		
Plate stripof four, with imprint and letter		

CM5 *Columbus soliciting aid from Isabella. From a painting by Brozik in the Metropolitan Museum of Art, New York*

CM5 (235)

5c brown (35,248,250)	65.	6.00
pale brown	65.	6.00
yellow brown	65.	6.00
Plate strip of three, with imprint	300.	
Plate strip of four, with imprint and letter	450.	
Plate block of six, with imprint	1,400.	

Plate block of eight, with imprint and letter	2,400.	
Double transfer	125.	25.
On cover		25.
FDC (Jan. 2, 1893)	17,500.	

CM6 *Columbus Welcomed at Barcelona. From a panel by Randolph Rogers in the bronze doors of the Capitol, Washington, D.C.*

CM6 (235)

6c dark lilac (4,707,550)	60.	17.50
dull purple	60.	17.50
Plate stripof three, with imprint	275.	
Plate stripof four, with imprint and letter	360.	
Plate block of six, with imprint	1,250.	
Plate block of eight, with imprint and letter	2,250.	
Double transfer	125.	
On cover	—	
FDC (Jan. 2, 1893)	22,500.	
a. red violet	—	

CM7 *Columbus Restored to Favor. From a painting by Francesco Jover*

CM7 (236)

8c brown purple (10,656,550)	50.	7.00
pale brown purple	50.	7.00
Plate strip of three, with imprint	225.	
Plate strip of four, with imprint and letter	300.	
Plate block of six, with imprint	750.	
Plate block of eight, with imprint and letter	1,150.	
Double transfer	75.	
On cover		25.

Earliest known use is March 3, 1893

CM8 *Columbus Presenting Natives. From a painting by Luigi Gregori at the University of Notre Dame, South Bend, Ind.*

CM8 (237)

10c black brown (16,516,950)	95.	5.50
dark brown	95.	5.50
gray black	95.	5.50
Plate strip of three, with imprint	475.	
Plate strip of four, with imprint and letter	650.	
Plate block of six, with imprint	2,800.	
Plate block of eight, with imprint and letter	4,250.	
Double transfer	175.	12.
Triple transfer	—	
On cover		35.
FDC (Jan. 2, 1893)	22,500.	

CM9 *Columbus Announcing his Discovery. From a painting by R. Baloca in Madrid, Spain*

CM9 *(238)*
15c deep bluish green *(1,576,950)*	175.	50.
dull green	175.	50.
Plate strip of three,with imprint	900.	
Plate strip of four, with imprint and letter	1,200.	
Plate block of six,with imprint	4,800.	
Plate block of eight, with imprint and letter	7,500.	
Double transfer	—	
On cover		250.

Earliest known use is Feb. 8, 1893

CM10 *Columbus at La Rabida. From a painting by R. Maso*

CM10 *(239)*
30c orange brown *(617,250)*	225.	65.
bright orange brown	225.	65.
Plate strip of three,with imprint	1,250.	
Plate strip of four, with imprint and letter	1,600.	
Plate block of six,with imprint	7,500.	
Plate block of eight, with imprint and letter	11,500.	
On cover		400.

Earliest known use is Feb. 8, 1893

CM11 *Recall of Columbus. From a painting by Augustus G. Heaton in the Capitol, Washington, D.C.*

CM11 *(240)*
50c slate black *(243,750)*	350.	125.
dull slate black	350.	125.
Plate strip of three,with imprint	1,750.	
Plate strip of four, with imprint and letter	2,500.	
Plate block of six,with imprint	12,000.	
Plate block of eight, with imprint and letter	17,500.	
Double transfer	—	
Triple transfer	—	
On cover		650.

Earliest known use is Feb. 8, 1893

CM12 *Isabella Pledging her Jewels. From a painting by Muñoz Degrain in the Hall of Legislature in Madrid, Spain*

CM12 *(241)*

$1 Venetian red *(55,050)*	1,000.	450.
pale venetian red	1,000.	450.
Plate strip of three,with imprint	5,250.	
Plate stripof four, with imprint and letter	7,250.	
Plate blockof six,with imprint	35,000.	
Plate block of eight, with imprint and letter	55,000.	
Double transfer	—	
On cover		2,850.

Earliest known use is Jan. 21, 1893

CM13 *Columbus in Chains. From a painting by K. Leutze, Germantown, Pennsylvania*

CM13 *(242)*
$2 brown red *(45,550)*	1,100.	400.
dark brown red		
Plate strip of three,with imprint	1,650.	
Plate strip of four, with imprint and letter	8,000.	
Plate block of six,with imprint	45,000.	
Plate block of eight, with imprint and letter	2,500.	
On cover		
FDC *(Jan. 2, 1893)*		65,000.

CM14 *Columbus Describing his Third Voyage. From a painting by Francesco Jover*

CM14 *(243)*
$3 bronze green *(27,650)*	1,700.	725.
pale bronze green	1,700.	725.
Plate strip of three,with imprint	8,500.	
Plate strip of four, with imprint and letter	14,000.	
Plate block of six,with imprint	65,000.	
Plate block of eight, with imprint and letter	85,000.	
On cover		4,000.
a. olive green	2,300.	850.

Earliest known use is April 4, 1893

CM15 *Queen Isabella and Columbus. Isabella from a painting in Madrid, Columbus by Lotto.*

CM15 *(244)*
$4 deep rose *(26,350)*	2,250.	1,000.
pale analine rose	2,250.	1,000.
Plate strip of three,with imprint	12,500.	
Plate strip of four, with imprint and letter	—	
Plate block of six,with imprint	—	

Plate block of eight, with
    imprint and letter   —
On cover   4,000.
a. rose carmine   3,000.   1,250.
Earliest known use is Jan. 6, 1893

CM16 *Profile of Columbus. From the sculpture of the commemorative half dollar.*

CM16 *(235)*
$5 black *(27,350)*   2,750.   1,100.
  gray black   2,750.   1,100.
  Plate strip of three,with imprint 14,000.
  Plate strip of four, with
    imprint and letter   20,000.
  Plate block of six,with imprint   —
  Plate block of eight, with
    imprint and letter   —
  On cover   5,000.
Earliest known use is Jan. 6, 1893

For stamps of these designs, but with '1992' instead of '1893' in the top-right corner see Nos. CM1456-61.

1898. Trans-Mississippi Issue, was released for the Trans-Mississippi Exposition, Omaha, NE, commemorating the settling of the Middle West. Jacques Marquette (CM17), a French Jesuit, founded a mission and in 1673 explored the Mississippi with Joliet. John Charles Fremont (CM20) mapped the Oregon Trail in 1842 and later surveyed railway routes in the Southwest.

    All denominations issued June 17. *Printed in intaglio by the Bureau of Engraving and Printing, Washington, D.C., on paper with double-line 'USPS' watermark.*

CM17 *Marquette Exploring the Mississippi. From a painting by Lamprecht.*

CM17 *(285)*
1c green *(70,993,400)*   22.50   4.75
  dark yellow green   22.50   4.75
  yellow green   22.50   4.75
  Plate pair, with imprint   75.
  Plate strip of three,with imprint   95.
  Plate block of four,with imprint   200.
  Plate block of six,with imprint   300.
  Margin block of four,with arrow   95.
  Double transfer   40.   7.50
  On cover   10.
  FDC *(June 17, 1898)*   12,500.

CM18 *Farming in the West, from a photograph.*

CM18 *(286)*
2c brown red *(159,720,800)*   19.   1.25
  pale brown red   19.   1.25
  Plate pair, with imprint   55.
  Plate strip of three,with imprint   85.
  Plate block of four,with imprint   175.
  Plate block of six,with imprint   240.
  Margin block of four,with arrow   85.
  Double transfer   35.   2.50
  Worn plate   25.   2.00
  On cover   2.50
  FDC *(June 17, 1898)*   11,500.
Earliest known use is June 16, 1898

CM19 *Indian Hunting Buffalo. From an engraving in Schoolcraft's* History of the Indian Tribes.

CM19 *(287)*
4c orange red *(94,924,500)*   100.   17.50
  orange   100.   17.50
  Plate pair, with imprint   250.   20.
  Plate strip of three,with imprint 450.   20.
  Plate block of four,with imprint 750.
  Plate block of six,with imprint 1250.
  Margin block of four,with arrow 500.
  On cover   75.
  FDC *(June 17, 1898)*   20,000.

CM20 *Fremont on Rocky Mountains. From old wood engraving.*

CM20 *(288)*
5c deep blue *(7,694,180)*   100.   17.50
  bright blue   100.   17.50
  dull blue
  Plate pair, with imprint   150.   17.50
  Plate strip of three,with imprint 250.
  Plate block of four, with imprint 700.
  Plate block of six,with imprint 1,250.
  Margin block of four,with arrow 450.
  On cover   75.
  FDC *(June 17, 1898)*   20,000.

CM21 *Troops Guarding Train. From a drawing by Frederic Remington.*

CM21 *(289)*
8c chocolate *(2,927,200)*   135.   32.50
  violet brown   135.   32.50

Plate pair, with imprint   350.
Plate strip of three,with imprint 500.
Plate block of four,with imprint 1,750.
Plate block of six,with imprint 2,500.
Margin block of four,with arrow 650.
On cover   150.
FDC *(June 17, 1898)*   25,000.
v. Horizontal pair, imperforate
   vertically between   15,000.
v1. Plate block of four,
   with imprint   65,000.

CM22 *Hardships of Emigration. From a painting by A.G. Heaton.*

CM22 *(290)*
10c violet black *(4,629,760)*   135.   17.50
  gray violet   135.   17.50
  Plate pair, with imprint   250.
  Plate strip of three,with imprint 525.
  Plate block of four,with imprint 1,750.
  Plate block of six,with imprint 2,750.
  Margin block of four,with arrow 750.
  On cover   100.
  FDC *(June 17, 1898)*   30,000.

CM23 *Western Mining Prospector. From a drawing by Frederic Remington.*

CM23 *(291)*
50c bronze green *(530,400)*   450.   130.
  dark bronze green   450.   130.
  Plate pair, with imprint   150.
  Plate strip of three,with imprint 2,000.
  Plate block of four,with imprint 10,250.
  Plate block of six,with imprint 16,000.
  Margin block of four,with arrow 2,250.
  On cover   1,500.
  FDC *(June 17, 1898)*   35,000.

CM24 *Western Cattle in a Storm. From a painting by John MacWhirter.*

CM24 *(292)*
$1 black *(56,900)*   950.   400.
  Plate pair, with imprint   2,750.
  Plate strip of three,with imprint 5,500.
  Plate block of four,with imprint 30,000.
  Plate block of six,with imprint 42,500.
  Margin block of four,with arrow 5,500.
  On cover   4,500.
  FDC *(June 17, 1898)*   20,000.

CM25 *Mississippi River Bridge at St. Louis, MO. From a photograph.*

CM25 *(293)*
$2 red brown *(56,200)*
  dark red brown   1,600.   650.
  Plate pair, with imprint   4,750.
  Plate strip of three,with imprint 7,500.
  Plate block of four,with imprint 65,000.
  Plate block of six,with imprint 100,000.
  Margin block of four,with arrow 10,500.
  On cover   60,000.

1901. Pan-American Issue commemorates the Pan-American Exposition at Buffalo, NY, promoting friendly relations among the countries of the New World. The stamps illustrating engineering achievements of the age were printed in two colors, and the first three denominations are known with inverted centers. The stamps were on sale only during the exposition, from May 1 to October 31. *Intaglio, perforated 12.*

CM26 *Navigation on the Great Lakes. (S.S. City of Alpena).*

CM26v1. inverted center.

CM26 *(294)*
1c emerald and black
   (91,401,500)   15.   2.75
  dark blue green and black   15.   2.75
  Plate strip of three,with imprint 100.
  Plate block of four, with
   imprint and arrow   —
  Plate strip of five (2 numbers),
   with imprint   175.
  Plate block of six, with imprint 275.
  Plate block of ten (2 numbers),
   with imprint   —
  Margin block of four, with
   imprint and arrow   125.
  Double transfer   22.50   2.75
  On cover   8.00
  FDC *(May 1, 1901)*   5,000.
  v. Center inverted
   (1,000 reported)   12,500.   6,000.
   Plate strip of 3,with imprint 45,000.
   On cover   18,500.

CM27 *Fast Rail Transportation. (Empire State Express).*

27v 2c inverted center, 158 stamps known to exist.

CM27 *(295)*
2c rose red and black

(209,759,700)	15.	1.00
carmine and gray black	15.	1.00
Plate strip of three,with imprint	85.	
Plate block of four, with imprint and arrow	—	
Plate strip of five (2 numbers), with imprint	200.	
Plate block of six, with imprint	275.	
Plate block of ten (2 numbers), with imprint	—	
Margin block of four, with imprint and arrow	100.	
Double transfer	30.	4.00
On cover		2.00
FDC *(May 1, 1901)*	2,750.	
v. Center inverted *(158 known)*	—	
Block of four	—	

CM28 *Electric Aautomobile.*

28v 4c inverted center.

CM28 *(296)*
4c orange brown and black

(5,737,100)	70.	12.50
red brown and black	70.	12.50
Plate strip of three, with imprint	350.	
Plate block of four, with imprint and arrow	—	
Plate strip of five (2 numbers), with imprint	600.	
Plate block of six,with imprint	2,500.	
Plate block of ten (2 numbers), with imprint	4,500.	
Margin block of four, with imprint and arrow	350.	
On cover		50.
FDC *(May 1, 1901)*	8,500.	
v. Center inverted *(206 known)*	—	
Plate strip of 4,with imprint	13,500.	
v1. Center inverted, overprinted "Specimen"	—	

CM29 *Bridge at Niagara Falls.*

CM29 *(297)*
5c gray blue and black

(7,201,300)	75.	12.50
dark gray blue and black	75.	12.50
Plate strip of three,with imprint	400.	
Plate block of four, with imprint and arrow	—	
Plate strip of five (2 numbers), with imprint	725.	
Plate block of six,with imprint	3,000.	
Plate block of ten (2 numbers), with imprint and arrow	5,250.	
Margin block of four, with imprint and arrow	425.	
On cover		55.
FDC *(May 1, 1901)*	16,000.	

CM30 *Canal Locks, Sault Ste. Marie.*

CM30 *(298)*
8c chocolate and black

(4,921,700)	100.	45.
purple brown and black	100.	45.
Plate strip of three,with imprint	500.	
Plate block of four, with imprint and arrow	—	
Plate strip of five (2 numbers), with imprint	900.	
Plate block of six,with imprint	4,500.	
Plate block of ten (2 numbers), with imprint	8,000.	
Margin block of four, with imprint and arrow	500.	
On cover		125.

CM31 *Fast Ocean Navigation* (S.S. St. Paul).

CM31 *(299)*
10c yellow brown and black

(5,043,700)	140.	22.50
dark yellow brown and black	140.	22.50
Plate strip of three,with imprint	750.	
Plate block of four, with imprint and arrow	—	
Plate strip of five (2 numbers), with imprint	1,400.	
Plate block of six,with imprint	7,000.	
Plate block of ten (2 numbers), with imprint	12,500.	
Margin block of four, with imprint and arrow	800.	
On cover		150.

1904. Louisiana Purchase Issue, prepared for the World's Fair at St. Louis, MO. commemorating the 1803 acquisition of the Louisiana Territory from France. All values were placed on sale April 30, the opening day of the fair.

Robert Livingston (CM32), was appointed minister to France in 1801. In 1803, President Jefferson (CM33) instructed him to negotiate with Napoleon for the purchase of New Orleans and the mouth of the Mississippi. James Monroe (CM34), former minister to France, was sent to aid in the negotiations. Francois de Barbe-Marbois, Napoleon's finance minister, astounded them by offering to sell the entire Louisiana Territory, an offer which they accepted without delay or authority. The price was $11,250,000; claims and interest accruals raised it to $27,000,000 — about 4c an acre. The territory (CM36) eventually became ten entire states and parts of three others. President McKinley (CM35) signed the Act of Congress approving the 1904 World's Fair but never lived to see it. In September 1901 he was assassinated while attending the Pan-American Exposition. *Intaglio, perforated 12.*

CM32 *Robert Livingston. From a painting by Gilbert Sullivan.*

CM32 *(323)*

1c green *(79,779,200)*	20.	3.50
dark green	20.	3.50
Plate pair, with imprint	65.	
Plate strip of three, with imprint	100.	
Plate block of four, with imprint	160.	
Plate block of six, with imprint	175.	
Margin block of four, with arrow	75.	
Diagonal line through left "1"	50.	10.
Double transfer	—	
On cover		75.
FDC *(April 30, 1904)*		6,500.

CM33 *Thomas Jefferson. From a painting attributed to Gilbert Stuart.*

CM33 *(324)*

2c carmine *(192,732,400)*	19.	1.25
bright carmine	19.	1.25
Plate pair, with imprint	75.	
Plate strip of three, with imprint	125.	
Plate block of four, with imprint	160.	
Plate block of six, with imprint	175.	
Margin block of 4, with arrow	100.	
On cover		6.00
FDC *(April 30, 1904)*		5,000.
v. Vertical pair, imperforate horizontally		—

CM34 *James Monroe. From a painting by Vanderlyn in New York City Hall.*

CM34 *(325)*

3c dark red violet *(4,542,600)*	60.	25.
Plate pair, with imprint	150.	
Plate strip of three, with imprint	275.	
Plate block of four, with imprint	550.	
Plate block of six, with imprint	800.	
Margin block of four, with arrow	325.	
Double transfer	—	
On cover		75.
FDC *(April 30, 1904)*		18,000.

CM35 *William McKinley.*

CM35 *(326)*

5c indigo *(6,926,700)*	75.	17.50
Plate pair, with imprint	200.	
Plate strip of three, with imprint	325.	
Plate block of four, with imprint	625.	
Plate block of six, with imprint	900.	
Margin block of four, with arrow	350.	
On cover		75.
FDC *(April 30, 1904)*		26,000.

CM36 *Map of Louisiana Purchase.*

CM36 *(327)*

10c red brown *(4,011,200)*	125.	25.
dark red brown	125.	25.
Plate pair, with imprint	325.	
Plate strip of three, with imprint	500.	
Plate block of four, with imprint	1,250.	
Plate block of six, with imprint	1,750.	
Margin block of four, with arrow	575.	
On cover		125.
FDC *(April 30, 1904)*		27,500.

1907. Jamestown Issue, was created for the Jamestown Exposition at Hampton Roads, VA, commemorating the 300th anniversary of the oldest permanent English settlement in America. In 1607, on their way to reattempt a settlement at Roanoke Island, three London Company ships with 105 men were blown off course and discovered the entrance to Chesapeake Bay. Sailing 50 miles up a river they named the James (for King James I), they began a settlement called Jamestown (CM38). Constant Indian trouble brought out the leadership qualities of Captain John Smith (CM37). Captured while foraging and condemned to death by the Indian chief Powhatan, Smith is said by legend to have been saved by the chief's beautiful daughter Pocahontas (CM39), Married to a settler named John Rolfe, she was received with royal honors in England, where she died in 1617. The 1c and 2c stamps were placed on sale April 25, 1907. The 5c value was first sold May 3, 1907. *Intaglio, perforated 12.*

CM37 *Captain John Smith. From a painting in the State Library, Virginia*

CM37 *(328)*
1c deep bluish green

(77,728,794)		17.50	3.00
dark green		17.50	3.00
Plate strip of three,with imprint	65.		
Plate block of six,with imprint	225.		
Margin block of four,with arrow	75.		
Double transfer		25.	8.00
On cover			12.50
FDC *(April 25, 1907)*			12,000.

CM38 *Founding of Jamestown. From a lost painting*

CM38 *(329)*
2c rose red *(149,497,994)*

		22.50	2.75
bright rose red		22.50	2.75
Plate strip of three, with imprint	75.		
Plate block of six, with imprint	325.		
Margin block of four, with arrow	90.		
Double transfer			6.00
On cover			7.50
FDC *(April 25, 1907)*			12,000.

CM39 *Pocahontas. From a painting in Norfolk, England*

CM39 *(330)*
5c indigo *(7,980,594)*

		85.	22.50
blue		85.	22.50
Plate strip of three,with imprint	300.		
Plate block of six,with imprint	1,900.		
Margin block of four,with arrow	350.		
Double transfer		125.	45.
On cover			75.

Earliest known use is May 10, 1907

1909. Lincoln Memorial Issue commemorated the 100th anniversary of the birth of Abraham Lincoln. As an experiment to counteract the shrinking caused by printing on wet paper, some rows of stamps were spearated by 3 mm spacing instead of the usual 2 mm. Some of the perforated stamps were printed on a 35-percent rag stock known as "bluish paper," which is actually grayish in appearance. *Intaglio, perforated 12 and imperforate.*

CM40-42 *Abraham Lincoln. From statue by St. Gaudens, Grant Park, Chicago.*

Perforated 12
CM40 *(367)*
2c carmine *(148,387,191)*

		5.00	1.75
bright carmine		5.00	1.75
Block of four (2 mm spacing)		25.	17.50
Block of four (3 mm spacing)		25.	17.50
Plate block of six,with imprint	125.		
Double transfer		12.50	5.00
On cover			9.00
FDC *(Feb. 12, 1909)*			500.

Imperforate
CM41 *(368)*
2c carmine *(1,273,900)*

		22.50	1,750.
Block of four (2 mm spacing)		100.	
Block of four (3 mm spacing)		100.	
Plate block of six, with imprint	225.		
Center line block		200.	
Margin block of four, with arrow	100.		
Double transfer		60.	30.
On cover			50.
FDC *(Feb. 12, 1909)*			17,000.

Bluish gray paper, perforated 12 (February 1909)
CM42 *(369)*
2c carmine *(637,000)*

		175.	195.
Block of four (2 mm spacing)		900.	750.
Block of four (3 mm spacing)		900.	750.
Plate block of six, with imprint	3,000.		
On cover			450.

1909. Alaska-Yukon Issue, released in connection with a Seattle, WA exposition, commemorating the development of the Alaska-Yukon-Pacific Territory. William H. Seward, secretary of state under Lincoln and Johnson, negotiated the purchase of Alaska from Russia, begun in 1859 but postponed by the Civil War. The treaty of March 30, 1867, set the purchase price at $7,200,000. The formal transfer was made October 18 at Sitka. *Intaglio, perforated 12 and imperforate.*

CM43, 44 *William Seward. From a drawing by Marcus W. Baldwin.*

Perforated 12
CM43 *(370)*
2c carmine *(152,887,311)*

		7.	1.50
bright carmine		7.	1.50
Plate block of six,with imprint	250.		
Double transfer		1,750.	6.00
On cover			7.50
FDC *(June 1, 1909)*			4,500.

Imperforate
CM44 *(371)*
2c carmine *(525,400)*

		30.	22.50
Plate block of six,with imprint	275.		
Center line block		175.	150.
Margin block of four,with arrow	150.	120.	
Double transfer		55.	35.
On cover			45.

Earliest known use is June 7, 1909

1909. Hudson-Fulton Issue commemorated historic voyages 200 years apart up the Hudson River to Albany. Henry Hudson, an English navigator commanding the Dutch East India Company ship, *Half Moon*, explored the river when he sailed into New York Bay September 3, 1609. Robert Fulton, aided by Robert Livingston (CM32), constructed the first practical steamship, named *Clermont* after Livingston's home, and steamed to Albany and back August 17-22, 1807. *Printed in intaglio, perforated 12 and imperforate.*

CM45 Half Moon *and* S.S. Clermont

Perforated 12
CM45 *(372)*

2c carmine *(72,634,631)*	10.	3.50
Plate block of six, with imprint	350.	
Double transfer	25.	7.50
On cover		800.

Imperforate
CM46 *(373)*

2c carmine *(216,480)*	35.	22.50
Plate block of six, with imprint	350.	
Center line block	275.	140.
Margin block of four, with arrow	175.	120.
Double transfer	55.	35.
On cover		45.
FDC *(Sept. 25, 1909)*		7,500.

1912-13. Panama-Pacific Issue commemorates Balboa's sighting of the Pacific Ocean in 1513; the opening of the Panama Canal in 1914: and the Panama-Pacific Exposition at San Francisco, CA, in 1915.

Balboa (CM47), Spanish governor of Darien (Panama), marched across the isthmus and from the peak of Mount Darien sighted the waters of "the South Sea" on September 25, 1513. Magellan named it the Pacific Ocean in 1520. A canal connecting the Atlantic and Pacific oceans (CM48), was built by the United States during 1904-14 at a cost of $336,650,000. San Francisco Bay (CM99) is said to have been sighted by Drake in 1579, but the city's site was discovered (CM 50) in 1770 by Don Gaspar de Portola, Spanish governor of the Californias, who, with the Franciscan missionary Junipero Serra (A116), led a 1,000-mile march establishing settlements from Lower California to Monterey. *Stamps issued on with single-line 'USPS' watermark. Printed in intaglio, perforated 12 (1913) and perforated 1919-15). (Quantities shown include both perforation types).*

CM47, 52 *Vasco Nuñez de Balboa (334.796.926)*

CM47 *(397)*

1c green *(334,796,926)*	13.50	1.25

yellow green	13.50	1.25
Plate block of six	150.	
Double transfer	25.	5.00
On cover		7.50
FDC *(Jan. 1, 1913)*		5,000.

CM48, CM53 *Panama Canal. From a model of the Pedro Miguel Locks (503,713,086)*

CM48 *(398)*

2c rose red	15.	.50
deep carmine	15.	.50
camine lake	15.	.50
Plate block of six	250.	
Double transfer	45.	5.00
On cover		4.00
FDC *(Jan. 18, 1913)*		2,000.

Earliest known use is January 17, 1913

CM49, CM54 *The Golden Gate. From a photograph. (29,088,726)*

CM49 *(399)*

5c blue	55.	8.00
dark blue	55.	8.00
Plate block of six	2,000.	
On cover		45.
FDC *(Jan. 1, 1913)*		22,000.

CM50-51, CM55 *Discovery of San Francisco Bay. From a painting by Charles F. Matthews, San Francisco Art Museum (16,968,365)*

CM50 *(400)*

10c orange yellow *(Jan. 1, 1913)*	100.	20.
Plate block of six	2,500.	
On cover		100.
FDC *(Jan. 1, 1913)*		17,500.

CM51 *(400A)*

10c orange *(August 1913)*	175.	15.
Plate block of six	8,250.	
On cover		125.

1914-15. Stamps with previous designs, *perforated 10.*

CM52 *(401)*

1c green	20.	5.25
dark green	20.	5.25
Plate block of six	300.	
On cover		30.

Earliest known use is December 21, 1914

CM53 *(402)*

2c rose red *(January 1915)*	60.	1.50
dark carmine	60.	1.50
red	60.	1.50

Plate block of six	1,300.	
On cover		12.50

CM54 *(403)*
5c blue	125.	13.50
dark blue	125.	13.50
Plate block of six	4,250.	
On cover		75.

Earliest known use is February 6, 1915

CM55 *(404)*
10c orange	750.	55.
Plate block of six	13,000.	
On cover		225.

Earliest known use is August 27, 1915

1919. Victory Issue commemorated the winning of World War I by the Allies. The design shows a female allegory of "Victory" and the U.S. flag flanked by the flags of Great Britain, Belgium, Italy and France. *Printed in intaglio, perforated 11.*

CM56 *"Victory" and Flags*

CM56 *(537)*
3c dark lilac *(99,585,200)*	7.50	3.00
Plate block of six	75.	
FDC *(March 3, 1919)*		200.
a. dark red lilac	350.	125.
Plate block of six	—	
b. pale red lilac	13.50	3.50
Plate block of six	—	
c. bright red lilac	40.	15.
Plate block of six	—	

1920. Pilgrim Tercentenary Issue marks the 300th anniversary of the landing of the Pilgrims at Plymouth, MA (CM58), in December 1620. Of the *Mayflower's* (CM57) 102 passengers. 41 Pilgrim "fathers" en route signed a compact (CM59) in which they pledged to adhere to the principles of self-government in the colony. *Printed in intaglio, perforated 11.*

CM57 *The* Mayflower. *From a watercolor by Harrison Eastman, Smithsonian Institution, Washington, D.C.*

CM57 *(548)*
1c green *(137,978,207)*	3.50	2.50
dark green	3.50	2.50
Plate block of six	35.	
Double transfer	—	
On cover		8.00
FDC *(Dec. 21, 1920)*		1,600.

CM58 *Landing of the Pilgrims. From an 1846 engraving by Burt based on a sketch by White.*

CM58 *(549)*
2c rose red *(196,037,327)*	5.25	1.75
carmine	5.25	1.75
rose	5.25	1.75
Plate block of six	50.	
On cover		5.00
FDC *(Dec. 21, 1920)*		1,500.

CM59 *Signing of the Compact. From a painting by Edwin White.*

CM59 *(550)*
5c deep blue *(11,321,607)*	35.	12.50
dark blue	35.	12.50
Plate block of six	375.	
On cover		30.
FDC *(Dec. 21, 1920)*		3,000.

1923. Harding Memorial Issue honored President Warren G. Harding, who died August 2 in San Francisco, CA. An Ohio newspaper editor elected to the U.S. Senate in 1914, he won the presidency in 1920 on a platform pledging a "return to normalcy." First President to visit Alaska, he died on the way home. The stamp was issued less than a month later. *Printed in intaglio.*

The printed design of the flat plate printing measures 19 x 21 7/8 mm. Small specks of black color usually are seen on the backs of these stamps, a characteristic of almost all flat-press-printed stamps.

CM60-63 *Warren G. Harding*

Flat plate printing. perforated 11.
CM60 *(610)*
2c black *(1,459,487,085)*	.60	.20
grayish black	.60	.20
Plate block of six	17.50	
Double transfer	3.00	.75
On cover		1.00
FDC *(Sept. 1, 1923)*		30.
v. Horizontal pair, imperforate vertically	1,500.	

Flat plate printing, imperforate.
CM61 *(611)*
2c black *(770,000)*	6.50	4.50
Plate block of six	90.	
Block of four, with arrow	40.	
Center line block of four	75.	
On cover		12.50
FDC *(Nov. 15, 1923)*		125.

The printed design of the rotary press printings measures 19 x 22 1/2 mm. Color specks are almost always absent from the backs of these stamps.

Rotary press printing, perforated 10
CM62 *(612)*

2c gray black *(99,950,300)*	15.	1.75
black	15.	1.75
Plate block of four	275.	
Gutter pair	450.	
On cover		6.00
FDC *(Sept. 12, 1923)*		175.

Rotary press printing, perforated 11
CM63 *(613)*

2c gray black	15,000.	

1924. Huguenot-Walloon Issue commemorated the 300th anniversary of the Walloon settlement of New York, and the restoration of a monument to earlier Huguenot settlements in the South.

During the religious wars of the 16th century, thousands of French and Belgian Protestants, known as Huguenots, settled in Holland, where they were called Walloons (foreigners). Although Dutch traders had visited Manhattan since 1613, the first Dutch immigrants were 30 Walloon families sent by the Dutch West India Company in 1624. Under Peter Minuit they bought Manhattan from the Indians and tried founding settlements all the way from the Delaware River to Fort Orange, now Albany (CM65). In 1562, French Huguenots unsuccessfully had tried a settlement at Port Royal, SC. In 1564 a colony was established at Fort Caroline (now Mayport) on the St. Johns River in Florida, and had a stone column erected bearing the French coat of arms. The colony was massacred in 1565 by the Spanish under Pedro Menendez de Aviles. This column was replaced and dedicated May 2, 1924. *Intaglio, perforated 11.*

CM64 *The New Netherland*

CM64 *(614)*

1c green *(51,378,023)*	2.75	2.75
dark green	2.75	2.75
Plate block of six	30.	
Double transfer	10.	6.50
On cover		7.00
FDC *(May 1, 1924)*		40.

CM65 *Landing of Walloons at Fort Orange. From* History of New York *by Martha Lamb*

CM65 *(615)*

2c carmine red *(77,753,423)*	5.00	2.00
Plate block of six	55.	
Double transfer	15.	4.25
On cover		5.00
FDC *(May 1, 1924)*		60.

CM66 *Monument to Huguenots at Mayport, Florida*

CM66 *(616)*

5c Prussian blue *(5,659,023)*	27.50	14.
dark blue	27.50	14.
Plate block of six	250.	
On cover (UPU rate)		30.
FDC *(May 1, 1924)*		85.
v. broken circle below right numeral "5"	65.	22.50

1925. Lexington-Concord Issue commemorated the 150th anniversary of the first armed conflicts of the American Revolution, which took place on April 19, 1775.

When Gen. Thomas Gage, colonial governor of Massachusetts, sent 800 troops to Lexington and Concord to destroy military supplies stored there by the colonists, Paul Revere made his famous ride on horseback to warn the colonists. Calling themselves the Minute Men (ready to fight on a minute's notice) (CM69), the colonists gathered on the Green at Lexington with the watchword, "If they mean to have a war, let it begin here" (CM68). Eight of the 70 Minute Men were killed; the rest fell back, and the British went on to Concord. In fighting on the North Bridge there, and continuing all the way back to the protection of naval guns at Charlestown Harbor, the British suffered 273 casualties; the colonists 93. Chosen to head a Continental Army, George Washington took command at Cambridge in July (CM67). *Intaglio, perforated 11.*

CM67 *Washington at Cambridge. From an engraving in the Cambridge Public Library*

CM67 *(617)*

1c green *(15,615,000)*	2.75	2.50
dark green	2.75	2.50
Plate block of six	40.	
On cover		5.00
FDC *(April 4, 1925)*		30.

CM68 *Battle of Lexington. Painting by Henry Sandham, Town Hall, Lexington, Massachusetts*

CM68 *(618)*

2c carmine red *(26,596,600)*	5.00	3.50
Plate block of six	65.	
On cover		7.50
FDC *(April 4, 1925)*		35.

CM69 *The Minute Man. From a statue by Daniel Chester French in Concord, the poetry by Ralph Waldo Emerson*

CM69 *(619)*

5c Prussian blue *(5,348,800)*	25.	14.
Plate block of six	225.	
On cover (UPU rate)		22.50
FDC *(April 4, 1925)*		85.
v. Line over head	65.	25.

1925. Norse-American Issue commemorated the 100th anniversary of the first Norwegian immigrants' arrival on the *Restaurationen* on October 9, 1825. Sagas tell of Norse exploration of the North American coast ca. 1000 A.D. *Intaglio, perforated 11.*

CM70 *Sloop* Restaurationen. *Adapted from a drawing of a sister ship*

CM70 *(620)*

2c carmine and black

(9,104,983)	4.00	3.00
dark carmine and black	4.00	3.00
Plate block of eight, with		
two numbers and arrow	200.	
Plate block of eight, with carmine		
number (only) and arrow	3,250.	
Center line block of four	27.50	
Margin block of four, with arrow	35.	
On cover		8.00
FDC *(May 18, 1925)*		20.

CM71 *Viking Ship. Built in Norway, by popular subscription, as a gift to the people of the United States*

CM71 *(621)*

5c indigo and black *(1,900,983)*	15.	12.50
Plate block of eight, with		
two numbers and arrow	575.	
Center line block of four	90.	
Margin block of four, with arrow	85.	
On cover (UPU rate)		22.50
FDC *(May 18, 1925)*		30.

1926. Sesquicentennial Issue, in connection with the Sesquicentennial Exposition at Philadelphia, PA, commemorated the 150th anniversary of the Declaration of Independence. *Intaglio, perforated 11.*

CM72 *The Liberty Bell. Designed from the entrance to the exposition*

CM72 *(627)*

2c carmine red *(307,731,900)*	2.50	.50
Plate block of six	35.	
Double transfer	—	
FDC *(May 10, 1926)*		10.

1926. Ericsson Memorial Issue honored John Ericsson, the Swedish-born engineer who built the ironclad *USS Monitor*, which engaged the Confederate ironclad *Virginia* (formerly *USS Merrimac*) off Hampton Roads, VA, in 1862. Ericsson's inventions include a screw propeller that revolutionized shipbuilding. The stamp shows a statue of him unveiled in Washington by the Crown Prince of Sweden. *Intaglio, perforated 11.*

CM73 *Statue of John Ericsson . Sculpted by James Earl Fraser, Washington D.C.*

CM73 *(628)*

5c slate violet *(20,280,500)*	6.00	2.50
Plate block of six	75.	
FDC *(May 29, 1929)*		25.

1926. White Plains Issue commemorated the 150th anniversary of the Battle of White Plains, NY, October 28, 1776. The British, attempting to outflank Washington's forces in upper Manhattan, caused him to withdraw his main force northward. In a sharp battle at White Plains, the British captured a key hill, but Washington escaped while they were awaiting reinforcements. *Intaglio, perforated 11.*

CM74 *Alexander Hamilton's battery. From a painting by E.L. Ward*

CM74 *(629)*

2c carmine red *(40,639,485)*	2.00	1.50
Plate block of six	40.	
FDC *(Oct. 18, 1926)*		8.00
v. Vertical pair, imperforated		
between	1,500.	

Sheets of 25 stamps with marginal inscription reading "International Philatelic Exhibition, Oct. 16 to 23, 1926, N.Y., U.S.A." Sheet size 161 x 149 mm.

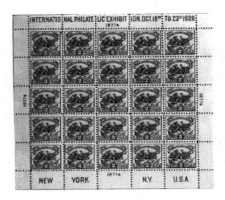

CM75 *White Plains souvenir sheet*

CM75

2c carmine red, sheet of 25

(107,398)	400.	425.

v.Dot over fist "S" of "States"
on stamp in position 9 of lower
left pane of plate 18774 or
position 11 of the lower left
pane of plate 18773. 425. 450.
FDC Full sheet *(Oct. 18, 1926)* 1,700.

1927. Vermont Sesquicentennial Issue

commemorated the 150th anniversary of the Battle of
Bennington and the independence of the State of
Vermont. In 1777, badly needing supplies at Saratoga,
NY, Burgoyne sent a force to capture Amercian military
stores at Bennington, VT. In a battle August 16th with
2,600 militiamen (the "Green Mountain Boys") under
Gen. John Stark, almost the entire British force was
killed or captured. *Intaglio, perforated 11.*

CM76 *Green Mountain Boy*

CM76 *(643)*
  2c carmine red *(39,974,900)* 1.25 1.00
    Plate block of six 40.
    FDC *(Aug. 3, 1927)* 6.00

1927. Burgoyne Campaign Issue

commemorated the
Battles of Bennington, Oriskany, Fort Stanwix and
Saratoga. On October 17, 1777, surrounded by a force
three times his own, Burgoyne surrendered to the
Americans. His 5,700 men went back to England, pledged
not to fight again in the war. *Intaglio, perforated 11.*

CM77 *Surrender of Gen. John
Burgoyne. From a painting by
Trumbull in the Capitol Rotunda,
Washington, D.C.*

CM77 *(644)*
  2c carmine red *(25,628,450)* 3.50 2.25
    Plate block of six 40.
    FDC *(Aug. 3, 1927)* 12.50

1928. Valley Forge Issue

recalled the 150th
anniversary of Washington's winter encampment at
Valley Forge, about 20 miles northwest of Philadelphia,
PA. Beaten at Brandywine and Germantown, desperately
short of food, clothing and supplies, the American troops
at Valley Forge showed courage in the darkest period of
American history. *Intaglio, perforated 11.*

CM78 *General Washington at Prayer. From
an engraving by John C. McRae*

CM78 *(645)*
  2c carmine red *(101,330,328)* 1.00 .50
    Plate block of six 25.
    FDC *(May 26, 1928)* 5.00

1928. Hawaiian Sesquicentennial Issue

marked the
150th anniversary of the arrival in the Hawaiian Islands
of English navigator Capt. James Cook. These makeshift
commemoratives, made by overprinting ordinary
definitive stamps (Nos. 476 and 479), disappointed
collectors who expected something more elaborate. The
overprints caused confusion; when some postal clerks
would not honor them because they thought they were
precancels. *Intaglio, perforated 11 x 10 1/2.*

CM79 2c overprint   Cm80 5c overprint

CM79 *(647)*
  2c carmine *(5,519,897)* 4.50 4.50
    Plate block of four 100.
    Vertical pair with wide spacing
      (28 mm rather than 18 mm) 100.
    FDC *(Aug. 13, 1928)* 20.

CM80 *(648)*
  5c blue *(1,459,897)* 12.50 12.50
    Plate block of four 200.
    FDC *(Aug. 13, 1928)* 20.

1928. Molly Pitcher Issue,

another two-line overprint
of No. 476, commemorated the 150th anniversary of the
Battle of Monmouth, NJ, June 28, 1778, and honored
Mary Ludwig Hays, whose husband was a cannoneer in
the battle. Called "Molly Pitcher" because she carried
water to the tired and wounded soldiers, she also took
her husband's place when he was overcome by the heat,
and manned his cannon throughout the rest of the
battle. (See also the 1978 10c postal card, No. PC73).
Intaglio, perforated 11.

CM81 *The 2c Molly Pitcher overprint*

CM81 *(646)*
  2c carmine *(9,779,896)* 1.00 1.25
    Plate block of four 25.
    Vertical pair with wide spacing
      (28 mm rather than 18 mm) 2,750.
    FDC *(Oct. 20, 1928)*

1928. The Aeronautics Conference Issue,

in
connection with the International Civil Aeronautics
Conference held December 12-14 in Washington,
commemorated the 25th anniversary of the first airplane
flight (December 17, 1903) by the Wright brothers at
Kitty Hawk, North Carolina. The plane (CM80), in
England for 20 years, was returned to the United States
in 1948 and is now on view at the Smithsonian
Institution in Washington, DC. *Intaglio, perforated 11.*

CM82 *Wright Airplane*

CM82 *(649)*
2c carmine red *(51,342,273)*	1.25	1.00
Plate block of six	12.50	
FDC *(Dec. 12, 1928)*		6.00

CM83 *Globe and Airplane*

CM83 *(650)*
5c Prussian blue *(10,319,700)*	5.00	3.00
Plate block of six	55.	
"Prairie dog" plate flaw (position 50 of bottom-lower left pane of plate 19658)	30.	
FDC *(Dec. 12, 1928)*		10.

1929. George Rogers Clark Issue commemorated the 150th anniversary of Clark's recapture of Fort Sackville (now Vincennes, Ind. from a force of British, Loyalists and Indians commanded by Col. Henry Hamilton. From winter quarters at Kaskaskia, Clark sent 40 men by boat, led another 130 across the flooded plains, tricked Hamilton's Indians into deserting, took the fort on February 25, and secured the Northwest for the colonists. *Intaglio, perforated 11.*

CM84 *Surrender of Fort Sackville. From a painting by Frederick C. Yohn*

CM84 *(651)*
2c carmine and black *(16,684,674)*	.60	.50
Plate block of six, with two numbers and "TOP"	12.50	
Plate block of ten, with red number only	—	
Margin block of four, with arrow	3.50	
Double transfer	5.50	3.00
FDC *(Feb. 25, 1929)*		30.

1929. Edison Commemorative Issue celebrated the 50th anniversary of the invention of the incandescent electric lamp by Thomas Alva Edison (CM287). *Issued in both flat and rotary press intaglio printings and as a rotary press coil stamp.*

CM85-87 *Edison's First Electric Lamp*

Flat press, perforated 11
CM85 *(654)*
2c carmine red *(31,679,200)*	.75	.75
Plate block of six	30.	
FDC *(June 5, 1929)*		40.

Rotary press, perforated 11 x 10 1/2
CM86 *(655)*
2c carmine red *(210,119,474)*	.75	.25
Plate block of four	35.	
FDC *(June 11, 1929)*		375.

Rotary press coil, perforated 10 vertically
CM87 *(656)*
2c carmine red *(133,530,000)*	12.50	1.50
Pair	22.50	7.00
Joint line pair	60.	40.
FDC *(June 11, 1929)*		375.

1929. Sullivan Expedition Issue notes the 150th anniversary of the campaign by Gens. John Sullivan and James Clinton against the Loyalists and Iroquois Indians ravaging Pennsylvania and New York frontier settlements. They defeated the Iroquois at Newtown (now Elmira), NY, August 29, 1779. *Intaglio, perforated 11.*

CM88 Mag. Gen. John Sullivan

CM88 *(657)*
2c carmine red *(51,451,880)*	.75	.75
Plate block of six	25.	
FDC *(June 17, 1929)*		2,750.

1929. Battle of Fallen Timbers Issue commemorated Gen. Anthony Wayne's defeat of Chief Little Turtle, August 1794, near what is now Toledo. His victory led to the settlement of Ohio. *Intaglio, perforated 11.*

CM89 *Gen. Wayne Memorial. Monument by Bruce W. Laville at Fallen Timbers Park, Ohio*

CM89 *(680)*
2c carmine red *(29,338,274)*	.75	.75
Plate block of six	25.	
FDC *(Sept. 14, 1929)*		35.

1929. Ohio River Canalization Issue saluted the Army Engineers' completion of America's most extensive canal system. Its 46 locks and dams provided a dependable 9-foot channel between Pittsburgh, PA, and Cairo, IL, a distance of 981 miles. *Intaglio, perforated 11.*

CM90 *Monongahela River Lock*

CM90 *(681)*

2c carmine red *(32,680,900)*	.50	.75
Plate block of six	17.50	35.
FDC *(Oct. 19, 1929)*		

1930. Massachusetts Bay Colony Issue commemorated the 300th anniversary of the arrival of the Puritans under Gov. John Winthrop. When the charter given to the Massachusetts Bay Company neglected to specify where its annual meetings were to be held, the company took advantage of the oversight by moving itself to New England as a self-governing commonwealth, the first in the New World. *Intaglio, perforated 11.*

CM91 *Seal of the Massachusetts Bay Colony*

CM91 *(682)*

2c carmine red *(74,000,774)*	.75	.45
Plate block of six	25.	
FDC *(April 8, 1930)*		35.

1930. Carolina-Charleston Issue commemorated the 260th anniversary of the Province of Carolina and 250th anniversary of the City of Charleston. In 1670, Gov. William Sayle and 150 colonists landed at Albemarle Point on the Ashley River, founding a settlement called Charles Town. In 1680 they moved into a walled city they had built at Oyster Point, present site of Charleston. This was the first permanent settlement in the Carolinas *Intaglio, perforated 11.*

CM92 *Colonial Governor and Indian*

CM92 *(683)*

2c carmine red *(25,215,574)*	1.25	1.00
Plate block of six	40.	
FDC *(April 10, 1930)*		35.

1930. Braddock's Field Issue commemorated the 175th anniversary of the Battle of the Wilderness in the French and Indian War. Advancing on Fort Duquesne (now Pittsburgh), Gen. Braddock's forces were defeated, and Braddock was killed. Lt. Col. George Washington, 23, commanding Braddock's colonials, led the remnant troops in a safe retreat. *Intaglio, perforated 11.*

CM93 *Col. George Washington. Monument by Frank Vittor, at Braddock's Field, PA*

CM93 *(688)*

2c carmine red *(25,609,470)*	1.00	1.00
Plate block of six	30.	
FDC *(July 9, 1930)*		30.

1930. Von Steuben Issue commemorated the 200th birthday of Baron Friedrich Wilhelm von Steuben, a Prussian officer who joined Washington at Valley Forge to serve as inspector general. Von Steuben reorganized and trained the army, lifted its morale, and fought at Monmouth and Yorktown. Naturalized in 1783, he was given 16,000 acres of land by New York State and an annual pension by Congress. *Intaglio, perforated 11.*

CM94 *Gen. von Steuben. From a memorial tablet by Karl Dautert, Magdeburg, Germany.*

CM94 *(689)*

2c carmine red *(66,487,000)*	.50	.50
Plate block of six	20.	
FDC *(Sept. 17, 1930)*		30.
v. Imperforate pair	—	
v. Imperforate plate block of six	—	

1931. Pulaski Issue tardily commemorated the 150th anniversary of the October 11, 1779, death of Count Casimir Pulaski, Polish patriot and hero of the American Revolution. Known as the Father of the U.S. Cavalry, he was mortally wounded leading a cavalry charge against the British at Savannah, GA. *Intaglio, perforated 11.*

CM95 *Gen. Casimir Pulaski. From an etching by H.B. Hall*

CM95 *(690)*

2c carmine red *(96,559,400)*	.25	.20
dark carmine red	.25	.20
Plate block of 6	12.50	
FDC *(Jan. 16, 1931)*		30.

1931. Red Cross Issue commemorated the 50th anniversary of the founding of the American Red Cross Society at Dansville, NY. Clara Barton (see CM309, CM1723) was its first president. The design of the stamp is adapted from the popular poster, *The Greatest Mother*, by Laurence Wilbur. *Intaglio, perforated 11.*

CM96 *Red Cross Nurse and Globe*

CM96 *(702)*

2c black and scarlet *(99,074,600)*	.25	.20
Plate block of four	2.00	
Margin block of 4, with arrow	—	
Double transfer	—	
FDC *(May 21, 1931)*		30.
v. Red (cross) omitted	—	

1931. Yorktown Issue commemorated the 150th anniversary of Lord Cornwallis' surrender at Yorktown, the last important battle of the Revolutionary War. When Lafayette's small force in Virginia was joined in June 1781 by Wayne and von Steuben, Cornwallis moved to Yorktown to maintain sea communication with Clinton's forces in New York. The sudden arrival of De Grasse's French fleet with 3,000 troops hemmed Cornwallis in completely. Washington, who had been preparing an attack on New York, suddenly marched his troops and the French forces of Rochambeau to Virginia, where, with almost 17,000 men, he began the siege of Yorktown. Cornwallis' attempt to escape across the York River by night was thwarted by a storm. On October 19 he surrendered almost 8,000 British and Hessian troops.

Flat press, two plate layouts used. Most panes have a straight edge along one side, but about 10 % of printing was from plates that permitted perforation all around, and thus these sheets have no straight edges. Perforated 11.

CM97 *Rochambeau, Washington, De Grasse. From painting s by J.D. Court and J. Trumbull and an engraving.*

CM97 *(703)*
2c carmine red and black

(25,006,400)	.35	.20
Plate block of four,two numbers 3.50		
Plate block of four, two numbers and arrow	—	
Plate block of six, two numbers, "TOP," and arrow	4.50	
Plate block of eight, two numbers, and "TOP"	—	
Center line block of four	—	
Margin block of four,with arrow	—	
Double transfer	—	
a. dark lake and black		
Plate block of four, two numbers	—	
b. lake and black	—	
v. Horizontal pair, imperforated vertically	—	
FDC	45.	

1932. Washington Bicentennial Issue commemorated the 200th birthday of George Washington, February 22, 1932, in Westmoreland County, VA. *Intaglio, perforated 11 x 10 1/2.*

CM98 *Washington. After miniature by Charles W. Peale, Metropolitan Museum of Art, New York, N.Y.*

CM 98 *(704)*
1/2c olive brown *(87,969,700)* .25 .20
Plate block of four 3.75
Broken circle (position 8 of
top-right pane of
plate No. 20560) —
FDC *(Jan. 1, 1932)* 17.50

CM99 *Washington. From bust by Jean A. Houdon, Mount Vernon, VA*

CM 99 *(705)*
1c yellow green *(1,265,555,100)* .25 .20
Plate block of four 3.75
Gripper cracks (top left and
top-right panes of
plate No. 20742)
FDC *(Jan. 1, 1932)* 17.50

CM100 *Washington at 40. After painting by Peale, Washington & Lee University, Lexington, VA.*

CM 100 *(706)*
1 1/2c yellow brown *(304,926,800)* .50 .20
Plate block of four 19.
FDC *(Jan. 1, 1932)* 17.50

CM101 *Washington at 64. After painting by Gilbert Stuart, Boston Museum, Boston, MA*

CM 101 *(707)*
2c carmine red *(4,222,198,300)* .25 .20
Plate block of four 2.00
Gutter pair —
Gripper cracks —
FDC *(Jan. 1, 1932)* 17.50

CM102 *Washington at 46. Painted by Peale at Valley Forge. West Chester State University, PA*

CM 102 *(708)*
3c slate purple *(456,198,500)* .50 .20
Plate block of four 15.
Broken top frame line
(position 8 of blottom-left
pane of plate No. 20847) —
Double transfer —
FDC *(Jan. 1, 1932)* 17.50

CM103 *Washington at 49. After painting by Polk, Rhinebeck, NY*

CM 103 *(709)*
4c yellow brown *(151,201,300)* .40 .20
Plate block of four 7.50
Broken bottom fram line
(position 100 of bottom-right
pane of plate No. 20568) —
Retouch in eyes (position 89 of
bottom-right pane of
plate No. 20568) —
Double transfer —
FDC *(Jan. 1, 1932)* 17.50

CM104 *Washington at 63. After painting by Peale, New-York Historical Society, N.Y.*

CM 104 *(710)*
5c Prussian blue *(170,656,100)*   1.75   .20
   Plate block of four   19.
   Cracked plate (position 80 of top-right
     pane of plate No. 20637)   —
   FDC *(Jan. 1, 1932)*   17.50

CM105 *Washington at 60. After a painting by John Trumbull, Yale University, New Haven, CT*

CM 105 *(711)*
6c orange *(111,739,400)*   3.50   .20
   Plate block of four   65.
   FDC *(Jan 1, 1932)*   17.50

CM106 *Washington at 48. After painting by Trumbull, Metropolitan Museum of Art, New York, N.Y.*

CM 106 *(712)*
7c black *(83,257,400)*   .40   .20
   Plate block of four   7.00
   Double transfer   —
   FDC *(Jan. 1, 1932)*   20.

CM107 *Washington at 66. After drawing by Charles Saint Memin, Brooklyn, N.Y.*

CM 107 *(713)*
8c bister *(96,506,100)*   3.00   .75
   Plate block of four   65.
   FDC *(Jan 1. 1932)*   20.

CM108 *Washington at 62. After drawing by W. Williams, Alexandria, VA*

CM 108 *(714)*
9c salmon *(75706,200)*   2.50   .20
   orange red   2.50   .20
   Plate block of four   40.
   FDC *(Jan. 1, 1932)*   20.

CM109 *Washington at 63. After portrait by Gilbert Stuart, Metropolitan Museum, New York, N.Y.*

CM 109 *(715)*
   10c orange yellow *(147,216,000)*   12.50   .20
   Plate block of four   125.
   FDC *(Jan. 1, 1932)*   20.

1932 Olympic Winter Games Issue honored the Third Wingert games, February 4-13 at Lake Placid, NY. *Printed in intaglio, perforated 11.*

CM110 *Ski Jumper*

CM 110 *(716)*
   2c carmine red *(51,102,800)*   .40   .25
   dark carmine red   .40   .25
   Plate block of six   12.50
   Cracked plate
   Recut (position 61 of top-right
     pane of plate No. 20823)
   'Snowball' (position 64 of top-right
     pane of plate No. 20815)
   FDC *(Jan. 25, 1932)*   25.

1932 Arbor Day Issue hailed the 60th anniversary of Arbor Day, observed in many individual states for the plating of trees. First celebrated in Nebraska, it was originated by Julius Sterling Morton, agriculturist, newspaper editor, Secretary of the Nebraska Territory, and national Secretary of Agriculture from 1893 to 1897. *Printed in intaglio, perforated 11 x 10 1/2*

CM111 *Children Planting Tree*

CM 111 *(717)*
2c carmine red *(100,869,300)*   .25   .20
   Plate block of four   7.00
   FDC *(April 22, 1932)*   15.

1932. Olympic Summer Games Issue honored the 10th Modern Olympic Games, held July 30-August 14 in Los Angeles, CA. The ancient games began in 776 B.C. and were banned in 394 A.D. Through the efforts of Pierre de Coubertin, French educator and sportsman, they were revived in 1896 in Greece. *Printed in intaglio, perforated 11 x 10 1/2.*

CM112 *Modern Athlete Preparing to Run*

CM112 *(718)*
3c reddish violet *(168,885,300)*   1.50   .20
   dark reddish violet   1.50   .20
   Plate block of four   15.
   Gripper cracks
   FDC *(June 15, 1932)*   25.

CM113 *Discus Thrower, by Myron, 5 B.C.*

CM113 *(719)*

5c blue *(52,376,100)*	2.25	.30
dark blue	2.25	.30
Plate block of four	27.50	
Gripper cracks		
FDC *(June 15, 1932)*		25.

1932. William Penn Issue commemorated the 250th anniversary of the arrival of William Penn (1644-1718) to found a colony. A Quaker at 18, Penn was imprisoned three times for religious nonconformity before he was 26. Inheriting a £16,000 claim against King Charles II, he asked for a grant of land in America and was given Pennsylvania in 1681. Landing October 24, 1682, at New Castle, Del., he organized the colony on a liberal basis guaranteeing freedom of conscience, made fair treaties with the Indians, laid out the city of Philadelphia and established the first successful postal system in America. *Intaglio, perforated 11.*

CM114 *Young William Penn. From a painting, Pennsylvania Historical Society, Philadelphia, PA.*

CM114 *(724)*

3c reddish violet *(49,949,000)*	.35	.25
Plate block of six	12.50	
Vertical pair, imperforate horizontally	—	
FDC *(Oct. 24, 1932)*		17.50

1933. Daniel Webster Issue commemorated the 150th anniversary of the birth of Daniel Webster and the 80th anniversary of his death. Famed orator, constitutional lawyer and statesman, Webster was elected four times to the Senate and twice appointed secretary of state. In 1840 he submitted a Senate resolution advocating reduced postal rates and the use of postage stamps in America. *Intaglio, perforated 11.*

CM115 *Daniel Webster. From a bust by Daniel Chester French, Franklin, N.H.*

CM115 *(725)*

3c reddish violet *(49,538,500)*	.35	.40
light violet	.35	.40
Plate block of six	20.00	
FDC *(Oct. 24, 1932)*		17.50

1933. Oglethorpe Issue commemorated the 200th anniversary of the founding of Georgia and the city of Savannah, and honored Gen. James Edward Oglethorpe. A philanthropist concerned with religious tolerance and the relief the debtors, Oglethorpe obtained a royal charter and led 120 immigrants in settling the colony. He successfully repulsed Spanish attacks and attempted a siege of St. Augustine, FL. *Intaglio, perforated 11.*

CM116 *Gen. James Edward Oglethorpe. From a painting at Oglethorpe University, Atlanta, GA*

CM116 *(726)*

3c reddish violet *(61,719,200)*	.35	.25
Plate block of six	14.	
FDC *(Feb. 12, 1933)*		17.50

1933. Newburgh Stamp commemorated the 150th anniversary of the Proclamation of Peace issued by Gen. George Washington from his headquarters at Newburgh, ending the Revolutionary War. *Perforated 10 1/2 x 11.*

CM117, CM142 *Washington's Headquarters at Newburgh, NY. From an engraving by James Smille*

CM117 *(727)*

3c reddish violet *(73,382,400)*	.25	.20
Plate block of four	6.00	
Block of four, horizontal gutter between	—	
Block of four, vertical gutter between	—	
Center block, with crossed gutters	—	
FDC *(Apr. 19, 1933)*		17.50

For ungummed stamps, see CM142.
Although not regularly issued that way, CM117 was also available in full sheets of 400 subjects.

1933. Century of Progress Issue commemorated the World's Fair held in Chicago, IL, to honor the 100th anniversary of its incorporation as a city. *Intaglio, perforated 10 1/2 x 11.*

CM118 *Fort Dearborn Blockhouse. From a painting by Dwight Benton*

CM118 *(728)*

1c yellow green *(348,266,800)*	.25	.20
Plate block of four	3.00	
Block of four, horizontal gutter between	—	
Block of four, vertical gutter between	—	
Center block, with crossed gutters	—	
Gripper cracks	—	
FDC *(May 25, 1933)*		17.50

CM119 *Federal Building at Fair*

CM119 *(729)*

3c reddish violet *(480,239,300)*	.25	.20
Plate block of four	3.00	
Block of four, horizontal		
gutter between	—	
Block of four, vertical		
gutter between	—	
Center block, with crossed		
gutters	—	
FDC *(May 25, 1933)*		17.50

Although not regularly issued that way, CM118 and CM119 were also available in full sheets of 400 subjects.

1933. Century of Progress Souvenir Sheets were issued in honor of the American Philatelic Society convention held in Chicago in August. Each sheet measures 134 x 120 mm, contains 25 ungummed, imperforate stamps, and is inscribed in the margin:

"PRINTED BY THE TREASURY DEPARTMENT, BUREAU OF ENGRAVING AND PRINTING—UNDER AUTHORITY OF JAMES A. FARLEY, POSTMASTER GENERAL, AT A CENTURY OF PROGRESS—IN COMPLIMENT TO THE AMERICAN PHILATELIC SOCIETY FOR ITS CONVENTION AND EXHIBITION— CHICAGO, ILLINOIS, AUGUST 1933."

CM120, CM156

CM120 *(730)*

1c yellow green, sheet of 25 *(456,704)*	35.	32.50
FDC *(Aug. 25, 1933)*		200.
Single stamp	.75	.20
FDC (single stamp)		15.

CM121, CM157

CM121 *(731)*

3c reddish violet, sheet of twenty-five		
(441,172)	30.	27.50
FDC *(Aug. 25, 1933)*		200.
Single stamp	.75	.50
FDC (single stamp)		15.

For Farley issue, see CM156 and CM157.

1933. NRA Issue publicized the National Recovery Administration, one of the first acts of the New Deal aimed at recovery from the Depression of the 1930's. The NRA was declared unconstitutional in 1935. In the original drawing for this stamp, the second figure was said by some to resemble President Roosevelt. A mustache was added since postal custom is against depicting a living person on a stamp. *Intaglio, perforated 10 1/2 x 11.*

CM122 *Workers Marching Forward. From a poster drawn by Rudolph L. Bortel*

CM122 *(732)*

3c reddish violet *(1,978,707,300)*	.25	.20
Plate block of four	2.00	
Gripper cracks		
Recut at right (position 47 of		
top-right pane of plate		
No. 21151)		
FDC *(Aug. 15, 1933)*		17.50

1933. Byrd Antarctic Stamp publicized the second expedition of Rear Adm. Richard E. Byrd to the South Pole. Flight routes used by Byrd, as well as proposed new routes, are indicated on the stamp. Letters mailed with this 3c stamp from the camp at Little America, Antarctica were subject to an additional service charge of 50c each. *Intaglio, perforated 11.*

CM123, CM143 *Globe with Antartic Routes*

CM123 *(733)*

3c blue *(5,735,944)*	.75	.60
Plate block of six	17.50	
Double transfer		
FDC *(Oct. 9, 1933)*		25.

For Farley issue, without gum, see CM143.

1933. Kosciuszko Issue commemorated Polish patriot Tadeusz Kosciuszko and the 150th anniversary of his naturalization as an American citizen. Gen. Kosciuszko fought throughout the Revolutionary War, served as aide to Washington, and laid out the fortifications of West Point. Afterward he led a rebellion that briefly liberated his native Poland from Russia. *Intaglio, perforated 11.*

CM124 *Gen. Tadeusz Kosciuszko. From a statue by Anton Popiel, Lafayette Park, Washington, D.C.*

CM124 *(734)*

5c blue *(45,137,700)*	.75	.35
Plate block of six	35.	
Cracked plate		
FDC *(Oct. 13, 1933)*		17.50
v. Horizontal pair, imperforate vertically		

1934. Byrd Souvenir Sheet honored the National Stamp Exhibition held in New York. It measured 87 x 93 mm, contained six imperforate stamps without gum. The margins of the sheets inscribed:

"PRINTED BY THE TREASURY DEPARTMENT, BUREAU OF ENGRAVING AND PRINTING — UNDER AUTHORITY OF JAMES A. FARLEY, POSTMASTER GENERAL — IN COMPLIMENT TO THE NATIONAL STAMP EXHIBITION OF 1934 — NEW YORK, N.Y. FEBRUARY 10-18, 1934."

CM125, CM158 *Globe with Antartic routes. Souvenir Sheet.*

CM125 *(735)*

3c blue, sheet of six *(811,404)*	17.50	16.50
FDC *(Feb. 10, 1934)*		75.
Single stamp	3.00	2.75
FDC (single stamp)		15.

For Farley issue, see CM158.

1934. Maryland Tercentenary Issue marked the 300th anniversary of the settlement of Maryland by about 200 colonists under a charter held by Cecilius Calvert, second Lord Baltimore, a Catholic. He made the colony a haven of religious tolerance. The *Ark* and the *Dove* were sailing vessels used in the voyage to America. *Intaglio, perforated 11.*

CM126 *The Ark and the Dove. From a drawing by Edwin Tunis*

CM126 *(736)*

3c carmine red *(46,258,300)*	.25	.20
Plate block of six	10.	
Double transfer (position 1 of top-left pane of plate No. 21190)	—	
FDC *(March 23, 1934)*		15.

1934. Mother's Day Issue commemorated the 20th anniversary of Woodrow Wilson's proclamation of the second Sunday in May as Mother's Day. The design shows the painting popularly known as "Whistler's Mother," a world symbol of motherhood, although the painter, James Abbott McNeill Whistler, called the picture simply *An Arrangement in Grey and Black.* Stamp issued in both rotary and flat-press printings. *Intaglio.*

CM127-128, CM144 *Whistler's Mother. From a painting by James McNeill Whistler, Louvre Museum, Paris, France*

Rotary press, perforated 11 x 10 1/2

CM127 *(737)*

3c reddish violet *(193,239,100)*	.25	.20
Plate block of four	1.25	
FDC *(May 2, 1934)*		15.

Flat press, perforated 11

CM128 *(738)*

3c reddish violet *(15,432,200)*	.25	.20
Plate block of six	5.00	
FDC *(May 2, 1934)*		1.00

For Farley issue, imperforate and without gum, see CM144.

1934. Wisconsin Tercentenary Issue memoralized the 300th anniversary of the arrival of the French explorer, Jean Nicolet, onto the shores of Green Bay in Lake Michigan. The first white man to reach that region, he appears in Chinese garb as he thought he was landing in China. *Intaglio.*

CM129, CM145 *Nicolet's Landing on Green Bay. From a painting by Edward W. Deming, Wisconsin Historical Society.*

CM129 *(739)*

3c reddish violet *(64,525,400)*	.25	.20
violet	.25	.20
Plate block of six	4.00	
FDC *(July 7, 1934)*		15.
v. Horizontal pair, imperforate vertically		
v1. Vertical pair, imperforate horizontally		

For Farley issue, imperforate and without gum, see CM145.

1934. National Parks Issue commemorated National Parks Year and publicized the great American park system. *Intaglio.*

CM130, CM146 *El Capitan, Yosemite (California)*

CM130 *(740)*
1c green *(84,896,350)*	.25	.20
light green	.25	.20
Plate block of six	1.50	
Recut	—	
FDC *(July 16, 1934)*		10.
v. Vertical pair, imperforate		
horizontally (with gum)	550.	

CM131, CM147 *Grand Canyon (Arizona)*

CM131 *(741)*
2c red *(74,400,200)*	.25	.20
Plate block of six	1.75	
Double transfer	—	
FDC *(July 24, 1934)*		10.
v. Horizontal pair, imperforate		
vertically (with gum)	350.	
v1. Vertical pair, imperforate		
horizontally (with gum)	400.	

CM132, CM148 *Mt. Rainier and Mirror Lake (Washington)*

CM132 *(742)*
3c reddish violet *(95,089,000)*	.25	.20
Plate block of six	2.00	
Recut	—	
FDC *(Aug. 3, 1934)*		10.
v. Vertical pair, imperforate		
horizontally (with gum)	450.	

CM133, CM149 *The Cliff Palace, Mesa Verde (Colorado)*

CM133 *(743)*
4c yellow brown *(19,178,650)*	.50	.35
light brown	8.00	
Plate block of six	—	
FDC *(Sept. 25, 1934)*		10.
v. Vertical pair, imperforate		
horizontally(with gum)	550.	

CM134, CM150 *Old Faithful, Yellowstone (Wyoming)*

CM134 *(744)*
5c light blue *(30,980,100)*	1.00	.75
blue	1.00	.75
Plate block of six	10.	
FDC *(July 30, 1934)*		10.
v. Horizontal pair, imperforate		
vertically (with gum)	475.	

CM135, CM151 *Crater Lake (Oregon)*

CM135 *(745)*
6c blue *(16,923,350)*	1.25	1.00
Plate block of six	20.	
FDC *(Sept. 5, 1934)*		22.50

CM136, CM152 *Great Head, Acadia (Maine)*

CM136 *(746)*
7c black *(15,988,250)*	1.00	.75
Plate block of six	12.50	
Double transfer	—	
FDC *(Oct. 2, 1934)*		10.
v. Horizontal pair, imperforate		
vertically (with gum)	550.	

CM137, CM153 *Great White Throne, Zion (Utah)*

CM137 *(747)*
8c gray green *(15,288,700)*	2.00	1.75
Plate block of six	20.	
FDC *(Sept. 18, 1934)*		10.

CM138, CM154 *Mt. Rockwell and Two Medicine Lake, Glacier (Montana)*

CM138 *(748)*
9c orange red *(17,472,600)*	2.00	.75
orange	2.00	.75
Plate block of six	20.	
FDC *(Aug. 27, 1934)*		10.

CM139, CM155 *Great Smoky Mountains (North Carolina)*

CM139 *(749)*
10c gray black *(18,874,300)*	3.25	1.25
gray	3.25	1.25
Plate block of six	30.	
FDC *(Oct. 8, 1934)*		10.

For Farley issues, imperforate and without gum, see CM146-CM155

1934. Trans-Mississippi Philitelic Exposition Issue
was released in honor of the Philatelic Exposition and
Convention held at Omaha, Neb. The sheet measured 94
x 99 mm, contained six imperforate, gummed 1c
National Parks stamps, and was inscribed in the margin:

"PRINTED BY THE TREASURY DEPARTMENT,
BUREAU OF ENGRAVING AND PRINTING—UNDER
AUTHORITY OF JAMES A. FARLEY, POSTMASTER
GENERAL — IN COMPLIMENT TO THE TRANS-
MISSISSIPPI PHILATELIC EXPOSITION AND
CONVENTION—OMAHA, NEBRASKA, OCTOBER 1934."

CM140, CM159 *El Capitan,
Yosemite (California)*

CM140 *(751)*

1c green, sheet of six *(793,551)*	14.	12.50
FDC *(Oct. 10, 1934)*		75.
a. Single stamp	2.00	1.75
FDC, single stamp		20.

*For Farley issue, imperforate and without gum, see
CM159.*

1934. American Philatelic Society Issue honored the
American Philatelic Society convention and exhibition
held at Atlantic City, NJ. The sheet measured 97 x 99
mm, contained six imperforate, gummed 3c National
Parks stamps, and was inscribed in the margin:

"PRINTED BY THE TREASURY DEPARTMENT,
BUREAU OF ENGRAVING AND PRINTING—UNDER
AUTHORITY OF JAMES A. FARLEY, POSTMASTER GENERAL
— IN COMPLIMENT TO THE AMERICAN PHILATELIC
SOCIETY FOR ITS CONVENTION AND EXHIBITION—
ATLANTIC CITY, NEW JERSEY, AUGUST 1934."

CM141, CM160 *Mt.
Rainier and Mirror Lake
(Washington)*

CM141 *(750)*

3c reddish violet, sheet of six *(511,391)*	40.	30.
FDC *(Aug. 28, 1934)*		75.
a. Single stamp	4.50	4.00
FDC, single stamp		20.

For Farley issue, imperforate and without gum, see CM160.

The Farley Issues (CM142-CM161)

The Farley Issues is a collective term commonly applied
to 20 stamps which were issued to the public as a direct
result of protests by collectors against the practice of
presenting to a few favored collectors full sheets of
stamps in forms not available to the general public.
Original "Farley Sheets"—signed by various government
officials, including Franklin D. Roosevelt, President;
Harold L. Ickes, Secretary of the Interior; and James A.
Farley, Postmaster General were given as philatelic
favorers to political friends.

The full sheets of the Farley Issues contained
four or more post office panes separated by spaces
(called gutters) or by guide lines and arrows (to guide the
cutting machine). Blocks showing two crossed gutters or
crossed lines are called "cross gutter" and "center line"
blocks, respectively.

All of the Farley stamps were issued ungummed.
In 1940 the Post Office Department gummed full sheets
of CM144-61 sent in by collectors for that purpose. With
the exception of CM142-43, all Farley stamps were
imperforate.

The Farley issues were first placed on sale March
15, 1935, at the Philatelic Agency in Washington, DC,
and were sold through June 15, 1935.

1935. Newburgh Farley Issue was printed in sheets of
400 stamps: 4 panes of 100 stamps, separated by
gutters. Newburgh Farley stamps differ slightly in color
from the original Newburgh issue (CM117); there seems
to be a tinge of blue in the violet. They usually are not
well-centered and the perforations are ragged. *Intaglio,
ungummed and perforated 10 1/2 x 11.*

CM142 *Block with horizontal
gutter*

CM142 *Cross gutter block*

CM142 *(752)*

3c reddish violet *(3,274,556)*	.25	20.
Plate block of four	16.50	
Block of four with		
arrow at top or bottom	15.	
Block of four with arrow at side	8.50	
Pair with vertical line	7.50	
Pair with horizontal line	4.00	
Center line block	50.	
FDC *(March 15, 1935)*		35.

1935. Byrd Farley Issue was printed in sheets of 200, so that arrows and guide lines along which the sheets normally were cut into panes of 50 before being sent to the post office, are complete. The stamps were issued *without gum and perforated 11.* Since it is virtually impossible to distinguish between a used copy of this and the original Byrd stamp (CM123), they must be considered interchangeable in used condition.

CM143 *Arrow block*

CM143 *Center line block*

CM143 *(753)*

3c blue *(2,040,760)*	.50	.45
Plate block of six	17.50	
Pair, with vertical line	2.00	
Pair, with horizontal line	40.	
Block of four, with arrow		
at top or bottom	85.	
Block of four, with arrow at side	4.00	
Center line block	90.	
FDC *(March 15, 1935)*		35.

1935. Mother's Day Farley Issue was printed in sheets of 200 with arrows and guide lines, identical in design to CM127, but issued *without gum* and *imperforate.*

CM144 *(754)*

3c reddish violet *(2,389,288)*	.60	.60
Plate block of six	18.50	
Block of four, with arrow		
at to or bottom	—	
Block of four with arrow at side	4.50	
Pair, with vertical line	1.75	
Pair, with horizontal line	2.25	
Center line block	10.	
FDC *(March 15, 1935)*		35.

1935. Wisconsin Farley Issue was printed in sheets of 200 with arrows and guide lines, identical in design to CM129, but issued *without gum* and *imperforate.*

CM145 *(755)*

3c reddish violet *(2,294,948)*	.60	.60
Plate block of six	18.50	
Block of four, with arrow		
at top or bottom	3.50	
Block of four with arrow at side	4.50	
Pair, with vertical line	1.75	
Pair, with horizontal line	2.25	
Center line block	10.	
FDC *(March 15, 1935)*		35.

1935. National Parks Farley Issues were printed in sheets of 200 with arrows and guide lines. The designs are identical to CM130-39, but the Farley versions were issued *without gum* and *imperforate.*

CM146 *(756)*

1c green *(3,217,636)*	.25	.20
Plate block of six	6.50	
Block of four, with		
arrow at top or bottom	1.25	
Block of four with arrow at sides	1.00	
Pair, with vertical line	.60	
Pair, with horizontal line	.45	
Center line block	4.50	
FDC *(March 15, 1935)*		30.

CM147 *(757)*

2c red *(2,746,640)*	.25	.20
Plate block of six	7.50	
Block of four, with		
arrow at top or bottom	1.50	
Block of four with arrow at sides	1.50	
Pair, with vertical line	.60	
Pair, with horizontal line	.65	
Center line block	5.00	
Double transfer	—	
FDC *(March 15, 1935)*		30.

CM148 *(758)*

3c reddish violet *(2,168,088)*	.50	.45
Plate block of six	17.50	
Block of four, with		
arrow at top or bottom	3.00	
Block of four with arrow at sides	3.75	
Pair, with vertical line	1.25	
Pair, with horizontal line	1.75	
Center line block	12.50	
FDC *(March 15, 1935)*		30.

CM149 *(759)*

4c yellow brown *(1,822,684)*	1.25	1.25
Plate block of six	22.50	
Block of four, with		
arrow at top or bottom	5.50	

Block of four with arrow at sides	6.50	
Pair, with vertical line	2.50	
Pair, with horizontal line	3.00	
Center line block	12.50	
FDC (March 15, 1935)		30.

CM150 (760)
5c light blue (1,724,576)	1.75	1.75
Plate block of six	27.50	
Block of four, with arrow at top or bottom	12.00	
Block of four with arrow at sides	10.	
Pair, with vertical line	5.25	
Pair, with horizontal line	4.25	
Center line block	20.	
Double transfer	—	
FDC (March 15, 1935)		30.

CM151 (761)
6c blue (1,647,696)		
Plate block of six	2.25	2.25
Block of four, with arrow at top or bottom	40.	
Block of four with arrow at sides	15.	
Pair, with vertical line	6.00	
Pair, with horizontal line	6.75	
Center line block	22.50	
FDC (March 15, 1935)		30.

CM152 (762)
7c black (1,682,948)	2.00	1.75
Plate block of six	37.50	
Block of four, with arrow at top or bottom	10.	
Block of four with arrow at sides	12.	
Pair, with vertical line	4.50	
Pair, with horizontal line	5.00	
Center line block	2.00	
Double transfer	—	
FDC (March 15, 1935)		30.

CM153 (763)
8c gray green (1,638,644)	2.00	2.00
Plate block of six	45.	
Block of four, with arrow at top or bottm	14.	
Block of four with arrow at sides	12.50	
Pair, with vertical line	6.50	
Pair, with horizontal line	5.00	
Center line block	22.50	
FDC (March 15, 1935)		30.

CM154 (764)
9c orange red (1,625,224)	2.00	2.00
Plate block of six	4750	
Block of four, with arrow at top or bottom	12.50	
Block of four with arrow at sides	14.	
Pair, with vertical line	12.50	
Pair, with horizontal line	10.	
Center line block	35.	
FDC (March 15, 1935)		30.

CM155 (765)
10c gray black (1,644,900)	4.00	3.50
Plate block of six	55.	
Block of four, with arrow at top or bottom	25.	
Block of four with arrow at sides	22.50	
Pair, with vertical line	12.50	
Pair, with horizontal line	10.	
Center line block	35.	
FDC (March 15, 1935)		30.

1935. Century of Progress Souvenir Sheet, Farley Issue, contained nine souvenir sheets of 25 stamps each, separated by gutters, issued *without gum* and *imperforate*. Identification of single stamps is possible only with stamps that come from the outside rows of the miniature sheets, in which the margins are wider than those from the regular sheets, CM120-21.

CM156 *Cross gutter block*

CM156 (766)
1c yellow green, pane of 25 (2,467,800)	22.50	22.50
Horizontal gutter block	—	
Vertical gutter block	—	
Cross-gutter block	12.50	
a. Single stamp	.75	.30
FDC (March 15, 1935)		40.

CM157 (767)
3c reddish violet, pane of 25 (2,147,856)	20.	20.
Horizontal gutter block	—	
Vertical gutter block	—	
Cross-gutter block	12.50	
a. Single stamp	.75	.30
FDC (March 15, 1935)		40.

1935. Byrd Souvenir Sheet, Farley Issue, contained 25 souvenir sheets of six stamps each, separated by gutters, issued *without gum* and *imperforate*.

Identification of single stamps is possible only if their margins are wider than those from the regular sheet, CM125.

CM158 (768)
3c blue, pane of six (1,603,200)	17.50	12.50
Horizontal gutter block	—	
Vertical gutter block	—	
Cross-gutter block	17.50	
a. Single stamp	2.75	2.25
FDC (March 15, 1935)		40.

1935. National Parks Souvenir Sheets, Farley Issue,

contained 20 souvenir sheets of six stamps each, separated by gutters, issued *without gum* and *imperforate*. Identification of single stamps is possible only if their margins are wider than those from the regular sheets CM140-41.

CM 159 *Pair with vertical gutter*

CM159 *(769)*

1c green, pane of six *(1,679,760)*	10.	9.00
Horizontal gutter block	—	
Vertical gutter block	—	
Cross-gutter block	12.50	
a. Single stamp	1.75	1.75
FDC *(March 15, 1935)*		40.

CM160 *(770)*

3c reddish violet, pane of six *(1,295,520)*	25.	20.
Horizontal gutter block	—	
Vertical gutter block	—	
Cross-gutter block	25.	
a. Single stamp	3.00	2.75
FDC *(March 15, 1935)*		40.

1935. Airmail Special Delivery Farley

was printed in sheets of 200 stamps with arrows and guide lines. It is listed in this section of the catalog because it always has been considered an integral part of the Farley Issues. *Intaglio, without gum, imperforate.*

CM161 *Line pair*

CM161 *(771)*

16c blue *(1,370,560)*	2.75	2.50
Plate block of six	70.	
Block of four, with arrow at top or bottom	13.50	
Block of four with arrow at sides	17.00	
Horizontal gutter block	—	
Vertical gutter block	—	
Center-line block	77.50	
FDC *(March 15, 1935)*		40.

1935. Connecticut Tercentenary Issue

commemorated the 300th anniversary of the settlement of Connecticut by dissatisfied members of the Massachusetts Bay Colony. The tree depicted is the oak in which the original Connecticut colony charter was hidden when it was demanded by the British in 1687. *Intaglio, perforated 11 x 10 1/2.*

CM162 *The Charter Oak. From a painting by Charles D. Brownell, State Library, Hartford, CT*

CM162 *(772)*

3c purple *(70,726,800)*	.25	.20
rose violet	.25	.20
Plate block of four	2.00	
Defect in cents sign (position 4 of top-right pane of plate No. 21395)	—	
FDC *(April 26, 1935)*		10.

For imperforates, see No. CM168

1935. California-Pacific Issue

commemorated the California-Pacific Exposition at San Diego, CA. *Intaglio, perforated 11 x 10 1/2.*

CM163 *View of the San Diego Exposition. From a sketch by Larrinague*

CM163 *(773)*

3c dark lilac *(100,839,600)*	.25	.20
Plate block of four	1.50	
Gutter pair	—	
FDC *(May 29, 1935)*		12.50

For imperforates, see No. CM168.

1935. Boulder Dam Issue

commemorates the dedication of the largest dam on the Colorado River. Built to supply power, water and flood control, its name was changed in 1933 to Boulder Dam, which appears on the stamp. Its original name, Hoover Dam, was restored in 1947. *Intaglio, perforated 11.*

CM164 *Boulder (Hoover) Dam*

CM164 *(774)*

3c dark lilac *(73,610,650)*	.25	.20
purple	.25	.20
Plate block of six	2.25	
FDC *(Sept. 30, 1935)*		15.

1935. Michigan Centennial Issue

commemorates the 100th anniversary of the admission of Michigan as the 26th state. *Intaglio, perforated 11 x 10 1/2.*

CM165 *Michigan State Seal*

CM165 *(775)*
3c dark lilac *(75,823,900)* .25 .20
  Plate block of four 1.50
  FDC *(Nov. 1, 1935)* 12.50
For imperforates, see No. CM168.

1936. Texas Centennial Issue commemorates the 100th anniversary of Texas independence, established after the Texans under Gen. Sam Houston defeated the Mexicans at the Battle of San Jacinto. The first Texas colony was founded by Stephen P. Austin under a Mexican charter in 1821. *Intaglio, perforated 11 x 10 1/2.*

CM166 *Sam Houston, Stephen F. Austin and The Alamo. From artwork by S. Salamo, T.A. Butler and F. Pauling*

CM166 *(776)*
3c dark lilac *(124,324,500)* .25 .20
  Plate block of four 1.50
  FDC *(March 2, 1936)* 15.
For imperforates, see No. CM168.

1936. Rhode Island Tercentenary Issue honors the 300th anniversary of the founding of Rhode Island as a haven of tolerance by Roger Williams. This was the only New England colony to tolerate a permanent Jewish community in the 17th century. *Intaglio, perforated 10 1/2 x 11.*

CM167 *Roger Williams, a statue by Franklin Simmons in Williams Park, Providence, R.I.*

CM167 *(777)*
3c dull purple *(67,127,650)* .25 .20
  rose violet .25 .20
  Plate block of four 1.50
  Gutter pair
  FDC *(May 4, 1936)* 10.

1936. TIPEX Souvenir Sheet was issued in compliment to the Third International Philatelic Exhibition held in New York City. The sheet measured 98 x 66 mm and contains one each of the Connecticut, California-Pacific, Michigan and Texas stamps. *Printed in intaglio, imperforate.* The sheet is inscribed in the margins:
  "PRINTED BY THE TREASURY DEPARTMENT, BUREAU OF ENGRAVING AND PRINTING—UNDER AUTHORITY OF JAMES A. FARLEY, POSTMASTER GENERAL—IN COMPLIMENT TO THE THIRD INTERNATIONAL PHILATELIC EXHIBITION OF 1936—NEW YORK, N. Y., MAY 9-17, 1936."

CM168 *Tipex Souvenir Sheet*

CM168 *(778)*
4x3c reddish purple, sheet of four
    (2,809,039) 2.75 2.50
  FDC *(May 9, 1936)* 17.50
  a. Any single from souvenir sheet .75 .60

1936. Arkansas Centennial Issue commemorated the 100th anniversary of the admission of Arkansas into the Union as the 25th state. *Intaglio, perforated 11 x 10 1/2.*

CM169 *Old State House in Little Rock, Ark.*

CM169 *(782)*
3c dark lilac *(72,992,650)* .25 .20
  Plate block of four 1.50
  FDC *(June 15, 1936)* 10.

1936. Oregon Territory Centennial Issue commemorated the 100th anniversary of the opening of the Oregon Territory, comprising the present states of Oregon, Washington, Idaho and parts of Montana and Wyoming. *Intaglio, perforated 11 x 10 1/2.*

CM170 *Map of Oregon Territory*

CM170 *(783)*
3c dark lilac *(74,407,450)* .25 .20
  Plate block of four 1.25
  Double transfer —
  FDC *(July 14, 1936)* 1.50

1936. Susan B. Anthony Issue honored the 16th anniversary of the ratification of the 19th Amendment, which granted suffrage to women. Anthony was a pioneer in temperance and social reform, and it was in part through her leadership and effort that women in the United States won the right to vote. *Intaglio, perforated 11 x 10 1/2.*

CM171 *Susan B. Anthony*

CM171 *(784)*
3c reddish purple *(269,522,200)* .25 .20
  Plate block of four 1.25
  FDC *(Aug 26, 1936)* 10.

1936-37. Army Issue honored the U.S. Army and paid tribute to its early leaders and heroes.

 CM172 *George Washington commanded the Continental Army throughout the Revolutionary War. (See CM98-CM109) Mount Vernon was his home in Virginia. Nathanial Greene led the patriot forces in the Southern theater. Both portraits are from Trumbull paintings.*

CM172 (785)

1c green *(105,196,150)*	.25	.20
Plate block of four	1.00	
FDC *(Dec. 15, 1936)*	7.50	

 CM173 *Andrew Jackson (from a statue by Belle Scholtz in the U.S. Hall of Fame) defeated the Creek Indians at Horseshoe Bend in 1814, and the British at New Orleans in 1815. The Hermitage was his Tennessee home. Winfield Scott (from a statue by Launt Thomas in the U.S. Soldiers' Home at Washington) fought gallantly at Chippewa and Lundy's Lane in the War of 1812 and led the U.S. Army in the Mexican War.*

CM173 (786)

2c rose red *(93,848,500)*	.25	.20
Plate block of four	1.00	
FDC *(Jan. 15, 1937)*	10.	

 CM174 *William Tecumseh Sherman has been called "the first moderm general." His march from Atlanta to the sea in the Civil war aimed at weakening his adversaires by the destruction of supplies rather than lives. Ulysses S. Grant split the Confederacy in two by capturing Vicksburg in 1863. After his successful Tennessee campaigns, he was given command under Lincoln of all Union forces and fought a war of attrition that brought the war to an end in 1865. Philip H. Sheridan, a cavalry commnader, distinguished himself at Chickamauga and Chattanooga, and commanded the army that laid waste to the Shenandoah Valley.*

CM174 (787)

3c dull purple *(87,741,150)*	.25	.20
Plate block of four	1.50	
FDC *(Feb. 18, 1937)*	7.50	

 CM175 *Robert E. Lee, whom Lincoln offered command of the Union field forces in 1861, resigned his commission instead to command the forces of Virginia. After his defeat at Gettysburg, July 1863, he fought bravely and brilliantly against hopeless odds, surrendering to Grant in 1865. Stratford Hall was his birthplace. Thomas J. Jackson, greatest of Lee's generals, won his nickname*

"Stonewall" by holding off strong Union assaults at the first Battle of Bull Run. After forcing back the Union troops at Chancellorsville, he was mistakenly shot by one of his own pickets.

CM175 (788)

4c slate *(35,794,150)*	.50	.20
Plate block of four	10.	
FDC *(March 23, 1937)*	7.50	

 CM176 *The U.S. Military Academy at West Point, New York, was established in 1802. Upon completion of a four-year course, cadets are eligible for commission as second lieutenants in the Army. Its graduates include all five generals pictured on CM174 and CM175. Among its civilian alumni were James Abbott McNeill Whistler (CM227) and Edgar Allan Poe (CM328).*

CM176 (789)

5c gray blue *(36,839,250)*	.75	.20
Plate Block of four	12.50	
FDC *(May 26, 1937)*	7.50	

1936-37. Navy Issue honored the U.S. Navy and paid tribute to early naval leaders and heroes. *Intaglio, perforated 11 x 10 1/2.*

 CM177 *John Paul Jones (from a painting by Peale) destroyed British ships, preyed upon the British coast and captured the man-of-war Serapis in a battle in which his own flagship Bonhomme Richard (shown) was sunk. John Barry (from a painting by Stuart) commanded the Lexington when he captured the first ship ever taken by a commanding officer of the U.S. Navy.*

CM177 (790)

1c green *(104,773,450)*	.25	.20
Plate block of four	1.00	
FDC *(Dec. 15, 1936)*	7.50	

 CM178 *Stephen Decatur (from a painting by Alonzo Chappel), fighting the Tripolitan pirates, effected the daring recapture of the frigate Philadelphia. He commanded the ship United States in the War of 1812. The stamp shows a contemporary warship under full sail. Thomas Macdonough (from a painting by Carl Becker) commanded the American fleet on Lake Champlain, where his brilliant victory over the British in 1814 saved New York and Vermont from invasion. The Saratoga was his flagship.*

CM178 (791)

2c rose red *(92,054,550)*	.25	.20
Plate block of four	1.00	
FDC *(Jan. 15, 1937)*	7.50	

CM179 *David Farragut (from a photograph by Brady) in 1862 destroyed the Confederate fleet at New Orleans. His foster brother David Dixon Porter aided him there and at Vicksburg; later, as superintendent of the U.S. Naval Academy, Porter greatly improved its organization and curriculum. The stamp mentions ships commanded and depicts a warship of the period.*

CM179 *(792)*

3c dull purple *(93,291,650)*	.25	.20
Plate block of four	1.50	
FDC *(Feb. 18, 1937)*		7.50

CM180 *William T. Sampson commanded North Atlantic Squadron which destroyed the Spanish fleet at Santiago, Cuba, in 1898 — sharing the victory with Winfield S. Schley, his second in command. Schley earlier had led the expedition that rescued the Arctic explorer Adolphus Greely in 1884. George Dewey, commanding the Asiatic Squadron, destroyed the Spanish fleet in the Philippines in 1898.*

CM180 *(793)*

4c slate *(34,521,950)*	.50	.20
Plate block of four	10.	
FDC *(March 23, 1937)*		7.50

CM181 *The U.S. Naval Academy at Annapolis, Maryland, was established in 1805. Upon completion of a four-year course, midshipmen are eligible for commissions as ensigns in the Navy. Its graduates include all three admirals pictured on CM180. The stamp pictures the Academy's seal and cadets of early days and the present.*

CM181 *(794)*

5c gray blue *(36,819,050)*	.75	.20
Plate block of four	12.50	
Gutter pair	—	
FDC *(May 26, 1937)*		7.50

1937. Northwest Ordinance Issue of 1787 marked the 150th anniversary of the adoption of the Northwest Ordinance by the Congress of the Confederation. The confederation's greatest achievement, it provided for the governing of the Northwest Territory, dividing it into five parts that are now Ohio, Indiana, Illinois, Wisconsin and Michigan. The Rev. Manasseh Cutler, a distinguished botanist, aided in drafting the ordinance and organizing the colonization. Rufus Putnam led the first settlers (see CM192), who founded Marietta, Ohio. *Intaglio, perforated 11 x 10 1/2.*

CM182 *Manasseh Cutler (from an engraving by J.C. Buttre), Rufus Putnam (from a Trumbull miniature), map of the Northwest Territory.*

CM182 *(795)*

3c dull purple *(84,825,250)*	.25	.20
Plate block of four	8.50	
FDC *(July 13, 1937)*		10.

1937. Virginia Dare Issue commemorated the 350th birthday of Virginia Dare, first child of English parentage born in America, at Roanoke Island off the North Carolina coast. Her grandfather, John White, leader of the expedition for Sir Walter Raleigh, returned to England for supplies a week after her birth in 1579. The Spanish War delayed his return until 1591, by which time the entire colony had mysteriously vanished. The stamps were printed 48 to the pane. *Flat plate printing, Intaglio, perforated 11.*

CM183 *Virginia Dare and parents. From a drawing by William A. Roache.*

CM183 *(796)*

5c light slate blue *(25,040,400)*	.25	.20
Plate block of six	8.50	
FDC *(Aug. 18, 1937)*		10.

1937. Society of Philatelic Americans Souvenir Sheet was issued in for the 43rd annual convention of the S.P.A. at Asheville, NC. It consisted of a single stamp, the 10c. Great Smokey Mountains National Park design (CM139), printed in blue green on a sheet measuring 67 x 78 mm. *Printed in intaglio, imperforate.* The margin is inscribed:

"PRINTED BY THE TREASURY DEPARTMENT, BUREAU OF ENGRAVING AND PRINTING—UNDER THE AUTHORITY OF JAMES A. FARLEY, POSTMASTER GENERAL—IN COMPLIMENT TO THE 43RD ANNUAL CONVENTION OF THE SOCIETY OF PHILATELIC AMERICANS — ASHEVILLE, N.C., AUGUST 26-28, 1937."

CM184 *SPA souvenir sheet*

CM184 *(797)*

10c blue green *(5,277,445)*	.75	.65
FDC *(Aug. 26, 1937)*		10.

1937. Constitution Sesquicentennial Issue marked the 150th anniversary of the signing of the U. S. Constitution. The Articles of Confederation having proved ineffectual, a convention was called in Philadelphia to revise and strengthen them. The convention, presided over by Washington, sat for four months in closed sessions, scrapping the Articles altogether and vigorously debating a new constitution point by point. On September 17, 1787, a final draft was signed by 39 of the 42 delegates present and sent to Congress for submission to the states. *In intaglio, perforated 11 x 10 1/2.*

CM185 *Adoption of the Constitution. From a painting by J.B. Sterns.*

CM185 *(798)*
3c bright purple *(99,882,300)* .25 .20
   Plate block of four 1.75
   FDC *(Sept. 17, 1937)* 7.50

1937. Hawaii Territory Issue honors Hawaii, which voluntarily joined the United States in 1898. King Kamehameha the Great (1737-1819) united the Hawaiian Islands under one rule and allowed the first foreign traders to settle there. *Intaglio, perforated 10 1/2 x 11.*

CM186 *Kamehameha I. From statue by T.R. Gould, Iolani Castle, Honolulu*

CM186 *(799)*
3c violet *(78,454,450)* .25 .20
   Plate block of four 1.50
   FDC *(Oct. 18, 1937)* 20.

1937. Alaska Territory Issue honors Alaska purchased from Russia in 1867 (see CM43). Mount McKinley, pictured on the stamp, is the highest North American peak. *Intaglio, perforated 10 1/2 x 11.*

CM187 *Mount McKinley*

CM187 *(800)*
3c violet *(77,004,200)* .25 .20
   Plate block of four 1.50
   Gutter pair
   FDC *(Nov. 12, 1937)* 15.

1937. Puerto Rico Territory Issue honors Puerto Rico, ceded to the United States by Spain after the Spanish-American War of 1898. The stamps shows the old Governor's Palace, in San Juan known as La Fortaleza. *Intaglio, perforated 10 1/2 x 11.*

CM188 *La Fortaleza Palace*

CM188 *(801)*
3c light reddish violet *(81,292,450)* .25 .20
   Plate block of four 1.50
   FDC *(Nov. 25, 1937)* 15.

1937. Virgin Islands Issue honored the Virgin Islands Territory, purchased from Denmark in 1917 to serve as a naval base for the defense of the Panama Canal. *Intaglio, perforated 10 1/2 x 11.*

CM189 *Harbor at Charlotte Amalie, St. Thomas, Virgin Islands*

CM189 *(802)*
3c lilac *(76,474,550)* .25 20
   Plate block of four .50
   Gutter pair
   FDC *(Dec. 15, 1937)* 15.

1938. Constitution Ratification Issue commemorated the 150th anniversary of the ratification of the Constitution of the United States. The endorsement of nine states was needed to make the Constitution effective. Maryland was the first state to ratify it. New Hampshire became the ninth (June 21, 1788).

CM190 *Colonial Court House, Williamsburg, VA*

CM190 *(835)*
3c violet *(73,043,650)* .50 .20
   Plate block of four 4.50
   FDC *(June 21, 1938)* 10.

1938. Swedes and Finns Issue commemorated the 300th anniversary of the settlement by Swedish and Finnish colonists of Fort Christina (now Wilmington, Del.). They were led by Peter Minuit, who was a leader in the earlier settlement of New York (see CM64). The stamps were printed 48 to the sheet. *Intaglio, perforated 11.*

CM191 *Landing of the Swedes and Finns. From a painting by Stanley M. Arthurs, Wilmington, Del.*

CM191 *(836)*
3c carmine purple *(58,564,368)* .25 .20
   Plate block of six 3.25
   FDC *(June 27, 1938)* 10.

1938. Northwest Territory Issue commemorated the 150th anniversary of the settlement of the Northwest Territory after the Northwest Ordinance of 1787 (see CM182). *Intaglio, perforated 11 x 10 1/2.*

CM192 *Colonization of the West. From a statue by Gutzon Borglum, Marietta, Ohio*

CM192 *(837)*
3c light reddish violet *(65,939,500)*   .25   .20
    violet   .25   .20
    Plate block of four   10.
    FDC *(July 15, 1938)*   10.

1938. Iowa Territory Issue commemorated the 100th anniversary of the establishment of the Iowa Territory, July 3, 1838. The stamp was placed on sale in Des Moines at the opening of the Iowa State Fair. The building pictured was the old Iowa capitol in Iowa city *Intaglio, perforated 11 x 10 1/2.*

CM193 *Old Capitol Building, Iowa City, Iowa.*

CM193 *(838)*
3c violet *(47,064,300)*   .25   .20
    Plate block of four   7.50
    Gutter pair   —
    FDC *(Aug. 24, 1938)*   10.

1939. Golden Gate Exposition Issue commemorated the international fair held in San Francisco, CA. The exposition's Tower of the Sun is shown. *Intaglio, perforated 10 1/2 x 11.*

CM194 *Tower of the Sun*

CM194 *(852)*
3c light reddish violet
    (114,439,600)   .25   .20
    Plate block of four   1.75
    FDC *(Feb. 18, 1939)*   *10.*

1939. New York World's Fair Issue commemorated the enormous fair and exhibition, "The World of Tomorrow," held in New York City during 1939-40. The Trylon and Perisphere served as a focal point for the fair. *Intaglio, perforated 10 1/2 x 11.*

CM195 *Trylon and Perisphere*

CM195 *(853)*
3c bluish violet *(101,699,550)*   .25   .20
    Plate block of four   2.25
    FDC *(April 1, 1939)*   12.

1939. Washington Inauguration Issue commemorated the 150th anniversary of George Washington's inauguration as first President of the United States. The oath of office was administered on the balcony of Federal Hall, at the corner of Wall and Broad Streets in New York City, by Robert Livingston, chancellor of New York State. *Intaglio, perforated 11.*

CM196 *Washington Taking the Oath of Office. From an engraving by Alonzo Chappel*

CM196 *(854)*
3c bright purple *(73,764,550)*   .25   .20
    Plate block of six   5.50
    FDC *(April 30, 1939)*   9.00

1939. Baseball Centennial Issue commemorated the 100th anniversary of this popular American sport. According to a story now generally held to be spurious, while attending school at Cooperstown, NY, in 1839, Abner Doubleday laid out the base and player pattern still used today. The National Baseball Hall of Fame and Museum at Cooperstown, was selected as the First Day site. *Intaglio, perforated 11 x 10 1/2.*

CM197 *Sandlot Baseball Game*

CM197 *(855)*
3c violet *(81,269,600)*   2.25   .20
    Plate block of four   11.
    FDC *(June 12, 1939)*   40.

1939. Panama Canal Issue commemorated the 25th anniversary of the opening of the Panama Canal (see CM48). Authorized by President Theodore Roosevelt, who arranged the requisite treaty with Panama in 1904, it was built under the direction of Col. George W. Goethals. *Intaglio, perforated 11.*

CM198 *Theodore Roosevelt, George W. Goethals and a ship in the Gaillard Cut of the Panama Canal*

CM198 *(856)*
3c deep reddish purple *(67,813,350)*   .50   .20
    Plate block of six   4.00
    FDC *(Aug. 15, 1939)*   10.

1939. Printing Tercentenary Issue recalled the 300th anniversary of printing in Colonial America. The press shown was brought to the colonies by the Rev. Joseph Glover, who died en route. Stephen Daye set up the press at Cambridge, MA. Its first publication, in March

1639, was a single sheet, "Oath of a Free-man." In 1640 it printed *The Bay Psalm Book,* the first American book in English. The press is now in the Harvard University Museum. *Intaglio, perforated 10 1/2 x 11.*

CM199 *Stephen Daye press*

CM199 *(857)*

3c violet *(71,394,750)*	.25	.20
Plate block of four	1.50	
FDC *(Sept. 25, 1939)*		8.00

1939. Four States Issue commemorated the 50th anniversary of the states of North Dakota, South Dakota, Montana and Washington. The stamp had three different first-day dates (November 2nd for the Dakotas, November 8th for Montana and November 11th for Washington) before being placed on general sale November 13. *Intaglio, perforated 11 x 10 1/2.*

CM200 *Map of North Dakota, South Dakota, Montana and Washington*

CM200 *(858)*

3c reddish purple *(66,835,000)*	.25	.20
Plate block of four	1.50	
FDC *(Nov. 2, 1939)*		7.50

1940. Famous Americans Series, issued over a nine-month period, paid tribute to America's men and women who have distinguished themselves and their country in their creative dedication to the betterment of all mankind. Honorees were chosen mainly through a poll conducted by the National Federation of Stamp Clubs. *Intaglio, perforated 10 1/2 x 11.*

Authors

CM201 *Washington Irving (1783-1859), America's first internationally accepted man of letters, is best remembered for his stories such as* The Legend of Sleepy Hollow *(see CM754) and* Rip Van Winkle.

CM201 *(859)*

1c emerald *(56,348,320)*	.25	.20
Plate block of four	1.25	
FDC *(Jan. 29, 1940)*		4.00

CM202 *James Fenimore Cooper (1789-1851) lives on through his adventure stories, notably* The Leather-Stocking Tales, *five novels about a pioneer scout named Natty Bumppo.*

CM202 *(860)*

2c carmine *(53,177,110)*	.25	.20
Plate block of four	1.25	
FDC *(Jan. 29, 1940)*		4.00

CM203 *Ralph Waldo Emerson (1803-82), New England philosopher, is known for the practical idealism of his essays and for poems such as* The Concord Hymn.

CM203 *(861)*

3c bright purple *(53,260,270)*	.25	.20
Plate block of four	1.25	
FDC *(Feb. 5, 1940)*		4.00

CM204 *Louisa May Alcott (1832-88), teacher, social reformer and Civil War nurse, wrote the spectacularly popular novel* Little Women *and many others.*

CM204 *(862)*

5c gray blue *(22,104,950)*	.40	.25
Plate block of four	12.	
FDC *(Feb. 5, 1940)*		5.00

CM205 *Samuel Langhorne Clemens (1835-1910) is known to the world as Mark Twain. His best-known character is Tom Sawyer, his greatest work* Adventures of Huckleberry Finn, *published in 1884.*

CM205 *(863)*

10c sepia *(13,201,270)*	2.25	1.75
Plate block of four	45.	
FDC *(Feb. 13, 1940)*		10.

Poets

CM206 *(864)*

1c emerald *(51,603,580)*	.25	.20
Plate block of four	2.00	
FDC *(Feb. 16, 1940)*		4.00

CM207 *John Greenleaf Whittier (1807-92), poet and abolitionist, is best remembered for his* Snow-Bound, The Barefoot Boy, Maude Muller *and* Barbara Frietchie.

CM207 *(865)*

2c carmine *(52,100,510)*	.25	.20
Plate block of four	2.00	
FDC *(Feb. 16, 1940)*		4.00

CM208 *James Russell Lowell (1819-91) also was a diplomat, teacher and satirist. His best-known works are* The Biglow Papers *and* The Vision of Sir Launfal.

CM208 *(866)*

3c bright purple *(51,666,580)*	.25	.20
Plate block of four	2.75	
FDC *(Feb. 20, 1940)*		4.00

CM209 *Walt Whitman (1819-92), poet of democracy and the individual, pioneered the free-verse form with a collection of poems called* Leaves of Grass, *first published in 1855.*

CM209 *(867)*

5c gray blue *(22,207,780)*	.45	.25
Plate block of four	12.	
FDC *(Feb. 20, 1940)*		5.00

CM210 *James Whitcomb Riley (1853-1916) wrote kindly, cheerful poems in Indiana dialect. His best-known works are* Little Orphan Annie *and* The Raggedy Man.

CM210 *(868)*

10c sepia *(11,835,530)*	2.25	1.75
Plate block of four	50.	
FDC *(Feb. 24, 1940)*		10.

Educators

CM211 *Horace Mann (1796-1859) founded the nation's first normal school and revolutionized the organization and teaching of the American public school system.*

CM211 *(869)*

1c emerald *(52,471,160)*	.25	.20
Plate block of four	2.75	
FDC *(Mar. 14, 1940)*		4.00

CM212 *Mark Hopkins (1802-87), for 36 years president of Williams College in Massachusetts, did much to raise American educational standards.*

CM212 *(870)*

2c carmine *(52,366,440)*	.25	.20
Plate block of four	1.25	
FDC *(Mar. 14, 1940)*		4.00

CM213 *Charles W. Eliot (1834-1926), president of Harvard, 1869-1909, made the school America's leading university and edited the* Harvard Classics, *commonly known as "Dr. Eliot's Five-Foot Shelf of Books."*

CM213 *(871)*

3c bright purple *(51,636,270)*	.25	.20
Plate block of four	2.75	
FDC *(Mar. 28, 1940)*		4.00

CM214 *Frances E. Willard (1839-1898), dean of women at Northwestern University, was a pioneer worker for the improvement of education for women.*

CM214 *(872)*

5c gray glue *(20,729,030)*	.40	.30
Plate block of four	12.	
FDC *(Mar. 28, 1940)*		5.00

CM215 *Booker T. Washington (1856-1910), born a slave, was America's leading Black educator. In 1881 he founded Tuskegee Normal and Industrial Institute.*

CM215 *(873)*

10c sepia *(14,125,580)*	2.50	1.75
Plate block of four	42.50	
FDC *(Apr. 7, 1940)*		10.

Scientists

CM216 *John James Audubon (1785-1851), ornithologist, painted birds from life. His* Birds of America, *published 1827-38, has been called "the most magnificant monument yet raised by art to science."*

CM216 *(874)*

1c emerald *(59,409,000)*	.25	.20
Plate block of four	1.25	
FDC *(Apr. 8, 1940)*		4.00

CM217 *Dr. Crawford W. Long (1815-78), a Georgia physician, is believed to have been the first surgeon to use ether as an anaesthetic in 1842.*

CM217 *(875)*

2c carmine *(57,888,600)*	.25	.20
Plate block of four	1.25	
FDC *(Apr. 8, 1940)*		4.00

CM218 *Luther Burbank (1849-1926), horticulturist, developed the Burbank potato and many new and better varieties of fruits, flowers and vegetables.*

CM218 *(876)*

3c bright purple *(58,273,180)*	.25	.20
Plate block of four	1.25	
FDC *(Apr. 17, 1940)*		4.00

CM219 *Dr. Walter Reed (1851-1902) led the experiments in Cuba establishing that yellow-fever is transmitted by a variety of mosquito, a discovery that made possible the virtual elimination of the disease.*

CM219 *(877)*

5c gray blue *(23,779,000)*	.50	.20
Plate block of four	7.75	
FDC *(Apr. 17, 1940)*		5.00

CM220 *Jane Addams (1860-1935), noted humanitarian, in 1889 founded Hull House, a social settlement to improve community life in the slums of Chicago. It was the first institution of its kind in the United States.*

CM220 *(878)*
10c sepia *(15,112,580)*   1.50   1.50
   Plate block of four   32.50
   FDC *(Apr. 26, 1940)*   6.00

Composers

CM221 *Stephen Collins Foster (1826-64), most popular of all American composers, wrote such songs as* O Susanna, Swanee River, Camptown Races, *and* Jeannie with the Light Brown Hair.

CM221 *(879)*
1c emerald *(57,322,790)*   .25   .20
   Plate block of four   .25   .20
   FDC *(May 3, 1940)*   4.00

CM222 *John Philip Sousa (1854-1932), a bandmaster and composer, was known as* The March King. *His most popular march is* The Stars and Stripes Forever.

CM222 *(880)*
2c carmine *(58,281,580)*   .25   .20
   Plate block of four   1.25
   FDC *(May 3, 1940)*   4.00

CM223 *Victor Herbert (1859-1924), Irish-born cellist and conductor, wrote many operettas, including* Babes in Toyland, The Red Mill *and* Naughty Marietta. *His best-known song is* Ah, Sweet Mystery of Life.

CM223 *(881)*
3c bright purple *(56,398,790)*   .25   .20
   Plate block of four   1.25
   FDC *(May 13, 1940)*   4.00

CM224 *Edward A. MacDowell (1861-1908), composed piano and orchestral works and songs. He is best known for his* Woodland Sketches *and* To a Wild Rose.

CM224 *(882)*
5c gray blue *(21,147,000)*   .75   .30
   Plate block of four   12.50
   FDC *(May 13, 1940)*   5.00

CM225 *Ethelbert Nevin (1862-1901), composed 70 songs, including* Narcissus, The Rosary, *and* Mighty Lak a Rose.

CM225 *(883)*
10c sepia *(13,328,000)*   5.00   2.00
   Plate block of four   50.
   FDC *(June 10, 1940)*   6.00

Artists

CM226 *Gilbert Charles Stuart (1755-1828) was one of the first eminent American painters. His portraits of contemporaries, especially Washington, have been used on many U.S. stamps.*

CM226 *(884)*
1c emerald *(54,389,510)*   .25   .20
   Plate block of four   1.00
   FDC *(Sept. 5, 1940)*   4.00

CM227 *James Abbott McNeill Whistler (1834-1903), a brilliant American painter and etcher, made his success in Europe. His portrait of his mother (see CM127) is his best-known work.*

CM227 *(885)*
2c carmine *(53,636,580)*   .25   .20
   Plate block of four   1.00
   FDC *(Sept. 5, 1940)*   4.00

CM228 *Augustus Saint-Gaudens (1848-1907), great Irish-born sculptor, is best known for his equestrian statue of Sherman in New York City , and hisstatue of Lincoln (CM).*

CM228 *(886)*
3c bright purple *(55,313,230)*   .25   .20
   Plate block of four   1.25
   FDC *(Sept. 16, 1940)*   4.00

CM229 *Daniel Chester French (1850-1931), New Hampshire sculptor, created* The Minute Man *(CM69) on Lexinton Green and the seated Abraham Lincoln in the Lincoln Memorial at Washington, D.C..*

CM229 *(887)*
5c gray blue *(21,720,580)*   .75   .30
   Plate block of four   11.
   FDC *(Sept. 16, 1940)*   5.00

CM230 *Frederic Remington (1861-1909) was a painter, illustrator and sculptor known for his depiction of lively action in Western scenes. His artwork on CM21, CM23,CM496 and CM993.*

CM230 *(888)*
10c sepia *(13,600,580)*   2.00   1.75
   Plate block of four   35.
   FDC *(Sept. 30, 1940)*   6.00

Inventors

CM231 *Eli Whitney (1765-1825) revolutionized the cotton industry in 1793 by inventing the cotton gin, a machine which separated cotton seed from the fiber 50 times faster than it could be done by hand.*

CM231 *(889)*
1c emerald *(47,599,580)* .25 .20
Plate block of four 2.00
FDC *(Oct. 7, 1940)* 4.00

CM232 *Samuel F.B. Morse (1791-1872), a portrait painter, invented the electric telegraph (CM266) and the telegraphic alphabet known as Morse Code.*

CM232 *(890)*
2c carmine *(53,766,510)* .25 .20
Plate block of four 1.25
FDC *(Oct. 7, 1940)* 4.00

CM233 *Cyrus Hall McCormick (1809-1884), in 1831 invented a reaping machine with all key features of the harvesting machines of today. It increased American farm output and settlement of the West.*

CM233 *(891)*
3c bright purple *(54,193,580)* .25 .20
Plate block of four 2.00
FDC *(Oct. 14, 1940)* 4.00

CM234 *Elias Howe (1819-67) invented the sewing machine in 1846, which revolutionized clothesmaking, lowered costs, increased qual;ity and eventually brought many women into American industry.*

CM234 *(892)*
5c gray blue *(20,264,580)* 1.25 .50
Plate block of four 17.50
FDC *(Oct. 14, 1940)* 7.50

CM235 *Alexander Graham Bell (1847-1922), whose interest in acoustics stemmed from his work in teaching the deaf, invented the telephone in 1876.*

CM235 *(893)*
10c sepia *(13,726,580)* 15. 3.25
Plate block of four 3.50
FDC *(Oct. 28, 1940)* 7.50

1940. Pony Express Stamp marked the 80th anniversary of the Central Overland California and Pike's Peak Express Company, the "Pony Express" that carried letters at $5 an ounce from St. Joseph, MO, to Sacramento, CA. Using 80 young riders, 420 horses, and 190 relay stations, it made the 1,900-mile trip in ten days (winter) or eight days (summer). *Intaglio, perforated 11 x 10 1/2.*

CM236 *Pony Express Rider*

CM236 *(894)*
3c chestnut *(46,497,400)* .35 .20
Plate block of four 3.50
FDC *(Apr. 3, 1940)* 7.50

1940. Pan-American Union Issue commemorated the 50th anniversary of the founding of the International Bureau of American Republics, now known as the Pan-American Union. It was created by the various republics of North, Central and South America for the development of trade relations and peace. *Intaglio, perforated 10 1/2 x 11.*

CM237 *Three Graces. From Bottivcelli's painting,* Spring.

CM237 *(895)*
3c lilac *(47,700,000)* .30 .20
Plate block of four 4.25
FDC *(April 14, 1940)* 5.00

1940. Idaho Statehood Issue commemorated the 50th anniversary of Idaho's admission as the 43rd state. The region, crossed by Lewis and Clark in 1806, was a part of the Oregon Territory (CM170) in 1848-63, before becoming Idaho Territory. *Intaglio, perforated 11 x 10 1/2.*

CM238 *State Capitol at Boise*

CM238 *(896)*
3c light reddish violet *(50,618,150)* .25 .20
Plate block of four 2.50
FDC *(July 3, 1940)* 5.00

1940. Wyoming Statehood Issue commemorated the 50th anniversary of Wyoming's admission as the 44th state. The state seal's central figure, a femal on a pedestal under the banner "Equal Rights," is a reminder that in Wyoming Territory women were given the right to vote in 1869. *Intaglio, perforated 10 1/2 x 11.*

CM239 *Wyoming State Seal*

CM239 *(897)*
3c purple brown *(50,034,400)* .25 .20
Plate block of four 2.25
FDC *(July 10, 1940)* 5.00

1940. Coronado Expedition Issue observed the 400th anniversary of the expedition by Francisco Vasquez de Coronado, seeking the fabled Seven Cities of Cibola. Coronado's men discovered the Grand Canyon, explored what is now Southern California and the Rio Grande, captured Zuni Indian settlements in New Mexico, and crossed the Arkansas River into Kansas. *Intaglio, perforated 11 x 10 1/2.*

CM240 *Coronado and His Captains. Painting by Gerald Cassidy*

CM240 *(898)*

3c reddish lilac *(60,943,700)*	.25	.20
Plate block of four	1.75	
FDC *(Sept. 7, 1940)*		5.00

1940. National Defense Issue focused attention upon the necessity for building an adequate national defense. Original sketches by President Roosevelt were the basis for the final designs. *Intaglio, perforated 11 x 10 1/2.*

CM 241 *The Statue of Liberty, rising 305 feet above the waters of New York Harbor, is the work of Alsatian*

sculptor Frederic Auguste Bartholdi (CM1163), who conceived the idea on a visit to the United States. A Centennial Gift from the People of France, it was up to America to supply the funds to build the pedistal, which was completed ten years later in 1886, after the effots of Pulitzer and his New York World newspaper. Its full name is "Liberty Enlightening the World"; and it has become a universal symbol of the freedom and security of democracy in America.

CM241 *(899)*

1c emerald *(6,081,409,300)*	.25	.20
Plate block of four	.50	
Cracked plate	—	
Gripper cracks	—	
Gutter pair	—	
FDC *(Oct. 16, 1940)*		5.00
v. Imperforate-between horizontal pair	—	
v1. Imperforate-between vertical pair	—	

CM242 *90mm anti-aircraft gun*

CM242 *(900)*

2c rose *(5,211,708,200)*	.25	.20
Plate block of four	.50	
Gutter pair	—	
FDC *(Oct. 16, 1940)*		5.00
v. Imperforate-between horizontal pair	—	

CM243 *Torch Symbolizing Enlightenment*

CM243 *(901)*

3c light reddish violet *(8,384,867,600)*	.25	.20
Plate block of four	.75	

Gutter pair	—	
FDC *(Oct. 16, 1940)*		5.00
v. Imperforate-between horizontal pair	—	

1940. Thirteenth Amendment Issue commemorated the abolition of slavery in the United States. President Lincoln's Emancipation Proclamation of 1863 freed only the slaves in states that had seceded from the Union, leaving the status of nearly a million others in northern and border states were unchanged. The Thirteenth Amendment, proclaimed in force December 18, 1865, abolished all involuntary servitude except as a punishment for crime. *Intaglio, perforated 10 1/2 x 11.*

CM244 *Emancipation Monument by Thomas Ball in Lincoln Park, Washington, D.C.*

CM244 *(902)*

3c violet *(44,389,550)*	.35	.20
Plate block of four	3.75	
FDC *(Oct. 20, 1940)*		7.50

1941. Vermont Statehood Issue commemorated the 150th anniversary of Vermont's admission into the Union as the 14th state. *Intaglio, perforated 11 x 10 1/2.*

CM245 *State Capitol at Montpelier, VT.*

CM245 *(903)*

3c violet *(54,574,550)*	.25	.20
Plate block of four	2.00	
FDC *(March 4, 1941)*		7.50

1942. Kentucky Statehood Issue commemorated the 150th anniversary of its admission as the 15th state. Kentucky was explored in 1767 by Daniel Boone who in 1775 led a party of settlers through the Cumberland Gap and over the Wilderness Road to erect a fort at what later became Boonesborough. *Intaglio, perforated 11 x 10 1/2.*

CM246 *Daniel Boone and Frontiersmen. Mural by Gilbert White, State Capitol, Frankfort, KY.*

CM246 *(904)*

3c reddish violet *(63,558,400)*	.25	.20
Plate block of four	1.25	
FDC *(June 1, 1942)*		5.00

1942. Win the War Issue, Following Pearl Harbor, replaced the 3c National Defense stamp (CM243) and symbolized the nation's war effort and its goal of victory. *Intaglio, perforated 11 x 10 1/2.*

CM247 *Victory Eagle*

CM247 *(905)*
  3c violet *(20,642,793,300)*   .25   .20
    light violet   .25   .20
    Plate block of four   .75
    Gutter pair   —
    FDC *(July 4, 1942)*   5.00
    a. purple   —

1942. Chinese Commemorative Issue honored five years of Chinese resistance to Japanese aggression. Chinese characters below the portrait of Sun Yat-sen, founder of the Republic, are Abraham Lincoln's words: "of the people, by the people, for the people." *Intaglio, perforated 11 x 10 1/2.*

CM248 *Abraham Lincoln, Map of China, Sun Yat-sen*

CM248 *(906)*
  5c Prussian blue *(21,272,800)*   .60   .30
    Plate block of four   12.
    FDC *(July 7, 1942)*   10.

1943. Allied Nations Issue commemorated the strength and unity with which nations of the free world were fighting to establish peace and freedom. *Intaglio, perforated 11 x 10 1/2.*

CM249 *Nations United for Victory*

CM249 *(907)*
  2c carmine *(1,671,564,200)*   .25   .20
    Plate block of four   .50
    Gutter pair   —
    FDC *(Jan. 14, 1943)*   5.00

1943. Four Freedoms Issue symbolized principles enunciated by President Roosevelt in the 1941 State of the Union message to Congress: freedom of speech and expression, freedom of worship, freedom from want, and freedom from fear. *Intaglio, perforated 11 x 10 1/2.*

CM250 *Liberty Bearing the Torch of Freedom and Enlightenment*

CM250 *(908)*
  1c emerald *(1,227,334,200)*   .25   .20
    Plate block of four   .60
    FDC *(Feb. 12, 1943)*   5.00

1943-44. Overrun Countries Series recognized the countries occupied by the Axis powers, which implied the free world's determination to liberate them.

For the first time since 1893, the Bureau of Engraving and Printing contracted with a private firm, the American Bank Note Co., so that the stamps could be printed in color. The frames of all values were engraved slate violet. The vignettes were printed by offset in two or three colors. *Flat-plate, Intaglio, perforated 12.*

CM251 *Flag of Poland*

CM251 *(909)*
  5c slate violet, scarlet, and black
    (19,999,646)   .25   .20
    'Poland' block of four   7.25
    'Poland' block of six, with
      guide markings   —
    FDC *(June 22, 1943)*   5.00

CM252 *Flag of Czechoslovakia*

CM252 *(910)*
  5c slate violet, blue, scarlet and black
    (19,999,646)   .25   .20
    'Czechoslovakia' block of four   4.00
    'Czechoslovakia' block of six,
      with guide markings   —
    FDC *(July 12, 1943)*   5.00

CM253 *Flag of Norway*

CM253 *(911)*
  5c slate violet, rose red, ultramarine and
    black *(19,999,616)*   .25   .20
    'Norway' block of four   1.75
    "Norway' block of six, with
      guide markings   —
    FDC *(July 27, 1943)*   5.00

CM254 *Flag of Luxembourg*

CM254 *(912)*
  5c slate violet, rose red, light blue and black
    (19,999,646)   .25   .20
    'Luxembourg' block of four   1.75
    'Luxembourg' block of six, with
      guide markings   —
    FDC *(Aug. 10, 1943)*   5.00

CM255 *Flag of Netherlands*

CM255 *(913)*
5c slate violet, scarlet, blue and black
(19,999,646)	.25	.20
'Netherlands' block of four	1.75	
'Netherlands block of six, with guide markings	—	
FDC *(Aug. 24, 1943)*		5.00

CM256 *Flag of Belgium*

CM256 *(914)*
5c slate violet, scarlet, greenish yellow and black *(19,999,646)*
	.25	.20
'Belgium' bock of four	1.75	
'Belgium' block of six, with guide markings	—	
FDC *(Sept. 14, 1943)*		5.00

CM257 *Flag of France*

CM257 *(915)*
5c slate violet, blue, red and black
(19,999,648)	.25	.20
'France' block of four	1.75	
'France' block of six, with guide markings	—	
FDC *(Sept. 28, 1943)*		5.00

CM258 *Flag of Greece*

CM258 *(916)*
5c slate violet, pale light blue and black
(14,999,646)	.50	.20
'Greece' block of four	15.	
'Greece' block of six, with guide markings	—	
FDC *(Oct. 12, 1943)*		5.00

CM259 *Flag of Yugoslavia*

CM259 *(917)*
5c slate violet, blue, rose red and black *(14,999,646)*
	.30	.20
'Yugoslavia' block of four	8.00	

'Yugoslavia' block of six, with guide markings —
'Yugoslavia' block of six, with guide markings	—	
FDC *(Oct. 26, 1943)*		5.00

CM260 *Flag of Albania*

CM260 *(918)*
5c slate violet, red and black
(14,999,646)	.30	.20
'Albania' block of four	8.00	
'Albania' block of six, with guide markings	—	
FDC *(Nov. 9, 1943)*		5.00

CM261 *Flag of Austria*

CM261 *(919)*
5c slate violet, red and black
(14,999,646)	.30	.20
'Austria' block of four	5.25	
'Austria' block of six, with guide markings	—	
FDC *(Nov. 23, 1943)*		5.00

CM262 *Flag of Denmark*

CM262 *(920)*
5c slate violet, scarlet and black
(14,999,646)	.30	.20
'Denmark' block of four	6.25	
'Denmark' block of six, with guide markings	—	
FDC *(Dec. 7, 1943)*		5.00

CM263 *Flag of Korea*

CM263 *(921)*
5c slate violet, scarlet, bright blue and gray *(14,999,646)*
	.30	.20
'Korea' block of four	5.25	
'Korea' block of six, with guide markings	—	
FDC *(Nov. 2, 1944)*		5.00
v. "KORPA" plate flaw	27.50	

1944. Transcontinental Railroad Issue marks the 75th anniversary of the completion of the first transcontinental railroad. A golden spike driven at Promitory Point, near Ogden, Utah on May 10, 1869, marked the meeting of the Union Pacific tracks from the west with the Central Pacific from the east. *Intaglio, perforated 11 x 10 1/2.*

CM264 *Golden Spike Ceremony. Mural By John McQuarrie, Union Pacific Station, Salt Lake City, Utah*

CM264 *(922)*
3c violet *(61,303,000)*   .30   .20
  Plate block of four   1.75
  FDC *(May 10, 1944)*   7.50

1944. Steamship Issue commemorated the 125th anniversary of the first steamship crossing of the Atlantic. The first-day date was National Maritime Day. The ship *Savannah*, sailing with an auxiliary steam engine, crossed from Savannah, GA, to Liverpool, England, in 19 days. *Intaglio, perforated 11 x 10 1/2.*

CM265 *S.S. Savannah. From ship model, Marine Museum, Newport News, VA.*

CM265 *(923)*
3c violet *(61,001,450)*   .25   .20
  Plate block of four   1.50
  FDC *(May 22, 1944)*   7.50

1944. Telegraph Centennial Issue commemorated the 100th anniversary of the first message sent by telegraph. The inventor, Samuel F.B. Morse (CM232), sent the historic words, "What hath God wrought!" from Washington, DC, to Baltimore, MD, where they were received by his associate, Alfred Vail. *Intaglio, perforated 11 x 10 1/2.*

CM266 *Telegraph Wires and Posts*

CM266 *(924)*
3c bright purple *(60,605,000)*   .25   .20
  Plate block of four   1.00
  FDC *(May 24, 1944)*   7.50

1944. Corregidor Issue paid tribute to the gallant resistance of Gen. Jonathan M. Wainwright's American and Philippine troops beseiged there by the Japanese in 1942. After the fall of Bataan, the surviving forces withdrew to Corregidor in Manila Bay and withstood the invaders for almost a month before surrendering May 6, 1942. *Intaglio, perforated 11 x 10 1/2.*

CM267 *Corregidor Island*

CM267 *(925)*
3c violet *(50,129,350)*   .25   .20
  Plate block of four   1.25
  FDC *(Sept. 27, 1944)*   7.50

1944. Motion Picture Issue commemorated the 50th anniversary of motion pictures and paid tribute to the cinema industry's contributions to the war effort. *Intaglio, perforated 11 x 10 1/2.*

CM268 *Motion Pictures for the Troops*

CM268 *(926)*
3c violet *(53,479,400)*   .25   .20
  Plate block of four   1.00
  FDC *(Oct. 31, 1944)*   7.50

1945. Florida Centennial Issue marked the 100th anniversary of Florida's admission as the 27th state. Explored by Juan Ponce de Leon in 1513, Florida was not settled by Europeans until 1565, when Pedro Menendez de Aviles set up a colony at St. Augustine, now the oldest city in the United States. West Florida was seized by the United States in 1813; East Florida was ceded by Spain in 1819. *Intaglio, perforated 11 x 10 1/2.*

CM269 *Gates of St. Augustine, State Seal and State Capitol*

CM269 *(927)*
3c bright purple *(61,617,350)*   .25   .20
  Plate block of four   .75
  FDC *(Mar. 3, 1945)*   7.50

1945. United Nations Conference Issue honored the conference in San Francisco at which the delegates of 50 nations met to draft the Charter of the United Nations Organization. President Roosevelt, who had invited them there, died 13 days before the conference. His words, "Toward United Nations, April 25, 1945," were inscribed on the stamp as a memorial to him. *Intaglio, perforated 11 x 10 1/2.*

CM270 *"Toward United Nations, April 25, 1945"*

CM270 *(928)*
5c ultramarine *(75,500 000)*   .25   .20
  Plate block of four   .75
  FDC *(Apr. 25, 1945)*   8.00

1945-46. Roosevelt Series paid tribute to President Franklin Delano Roosevelt (1882-1945), who died April 12, 1945. The only American for whom the "no third term" tradition was set aside, he was elected to the presidency four times. First taking office in a time of grave economic depression, he began the vast economic and social program known as the New Deal. He gave substantial support to Great Britain after the fall of France in 1940, wrote (with British Prime Minister Winston S. Churchil) the Atlantic Charter in 1941, defined the Four Freedoms (CM250), helped lead the fight to victory in World War II and called the conference which was to organize the United Nations. Thirteen days before it opened, he died of a cerebral hemorrhage at the 'Summer White House' in Warm Springs, GA (CM272), where he had set up a foundation for children who had, like himself, been stricken by infantile paralysis. He was buried in the garden of his home at Hyde Park, NY. (CM271)

An ardent stamp collector for 56 years, Roosevelt added greatly to the popularity of the hobby and suggested the designs of a number of postage stamps issued during his presidency. "I owe my life to my hobbies," he said, "especially stamp collecting." Many countries have honored him on their postage stamps. *Intaglio, perforated 11 x 10 1/2.*

CM271 *Roosevelt and Hyde Park*

CM271 *(930)*
  1c blue green *(128,140,000)*   .25   .20
    Plate block of four   .50
    FDC *(July 26, 1945)*   4.00
    p. printed on thin,translucent paper —

CM272 *Roosevelt and "Little White House" at Warm Springs, Ga.*

CM272 *(931)*
  2c carmine red *(67,255,000)*   .25   .20
    Plate block of four   .50
    FDC *(Aug. 24, 1945)*   4.00

CM273 *Roosevelt and the White House*

CM273 *(932)*
  3c lilac *(138,870,000)*   .25   .20
    Plate block of four   .50
    FDC *(July 27, 1945)*   4.00

CM274 *Roosevelt , Globe and Four Freedoms*

CM274 *(933)*
  5c light blue *(76,455,400)*   .25   .20
    Plate block of four   .75
    FDC *(Jan. 30, 1946)*   3.00

1945-46. Armed Forces Series of five stamps paid tribute to the nation's fighting forces and Merchant Marine for their valiant efforts toward victory in World War II.

1945. Marine Commemorative, honored the U.S. Marine Corps. The design, is taken from the famous photograph by Joseph Rosenthal of the Associated Press, showing the Marines raising the American Flag on Mount Suribachi on the Japanese island of Iwo Jima. The color was intended to match that of the Marine uniform. *Intaglio, perforated 10 1/2 x 11.*

CM275 *U.S. Marines Raising the Flag on Mount Suribachi, Iowa Jima*

CM275 *(929)*
  3c dark yellow green
    (137,321,000)   .25   .20
    Plate block of four   .75
    FDC *(July 11, 1945)*   7.50

1945. Army Commemorative honored the U.S. Army, particularly the infantry, in World War II. The design was devised from a group of photographs of the 28th Division marching through Paris. The color was selected to match the olive-drab uniform of the Army. *Intaglio, perforated 11 x 10 1/2.*

CM276 *U.S. Infantry, Bombers and L' Arc de Triomphe, Paris, France*

CM276 *(934)*
  3c brown olive *(128,357,750)*   .25   .20
    Plate block of four   .65
    FDC *(Sept. 28, 1945)*   7.50

1945. Navy Commemorative honored the U.S. Navy in World War II. The design reproduces an official Navy photograph made at the Corpus Christi Naval Air Station. The color was selected to match the blue uniform of the Navy. *Intaglio, perforated 11 x 10 1/2.*

CM277 *U.S. Sailors*

CM277 *(935)*
  3c blue *(138,863,000)*   .25   .20
    Plate block of four   .65
    FDC *(Oct. 27, 1945)*   7.50

1945. Coast Guard Commemorative honored the U.S. Coast Guard service in World War II. The nation's oldest uniformed service, the Coast Guard participated in every major invasion of the war. *Intaglio, perforated 11 x 10 1/2.*

CM278 *Coast Guard Landing Craft and Supply Ship*

CM278 *(936)*
  3c blue green *(111,616,700)*   .25   .20
    Plate block of four   .65
    FDC *(Nov. 10, 1945)*   7.50

1946. Merchant Marine Commemorative honored the achievements of the U.S. Merchant Marine in World War II. Photographs of two Liberty Ships, the *James Madison* and the *John W. Troy*, were used in the composite design. *Intaglio, perforated 11 x 10 1/2.*

CM279 *Liberty Ship and Goods*

CM279 *(939)*
3c blue green *135,927,000)*   .25   .20
    Plate block of four   .65
    FDC *(Feb. 26, 1946)*   7.50

1945. Alfred E. Smith Issue honored the colorful and popular American who rose from humble beginnings to serve four terms as governor of New York. Known as "The Happy Warrior," he was the Democratic candidate for president in 1928, but was defeated by Herbert Hoover. He died in 1944. *Intaglio, perforated 11 x 10 1/2.*

CM280 *Alfred E. Smith*

CM280 *(937)*
3c dark lilac *(308,587,700)*   .25   .20
    Plate block of four   .55
    Gutter pair   —
    FDC *(Nov. 26, 1945)*   5.00

1945. Texas Statehood Issue commemorated the 100th anniversary of Texas as the 28th state. A former Mexican state whose American settlers revolted in 1836 and set up a republic (CM166), Texas was granted Congressional authority to divide its vast territory into as many as five states of "convenient size" and "sufficient population" without further permission of Congress. *Intaglio, perforated 11 x 10 1/2.*

CM281 *U.S. and Texas Flags and the "Lone Star"*

CM281 *(938)*
3c Prussian blue *(170,640,000)*   .25   .20
    Plate block of four   .55
    FDC *(Dec. 29, 1945)*   5.00

1946. Honorable Discharge Stamp honored the members of the armed forces who were returning to civilian life after having served their country in World War II. *Intaglio, perforated 11 x 10 1/2.*

CM282 *Honorable Discharge Emblem*

CM282 *(940)*
3c violet *(269,339,100)*   .25   .20
    Plate block of four   .55
    FDC *(May 9, 1946)*   5.00

1946. Tennessee Statehood Issue commemorated the 150th anniversary of Tennessee as the 16th state. First settled in 1757 as part of North Carolina, it was ceded in 1784 to the federal government, which gave it neither administration nor protection. Settlers under John Sevier set up the independent State of Franklin in 1785-88, and later served as first governor of Tennessee. *Intaglio, perforated 11 x 10 1/2.*

CM283 *Capitol at Nashville, Andrew Jackson and John Sevier*

CM283 *(941)*
3c violet *(132,274,500)*   .25   .20
    Plate block of four   .55
    FDC *(June 1, 1946)*   3.00

1946. Iowa Statehood Issue commemorated the 100th anniversary of Iowa's admission as the 29th state *Intaglio, perforated 11 x 10 1/2.*

CM284 *Iowa map and Flag*

CM284 *(942)*
3c Prussian blue *(132,430,000)*   .25   .20
    Plate block of four   .55
    FDC *(Aug. 3, 1946)*   3.00

1946. Smithsonian Instutition Issue commemorated the 100th anniversary of its establishment at Washington, D.C. James Smithson, an English chemist, willed more than £100,000 as a gift to the United States for "an establishment for the increase and diffusion of knowledge among men." Today it includes a great library and several museums, including the National Postal Museum, (CM1589-92). *Intaglio, perforated 11 x 10 1/2.*

CM285 *Smithsonian Institution*

CM285 *(943)*
3c brown purple *(139,209,500)*   .25   .20
    Plate block of four   .55
    FDC *(Aug. 10, 1946)*   3.00

1946. Kearny Expedition Issue commemorated the 100th anniversary of the march of Gen. Stephen W. Kearny's Army of the West from Fort Leavenworth to New Mexico. Kearny's unopposed entry into Santa Fe on August 18, 1846, ended the Mexican War and established New Mexico as a part of the United States. *Intaglio, perforated 11 x 10 1/2.*

CM286 *Capture of Santa Fe. From a painting by Kenneth M. Chapman*

CM286 *(944)*

3c brown purple *(114,684,450)*	.25	.20
Plate block of four	.55	
FDC *(Oct. 16, 1946)*		3.00

1947. Thomas A. Edison Issue commemorated the 100th anniversary of the birth of America's greatest practical scientist. Thomas Alva Edison's more than 1,200 inventions include the incandescent electric bulb (CM85), the automatic telegraph repeater, teleprinter, mimeograph, phonograph, microphone, Ediphone, storage battery, electric dynamo, electric automobile, electric locomotive, carbon telephone transmitter, many motion picture developments, and telegraphic communication with moving trains. *Intaglio, perforated 10 1/2 x 11.*

CM287 *Thomas A. Edison*

CM287 *(945)*

3c bright purple *(156,540,510)*	.25	.20
Plate block of four	.55	
FDC *(Feb. 11, 1947)*		3.00

1947. Joseph Pulitzer Issue commemorated the 100th anniversary of the birth of Joseph Pulitzer, the Hungarian-born journalist who published the *St. Louis Post-Dispatch* and the *New York World*. It was a drive by Pulitzer's *World* that raised the funds to build the base for the Statue of Liberty. He founded and endowed the Columbia School of Journalism, which awards annual Pulitzer Prizes in journalism and letters. *Intaglio, perforated 11 x 10 1/2.*

CM288 *Joseph Pulitzer and the Statue of Liberty*

CM288 *(946)*

3c dark lilac *(120,452,600)*	.25	.20
Plate block of four	.55	
FDC *(Apr. 10, 1947)*		3.00

1947. Postage Stamp Centenary Issue marked the 100th anniversary of the first regular issue postage stamps. *Intaglio, perforated 11 x 10 1/2.*

CM289 *Washington and Franklin and New Methods of Carrying the Mail*

CM289 *(947)*

3c blue *(127,104,300)*	.25	.20
Plate block of four	.55	
FDC *(May 17, 1947)*		3.00

1947. CIPEX Souvenir Sheet was an imperforate, flat-plate souvenir sheet featuring reproductions of the two stamps of the 1847 issue produced for the Centenary International Philatelic Exhibition. Stamps cut out of the sheet are valid for postage and sometimes are mistaken for the 1847 originals by those who have not checked the colors. The reproduced 5c Franklin is light blue instead of the original red brown and 10c Washington reproduction isis Venetian red instead of black. The sheet is inscribed in the margin:

"PRINTED BY THE TREASURY DEPARTMENT, BUREAU OF ENGRAVING AND PRINTING—UNDER AUTHORITY OF ROBERT E. HANNEGAN, POSTMASTER GENERAL — IN COMPLIMENT TO THE CENTENARY INTERNATIONAL PHILATELIC EXHIBITION.—NEW YORK, N.Y., MAY 17-25, 1947."

Printed in intaglio, imperforate.

CM290 *CIPEX Souvenir Sheet*

CM290 *(948)*

15c complete sheet of two stamps		
(10,299,600)	.75	.65
a. 5c light blue, from sheet	.30	.25
b. 10c Venetian red, from sheet	.45	.25
FDC *(May 19, 1947)*		4.00

1947. The Doctors' Issue paid tribute to the physicians of America. *Intaglio, perforated 11 x 10 1/2.*

CM 291 *The Doctor. From a painting by Sir Luke Fildes*

CM291 *(949)*

3c brown purple *(132,902,000)*	.25	.20
Plate block of four	.75	
FDC *(June 9, 1947)*		7.00

1947. Utah Issue commemorated the 100th anniversary of the settlement of Utah by the Mormons under Brigham Young. Driven out of the Mid-West by religious persecution, members of the Church of Jesus Christ of Latter-Day Saints made a mass migration to the valley of the Great Salt Lake and founded a territory called Deseret, which in 1850 became the Utah Territory. *Intaglio, perforated 11 x 10 1/2.*

CM292 *Pioneers Entering the Valley of Great Salt Lake, Utah.*

CM292 *(950)*
3c violet *(131,968,000)*   .25   .20
    Plate block of four   .75
    FDC *(July 24, 1947)*   3.00

1947. U.S. Frigate Constitution Issue commemorated the 150th anniversary of the launching of the great fighting ship *Constitution*. Ordered dismantled in 1830, she was saved by public sentiment aroused by Oliver Wendell Holmes' poem *Old Ironsides*. *Intaglio, perforated 11 x 10 1/2.*

CM293 *Drawing of U.S. frigate* Constitution

CM293 *(951)*
3c blue green *(131,488,000)*   .25   .20
    Plate block of four   .55
    FDC *(Oct. 21, 1947)*   3.50

1947. Everglades National Park Issue commemorated the dedication of the park on December 6. The park contains more than a million acres of subtropical land in southern Florida, with extensive watercourses and profuse bird life. *Intaglio, perforated 10 1/2 x 11.*

CM294 *Great White Heron and Map of Florida*

CM294 *(952)*
3c emerald *(122,362,000)*   .25   .20
    Plate block of four   .75
    FDC *(Dec. 5, 1947)*   3.00

1948. George Washington Carver Issue memorialized the fifth anniversary of the death of the agricultural chemist. Born in slavery, and illiterate until he was almost 20, Dr. Carver spent 47 years as director of agricultural research at Tuskegee Institute, discovered hundreds of industrial uses for the peanut, sweet potato and soybean, aided Southern agriculture, and developed a new cotton strain known as Carver's Hybrid. *Intaglio, perforated 10 1/2 x 11.*

CM295 *George Washington Carver*

CM295 *(953)*
3c bright purple *(121,548,000)*   .25   .20
    Plate block of four   .55
    FDC *(Jan. 5, 1948)*   4.00

1948. California Gold Centennial Issue celebrated the 100th anniversary of the discovery of gold by James W. Marshall at Sutter's Mill in California. News of the discovery brought 100,000 gold-seeking "Forty-Niners," to the state from all parts of the world. *Intaglio, perforated 11 x 10 1/2.*

CM296 *Sutter's Mill, CA.*

CM296 *(954)*
    3c violet *(131,109,500)*   .25   .20
    Plate block of four   .55
    FDC *(Jan. 24, 1948)*   2.00

1948. Mississippi Territory Issue commemorated the 150th anniversary of the establishment of the Mississippi Territory, comprising the present states of Mississippi and Alabama. Winthrop Sargent was its first governor. *Intaglio, perforated 11 x 10 1/2.*

CM297 *Map and Original Seal of the Territory and Sargent*

CM297 *(955)*
    3c brown purple *(122,650,500)*   .25   .20
    Plate block of four   .55
    FDC *(Apr. 7, 1948)*   2.00

1948. Four Chaplains Issue honored the heroic chaplains—George L. Fox, Clark V. Poling, John P. Washington and Alexander D. Goode—who sacrificed themselves for their comrades when the S.S. *Dorchester* sank on February 3, 1943. Two ministers, a priest, and a rabbi, they gave up their life preservers so that others might live. *Intaglio, perforated 11 x 10 1/2.*

CM298 *Four chaplains and the Sinking S.S.* Dorchester

CM298 *(956)*
    3c black *(121,953,500)*   .25   .20
    Plate block of four   .55
    FDC *(May 28, 1948)*   2.00

1948. Wisconsin Centennial Issue commemorated the 100th anniversary of Wisconsin's admission as the 30th state. First explored by Jean Nicolet in 1634, it was surrendered by France to the British in 1760 and ceded by the British to the United States in 1783. It was part of the Northwest, Indiana, Illinois, and Michigan Territories before becoming the Wisconsin Territory in 1836. *Intaglio, perforated 11 x 10 1/2.*

CM299 *Scoll with Map of Wisconsin and State Capitol at Madison*

CM299 *(957)*
3c violet *(115,250,000)* .25 .20
   Plate block of four .75
   FDC *(May 29, 1948)* 2.00

1948. Swedish Pioneers Issue hailed the 100th anniverseary of the arrival of Swedish pioneers in the Mid-west. The 12 stars on the stamp represent the 12 states in which the immigrants settled. *Intaglio, perforated 11 x 10 1/2.*

CM300 *Swedish Pioneer and Covered Wagon*

CM300 *(958)*
5c blue *(64,198,500)* .25 .20
   Plate block of four .75
   FDC *(June 4, 1948)* 2.00

1948. The Progress of Women Issue observed the 100th anniversary of the first woman's rights convention, held at Seneca Falls, NY, July 19-20, 1848. The convention, called by pioneer feminists Elizabeth Stanton and Lucretia Mott, began the women's suffrage movement to which both devoted the rest of their lives. Carrie Chapman Catt led the suffrage campaign to its final victory in 1920, when the 19th Amendment gave women the vote. *Intaglio, perforated 11 x 10 1/2.*

CM301 *Elizabeth Stanton, Carrie Chapman Catt, and Lucretia Mott*

CM301 *(959)*
3c violet *(117,642,500)* .25 .20
   Plate block of four .55
   FDC *(July 19, 1948)* 2.00

1948. William Allen White Issue honored the distinguished editor of the *Emporia Gazette*, from 1896, when his editorial "What's the Matter with Kansas?" attracted nationwide attention, until his death in 1944. White was known for his intellectual greatness and honesty, and he made the *Gazette* one of the most notable newspapers in American history. *Intaglio, perforated 10 1/2 x 11.*

CM302 *Wiliam Allen White*

CM302 *(960)*
3c bright purple *(77,649,000)* .25 .20
   Plate block of four .55
   FDC *(July 31, 1948)* 2.00

1948. United States - Canada Friendship Issue commemorated a century of friendship between the United States and Canada. The 3,000-mile frontier between the two countries is the longest undefended border in the world. *Printed in intaglio, perforated 11 x 10 1/2.*

CM303 *The Niagara Gorge Railway Suspension Bridge joining the United States and Canada*

CM303 *(961)*
3c blue *(113,474,500)* .25 .20
   Plate block of four .55
   FDC *(Aug. 2, 1948)* 2.00

1948. Francis Scott Key Issue honored the author of our national anthem, *The Star Spangled Banner*. Negotiating the exchange of an American held by the British fleet off Baltimore, Key was detained aboard a warship while the British bombarded Fort McHenry on September 13, 1814. After the fort endured a 25-hour bombardment of more than 1,500 shells, Key was thrilled to see the Amercian flag still flying over the parapet. The verses were written there on the back of an envelope, published as *The Defense of Fort McHenry*, and set to an old English tune, *To Anacreon in Heaven*. The song was made the U.S. national anthem March 3, 1931. *Intaglio, perforated 11 x 10 1/2.*

CM304 *Francis Scott Key and Amercian Flags*

CM304 *(962)*
3c carmine *(120,868,500)* .25 .20
   Plate block of four .55
   FDC *(Aug. 9, 1948)* 2.00

1948. American Youth Issue paid tribute to the young people of America, and was a part of the celebration of Youth Month. *Intaglio, perforated 11 x 10 1/2.*

CM305 *Girl and Boy*

CM305 *(963)*
3c blue *(77,800,500)* .25 .20
   Plate block of four .55
   FDC *(Aug. 11, 1948)* 2.00

1948. Oregon Territory Issue commemorated the 100th anniversary of the signing of the Oregon Bill by Presiden James Polk. The bill, passed after seven months' wrangling between slavery and anti-slavery elements in Congress, established a non-slaveholding Oregon Territory. Jason Lee, a Methodist minister, had petitioned Congress for territorial status as early as 1836. Dr. John McLoughlin, who founded Fort Vancouver in 1824 and for 22 years served as administrator for the Hudson's Bay Company, is known as the "Father of Oregon." *Intaglio, perforated 11 x 10 1/2.*

CM306 *John McLoughlin, Jason Lee, and Wagon on Oregon Trail*

CM306 *(964)*
3c Venetian red *(52,214,000)* .25 .20
Plate block of four .55
FDC *(Aug. 14, 1948)* 2.00

1948. Harlan Fiske Stone Issue honored the great American jurist, appointed to the U.S. Supreme Court by President Calvin Coolidge in 1925. Stone was named 12th chief justice of the United States by President Franklin D. Roosevelt in 1941, and served until his death in 1946. *Intaglio, perforated 10 1/2 x 11.*

CM307 *Harlan Fiske Stone*

CM307 *(965)*
3c bright purple *(53,958,100)* .25 .20
Plate block of four .75
FDC *(Aug. 25, 1948)* 2.00

1948. Palomar Mountain Observatory Issue commemorated the dedication of the world's largest telescope on Palomar Mountain, 66 miles north of San Diego, CA. The 200-inch reflecting telescope, named in honor of the astronomer George Ellery Hale, penetrates a billion light years into the sky. *Intaglio, perforated 10 1/2 x 11.*

CM308 *Palomar Mountain Obseratory*

CM308 *(966)*
3c blue *(61,120,010)* .25 .20
Plate block of four 1.00
FDC *(Aug. 30, 1948)* 2.00
v. Vertical pair, imperforate
between —

1948. Clara Barton Issue honored the founder of the American Red Cross (CM96, CM358). A humanitarian, Miss Barton organized supply and nursing services for Union casualties in the Civil War (CM1723), successfully campaigned for an American society of the International Red Cross, and served as its first president, 1882-1904. *Intaglio, perforated 11 x 10 1/2.*

CM309 *Clara Barton and Red Cross*

CM309 *(967)*
3c carmine *(57,823,000)* .25 .20
Plate block of four .60
FDC *(Sept. 7, 1948)* 2.00

1948. Poultry Industry Centennial Issue marked the 100th anniversary of the establishment of the American poultry industry. *Intaglio, perforated 11 x 10 1/2.*

CM310 *Light Brahma Rooster.*

CM310 *(968)*
3c sepia *(52,975,000)* .25 .20
Plate block of four .60
FDC *(Sept. 9, 1948)* 2.00

1948. Gold Star Mothers Issue honored mothers of those members of the armed forces who lost their lives in both World Wars. *Intaglio, perforated 10 1/2 x 11.*

CM311 *Gold Star and Palm Branch*

CM311 *(969)*
3c yellow *(77,149,000)* .25 .20
Plate block of four .60
FDC *(Sept. 21, 1948)* 2.00

1948. Fort Kearny Issue commemorated the 100th anniverseary of the establishment of Fort Kearny, Neb., an important frontier post in protecting settlers. *Intaglio, perforated 11 x 10 1/2.*

CM312 *Fort Kearny and Pioneers*

CM312 *(970)*
3c violet *(58,332,000)* .25 .20
Plate block of four .60
FDC *(Sept. 22, 1948)* 2.00

1948. Volunteer Fireman Issue commemorated the 300th anniversary of the organization of America's first volunteer fire department in New Amsterdam (now New York City) by Peter Stuyvesant, director-general of the Dutch colony of New Netherland. *Intaglio, perforated 11 x 10 1/2.*

CM313 *Peter Stuyvesant and Fire Engines*

CM313 *(971)*
3c rose carmine *(56,228,000)* .25 .20
Plate block of four .60
FDC *(Oct. 4, 1948)* 2.00

1948. Indian Centennial Issue commemorated the arrival of the Five Civilized Indian Tribes in the Indian Territory, which later became the State of Oklahoma.

The Cherokee, Choctaw, Chickasaw, Muskogee (Creek), and Seminole tribes were called "civilized" because of their willingness to adopt the ways of white culture. *Intaglio, perforated 11 x 10 1/2.*

CM314 *Map of Oklahoma and the Seals of the Five Civilized Tribes*

CM314 *(972)*
3c brown *(57,832,000)*	.25	.20
Plate block of four	.60	
FDC *(Oct. 15, 1948)*		2.00

1948. Rough Riders Issue marked the 50th anniversary of the First U.S. Volunteer Cavalry Regiment, composed of cowboys and adventurous young Easterners, and known as the Rough Riders. Commanded by Col. Leonard Wood and Lt. Col. Theodore Roosevelt, they fought a spectacular dismounted action in the Battle of San Juan Hill, Cuba (July 1, 1898), seizing the heights and exposing Santiago and the Spanish fleet to artillery bombardment. Capt. William "Bucky" O'Neill, killed in the battle, was one of 1,572 American casualties. *Intaglio, perforated 11 x 10 1/2.*

CM315 *Capt. William O'Neill on Horse. From statue by Solon H. Borglum, Prescott, AZ*

CM315 *(973)*
3c brown purple *(53,875,000)*	.25	.20
Plate block of four	.60	
FDC *(Oct. 27, 1948)*		2.00

1948. Juliette Low Issue honored the Girl Scouts of America and the memory of founder Juliette Gordon Low, who organized its first troop in Savannah, GA, in 1912. *Intaglio, perforated 11 x 10 1/2.*

CM316 *Juliette Gordon Low and Girl Scout Emblem*

CM316 *(974)*
3c blue green *(63,834,000)*	.25	.20
Plate block of four	.60	
FDC *(Oct. 28, 1948)*		1.00

1948. Will Rogers Issue memorialized America's beloved cowboy philosopher and humorist. A part-Indian native of Oklahoma, Rogers began as a vaudeville entertainer, delivering humorous monologues while doing lasso tricks. As a lecturer, movie actor and newspaper columnist, he was known for his shrewd but kindly commentary on current events. He died in an airplane crash at Point Barrow, Alaska, in 1935 with his friend Wiley Post (A96-97), holder of the 'round-the-world flight record (See also CM929). *Intaglio, perforated 10 1/2 x 11.*

CM317 *Will Rogers*

CM317 *(975)*
3c bright purple *(67,162,200)*	.25	.20
Plate block of four	.60	
FDC *(Nov. 4, 1948)*		1.00

1948. Fort Bliss Centennial Issue commemorated the 100th anniversary of Fort Bliss, TX, largest cavalry post in America and later a center for guided-missile training. *Intaglio, perforated 10 1/2 x 11.*

CM318 *Fort Bliss and Rocket Launch*

CM318 *(976)*
3c chestnut *(64,561,000)*	.35	.20
Plate block of four	1.50	
FDC *(Nov. 5, 1948)*		1.00

1948. Moina Michael Issue honored the originator of the Memorial Poppy. John McCrae's poem, *In Flanders Fields*, spoke of wild poppies growing in the cemeteries of the dead of World War I. By an annual Memorial Day sale of poppies made by disabled veterans, Moina Michael used this symbol of the dead to assist the living. *Intaglio, perforated 11 x 10 1/2.*

CM319 *Moina Michael and Poppies*

CM319 *(977)*
3c rose carmine *(64,079,500)*	.25	.20
Plate block of four	.55	
FDC *(Nov. 9, 1948)*		1.00

1948. Gettysburg Address Issue commemorated the 85th anniversary of the brief speech with which Abraham Lincoln, dedicated the military cemetery at Gettysburg, PA, (CM174), November 19, 1863. The 11 sentences, which Lincoln said "the world will little note nor long remember," have since been recognized as one of the noblest and most eloquent orations in the English language. *Intaglio, perforated 11 x 10 1/2.*

CM320 *Abraham Lincoln. From the statue by Daniel Chester French, State Capitol, Lincoln, Neb.*

CM320 *(978)*
3c light blue *(63,388,000)*	.25	.20
Plate block of four	.55	
FDC *(Nov. 19, 1948)*		1.00

1948. American Turners Issue recalled the centennial of the formation in Cincinnati, of an association of gymnasts and athletes, known as the American Turners Society, which comes from the German "turnverein," meaning an exercise club. The organizer was Friedrich Hecker, a German refugee. *Intaglio, perforated 10 1/2 x 11.*

CM321 *American Turners Emblem*

CM321 *(978)*
3c carmine *(62,285,000)*   .25   .20
   Plate block of four   .80
   FDC *(Nov. 20, 1948)*   1.00

1948. Joel Chandler Harris Issue commemorated the 100th anniversary of the birth of the Georgia journalist and author of *Uncle Remus* and *Br'er Rabbit*. His stories, written for children, also are treasured by adults for their insights into human nature. The richness of their background and humor make them the greatest works in the school of folk literature. *Intaglio, perforated 10 1/2 x 11.*

CM322 *Joel Chandler Harris*

CM322 *(979)*
3c bright purple *(57,492,610)*   .25   .20
   Plate block of four   .60
   FDC *(Dec. 9, 1948)*   1.00

1949. Minnesota Territory Issue commemorated the 100th anniversary of the Minnesota Territory, with Alexander Ramsey as its first governor. It encompassed part of the Northwest Territory and part of the Louisiana Purchase. *Intaglio, perforated 11 x 10 1/2.*

CM323 *Pioneer and Ox Cart*

CM323 *(981)*
3c blue green *(99,190,000)*   .25   .20
   Plate block of four   .55
   FDC *(March 3, 1949)*   1.00

1949. Washington and Lee University Issue commemorated the 200th anniversary of the founding of Agusta Academy at Lexington, VA. In 1776, as a patriotic gesture, it was renamed Liberty Hall Academy. In 1798, endowed with $50,000 by George Washington, it became Washington Academy. It was renamed Washington and Lee University in 1871 after the death of its president, Gen. Robert E. Lee (CM175). *Intaglio, perforated 11 x 10 1/2.*

CM324 *George Washington, University, and Robert E. Lee*

CM324 *(982)*
3c bright blue *(104,790,000)*   .25   .20
   Plate block of four   .55
   FDC *(April 12, 1949)*   1.00

1949. Puerto Rico Election Issue celebrated Puerto Rico's first gubernatorial election, November 2, 1948. Acquired from Spain in 1898, the island was an unorganized territory until 1917, when its residents were made U.S. citizens. A bill signed by Presisent Harry Truman in 1947 gave it the right to choose its own chief executive by popular vote. Luis Muñoz Marin (927), its first elected governor, was sworn into office January 2, 1949. *Intaglio, perforated 11 x 10 1/2.*

CM325 *Puerto Rican Farmer with Cog Wheel and Ballot Box*

CM325 *(983)*
3c dull green *(108,805,000)*   .25   .20
   Plate block of four   .55
   FDC *(April 27, 1949)*   1.00

1949. Annapolis Tercentenary Issue marked the 300th anniversary of the founding of Annapolis by the colonists of Lord Baltimore's Maryland Plantation (CM126). Named for Queen Anne of England, it is the site of the U.S. Naval Academy (CM181). *Intaglio, perforated 11 x 10 1/2.*

CM326 *Map of 11718 and Seal of Lord Baltimore*

CM326 *(984)*
3c turquoise green *(107,340,000)*   .25   .20
   Plate block of four   .55
   FDC *(May 23, 1949)*   1.00

1949. GAR issue commemorated the 83rd and final encampment, August 28 at Indianapolis, IN, of the Civil War Union-veterans' organization known as the Grand Army of the Republic. Founded in 1866 by Benjamin Franklin Stevenson its members had included five presidents of the United States. *Intaglio, perforated 11 x 10 1/2.*

CM327 *Union Soldier and GAR Veteran*

CM327 *(985)*
3c carmine *(117,020,000)*   .25   .20
   Plate block of four   .55
   FDC *(Aug. 19, 1949)*   1.00

1949. Edgar Allan Poe Issue commemorated the 100th anniversary of the death of a world-renowned American writer. Born 1809 in Richmond, he was expelled from the University of Virginia for bad debts and from the U.S. Military Academy for disobedience and neglect of duty, and went on to a brilliant but erratic career. Now recognized as one of the world's great lyric poets, he also was one of the originators of the modern detective story. *Intaglio, perforated 10 1/2 x 11.*

CM328 *Edgar Allan Poe*

CM328 *(986)*

3c bright purple *(122,633,000)*	.25	.20
Plate block of four	.65	
Top inner frame line missing (position 42of bottom-left pane of plate 24143)	—	
FDC *(Oct. 7, 1949)*		1.00

1950. American Bankers Association Issue commemorats the 75th anniversary of its founding at Saratoga Springs, NY. The group made valuable contributions to the growth and development of American industry and life. *Intaglio, perforated 11 x 10 1/2.*

CM329 *Areas of Banking Service*

CM329 *(987)*

3c green *(130,960,000)*	.25	.20
Plate block of four	.55	
FDC *(Jan. 3, 1950)*		1.00

1950. Samuel Gompers Issue commemorated the 100th anniversary of the birth of the British-born labor leader who helped to found the American Federation of Labor and served as its president from 1886 until his death in 1924. Acknowledged leader of the American labor movement, Gompers concentrated it on the betterment of wages, hours and working conditions. *Intaglio, perforated 10 1/2 x 11.*

CM330 *Samuel Gompers*

CM330 *(988)*

3c bright purple *(128,478,000)*	.25	.20
Plate block of four	.55	
FDC *(Jan. 27, 1950)*		1.00

1950. National Capital Sesquicentennial Series, of four stamps commemorated the 150th anniversary of the establishment of the national capital at Washington, D.C. First national capital in the world expressly planned and built for that purpose, its site was chosen by George Washington, who appointed the French engineer Pierre Charles L'Enfant to plan the city. *Printed by intaglio, perforated 10 1/2 x 11 (CM 331) or 11x10 1/2 (CM332-34).*

CM331*Statue of Capitol Dome Freedom Statue by Thomas Crawford*

CM331 *(989)*

3c light blue *(132,090,000)*	.25	.20
Plate block of four	.60	
FDC *(April 20, 1950)*		1.00

 CM332 *Executive Mansion, shich Congress in 1902 officially designated The White House, was designed in 1792 by James Hoban (CM994-95), who is believed to have patterned it after the Duke of Leinster's palace in Dublin. Its sandstone walls were painted white after the British burned it in 1814. It was enlarged by William Howard Taft and by both Roosevelts. In 1951-52, in bad disrepair, it was completely reconstructed within its original walls during the presidency of Harry Truman.*

CM332 *(990)*

3c dull green *(130,050,000)*	.25	.20
Plate block of four	.65	
FDC *(June 12, 1950)*		1.00

 CM333 *The Supreme Court Building*

CM333 *(991)*

3c bluish violet *(131,350,000)*	.25	.20
Plate block of four	.60	
FDC *(Aug. 2, 1950)*		1.00

 CM334 *The U.S. Capitol is the seat of the Congress. Designed by William Thornton, it was built during 1793-1800, restored in 1814-17 after being burned by British troops in the War of 1812, and greatly enlarged in 1861-65, when the dome also was added.*

CM334 *(992)*

3c bright purple *(129,980,000)*	.25	.20
Plate block of four	.80	
Gripper cracks		
FDC *(Nov. 22, 1950)*		1.00

1950. Railroad Engineers Issue paid tribute to American railway and pictured their fabled hero, "Casey" Jones. Born John Luther Jones in 1864, he acquired the nickname "Casey" for having lived at one time in Cayce, KY. A railroader from boyhood, he spent the last 10 years of his life as an engineer with the Illinois Central Railroad. The "big eight-wheeler" in which he won his fame was a part of the Cannonball Express between Chicago and New Orleans, and Jones' run was between Canton, MI, and Memphis, TN. He was killed April 30, 1900, when his train crashed into the rear of a freight train near Vaughn, MI, and the ballad about the wreck is known throughout America. *Intaglio, perforated 11 x 10 1/2.*

CM335 *"Casey" Jones, Steam and Diesel Locomotives*

CM335 *(993)*

3c brown purple *(122,315,000)*	.25	.20
Plate block of four	.60	
FDC *(April 29, 1950)*		1.00

1950. Kansas City Centennial Issue commemorated the 100th anniversary of the incorporation of Kansas City, MO. The "Gateway to the West," was first settled by a French fur trapper named Louis Barthelot. *Intaglio, perforated 11 x 10 1/2.*

CM336 *Kansas City in 1950 and Westport Landing in 1850*

CM336 *(994)*

3c violet *(122,170,000)*	.25	.20
Plate block of four	.55	
FDC *(June 3, 1950)*		1.00

1950. Boy Scouts Issue honored the 40th anniversary of the Boy Scouts of America, and the second National Jamboree at Valley Forge, PA. The organization (CM454, CM1173) was incorporated February 8, 1910, formed by uniting Ernest Thompson Seton's *Woodcraft Indians* with Daniel Beard's *Sons of Daniel Boone*, with ideas from the English program of Robert Baden-Powell. *Intaglio, perforated 11 x 10 1/2.*

CM337 *Scouts, Statue of Liberty, and Scout badge*

CM337 *(995)*

3c sepia *(131,635,000)*	.25	.20
Plate block of four	.60	
FDC *(June 30, 1950)*		1.00

1950. Indiana Territory Sesquicentennial Issue marked the 150th anniversary of the Indiana Territory. William Henry Harrison, later a military hero and ninth president, was the territory's first governor. *Intaglio, perforated 11 x 10 1/2.*

CM338 *Gov. William Henry Harrison and First Capitol at Vincennes*

CM338 *(996)*

3c light blue *(121,860,000)*	.25	.20
Plate block of four	.55	
FDC *(July 4, 1950)*		1.00

1950. California Statehood Centennial Issue commemorated the 100th anniversary of California's admission as the 31st state. First settled by the Spaniards under Gaspar de Portola, the territory was ceded to the United States by Mexico in 1848. Its development was greatly accelerated by the discovery of gold that year at Sutter's Mill (CM296). *Intaglio, perforated 11 x 10 1/2.*

CM339 *Gold Miner, Pioneers and S.S> Oregon*

CM339 *(997)*

3c yellow *(121,120,000)*	.25	.20
Plate block of four	.55	
FDC *(Sept. 9, 1950)*		1.00

1951. Confederate Veterans Issue commemorated the final reunion, May 30 at Norfolk, VA, of the Veterans of the Confederacy, organized in New Orleans in 1889. *Intaglio, perforated 11 x 10 1/2.*

CM340 *Confederate Soldier and Veteran*

CM340 *(998)*

3c gray *(119,120,000)*	.25	.20
Plate block of four	.60	
FDC *(May 30, 1951)*		1.00

1951. Nevada Centennial Issue commemorated the first settlement of Nevada in 1851. The discovery of the Comstock Lode in 1856 led to rapid development of the territory; by 1863 it had 40,000 inhabitants and was producing as much as $30,000,000 worth of silver a year. Nevada was admitted to statehood in 1864. *Intaglio, perforated 11 x 10 1/2.*

CM341 *Carson Valley Homestead*

CM341 *(999)*

3c light olive green *(112,125,000)*	.25	.20
Plate block of four	.55	
FDC *(July 14, 1951)*		1.00

1951. Detroit Issue noted the 250th anniversary of the landing of Antoine de la Mothe Cadillac, at what is now Detroit, with a charter from King Louis XIV of France. Established by Cadillac as a military post to protect his fur trade, Detroit became the automotive capital of the world. *Intaglio, perforated 11 x 10 1/2.*

CM342 *Landing of Cadillac at Detroit, Modern Skyline*

CM342 *(1000)*
   3c light blue *(114,140,000)*   .25   .20
     Plate block of four   .55
     FDC *(July 24, 1951)*   1.00

1951. Colorado Statehood Issue commemorated the 75th anniversary of Colorado's admission as the 38th state. Formed of lands that were once part of the Louisiana Purchase and of the Texas and Mexican cessions, it became a territory in 1861. *Intaglio, perforated 11 x 10 1/2.*

CM343 *Capitol at Denver, Mount of the Holy Cross, Bronco Buster.*

CM343 *(1001)*
   3c violet blue *(114,490,000)*   .25   .20
     Plate block of four   .55
     FDC *(Aug. 1, 1951)*   1.00

1951. American Chemical Society Issue marks the 75th anniversary of the American Chemical Society. *Intaglio, perforated 11 x 10 1/2.*

CM344 *ACS Emblem, Industrial Chemical Equiptment*

CM344 *(1002)*
   3c brown purple *(117,200,000)*   .25   .20
     Plate block of four   .55
     FDC *(Sept. 4, 1951)*   1.00

1951. Battle of Brooklyn Issue commemorated the 175th anniversary of the Battle of Long Island, August 27, 1776. British and Hessian troops, under Clinton, Howe, Percy, Cornwallis and DeHesiter, attacked the American fortifications at what is now Prospect Park in Brooklyn, overpowered the desperate Americans and captured their commander, Gen. John Sullivan (CM88). General Washington arrived late in the day with additional troops, saw the futility of making a stand, and withdrew the remaining American forces in a skillful night retreat. *Intaglio, perforated 11 x 10 1/2.*

CM345 *Gen. George Washington Evacuating the Army*

CM345 *(1003)*
   3c violet *(16,130,000)*   .25   .20
     Plate block of four   .60
     FDC *(Dec. 10, 1951)*   1.00

1952. Betsy Ross Issue celebrated the 200th birthday of Betsy Ross, the Philadelphia upholsterer, whom the Continental Congress engaged in 1777 to make the first American flag. The legend that she designed the original Stars and Stripes generally is disputed, and the credit given to Francis Hopkinson, one of the signers of the Declaration of Independence. *Intaglio, perforated 11 x 10 1/2.*

CM346 *Birth of Our Nation's Flag. From a painting by C.H. Weisgerber*

CM346 *(1004)*
   3c carmine red *(116,175,000)*   .25   .20
     Plate block of four   .55
     FDC *(Jan. 2, 1952)*   1.00

1952. 4-H Club Issue honored the farm youth organization whose emblem - the letter H on each leaf of a four-leaf clover - signifies the 4-H pledge: "I pledge— My Head to clear thinking. My Heart to great Loyalty. My Hands to larger service. My Health to better living, for my club, my community, and my country." *Intaglio, perforated 11 x 10 1/2.*

CM347 *American Farm, 4-H Emblem and Members*

CM347 *(1005)*
   3c blue green *(115,945,000)*   .25   .20
     Plate block of four   .55
     FDC *(Jan. 15, 1952)*   1.00

1952. American Railroads Issue commemorated the 125th anniversary of the chartering of the B & O Railroad by the Maryland Legislature. The first passenger railroad in the United States, it was begun on July 4, 1828 with Charles Carroll of Carrollton in attendance, the last living signer of the Declarition of Independence. The first 14-mile section opened to horse-drawn traffic May 24, 1830. *Intaglio, perforated 11 x 10 1/2.*

CM348 *Charter, Horse-Drawn Car, Tom Thumb and Modern Diesel*

CM348 *(1006)*
   3c light blue *(112,540,000)*   .25   .20
     Plate block of four   .55
     FDC *(Feb. 28, 1952)*   1.00

1952. AAA Issue commemorated the 50th anniversary of the American Automobile Association (the Tripple-A) and honored its contribution to motoring safety and convenience. *Intaglio, perforated 11 x 10 1/2.*

CM349 *Children and Crossing Guard, Automobiles of 1902 and 1952*

CM349 *(1007)*
3c blue *(117,415,000)* .25 .20
   Plate block of four .55
   FDC *(March 4, 1952)* 1.00

1952. NATO Issue commemorated the third anniversary of the signing of the North Atlantic Treaty Organization, in which the United States, Canada and 10 Western European nations pledged that an armed attack against any of them would be considered an attack against all. *Intaglio, perforated 11 x 10 1/2.*

CM350 *The Torch of Liberty, Globe*

CM350 *(1008)*
3c violet *(2,899,580,000)* .25 .20
   Plate block of four .55
   FDC *(April 4, 1952)* 1.00
   v. thin, translucent paper

1952. Grand Coulee Dam Issue commemorated 50 years of federal cooperation in developing western rivers, and paid tribute to the world's largest concrete dam, the Grand Coulee, built and operated by the Bureau of Reclamation on Washington's Columbia River. *Intaglio, perforated 11 x 10 1/2.*

CM351 *Grand Coulee Dam Spillway*

CM351 *(1009)*
3c blue green *(114,540,000)* .25 .20
   Plate block of four .55
   FDC *(May 15, 1952)* 1.00

1952. Lafayette Issue commemorated the 175th anniversary of the arrival in America of Marquis de Lafayette (CM409, CM866) to fight for American freedom. Commissioned a major general at 20 by the Continental Congress, he fought valiantly at Brandywine and Monmouth and in the Virginia campaign ending in the British surrender at Yorktown (CM97). After the war he was a significant figure in the French Revolution. He returned briefly to the United States in 1784 and again for a triumphant tour in 1824. *Intaglio, perforated 11 x 10 1/2.*

CM352 *Lafayette, Flags of the United States and France*

CM352 *(1010)*
3c bright blue *(113,135,000)* .25 .20
   Plate block of four .55
   FDC *(June 13, 1952)* 1.00

1952. Mount Rushmore Memorial Issue marked the 25th anniversary of the dedication of the monument in the Black Hills of South Dakota. The first such memorial authorized by the government, it was financed by South Dakota. The sculptor Gutzon Borglum designed and carved the enormous heads of Washington, Jefferson, Lincoln and Roosevelt from the solid rock of the mountain. *Intaglio, perforated 10 1/2 x 11.*

CM353 *Mount Rushmore*

CM353 *(1011)*
3c blue green *(116,255,000)* .25 .20
   Plate block of four .55
   FDC *(Aug. 11, 1952)* 1.00

1952. Engineering Centennial Issue commemorated the 100th anniversary of the American Society of Civil Engineers. The George Washington Bridge in New York City, shown on the stamp, was chosen as a symbol of the great engineering projects for which society members are responsible. *Intaglio, perforated 11 x 10 1/2.*

CM354 *The George Washington Bridge and an Old Covered Bridge*

CM354 *(1012)*
3c ultramarine *(113,860,000)* .25 .20
   Plate block of four .55
   FDC *(Sept. 6, 1952)* 1.00

1952. Service Women Issue honors women in the U.S. armed services. More than 40,000 women served in World War II and contributed immeasurably to Allied victory. *Intaglio, perforated 11 x 10 1/2.*

CM355 *Marine Corp., Army, Navy and Air Force Service women*

CM355 *(1013)*
3c blue *(124,260,000)* .25 .20
   Plate block of four .55
   FDC *(Sept. 11, 1952)* 1.00

1952. Gutenberg Bible Issue commemorated the 500th anniversary of the first european book published from movable type, attributed to Johann Gutenberg of Mainz, Germany. Movable type replaced the tedious and costly process of hand copying. It made books available to many people, thus spreading knowledge on an unprecedented scale. *Intaglio, perforated 11 x 10 1/2.*

CM356 *Gutenberg Showing a Proof to the Elector of Mainz. From a mural by Edward Laning in the New York Public Library*

CM356 *(1014)*
    3c violet *(115,735,000)* .25 .20
      Plate block of four .55
      FDC *(Sept. 30, 1952)* 1.00

1952. Newspaperboys of America Issue recognized the America's newsboys and the value of their early business training. It also complimented the meeting of the International Circulation Managers Association, at Philadelphia, PA, in October. *Intaglio, perforated 11 x 10 1/2.*

CM357 *Paperboy, Tourch of "Free Enterprise" and Neighborhood*

CM357 *(1015)*
    3c violet *(115,430,000)* .25 .20
      Plate block of four .55
      FDC *(Oct. 4, 1952)* 1.00

1952. International Red Cross Issue honored the humanitarian society founded by Jean Henri Dunant and others in 1864. Its headquarters in Geneva, Switzerland, provides an exchange for all the Red Cross societies of the world. Maintaining strict neutrality, the organization extends relief to civilian victims of war, furnishes aid to war prisoners and monitors their treatment by their captors. (See also CM96, CM525 and CM969) *Intaglio, perforated 11 x 10 1/2.*

CM358 *Red Cross Enlightening the World*

CM358 *(1016)*
    3c ultramarine and scarlet .25 .20
      (136,220,000)
      Plate block of four .55
      FDC *(Nov. 21, 1952)* 1.00

1953. National Guard Issue honors the oldest military organization in the United States, a service older than the nation itself (C110). The guard, under state control except in war, has served with distinction in every national conflict. In peacetime, it aids in disasters such as floods, forest fires and hurricanes. *Intaglio, perforated 11 x 10 1/2.*

CM359 *National Guard in War and Peace*

CM359 *(1017)*
    3c light blue *(114,894,600)* .25 .20
      Plate block of four .55
      FDC *(Feb. 23, 1953)* 1.00

1953. Ohio Sesquicentennial Issue commemorated the 150th anniversary of Ohio as the 17th state. A part of the Northwest Territory, Ohio became a state March 1,

1803, with Chillicothe as its capital. Columbus has been the capital since 1817. Ohio has given the nation eight presidents, and its history is reflected in many U.S. stamps. *Intaglio, perforated 11 x 10 1/2.*

 CM360 *Ohio Map and Seal*

CM360 *(1018)*
    3c sepia *(117,706,000)* .25 .20
      Plate block of four .55
      FDC *(March 2, 1953)* 1.00

1953. Washington Territory Issue commemorated the 100th anniversary of the Washington Territory. Visited by the Lewis and Clark Expedition in 1803, it first was settled in 1811. *Intaglio, perforated 11 x 10 1/2.*

CM361 *Centennial Crest, Pioneer and Vista*

CM361 *(1019)*
    3c blue green *(114,190,000)* .25 .20
      Plate block of four .55
      FDC *(March 2, 1853)* 1.00

1953. Louisiana Purchase Issue commemorated the 150th anniversary of the Louisiana Purchase from France. (See CM32-CM36.) *Intaglio, perforated 11 x 10 1/2.*

CM362 *Monroe, Livingston and de Barbe-Marbois Signing Transfer. From the sculpture by Karl Bitter in the Jefferson Memorial, St. Louis, Mo.*

CM362 *(1020)*
    3c brown purple *(113,990,000)* .25 .20
      Plate block of four .55
      FDC *(April 30, 1953)* 1.00

1953. Opening of Japan Issue commemorated the centennial of negotiations between Commodore Matthew C. Perry and representatives of the emperor of Japan, leading to the Treaty of Kanagawa in 1854. Japan, isolated since the early 17th century, agreed to open two ports to U.S. trade and make provision for shipwrecked American seamen. In 1858 Japan opened additional ports, granted residence rights to Americans, and exchanged diplomatic representatives. *Intaglio, perforated 11 x 10 1/2.*

CM363 *Commodore Perry and Vessels in Tokyo Bay*

CM363 *(1021)*
    5c blue green *(89,289,600)* .25 .20
      Plate block of four .75
      FDC *(July 14, 1953)* 1.00

1953. American Bar Association Issue honored the organization's 75th anniversary and its efforts in securing uniform state laws, promoting sound legislation and advancing the administration of justice. *Intaglio, perforated 11 x 10 1/2.*

CM364 *Wisdom, Justice, Divine Inspiration and Truth. Frieze on a wall of the Supreme Court.*

CM364 *(1022)*
3c light reddish violet

(114,865,000)		.25	.20
Plate block of four		.75	
FDC (Aug. 24, 1953)			1.00

1953. Sagamore Hill Issue commemorated its dedication as a national shrine, June 14th. Sagamore Hill was the Oyster Bay, NY, home of Theodore Roosevelt and it was there that Roosevelt died on January 6, 1919. *Intaglio, perforated 11 x 10 1/2.*

CM365 *Sagamore Hill Home of Theodore Roosevelt*

CM365 *(1023)*
3c green *(115,780,000)* .25 .20
Plate block of four .55
FDC *(Sept. 14, 1953)* 1.00

1953. Future Farmers of America Issue honored the 25th anniversary of the founding of the Future Farmers of America under the auspices of the U.S. Office of Education. *Intaglio, perforated 11 x 10 1/2.*

CM366 *Future Farmer and Farmland*

CM366 *(1024)*
3c bright blue *(115,244,600)* .25 .20
Plate block of four .55
FDC *(Oct. 13, 1953)* 1.00

1953. Trucking Industry Issue marked the 50th anniversary of the American Trucking Association and its convention in Los Angeles. *Intaglio, perforated 11 x 10 1/2.*

CM367 *Truck, Farm and City*

CM367 *(1025)*
3c violet *(123,709,600)* .25 .20
Plate block of four .55
FDC *(Oct. 27, 1953)* 1.00

1953. General Patton Issue honored Gen. George S. Patton, Jr., and the armored forces of the U.S. Army. Patton was a hero of the Battle of the Bulge in World War II. *Intaglio, perforated 11 x 10 1/2.*

CM368 *Gen. Patton and Patton Tanks in Action*

CM368 *(1026)*
3c bluish violet *(114,789,600)* .25 .20
Plate block of four .65
FDC *(Nov. 11, 1953)* 1.00

1953. New York City Tercentenary Issue commemorated the 300th anniversary of the incorporation of Niew Amsterdam as a city, February 2, 1653. *Intaglio, perforated 11 x 10 1/2.*

CM369 *Dutch Ship and New Amsterdam, Modern New York City Skyline*

CM369 *(1027)*
3c bright purple *(115,759,600)* .25 .20
Plate block of four .55
FDC *(Nov. 20, 1953)* 1.00

1953. Gadsden Purchase Issue commemorated the 100th anniversary of the purchase of territory from Mexico to add territory to the states of Arizona and New Mexico and settle a dispute dating from the Guadelupe-Hildalgo Treaty of 1848. *Intaglio, perforated 11 x 10 1/2.*

CM370 *Gadsen Purchase Map and Pioneers*

CM370 *(1028)*
3c Venetian red *(115,759,600)* .25 .20
Plate block of four .55
FDC *(Dec. 30, 1953)* 1.00

1954. Columbia University Issue commemorated the 200th anniversary of King's College, which closed during the Revolution to reopen as Columbia College. It now includes many colleges such as Teacher's College, Barnard College, and schools of medicine, pharmacy, engineering, law, architecture, and journalism among others. Located in New York City, it is one of the oldest and largest U.S. universities. *Intaglio, perforated 11 x 10 1/2.*

CM371 *Low Memorial Library*

CM371 *(1029)*
3c cobalt blue *(118,540,000)* .25 .20
Plate block of four .55
FDC *(Jan. 4, 1954)* 1.00

1954. Nebraska Territorial Centennial Issue honors the centennial of the Nebraska Territory, under the Kansas-Nebraska Bill. *Intaglio, perforated 11 x 10 1/2.*

CM372 *Mitchell Pass, Scotts Bluff and The Sower. From a statue by Lee Lawrie from a painting by Millet*

CM372 *(1060)*
3c violet *(115,810,000)* .25 .20
  Plate block of four .55
  FDC *(May 7, 1954)* 1.00

1954. Kansas Territorial Centennial Issue commemorated the centennial of the Kansas Territory from unorganized Indian reservations. The Kansas-Nebraska bill repealed the 1820 Missouri Compromise that had drawn a line north of which slavery could not exist. The politicians intended Kansas to be a slave state and Nebraska free, by "popular sovereignty." The rivalry for settling the status of these two new territories was one of the direct causes of the War Between the States. *Intaglio, perforated 11 x 10 1/2.*

CM373 *Wagon Train and Wheat Field*

CM373 *(1061)*
3c salmon *(113,603,700)* .25 .20
  Plate block of four .55
  FDC *(May 31, 1954)* 1.00

1954. George Eastman Issue commemorated the 100th birthday of George Eastman at Waterville, NY. At an early age he went to Rochester where he gained fame as an inventor and philanthropist. His inventions made photography possible for virtually everyone, and his invention of transparent film created motion pictures. He gave $100 million to educational and musical institutions and dental clinics around the world. He was a proponent of the Community Chest, and profit sharing with employees. *Intaglio, perforated 10 1/2 x 11.*

CM374 *George Eastman*

CM374 *(1062)*
3c brown purple *(121,100,000)* .25 .20
  Plate block of four .55
  FDC *(July 12, 1954)* 1.00

1954. Lewis and Clark Expedition Issue commemorated the trip made by Meriwether Lewis and William Clark, (brother of George Rogers Clark) at the request of President Jefferson to secure more information about the country west of the Mississippi. The party of thirty made its way overland to Oregon and the Pacific Ocean, leaving St. Louis in May 1804, and returning in 1806 after having been given up as lost. They owed much of the success of the venture to Sacagawea (Birdwoman), a Shoshone Indian woman who acted as their guide (CM1690). *Intaglio, perforated 11 x 10 1/2.*

CM375 *Lewis and Clark from a statue by Charles Keck at Charlottesville, Va., and Sacagawea from a statue by Leonard Crunekle at Bismark, N.D.*

CM375 *(1063)*
3c brown *(116,078,150)* .25 .20
  Plate block of four .55
  FDC *(July 8, 1954)* 1.00

1955. Pennsylvania Academy of Fine Arts Issue honored the 150th anniversary of that institution. The design of the stamp is a reproduction of the painting *Peale in his Museum*, a self-portrait of Charles Willson Peale (1741-1827), now in the collection of the Pennsylvania Academy, of which Peale was one of the founders. *Intaglio, perforated 10 1/2 x 11.*

CM376 *Charles Wilson Peale in His Museum*

CM376 *(1064)*
3c brown purple *(116,139,800)* .25 .20
  Plate block of four .55
  FDC *(Jan. 15, 1955)* 1.00

1955. First Land-Grant Colleges Issue commemorated the centennial of the establishment of Michigan State University and Pennsylvania State University. Land grants, originally intended for settlers and homesteaders, were extended in 1854 to various groups for services for the national welfare. *Intaglio, perforated 11 x 10 1/2.*

CM377 *Open Book and Symblols of Agriculture, Mining, Chemistry, Engineering*

CM377 *(1065)*
3c emerald green *(120,484,800)* .25 .20
  Plate block of four .55
  FDC *(Feb. 12, 1955)* 1.00

1955. Rotary International Issue marked the 50th anniversary of the organization founded February 23, 1905, by Chicago lawyer Paul P. Harris. Rotary became national in 1910, international in 1912. It is an organization of business and professional men founded to further the ideal of service to others in all relationships. *Intaglio, perforated 11 x 10 1/2.*

CM378 *Rotary Insignia, Globe and Torch*

CM378 *(1066)*
  8c deep blue *(53,854,750)*   .25   .20
    Plate block of four   1.95
    FDC *(Feb. 23, 1955)*   1.00

1955. The Armed Forces Reserve Issue honored the Reserves of all the U.S. armed forces. *Intaglio, perforated 11 x 10 1/2.*

CM379 *Marines, Coast Guard, Army, Navy and Air Force Reservists*

CM379 *(1067)*
  3c bright purple*(176,075,000)*   .25   .20
    Plate block of four   .55
    FDC *(May 21, 1955)*   1.00

1955. Old Man of the Mountain Issue commemorated the sesquicentennial of the discovery of New Hampshire's famous landmark of that name (see also CM1312.) Also called "The Great Stone Face," it was immortalized in prose by Hawthorne. *Intaglio, perforated 10 1/2 x 11.*

CM380 *Old Man of the Mountain (as seen from Franconia, N.H.)*

CM380 *(1068)*
  3c blue green *(125,944,400)*   .25   .20
    Plate block of four   .55
    FDC *(June 21, 1955)*   1.00

1955. Soo Locks Centennial Issue was released in conjunction with the opening of the Soo Locks Exposition at Sault Ste. Marie, MI, celebrating a century of Great Lakes transportation. *Intaglio, perforated 11 x 10 1/2.*

CM381 *Map of the Great Lakes and Freighter*

CM381 *(1069)*
  3c blue *(122,284,600)*   .25   .20
    Plate block of four   .55
    FDC *(June 28, 1955)*   1.00

1955. Atoms for Peace Issue symbolized the intention of the United States to put atomic energy to peaceful uses. The stamp features the words "To find the way by which the inventiveness of man shall be consecrated to his life" from President Eisenhower's speech before the U.N. General Assembly on December 8, 1953. *Intaglio, perforated 11 x 10 1/2.*

CM382 *Atomic Emblem and Hemispheres*

CM382 *(1070)*
  3c deep blue *(133,638,850)*   .25   .20
    Plate block of four   .55
    FDC *(July 28, 1955)*   1.00

1955. Fort Ticonderoga Bicentennial Issue marked the building of the fort in 1755 by the French, who named it Fort Carillon. During the French & Indian War it was unsuccessfully attacked by Abercrombie in 1758, but a year later was captured by Lord Amherst. Ethan Allen and his Green Mountain Boys (see CM76) took the fort at the outbreak of the Revolution (1775). *Intaglio, perforated 11 x 10 1/2.*

Plan of Fort Ticonderoga Officer and Cannon

CM383 *(1071)*
  3c dark red brown *(118,664,600)*   .25   .20
    Plate block of four   .55
    FDC *(Sept. 18, 1955)*   1.00

1955. Andrew Mellon Issue commemorated the 100th anniversary of the birth of Mellon (1855-1937), Secretary of the Treasury under Harding, Coolidge and Hoover. He negotiated the payments of war debts owed to the United States, and reduced internal debt and income taxes. He later served as ambassador to England. He donated a gallery and his very valuable art collection to the United States. *Intaglio, perforated 10 1/2 x 11.*

CM384 *Andrew W. Mellon, Portrait by O. Birely*

CM384 *(1072)*
  3c carmine red *(112,434,000)*   .25   .20
    Plate block of four   .55
    FDC *(Dec. 20, 1955)*   1.00

1956. Franklin 250th Anniversary Issue commemorated the birth of the great inventor, writer and public official Benjamin Franklin (see 524). *Intaglio, perforated 10 1/2 x 11.*

CM385 *Franklin Taking Electricity from the Sky. Benjamin West painting.*

CM385 *(1073)*
3c carmine *(129,384,550)*   .25   .20
    Plate block of four   .55
    FDC *(Jan. 17, 1956)*   1.00

1956. Booker T. Washington Issue commemorated the 100th anniversary of the great educator's birth (CM215). *Intaglio, perforated 11 x 10 1/2.*

CM386 *Log Cabin*

CM386 *(1074)*
3c deep blue *(121,184,600)*   .25   .20
    Plate block of four   .55
    FDC *(April 5, 1956)*   1.00

1956. FIPEX Issue celebrated the Fifth International Philatelic Exhibition (April 28 to May 6, 1956). Stamp, photography and auto exhibitions, held simultaneously, opened the newly completed New York Coliseum at Columbus Circle, New York City. *Intaglio, perforated 11 x 10 1/2.*

CM387 *New York Coliseum and Columbus Monument*

CM387 *(1076)*
3c violet *(119,784,200)*   .25   .20
    Plate block of four   .55
    FDC *(April 30, 1956)*   1.00

1956. Fifth International Philatelic Exhibition (FIPEX) Souvenir Sheet pictured two oversize versions of stamps from the Liberty definative series (see 573, 578) and measure 108 x 73 mm. *Flat plate printing, intaglio, imperforate.*

CM388 *FIPEX Souvenir Sheet*

CM388 *(1075)*
11c Complete sheet of two stamps
    (9,802,025)   2.50   2.00
    FDC *(April 28, 1956)*   2.50
    a. 3c dark violet, from sheet   .80
    b. 8c deep blue and rose, from sheet   1.00

1956. Wildlife Conservation Series highlights the importance of protecting wildlife. *Intaglio, perforated 11 x 10 1/2.*

CM389 *Wild Turkey, early America's most popular game bird, almost extinct in 1910 and now making a comeback*

CM389 *(1077)*
3c brown purple *(123,159,400)*   .25   .20
    Plate block of four   .55
    FDC *(May 5, 1956)*   1.00

CM390 *Pronghorn Antelope Buck and Two Does. This species had dwindled to only 17,000, but multiplied rapidly under protection and now is widely hunted.*

CM390 *(1078)*
3c sepia *(123,138,800)*   .25   .20
    Plate block of four   .55
    FDC *(June 22, 1956)*   1.00

CM391 *King Salmon Migrating to Spawning Ground. Construction of fish ladders and elevators, and elimination of log jams and high waterfalls aids salmon migration and reproduction.*

CM391 *(1079)*
3c blue green *(109,275,000)*   .25   .20
    Plate block of four   .55
    FDC *(Nov. 9, 1956)*   1.00

1956. Pure Food and Drug Laws Issue commemorated the 50th anniversary of their passage. Harvey W. Wiley (1844-1930) was a chemist and teacher who single-handedly devoted himself to the cause of pure food. While chief of the Bureau of Chemistry in the U.S. Department of Agriculture he secured passage of the 1906 laws, which required government inspection and accurate labeling of foods and drugs. Wiley was the author of hundreds of scientific papers and pamphlets. *Intaglio, perforated 10 1/2 x 11.*

CM392 *Harvey W. Wiley*

CM392 *(1080)*
3c blue green *(112,932,200)*   .25   .20
    Plate block of four   .55
    FDC *(June 26, 1956)*   1.00

1956. Wheatland Issue honored President James Buchanan and his Pennsylvania home Wheatland. *Intaglio, perforated 11 x 10 1/2.*

CM393 *Wheatland, Lancaster, Pa.*

CM393 *(1081)*
3c black brown *(125,475,000)*   .25   .20
   Plate block of four   .55
   FDC *(Aug. 5, 1956)*   1.00

1956. Labor Day Issue celebrated the national holiday honoring workers. The movement for a Labor Holiday was begun by the Knights of Labor, who paraded on the first Monday of September in 1882-84. The holiday first was recognized by Oregon (1887) then by New York, New Jersey and Colorado, and by the U.S. Congress in 1894. *Intaglio, perforated 10 1/2 x 11.*

CM394 *"Labor Is Life" Mural by L. Winter in AFL-CIO headquarters building, Washington, D.C.*

CM394 *(1082)*
3c deep blue *(117,855,000)*   .25   .20
   Plate block of four   .55
   FDC *(Sept. 3, 1956)*   1.00

1956. Nassau Hall Issue commemorated the 200th anniversary of the oldest building at Princeton University. Named for William of Nassau (later King William III of England), it was at its' completion the largest academic building in the American colonies. In 1783, in Nassau Hall, Congress formally thanked George Washington for his leadership in the Revolutionary War. *Intaglio, perforated 11 x 10 1/2.*

CM395 *Nassau Hall. From the Dawkins engraving of 1764.*

CM395 *(1083)*
3c black on orange *(122,100,000)*   .25   .20
   Plate block of four   .55
   FDC *(Sept. 22, 1956)*   1.00

1956. Devils Tower Issue commemorated the 50th anniversary of the establishment of the 1,200-acre area as the first U.S. national monument. The natural 600-foot rock formation is the eroded core of a long-extinct volvano. *Intaglio, perforated 10 1/2 x 11.*

CM396 *Devils Tower National Monument, Wyoming*

CM396 *(1084)*
3c lilac *(118,180,000)*   .25   .20
   Plate block of four   .55
   Gutter pair
   FDC *(Sept. 24, 1956)*   1.00

1956. Children's Issue featured the theme "Friendship—The Key to World Peace," and promoted friendship among children throughout the world. The stamp design, by Ronald Dias, a 1956 high school graduate, was selected in a nationwide competition. *Intaglio, perforated 11 x 10 1/2.*

CM397 *Children of the World and Key of Friendship*

CM397 *(1085)*
3c blue *(100,975,000)*   .25   .20
   Plate block of four   .55
   FDC *(Dec. 15, 1956)*   1.00

1957. Alexander Hamilton Bicentennial Issue commemorated the 200th anniversary of the birth of this great patriot. The first secretary of the treasury and one of the signers of the Constitution. *Intaglio, perforated 11 x 10 1/2.*

CM398 *Alexander Hamilton and Federal Hall, New York, N.Y.*

CM398 *(1086)*
3c rose red *(115,299,450)*   .25   .20
   Plate block of four   .55
   FDC *(Jan. 11, 1957)*   1.00

1957. Anti-Polio Issue is a tribute to those who helped fight this dreaded disease, from children who contributed pennies to scientists who devoted their lives to the battle against a terrifying affliction. Issue marked 20th anniversary of the National Foundation for Infantile Paralysis and the March of Dimes. *Intaglio, perforated 10 1/2 x 11.*

CM399 *Boy, Girl and Allegorical Figure with Shield Caduceus*

CM399 *(1087)*
3c bright purple *(186,949,250)*   .25   .20
   Plate block of four   .55
   FDC *(Jan. 15, 1957)*   1.00

1957. Coast and Geodetic Survey Issue commemorated the 150th anniversary of this government service, devoted to charting and surveying America's coasts and harbors and land masses. *Intaglio, perforated 11 x 10 1/2.*

CM400 *Coast and Geodestic Survey Flag and Ships*

CM400 *(1088)*
3c deep blue *(115,235,000)* .25 .20
Plate block of four .55
FDC *(Feb. 11, 1957)* 1.00

1957. Architects of America Issue honored the centennial of the founding of the American Institute of Architects, and its members who create buildings, structures and communities of lasting beauty and usefulness. *Intaglio, perforated 11 x 10 1/2.*

CM401 *Corinthian Capitol and Modern Pillar*

CM401 *(1089)*
3c rose lilac *(106,647,500)* .25 .20
Plate block of four .55
FDC *(Feb. 23, 1957)* 1.00

1957. Steel Industry in America Issue marked the centennial of this great industry, which has contributed to our social progress, economic welfare and comforts in our daily lives. *Intaglio, perforated 10 1/2 x 11.*

CM402 *Eagle and Pouring Ladle*

CM402 *(1090)*
3c bright blue *(112,010,000)* .25 .20
Plate block of four .55
FDC *(May 22, 1957)* 1.00

1957. International Naval Review Issue commemorated the Jamestown Festival and the naval review. Its theme was "Freedom of the Seas," and it was the largest representation of nations in an event of this type. *Intaglio, perforated 11 x 10 1/2.*

CM403 *Aircraft Carrier and Jamestown Festival Emblem*

CM403 *(1091)*
3c blue green *(118,399,600)* .25 .20
Plate block of four .55
FDC *(June 10, 1957)* 1.00

1957. Oklahoma Statehood Issue celebrated the 50th anniversary of statehood, growth and progress of a land that was once the Indian Territory. *Intaglio, perforated 11 x 10 1/2.*

CM404 *Arrow, Atom and Oklahoma Map*

CM404 *(1092)*
3c bright blue *(102,209,500)* .25 .20
Plate block of four .55
FDC *(June 14, 1957)* 1.00

1957. Teachers of America Issue honored the National Eduation Association and the teaching profession that has contributed to the development of America through our school systems. *Intaglio, perforated 11 x 10 1/2.*

CM405 *Teacher, Students and Globe*

CM405 *(1093)*
3c brown purple *(103,045,000)* .25 .20
Plate block of four .70
FDC *(July 1, 1957)* 1.00

1957. Amercian Flag Issue salutes "Old Glory," symbol of freedom throughout the world. *Intaglio (Giori Press), perforated 11.*

CM406 *48-Star American Flag*

CM406 *(1094)*
4c deep blue and carmine
(84,054,400) .25 .20
Plate block of four .55
FDC *(July 4, 1957)* 1.00

1957. *Virginia of Sagadahock* Issue commemorated the 350th anniversary of shipbuilding in the United States, and featured the first American built-ship to participate in world commerce. *Intaglio, perforated 10 1/2 x 11.*

CM407 *Virginia of Sagadahock and state Seal of Maine*

CM407 *(1095)*
3c violet *(126,266,000)* .25 .20
Plate block of four .55
FDC *(Aug. 15, 1957)* 1.00

1957. Ramon Magsaysay Issue was the first of a new five-year-long series honoring Champions of Liberty and freedom fighters of other nations. A man of humble birth, Magsaysay became president of the Philippines. (See also CM 419-20, CM 423-24, CM 434-35, CM445-46, CM456-57, CM474-75, CM477-78 and CM483-84.) *Intaglio (Giori Press), perforated 11.*

CM408 *Ramon Magsaysay*

CM408 *(1096)*
8c scarlet, deep ultramarine, and ocher
(39,489,600)   .25   .20
Plate block of four, 2 numbers   .75
v.Plate block of four, deep
     ultramarine number omitted   —
FDC *(Aug. 11, 1957)*   1.00

1957. Lafayette Issue commemorated the 200th birthday of the French officer who came to America in 1777 and helped the fight for independence. *Intaglio, perforated 10 1/2 x 11.*

CM409 *Lafayette, Flintlock Rifle and Sword*

CM409 *(1097)*
3c brown purple *(122,990,000)*   .25   .20
Plate block of four   .55
FDC *(Sept. 6, 1957)*   1.00

1957. Wildlife Conservation Issue brought to the attention of the American public the need to protect and preserve wildlife resources. This, the fourth in the series (see CM389-CM391), portrays the whooping crane, which at the time was almost extinct. *Intaglio, (Giori Press), perforated 11.*

CM410 *Whooping Cranes*

CM410 *(1098)*
3c gray blue, yellow, and blue green
(174,372,800)   .25   .20
Plate block of four   .55
FDC *(Nov. 22, 1957)*   1.00

1957. Flushing Remonstrance Issue recalled a 1657 demonstration for religious freedom and liberty by the citizens of Flushing, NY. *Intaglio, perforated 10 1/2 x 11.*

CM411 *Bible, Hat, Pen and Inkwell*

CM411 *(1099)*
3c brown black *(114,365,000)*   .25   .20
Plate block of four   .55
FDC *(Dec. 27, 1957)*   1.00

1958. Garden and Horticultural Issue marked the 100th birthday of Liberty Hyde Bailey, famous botanist, author, and teacher whose horticultural achievements contributed to American prosperity. *Intaglio, perforated 10 1/2 x 11.*

CM412 *Allegory of the Good Earth with Horn of Plenty*

CM412 *(1100)*
3c dull green *(122,765,200)*   .25   .20
Plate block of four   .55
FDC *(March 15, 1958)*   1.00

1958. Brussels Universal and International Exhibition Issue pay tribute to the World's Fair and U.S. participation in it. *Intaglio, perforated 11 x 10 1/2.*

CM413 *U.S. Fair Pavilion*

CM413 *(1104)*
3c brown purple *(113,660,200)*   .25   .20
Plate block of four   .55
FDC *(April 17, 1958)*   1.00

1958. James Monroe Issue commemorated the 200th birthday of the fifth president of the United States. *Intaglio, perforated 11 x 10 1/2.*

CM414 *James Monroe. From a portrait by Gilbert Stuart*

CM414 *(1105)*
3c violet *(120,196,580)*   .25   .20
Plate block of four   .55
FDC *(April 28, 1958)*   1.00

1958. Minnesota Statehood Centennial Issue commemorated the 100th anniversary of Minnesota's admission as the 32nd state. *Intaglio, perforated 11 x 10 1/2.*

CM415 *Minnesota Lakes*

CM415 *(1106)*
3c emerald green *(120,805,200)* .25 .20
    Plate block of four .55
    FDC *(May 11, 1958)* 1.00

1958. International Geophysical Year Issue paid tribute to geophysicists in more than 60 countries who pool their knowledge for mankind's welfare in exploring outer space and the oceans and Earth. *Intaglio, (Giori Press), perforated 11.*

CM416 *Detail from Michelangelo's The Creation of Adam and Solar Surface*

CM416 *(1107)*
3c black and red *(125,815,200)* .25 .20
    Plate block of four .55
    FDC *(May 31, 1958)* 1.00

1958. Gunston Hall Bicentennial Issue honors the completion of the home of George Mason, Revolutionary patriot and friend of George Washington. The house, about 15 miles south of Alexandria, VA, was opened to the public in 1952. *Intaglio, perforated 11 x 10 1/2.*

CM417 *Gunston Hall*

CM417 *(1108)*
3c dull green *(108,415,200)* .25 .20
    Plate block of four .55
    FDC *(June 12, 1958)* 1.00

1958. Mackinac Straits Bridge Issue marked the formal opening and dedication of the suspension span that connects St. Ignace and Mackinaw City, in Michigan's Upper and Lower Peninulas. *Intaglio, perforated 10 1/2 x 11.*

CM418 *Ore Boat under Mackinac Bridge*

CM418 *(1109)*
3c turquoise blue *(107,195,200)* .25 .20
    Plate block of four .55
    FDC *(June 25, 1958)* 1.00

1958. Simon Bolívar Issue — The first two-stamp installment in the Champions of Liberty series honors the South American freedom fighter known as "The Liberator" who dedicated his life to bringing happiness, social security and political stability to his countrymen.

CM419-20 *Simon Bolívar. From portrait by Acevedo Bernal*

Intaglio, perforated 10 1/2 x 11
CM419 *(1110)*
4c olive buff *(115,745,280)* .25 .20
    Plate block of four .60
    FDC *(July 24, 1958)* 1.00

Intaglio, (Giori Press), perforated 11
CM420 *(1111)*
**8c scarlet, deep ultramarine and
    deep ocher** *(39,743,640)* .25 .20
    Plate block of four, two numbers —
    v. Plate block of four, ocher
        number only —
    FDC *(July 25, 1958)* 1.00

1958. Atlantic Cable Centennial Issue commemorated the linking by cable of the eastern and western hemispheres in 1858. The first formal messages were exchanged by President Buchanan and Queen Victoria. *Intaglio, perforated 11 x 10 1/2.*

CM421 *Globe, Neptune and Mermaid*

CM421 *(1112)*
4c red violet *(114,570,200)* .25 .20
    Plate block of four .60
    FDC *(Aug. 15, 1958)* 1.00

1958. Lincoln Sesquicentennial Series consisted of four denominations inssued in 1858-59 (CM422, CM430-32) commemorating the cirth of the 16th president of the United States, This first stamp in the series also marked 100th anniversary of the Lincoln-Douglas debates held as part of the 1859 campaign for U.S. Senator. Although Douglas was re-elected, Lincoln gained national prominence and two years later was elected to the presidency. *Intaglio, perforated 11 x 10 1/2.*

CM422 *Lincoln and Douglas Debating*

CM422 *(1115)*
4c brown *(114,860,200)* .25 .20
    Plate block of four .85
    FDC *(Aug. 27, 1958)* 1.00

1958. Lajos Kossuth Issue — The third honoree in the Champions of Liberty series — honored the famous Hungarian patriot who fought to liberate Hungary from Austrian control. He lived in exile until his death in 1894, never giving up hope that some day his beloved country would be free.

CM423-24 *Lajos Kossuth. From a photo taken in the United States in 1852*

Intaglio, perforated 10 1/2 x 11
CM423 *(1117)*
  4c dull green *(120,561,280)*   .25   .20
    Plate block of four   .60
    FDC *(Sept. 19, 1958)*   1.00

Intaglio, (Giori Press), perforated 11
CM424 *(1118)*
  8c scarlet, deep ultramarine, and
      deep ochre *(44,064,576)*   .25   .20
    Plate block of four   1.30
    FDC *(Sept. 19, 1958)*   1.00

1958. Journalism and Freedom of the Press Issue
marked the 50th anniversary of the establishment of the world's first school of journalism at the University of Missouri. *Intaglio, perforated 10 1/2 x 11.*

CM425 *Symbols of a Free Press*

CM425 *(1119)*
  4c gray black *(118,390,200)*   .25   .20
    Plate block of four   .60
    FDC *(Sept. 22, 1958)*   1.00

1958. Overland Mail Centennial Issue honored the pioneer mail service established in 1858 "The Great Overland Mail Route" it started its run from Memphis and St. Louis and went to San Francisco, and was important in the settlement of the Southwest. *Intaglio, perforated 11 x 10 1/2.*

CM426 *Overland Mail Coach and Map of Route*

CM426 *(1120)*
  4c orange red *(125,770,200)*   .25   .20
    Plate block of four   .60
    FDC *(Oct. 10, 1958)*   1.00

1958. Noah Webster Bicentennial Issue
commemorated the 200th birthday of the noted lexicographer. He fought for American independence in the Revolutionary War, and his *Elementary Spelling Book* sold a million copies. *Intaglio, perforated 10 1/2 x 11.*

CM427 *Noah Webster. From a painting by James Herring*

CM427 *(1121)*
  4c magenta *(114,114,280)*   .25   .20
    Plate block of four   .60
    FDC *(Oct. 16, 1958)*   1.00

1958. Forest Conservation Issue honored the 100th birthday of Theodore Roosevelt, one of the first leaders in the movement to preserve the nation's natural resources. *Intaglio, (Giori Press), perforated 11.*

CM428 *Forest and Deer*

CM428 *(1122)*
  4c deep green, yellow, and brown
      (156,600,200)   .25   .20
    Plate block of four   .60
    FDC *(Oct. 28, 1958)*   1.00

1958. Fort Duquesne Bicentennial Issue
commemorated the 200th anniversary of the historic site that was so important in the conflict between England and France for control of North America. *Intaglio,*

CM429 *Composite drawing showing Gen. Forbes, Col. Washington, and Col. Henry Bouquet*

perforated 11 x 10 1/2.
CM429 *(1123)*
  4c light blue *(124,200,200)*   .25   .20
    Plate block of four   .60
    FDC *(Nov. 25, 1958)*   1.00

1959. Lincoln Sesquicentennial Issue consisted of three additional commemoratives as well as the one issued in 1958 (CM422). Each of the four stamps represents a different form of art — oil painting, sculpture, print and pastel drawing adapted to a stamp form.

CM430 *Beardless Lincoln. Painting by George P.A. Healy*

Intaglio, perforated 10 1/2 x 11.
CM430 *(1113)*
  1c deep green *(120,400,200)*   .25   .20
    Plate block of four   .45
    FDC *(Feb. 12, 1959)*   1.00

CM431 Head of Lincoln. *sculpture by Gutzon Borglum*

CM431 *(1114)*
  3c deep plum *(91,160,200)*   .25   .20
    Plate block of four   .60
    FDC *(Feb. 27, 1959)*   1.00

CM432 Lincoln Statue. *By Daniel Chester French, taken from a line and pastel drawing by Fritz Busse*

Intaglio, perforated 11 x 10 1/2.
CM432 *(1116)*
  4c blue *(126,500,000)*   .25   .20
    Plate block of four   1.25
    FDC *(May 30, 1959)*   1.00

1959. Oregon Statehood Issue commemorated the 100th anniversary of Oregon's admission as a state

CM433 *Mount Hood and Covered Wagon*

Intaglio, perforated 11 x 10 1/2.
CM433 *(1124)*
  4c blue green *(120,740,200)*   .25   .20
    Plate block of four   .60
    FDC *(Feb. 14, 1959)*   1.00

1959. José de San Martin Issue— the fourth of the Champions of Liberty— paid tribute to the "hero of the Andes," a great general who fought for freedom in his native Argentina and other South American nations.

CM434-35 *Portrait of José de San Martin. From a print provided by the Library of Congress*

Intaglio, perforated 10 1/2 x 11.
CM434 *(1125)*
  4c blue *(113,623,280)*   .25   .20
    Plate block of four   .60
    FDC *(Feb. 25, 1959)*   1.00
    v. horizontal pair, imperforate
      between

Intaglio, (Giori Press), perforated 11
CM435 *(1126)*
  8c carmine, blue, and ocher
       (45,569,088)   .25   .20
    Plate block of four   1.25
    FDC *(Feb. 25, 1959)*   1.00

1959. NATO Issue honors the 10th anniversary of the North Atlantic Treaty Organization, binding 15 nations "to safeguard the freedom, common heritage and civilization of their people, founded on the principles of democracy, individual liberty and the rule of law." *Intaglio, perforated 10 1/2 x 11.*

CM436 *NATO Emblem*

CM436 *(1127)*
  4c blue *(122,493,280)*   .25   .20
    Plate block of four   .60
    FDC *(April 1, 1959)*   1.00

1959. Arctic Explorations Issue marked the conquest of the north polar regions and commemorated the 50th anniversary of Adm. Peary's expedition. The nuclear-powered aubmarine, USS *Nautilis*, joined the anniversary celebration, making the first underwater crossing of the North Pole. *Intaglio, perforated 11 x 10 1/2.*

CM437 *Dog team and USS* Nautilis

CM437 *(1128)*
  4c turquoise blue *(131,260,200)*   .25   .20
    Plate block of four   .60
    FDC *(April 6, 1959)*   1.00

1959. Peace through Trade Issue was released in association with the 17th Congress of the International Chamber of Commerce, held in Washington, D.C., from April 19 to 25. *Intaglio, perforated 11 x 10 1/2.*

CM438 *Globe and Laurel Spray*

CM438 *(1129)*
  8c brown purple *(47,125,200)*   .25   .20
    Plate block of four   .60
    FDC *(April 20, 1959)*   1.00

1959. Silver Centennial Issue commemorated the 100th anniversary of the discovery of the Comstock Lode, which produced about $300,000,000 worth of silver in its first 20 years. *Intaglio, perforated 11 x 10 1/2.*

CM439 *Henry Comstock and miners*

CM439 *(1130)*
4c black *(123,105,000)*   .25   .20
    Plate block of four   .60
    FDC *(June 8, 1959)*   1.00

1959. St. Lawrence Seaway Issue commemorated the opening of a new link joining the United States and Canada in friendship and commerce, and providing a source of electric energy for both countries. Canada issued a commemorative stamp on the same day (Canada 480). Artists of both nations contributed to the design of both stamps, which are identical in design except for captions and denominatioins. *Intaglio, (Giori Press), perforated 11.*

CM440 *Linked Eagle and Maple Leaf over Great Lakes*

CM440 *(1131)*
4c blue and red *(126,105,050)*   .25   .20
    Plate block of four   .60
    Gutter pair   —
    FDC *(June 26, 1959)*   1.00

1959. 49-Star Flag Issue commemorated the admission of Alaska as the 49th state. *Intaglio, (Giori Press), perforated 11.*

CM441 *49-Star American Flag*

CM441 *(1132)*
4c deep blue and carmine
        (209,170,000)   .25   .20
    Plate block of four   .60
    FDC *(July 4, 1959)*   1.00

1959. Soil Conservation Issue was a tribute to the effort to prevent erosion and conserve soil, vital to successful farming and ranching. *Intaglio, (Giori Press), perforated 11.*

CM442 *Soil Conservation Methods*

CM442 *(1133)*
4c blue green and yellow orange
        (120,835,000)   .25   .20
    Plate block of four   .60
    FDC *(Aug. 26, 1959)*   1.00
    v. Orange brown omitted   5,280.

1959. Petroleum Industry Centennial Commemorative marked the 100th anniversary of the completion of the first oil well at Titusville, Pa., by Edwin L. Drake. *Intaglio, perforated 10 1/2 x 11.*

CM443 *Oil Derrick*

CM443 *(1134)*
4c brown *(115,715,000)*   .25   .20
    Plate block of four   .60
    FDC *(Aug. 27, 1959)*   1.00

1959. Dental Health Issue honored the centennial of the American Dental Association. *Intaglio, perforated 11 x 10 1/2.*

CM444 *Children playing and smiling girl with feather-cut hair style*

CM444 *(1135)*
4c dark green *(118,445,000)*   .25   .20
    Plate block of four   .90
    FDC *(Sept. 14, 1959)*   1.00

1959. Ernst Reuter Issue — fifth in the Champions of Liberty series — honored Ernst Reuter (1889-1953). He was persecuted and imprisoned by the Nazis, went into exile and after World War II returned to help rebuild his country. He was elected mayor of Berlin in 1947, holding that office until his death.

CM445-46 *Ernst Reuter*

Intaglio, perforated 10 1/2 x 11.
CM445 *(1136)*
4c black *(111,685,000)*   .25   .20
    Plate block of four   .60
    FDC *(Sept. 29, 1959)*   1.00

Intaglio, (Giori Press), perforated 11
CM446 *(1137)*
8c carmine, blue and ocher
        (43,099,200)   .25   .20
    Plate block of four   1.25
    FDC *(Sept. 29, 1959)*   1.00

1959. Ephraim McDowell Issue paid tribute to a famous American who performed the first successful abdominal operation of its kind in the world at Danville, Ky., in 1809. *Intaglio, perforated 10 1/2 x 11.*

CM447 *Ephraim McDowell,*

CM447 *(1138)*
4c brown purple *(115,444,000)* .25 .20
   Plate block of four .65
   FDC *(Dec. 3, 1959)* 1.00
   v. Vertical pair, imperforate
      between 400.
   v1. Vertical pair, imperforate
      horizontally 300.

1960-61. American Credo Series of bicolored stams enshrins the enduring, inspiring words of great Americans. *Intaglio, (Giori Press), perforated 11.*

CM448 *"Observe good faith and justice toward all nations."* George Washington

CM448 *(1139)*
4c deep blue and carmine *(126,470,000)*.25 .20
   Plate block of four .65
   FDC *(Jan. 20, 1960)* 1.00

CM449 *"Fear to do ill, and you need fear nought else."*

CM449 *(1140)*
4c brown bister and emerald
     (124,460,000) .25 .20
   Plate block of four .65
   FDC *(March 31, 1960)* 1.00

CM450 *"I have sworn hostility against every form of tyranny over the mind of man."* Thomas Jefferson

CM450 *(1141)*
4c gray and scarlet *(115,445,000)* .25 .20
   Plate block of four .65
   FDC *(May 18, 1960)* 1.00

CM451 *"And this be our motto, in God is our Trust."* Francis Scott Key

CM451 *(1142)*
4c carmine red and deep blue
     (122,060,000) .25 .20
   Plate block of four .65
   FDC *(Sept. 14, 1960)* 1.00

CM452 *"Those who deny freedom to others deserve it not for themselves."* Abraham Lincoln

CM452 *(1143)*
4c bright purple and green
     (120,540,000) .25 .20
   Plate block of four .90
   FDC *(Nov. 19, 1960)* 1.00

CM453 *"Give me liberty or give me death."* Patrick Henry

CM453 *(1144)*
4c green and brown *(113,075,000)* .25 .20
   Plate block of four .90
   Gutter pair —
   FDC *(Jan. 11, 1961)* 1.00

1960. Boy Scouts of America Golden Jubilee Issue commemorated the 50th anniversary of the Boy Scout movement in America. Norman Rockwell designed the stamp. *Intaglio, (Giori Press), perforated 11.*

CM454 *Boy Scout Giving the Sign*

CM454 *(1145)*
4c red, deep blue and deep ocher
     (139,325,000) .25 .20
   Plate block of four .90
   FDC *(Feb. 8, 1960)* 1.00

1960. Winter Olympic Games Issue marked the eighth Winter Games at Squaw Valley, Ca. It was the second time this important athletic contest was held in the United States (see CM110). *Intaglio, perforated 10 1/2 x 11.*

CM455 *Olympic Emblem and Snowflake*

CM455 *(1146)*
4c turquoise blue *(124,445,000)* .25 .20
   Plate block of four .60
   FDC *(Feb. 18, 1960)* 1.00

1960. Thomas G. Masaryk Issue — sixth in the Champions of Liberty series — honored the memory of the first president of Czechoslovakia, who rose from humble origin to lead the movement for an independent Czechoslovakia. The two stamps were issued on the 41st anniversary of the republic.

CM456-57 *Thomas G. Masaryk*

Intaglio, perforated 10 1/2 x 11.
CM456 *(1147)*
  4c blue *(113,792,000)*   .25   .20
    Plate block of four   .60
    v. Vertical pair, imperforate
      between   3,250.
    FDC *(March 7, 1960)*   1.00

Intaglio, (Giori Press), perforated 11
CM457 *(1148)*
  8c carmine, deep blue and ocher
      (44,215,200)   .25   .20
    Plate block of four   1.10
    v. Horizontal pair, imperforate
      between   —
    FDC *(March 7, 1960)*   1.00

1960. World Refugee Year Issue focused attention on the world's homeless and destitute; and the importance of universal participation in aiding them. *Intaglio, perforated 11 x 10 1/2.*

CM458 *Family Facing Doorway to a New Life*

CM458 *(1149)*
  4c gray black *(113,195,000)*   .25   .20
    Plate block of four   .60
    FDC *(April 7, 1960)*   1.00

1960. Water Conservation Issue issued in conjunction with the Seventh National Watershed Congress, emphasized the importance of conserving this precious natural resource. *Intaglio, (Giori Press), perforated 11.*

CM459 *Watershed and Dependent Farm and Factories*

CM459 *(1150)*
  4c blue, green and orange brown
      (120,570,000)   .25   .20
    Plate block of four   .60
    FDC *(April 18, 1960)*   1.00

1960. SEATO Issue commemorats the South East Asia Treaty Organization Conference (May 31-June 3) and the organization's efforts on behalf of peace and freedom. This defensive alliance of nations includes Australia, France, New Zealand, Pakistan, Philippines, Thailand, United Kingdom and the United States. *Intaglio, perforated 10 1/2 x 11.*

CM460 *SEATO Emblem*

CM460 *(1151)*
  4c blue *(115,353,000)*   .25   .20
    Plate block of four   .60
    FDC *(May 31, 1960)*   1.00
    v. Vertical pair, imperforate
      between   150.

1960. American Women Issue emphasized the important contributions American women have made to the social, spiritual, economic and political progress of our nation. *Intaglio, perforated 11 x 10 1/2.*

CM461 *Mother, Daughter, and Open Book*

CM461 *(1152)*
  4c violet *(111,080,000)*   .25   .20
    Plate block of four   .60
    FDC *(June 2, 1960)*   1.00

1960. 50-Star Flag Issue commemorated the admission of Hawaii as the 50th state. *Intaglio, (Giori Press), perforated 11.*

CM462 *50-Star American Flag*

CM462 *(1153)*
  4c deep blue and scarlet
      (153,025,000)   .25   .20
    Plate block of four   .60
    FDC *(July 4, 1960)*   1.00

1960. Pony Express Centenary Issue commemorated the contribution to our nation's progress by this pioneer transportation service , which provided a faster mail service vitally needed at the time. A stamped envelope (EN844) also was issued in conjunction with this event (See also CM236). *Intaglio, perforated 11 x 10 1/2.*

CM463 *Pony Express Rider and Map of Route*

CM463 *(1154)*
  4c sepia *(119,665,000)*   .25   .20
    Plate block of four   .70
    FDC *(July 19, 1960)*   1.00

1960. Employ the Handicapped Issue focused on the need to promote employment of physically handicapped people who could be trained for gainful activity in American industry. *Intaglio, perforated 10 1/2 x 11.*

CM464 *Drill Press Operator in Wheelchair*

CM464 *(1155)*
4c blue *(117,855,000)* .25 .20
Plate block of four .60
FDC *(Aug. 28, 1960)* 1.00

1960. Fifth World Forestry Congress Issue paid tribute to the 2,000 foresters from more than 60 nations who gathered to explore the many uses of forest land. The congress was sponsored by the Food and Agriculture Organization of the United Nations. *Intaglio, perforated 10 1/2 x 11.*

CM465 *Seal of World Forestry Congress*

CM465 *(1156)*
4c blue green *(118,185,000)* .25 .20
Plate block of four .60
FDC *(Aug. 29, 1960)* 1.00

1960. Mexican Independence Issue marked the 150th anniversary of the Republic of Mexico. Mexico issued an identical stamp on the same day, (Mexico 1373) different only in captions and denomination. *Intaglio, (Giori Press), perforated 11.*

CM466 *Freedom Bell of the National Palace, Mexico City*

CM466 *(1157)*
4c deep green and carmine red
(112,260,000) .25 .20
Plate block of four .60
FDC *(Sept. 16, 1960)* 1.00

1960. United States of America-Japan Centennial Issue commemorated the 100th anniversary of the first treaty between the two countries to promote good will and understanding. *Intaglio, (Giori Press), perforated 11.*

CM467 *Washington Monument and Cherry Blossoms*

CM467 *(1158)*
4c light blue and carmine
(125,010,000) .25 .20
Plate block of four .65
FDC *(Sept. 28, 1960)* 1.00

1960. Ignace Jan Paderewski Issue — seventh in the Champions of Liberty series — honored the world-famous statesman, pianist and Polish patriot.

CM468-69 *Ignace Jan Paderewski*

Intaglio, perforated 10 1/2 x 11.
CM468 *(1159)*
4c blue *(119,798,000)* .25 .20
Plate block of four .60
FDC *(Oct. 8, 1960)* 1.00

Intaglio, (Giori Press), perforated 11
CM469 *(1160)*
8c red, blue and ocher
(42,696,000) .25 .20
Plate block of four 1.10
FDC *(Oct. 8, 1960)* 1.00

1960. Robert A. Taft Issue honored the memory of a great American who served his country as a senator from 1939 until his death on July 31, 1953. A native of Ohio, he distinguished himself as Senate majority leader. *Intaglio, perforated 10 1/2 x 11.*

CM470 *Robert A. Taft*

CM470 *(1161)*
4c violet *(115,171,000)* .25 .20
Plate block of four .60
FDC *(Oct. 10, 1960)* 1.00

1960. Wheels of Freedom Issue was issued as a tribute to the automotive industry. It was released in conjunction with the National Automobile Show in Detroit. *Intaglio, perforated 11 x 10 1/2.*

CM471 *Hemispheres and steering wheel, symbol of automobile industry*

CM471 *(1162)*
4c blue *(109,695,000)* .25 .20
Plate block of four .60
FDC *(Oct. 15, 1960)* 1.00

1960. Boys' Club of America Issue commemorated the 100th anniversary of the movement that provided excellent recreational facilities for the underprivileged. *Intaglio, (Giori Press), perforated 11.*

CM472 *American youth*

CM472 *(1163)*
4c deep blue, black and red
     (123,690,000) .25 .20
Plate block of four .60
FDC *(Oct. 18, 1960)* 1.00

1960. First Automated Post Office Issue commemorated the establishment of the first fully automated post office at Providence, RI. Considered a milestone in postal progress, the specially created machinery was expected to speed mail delivery. *Intaglio, (Giori Press), perforated 11.*

CM473 *Automated post office*

CM473 *(1164)*
4c deep blue and scarlet *(127,970,000)* .25 .20
Plate block of four .60
FDC *(Oct. 20, 1960)* 1.00

1960. Baron Karl Gustaf Emil Mannerheim Issue — the eighth of the Champions of Liberty series — honored the great Finnish soldier, statesman and leader for his heroic devotion to his country, in peace and war. Born in Askainen, June 4, 1867, he rose to the rank of marshal and led Finnish forces three times in his country's struggle for independence. He served twice as Finland's chief of state.

CM474-75 *Karl Gustaf Emil Mannerheim*

Intaglio, perforated 10 1/2 x 11.
CM474 *(1165)*
4c blue *(124,796,000)* .25 .20
Plate block of four .60
FDC *(Oct. 26, 1960)* 1.00

Intaglio, (Giori Press), perforated 11
CM475 *(1166)*
8c red, blue and ocher
     (42,076,800) .25 .20
Plate block of four 1.10
FDC *(Oct. 26, 1960)* 1.00

1960. Campfire Girls Issue commemorated the Golden Jubilee Convention celebration of the organization that was created in 1910 for girls seven to 18 years of age. *Intaglio, (Giori Press), perforated 11.*

CM476 *Campfire Girls Insignia*

CM476 *(1167)*
4c blue and red *(116,215,000)* .25 .20
Plate block of four .60
FDC *(Nov. 1, 1960)* 1.00

1960. Giuseppe Garibaldi Issue — the ninth of the Champions of Liberty series — commemorated Italy's great patriot and fighter for freedom. A born leader, Garibaldi helped unify Italy and fought for the cause of liberty in South America and Europe.

CM477-78 *Giuseppe Garibaldi*

Intaglio, perforated 10 1/2 x 11.
CM477 *(1168)*
4c green *(126,252,000)* .25 .20
Plate block of four .60
FDC *(Nov. 2, 1960)* 1.00

Intaglio, (Giori Press), perforated 11
CM478 *(1169)*
8c red, blue and ocher
     (42,746,400) .25 .20
Plate block of four 1.10
FDC *(Nov. 2, 1960)* 1.00

1960. Walter F. George Issue honored the distinguished public servant who served as a senator from Georgia and as special assistant for President Eisenhower to NATO in 1957. *Intaglio, perforated 10 1/2 x 11.*

CM479 (1170)
4c violet (124,117,000) .25 .20
 Plate block of four .60
 FDC (Nov. 5, 1960) 1.00

1960. John Foster Dulles Issue paid tribute to a famous American who died while serving as Secretary of State. His long distinguished career included service as secretary to the Hague Peace Conference in 1907 and as U.S. Senator from New York. *Intaglio, perforated 10 1/2 x 11.*

CM480 *John Foster Dulles*

CM480 (1171)
4c violet (177,187,000) .25 .20
 Plate block of four .60
 FDC (Dec. 6, 1960) 1.00

1960. Andrew Carnegie Issue honored the industrialist on his 125th birthday and the 50th anniversary of the establishment of the Carnegie Endowment for International Peace. Born in Scotland, Carnegie came to the United States as a young boy and became one of the great leaders of world industry. He devoted a good portion of his life and wealth to the cause of social and educational advancements and the promotion of international peace. In 1910, in an effort to abolish the horrors of war, he founded the Carnegie Endowment for International Peace with a gift of $10 million. *Intaglio, perforated 10 1/2 x 11.*

CM481 *Andrew Carnegie*

CM481 (1172)
4c claret (119,840,000) .25 .20
 Plate block of four .60
 FDC (Nov. 25, 1960) 1.00

1960. Echo I Issue commemorated the world's first communications satellite launched by NASA into orbit on August 12, 1960. *Intaglio, perforated 11 x 10 1/2.*

CM482 *Echo I satellite in orbit*

CM482 (1173)
4c violet (125,290,000) .25 .20
 Plate block of four 1.00
 FDC (Dec. 15, 1960) 1.00

1961. Mahatma Gandhi Issue — the tenth and final Champions of Liberty issue — honored the Indian who led his country to freedom. A physically frail man, he

endured many hardships that inspired his countrymen to work non-violently for independence, equality and social justice.

CM483-84 *Mahatma Gandhi*

Intaglio, perforated 10 1/2 x 11.
CM483 (1174)
4c red orange (112,966,000) .25 .20
 Plate block of four .60
 FDC (Jan. 26, 1961) 1.00

Intaglio, (Giori Press), perforated 11
CM484 (1175)
8c red, blue and ocher
 (41,644,200) .25 .20
 Plate block of four 1.20
 FDC (Jan. 26, 1961) 1.00

1961. Range Conservation Issue was released in conjunction with the annual meeting of the American Society of Range Management, devoted to conservation, forestry, livestock and land management. *Intaglio, (Giori Press), perforated 11.*

CM485 "The Trail Boss" *and Cattle Grazing*

CM485 (1176)
4c blue, orange and indigo
 (110,850,000) .25 .20
 Plate block of four .60
 FDC (Feb. 2, 1961) 1.00

1961. Horace Greeley Issue honored the publisher and editor who advised the youth of America to "Go West, young man, go West." He established the *New York Tribune* in 1841. *Intaglio, perforated 10 1/2 x 11.*

CM486 *Horace Greeley*

CM486 (1177)
4c violet (98,616,000) .25 .20
 Plate block of four .60
 FDC (Feb. 3, 1961) 1.00

1961-65. Civil War Centennial Series saluted the 100th anniversary of the bloodiest conflict in the nation's history with one centennial stamp for each of the war's five years.

1961. Fort Sumter Issue marked the 100th anniversary of the assault and capture of the Charleston fort by South Carolina. This attack committed the Confederate states to war. *Intaglio, perforated 11 x 10 1/2.*

CM487 *Costal Gun at Fort Sumter*

CM487 *(1178)*
4c green *(101,125,000)* .25 .20
Plate block of four 1.65
FDC *(April 12, 1961)* 1.00

1962. Battle of Shiloh Issue commemorates the valiant stand of Confederate troops under Gen. Albert S. Johnston and Union soldiers under Gen. Ulysses S. Grant in the fields of Tennessee (See also CM1725). *Intaglio, perforated 11 x 10 1/2.*

CM488 *Infantryman in Action*

CM488 *(1179)*
4c black on pink
(124,865,000) .25 .20
Plate block of four 1.10
FDC *(April 7, 1962)* 1.00

1963. Battle of Gettysburg Issue honored the heroes of one of the most important battles of the Civil War, which was fought July 1-3, 1863 in eastern Pennsylvania (See also CM1740). *Intaglio, (Giori Press), perforated 11.*

CM489 *Union and Confederate Soldiers Fighting*

CM489 *(1180)*
5c gray and blue *(79,905,000)* .25 .20
Plate block of four 1.75
FDC *(July 1, 1963)* 1.00

1964. Battle of the Wilderness Issue saluted the fierce battle between the armies of Grant and Lee that took place in densely wooded terrain near Fredericksburg, VA. *Intaglio, (Giori Press), perforated 11.*

CM490 *Artillery in Action*

CM490 *(1181)*
5c brown, purple and black *(125,410,000)*.25 .20
Plate block of four 1.50
FDC *(May 5, 1964)* 1.00

1965. Appomattox Issue celebrated the end of the War between the States. It was at Appomattox Court House, VA, on Sunday, April 9, 1865, that the Confederate

Army under the command of Gen. Robert E. Lee surrendered to Gen. Ulysses S. Grant and the Union forces. *Intaglio, (Giori Press), perforated 11.*

CM491 *Civil War Soldier and Rifles*

CM491 *(1182)*
5c blue and black
(112,845,000) .25 .20
Plate block of four 3.75
FDC *(April 9, 1965)* 1.00
v. Horizontal pair, imperforate vertically

1961. Kansas Statehood Centennial Issue marks 100 years of statehood for Kansas admitted in 1861 as the 34th state. *Intaglio, (Giori Press), perforated 11.*

CM492 *Sunflower, Pioneers and Fort*

CM492 *(1183)*
4c brown, lake and green on yellow paper
(106,210,000) .25 .20
Plate block of four .60
FDC *(May 10, 1961)* 1.00

1961. George William Norris Issue honors the Nebraska senator on his100th birthday. Among his many achievements was a key role in the creation of the Tennessee Valley Authority. *Intaglio, perforated 11 x 10 1/2.*

CM493 *George W. Norris and Norris Dam*

CM493 *(1184)*
4c blue green *(110,810,000)* .25 .20
Plate block of four .60
FDC *(July 11, 1961)* 1.00

1961. Naval Aviation Issue salutes the Golden Jubilee of the Navy's participation and development in aviation. *Intaglio, perforated 11 x 10 1/2.*

CM494 *Naval Air Wings and First Naval Airplane (1911 Curtiss A-1)*

CM494 *(1185)*
4c blue *(116,995,000)* .25 .20
Plate block of four .65
Gutter pair —
FDC *(Aug. 20, 1961)* 1.00

1961. Workman's Compensation Issue marks the 50th anniversary of the first U.S. legislation to compensat workers injured on the job. The Wisconsin law of 1911 set a pattern that was followed by nine other states that year. *Intaglio, perforated 10 1/2 x 11.*

CM495 *Factory and Family in Scales of Justice*

CM495 *(1186)*
4c ultramarine on bluish paper

(121,015,000)	.25	.20
Plate block of four	.60	
v. Plate block of four, plate number inverted	—	
FDC (Sept. 4, 1961)		1.00

1961. Frederic Remington Issue first stamp in a continuing Fine Arts series, honored the 100th birthday of this American artist of the West (CM230) who won fame for his paintings and sculptures of North American Indians, U.S. soldiers and cowboys on the western plains (See also CM993). *Intaglio, (Giori Press), perforated 11.*

CM496 *Detail from* The Smoke Signal *by Remington (left side of painting)*

CM496 *(1187)*

4c blue, red and yellow (111,600,000)	.25	.20
Plate block of four	.65	
FDC (Oct. 4, 1961)		1.00

1961. 50th Anniversary of the Republic of China Issue bears the portrait of Sun Yat-sen (1866-1925), the founder of the republic who fought against dynastic rule for the freedom of China. (See also CM248) *Intaglio, perforated 10 1/2 x 11.*

CM497 *Sun Yat-Sen*

CM497 *(1188)*
4c blue (110,620,000)

4c blue (110,620,000)	.25	.20
Plate block of four	.85	
FDC (Oct. 10, 1961)		1.00

1961. Naismith-Basketball Issue commemorated the 100th birthday of Dr. James A. Naismith (1861-1939), Canadian-born inventor of basketball. An athletic instructor at the YMCA, Naismith saw the need for a fast-moving, exciting indoor sport that could be played in the winter. In 1891 he founded the game, which today draws millions of participants and spectators. *Intaglio, perforated 10 1/2 x 11.*

CM498 *Basketball, Hand and Net*

CM498 *(1189)*

4c brown (109,110,000)	.25	.20
Plate block of four	1.00	
FDC (Nov. 6, 1961)		1.00

1961. Nursing Issue honored the 100th anniversary of the nursing profession in the United States. An urgent need for skilled nurses was created by the Civil War. The training programs then established laid the foundations for the profession, which thousands American women enter each year. *Intaglio, (Giori Press), perforated 11.*

CM499 *Nurse Lighting Candle*

CM499 *(1191)*
4c blue, black, orange and flesh

(145,350,000)	.25	.20
Plate block of four	.60	
FDC (Dec. 28, 1961)		1.00

1962. New Mexico Statehood Issue commemorated the 50th anniversary of its admission as the 47th state. (See CM286) *Intaglio, (Giori Press), perforated 11.*

CM500 *Shiprock Mesa*

CM500 *(1192)*
4c light blue, bister and brown purple

(112,870,000)	.25	.20
Plate block of four	.60	
FDC (Jan. 6, 1962)		1.00

1962. Arizona Statehood Issue marks the 50th anniversary of the admissionof the 48th state. *Intaglio, (Giori Press), perforated 11.*

CM501 *Giant Saguaro Cactus in Bloom at Night*

CM501 *(1192)*
4c scarlet, deep blue and green
(121,820,000)   .25   .20
Plate block of four   .60
FDC *(Feb. 14, 1962)*   1.00

1962. Project Mercury Issue paid tribute to the successful three-orbit flight of Lt. Col. John H. Glenn, Jr. The stamp was released at the moment the flight was completed — the first time the United States honored a historic event with an unannounced, simultaneous commemorative. Glenn, the first American astronaut to orbit the earth, traveled at 17,500 miles per hour in his Mercury capsule, *Friendship 7. Intaglio, (Giori Press), perforated 11.*

CM502 *Mercury Capsule Circling Earth*

CM502 *(1193)*
4c deep blue and yellow(289,240,000) .25   .20
Plate block of four   .80
FDC *(Feb. 20, 1962)*   1.00

1962. Malaria Eradication Issue pledged U.S. support to the World Health Organization in its campaign to eliminate malaria, a disease that claims countless lives each year. *Intaglio, (Giori Press), perforated 11.*

CM503 *United States Seal and WHO Emblem*

CM503 *(1194)*
4c blue and bister *(120,155,000)*   .25   .20
Plate block of four   .60
FDC *(March 30, 1962)*   1.00

1962. Charles Evans Hughes Issue honors the 100th birthday of this statesman-jurist (1862-1948). Hughes served as governor of New York, secretary of state under President Harding and as Chief Justice of the U.S. Supreme Court (1930-41). *Intaglio, perforated 10 1/2 x 11.*

CM504 *Charles Evans Hughes*

CM504 *(1195)*
4c black on yellow paper *(124,595,000)* .25   .20
Plate block of four   .60
FDC *(April 11, 1962)*   1.00

1962. Seattle World's Fair Issue marks the International Exposition held in Seattle, WA. April 21-Oct. 21, 1962. This was America's first space-age world's fair, with the 550-foot-high Space Needle as its most distinctive structure and symbol. *Intaglio, (Giori Press), perforated 11.*

CM505 *Space Needle and Monorail*

CM505 *(1196)*
4c red and deep blue *(147,310,000)*   .25   .20
Plate block of four   .60
FDC *(April 25, 1962)*   1.00

1962. Louisiana Statehood Commemorative marks the 150th anniversary of the admission of Louisiana as the 18th state. *Intaglio, (Giori Press), perforated 11.*

CM506 *Mississippi Riverboat*

CM506 *(1197)*
4c gray green, blue and vermilion
(118,690,000)   .25   .20
Plate block of four   .60
FDC *(April 30, 1962)*   1.00

1962. Homestead Act Issue commemorates the 100th anniversary of the act signed by Abraham Lincoln that opened the Great Plains to settlers. A homesteader could acquire 160 acres by living and working on the land for five years. *Intaglio, perforated 11 1/4 x 10 1/2.*

CM507 *Sod Hut and Homesteaders*

CM507 *(1198)*
4c slate blue *(122,730,000)*   .25   .20
Plate block of four   .60
FDC *(May 20, 1962)*   1.00

1962. Girl Scouts of America Issue commemorates the 50th anniversary of the movement, which has grown into an organization of millions. (See CM316). *Intaglio, perforated 11 1/4 x 10 1/2.*

CM508 *Girl Scout, American Flag*

CM508 *(1199)*
4c red *(126,515,000)*	.25	.20
Plate block of four	.60	
Gutter pair	—	
FDC *(July 24, 1962)*		1.00

1962. Brien McMahon Issue pays tribute to the Conneticut senator who saw the vast potential of the atom for medical, industrial and scientific purposes. McMahon (1903-1952) succeeded in forming the Atomic Energy Commission. (See also CM382) *Intaglio, perforated 11 1/4 x 10 1/2.*

CM509 *James O'Brien McMahon and Atomic Symbol*

CM509 *(1200)*
4c violet *(130,960,000)*	.25	.20
Plate block of four	.60	
FDC *(July 28, 1962)*		1.00

1962. National Apprenticeship Issue marked the 25th anniversary of the program, under which the U.S. Department of Labor, unions and management join in sponsoring apprenticeship training. *Intaglio, perforated 11 1/4 x 10 1/2.*

CM510 *Young Hand Receiving Micrometer*

CM510 *(1201)*
4c black on buff *(120,055,000)*	.25	.20
Plate block of four	.60	
FDC *(Aug. 31, 1962)*		1.00

1962. Sam Rayburn Issue honored the Texan who served as a Congressman from 1913 until 1961. Rayburn was Speaker of the House of Representatives for 17 years, longer than any other. *Intaglio, (Giori Press), perforated 11.*

CM511 *Sam Rayburn and Capitol Dome*

CM511 *(1202)*
4c brown and blue *(120,715,000)*	.25	.20
Plate block of four	.60	
FDC *(Sept. 16, 1962)*		1.00

1962. Dag Hammarskjöld Issue honored the secretary-general of the United Nations who lost his life while on a peace mission in Africa. *Intaglio, (Giori Press), perforated 11.*

CM512-13 *Dag Hammarskjöld and U.N. Building*

CM512 *(1203)*
4c black, brown and yellow		
(121,440,000)	.25	.20
Plate block of four	.60	
FDC *(Oct. 23, 1962)*		1.00

1962. Dag Hammarskjold Special Issue. Shortly after the commemorative was released. a yellow-inverted error was discovered by collectors in New Jersey and Ohio. The Post Office Department deliberately reprinted this error — the first U.S. invert error since the 24c Jenny airmail of 1918. Only the yellow is inverted and there are three distinct varieties: Type I—the non-yellow strip at left is 3.5 mm wide; Type II—the non-yellow at left is 11-11.5 mm wide; and, Type III—the non-yellow strip at left is 9.75 mm wide. *Intaglio, (Giori Press), perforated 11.*

CM513 *(1204)*
4c black, brown and yellow		
(40,270,000)	.25	.20
Type I	.55	.25
FDC *(Nov. 16, 1962)*		1.00
Type II	.55	.25
FDC *(Nov. 16, 1962)*		1.00
Type III	.55	.25
FDC *(Nov. 16, 1962)*		1.00

1962. Higher Education Issue commemorated the centennial of the law creating land-grant colleges and universities and pointed out the role higher education has played in the development of the United States (See also CM377). *Intaglio, (Giori Press), perforated 11.*

CM514 *Lamp of Learning and U.S. Map*

CM514 *(1206)*
4c blue, green and black *(120,035,000)*	.25	.20
Plate block of four	.65	
FDC *(Nov. 14, 1962)*		1.00

1962. Winslow Homer Commemorative honors the American artist who painted *Breezing Up*, on display in the National Gallery of Art in Washington, D.C. This is the second issue in the Fine Arts series. *Intaglio, (Giori Press), perforated 11.*

CM515 Breezing Up *by Winslow Homer*

CM515 *(1207)*
4c multicolored *(117,870,000)*   .25   .20
     Plate block of four   .65
     v. Horizontal pair, imperforate
       between   6,750.
     FDC *(Dec. 15, 1962)*   1.00

1963. Carolina Charter Issue commemorates the 300th anniversary of the granting of the charter by Charles II to eight supporters who helped him regain the English throne. The land grant covered 1.5 million square miles. *Intaglio, (Giori Press), perforated 11.*

CM516 *Charter and Quill Pen*

CM516 *(1230)*
5c dark carmine and brown
     (129,445,000)   .25   .20
     Plate block of four   .65
     FDC *(April 6, 1963)*   1.00

1963. Food for Peace Issue pays tribute to the World Food Congress and joins nearly 150 other nations and territories in publicizing the international Freedom from Hunger campaign on stamps. *Intaglio, (Giori Press), perforated 11.*

CM517 *Stalk of Wheat*

CM517 *(1231)*
5c green, yellow and red
     (135,620,000)   .25   .20
     Plate block of four   .65
     FDC *(June 4, 1963)*   1.00

1963. West Virginia Statehood Centennial Issue commemorated the 100th anniversary of the admission of the Mountain State to the union during the Civil War. *Intaglio, (Giori Press), perforated 11.*

CM518 *Map and State Capitol West Virginia*

CM518 *(1232)*
5c green, red and black
     (June 20, 1963)   .25   .20
     Plate block of four   .65
     FDC *(June 20, 1963)*   1.00

1963. Emancipation Proclamation Issue commemorated the centennial of President Lincoln's action to abolish slavery in the United States. *Intaglio, (Giori Press), perforated 11.*

CM519 *Broken Chains*

CM519 *(1233)*
5c bright blue, scarlet and indigo
     (132,435,000)   .25   .20
     Plate block of four   .85
     FDC *(Aug. 16, 1963)*   1.00

1963. Alliance for Progress Issue marks the second anniversary of an inter-American program for peaceful coexistence and economic improvement. Other members of the Organization of American States to issue stamps honoring the event include Argentina, Bolivia, Costa Rica, Uruguay and Canal Zone. *Intaglio, (Giori Press), perforated 11.*

CM520 *Torch of Progress*

CM520 *(1234)*
5c bright blue and green
     (135,520,000)   .25   .20
     Plate block of four   .65
     FDC *(Aug. 17, 1963)*   1.00

1963. Cordell Hull Issue paid tribute to the secretary of state during the administration of Franklin Roosevelt, from 1933 until 1944. He was awarded the Nobel Peace Prize in 1945. *Intaglio, perforated 10 1/2 x 11.*

CM521 *Cordell Hull*

CM521 *(1235)*
5c blue green *(131,420,000)*   .25   .20
     Plate block of four   .65
     FDC *(Oct. 5, 1963)*   1.00

1963. Eleanor Roosevelt Issue celebrates the 79th birthday of Franklin D. Roosevelt's widow who died in 1962. A champion of liberty and a formidable fighter for human rights. The likeness on the stamp was taken from a photograph she liked best. *Intaglio, perforated 11 x 10 1/2.*

CM522 *Eleanor Roosevelt*

CM522 *(1236)*
5c purple *(133,170,000)*   .25   .20
     Plate block of four   .65
     FDC *(Oct. 11, 1963)*   1.00

1963. National Academy of Science Issue saluted this organization on its 100th anniversary. Abraham Lincoln signed into law the legislation that created the academy, which was originally composed of 50 American scientists. *Intaglio, (Giori Press), perforated 11.*

CM523 *Astral Belt Over Globe*

CM523 *(1237)*
5c turquoise, blue and black
(139,195,000)   .25   .20
Plate block of four   .65
FDC *(Oct. 14, 1963)*   1.00

1963. City Mail Delivery Issue marked the centennial of the service begun at the suggestion of Postmaster General Montgomery Blair, who convinced Congress to pass a law providing for the free delivery of city mail. Designed by Norman Rockwell, this commemorative is considered the first expression of humor on a U.S. stamp. It was also the first U.S. issue fully tagged with an invisible compount that reacts to ultraviolet light in automated mail handling equipment. *Intaglio, (Giori Press), perforated 11.*

CM524 *Postman flanked by boy and dog*

CM524 *(1238)*
5c red, gray and blue, *tagged*
(128,450,000)   .25   .20
Plate block of four   .65
FDC *(Oct. 26, 1963)*   1.00
zo. Tagging omitted   —

1963. International Red Cross Issue marks the centennial of the organization and salutes the Red Cross for its participation in the Cuban prisoner exchange program. *Intaglio, (Giori Press), perforated 11.*

CM525 *Cuban Refugees on* S.S. Morning Light

CM525 *(1239)*
5c deep gray and red
(116,665,00)   .25   .20
Plate block of four   .65
FDC *(Oct. 29, 1963)*   1.00

1963. John James Audubon Issue honors the great American artist and ornithologist. This is the third in the Fine Arts series and is the second time Audubon has been honored with a stamp (see CM216). *Intaglio, (Giori Press), perforated 11.*

CM526 *Audubon's* Columbia Jays

CM526 *(1241)*
5c multicolored *(175,175,000)*   .25   .20
Plate block of four   .80
FDC *(Dec. 7, 1963)*   1.00

1964. Sam Houston Issue salutes the first president of the Republic of Texas, commander of the army that defeated Santa Ana in 1836 and thus gained independence for the Lone Star state. (See also CM166, CM168.) *Intaglio, perforated 10 1/2 x 11.*

CM527 *Sam Houston*

CM527 *(1242)*
5c black *(125,995,000)*   .25   .20
Plate block of four   .85
FDC *(Jan. 10, 1964)*   1.00

1964. Charles M. Russell Issue honors the 100th anniversary of the artist's birth with the fourth stamp in the Fine Arts series. Famous for his Western themes, Russell's art have themes of gunmen, longhorn steers, broncos and dancehall girls. *Intaglio, (Giori Press), perforated 11.*

CM528 *Russell's* Jerked Down

CM528 *(1243)*
5c multicolored *(128,025,000)*   .25   .20
Plate block of four   .85
FDC *(March 19, 1964)*   1.00

1964. New York World's Fair Issue commemorated the opening of the international exposition dedicated to "Peace Through Understanding." Approximately 175 separate pavilions and other structures presented the achievements of more than 509 nations, states and major industries. *Intaglio, perforated 11 x 10 1/2.*

CM529 *Unisphere and World Fair Mall*

CM529 *(1244)*
 5c green *(145,700,000)*   .25   .20
  Plate block of four   .85
  FDC *(April 22, 1964)*   1.00

1964. John Muir Issue honored the naturalist and conservationist whose efforts helped save California's priceless forests. *Intaglio, (Giori Press), perforated 11.*

CM530 *John Muir and Redwoods*

CM530 *(1245)*
 5c brown, green, brownish gray and
    olive green *(120,310,000)*   .25   .20
  Plate block of four   .85
  FDC *(April 29, 1964)*   1.00

1964. John F. Kennedy Memorial Issue pays tribute to the 35th president of the United States, assassinted November 22, 1963. Many nations mourned his passing and issued stamps in his memory. Although Boston was the official First Day city, the stamp was released nation wide that same day. *Intaglio, perforated 11 x 10 1/2.*

CM531 *John F. Kennedy and Eternal Flame*

CM531 *(1246)*
 5c gray blue *(500,000,000)*   .25   .20
  Plate block of four   1.85
  FDC *(May 29, 1964)*   1.00

1964. New Jersey Tercentenary Issue marks the 300th anniversary of the colonization of the Garden State by the British. The stamp was first issued in Elizabeth, the state's first capital and oldest city. *Intaglio, perforated 10 1/2 x 11.*

CM532 *Philip Carteret at Elizabethtown*

CM532 *(1247)*
 5c ultramarine *(123,845,000)*   .25   .20
  Plate block of four   .65
  FDC *(June 15, 1964)*   1.00

1964. Nevada Statehood Issue commemorats the centenary of the entry of Nevada as the 36th state. *Intaglio, (Giori Press), perforated 11.*

CM533 *Virginia City and Map of Nevada*

CM533 *(1248)*
 5c multicolored *(122,825000)*   .25   .20
  Plate block of four   .65
  FDC *(July 22, 1964)*   1.00

1964. Register and Vote Issue encouroges all eligible Americans to take part in the forthcoming election and was endorsed by both the Democratic and Republican parties. *Intaglio, (Giori Press), perforated 11.*

CM534 *U.S. Flag*

CM534 *(1249)*
 5c blue and red *(325,000,000)*   .25   .20
  Plate block of four   .65
  FDC *(Aug. 1, 1964)*   1.00

1964. William Shakespeare Issue commemorates the 400th birthday of the Bard of Avon. His contribution to the world included such masterpieces as *Romeo & Juliet, Hamlet, Othello, Macbeth* and *King Lear. Intaglio, perforated 10 1/2 x 11.*

CM535 *William Shakespeare*

CM535 *(1250)*
 5c brown on tan paper *(123,245,000)*   .25   .20
  Plate block of four   .65
  FDC *(Aug. 14, 1964)*   1.00

1964. Doctors Mayo Issue honor the birth of William J. Mayo and his brother Charles H. Mayo and the 50th anniversary of the founding of the world-famous Mayo Clinic in Rochester, MN. *Intaglio, perforated 10 1/2 x 11.*

CM536 *Statue of the Mayo Brothers*

CM536 *(1251)*
 5c green *(123,355,000)*   .25   .20
  Plate block of four   1.50
  FDC *(Sept. 11, 1964)*   1.00

1964. American Music Issue commemorates the 50th anniversary of the American Society of Composers, Authors and Publishers. *Intaglio, (Giori Press), perforated 11.*

CM537 *Lute and Horn, Music Score, Oak and Laurel*

CM537 *(1252)*
5c red, gray and blue on granite paper

	(126,370,000)	.25	.20
Plate block of four		.85	
v.blue omitted		1,000.	
FDC *(Oct. 15, 1964)*			1.00

1964. Homemakers Issue commemorates the 50th anniversary of the Smith-Lever Act that improved home life in America and was issued in conjunction with the annual meeting of the National Extension Homemakers Council. This is the first time the Bureau of Engraving and Printing combined offset and intaglio printing on a stamp, a method used by the American Bank Note Company to print the Overrun Countries stamps (CM251-63). *Intaglio (Giori Press) and offset, perforated 11.*

CM538 *Needlepoint Sampler of American Farm Scene*

CM538 *(1253)*
5c multicolored on buff *(121,250,000)* .25 .20

Plate block of four	.85	
FDC *(Oct. 26, 1964)*		1.00

1964. Verrazano-Narrows Bridge Issue marks the dedication of what was the longest single suspension bridge in the world. Named for the Florentine explorer who discovered New York Bay in 1524, the span links Staten Island and Brooklyn, NY. *Intaglio, perforated 10 1/2 x 11.*

CM539 *Verrazano-Narrows Bridge and Map*

CM539 *(1258)*
5c green *(125,005,000)* .25 .20

Plate block of four	.65	
FDC *(Nov. 21, 1964)*		1.00

1964. Abstract Art Issue is the fifth in the series of Fine Arts commemoratives. It is based on a lithograph by the late Stuart Davis. *Intaglio, (Giori Press), perforated 11.*

CM540 Melange of Squiggles *by Stuart Davis*

CM540 *(1259)*
5c blue, black and red *(125,800,000)* .25 .20

Plate block of four	.65	
FDC *(Dec. 2, 1964)*		1.00

1964. Amateur Radio Operators Issue paid tribute to the nation's 250,000 "hams" and their long record of service to the country in emergencies and marks the 50th anniversary of the American Radio Relay League. *Intaglio, perforated 10 1/2 x 11.*

CM541 *Radio Dial and Wave*

CM541 *(1260)*
5c purple *(122,230,000)* .25 .20

Plate block of four	.90	
FDC *(Dec. 15, 1964)*		1.00

1965. Battle of New Orleans Issue salutes 150 years of peace between England and the United States and the sesquicentennial of the famous battle between American forces under Gen. Andrew Jackson and the British troops led by Sir Edward Packenham. *Intaglio, (Giori Press), perforated 11.*

CM542 *Gen. Andrew Jackson Leading Troops in Battle and Sesquicentennial Medal*

CM542 *(1261)*
5c carmine, blue and slate

	(115,695,000)	.25	.20
Plate block of four		.65	
FDC *(Jan. 8, 1965)*			1.00

1965. Sokol Centennial - Physical Fitness Issue paid tribute to the program initiated by the President Kennedy and the 100th anniversary of the Sokol educational and physical fitness organization. *Intaglio, (Giori Press), perforated 11.*

CM543 *Discus Thrower*

CM543 *(1262)*
5c lake and deep slate *(115,095,000)* .25 .20

Plate block of four	.65	
FDC *(Feb. 15, 1965)*		1.00

1965. Crusade Against Cancer Issue publicizes the importance of medical checkups and prompt treatment and salutes the efforts of those dedicated to the eradicating cancer. *Intaglio, (Giori Press), perforated 11.*

CM544 *Stethoscope and Microscope*

CM544 *(1263)*
5c reddish violet, black and red
(116,560,000) .25 .20
Plate block of four .65
FDC *(April 1, 1965)* 1.00

1965. Winston Churchill Memorial Issue honors the World War II British leader, (1874-1965). *Intaglio, perforated 10 1/2 x 11.*

CM545 *Winston Churchill*

CM545 *(1264)*
5c black *(125,180,000)* .25 .20
Plate block of four .65
FDC *(May 13, 1965)* 1.00

1965. Magna Carta Issue commemorates the 750th anniversary of the document by King John that became the first detailed statement of English feudal law esteemed by many as a cornerstone of later British and American law. *Intaglio, (Giori Press), perforated 11.*

CM546 Triumph of the People over the King. *Symbolic design by Brook Temple*

CM546 *(1265)*
5c black, yellow and reddish-violet
(120,135,000) .25 .20
Plate block of four (two numbers) .65
v. Plate block of four, black
plate number omitted —
FDC *(June 15, 1965)* 1.00

1965. International Cooperation Year Issue commemorates the 20th anniversary of the United Nations. The United States and other U.N. member nations, issued stamps dedicated to the theme, and the United Nations issued a set of two stamps and a souvenir sheet on the same day as this U.S. stamp. *Intaglio, (Giori Press), perforated 11.*

CM547 *Interrnational Cooperation Year Emblem*

CM547 *(1266)*
5c turquoise blue and slate
(115,405,000) .25 .20
Plate block of four .65
FDC *(June 26, 1965)* 1.00

1965. Salvation Army Issue marks the 100th anniversary of this non-sectarian international organization. Founded in London by William Booth in 1865, the Salvation Army was first established in the United States in 1880. *Intaglio, (Giori Press), perforated 11.*

CM548 *Salvation Army*

CM548 *(1267)*
5c red, black and deep blue
(115,855,000) .25 .20
Plate block of four .65
FDC *(July 2, 1965)* 1.00

1965. Dante Alighieri Issue marks the 700th birthday of Italy's poet who wrote *The Divine Comedy. Intaglio, perforated 10 1/2 x 11.*

CM549 *Dante Alighieri. Adopted from a 16th-century painting.*

CM549 *(1268)*
5c carmine red on light venetian red paper
(115,340,000) .25 .20
Plate block of four .65
FDC *(July 17, 1965)* 1.00

1965. Herbert Hoover Issue paid tribute to the 31st president of the United States who died October 20, 1964. He was a talented mining engineer and served the country in many capacities, including secretary of commerce under Harding. *Intaglio, perforated 10 1/2 x 11.*

CM550 *Herbert Hoover*

CM550 *(1269)*
5c red *(114,840,000)* .25 .20
Plate block of four .65
FDC *(Aug. 10, 1965)* 1.00

1965. Robert Fulton Issue commemorated the 200th
birthday of the inventor who built the first successful
steamship, *The Clermont*, in 1807. *Intaglio, (Giori Press),
perforated 11.*

CM551 *Robert Fulton and* The
Clermont

CM551 *(1270)*
5c blue and black *(116,140,000)* .25 .20
Plate block of four .65
FDC *(Aug. 19, 1965)* 1.00

1965. European Settlement Issue commemorated the
400th anniversary of the establishment by Spanish
colonists of a permanent settlement in Florida in
September 1565. Spain released a joint issue marking this
event (Spain 1715). *Intaglio, (Giori Press), perforated 11.*

CM552 *Spanish Explorer and Ships*

CM552 *(1271)*
5c yellow, red and black *(116,900,000)* .25 .20
Plate block of four .65
v. Yellow omitted 400.
FDC *(Aug. 28, 1965)* 1.00

1965. Traffic Safety Issue called attention to the
urgent need to reduce automotive accidents. *Intaglio,
(Giori Press), perforated 11.*

CM553 *Traffic Signal*

CM553 *(1272)*
5c green, black and red *(114,085,000)* .25 .20
Plate block of four .65
FDC *(Sept. 3, 1965)* 1.00

1965. John Singleton Copley Issue is the sixth stamp
in the Fine Arts series. Features a portrait of the artist's
daughter, part of a family group painted in 1776 by
Copley. The original now hangs in the National Gallery of
Art, Washington, D.C. *Intaglio, (Giori Press), perforated 11.*

CM554 *Elizabeth Clarke Copley*

CM554 *(1273)*
5c black and tones of brown and olive
(114,880,000) .25 .20
Plate block of four .65
FDC *(Sept. 17, 1965)* 1.00

1965. International Telecommunication Union Issue
commemorated the 100th anniversary of this
international organization created in 1865 to develop
electronic communication among nations. *Intaglio, (Giori
Press), perforated 11.*

CM555 *World Map and Radio Wave*

CM555 *(1274)*
11c yellow, red and black *(26,995,000)* .25 .20
Plate block of four 5.50
FDC *(Oct. 6, 1965)* 1.00

1965. Adlai Stevenson Memorial Issue pays tribute to
the late U.S. ambassador to the United Nations and
former presidential candidate. *Intaglio (Giori Press) and
offset, perforated 11.*

CM556 *Adlai Stevenson, U.N. Wreath and
U.S. Colors*

CM556 *(1275)*
5c light blue gray, black, red and blue
(128,495,000) .25 .20
Plate block of four .65
FDC *(Oct. 23, 1965)* 1.00

1966. Migratory Bird Treaty Issue marked the 50th
anniversary of cooperation between the United States
and Canada in protecting birds. *Intaglio, (Giori Press),
perforated 11.*

CM557 *Birds Over the Great Lakes*

CM557 *(1306)*
5c red, blue and light blue
(116,835,000) .25 .20
Plate block of four .65
FDC *(March 16, 1966)* 1.00

1966. Humane Treatment of Animals Issue paid tribute to The American Society for the Prevention of Cruelty to Animals, founded in 1866 by Henry Bergh. *Intaglio (Giori Press) and offset, perforated 11.*

CM558 *"Babe" the Dog*

CM558 *(1307)*
5c reddish brown and black

(117,470,000)	.25	.20
Plate block of four	.65	
FDC *(April 9, 1966)*		1.00

1966. Indiana Statehood Issue marked the 150th anniversary of the admission to the union. The event was officially celebrated at Corydon, the first capital of Indiana. *Intaglio, (Giori Press), perforated 11.*

CM559 *Map of Indiana and Old Capitol*

CM559 *(1308)*
5c blue, yellow and brown

(123,770,000)	.25	.20
Plate block of four	.65	
FDC *(April 16, 1966)*		1.00

1966. American Circus Issue saluted the Big Top and those who bring fun and thrills to audiences throughout the nation. *Intaglio, (Giori Press), perforated 11.*

CM560 *Circus Clown*

CM560 *(1309)*
5c red, blue, pink and black

131,270,000)	.25	.20
Plate block of four	.90	
FDC *(May 2, 1966)*		1.00

1966. Sixth International Philatelic Exhibition Issue commemorated the show, held in Washington, D.C., May 21-30. This commemorative stamp, souvenir sheet and airmail postal card were issued to mark the event. *Intaglio (Giori Press) and offset, perforated 11.*

CM561 *Envelope with Stamps*

CM561 *(1310)*
5c multicolored *(122,285,000)*   .25   .20

Plate block of four	.65	
FDC *(May 21, 1966)*		1.00

1966. SIPEX Souvenir Sheet, dedicated to stamp collectors also featurs the words "Discover America," the theme of President Johnson's program to stimulate travel and tourism in the United States. *Intaglio (Giori Press) and offset, imperforate.*

CM562
Envelope and Capitol Scene

CM562 *(1311)*
5c multicolored *(14,680,000)*   .30   .25

FDC *(May 23, 1966)*		1.00

1966. Bill of Rights Issue commemorated the 175th anniversary of the first 10 amendments to the U.S. Constitution. The stamp was designed by Herbert L. Block, renowned editorial cartoonist. *Intaglio, (Giori Press), perforated 11.*

CM563 *"Freedom Conquers Tyranny"*

CM563 *(1312)*
5c red and blue

(114,160,000)	.25	.20
Plate block of four	.65	
FDC *(July 1, 1966)*		1.00

1966. Polish Millennium Issue commemorated the 1,000th anniversary of in Poland and pays tribute to the longstanding friendship between Americans and the Polish people. *Intaglio, perforated 10 1/2 x 11*

CM564 *Polish Eagle*

CM564 *(1313)*
5c red *(126,475,000)*   .25   .20

Plate block of four	.65	
FDC *(July 30, 1966)*		1.00

1966. National Park Service Issue paid tribute to the 50th anniversary of the National Park Service. Although the national park system dates back to 1872, it was first established as a bureau under the Department of Interior August 25, 1916. *Intaglio (Giori Press) and offset, perforated 11.*

CM565 *National Park Emblem*

CM565 *(1314)*

5c multicolored *(119,535,000)*	.25	.20
Plate block of four	.80	
FDC *(Aug. 25, 1966)*		1.00
z. Tagged	.30	.25
Plate block of four, tagged	2.00	
FDC, tagged *(Aug. 26, 1966)*		1.00
z1. Tagged after perforating	—	
Plate block of four, with untagged left margin	—	
FDC (Washington, D.C.) *(Aug. 26, 1966)*		—
z2. Tagging inverted		
Plate block of four	—	
z3. Error (untagged), plate-block-side margin strip of 20 with plate, Zip, With tagged and untagged errors on same piece	—	

Stamps tagged after perforation can be distinguished by a grid of tagging which connects the perforation holes on the gummed side of unused stamps and perforation-sized disc-like blemishes in the tagging on the face of the stamps. Untagged gripper margins, about 3/8-inch in width, were intended to appear in left sheet margins, but some sheets were put through the offset tagging press with the underlying design inverted, resulting in errors with tagging absent in the opposite margins.

Values shown for the untagged errors are for strips of at least five stamps with both tagged and untagged specimens on a single piece.

For more information on tagging, see the introduction.

1966. Marine Corps Reserve Issue celebrates the 50th anniversary of the military organization. *Intaglio (Giori Press) and offset, perforated 11.*

CM566 *U.S. Marines 1775-1966*

CM566 *(1315)*

5c black, olive, red and blue *(125,110,000)*	.25	.20
Plate block of four	.65	

FDC *(Aug. 29, 1966)*		1.00
z. Tagged	.30	.25
Plate block of four, tagged	2.00	
FDC, tagged *(Aug. 29, 1966)*		1.00
z1. Error (untagged), strip of five showing both tagged and untagged on same piece.	—	
v. Black and olive omitted	15,400.	

1966. General Federation of Women's Clubs Issue commemorated 75 years of service ranging from aiding school dropouts to aiding international understanding, and the millions of women who are members of the clubs and associate organizations. *Intaglio, (Giori Press), perforated 11.*

CM567 *Women of 1890's and 1960's*

CM567 *(1316)*

5c pink, blue and black *(114,853,000)*	.25	.20
Plate block of four	.65	
FDC *(Sept. 12, 1966)*		1.00
z. tagged	.30	.25
Plate block of four	2.00	
FDC *(Sept. 13, 1966)*		1.00

1966. Johnny Appleseed Issue, the inaugural stamp in the American Folklore series, honors John Chapman, eccentric nurseryman who devoted his life to planting apple trees in Pennsylvania, Ohio and Indiana It is reputed that he covered over 100,000 square miles before his death in 1845. *Intaglio, (Giori Press), perforated 11.*

CM568 *Johnny Appleseed and Fruit*

CM568 *(1317)*

5c black, red and green *(124,290,000)*	.25	.20
Plate block of four	.65	
FDC *(Sept. 24, 1966)*		1.00
z. tagged	.30	.25
Plate block of four	2.00	
FDC *(Sept. 26, 1966)*		1.00

1966. Beautification of America Issue publicized the campaign to restore and enhance the beauty of the country. *Intaglio, (Giori Press), perforated 11.*

CM569 *Jefferson Memorial and Cherry Blossoms*

CM569 *(1318)*
> **5c black, green and pink** *(128,460,000)* .25   .20
>> Plate block of four   .65
>> FDC *(Oct. 5. 1966)*   1.00
>> z. tagged   .30   .25
>>> Plate block of four   2.00
>>> FDC *(Oct. 5, 1966)*   1.00
>> z1. Tagged after perforating   —
>>> Plate block of four, untagged
>>> right margin   —
>> z2. Tagged after perforating (error),
>>> untagged *left* sheet margin   —
>>> Plate block of four   —

1966. Great River Road Issue publicizes the longest parkway in the world, stretching from Kenora, Canada southward to New Orleans, a distance of 5,600 miles. *Intaglio (Giori Press) and offset, perforated 11.*

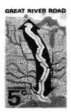

CM570 *Map of Mississippi River and Road*

CM570 *(1319)*
> **5c salmon, blue, olive yellow and yellow**
>> **green** *(127,585,000)*   .25   .20
>> Plate block of four   .65
>> FDC *(Oct. 21, 1966)*   1.00
>> z. tagged   .30   .25
>>> Plate block of four   2.00
>>> FDC *(Oct. 22, 1966)*

1966. U.S. Savings Bond Issue salutes 25 years of bond sales and also carries the message, "We Appreciate our Servicemen." *Intaglio (Giori Press) and offset, perforated 11.*

CM571 *Statue of Liberty and U.S. Flag*

CM571 *(1320)*
> **5c red, blue and black** *(115,875,000)*   .25   .20
>> Plate block of four   .75
>> FDC *(Oct. 26, 1966)*   1.00
>> v. Red, black and dark
>>> blue omitted   5,000.
>> v1. Dark blue omitted   —
>> z. tagged   .30   .25
>>> Plate block of four   2.00
>>> FDC *(Oct. 27, 1966)*

1966. Mary Cassatt Issue the seventh in the Fine Arts series, pays tribute to the American painter whom many

critics regard as the greatest female artist. She is the only American, besides Whistler, to have her work hang in the Louvre. *Intaglio, (Giori Press), perforated 11.*

CM572 The Boating Party

CM572 *(1322)*
> **5c multicolored** *(114,015,000)*   .25   .20
>> Plate block of four   .75
>> FDC *(Nov. 17, 1966)*   1.00
>> z. tagged   .30   .25
>>> Plate block of four   —
>>> FDC *(Nov. 17, 1966)*   —

1967. National Grange Issue commemorates the 100th anniversary of the farmer's organization founded by Oliver H. Kelley to help farmers develop economically and culturally. Its sphere of activities has broadened and now include scholarships and aid to undeveloped. *Intaglio, (Giori Press), perforated 11.*

CM573 *Grange Poster of 1870*

CM573 *(1323)*
> **5c brownish orange, green, orange and**
>> **black,** tagged *(121,105,000)*   .25   .20
>> Plate block of four   .65
>> FDC *(April 17, 1967)*   1.00
>> zo. Tagging omitted   —

1967. Canada Centennial Issue commemorated the 100th annivesary of Canada's Confederation. The stamp was first sold at the U.S. pavilion at Expo 67 in Montreal. *Intaglio, (Giori Press), perforated 11.*

CM574 *Abstract Canadian Landscape*

CM574 *(1324)*
> **5c blue, green, dark blue and olive green,**
>> tagged *(132,045,000)*   .25   .20
>> Plate block of four   .65
>> FDC *(May 25, 1967)*   1.00
>> zo. Tagging omitted   —

1967. Erie Canal Sesquicentennial Issue celebrates the engineering feat that linked Lake Erie with New York City. This 363-mile man-made waterway contributed to the economic development of the young nation. *Intaglio (Giori Press) and offset, perforated 11.*

CM575 *Canal Boat*

CM575 *(1325)*
5c dark blue, light blue, black and red,
        tagged *(118,780,000)*   .25   .20
        Plate block of four   .65
        FDC *(July 4, 1967)*   1.00
        zo. Tagging omitted   —

1967. Lions International Issue salutes the world's largest volunteer service organization on its 50th anniversary. The theme of the stamp, "Search for Peace," was that of an essay contest sponsored by the Lions. *Intaglio, (Giori Press), perforated 11.*

CM576 *Dove of Peace and Olive Branch*

CM576 *(1326)*
5c red, blue and black on granite paper,
        tagged *(121,985,000)*   .25   .20
        Plate block of four   .80
        FDC *(July 5, 1967)*   1.00
        zo. Tagging omitted   —

1967. Henry David Thoreau Issue honors the 19th-century essayist on his 150th birthday. His writings reflect his love of nature and his belief in the dignity of all man. *Intaglio, (Giori Press), perforated 11.*

CM577 *Henry David Thoreau*

CM577 *(1327)*
5c red, black and green, tagged
        (111,850,000)   .25   .20
        Plate block of four   .65
        FDC *(July 12, 1967)*   1.00
        zo. Tagging omitted   —

1967. Nebraska Statehood Issue marks the centennial of the State's entry into the union. *Intaglio (Giori Press) and offset, perforated 11.*

CM578 *Cattle and corn*

CM578 *(1328)*
5c yellow, green and brown, tagged
        (117,225,000)   .25   .20
        Plate block of four   .65
        FDC *(July 29, 1967)*   1.00
        zo. Tagging omitted   —

1967. Voice of America Issue pays tribute to the radio branch of the U.S. Information Agency on its 25th anniversary. *Intaglio, (Giori Press), perforated 11.*

CM579 *Radio Tower Transmitting*

CM579 *(1329)*
5c red, blue and black, tagged
        (111,515,000)   .25   .20
        Plate block of four   .65
        FDC *(Aug. 1, 1967)*   1.00
        zo. Tagging omitted   —

1967. Davy Crockett Issue, the second stamp in the American Folkfore seres, honors the Tennessee backwoodsman who gained fame as a trapper, hunter, soldier, public official and died at the Alamo. *Intaglio (Giori Press) and offset, perforated 11.*

CM580 *Davy Crockett*

CM580 *(1330)*
5c green, black and yellow, tagged
        (114,270,000)   .25   .20
        Plate block of four   .85
        FDC *(Aug. 17, 1967)*   1.00
        v. Green omitted   —
        v1. green and black omitted   —
        v2. green and yellow omitted   —
        v3. Vertical pair, imperforate
           between   —
        zo. Tagging omitted   —

1967. Space Twins Issue salutes America's achievements in space. For the first time, the United States printed two se-tenant stamp that blend into one complete design. *Intaglio (Giori Press) and offset, perforated 11.*

CM581-82 *Spacewalking Astronaut and Gemini Capsule*

CM581 *(1331)*
5c dark blue, black, light blue and red
        tagged *(120,865,000)*   1.00   .35

CM582 *(1332)*
5c dark blue, red and blue green,

tagged	1.00	.35
Se-tenant pair, CM581-82	2.00	1.50
Plate block of four	—	
FDC, single *(Sept. 29, 1967)*		—
FDC, pair		—
zo. Tagging omitted, any single	—	
zoy. Tagging omitted, pair	—	

1967. Urban Planning Issue publicizes the need to improve and develop American cities. *Intaglio, (Giori Press), perforated 11.*

CM583 *Overhead View of Model City*

CM583 *(1333)*
5c dark blue, light blue and black

tagged *(110,675,000)*	.25	.20
Plate block of four	.65	
FDC *(Oct. 2, 1967)*		1.00
zo. Tagging omitted	—	

1967. Finland Independence Issue honors the 50th anniversary of Finnish sovereignty. *Printed by intaglio (Giori Press), perforated 11.*

CM584 *Finnish Coat of Arms*

CM584 *(1334)*
5c blue, tagged *(110,670,000)*

	.25	.20
Plate block of four	.65	
FDC *(Oct. 6, 1967)*		1.00
zo. Tagging omitted	—	

1967. Thomas Eakins Issue, the eighth stamp in the Fine Arts series, honors an American artist who gained fame for his paintings of athletic events, portraits and early American life. A professor of anatomy at the Pennsylvania Academy of Fine Arts, Eakins' thorough knowledge of this subject is reflected in his works. The first U.S. postage stamp using the *gravure* method. The issue was printed by the Photogravure and Color Co., Moonachie, NJ. *Perforated 12.*

CM585 The Biglin Brothers Racing

CM585 *(1335)*
5c gold and multicolored, tagged

(113,825,000)	.25	.20
Plate block of four	.65	
FDC *(Nov. 2, 1967)*		1.00
zo. Tagging omitted	—	

1967. Mississippi Statehood Issue honors the 150th anniversary of the Magnolia State's entry into the union. *Intaglio, (Giori Press), perforated 11.*

CM586 *Magnolia Blossom*

CM586 *(1337)*
5c green blue, blue green and brown

tagged *(113,330,000)*	.25	.20
Plate block of four	.75	
FDC *(Dec. 11, 1967)*		1.00
zo. Tagging omitted		

1968. Illinois Statehood Issue marks the 150th anniversary of the State's entery into the Union. *Intaglio (Giori Press) and offset, perforated 11.*

CM587 *Illinois Farm Scene*

CM587 *(1339)*
6c multicolored, tagged

(141,350,000)	.25	.20
Plate block of four	.85	
FDC *(Feb. 12, 1968)*		1.00
zo. Tagging omitted	—	

1968. Hemisfair '68 Issue celebrated the international exposition that opened in San Antonio, TX, April 6th. The theme was "The Confluence of Civilizations in the Americas," and the stamp also commemorated the 250th anniversary of San Antonio. *Intaglio (Giori Press) and offset, perforated 11.*

CM588 *North and South America with Lines converging on San Antonio*

CM588 *(1340)*
6c blue, pink and white, tagged

(117,470,600)	.25	.20
Plate block of four	.85	
FDC *(March 30, 1968)*		1.00
v. White omitted	1,400.	

1968. Support Our Youth Issue honored the Benevolent and Protectorate Order of Elks centennial year and the expansion of its youth service program. *Intaglio, (Giori Press), perforated 11.*

CM589 *Young Americans*

CM589 *(1342)*
6c red and blue, tagged

(147,120,000)	.25	.20
Plate block of four	.85	
FDC *(May 1, 1968)*		1.00
zo. Tagging omitted	—	

1968. Law and Order Issue publicized the work of the law enforcement officer as a protector and friend of the people. *Intaglio, (Giori Press), perforated 11.*

CM590 *Policeman and young friend*

CM590 *(1343)*
6c red, blue and black, tagged

(130,125,000)	.25	.20
Plate block of four	.85	
FDC *(May 17, 1968)*		1.00
zo. Tagging omitted	—	

1968. Register and Vote Issue supports the efforts of the American Heritage Foundation and others in making the public aware of its civic obligation to vote. *Intaglio (Giori Press) and offset, perforated 11.*

CM591 *Eagle Weathervane*

CM591 *(1344)*
6c gold and black, tagged *(158,070,000)* .25   .20

Plate block of four	.85	
FDC *(June 27, 1968)*		1.00
zo. Tagging omitted	—	

1968. Historic Flags Issue saluted ten banners from America's struggle for independence. Nine of the flags were selected because of their important roles in the Revolutionary War period. One flag, the one flown at Fort McHenry, inspired Francis Scott Key to write the *Star Spangled Banner* during the War of 1812. *Intaglio (Giori Press) and offset, perforated 11.*

CM592 *Fort Moultrie Flag (1776)*

CM592 *(1345)*
6c blue, tagged *(228,040,000)*   .40   .30

CM593 *Fort McHenry Flag (1795-1818)*

CM593 *(1346)*
6c red and blue, tagged   .40   .30

CM594 *Washington's Cruisers Flag (1775)*

CM594 *(1347)*
6c green and blue, tagged   .40   .30

CM595 *Bennington Flag (1777)*

CM595 *(1348)*
6c red and blue, tagged   .40   .30

CM596 *Rhode Island Flag (1775)*

CM596 *(1349)*
6c gold and blue, tagged   .40   .30

CM597 *First Stars and Stripes (1777)*

CM597 *(1350)*
6c red and blue, tagged   .40   .30

CM598 *Bunker Hill Flag (1775)*

CM598 *(1351)*
6c red, green and blue,tagged   .40   .30

CM599 *Grand Union Flag (1776)*

CM599 *(1352)*
6c red and blue, tagged   .40   .30

CM600 *Philadelphia Light Horse Flag (1775)*

CM600 *(1353)*
6c multicolored, tagged   .40   .30

CM601 *First Navy Jack (1775)*

CM601 *(1354)*
6c red, gold and blue, tagged   .40   .30
Plate block of 20   7.50
Se-tenant strip of ten
  (CM592-60)   3.50   4.00
FDC, any single   1.00
  (July 4, 1968)
zo. Tagging omitted, any single   —
zoy. Tagging omitted se-tenant
  strip of 10   —
Because the plate number is attached to a vertical column of 10 different stamps, plate block of 20 is listed.

1968. Walt Disney Issue hails the creative genius who brought a new dimension to entertainment with his animated cartoons, full-length films and theme parks. The creator of Mickey Mouse, Donald Duck and other lovable characters, built a multi-million dollar entertainment empire. *Gravure by Achrovure Division of Union-Camp Corporation, Englewood, N.J., perforated 12.*

CM602 *Walt Disney and Cartoon Children*

CM602 *(1355)*
6c multicolored, tagged
  (153,015,000)   .25   .20
Plate block of four   2.10
FDC *(Sept. 11, 1968)*   1.00
v. Horizontal pair, imperforate
  between   5,000.
v1. Imperforate pair   675.
v2. Vertical pair, imperforate
  horizontally   700.
v3. Black omitted   2,150.
v4. Blue omitted   2,150.
v5. Yellow omitted   750.
zo. Tagging omitted   —

1968. Father Jacques Marquette Issue honors the French explorer-missionary (CM17) who in 1668 established what is considered the oldest permanent settlement in Michigan. *Intaglio (Giori Press) and offset, perforated 11.*

CM603 *Jacques Marquette and Louis Joliet in canoe*

CM603 *(1356)*
6c black, green and brown, tagged
  (132,560,000)   .25   .20
Plate block of four   .85
FDC *(Sept. 20, 1968)*   1.00
zo. Tagging omitted   —

1968. Daniel Boone Issue, the third commemorative in the American Folklore series, recalls the frontiersman whose exploits inspired historians and fiction writers to record the remarkable achievements of this heroic hunter, trapper, soldier and public servant. *Intaglio (Giori Press) and offset, perforated 11.*

CM604 *Pipe Tomahawk, Powder Horn, Rifle, and Knife*

CM604 *(1357)*
6c red brown, brown, yellow and black
  tagged *(130,385,000)*   .25   .20
Plate block of four   .85
FDC *(Sept. 26, 1968)*   1.00
zo. Tagging omitted   —

1968. Arkansas River Navigation Issue pays tribute to this important waterway and the economic potential of the $1.2 billion project. *Intaglio (Giori Press) and offset, perforated 11.*

CM605 *Ship's Wheel and Transmission Tower*

CM605 *(1358)*
6c blue, black and dark blue, tagged
  (132,265,000)   .25   .20
Plate block of four   .85
FDC *(Oct. 1, 1968)*   1.00
zo. Tagging omitted   —

1968. Leif Erikson Issue honored the 11th century Norseman, whose navigational skills and daring brought him to the Americas 500 years before Christopher Columbus. *Intaglio (Giori Press) and offset, perforated 11.*

CM606 *Statue by A. Stirling Calder Leif Erikson.*

CM606 *(1359)*

6c brown *(128,710,000)*	.25	.20
Plate block of four	.85	
FDC *(Oct. 9,1968)*		1.00

1968. Cherokee Strip Issue marks the 75th anniversary of the historic land run by more than 100,000 would-be homesteaders into northern Oklahoma, competing for the 40,000 available homesites. *Rotary press printing, perforated 11.*

 CM607 *Racing for Homesteads*

CM607 *(1360)*

6c brown, tagged *(124,775,000)*	.25	.20
Plate block of four	.85	
FDC *(Oct. 15, 1968)*		1.00
zo. Tagging omitted	—	

1968. John Trumbull Issue, ninth stamp in the Fine Arts series honors an artist noted for his paintings of Revolutionary War scenes. The design come from an original painting at Yale University, New Haven, CT. *Intaglio (Giori Press) and offset, perforated 11.*

 CM608 *Liet. Thomas Grosvenor and Peter Salem. Detail from the Battle of Bunker's Hill.*

CM608 *(1361)*

6c multicolored, tagged *(128,295,000)*	.25	.20
Plate block of four	.90	
FDC *(Oct. 18, 1968)*		1.00
zo. Tagging omitted	—	

1968. Waterfowl Conservation Issue pointed out the need for protecting waterfowl and their habitats. *Intaglio (Giori Press) and offset, perforated 11.*

 CM609 *Wood Ducks in Flight*

CM609 *(1362)*

6c multicolored *(142,245,000)*	.25	.20
Plate block of four	1.10	
FDC *(Oct. 24, 1968)*		1.00
v. Dark blue and red omitted	1,250.	
v1. Vertical pair, imperforate between	525.	

1968. American Indian Issue was repleased in conjunction with the dedication of the National Portrait Gallery in Washington, D.C. A portrait of the stamp subject, Chief Joseph, hangs in the gallery, which is part of the Smithsonian Institution. *Intaglio and offset, perforated 11.*

 CM610 *Chief Joseph. Painting by Cyrenius Hall.*

CM610 *(1364)*

6c multicolored, tagged *(125,100,000)*	.25	.20
Plate block of four	1.10	
FDC *(Nov. 4, 1968)*		1.00
zo. Tagging omitted	—	

1969. Beautification of America Issue encouraged the participation of all Americans in a nationwide natural beauty campaign. Four se-tenant stamp designs appear in the same pane of 50 stamps. *Printed by intaglio (Giori Press), perforated 11.*

 CM611 *Azaleas, Tulips and Capitol Building*

CM611 *(1365)*

6c multicolored, tagged *(102,570,000)*	.30	.25

 CM612 *Daffodils, Washington Monument and Potomac River*

CM612 *(1366)*

6c multicolored, tagged	.30	.25

 CM613 *Highway, Poppies and Lupines*

CM613 *(1367)*

6c multicolored, tagged	.30	.25

 CM614 *Flowering Crabapples on Tree-Lined Street*

CM614 *(1368)*

6c multicolored, tagged	.30	.25
Plate block of four	2.50	
Se-tenant block of four	2.00	
FDC *(Jan. 16, 1969)*		1.00
zo. Tagging omitted, any single	—	
zoy. Tagging omitted, se-tenant block of four	—	

1969. American Legion Issue saluted the 50th anniversary of the veterans' organization incorporated by an Act of Congess and signed by Woodrow Wilson on September 16, 1919. *Intaglio (Giori Press) and offset, perforated 11.*

CM615 *Eagle with Olive Branch. From the Great Seal of the United States*

CM615 *(1369)*
  6c red, black and blue, tagged

(148,770,000)	.25	.20
Plate block of four	.85	
FDC *(March 15, 1969)*		1.00
zo. Tagging omitted	—	

1969. Grandma Moses Issue honored the grand old lady of American painting, who took up art at the age of 76 and continued until her death at 101. *Intaglio (Giori Press) and offset, perforated 11.*

CM616 *July Fourth. Detail from a Grandma Moses painting.*

CM616 *(1370)*
  6c multicolored, tagged *(139,475,000)* .25   .20

Plate block of four	.85	
FDC *(May 1, 1969)*		1.00
v. Black and Prussian blue omitted	850.	
v1. Horizontal pair, imperforate between	225.	
zo. Tagging omitted	—	

1969. Apollo 8 Issue commemorated a vital space mission prior to the moon landing. *Intaglio, (Giori Press), perforated 11.*

CM617 *Earth Rising Over Lunar Surface*

CM617 *(1371)*
  6c gray, deep blue and blue, tagged

(187,165,000)	.25	.20
Plate block of four	1.30	
FDC *(May 5, 1969)*		1.00
zo. Tagging omitted	—	

Note: imperforate varieties, from printer's waste, exist.

1969. W.C. Handy Issue honored the memory of the great AfrIcan-American composer and jazz musician who composed such immortal hits as *The St. Louis Blues, The Memphis Blues* and *The Beale Street Blues.Intaglio (Giori Press) and offset, perforated 11.*

CM618 *W.C. Handy and Horn*

CM618 *(1372)*
  6c multicolored, tagged *(125,555,000)* .25   .20

Plate block of four	1.30	
FDC *(May 17, 1969)*		1.00
zo. Tagging omitted	—	

1969. Settlement of California Issue commemorated the 200th anniversary of european settlement inthe state. On July 16, 1769, a Spanish expedition led by Capt. Gaspar de Portola entered San Diego, which became the first european settlement in California. *Intaglio (Giori Press) and offset, perforated 11.*

CM619 *Mission Bells at Carmel, Calif.*

CM619 *(1373)*
  6c multicolored, tagged *(144,425,000)* .25   .20

Plate block of four	.85	
FDC *(July 16, 1969)*		1.00
zo. Tagging omitted	—	

1969. John Wesley Powell Issue honored the eminent geologist, who in 1869 explored the Colorado River. *Intaglio (Giori Press) and offset, perforated 11.*

CM620 *Maj. Powell Leading Colorado River Expedition*

CM620 *(1374)*
  6c multicolored, tagged *(133,100,000)* .25   .20

Plate block of four	.85	
FDC *(Aug. 1, 1969)*		1.00
zo. Tagging omitted	—	

1969. Alabama Statehood Issue marked the 150th anniversary of the entry of Alabama into the Union. *Intaglio (Giori Press) and offset, perforated 11.*

CM621 *Camelia and Yellow-Shafted Flicker*

CM621 *(1375)*
6c multicolored, tagged *(136,900,000)* .25   .20
    Plate block of four   .85
    FDC *(Aug. 2, 1969)*   1.00
    zo. Tagging omitted   —

1969. 11th International Botanical Congress Issue
saluted the first international meeting of botanists held
in the United States. Four se-tenant stamp designs
appear in the same pane of 50 stamps, each design
represents a region of the country. *Intaglio (Giori Press)
and offset, perforated 11.*

CM622 *Douglas Fir*

CM623 *Lady's-Slipper*

CM624 *Ocotillo*

CM625 *Franklinia*

CM622 *(1376)*
6c multicolored, tagged *(158,695,000)* .30   .25
CM623 *(1377)*
6c multicolored, tagged   .30   .25
CM624 *(1378)*
6c multicolored, tagged   .30   .25
CM625 *(1379)*
6c multicolored, tagged   .30   .25
    Plate block of four   2.75
    y. Se-tenant block of four   2.25   2.50
    FDC *(Aug. 23, 1969)*   1.00

1969. Dartmouth College Case Issue commemorated
the 150th anniversary of the legal decision that
protected college charters and reasserted the sanctity of
contracts. Daniel Webster won the case before the U.S.
Supreme Court. *Intaglio, perforated 10 1/2 x 11.*

CM626 *Daniel Webster and Dartmouth Hall*

CM626 *(1380)*
6c green, tagged *(124,075,000)*   .25   .20
    Plate block of four   .95
    FDC *(Sept. 22, 1969)*   1.00

1969. Professional Baseball Issue marked the 100th
anniversary of the use of salaried players on a baseball
team. The Red Stockings of Cincinnati, Ohio, in 1869
became the first club to pay its team members. *Intaglio
(Giori Press) and offset, perforated 11.*

CM627 *Player at bat*

CM627 *(1381)*
6c yellow, red, black and green
    tagged *(129,925,000)*   1.25   .20
    Plate block of four   4.95
    FDC *(Sept. 24, 1969)*   1.00
    v. Black omitted   950.

1969. Intercollegiate Football Issue celebrated the
100th anniversary of the popular college sport that
started November 6, 1869, when Rutgers defeated
Princeton. *Intaglio and offset, perforated 11.*

CM628 *Coach and Football Player*

CM628 *(1382)*
6c red and green, tagged *(129,860,000)* .45   .20
    Plate block of four   2.00
    FDC *(Sept. 26, 1969)*   1.00
    zo. Tagging omitted   —
*The intaglio portion of CM628 was printed on a rotary
press normally used for currency.*

1969. Dwight D. Eisenhower Issue paid tribute to the
West Point graduate who went on to become a five-star
general and the Supreme Allied Commander in Europe
during World War II. He also served as the 34th
president. *Intaglio, (Giori Press), perforated 11.*

CM629 *Dwight D. Eisenhower and flag*

CM629 *(1383)*
6c blue, black and reddish purple,
    tagged *(138,976,000)*   .25   .20
    Plate block of four   .85
    FDC *(Oct. 14, 1969)*   1.00
    zo. Tagging omitted   —

1969. Hope for the Crippled Issue encouraged aid in
research and therapy for the handicapped. *Intaglio (Giori
Press) and offset, perforated 11.*

CM630 *Child Rising from Wheelchair*

CM630 *(1385)*
  6c multicolored, tagged *(124,565,000)* .25   .20
    Plate block of four   .85
    FDC *(Nov. 20, 1969)*   1.00
    zo. Tagging omitted   —

1969. William M. Harnett Issue honored an artist noted for his realistic work. *Intaglio (Giori Press) and offset, perforated 11.*

CM631 *Still life* Old Models

CM631 *(1386)*
  6c multicolored, tagged *(124,729,600)* .25   .20
    Plate block of four   .85
    FDC *(Dec. 3, 1969)*   1.00

1970. Natural History Issue commemorated the centenary of the American Museum of Natural History in New York City. Four se-tenant stamp designs appear in the same 32-image pane. *Intaglio (Giori Press) and offset, perforated 11.*

CM632 *American Bald Eagle. Detail from a display in The American Museum of Natural History*

CM633 *Herd of African Elephants. A display in Carl Akeley Memorial Hall*

CM634 *Northwest Coast Canoe (Haida Indians). The figures in the canoe represent a Tlingit chief and his party on their way to a marriage ceremony.*

CM635 *Jurassic Dinosaurs. From a mural at Yale University's Peabody Museum of Natural History*

CM632 *(1387)*
  6c multicolored, tagged *(201,794,600)* .25   .20
CM633 *(1388)*
  6c multicolored, tagged   .25   .20
CM634 *(1389)*
  6c multicolored, tagged   .25   .20
CM635 *(1390)*
  6c multicolored, tagged   .25   .20
    Plate block of four   1.00
    y. Se-tenant block of four
      (CM632-35)
    FDC *(May 6, 1970)*   1.00
    zo. Tagging omitted, any single —
    zoy. Tagging omitted, block of four —

1970. Maine Statehood Issue honred the 150th anniversary of itsentry into the Union. *Intaglio (Giori Press) and offset, perforated 11.*

CM636 The Lighthouse at Two Lights, *Painted by Edward Hopper's oil painting in New York's Metropolitan Museum of Art*

CM636 *(1391)*
  6c multicolored, tagged *(171,850,000)* .25   .20
    Plate block of four   1.00
    FDC *(July 9, 1970)*   1.00
    zo. Tagging omitted   —

1970. Wildlife Conservation Issue reminds Americans of the continuing need to protect wildlife. Issued in Custer, SD, near Custer State Park, home to the largest buffalo herd in the country. *Intaglio, perforated 11 x 10 1/2.*

CM637 *American Bison*

CM637 *(1392)*
  6c black on tan *(142,205,000)*   .25   .20
    Plate block of four   1.00
    FDC *(July 20, 1970)*   1.00

1970. Edgar Lee Masters Issue, first in an American Poets series, paid tribute to the author of *Spoon River Anthology.* Its ruthless exposure of small-town mores won instant acclaim as well as outraged criticism. *Intaglio (Giori Press) and offset, perforated 11.*

CM638 *Edgar Lee Masters*

CM638 *(1405)*
  6c black, tagged *(137,660,000)*   .25   .20
    Plate block of four   .85
    FDC *(Aug. 22, 1970)*   1.00
    zo. Tagging omitted   —

1970. The 50th Anniversary of Woman Suffrage Issue celebrated the ratification of the 19th Amendment which gave women the right to vote. *Intaglio, (Giori Press), perforated 11.*

CM639 *Suffrograttes of 1920 and Modern Votes*

CM639 *(1406)*
6c blue, tagged *(135,125,000)*	.25	.20
Plate block of four	.85	
FDC *(Aug. 25, 1970)*		1.00

1970. South Carolina Issue marks the 300th anniversary of the state's first permanent european settlement, established by the English at Charles Town (now Charleston). *Intaglio (Giori Press) and offset, perforated 11.*

CM640 *Aspects of South Carolina.*

CM640 *(1407)*
6c brown, black and red, tagged *(135,895,000)*	.25	.20
Plate block of four	.85	
FDC *(Sept. 12, 1970)*		1.00

1970. Stone Mountain Memorial Issue commemorated the Georgia granite carving that has become one of the great wonders of the world. The memorial carving shows the mounted figures of Robert E. Lee, Jefferson Davis and Stonewall Jackson. *Intaglio, (Giori Press), perforated 11.*

CM641 *Stone Mountain Memorial*

CM641 *(1408)*
6c gray black, tagged *(132,675,000)*	.25	.20
Plate block of four	1.10	
FDC *(Sept. 19, 1970)*		1.00

1970. 150th Anniversary of Fort Snelling Issue commemorates the importance of this outpost in settling the Northwestern United States. The fort was named after Col. Joshiah Snelling. *Intaglio (Giori Press) and offset, perforated 11.*

CM642 *Fort Snelling and surrounding area*

CM642 *(1409)*
6c multicolored, tagged *(134,795,000)*	.25	.20
Plate block of four	.85	
FDC *(Oct. 17, 1970)*		1.00
zo. Tagging omitted	—	

1970. Anti-Pollution Issue emphasizes the importance of our ecology. Four se-tenant designs appear in the pane. *Printed in gravure by the Bureau of Engraving and Printing at Guilford Graphics, Inc., perforated 11 x 10 1/2.*

CM643 *Save Our Soil*   CM644 *Save Our Cities*

CM645 *Save Our Water*   CM646 *Save Our Air*

CM643 *(1410)*
6c multicolored, tagged *(161,600,000)*	.25	.20

CM644 *(1411)*
6c multicolored, tagged	.25	.20

CM645 *(1412)*
6c multicolored, tagged	.25	.20

CM646 *(1413)*
6c multicolored, tagged	.25	.20
Plate block of four	3.50	
Se-tenant block of four	—	
FDC *(Oct. 28, 1970)*		1.00

1970. United Nations Issue marks the 25th anniversary of the international organization, chartered in San Francisco on June 26, 1945. *Intaglio (Giori Press) and offset, perforated 11.*

CM647 *"Peace, Justice, and Progress"*

CM647 *(1419)*
6c black, red and blue, tagged *(127,610,000)*	.25	.20
Plate block of four	.85	
Gutter pair	—	
FDC *(Nov. 20, 1970)*		1.00
zo. Tagging omitted	—	

1970. Landing of the Pilgrims Issue commemorates the 350th anniversary of the arrival of the *Mayflower* and the landing of the Pilgrims at Plymouth, MA. *Intaglio (Giori Press) and offset, perforated 11.*

CM648 Mayflower *and Pilgrims*

CM648 *(1420)*
  6c multicolored, tagged *(129,785,000)* .25   .20
    Plate block of four   .85
    FDC *(Nov. 21, 1970)*   1.00
    v.Orange and yellow
      omitted   950.

1970. U.S. Servicemen Issue pays tribute to the Disabled American Veterans, Prisoners of War and those missing and killed in action. Two se-tenant stamp designs alternate in the pane. *Intaglio (Giori Press) and offset, perforated 11.*

CM649 *Crest of Disabled American Veterans*

CM650 *Honorng U.S. Servicemen*

CM649 *(1421)*
  6c multicolored, tagged *(134,380,000)* .25   .20
CM650 *(1422)*
  6c dark blue, black and red, tagged   .25   .20
    Plate block of four   1.30
    y. Se-tenant pair   .50
    FDC *(Nov. 24, 1970)*   1.00
    zo. Tagging omitted, single   —
    zoy. Tagging omitted, se-tenant pair —

1971. American Wool Issue commemorates the 450th anniversary of the introduction of sheep in America. *Intaglio (Giori Press) and offset, perforated 11.*

CM651 *Ewe and Lamb*

CM651 *(1423)*
  6c multicolored, tagged *(135,305,000)* .25   .20
    Plate block of four   .85
    FDC *(Jan. 19, 1971)*   1.00
    zo. Tagging omitted   —

1971. Douglas MacArthur Issue honors the soldier who rose to the rank of five-star general and was supreme commander in Tokyo for the Allied Powers. *Intaglio, (Giori Press), perforated 11.*

CM652 *Douglas MacArthur*

CM652 *(1424)*
  6c red, blue and black, tagged
      (134,840,000)   .25   .20
    Plate block of four   .85
    FDC *(Jan. 26, 1971)*   1.00
    zo. Tagging omitted   —

1971. Blood Donors Issue points out the need for more Americans to increase their participation. *Intaglio (Giori Press) and offset, perforated 11.*

CM653 *Giving Blood Saves Lives*

CM653 *(1425)*
  6c red and blue, tagged *(130,975,000)* .25   .20
    Plate block of four   .85
    FDC *(March 12, 1971)*   1.00
    zo. Tagging omitted   —

1971. Missouri Statehood Issue honors the 150th anniversary of entry into the Union of the "Show Me" state. *Gravure (Andreotti Press), perforated 11 x 10 1/2.*

CM654 Independence and the Opening of the West. *Detail of a mural by Thomas Hart Benton.*

CM654 *(1426)*
  8c multicolored, tagged *(161,235,000)* .25   .20
    Plate block of 12   3.25
    FDC *(May 8, 1971)*   1.00
    zo. Tagging omitted   —

1971. Wildlife Conservation Issue stressed the importance of preserving nature's creations from extinction. Four different representatives of wildlife are featured in the sheet of 32 stamps. *Intaglio (Giori Press) and offset, perforated 11.*

CM655 *Polar bear*   CM656 *Condor*

CM657 *Alligator*   CM658 *Trout*

CM655 *(1429)*
  8c multicolored, tagged *(175,680,000)* .25   .20
CM656 *(1430)*
  8c multicolored, tagged   .25   .20

CM657 *(1427)*
8c multicolored, tagged   .25   .20
CM658 *(1428)*
8c multicolored, tagged   .25   .20
    Plate block of four   1.20
    Se-tenant block of four   .75
    FDC *(June 12, 1971)*   1.00
    v. Red omitted, block of four   9,500.
    v. Light green and dark green
       omitted, block of four   4,500.
    xo. Tagging omitted, any single   —
    xoy. Tagging omitted, se-tenant
       block of four   —

1971. Antarctic Treaty Issue marked the 10th anniversary of the treaty that pledged 12 nations to scientific cooperation and peaceful use of Antartica: Argentina, Australia, Belgium, Chile, France, Japan, New Zealand, Norway, South Africa, Soviet Union, United Kingdom and United States. *Intaglio, (Giori Press), perforated 11.*

CM659 *Antarctic Treaty Emblem*

CM659 *(1431)*
8c red and dark blue, tagged
       (138,700,000)   .25   .20
    Plate block of four   1.00
    FDC *(June 23, 1971)*   1.00
    zo. Tagging omitted   —

1971. American Revolution Bicentennial Issue commemorates the struggle that led to the birth of the United States, and is the first in a series of stamps to pay tribute to the men, women, places and events of the Revolutionary War. *Intaglio (Giori Press) and offset, perforated 11.*

CM660 *American Revolution Bicentennial Symbol*

CM660 *(1432)*
8c gray, red, blue and black, tagged
       (138,165,000)   .25   .20
    Plate block of four   1.10
    FDC *(July 4, 1971)*   1.00
    v. Gray (top ledgend) omitted   1,250.
    v1. Black and gray omitted   700.

1971. Space Achievements Decade Issue marks 10 years of extraordinary accomplishments in space. *Intaglio (Giori Press) and offset, perforated 11.*

CM661 *Landing Craft on Moon's surface*

CM662 *Astronauts in Lunar Rover*

CM661 *(1434)*
8c multicolored, tagged *(176,295,000)* .25   .20
    v. Blue and red omitted   600.
CM662 *(1435)*
8c multicolored, tagged   .25   .20
    y. Se-tenant pair, CM661-62   .50
    Plate block of four   1.15
    FDC *(Aug. 2, 1971)*   1.00
    v. Blue and red omitted   600.
    y. Se-tenant pair, blue and
       red omitted   1,500.
    zo. Tagging omitted, any single   —
    zoy. Se-tenant pair, tagging omited —

1971. John Sloan Issue honors the artist on the centennial of his birth at Lock Haven, PA. *Intaglio (Giori Press) and offset, perforated 11.*

CM663 The Wake of the Ferry, *Phillips Gallery, Washington, D.C.*

CM663 *(1433)*
8c multicolored, tagged *(152,125,000)* .25   .20
    Plate block of four   1.00
    FDC *(Aug. 2, 1971)*   1.00
    zo. Tagging omitted   —

1971. American Poets Issue honors Emily Dickinson (1830-86), who was born in Amherst, MA. Only after she died was her poetry widely published and acclaimed. *Intaglio (Giori Press) and offset, perforated 11.*

CM664 *Emily Dickinson*

CM664 *(1436)*
8c multicolored, tagged *(142,845,000)* .25   .20
    Plate block of four   1.00
    FDC *(Aug. 28, 1971)*   1.00
    v. Black and olive omitted   850.
    v1. Pale rose omitted   7,500.
    zo. Tagging omitted   —

1971. San Juan Issue marked the 450th anniversary of the founding of the Puerto Rican city. *Intaglio (Giori Press) and offset, perforated 11.*

CM665 *Battlement at El Morro Castle*

CM665 *(1437)*
  8c multicolored, tagged *(148,755,000)* .25   .20
    Plate block of four   1.00
    FDC *(Sept. 12, 1971*   1.00
    zo. Tagging omitted   —

1971. Prevention of Drug Abuse Issue publicizes drug addiction as a national menace of concern to every American. *Gravure (Andreotti Press), perforated 10 1/2 x 11.*

CM666 *Drug Addict*

CM666 *(1438)*
  8c blue, deep blue and black, tagged
       (139,080,000)   .25   .20
    Plate block of six   1.50
    FDC *(Oct. 5, 1971)*   1.00
    zo. Tagging omitted   —

1971. CARE Issue honors the 25th anniversary of the American-Canadian Cooperative for American Relief Everywhere. *Intaglio, (Giori Press), perforated 11.*

CM667 *Hands and CARE Emblem*

CM667 *(1439)*
  8c black, blue, violet and red lilac,
      tagged *(130,755,000)*   .25   .20
    Plate block of eight   1.95
    FDC *(Oct. 27, 1971)*   1.00
    a. Black omitted   4,750.
    zo. Tagging omitted   —

1971. Historic Preservation Issue pays tribute to important artifacts of America's past. *Intaglio (Giori Press) and offset, perforated 11.*

CM668 *Decatur House, Washington, D.C.*

CM668 *(1440)*
  8c brown and dark beige on buff, tagged
      (170,208,000)   .25   .20

CM669 *Whaling Ship* Charles W. Morgan, Mystic, *Conn.*

CM669 *(1441)*
  8c brown and dark beige on buff,
      tagged   .25   .20

CM670 *Cable Car, San Francisco, Calif.*

CM670 *(1442)*
  8c brown and dark beige on buff,
      tagged   .25   .20

CM671 *San Xavier del Bac Mission, Tucson, Ariz.*

CM671 *(1443)*
  8c brown and dark beige on buff,
      tagged   .25   .20
    Plate block of four   1.20
    y. Se-tenant block of four
      (CM668-71)   .75
    FDC *(Oct. 29, 1971)*   1.00
    v. Brown omitted (any single) —
    v1. Dark beige omitted (any single) —
    vy. Brown omitted, se-tenant
      block of four   2,600.
    v1y. Dark beige omitted, se-tenant
      block of four   —
    zo. Tagging omitted, any single —
    voy. Tagging omitted, se-tenant
      block of four   —

1972. American Poets Issue honors Sidney Lanier, who had a distinguished career as a lawyer, teacher, musician and poet. Born in Macon, GA, he died at the age of 39. *Intaglio, (Giori Press), perforated 11.*

CM672 *Sidney Lanier*

CM672 *(1446)*
8c black, reddish brown and blue

tagged *(137,355,000)*	.25	.20
Plate block of four	1.00	
FDC *(Feb. 3, 1972)*		1.00
zo. Tagging omitted	—	

1972. Peace Corps Issue pays tribute to a government organization created to aid developing countries. *Gravre (Andreotti Press), perforated 10 1/2 x 11.*

CM673 *Flag and Doves. From poster by David Battle*

CM673 *(1447)*
8c dark blue, light blue and red, tagged

(150,400,000)	.25	.20
Plate block of six	1.60	
FDC *(Feb. 11, 1972)*		1.00
zo. Tagging omitted	—	

1972. National Parks Centennial Series, released over a five-month period consists of eight stamps (one is an airmail stamp, A82), marking the centennial of the establishment of the first national park in the world, Yellowstone National Park. *Intaglio (Giori Press) and offset, perforated 11.*

CM674 *Old Faithful, Yellowstone Park*

CM674 *(1453)*
8c multicolored, tagged *(164,096,000)* .25 .20

Plate block of four	1.00	
FDC *(March 1, 1972)*		1.00
zo. Tagging omitted	—	

CM675		CM676
CM677		CM678

CM675-78 *Cape Hatteras National Seashore*

CM675 *(1448)*
2c multicolored, tagged *(172,730,000)* .25 .20
CM676 *(1449)*
2c multicolored, tagged .25 .20

CM677 *(1450)*
2c multicolored, tagged .25 .20
CM678 *(1451)*
2c multicolored, tagged .25 .20

Plate block of four	.60	
y. Se-tenant block of four (CM675-78)		
FDC *(April 5, 1972)*		1.00
v. Black omitted (any single)	—	
vy. Black omitted, se-tenant block of four	2,750.	
zo. Tagging omitted, any single	—	
zoy. Tagging omitted, se-tenant block of four	—	

CM679 *Theater at Wolf Trap Farm, Va.*

CM679 *(1452)*
6c multicolored, tagged *(104,090,000)* .25 .20

Plate block of four	.85	
FDC *(June 26, 1972)*		1.00
zo. Tagging omitted	—	

CM680 *Mount McKinley, Alaska*

CM680 *(1454)*
15c multicolored, tagged *(53,920,000)* .25 .20

Plate block of four	1.90	
FDC *(July 28, 1972)*		1.00
zo. Tagging omitted	—	

1972. Family Planning Issue reminds people of the need for planning to have a better America and a better world. *Intaglio, (Giori Press), perforated 11.*

CM681 *Planned Family*

CM681 *(1455)*
8c multicolored, tagged *(153,025,000)* .25 .20

Plate block of four	1.10	
FDC *(March 18, 1972)*		1.00
v. Dark brown omitted	9,350.	
v1. Dark brown and olive omitted	—	
v2. Yellow omitted	—	
zo. Tagging omitted	—	

1972. Colonial American Craftsmen Issue, part of the American Revolution Bicentennial Series commemorates the contributions of Colonial artisans to the early development of America. *Intaglio, perforated 11 x 10 1/2.*

CM682 *Glass maker*   CM683 *Silversmith*

CM684
Wigmaker   CM685 *Hatter*

CM682 *(1456)*
  8c deep brown on buff paper, tagged
          (201,890,000)   .25   .20
CM683 *(1457)*
  8c deep brown on buff paper, tagged .25   .20
CM684 *(1458)*
  8c deep brown on buff paper, tagged .25   .20
CM685 *(1459)*
  8c deep brown on buff paper, tagged .25   .20
      Plate block of four   1.25
      y. Se-tenant block of four,
          (CM682-85)   .75
      FDC *(July 4, 1972)*   1.00
      zo. Tagging omitted, any single   —
      zoy. Tagging omitted, se-tenant
          block of four   —

1972. Olympic Games Issue saluted international athletic meets in Sapporo, Japan (Winter Games) and Munich, Germany (Summer Games) (See also A837). *Gravure (Andreotti Press), perforated 11 x 10 1/2. (See A83).*

CM686 *Cycling*

CM686 *(1460)*
  6c multicolored, tagged *(67,335,000)* .25   .20
      Plate block of ten   2.10
      Plate flaw, broken red ring
          (position 43 of top-left
          pane of plate No. 33313)   —
      FDC *(Aug. 17, 1972)*   1.00

CM687 *Bobsled Racing*

CM687 *(1461)*
  8c multicolored, tagged *(96,240,000)* .25   .20
      Plate block of ten   2.75
      FDC *(Aug. 17, 1972)*   1.00
      zo. Tagging omitted   —

CM688 *Foot Racing*

CM688 *(1462)*
  15c multicolored, tagged *(46,340,000)* .25   .20
      Plate block of ten   5.25
      FDC *(Aug. 17, 1972)*   1.00

1972. Parent-Teachers Association Issue salutes the 75th anniversary of an organization dedicated to improving educational methods furthering development of young minds. *Gravure (Andreotti Press), perforated 11 x 10 1/2.*

CM689 *Blackboard, symbol of education*

CM689 *(1463)*
  8c yellow and black, tagged
          (180,155,000)   .25   .20
      Plate block of four   1.00
      Plate block, yellow inverted   —
      FDC *(Sept. 15, 1972)*   1.00
      zo. Tagging omitted   —

1972. Wildlife Conservation Issue showcases the importance and beauty of nature's creatures. *Intaglio (Giori Press) and offset, perforated 11.*

CM690 *Fur Seal*   CM691 *Cardinal*

CM692 *Brown pelican*   CM693 *Bighorn sheep*

CM690 *(1464)*
  8c multicolored, tagged *(198,364,800)* .25   .20
CM691 *(1465)*
  8c multicolored, tagged   .25   .20
CM692 *(1466)*
  8c multicolored, tagged   .25   .20
CM693 *(1467)*
  8c multicolored, tagged   .25   .20
      Plate block of four   1.10
      y. Se-tenant block of four,
          CM690-93
      FDC *(Sept. 20, 1972)*   1.00
      v. Brown omitted   —

vy. Se-tenant block of four,
  brown omitted 4,500.
v1. Green and blue omitted —
v1y. Se-tenant block of four,
  Green and blue omitted 4,500.
v2. Red and brown omitted —
v2y. Se-tenant block of four,
  Red and brown omitted 4,500.

1972. Mail Order Centennial Issue marked the 100th anniversary of the introduction of merchandising by mail. *Gravure (Andreotti Press), perforated 11 x 10 1/2.*

CM694 *Rural Post Office Store*

CM694 *(1468)*
  8c multicolored, tagging *(185,490,000)* .25   .20
  Plate block of 12 3.00
  FDC *(Sept. 27, 1972)* 1.00
Tagging on this issue typically consists of a vertical bar, 10 mm wide.

1972. Osteopathic Medicine Issue marks the 75th anniversary of the American Osteopathic Associaiton established by Dr. Andrew Still. *Gravure (Andrcotti Press), perforated 10 1/2 x ll.*

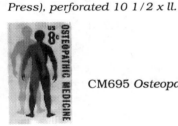

CM695 *Osteopathic Medicine*

CM695 *(1469)*
  8c multicolored, tagged *(162,335,000)* .25   .20
  Plate block of six 1.60
  FDC *(Oct 9, 1972)* 1.00

1972. Tom Sawyer Issue, the fourth stamp in the American Folklore Series, recalls the exciting, carefree adventures of the fictional mischievous boy created by Mark Twain (see CM205). *Intaglio (Giori Press) and offset, perforated 11.*

CM696 *Tom Sawyer. Painted by Norman Rockwell.*

CM696 *(1470)*
  8c multicolored, tagged *(162,789,950)* .25   .20
  Plate block of four 1.10
  FDC *(Oct. 13, 1972)* 1.00
  v. Black and red omitted 2,250.
  v1. Yellow and tan omitted 2,100.

v2. Horizontal pair, imperforate
  between —
zo. Tagging omitted —

1972. Pharmacy Issue saluted the nation's druggists and their contribution to keeping Americans healthy. *Intaglio (Giori Press) and offset, perforated 11.*

CM697 *Bowl of Hygeia, Mortar and Pestle*

CM697 *(1473)*
  8c multicolored, tagged *(165,895,000)* .25   .20
  Plate block of four 1.75
  FDC *(Nov. 10, 1972)* 1.00
  v. Blue omitted 2,000.
  v1. Blue and orange omitted 875.
  v2. Orange omitted 2,000.
  zo. Tagging omitted —

1972. Stamp Collecting Issue paid tribute to the nation's stamp collectors and the hobby of philately. *Intaglio (Giori Press) and offset, perforated 11.*

CM698 *First U.S. Stamp Under magnifying Glass*

CM698 *(1474)*
  8c multicolored, tagged *(166,508,000)* .25   .20
  Plate block of four 1.00
  FDC *(Nov. 17, 1972)* 1.00
  v. Black omitted 900.
  zo. Tagging omitted —

1973. Love Stamp was issued for use on birthdays, anniversaries and other occasions when special sentiments are being sent. *Gravure (Andreotti Press), (Andreotti Press), perforated 11 x 10 1/2.*

CM699 Love Sculpture *by Robert Indiana*

CM699 *(1475)*
  8c red, green, violet and blue, tagged
    (330,055,000) .25   .20
  Plate block of six 1.50
  FDC *(Jan. 26, 1973)* 1.00

1973. Rise of the Spirit of Independence Issue remarks on the role of communications in spurring the American revolution. *Intaglio (Giori Press) and offset, perforated 11.*

CM700 *Pamphlets Printed by Press*

CM700 *(1476)*
8c blue, greenish black and red,
       tagged *(166,005,000)*   .25   .20
       Plate block of four   1.00
       FDC *(Feb. 16, 1973)*   1.00
       zo. Tagging omitted   —

CM701 *Posting a Broadside*

CM701 *(1477)*
8c black, orange and ultramarine,
       tagged *(163,050,000)*   .25   .20
       Plate block of four   1.00
       FDC *(April 13, 1973)*   1.00
       Gutter pair   —
       zo. Tagging omitted   —

CM702 *Coloial Post Rider*

CM702 *(1478)*
8c blue, black, red and green, tagged
       (159,005,000)   .25   .20
       Plate block of four   1.00
       FDC *(June 22, 1973)*   1.00
       zo. Tagging omitted   —

CM703 *Drummer Summoning Minutemen*

CM703 *(1479)*
8c blue, black, yellow and red, tagged
       (147,295,000)   .25   .20
       Plate block of four   1.00
       FDC *(Sept. 28, 1973)*   1.00
       zo. Tagging omitted   —

1973. George Gershwin Issue honors the American composer who created music for over 400 songs, including *Rhapsody in Blue* and *Porgy and Bess* (CM1586), a folk opera. *Gravure (Andreotti Press), perforated 11.*

CM704 *George Gershwin and Porgy and Bess Montage*

CM704 *(1484)*
8c multicolored *(139,152,000)*   .25   .20
       Plate block of 12   3.25
       FDC *(Feb. 27, 1973)*   1.00
       v. Vertical pair, imperforate
         horizontally   —

1973. Nicolaus Copernicus Issue pays tribute to the father of modern astronomy on the 500th anniversary of his birth. *Intaglio (Giori Press) and offset, perforated 11.*

CM705 *Nicolaus Copernicus*

CM705 *(1488)*
8c black and yellow, tagged
       (159,475,000)   .25   .20
       Plate block of four   1.10
       FDC *(April 23, 1973)*   1.00
       v. Engraved black omitted   1,300.
       v1. Yellow omitted   1,000.
       zo. Tagging omitted   —
The yellow may be removed chemically. Competent expertization is recommended of CM705v1.

1973. Postal People Issue saluted the 700,000 employees of the U.S. Postal Service. Ten different stamps in a pane of 50 depict some of the services performed by postal employees, with text describing those activities printed on the reverse side of the stamp, under the gum, a U.S. stamp first. *Gravure (Andreotti Press), perforated 10 1/2 x 11.*

CM706 *(1489)*
8c multicolored, tagged *(486,020,000)* .25   .20
CM707 *(1490)*
8c multicolored, tagged   .25   .20
CM708 *(1491)*
8c multicolored, tagged   .25   .20
CM709 *(1492)*
8c multicolored, tagged   .25   .20

CM706   CM707   CM708   CM709   CM710   CM711   CM712   CM713   CM714   CM715
CM706-CM715 *Postal people performing services*

CM710 *(1493)*
8c multicolored, tagged   .25   .20
CM711 *(1494)*
8c multicolored, tagged   .25   .20
CM712 *(1495)*
8c multicolored, tagged   .25   .20
CM713 *(1496)*
8c multicolored, tagged   .25   .20
CM714 *(1497)*
8c multicolored, tagged   .25   .20
CM715 *(1498)*
8c multicolored, tagged   .25   .20
   Plate block of 20   5.50
   y. Se-tenant strip of 10,
      CM706-15   4.00
   FDC *(April 30, 1973)*   3.00
   zo. Tagging omitted, any single   —
   zoy. Tagging omitted,
      se-tenant strip of 10   —
Tagging consists of a 1/2 inch high horizontal band.

1973. Harry S Truman Issue honors the 33rd president of the United States, who died December 26, 1972. *Intaglio, (Giori Press), perforated 11.*

CM716 *Harry S Truman, From a photograph by Leo Stern*

CM716 *(1499)*
8c red, black and blue, tagged
      (157,052,800)   .25   .25
   Plate block of four   1.10
   FDC *(May 8, 1973)*   1.00
   zo. Tagging omitted   —

1973. Boston Tea Party Issue uses four differebt se-tenant designs to form a single scene depicting this historical event that preceded the war of independence. *Intaglio (Giori Press) and offset, perforated 11.*

   CM717   CM718

CM717-20
*Boston Tea
Party*

   CM719   CM720

CM717 *(1480)*
8c multicolored, tagged *(196,275,000)* .25   .20
CM718 *(1481)*
8c multicolored, tagged   .25   .20
CM719 *(1482)*
8c multicolored, tagged   .25   .20
CM720 *(1483)*
8c multicolored, tagged   .25   .20
   Plate block of four   1.15
   y. Se-tenant block of four,
      CM717-20   .75
   FDC *(July 4, 1973)*   2.00
   vy. Se-tenant block of four,
      intaglio black omitted   1,500.
   vy1. Se-tenant block of four,
      intaglio black omitted   500.
   zo. Tagging omitted, any single   —
   zoy. Se-tenant block of four,
      tagging omitted   —

1973. Progress in Electronics Issue commemorates advances and developments in electronic communications. (See also A84). *Intaglio (Giori Press) and offset, perforated 11.*

CM721 *Marconi Spark Coil and Gap*

CM721 *(1500)*
6c multicolored, tagged *(53,005,000)*   .25   .20
   Plate block of four   .85
   FDC *(July 10, 1973)*   1.00
   zo. Tagging omitted   —

CM722 *Transisitors and Electronic Circuit*

CM722 *(1501)*
8c multicolored, tagged *(159,775,000)* .25   .20
   Plate block of four   1.00
   FDC *(July 10, 1973)*   1.00
   a. Black (inscription) omitted   650.
   b. Lilac and tan (background)
      omitted   1,300.
   zo. Tagging omitted   —

CM723 *Radio and Television Components*

CM723 *(1502)*
15c multicolored, tagged *(39,005,000)* .25   .20
   Plate block of four   1.85
   FDC *(July 10, 1973)*   1.00
   v. Black omitted   1,500.

1973. Robinson Jeffers Issue pays tribute to the poet whose works were mainly allegories influenced by his love of the classical Greek and Roman tragedies. *Gravure (Andreotti Press), perforated 11.*

CM724 *Robinson Jeffers and Children with Burrow*

CM724 *(1485)*
8c multicolored, tagged *(128,048,000)* .25   .20
   Plate block of 12   3.00
   FDC *(Aug. 13, 1973)*   1.00
   v. Vertical pair, imperforate
     horizontally   —

1973. Lyndon B. Johnson Issue honored the 36th president of the United States, who died January 22, 1973. *Gravure (Andrecotti Press), perforated 11.*

CM725 *Lyndon B. Johnson*

CM725 *(1503)*
8c multicolored *(152,624,000)*   .25   .20
   Plate block of 12   3.50
   FDC *(Aug. 27, 1973)*   1.00
   v. Horizontal pair, imperforate
     vertically   —

1973. Henry O. Tanner Issue salutes the artist who studied art under Thomas Eakins. Many of his works were based on Biblical themes. *Gravure (Andreotti Press), perforated 11.*

CM726 *Henry O. Tanner, Palette and Rainbow*

CM726 *(1486)*
8c multicolored, tagged *(146,008,000)* .25   .20
   Plate block of 12   3.00
   FDC *(Sept. 10, 1973)*   1.00

1973. Willa Cather Issue salutes a novelist who won a 1922 Pulitzer Prize. *Gravure (Andreotti Press), perforated 11.*

CM727 *Willa Cather, Pioneers and Covered Wagon*

CM727 *(1487)*
8c multicolored, tagged *(139,608,000)* .25   .20
   Plate block of 12   3.00
   FDC *(Sept. 20, 1973)*   1.00
   v. Vertical pair, imperforate
     horizontally   —

1973. Rural America Issue, first of a series of three stamps, saluted the 100th anniversary of the introduction of Aberdeen Angus cattle into the United States (See also CM751-52F). *Intaglio (Giori Press) and offset, perforated 11.*

CM728 *Angus Cattle and Longhorn Cattle on Prairie*

CM728 *(1504)*
8c multicolored, tagged *(145,430,000)* .25   .20
   Plate block of four   1.00
   FDC *(Oct. 5, 1973)*   1.00
   v. Green and red brown omitted 975.
   v1. Vertical pair, imperforate
     between   —
   zo. Tagging omitted   —

1974. Veterans of Foreign Wars Issue saluted the men and women in America's military service since the Revolutionary War. *Intaglio, (Giori Press), perforated 11.*

CM729 *VFW Emblem*

CM729 *(1525)*
10c red and blue, tagged *(145,430,000)* .25   .20
   Plate block of four   1.30
   FDC *(March 11, 1974)*   1.00
   zo. Tagging omitted   —

1974. Robert Frost Issue honors the New England poet (1873-1963) and four-time winner of the Pulitzer Prize. *Intaglio, perforated 10 1/2 x 11.*

CM730 *Robert Frost*

CM730 *(1526)*
10c black, tagged *(145,235,000)*   .25   .20
   Plate block of four   1.30
   FDC *(March 26, 1974)*   1.00

1974. Expo '74 World's Fair Issue featured the theme "Preserve the Environment," ,e,prab;y rendered by Peter Max in his images Cosmic Jumper and Smiling Sage. *Gravure (Andreotti Press), perforated 11.*

CM731 *Expo '74*

CM731 *(1527)*
10c multicolored, tagged *(135,052,000)* .25 .20
   Plate block of 12 4.25
   FDC *(April 18, 1974)* 1.00

1974. Horse Racing Issue commemorats the 100th running of the Kentucky Derby. *Gravure (Andreotti Press), perforated 11 x 10 1/2.*

CM732 *Horses at the Turn*

CM732 *(1528)*
10c multicolored, tagged *(156,750,000)* .25 .20
   Plate block of 12 3.75
   FDC *(May 4, 1974)* 1.00
   v. Blue "Horse Racing"
      omitted 900.
   b. Red "U.S. Postage 10 cents"
      omitted —
   zo. Tagging omitted —

Beware of stamps with minute traces of red being offered as CM732b. They are printing freeks, and do not have comparable value to a full color-omitted error.

1974. Skylab Project Issue paid tribute to the Skylab I program, devoted to experimentation in space.

CM733 *Skylab*

CM733 *(1529)*
10c multicolored, tagged *(164,670,000)* .25 .20
   Plate block of four 1.30
   FDC *(May 14, 1974)* 1.00
   v. Vertical pair, imperforate
      between —
   zo. Tagging omitted —

1974. Universal Postal Union Issue marked the centenary of the international organization that helped standardize mail rates and expedite mail delivery worldwide. *Gravure (Andreotti Press), perforated 11.*

CM734 *(1530)*
10c multicolored, tagged *(190,1546,800)* .25 .20
CM735 *(1531)*
10c multicolored, tagged .25 .20
CM736 *(1532)*
10c multicolored, tagged .25 .20
CM737 *(1533)*
10c multicolored, tagged .25 .20
CM738 *(1534)*
10c multicolored, tagged .25 .20
CM739 *(1535)*
10c multicolored, tagged .25 .20

CM734   CM735   CM736   CM737

CM738   CM739   CM740   CM741

CM734: Lady Writing a Letter *by Terboch; CM735:* Still Life *by Chardin; CM736:* Mrs. John Douglas *by Gainsborough; CM737:* Don Antonio Noriega *by Goya; CM738:* Portrait of Michelangelo *by Raphael; CM739;* Five Feminine Virtues *by Hokusai; CM740:* Old Scraps (Old Letter Rack) *by Peto; CM741:* The Lovely Reader *by Liotard*

CM740 *(1536)*
10c multicolored, tagged .25 .20
CM741 *(1537)*
10c multicolored, tagged .25 .20
   Plate block of ten 3.50
   Se-tenant block or strip
      of eight, CM734-41 2.00
   FDC *(June 6, 1974)* 1.00
   v. Se-tenant block or strip of eight
      imperforate vertically —

1974. Mineral Heritage Issue focused attention to the outstanding contributions minerals have made to making the United States a leader among nations. *Intaglio (Giori Press) and offset, perforated 11.*

CM743 Petrified wood

CM742 *Amethyst*

CM745 *Tourmaline*

CM744 *Rhodochrosite*

CM742 *(1540)*
10c multicolored, tagged *(167,212,800)* .25 .20
    v. Light blue and yellow omitted —
CM743 *(1538)*
10c multicolored, tagged .25 .20
    v. Light blue and yellow omitted —
CM744 *(1541)*
10c multicolored, tagged .25 .20
    v. Light blue omitted —
    v1. Black and red omitted —
CM745 *(1539)*
10c multicolored, tagged .25 .20
    v. Light blue and omitted —
    v1.Black and purple omitted —
    Plate block of four 1.00
    Se-tenant block or strip
      of four —
    FDC *(June 13, 1974)*
    vy. Se-tenant block or stripof four,
      light blue and yellow omitted 2,000.
    zo. Tagging omitted, any single —
    zoy. Se-tenant block or strip of four,
      tagging omitted —

1974. Settlement of Kentucky Issue saluted the 200th anniversary of the founding of Fort Harrod, the first British settlement west of the Allegheny Mountains. *Intaglio (Giori Press) and offset, perforated 11.*

CM746 *Settlers at Fort Harrod*

CM746 *(1542)*
10c multicolored, tagged
      (156,265,000) .25 .20
    Plate block of four 1.30
    FDC *(June 15, 1974)* 1.00
    v. Offset dull black omitted 800.
    v1. Green and black (intaglio
      and offset) and blue omitted 4,250.
    v2. Green intaglio and offset
      black omitted —
    v3. Intaglio green omitted —
    zo. Tagging omitted —

1974. The First Continental Congress Issue commemorated the 200th anniversary of the assemblage that paved the way for the creation of the United States. *Intaglio, (Giori Press), perforated 11.*

CM747 *(1543)*
10c dark blue and red, tagged
      (195,585,000) .25 .20
CM748 *(1544)*
10c red and dark blue, tagged .25 .20

CM747      CM749

CM750   CM748

CM747 *Carpenters' Hall*, CM748 *Independence Hall*, CM749 *Quote from First Continental Congress*, CM750 *Quote from Declaration of Independence*

CM749 *(1545)*
10c gray, dark blue and red, tagged .25 .20
CM750 *(1546)*
10c gray, dark blue and red, tagged .25 .20
    Plate block of four 1.40
    y. Se-tenant block of four,
      CM747-50 .75
    FDC *(July 4, 1974)* 1.00
    zo. Tagging omitted, any single —
    zoy. Se-tenant block of four,
      tagging omitted —

1974. Rural America Issue, the second and third stamps completing this series, commemorated the 100th anniversary of the founding of the Chautauqua Institution, which developed into a teachers' training center for Sunday school and, later, public school, and also marked the 100th anniversary of hard winter wheat. *Intaglio (Giori Press) and offset, perforated 11.*

CM751 *Chautauqua Tent*

CM751 *(1505)*
10c multicolored, tagged *(151,335,000)* .25 .20
    Plate block of four 1.30
    FDC *(Aug. 6, 1974)* 1.00

CM752 *Winter Wheat and Train*

CM752 *(1506)*
10c multicolored, tagged *(141,085,000)* .25 .20
    Plate block of four 1.30
    FDC *(Aug. 16, 1974)* 1.00
    v. Black and intaglio blue
      omitted 875.
    zo. Tagging omitted —

1974. Energy Conservation Issue focused attention upon the national fuel shortage and the need to save energy. *Intaglio (Giori Press) and offset, perforated 11.*

CM753 *Energy Conservation*

CM753 *(1547)*
10c multicolored, tagged *(148,850,000)* .25 .20
  Plate block of four 1.30
  FDC *(Sept. 23, 1974)* 1.00
  v. Blue and orange omitted 950.
  v1. Green omitted 875.
  c2. Orange and green omitted 800.
  zo. Tagging omitted —

1974. Legend of Sleepy Hollow Issue is the fifth in the American Folklore series and commemorates Washington Irving's *Legend of Sleepy Hollow.Intaglio (Giori Press) and offset, perforated 11.*

CM754 *Headless Horseman pursuing Ichabod Crane*

CM754 *(1548)*
10c dark blue, black, orange and yellow,
  tagged *(157,270,000)* .25 .20
  Plate block of four 1.30
  FDC *(Oct. 10, 1974)* 1.00

1974. Help for Retarded Children Issue encourages efforts to help mentally retarded persons. *Intaglio, (Giori Press), perforated 11.*

CM755 *Retarded Girl and Helping Hand*

CM755 *(1549)*
10c light and dark brown, tagged
  (150,245,000) .25 .20
  Plate block of four 1.30
  FDC *(Oct. 12, 1974)* 1.00
  zo. Tagging omitted —

1975. American Arts Issue, the final stamp in a series begun in 1961 (CM496) commemorated Benjamin West, first American-born painter to gain an international reputation working abroad. *Gravure (Andreotti Press), perforated 10 1/2 x 11.*

CM756 *Self Portrait , Benjamin West*

CM756 *(1553)*
10c multicolored, tagged *(156,995,000)* .25 .20
  Plate block of ten 3.25
  FDC *(Feb. 10, 1975)* 1.00

1975. Pioneer Space Issue salutes the unmanned Pioneer space mission, which probed the planet Jupiter in 1973-74. *Printed by intaglio (Giori Press) and offset, perforated 11.*

CM757 *Pioneer 10 and Jupiter*

CM757 *(1556)*
10c dark blue, yellow and red, tagged
  (173,685,000) .25 .20
  Plate block of four 1.30
  FDC *(Feb. 28, 1975)* 1.00
  v. Intaglio blue omitted 950.
  v1. Red and yellow omitted 1,350.
  zo. Tagging omitted —
Imperforate varieties came from printer's waste.

1975. Collective Bargaining Issue commemorated the 40th anniversary of collective bargaining law in the Wagner Act, which stabilized labor-management relations in the United States. *Gravure (Andreotti Press), perforated 11.*

CM758 *Collective Bargaining*

CM758 *(1558)*
10c multicolored, tagged *(153,355,000)* .25 .20
  Plate block of eight 2.50
  FDC *(March 13, 1975)* 1.00
Imperforate varieties came from printer's waste.

1975. Contributors to the Cause Issue honors four heroes of the American Revolution. Emerald green inscriptions on the back of the stamptelling the story of each individual are printed under the gum. *Gravure (Andreotti Press), perforated 11 x 10 1/2.*

CM759 *Sybil Ludington, Youthful Heroine*

CM759 *(1559)*
8c multicolored, tagged *(63,205,000)* .25 .20
  Plate block of ten 2.50
  FDC *(March 25, 1975)* 1.00
  v. Inscription on back omitted 250.

CM760 *Salem Poor, Gallant Soldier*

CM760 *(1560)*
10c multicolored, tagged *(157,865,000)* .25 .20
Plate block of ten 3.25
FDC *(March 25, 1975)* 1.00
v. Inscription on back omitted 250.

CM761 *Haym Solomon, Financial Hero*

CM761 *(1561)*
10c multicolored, tagged *(166,810,000)* .25 .20
Plate block of ten 3.25
FDC *(March 25, 1975)* 1.00
v. Inscription on back omitted 250.
v1. Red omitted 275.

CM762 *Peter Francisco, Fighter Extraordinary*

CM762 *(1562)*
18c multicolored, tagged *(44,825,000)* .25 .20
Plate block of ten 6.25
FDC *(March 25, 1975)* 1.00

1975. Mariner Space Issue honored the Mariner 10 unmanned space mission to Venus and Mercury. *Intaglio (Giori Press) and offset, perforated 11.*

CM763 *Mariner 10, Venus and Mercury*

CM763 *(1557)*
10c black, red, ultramarine and bister
tagged *(158,600,000)* .25 .20
Plate block of four 1.30
FDC *(April 4, 1975)* 1.00
v. Red omitted 575.
v1. Ultramarine and bister omitted 1,750.
zo. Tagging omitted —

1975. Lexington and Concord Issue commemorated these 1775 battles, the first of the Revolutionary War. *Gravure (Andreotti Press), perforated 11.*

CM764 *Lexington and Concord. Based on painting Birth of Liberty by Henry Sandham*

CM764 *(1563)*
10c multicolored, tagged *(114,028,000)* .25 .20
Plate block of 12 3.75
FDC *(April 19, 1975)* 1.00
v. Vertical pair, imperforate horizontally —

1975. Paul Laurence Dunbar Issue honors the African-American poet. *Gravure (Andreotti Press), perforated 11.*

CM765 *Paul Laurence Dunbar*

CM765 *(1554)*
10c multicolored, tagged *(146,365,000)* .25 .20
Plate block of ten 3.25
FDC *(May 1, 1975)* 1.00
v. Imperforate pair —

1975. D.W. Griffith Issue of the American Art series and commemorates motion picture pioneer D.W. Griffith. *Intaglio (Giori Press) and offset, perforated 11.*

CM766 *D.W. Griffith Motion Picture Camera*

CM766 *(1555)*
10c multicolored, tagged *(148,805,000)* .25 .20
Plate block of four 1.30
FDC *(May 27, 1975)* 1.00
v. Intaglio dark brown omitted 650.

1975. Bunker Hill Issue commemorates the 200th anniversary of the Battle of Bunker Hill. *Gravure (Andreotti Press), perforated 11.*

CM767 *Bunker Hill 1775. Detail from the painting* The Battle of Bunker Hill *by John Trumbull*

CM767 *(1556)*
10c multicolored, tagged *(139,928,000)* .25 .20
Plate block of 12 1.30
FDC *(June 17, 1975)* 1.00

1975. Military Services Bicentennial Issue honored the 200th anniversary year of the U.S. military services. Designs depict uniforms worn by the Continental Army, Navy, Marines and Militia during the Revolutionary War. *Gravure (Andreotti Press), perforated 11.*

CM768
Soldier

CM769
Sailor

CM770
Marine

CM771
Militiaman

CM768 *(1565)*
10c multicolored, tagged *(179,855,000)* .25   .20
CM769 *(1566)*
10c multicolored, tagged   .25   .20
CM770 *(1567)*
10c multicolored, tagged   .25   .20
CM771 *(1568)*
10c multicolored, tagged   .25   .20
    Plate block of 12   4.25
    y. Se-tenant block of four,
      CM768-71   .75
    FDC *(July 4, 1975)*   1.00

1975. Apollo Soyuz Issue honored the first combined space mission between the United States and Soviet Union. The se-tenant designs used by both nations are identical except for language and denomination (Russia Nos. 4472-4473). *Gravure (Andreotti Press), perforated 11.*

CM772 *Spacecraft in Docked Position*

CM773 *Spacecraft Prior to Docking*

CM772 *(1569)*
10c multicolored, tagged *(161,863,200)* .25   .20
CM773 *(1570)*
10c multicolored, tagged   .25   .20
    Plate block of 12   4.00
    y. Se-tenant pair, CM 772-73   .45
    Gutter pair   —
    FDC *(July 15, 1975)*   1.00
    v. Vertical pair, imperforate
      horizontally   —
    zo. Tagging omitted, either single   —
    zoy. Se-tenant pair, tagging omitted   —

1975. World Peace Through Law Issue was a prelude to the Seventh World Law Conference of the World Peace Through Law Center and commemorates man's effort toward the universal goal of a peaceful world order with justice. *Intaglio (Giori Press), perforated 11.*

CM774 *Olive Branch, Globe, Gavel and Law Book*

CM774 *(1576)*
10c green, gray blue and brown, tagged
    (146,615,000)   .25   .20
    Plate block of four   1.35
    FDC *(Sept. 29, 1975)*   1.00
    v. Horizontal pair, imperforate
      vertically   —
    zo. Tagging omitted   —

1975. International Women's Year Issue celebrated the significance of women. *Gravure (Andreotti Press), perforated 11 x 10 1/2.*

CM775 *Stylized Dove, Globe and Gender Sign*

CM775 *(1571)*
10c blue, orange and dark blue, tagged
    (145,640,000)   .25   .20
    Plate block of six   1.90
    FDC *(Aug. 26, 1975)*   1.00

1975. U.S. Postal Service Bicentennial Issue commemorated the 200th anniversary of Postal Service in the U.S. *Gravure (Andreotti Press), perforated 11 x 10 1/2.*

CM776

CM777

CM778

CM779

CM776 *Stagecoach and Modern Trailer Truck,* CM777 *Early and modern locomotives,* CM778 *Early Mail Plane and Jumbo Jet,* CM779 *Satellite for Mailgram Transmitions*

CM776 *(1572)*
10c multicolored, tagged *(168,655,000)* .25   .20
CM777 *(1573)*
10c multicolored, tagged   .25   .20
CM778 *(1574)*
10c multicolored, tagged   .25   .20

CM779 *(1575)*

10c multicolored, tagged	.25	.20
Plate block of 12	4.25	
y. Se-tenant block of four		
CM776-79	1.25	
FDC *(Sept. 3, 1975)*		1.00
vy. Se-tenant block of four,		
red "10c" omitted	7,500.	

1975. Banking and Commerce Issue focused on the importance of these commercial activities in the nation's development *Intaglio (Giori Press) and offset, perforated 11.*

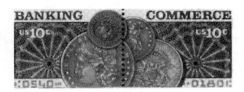

CM780-81 *Gold coins and Currency*

CM780 *(1577)*

10c multicolored, tagged *(146,196,000)*	.25	.20

CM781 *(1578)*

10c multicolored, tagged	.25	.20
Plate block of four	1.50	
y. Se-tenant pair, CM 780-81	.75	.50
FDC *(Oct. 6, 1975)*		2.00
vy. Se-tenant pair, brown and blue		
(offset) omitted	2,500.	
v1y. Se-tenant pair, brown,		
blue and yellow		
(offset) omitted	2,750.	

1976. Spirit of '76 Issue reproduces a classic image of the American Revolution. *Gravure (Andreotti Press), perforated 11.*

CM782   CM783   CM784

CM782-84 *Revolutionary War fife and drum trio, printing by Archibald M. Willard*

CM782 *(1629)*

13c multicolored, tagged *(219,455,000)*	.25	.20

CM783 *(1630)*

13c multicolored, tagged	.25	.20

CM784 *(1631)*

13c multicolored, tagged	.25	.20
Plate block of 12	5.00	
y. Se-tenant strip of three,		
CM 782-84	.75	1.00
FDC *(Jan. 1, 1976)*		1.00
v. Vertical pair, CM 784,		
imperforate	—	
v1. Se-tenant strip of three,		
imperforate	—	

1976. INTERPHIL Issue commemorates the Seventh International Philatelic Exhibition, May 29-June 6, 1976, in Philadelphia, PA. *Intaglio (Giori Press) and offset, perforated 11.*

CM785 *Interphil 76*

CM785 *(1632)*

13c blue, red and ultramarine, tagged		
(157,825,000)	.25	.20
Plate block of four	1.60	
FDC *(Jan. 17, 1976)*		1.00

1976. 50-State Flag Issue included in one sheet the flag of every state, arranged in order of its admission to the union. *Gravure (Andreotti Press), perforated 11, all stamps multicolored.*

CM786-CM835 State Flags

CM786 *(1633)*

13c Delaware, tagged *(436,005,000)*	.55	.40

CM787 *(1634)*

13c Pennsylvania, tagged	.55	.40

CM788 *(1635)*

13c New Jersey, tagged	.55	.40

CM789 *(1636)*

13c Georgia, tagged	.55	.40

CM790 *(1637)*

13c Connecticut, tagged	.55	.40

CM791 *(1638)*		
13c **Massachusetts**, tagged	.55	.40
CM792 *(1639)*		
13c **Maryland**, tagged	.55	.40
CM793 *(1640)*		
13c **South Carolina**, tagged	.55	.40
CM794 *(1641)*		
13c **New Hampshire**, tagged	.55	.40
CM795 *(1642)*		
13c **Virginia**, tagged	.55	.40
CM796 *(1643)*		
13c **New York**, tagged	.55	.40
CM797 *(1644)*		
13c **North Carolina**, tagged	.55	.40
CM798 *(1645)*		
13c **Rhode Island**, tagged	.55	.40
CM799 *(1646)*		
13c **Vermont**, tagged	.55	.40
CM800 *(1647)*		
13c **Kentucky**, tagged	.55	.40
CM801 *(1648)*		
13c **Tennessee**, tagged	.55	.40
CM802 *(1649)*		
13c **Ohio**, tagged	.55	.40
CM803 *(1650)*		
13c **Louisiana**, tagged	.55	.40
CM804 *(1651)*		
13c **Indiana**, tagged	.55	.40
CM805 *(1652)*		
13c **Mississippi**, tagged	.55	.40
CM806 *(1653)*		
13c **Illinois**, tagged	.55	.40
CM807 *(1654)*		
13c **Alabama**, tagged	.55	.40
CM808 *(1655)*		
13c **Maine**, tagged	.55	.40
CM809 *(1656)*		
13c **Missouri**, tagged	.55	.40
CM810 *(1657)*		
13c **Arkansas**, tagged	.55	.40
CM811 *(1658)*		
13c **Michigan**, tagged	.55	.40
CM812 *(1659)*		
13c **Florida**, tagged	.55	.40
CM813 *(1660)*		
13c **Texas**, tagged	.55	.40
CM814 *(1661)*		
13c **Iowa**, tagged	.55	.40
CM815 *(1662)*		
13c **Wisconsin**, tagged	.55	.40
CM816 *(1663)*		
13c **California**, tagged	.55	.40
CM817 *(1664)*		
13c **Minnesota**, tagged	.55	.40
CM818 *(1665)*		
13c **Oregon**, tagged	.55	.40
CM819 *(1666)*		
13c **Kansas**, tagged	.55	.40
CM820 *(1667)*		
13c **West Virginia**, tagged	.55	.40
CM821 *(1668)*		

13c **Nevada**, tagged	.55	.40
CM822 *(1669)*		
13c **Nebraska**, tagged	.55	.40
CM823 *(1670)*		
13c **Colorado**, tagged	.55	.40
CM824 *(1671)*		
13c **North Dakota**, tagged	.55	.40
CM825 *(1672)*		
13c **South Dakota**, tagged	.55	.40
CM826 *(1673)*		
13c **Montana**, tagged	.55	.40
CM827 *(1674)*		
13c **Washington**, tagged	.55	.40
CM828 *(1675)*		
13c **Idaho**, tagged	.55	.40
CM829 *(1676)*		
13c **Wyoming**, tagged	.55	.40
CM830 *(1677)*		
13c **Utah**, tagged	.55	.40
CM831 *(1678)*		
13c **Oklahoma**, tagged	.55	.40
CM832 *(1679)*		
13c **New Mexico**, tagged	.55	.40
CM833 *(1680)*		
13c **Arizona**, tagged	.55	.40
CM834 *(1681)*		
13c **Alaska**, tagged	.55	.40
CM835 *(1682)*		
13c **Hawaii**, tagged	.55	.40
FDC, any single *(Feb.23, 1976)*		1.00
FDC, pane of 50		15.00

1976. Telephone Centennial Issue honored the 100th anniversary of the first telephone call by Alexander Graham Bell (CM235). *Printed by intaglio (Giori Press), perforated 11.*

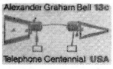

CM836 *Patent Application of Bell's 1876 Telelphone*

CM836 *(1683)*
13c black, purple and red on tan paper

tagged *(159,915,000)*	.25	.20
Plate block of four	1.60	
FDC *(March 10, 1976)*		1.00

1976. Commercial Aviation Issue saluted the 50th anniversary of the first contract airmail flights. The stamp depicts a Ford-Pullman monoplane and a Laird Swallow biplane. *Gravure (Andreotti Press), perforated 11.*

CM837 *Early Contract Airmail Planes*

CM837 *(1684)*

13c multicolored, tagged *(156,960,000)*	.25	.20
Plate block of ten	4.70	
FDC *(March 19, 1976)*		1.00

1976. Chemistry Issue pays tribute to that science and salutes the 100th anniversary of the American Chemical Society. *Gravure (Andreotti Press), perforated 11.*

CM838 *Laboratory Flasks, Computer Tape*

CM838 *(1685)*

13c multicolored, tagged *(158,470,000)* .25		.20
Plate block of 12	4.70	
Gutter pair		
FDC *(April 6, 1976)*		1.00

1976. Bicentennial Souvenir Sheets, issued to coincide with the Seventh International Philatelic Exhibition, held in Philadelphia, PA, May 29-June 6. Each contained five stamps of the same denomination. *Printed by offset, perforated 11.*

CM839 *Surrender of Cornwallis at Yorktown by John Trumbull (five 13c stamps)*

CM839 *(1686a-e)*

65c multicolored, tagged *(1,990,500)* 4.75		4.50
FDC *(May 29, 1976)*		10.00
a. 13c two British officers	.95	.90
b. 13c Gen. Benjamin Lincoln	.95	.90
c. 13c Gen. George Washington	.95	.90
d. 13c John Trumbull, Col. Cobb, von Steuben, Lafayette and Thomas Nelson	.95	.90
e. Alexander Hamilton, John Laurens, and Walter Stewart	.95	.90
v. "USA/13c" omitted on CM839b, CM839c and CM839d, imperforate	500.	
v1. "USA/13c" omitted on CM839b, CM839c and CM839d	900.	
v2. "USA/13c" omitted on CM839a and CM839e	500.	
v3. "USA/13c" omitted on CM839c and CM839d	500.	
v4. "USA/13c" omitted on CM839e	600.	
v5. "USA/13c" double on CM839b	—	
v6. Tagging and "USA/13c" omitted, imperforate	—	
zo. Tagging omitted	—	
zov. Tagging omitted, imperforate	—	

CM840 *(1687a-e)*

90c multicolored, tagged *(1,983,000)*	6.00	5.75
FDC *(May 29, 1976)*		10.00

CM840 *Declaration of Independence by John Trumbull (five 18c stamps)*

a. 18c John Adams, Roger Sherman, and Robert Livingston	1.35	1.30
b. 18c Jefferson and Franklin	1.35	1.30
c. 18c Thomas Nelson, Jr., Francis Lewis, John Witherspoon and Samuel Huntington	1.35	1.30
d. 18c John Hancock and Charles Thompson	1.35	1.30
e. 18c George Read, John Dickenson and Edward Rutledge	1.35	1.30
v. Black omitted in design	1,250.	
v1. Design and marginal inscriptions omitted	—	
v2. "USA/18c" and tagging omitted, imperforate	—	
v3. "USA/18c" omitted on CM840a and CM840c	600.	
v4. "USA/18c" omitted on CM840b, CM840d,and CM840e	500.	
v5. "USA/18c" omitted on CM840d	550.	
v6. "USA/18c" omitted on CM840b and CM840e	550.	
zo. Tagging omitted	—	

CM841 *Washington crossing the Delaware by E. Leutze and E. Johnson (five 24c stamps)*

CM841 *(1688a-e)*

$1.20 multicolored, tagged *(1,953,000)* 8.25		8.00
FDC *(May 29, 1976)*		10.00
a. 24c Boatsman	1.80	1.70
b. 24c Gen. George Washington	1.80	1.70
c. 24c Flag bearer	1.80	1.70
d. 24c Men in boat	1.80	1.70
e. 24c Men on shore	1.80	1.70
v. Design and marginal inscription omitted	—	
v1. "USA/24c" omitted, imperforate	—	
v2. "USA/24c" omitted on CM841a, CM841b and CM841c	600.	
v3. "USA/24c" omitted on CM841d and CM841e	550.	

v4. "USA/24c" of CM841d and
CM841e inverted 500.
zo. Tagging omitted —
zov Tagging omitted, imperforate —

CM842 *Washington Reviewing Army at Valley Forge by William T. Trego (five 31c stamps)*

CM842 *(1689a-e)*
$1.55 multicolored, tagged

(1,903,000)	10.75	10.50
FDC *(May 29, 1976)*		10.00
a. 31c Two officers	2.25	2.15
b. 31c Gen. George Washington	2.25	2.15
c. 31c Officer on black horse	2.25	2.15
d. 31c Officer and white horse	2.25	2.15
e. 31c Three foot soldiers	2.25	2.15

v. Black omitted in design —
v1. "USA/31c" omitted, imperforate—
v2. "USA/31c" omitted on CM842a,
CM842b and CM842e —
v3. "USA/31c" and tagging omitted
on CM842a, CM842b and
CM842e, imperforate —
v4. "USA/31c" omitted on CM842a
and CM842c 550.
v5. "USA/31c" and tagging omitted
on CM842a and CM842c,
imperforate —
v6. "USA/31c" omitted on CM842b,
CM842d and CM842e 550.
v7. "USA/31c" and tagging omitted
on CM842b, CM842d and
CM842e, imperforate —
v8. "USA/31c" omitted on CM842b
and CM842d —
v9. "USA/31c" omitted on CM842d
and CM842e 1,250.
v10. "USA/31c" omitted on
CM842e 550.
z11. Imperforate, tagging omitted —

1976. Benjamin Franklin Issue honors America's first postmaster general, appointed by the Continental Congress. *Intaglio (Giori Press) and offset, perforated 11.*

CM843 *Benjamin Franklin and North American Map*

CM843 *(1690)*
13c multicolored, tagged *(164,890,000)* .25 .20
Plate block of four 1.60
FDC *(June 1, 1976)* 1.00

v. Light blue omitted 275.
zo. Tagging omitted —

1976. Declaration of Independence Issue celebrates the anniversary of the approval of the document on July 4, 1976, by the members of the Continental Congress. *Gravure (Andreotti Press), perforated 11.*

CM844   CM845   CM846   CM847

CM844-47 The Declaration of Independence, *painting by John Trumbull*
CM844 *(1691)*
13c multicolored, tagged *(208,035,000)* .25 .20
CM845 *(1692)*
13c multicolored, tagged .25 .20
CM846 *(1693)*
13c multicolored, tagged .25 .20
CM847 *(1694)*
13c multicolored, tagged .25 .20
Plate block of 16 11.
y. Se-tenant strip of four, CM844-47 1.00 1.00
FDC *(July 4, 1976)* 2.00
FDC, any single 1.00

1976. Olympic Games Issue salutes the 1976 Winter Games in Innsbruck, Austria and the Summer Games in Montreal. Canada. *Gravure (Andreotti Press), perforated 11.*

CM848 *Diving*   CM849 *Skiing*
CM850 *Running*   CM851 *Skating*

CM848 *(1695)*
13c multicolored, tagged *(185,715,000)* .25 .20
CM849 *(1696)*
13c multicolored, tagged .25 .20
CM850 *(1697)*
13c multicolored, tagged .25 .20
CM851 *(1698)*
13c multicolored, tagged .25 .20
Plate block of 12 6.50
y. Se-tenant block of four 1.25 1.50

FDC *(July 16, 1976)*   1.00
v. Imperforate se-tenant
   block of four   —

1976. Clara Maass Issue honors the 100th birthday of the nurse who gave her life during yellow fever research. *Gravure (Andreotti Press), perforated 11.*

CM852 *Nurse Clara Maass and Hospital Pin*

CM852 *(1699)*
   13c multicolored, tagged *(130,592,000)* .25   .20
     Plate block of 12   5.75
     FDC *(Aug. 18, 1976)*   1.00
     v. Horizontal pair, imperforate
       vertically   —

1976. Adolph S. Ochs Issue commemorates the 125th anniversary of *The New York Times.* Ochs was the publisher of the *Times* from 1896 until his death in 1935. *Printed by intaglio (Giori Press), perforated 11.*

CM853 *Adolph S. Ochs. From portrait by S.J. Woolf.*

CM853 *(1700)*
   13c gray and black, tagged
     (158,332,800)   .25   .20
     Plate block of four   1.60
     FDC *(Sept. 18, 1976)*   1.00

1977. Washington at Princeton Issue commemorates the American victory at Princeton, NJ, over the British lead by Lord Cornwallis. *Gravure (Andreotti Press), perforated 11.*

CM854 *George Washington. Painting by Charles Willson Peale*

US Bicentennial 13c

CM854 *(1704)*
   13c multicolored, tagged *(150,328,000)* .25   .20
     Plate block of ten   3.95
     FDC *(Jan. 3, 1977)*   1.00
     v. Horizontal pair, imperforate
       vertically   —

1977. Sound Recording Centennial Issue pays tribute to a century of progress in the field of sound recording. *Intaglio (Giori Press) and offset, perforated 11.*

CM855 *Early Sound Recorder*

CM855 *(1705)*
   13c multicolored, tagged *(176,830,000)* .25   .20
     Plate block of four   1.60
     FDC *(March 23, 1977)*   1.00

1977. Pueblo Indian Art Issue, first installment in the all-se-tenant American Folk Art series showcases the artistic achievements of the Pueblo Indians in the craft of pottery. *Gravure (Andreotti Press), perforated 11.*

CM856 *Zia Pueblo*      CM857 *San Ildefonso Pueblo*

CM858 *Hopi Pueblo*   CM859 *Acoma Pueblo*

CM856 *(1708)*
   13c multicolored, tagged *(195,976,000)* .25   .20
CM857 *(1709)*
   13c multicolored, tagged
CM858 *(1706)*
                   .25   .20
   13c multicolored, tagged   .25   .20
CM859 *(1707)*
   13c multicolored, tagged   .25   .20
     Plate block of 10   4.50
     y. Se-tenant block or strip of four .75
     FDC *(April 13, 1977)*   1.00
     v. St-tenant block or strip of four,
       imperforate vertically   —

1977. 50th Anniversary of Transatlantic Flight Issue commemorated the epic solo flight of Charles A. Lindbergh's across the Atlantic Ocean (see A10). *Gravure (Andreotti Press), perforated 11.*

CM860 *The Spirit of St. Louis over the Atlantic Ocean*

CM860 *(1710)*
   13c multicolored, tagged *(208,820,000)* .25   .20
     Plate block of 12   4.75
     FDC *(May 20, 1977)*   1.00
     v. Imperforate pair   —
Privately applied overprints on this stamp have no official status.

1977. Colorado Statehood Centennial Issue

celebrates Colorado as the 38th state. *Gravure (Andreotti Press), perforated 11.*

CM861 *Columbine and Mountain Peak*

CM861 *(1711)*
  13c multicolored, tagged *(190,005,000)* .25   .20
    Plate block of 12   4.75
    FDC *(May 21, 1977)*   1.00
    v. Horizontal pair, imperforate
      between   —
    v1. Horizontal pair, imperforate
      vertically   —
    v2 Perforated 11 1/4   —

1977. Butterfly Issue

commemoratives display representatives of different regions of the United States. *Gravure (Andreotti Press), perforated 11.*

CM862 *Swallowtail*   CM863 *Checkerspot*

CM864 *Dogface*   CM865 *Orange-Tip*

CM862 *(1712)*
  13c multicolored, tagged *(219,830,000)* .25   .20
CM863 *(1713)*
  13c multicolored, tagged   .25   .20
CM864 *(1714)*
  13c multicolored, tagged   .25   .20
CM865 *(1715)*
  13c multicolored, tagged   .25   .20
    Plate block of 12   5.50
    y. Se-tenant block of four,
      CM1712-1715   1.00   .80
    FDC *(June 6, 1977)*   1.00
    v. Se-tenant block of four,
      imperforate horizontally   —

1977. Lafayette Issue

marks the 200th anniversary of Marquis de Lafayette's landing on the coast of South Carolina, north of Charleston. *Intaglio, (Giori Press), perforated 11.*

CM866 *Marquis de Lafayette*

CM866 *(1716)*
  13c blue, black and red *(159,852,000)* .25   .20
    Plate block of four   1.60
    FDC *(June 13, 1977)*   1.00

1977. Skilled Hands of Independence Issue

salutes representatives of four American industries — blacksmiths, wheelwrights, leatherworkers and seamstresses — who contributed to winning the Revolutionary War. *Gravure (Andreotti Press), perforated 11.*

CM867   CM868
Seamstress   *Blacksmith*

CM869 *Wheelwright*   CM870 *Leatherworker*

CM867 *(1717)*
  13c multicolored, tagged *(188,310,000)* .25   .20
CM868 *(1718)*
  13c multicolored, tagged   .25   .20
CM869 *(1719)*
  13c multicolored, tagged   .25   .20
CM870 *(1720)*
  13c multicolored   .25   .20
    Plate block of 12   5.50
    y. Se-tenant block of four,
      CM 1717-1720   1.00   .80
    FDC *(July 4, 1977)*   1.00

1977. Peace Bridge Issue

marked the 50th anniversary of the Peace Bridge between Buffalo (Fort Porter) NY, and Fort Erie, Ontario, Canada. *Intaglio, perforated 11 x 10 1/2.*

CM871 *Dove Over Peace Bridge*

CM871 *(1721)*
  13c blue, tagged *(163,625,000)*   .25   .20
    Plate block of four   1.60
    FDC *(Aug. 4, 1977)*   1.00

1977. Herkimer at Oriskany Issue honors Gen. Nicholas Herkimer's contribution to the American War for Independence and the 200th anniversary of the Battle of Oriskany. *Gravure (Andreotti Press), perforated 11.*

CM872 *Wounded Gen. Herkimer at Battle of Oriskany*

CM872 *(1722)*

13c multicolored, tagged *(156,296,000)* .25		.20
Plate block of ten	3.95	
FDC *(Aug. 6, 1977)*		1.00

1977. Alta California Issue commemorates the bicentennial of the first Spanish civil settlement in Alta (northern) California. *Intaglio (Giori Press) and offset, perforated 11.*

CM873 *Spansih Colonial Farms*

CM873 *(1725)*

13c multicolored, tagged *(154,495,000)* .25		.20
Plate block of four	1.60	
FDC *(Sept. 9, 1977)*		1.00

1977. Articles of Confederation Issue marked the 200th anniversary of the drafting of the Articles of Confederation in 1777. *Intaglio (Giori Press), perforated 11.*

CM874 *Drafting the Articles of Confederation*

CM874 *(1726)*

13c red and dark brown on cream paper, tagged *(168,050,000)*	.25	.20
Plate block of four	1.60	
FDC *(Sept. 30, 1977)*		1.00
zo. Tagging omitted	—	

1977. Talking Pictures Issue marks 50 years since the introduction of sound in films. *The Jazz Singer,* starring Al Jolson, is accepted as the first feature-length talking picture. *Intaglio (Giori Press) and offset, perforated 11.*

CM875 *Early Projector and Phonograph*

CM875 *(1727)*

13c multicolored, tagged *(156,810,000)* .25		.20
Plate block of four	1.60	
FDC *(Oct. 6, 1977)*		1.00

1977. Surrender at Saratoga marked the surrender of British Gen. John Burgoyne to Gen. Horatio Gates in 1777 (See CM77). *Printed by Gravure (Andreotti Press), perforated 11.*

CM876 *Surrender of Burgoyne. Painted by John Trumbell.*

CM876 *(1728)*

13c multicolored *(153,736,000)*	.25	.20
Plate block of 10	4.00	
FDC *(Oct. 7, 1977)*		1.00

1977. Energy Issue stresses the importance of conserving energy and developing new sources. Gravure (Andreotti Press), perforated 11.

CM876A *(1723)*

13c multicolored, tagged *(Oct. 20, 1977)*	.25	.20
13c multicolored, tagged	.25	.20
Plate block of twelve	5.00	
y. Se-tenant pair CM876A and CM876B	.50	

1978. The Carl Sandburg Issue honored "The Poet of the People" on the 100th anniversary of his birth. He won the Pulitzer Prize three times for his works. Intaglio (Giori Press), perforated 11.

CM877 *Carl Sandburg*

CM877 *(1731)*

13c brown and black, tagged *(156,560,000)*	.25	.20
Plate block of four	1.60	
FDC *(Jan. 6, 1978)*		1.00
v. Brown omitted		

1978. Captain Cook Issue , featuring two stamps oriented differently in the same sheet, marks the 200th anniversary of the explorer's arrival in Hawaii and Alaska. Intaglio *(Giori Press), perforated 11.*

CM878 *Capt. James Cook*
CM879 *Cook's ships* Resolution *and* Discovery

CM878 *(1732)*

13c blue, tagged *(202,155,000)*	.25	.20
FDC *(Jan. 20, 1978)*		1.00

CM879 *(1733)*

13c green, tagged	.25	.20
Plate block of four, CM878 or CM879	1.60	
Pate block of 20, 10 each CM878-79	4.00	
Se-tenant pair CM878-79	.50	
FDC *(Jan. 20, 1978)*		1.00
FDC, Se-tenant pair		2.00
v. Se-tenant pair, imperforate between	—	
v1. Vertical pair (CM879), imperforate horizontally	—	

1978. Harriet Tubman Issue, first stamp in the long-running Black Heritage series, honors the woman known as the "Moses of her People." Born into slavery, she is credited with helping more than 300 slaves to escape via the "Underground Railway."(See also CM1731) *Gravure(Andreotti Press), perforated 10 1/2 x 11.*

CM880 *Harriet Tubman*

CM880 *(1744)*

13c multicolored, tagged *(156,525,000)*	.25	.20
Plate block of 12	6.50	
FDC *(Feb. 1, 1978)*		1.00

1978. American Quilts Issue., the scond se-tenant set in the American Folk Art series, shows four different-basket design quilt patterns. *Gravure(Andreotti Press), perforated 11.*

CM881   CM882

CM883   CM884

CM881 *(1745)*

13c multicolored, tagged *(165,182,000)*	.25	.20

CM882 *(1746)*

13c multicolored, tagged	.25	.20

CM883 *(1747)*

13c multicolored, tagged	.25	.20

CM884 *(1748)*

13c multicolored, tagged	.25	.20
Plate block of 12	5.50	
y. Se-tenant block of four CM881-84	1.00	.95
FDC *(May 8, 1978)*		2.00

1978. American Dance Issue. celebrates various styles of popular dancing. *Gravure (Andreotti Press), perforated 11.*

CM886 *Theater*

CM885 *Ballet*   CM888 *Modern*

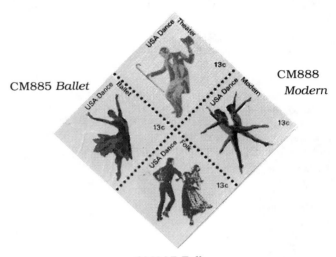

CM887 *Folk*

CM885 *(1749)*

13c multicolored, tagged *(157,598,400)*	.25	.20

CM886 *(1750)*

13c multicolored, tagged	.25	.20

CM887 *(1751)*

13c multicolored, tagged	.25	.20

CM888 *(1752)*

13c multicolored, tagged	.25	.20
Plate block of 12	5.50	
Se-tenant block of four CM885-88	1.50	.95
FDC *(April 26, 1978)*		2.00

1978. French Alliance Issue marks the 200th anniversary of the signing of the French Alliance in 1778. *Intaglio (Giori Press) and offset, perforated 11.*

CM889 *King Louis XVI and Benjamin Franklin. Porcelian statuette by Charles Gabriel Sauvage*

CM889 *(1753)*

13c blue, black, and red, tagged *(102,856,000)*	.25	.20
Plate block of four	1.60	
FDC *(May 4, 1978)*		1.00

1978. George Papanicolaou Issue commemorates the noted cancer researcher for his development of an early cancer detection procedure, the use of which has saved the lives of thousands of women. *Intaglio, perforated 10 1/2 x 11.*

CM890 *Dr, Papanixolaou and Microscope*

CM890 *(1754)*

13c brown, tagged *(152,270,000)*	.25	.20
Plate block of four	2.10	
FDC *(May 18, 1978)*		1.00

1978. Jimmie Rodgers Issue, the first stamp in the Performing Artists series, commemorates the country and western singer known as the "Singing Brakeman" and "Father of Country Music" and the first person inducted into the Country Music Hall of Fame in 1967. *Gravure(Andreotti Press), perforated 11.*

CM891 *Jimmie Rodgers*

CM891 *(1755)*

13c multicolored, tagged *(94,600,000)*	.25	.20
Plate block of 12	5.00	
FDC *(May 24, 1978)*		1.00

1978. Canadian International Philatelic Exhibition Souvenir Sheet commemorates the 1978 CAPEX stamp shown in Toronto, Canada. The souvenir sheet contains eight perforated stamps depicts animals and birds indigenous to the United States and Canadia. *Intaglio (Giori Press) and offset, perforated 11.*

CM892 *CAPEX souvenir sheet*

CM892 *(1757)*

$1.04 multicolored *(10,400,000)*	275.	
Souvenir sheet with plate number		
attached	3.25	2.25
a. 13c Cardinal, tagged	.25	.20
b. 13c Mallard, tagged	.25	.20
c. 13c Canada Goose, tagged	.25	.20
d. 13c Blue Jay, tagged	.25	.20
e. 13c Moose, tagged	.25	.20
f. 13c Chipmunk, tagged	.25	.20
g. 13c Red Fox, tagged	.25	.20
h. 13c Raccoon, tagged	.25	.20
y. Se-tenant block of eight CM892 a-h	3.00	
v. Yellow, green, red, brown, blue and offset black omitted	7,000.	
v1. Strip of four, imperforate vertically	5,000.	

1978. Photography Issue celebrates the colorful, popular art form. *Gravure (Andreotti Press), perforated 11.*

CM893 *Camera, Fritters and Photo Equiptment*

CM893 *(1758)*

15c multicolored, tagged *(161,228,000)*	.30	.20
Plate block of 12	5.75	
FDC *(June 26, 1978)*		1.00

1978. George M. Cohan Issue, second stamp in the Performing Artists series, marked the 100th birthday of George M. Cohan, a patriotic and world-renowned actor, popular song writer, playwright and producer. *Gravure (Anreotti Press), perforated 11.*

CM894 *George M. Cohan*

CM894 *(1756)*

15c multicolored, tagged *(151,570,000)*	.30	.20
Plate block of 12	5.75	
FDC *(July 3, 1978)*		1.00

1978. Viking Missions Issue commemorates the historic Viking space voyages; issued on the second anniversary of the landing of Viking I on Mars. *Intaglio (Giori Press) and offset, perforated 11.*

CM895 *Viking I Lander and Mars*

CM895 *(1759)*

15c multicolored, tagged *(158,880.000)*	.30	.20
Plate block of four	2.25	
FDC *(July 20, 1978)*		1.00

1978. Wildlife Conservation Issue features four species of owls native to the United States. *Intaglio (Giori Press) and offset, perforated 11.*

CM896 *Great Gray Owl*

CM897 *Saw Whet Owl*

CM898 *Barred Owl*

CM899 *Great Horned Owl*

CM896 *(1760)*
15c multicolored, tagged
    (186,550,000) | .30 | .20

CM897 *(1761)*
15c multicolored, tagged | .30 | .20

CM898 *(1762)*
15c multicolored, tagged | .30 | .20

CM899 *(1763)*
15c multicolored, tagged | .30 | .20
    Plate block of four | 2.00
    y. Se-tenant block of
        four CM896-99 | 1.50 | 1.00
    FDC *(Aug. 26, 1978)* | | 2.00

1978. American Trees Issue highlighted four different trees native to the United States and reflected a variety in both appearance and geographic location. *Gravure, perforated 11.*

CM900 *Giant Sequoia*

CM901 *Eastern White Pine*

CM902 *White Oak*

CM903 *Gray Birch*

CM900 *(1764)*
15c multicolored, tagged
    (168,136,000) | .30 | .20

CM901 *(1765)*
15c multicolored, tagged | .30 | .20

CM902 *(1766)*
15c multicolored, tagged | .30 | .20

CM903 *(1767)*
15c multicolored, tagged | .30 | .20
    Plate block of 12 | 6.00
    y. Se-tenant block of four
        CM900-03 | 1.25 | 1.00
    FDC *(Oct. 9, 1978)* | | 2.00
    vy. Se-tenant block of four,
        imperforate horizontally 12,250.

1979. Robert F. Kennedy Issue honors the assassinated U.S. senator and presidential hopeful. *Intaglio, perforated 11.*

CM904 *Robert F. Kennedy*

CM904 *(1770)*
15c blue, tagged *(159,297,000)* | .30 | .20
    Plate block of four | 1.80
    FDC *(Jan. 12, 1979)* | | 1.00
    za. Tagging omitted | —

1979. Martin Luther King Jr. Issue honors the civil rights leader and his role in the struggle for racial equality. Black Heritage series. *Gravure (Andreotti Press), perforated 11.*

CM905 *Martin Luther King Jr.*

CM905 *(1771)*
15c multicolored, tagged | .30 | .20
    (166,435,000)
    Plate block of 12 | 6.25
    FDC *(Jan. 13, 1979)* | | 1.00
    v. Imperforate pair | 1,750.

1979. International Year of the Child Issue commemorates the declaration by the U.N. General Assembly of 1979 as a year of concern for the condition and well being of the children of the world. *Intaglio, perforated 11.*

CM906 *Portraits of Four Children*

CM906 *(1772)*
15c light and dark brown, tagged
    (162,535,000) | .30 | .20
    Plate block of four | 1.80
    FDC *(Feb. 15, 1979)* | | 1.00

1979. John Steinbeck Issue, the first Literary Arts series, honors the novelist who won the Pulitzer Prize in 1940 and the Nobel Prize for Literature in 1962. *Intaglio, perforated 10 1/2 x 11.*

CM907 *John Steinbeck. From photograph by Philippe Halsman*

CM907 *(1773)*
  15c dark blue, tagged *(155,000,000)* .30   .20
    Plate block of four   1.80
    FDC *(Feb. 27, 1979)*   1.00

1979. Albert Einstein Issue honors the physicist, philosopher and humanitarian who is best known as the creator of the special and general theories of relativity. *Intaglio, perforated 10 1/2 x 11.*

CM908 *Albert Einstein. From photograph by Hermann Landshoff*

CM908 *(1774)*
  15c brown, tagged *(157,310,000)*   .30   .20
    Plate block of four   1.80
    Gutter pair, vertical   —
    FDC *(March 4, 1979)*   1.00

1979. Pennsylvania Toleware Issue, the third se-tenant installment in the American Folk Art series, depicts four of Pennsylvania Toleware, work well known for its colorful design motifs. *Gravure (Andreotti Press), perforated 11.*

CM909 *Coffee Pot with Straight Spout*

CM910 *Tea Caddy*

CM911 *Sugar Bowl with lid*

CM912 *Coffee Pot with Gooseneck Spout*

CM909 *(1775)*
  15c multicolored, tagged *(174,096,000)* .30   .20
CM910 *(1776)*
  15c multicolored, tagged   .30   .20

CM911 *(1777)*
  15c multicolored, tagged   .30   .20
CM912 *(1778)*
  15c multicolored, tagged   .30   .20
    Plate block of 12   5.00
    y. Se-tenant block of four
      CM909-12   1.50   1.00
    FDC *(April 19, 1979)*   2.00
    vy. Se-tenant block of four,
      imperforate horizontally 4,000.

1979. American Architecture Issue, the first of four se-tenant quartets on this subject designed by Walter D. Richards, commemorates successful early American architecture of enduring beauty, strength and usefulness. *Intaglio (Giori Press), perforated 11.*

CM913 *Virginia Rotunda, designed by Thomas Jefferson*

CM914 *Baltimore Cathedral, designed by Benjamin Latrobe*

CM915 *Boston State House, designed by Charles Bulfinch*

CM916 *Philadelphia Exchange, designed by William Strickland*

CM913 *(1779)*
  15c black and dark red, tagged   .30   .20
    (164,793,000)
CM914 *(1780)*
  15c black and dark red, tagged   .30   .20
CM915 *(1781)*
  15c black and dark red, tagged   .30   .20
CM916 *(1782)*
  15c black and dark red, tagged   .30   .20
    Plate block of four   2.50
    y. Se-tenant block of four
      CM913-16   1.50   1.00
    FDC *(June 4, 1979)*   2.00

1979. Endangered Flora Issue portrays four of the more than 1,700 plant species in the United States that are seriously threatened with extinction. *Gravure (Andreotti Press), perforated 11.*

CM917 *Persistent Trillium*

CM918 *Hawaiian Wild Broadbean*

CM919 *Contra Costa Wallflower*

CM920 *Antioch Dunes Evening Primrose*

CM917 *(1783)*
15c multicolored, tagged
    (163,055,000) .30 .20
CM918 *(1784)*
15c multicolored, tagged .30 .20

CM919 *(1785)*
15c multicolored, tagged .30 .20
CM920 *(1786)*
15c multicolored, tagged .30 .20
    Plate block of 12 6.50
    FDC *(June 7, 1979)* 1.00
    Horizontal gutter
      block of four —
    y. Se-tenant block of four
      CM917-20 2.00 1.00
    vy. Imperforate se-tenant
      block of four 600.

1979. Seeing Eye Dog Issue commemorates the 50th anniversary of the first guide dog program in the United States, founded by Dorothy Harrison. Gravure (Combination Press), perforated 11.

CM921 *German Shepherd Leading Man*

CM921 *(1787)*
15c multicolored, tagged *(161,860,000)* .30 .20
    Plate block of 20 9.00
    FDC *(June 15, 1979)* 1.00
    v. Imperforate pair 425.
    zo. Tagging omitted —

1979. Special Olympics Issue honors the international program of sports training, physical fitness and athletic competition for mentally retarded children and adults. *Gravure (Andrecotti Press), perforated 11.*

CM922 *Child with -Special Olympic Medal*

CM922 *(1788)*
15c multicolored, tagged *(165,775,000)* .30 .20
    Plate block of 10 4.50
    FDC *(Aug. 9, 1979)* 1.00

1979. 1980 Olympic Series begins with this 10c value featuring a decathlon competitor, the first of 10 commemorative stamps to be issued honoring the 1980 Olympic Games held in Lake Placid,N.Y., and Moscow. The United States and many other nations boycotted the

Moscow Summer Games to protest the Soviet invasion of Afghanistan. (See also CM925-28, CM932-35A and A95.) *Gravure, perforated 11.*

CM923 *Decathlete Throwing Javelin*

CM923 *(1790)*
10c multicolored, tagged *(67,195,000)* .25 .25
    Plate block of 12 4.50
    FDC *(Sept. 5, 1979)* 1.00

1979. John Paul Jones Issue honors the naval hero of the American Revolution. On the 200th anniversary of his victory over the British in the 1779 battle between *Bonhomme Richard* and *HMS Serapis.* This stamp was the first to be printed privately under terms of a contract awarded by the U.S. Postal Service in 1978. *Gravure by J.W. Fergusson and Sons, Richmond, V.A., with perforating, cutting and final processing by American Bank Note Co., New York, N.Y. Perforated 11 x 12*

CM924, 24B *John Paul Jones. Based on portrait by Charles Willson Peale*

CM924 *(1789)*
15c multicolored, tagged *(160,000,000,*
    all perforation types) .30 .20
    Plate block of 10 4.50
    FDC *(Sept. 23, 1979)* 1.00
    v. Vertical pair, imperforate
      horizontally 65.
Perforated 11
CM924A *(1790)*
15c multicolored, tagged .75 .25
    Plate block of 10 8.50
    FDC *(Sept. 23, 1979)* 1.00
    v. Vertical pair, imperforate
      horizontally 140.

Perforated 12
CM924B
15c multicolored, tagged 2,300 1,000
    v. Vertical pair, imperforate
      horizontally 175.

1979. 1980 Olympic Series Issue includes the four commemoratives for events of the Summer Olympic Games. *Gravure, perforated 11.*

CM925 *Women Runners*   CM926 *Women Swimmers*

CM927 *Pair of Rowers*   CM928 *Horse and Rider*

CM925 *(1791)*
15c multicolored, tagged *(186,905,000)* .25   .20
CM926 *(1792)*
15c multicolored, tagged   .25   .20
CM927 *(1793)*
15c multicolored, tagged   .25   .20
CM928 *(1794)*
15c multicolored, tagged   .25   .20
   Plate block of 12   6.50
   y. Se-tenant block of four
     CM925-28   1.50   1.10
   FDC *(Sept. 28, 1979)*   2.00
   vy. Se-tenant block of four,
     imperforate   1,500.
   v1. Vertical pair, imperforate
     (either)   650.

1979. Will Rogers Issue, third stamp in the Performing Artists series, honors the American humorist on the 100th anniversary of his birth. (See also CM267.) *Gravure (Andrecotti Press), perforated 11.*

CM929 *Will Rogers*

CM929 *(1801)*
15c multicolored, tagged *(161,290,000)* .30   .20
   Plate block of 12   6.00
   FDC *(Nov. 4, 1979)*   1.00
   v. Imperforate pair   225.

1979. Vietnam Veterans Issue pays tribute to the veterans of the war in Southeast Asia. *Gravure (Andreotti Press), perforated 11.*

   CM930 *Vietnam Service Ribbon*

CM930 *(1802)*
15c multicolored, tagged*(172,740,000)* .30   .20
   Plate block of 10   5.95
   FDC *(Nov. 11, 1979)*   1.00

1980. W.C. Fields Issue honors the juggler, actor and comedian on the 100th anniversary of his birth. Performing Artists series. *Gravure, perforated 11.*

   CM931 *W.C. Fields*

CM931 *(1803)*
15c multicolored, tagged *(168,995,000)* .30   .20
   Plate block of 12   6.00
   FDC *(Jan. 29, 1980)*   1.00
   v. Imperforate pair   —

1980. 1980 Olympics Series includes four commemoratives for events from the Winter Games, and honors the 13th Winter Games at Lake Placid, New York. *Gravure, perforated 11.*

CM932, CM932A *Speed Skater*   CM934, CM934A *Downhill Skier*

CM933, CM933A *Ski Jumper*   CM935, CM935A *Hockey Goaltender*

Perforated 11 x 10 1/2
CM932 *(1795)*
15c multicolored, tagged *(208,295,000,*
    both perforation types)   .30   .20
CM933 *(1796)*
15c multicolored, tagged   .30   .20
CM934 *(1797)*
15c multicolored, tagged   .30   .20
CM935 *(1798)*
15c multicolored, tagged   .30   .20
   Plate block of 12   6.50
   y. Se-tenant block of four
     CM932-35   1.50   1.10
   FDC *(Feb. 1, 1980)*   2.00
Perforated 11
CM932A *(1795a)*
15c multicolored, tagged   .80   .75
CM933A *(1796a)*
15c multicolored, tagged   .80   .75
CM934A *(1797a)*
15c multicolored, tagged   .80   .75
CM935A *(1798a)*
15c multicolored, tagged   .80   .75
   Plate block of 12   14.00
   y. Se-tenant block of four
     CM932-35   4.00   4.00

1980. Benjamin Banneker Issue honors a pioneer American scientist and mathematician. Born free in 1731, he became both a noted astronomer and surveyor. Black Heritage series. *Gravure by J.W. Fergusson and Sons for American Bank Note Co., perforated 11.*

CM936 *Benjamin Banneker*

CM936 *(1804)*

15c multicolored, tagged *(160,000,000)*	.30	.20
Plate block of 12	5.50	
FDC *(Feb. 15, 1980)*		1.00
v. Horizontal pair, imperforate		
vertically	50.	

Imperforates with misregistered colors from printers' waste exist, and have been fraudulently perforated to simulate CM936v. Genuine examples of this error have colors correctly registered.

1980. National Letter Writing Issue focuses attention on the importance of letter writing. Three sets of vertical pairs. *Gravure, perforated 11.*

CM937-38 *"Letters Preserve Memories" and "P.S. Write Soon"*

CM939-40 *"Letters Lift Spirits" and "P.S. Write Soon"*

CM941-42 *"Letters Shape Opinions" and "P.S. Write Soon"*

CM937 *(1805)*

15c multicolored, tagged *(232,134,00)*	.30	.20

CM938 *(1806)*

15c multicolored, tagged	.30	.20

CM939 *(1807)*

15c multicolored, tagged	.30	.20

CM940 *(1808)*

15c multicolored, tagged	.30	.20

CM941 *(1809)*

15c multicolored, tagged	.30	.20

CM942 *(1810)*

15c multicolored, tagged	.30	.20
Plate block of 36	19.50	
y. Se-tenant vertical strip		
of six CM937-42	2.00	
FDC *(Feb. 25, 1980)*		2.00

1980. Frances Perkins Issue honors the first woman to serve as a member of a U.S. presidential cabinet. Perkins served as Franklin Roosevelt's Secretary of Labor. *Intaglio, perforated 10 1/2 x 11.*

CM943 *Frances Perkins*

CM943 *(1821)*

15c blue, tagged *(163,510,000)*	.30	.20
Plate block of four	1.95	
FDC *(April 10, 1980)*		1.00

1980. Emily Bissell Issue celebrates the crusader against tuberculosis who introduced Christmas seals to the United States. *Intaglio, perforated 11.*

CM944 *Emily Bissell*

CM944 *(1823)*

15c black and red, tagged *(95,695,000)*	.30	.20
Plate block of four	1.80	
FDC *(May 31, 1980)*		1.00
v. Vertical pair, imperforate		
horizontally	350.	

1980. Helen Keller and Anne Sullivan Issue commemorates blind, deaf author and lecturer Helen Keller, and her teacher, Anne Sullivan. *Offset and intaglio, perforated 11.*

CM945 *Helen Keller and Anne Sullivan*

CM945 *(1824)*

15c multicolored, tagged *(153,975,000)*	.30	.20
Plate block of four	1.80	
FDC *(June 27, 1980)*		1.00

1980. Veterans Administration Issue marks the 50th anniversary of the Veterans Administration. *Gravure by J.W. Fergusson and Sons for American Bank Note Co., perforated 11.*

CM946 *Veterans Administration Emblem*

CM946 *(1825)*
  15c red and dark blue, tagged

(160,000,000)	.30	.20
Plate block of four	1.80	
FDC *(July 21, 1980)*		1.00
v. Horizontal pair, imperforate vertically	475.	

1980. Bernardo de Galvez Issue honors Gen. de Galvez, governor of Spanish Louisiana during the American Revolution, and a major contributor to the winning of the war. *Intaglio and offset, perforated 11.*

CM947 *Bernardo de Golvez From statue in Spanish Plaza, Mobile, Ala.*

CM947 (1826)
  15c multicolored, tagged *(103,850,000)* .30   .20

Plate block of four	1.80	
FDC *(July 23, 1980)*		1.00
v. Blue, brown, red and yellow omitted	13.50	
v1. Red, brown and blue omitted	7.50	

1980. Coral Reefs Issue showcases corals found in the waters of the United States, its territories and possessions. *Gravure, perforated 11.*

CM948 *Brain Coral, U.S. Virgin Islands*

CM949 *Elkhorn Coral, Florida*

CM950 *Chalice Coral, American Samoa*

CM951 *Finger Coral, Hawaii*

CM948 *(1827)*
  15c multicolored, tagged *(204,715,000)* .30   .20
CM949 *(1828)*
  15c multicolored, tagged   .30   .20
CM950 *(1829)*
  15c multicolored, tagged   .30   .20
CM951 *(1830)*
  15c multicolored, tagged   .30   .20

Plate block of 12	6.00	
y. Se-tenant block of four CM948-51	1.50	
FDC *(Aug. 26, 1980)*		2.00
v. Se-tenant block of four, imperforate	1,200.	
v1. Se-tenant block of four, imperforate between vertically	3,750.	
v2. Se-tenant block of four, imperforate vertically	2,975.	

1980. Organized Labor Issue honors the American labor movement, an integral part of the history of democracy and freedom in the United States. *Gravure, perforated 11.*

CM952 *Bald Eagle*

CM952 *(1852)*
  15c multicolored, tagged *(166,545,000)* .30   .20

Plate block of 12	5.50	
FDC *(Sept. 1, 1980)*		1.00
v. Imperforate pair	375.	

1980. Edith Wharton Issue honors the Pulitzer Prize-winning author of *The Age of Innocence.* and other novels, as well as short stories and poetry. Literary Arts series. *Intaglio, perforated 10 1/2 x 11.*

CM953 *Edith Wharton*

CM953 *(1832)*
  15c purple, tagged *(163,310,000)* .30   .20

Plate block of four	2.00	
FDC *(Sept. 5, 1980)*		1.00

1980. Education in America Issue commemorates American education and calls attention to the newly established U.S. Education Department. *Gravure by J.W. Fergusson and Sons for the American Bank Note Co., perforated 11*

CM954 Homage to the Square: Glow. *Acrylic printing by Josef Albers*

CM954 *(1833)*
  15c multicolored, tagged *(160,000,000)* .30   .20
    Plate block of six   3.50
    FDC *(Sept. 12, 1980)*   1.00
    v. Horizontal pair, imperforate
      vertically   225.

1980. Northwest Indian Masks Issue features four carved masks representing the craftsmanship of tribes in the Pacific Northwest coastal region. American Folk

CM955 *Heiltsuk Bella Bella Mask*

CM956 *Chilkat Tlingit Mask*

CM957 *Tlingit Mask*

CM958 *Bella Coola Mask*

Art series. *Gravure, perforated 11.*

CM955 *(1834)*
  15c multicolored, tagged *(152,404,000)* .30 .20
CM956 *(1835)*
  15c multicolored, tagged   .30 .20
CM957 *(1836)*
  15c multicolored, tagged   .30 .20
CM958 *(1837)*
  15c multicolored, tagged   .30 .20
    Plate block of 10   7.00
    y. Se-tenant block of four
      CM955-58   2.25 1.50
    FDC *(Sept. 25, 1980)*   2.00

1980. American Architecture Issue, second of four se-tenant quartets, representing 19th-century architecture of enduring beauty, strength and usefulness. *Intaglio (Gioro Press), perforated 11.*

CM959 *(1838)*
  15c black and red, tagged *(152,720,000)* .30 .20
CM960 *(1839)*
  15c black and red, tagged   .30 .20

CM959 *Smithsonian Institution in Washington, D.C., designed by James Renwick*

CM960 *Trinity Church in Boston, designed by Henry Hobson Richardson*

CM961 *Pennsylvania Academy of Fine Arts in Philadelphia, designed by Frank Furness*

CM962 *Lyndhurst at Tarr at Tarrytown, New York, designed by Alexander Jackson Davis*

CM961 *(1840)*
  15c black and red, tagged   .30 .20
CM962 *(1841)*
  15c black and red, tagged   .30 .20
    Plate block of four   2.50
    y. Se-tenant block of four
      CM959-62   2.25 1.50
    FDC *(Oct. 9, 1980)*   2.00

1981. Everett Dirksen Issue commemorates a public servant first elected from Illinois to the U.S. House of Representatives in 1932, then to the U.S. Senate in 1950, where he served until his death in 1969. Dirksen was noted for his oratory and attention to legislative detail. *Intaglio, perforated 11.*

CM963 *Everett Dirksen*

CM963 *(1874)*
  15c gray, tagged *(160,155,000)*   .30 .20
    Plate block of four   2.50
    FDC *(Jan. 4, 1981)*   1.00

1981. Whitney Moore Young Issue honors ted civil rights leader who was executive direc le National Urban League at his death. You an author, former dean of the Atlanta Sc ocial Work and a recipient of the Medal of Freed ck Heritage series. *Gravure, perforated 11.*

CM964 *Whitney M. Young*

CM964 *(1875)*
  15c multicolored, tagged *(159,505,000)* .30   .20
    Plate block of four   1.80
    FDC *(Jan. 30, 1981)*   1.00

1981. Flower Issue features the designs of four flowers cultivated in the United States, reproduced from original paintings by Lowell Nesbitt in se-tenant form. *Gravure, perforated 11.*

CM965
Rose

CM966
Camellia

CM967
Dahlia

CM968 *Lily*

CM965 *(1876)*
  18c multicolored, tagged *(210,633,000)* .30   .20
CM966 *(1877)*
  18c multicolored, tagged   .30   .20
CM967 *(1878)*
  18c multicolored, tagged   .30   .20
CM968 *(1879)*
  18c multicolored, tagged   .30   .20
    Plate block of four   2.60
    y. Se-tenant block of four
        CM 965-68   2.00   1.50
    FDC *(April 23, 1981)*   2.00

1981. American Red Cross Issue marks the centennial of the organization and honors the thousands of Red Cross volunteers who have given freely of their time to help people throughout the country. *Gravure, perforated 10 1/2 x 11.*

CM969 *Nurse and Baby*

CM969 *(1910)*
  18c multicolored, tagged *(165,175,000)* .30   .20
    Plate block of four   2.80
    FDC *(May 1, 1981)*   1.00

1981. Savings and Loans Issue marks the sesquicentennial of the first savings and loan organization in the United States, and emphasizes the importance of thrift and home ownership. *Gravure, perforated 11.*

CM970 *Savings and Loan Building, Coin Bank*

CM970 *(1911)*
  18c multicolored, tagged *(107,240,000)* .30   .20
    Plate block of four   2.50
    FDC *(May 8, 1981)*   1.00

1981. Space Achievement Issue salutes the U.S. accomplishments and technology in space research. *Gravure, perforated 11.*

CM971   CM975   CM976   CM973

CM972   CM977   CM978   CM974

CM971 *Astronaut on Moon,* CM972 *Pioneer II and Saturn,* CM973 *Skylab and Sun,* CM974 *Hubble Space Telescope* CM975*Space Shuttle in orbit,* CM976 *Space Shuttle with Arm deployed,* CM977 *Space Shuttle at Launch,* CM978 *Space Shuttle prior to Landing*

CM971 *(1912)*
  18c multicolored, tagged *(337,819,000)* .30   .20
CM972 *(1913)*
  18c multicolored, tagged   .30   .20
CM973 *(1914)*
  18c multicolored, tagged   .30   .20
CM974 *(1915)*
  18c multicolored, tagged   .30   .20
CM975 *(1916)*
  18c multicolored, tagged   .30   .20
CM976 *(1917)*
  18c multicolored, tagged   .30   .20
CM977 *(1918)*
  18c multicolored, tagged   .30   .20
CM978 *(1919)*
  18c multicolored, tagged   .30   .20
    Plate block of eight   6.00
    y. Se-tenant block of eight
        CM971-78   5.00   4.00
    v. Se-tenant block of eight,
        imperforate   9,500.

1981. Professional Management Issue marks the 100th anniversary of professional management education in the United States, and honored Joseph Wharton, founder of the Wharton School of Business. *Gravure, perforated 11.*

CM979 *Joseph Wharton*

CM979 *(1920)*
  18c blue and black, tagged *(99,420,000)* .30   .20
    Plate block of four   2.40
    FDC *(June 18, 1981)*   1.00

1981. Save Wildlife Habitats Issue focuses on the necessity for the preservation of the natural environment of our native birds and mammals. *Gravure, perforated 11.*

CM980 *Blue Heron*

CM981 *Badger*

CM982 *Grizzly Bear*

CM983 *Ruffed Grouse*

CM980 *(1921)*
  18c multicolored, tagged *(178,930,000)* .30   .20
CM981 *(1922)*
  18c multicolored, tagged   .30   .20
CM982 *(1923)*
  18c multicolored, tagged   .30   .20
CM983 *(1924)*
  18c multicolored, tagged   .30   .20
    Plate block of four   2.50
    y. Se-tenant block of four
        CM980-83   2.25   1.50
    FDC *(June 26, 1981)*   2.00

1981. Disabled Persons Issue hails the International Year of Disabled Persons designated by the U.N., and in the worldwide effort to promote education, prevention of impairments and rehabilitation. *Gravure, perforated 11.*

CM984 *Disabled Man Using Microscope*

CM984 *(1925)*
  18c multicolored, tagged *(100,265,00)* .30   .20
    Plate block of four   2.40
    FDC *(June 29, 1981)*   1.00

    v. Vertical pair, imperforate
      horizontally   2,750.

1981. Edna St. Vincent Millay Issue honors the poet and author who received, among other awards, the Pulitzer Prize for Poetry in 1923. *Offset and intaglio, perforated 11.*

CM985 *Edna St. Vincent Millay. From miniature painting by Glenora Case Richards*

CM985 *(1926)*
  18c multicolored, tagged *(99,615,000)* .30   .25
    Plate block of four   2.40
    FDC *(July 10, 1981)*   1.00
    v. Intaglio block (inscriptions)
      omitted   525.

1981. Alcoholism Issue conveys the message that alcoholism is a treatable disease. *Intaglio, perforated 11.*

CM986 *Alcoholism - You Can Beat It!*

CM986 *(1927)*
  18c blue and black, tagged *(97,535,000)* .65   .20
    Plate block of 20   40.00
    FDC *(Aug. 19, 1981)*   1.00
    v. Imperforate pair   425.
    v1. Vertical pair, imperforate
      horizontally   1,850.

1981. American Architecture Issue, the third of four quartets or se-tenant this subject, features examples of successful work by late 19th and early 20th century American architects. *Intaglio, perforated 11.*

CM987 *New York University Library, by Stanford White*

CM988 *Biltmore House, Asheville, N.C. by Richard Morris Hunt*

CM989 *Palace of Arts, San Francisco, Calif. by Bernard Maybeck*

CM990 *Bank, Owatonna, Minn., by Louis Sullivan*

CM987 *(1928)*
18c black and red, tagged *(167,308,000)* .30   .20
CM988 *(1929)*
18c black and red, tagged   .30   .20
CM989 *(1930)*
18c black and red, tagged   .30   .20
CM990 *(1931)*
18c black and red, tagged   .30   .20
          Plate block of four   3.00
          y. Se-tenant block of
              four CM987-90   2.75
          FDC *(Aug. 28, 1981)*   2.00

1981. Bobby Jones and Babe Zaharias Issues
inaugurated the American Sports Series honoring
famous American athletes. In 1930 Bobby Jones became
the only golfer in history to win the Grand Slam of Golf .
Babe Zaharias, one of the greatest athletes of the first
half of the 20th century, won virtually every women's
golf title, both as an amateur and as a professional.
Intaglio, perforated 10 1/2 x 11.

CM991 *Bobby Jones*

CM991 *(1933)*
18c green, tagged *(99,170,000)*   .30   .20
          Plate block of four   7.75
          FDC *(Sept. 22, 1981)*   1.00

CM992 *Babe Zaharias*

CM992 *(1932)*
18c light violet, tagged *(101,625,000)* .30   .20
          Plate block of four   4.00
          FDC *(Sept. 22, 1981)*   1.00

1981. Frederic Remington Issue again honors the
American painter, illustrator and sculptor. *Offset and
intaglio, perforated 11.*

CM993 *Frederic Remington's
Coming Through the Rye*

CM993 *(1934)*
18c multicolored, tagged *(101,155,000)* .30   .20
          Plate block of four   2.40
          FDC *(Oct. 9, 1981)*   1.00
          v. Brown omitted   550.
          v1. Vertical pair, imperforate
              between   250.

1981. James Hoban Issues honors the Irish-American
architect of the White House. The Irish Postal
Administration and the U.S. Postal Service jointly issued
stamps identical in design except for country
designation and denomination (Ireland 528). The issue
was released by the USPS in two denominations: the
lower to accommodate the then-current first-class letter
rate; and the higher to accommodate the rate that went
into effect a little more than two weeks following the
release of the stamps. *Gravure, perforated 11.*

CM994-CM995 *James Hoban and
White House*

CM994 *(1935)*
18c multicolored, tagged *(101,200,000)* .30   .20
          Plate block of four   2.40
          FDC *(Oct. 13, 1981)*   1.00

CM995 *(1936)*
20c multicolored, tagged *(167,360,000)* .35   .20
          Plate block of four   2.50
          FDC *(Oct. 13, 1981)*   1.00

**1981. Battle of Yorktown and the Battle of the
Virginia Capes Issue** commemorates the bicentennial of
the two battles. The Battle of the Virginia Capes of Sept.
5, 1781, prevented the British fleet from aiding British
troops, a critical turning point in the Revolutionary War.
The Battle of Yorktown, Oct. 16-19, ending with the
surrender of the British, marked the end of the final
battle of the war. *Offset and intaglio, perforated 11.*

CM996 *Map of Yorktown*

CM997 *Map of Virginia Capes*

CM996 *(1937)*
18c multicolored, tagged *(162,420,000)* .30   .20
          v. Intalglio back
              (inscriptions) omitted   175.
          zo. Tagging omitted   —

CM997 *(1938)*
18c multicolored, tagged   .30   .20
          Plate block of four   3.00
          y. Se-tenant pair CM996-97
          FDC *(Oct. 16, 1981)*   1.00
          v. Intalglio black
              (inscriptions) omitted   175.
          vy. Se-tenant pair, Intaglio black
              (inscriptions) omitted   425.
          zo. Tagging omitted   —
          zoy. Se-tenant pair, tagging omitted —

1981. John Hanson Issue commemorates the American Revolutionary leader elected first president of the Continental Congress Nov. 5, 1781. Elected "President of the United States in Congress Assembled," and often considered the first president of the United States, Hanson was a congressional presiding officer and had none of the powers of the president under the Constitution. *Gravure, perforated 11.*

CM998 *John Hanson*

CM998 *(1941)*
20c multicolored, tagged *(167,130,000)* .30   .20
FDC *(Nov. 5, 1981)*   1.00

1981. Desert Plants Issue depicts four plants that grow in the arid American West. Three are in the cactus family, and the agave is a succulent plant of the amaryllis family. *Offset and intaglio, perforated 11.*

CM1000

CM999   CM1001   CM1002

CM999 *Barrel cactus*, CM1000 *Agave*, CM1001 *Beavertail cactus*, CM1002 *Saguaro*

CM999 *(1942)*
20c multicolored, tagged *(191,560,000)* .35   .20
CM1000 *(1943)*
20c multicolored, tagged   .35   .20
CM1001 *(1944)*
20c multicolored, tagged   .35   .20
CM1002 *(1945)*
20c multicolored, tagged   .35   .20
    v. Vertical pair (CM1002), imperforate
    Plate block of four   3.25
    FDC *(Dec. 11, 1981)*   2.00
    y. Se-tenant block of
       four C999-1002   2.00
    vy. Se-tenant block of four,
       intaglio brown omitted   8,000.

1982. Franklin D. Roosevelt Issue commemorates the 100th birthday of the 32nd president of the United States, the only president to be elected four times, Roosevelt was inaugurated in 1933 and served as president through the New Deal era and World War II until his death in April 1945. *Intaglio, perforated 11.*

CM1003 *Franklin D. Roosevelt*

CM1003 *(1950)*
20c blue, tagged *(163,939,200)*   .35   .20
    Plate block of four   2.50
    FDC *(Jan. 30, 1982)*   1.00

CM1004-04A *Love In Blooms* "L": miniature poppy; "O": painted daisies and miniature pansies; "V": cornflower; "E": coralbells

1982 Love Issue celebrates special occasions, such as birthdays, anniversaries, weddings and other special sentiments. Flowers form the letters "L": miniature poppy; "O" : painted daisies and miniature pansies; "V" : cornflower; "E" : corabells. *Gravure, perforated 11 x 10 1/2.*

Perforated 11
CM1004 *(1951)*
20c multicolored, tagged   .35   .20
    Plate block of four   3.25

Perforated 11 x 10 1/2
CM1004A *(1951a)*
20c multicolored, tagged   1.00   .25
    Plate block of four   5.50
    FDC *(Feb. 1, 1982)*   1.00
    v. Blue omitted   225.
    v1. Imperforate pair   275.

CM1005 *George Washington*

1982 George Washington Issue commemorates the 250th anniversary of his birth. *Gravure, perforated 11.*

CM1005 *(1952)*
20c multicolored, tagged *(180,700,000)* .35   .20
    Plate block of four   2.75
    FDC *(Feb. 22, 1982)*   1.00

1982. State Birds and Flowers Issue commemorates the official birds and flowers of all 50 states. Arranged in alphabetical order in the pane, from top-left to bottom right, these stamps were designed by the father-and-son team of Arthur and Alan Singer. Arthur, the father, created the birds designs and Alan contributed the flower designs. *Gravure.*
Perforated 10 1/2 x 11

CM1019 (1966)		
20c Indiana, tagged	1.00	.50
CM1020 (1967)		
20c Iowa, tagged	1.00	.50
CM1021 (1968)		
20c Kansas, tagged	1.00	.50
CM1022 (1969)		
20c Kentucky, tagged	1.00	.50

CM1006 (1953)				CM1023 (1970)		
20c Alabama, tagged (666,950,000)	1.00	.50		**20c Louisiana,** tagged	1.00	.50
CM1007 (1954)				**CM1024** (1971)		
20c Alaska, tagged	1.00	.50		**20c Maine,** tagged	1.00	.50
CM1008 (1955)				**CM1025** (1972)		
20c Arizona, tagged	1.00	.50		**20c Maryland,** tagged	1.00	.50
CM1009 (1956)				**CM1026** (1973)		
20c Arkansas, tagged	1.00	.50		**20c Massachusetts,** tagged	1.00	.50
CM1010 (1957)				**CM1027** (1974)		
20c California, tagged	1.00	.50		**20c Michigan,** tagged	1.00	.50
CM1011 (1958)				**CM1028** (1975)		
20c Colorado, tagged	1.00	.50		**20c Minnesota,** tagged	1.00	.50
CM1012 (1959)				**CM1029** (1976)		
20c Connecticut, tagged	1.00	.50		**20c Mississippi,** tagged	1.00	.50
CM1013 (1960)				**CM1030** (1977)		
20c Delaware, tagged	1.00	.50		**20c Missouri,** tagged	1.00	.50
CM1014 (1961)				**CM1031** (1978)		
20c Florida, tagged	1.00	.50		**20c Montana,** tagged	1.00	.50
CM1015 (1962)				**CM1032** (1979)		
20c Georgia, tagged	1.00	.50		**20c Nebraska,** tagged	1.00	.50
CM1016 (1963)				**CM1033** (1980)		
20c Hawaii, tagged	1.00	.50		**20c Nevada,** tagged	1.00	.50
CM1017 (1964)				**CM1034** (1981)		
20c Idaho, tagged	1.00	.50		**20c New Hampshire,** tagged	1.00	.50
CM1018 (1965)				**CM1035** (1982)		
20c Illinois, tagged	1.00	.50		**20c New Jersey,** tagged	1.00	.50

CM1036 *(1983)*		
20c New Mexico, tagged	1.00	.50
CM1037 *(1984)*		
20c New York, tagged	1.00	.50
CM1038 *(1985)*		
20c North Carolina, tagged	1.00	.50
CM1039 *(1986)*		
20c North Dakota, tagged	1.00	.50
CM1040 *(1987)*		
20c Ohio, tagged	1.00	.50
CM1041 *(1988)*		
20c Oklahoma, tagged	1.00	.50
CM1042 *(1989)*		
20c Oregon, tagged	1.00	.50
CM1043 *(1990)*		
20c Pennsylvania, tagged	1.00	.50
CM1044 *(1991)*		
20c Rhode Island, tagged	1.00	.50
CM1045 *(1992)*		
20c South Carolina, tagged	1.00	.50
CM1046 *(1993)*		
20c South Dakota,tagged	1.00	.50
CM1047 *(1994)*		
20c Tennessee, tagged	1.00	.50
CM1048 *(1995)*		
20c Texas, tagged	1.00	.50
CM1049 *(1996)*		
20c Utah, tagged	1.00	.50
CM1050 *(1997)*		
20c Vermont, tagged	1.00	.50
CM1051 *(1998)*		
20c Virginia, tagged	1.00	.50
CM1052 *(1999)*		
20c Washington, tagged	1.00	.50
CM1053 *(2000)*		
20c West Virginia, tagged	1.00	.50
CM1054 *(2001)*		
20c Wisconsin, tagged	1.00	.50
CM1055 *(2002)*		
20c Wyoming, tagged	1.00	.50
y. Se-tenant pane of 50	45.	
FDC *(April 14, 1982)*		1.00
FDC, pane of 50		15.
v. Imperforate pane of 50	23,150.	

Because most plate block collectors consider that a plate block contains at least one copy of each stamp in the issue, a plate block of the State Birds and Flowers Issue is considered to be a full pane of 50 stamps.

Perforated 11

CM1006A *(1953a)*		
20c Alabama, tagged	1.00	.50
CM1007A *(1954a)*		
20c Alaska, tagged	1.00	.50
CM1008A *(1955a)*		
20c Arizona, tagged	1.00	.50
CM1009A *(1956a)*		
20c Arkansas, tagged	1.00	.50
CM1010A *(1957a)*		
20c California, tagged	1.00	.50

CM1011A *(1958a)*		
20c Colorado, tagged	1.00	.50
CM1012A *(1959a)*		
20c Connecticut, tagged	1.00	.50
CM1013A *(1960a)*		
20c Delaware, tagged	1.00	.50
CM1014A *(1961a)*		
20c Florida, tagged	1.00	.50
CM1015A *(1962a)*		
20c Georgia, tagged	1.00	.50
CM1016A *(1963a)*		
20c Hawaii, tagged	1.00	.50
CM1017A *(1964a)*		
20c Idaho, tagged	1.00	.50
CM1018A *(1965a)*		
20c Illinois, tagged	1.00	.50
CM1019A *(1966a)*		
20c Indiana, tagged	1.00	.50
CM1020A *(1967a)*		
20c Iowa, tagged	1.00	.50
CM1021A *(1968a)*		
20c Kansas, tagged	1.00	.50
CM1022A *(1969a)*		
20c Kentucky, tagged	1.00	.50
CM1023A *(1970a)*		
20c Louisiana, tagged	1.00	.50
CM1024A *(1971a)*		
20c Maine, tagged	1.00	.50
CM1025A *(1972a)*		
20c Maryland, tagged	1.00	.50
CM1026A *(1973a)*		
20c Massachusetts, tagged	1.00	.50
CM1027A *(1974a)*		
20c Michigan, tagged	1.00	.50
CM1028A *(1975a)*		
20c Minnesota, tagged	1.00	.50
CM1029A *(1976a)*		
20c Mississippi, tagged	1.00	.50
CM1030A *(1977a)*		
20c Missouri, tagged	1.00	.50
CM1031A *(1978a)*		
20c Montana, tagged	1.00	.50
CM1032A *(1979a)*		
20c Nebraska, tagged	1.00	.50
CM1033A *(1980a)*		
20c Nevada, tagged	1.00	.50
CM1034A *(1981a)*		
20c New Hampshire, tagged	1.00	.50
CM1035A *(1982a)*		
20c New Jersey, tagged	1.00	.50
CM1036A *(1983a)*		
20c New Mexico, tagged	1.00	.50
CM1037A *(1984a)*		
20c New York, tagged	1.00	.50
CM1038A *(1985a)*		
20c North Carolina, tagged	1.00	.50
CM1039A *(1986a)*		
20c North Dakota, tagged	1.00	.50
CM1040A *(1987a)*		
20c Ohio, tagged	1.00	.50

CM1041A *(1988a)*
20c **Oklahoma,** tagged   1.00   .50
CM1042A *(1989a)*
20c **Oregon,** tagged   1.00   .50
CM1043A *(1990a)*
20c **Pennsylvania,** tagged   1.00   .50
CO1044A *(1991a)*
20c **Rhode Island,** tagged   1.00   .50
CM1045A *(1992a)*
20c **South Carolina,** tagged   1.00   .50
CM1046A *(1993a)*
20c **South Dakota,** tagged   1.00   .50
CM1047A *(1994a)*
20c **Tennessee,** tagged   1.00   .50
CM1048A *(1995a)*
20c **Texas,** tagged   1.00   .50
CM1049A *(1996a)*
20c **Utah,** tagged   1.00   .50
CM1050A *(1997a)*
20c **Vermont,** tagged   1.00   .50
CM1051A *(1998a)*
20c **Virginia,** tagged   1.00   .50
CM1052A *(1999a)*
20c **Washington,** tagged   1.00   .50
CM1053A *(2000a)*
20c **West Virginia,** tagged   1.00   .50
CM1054A *(2001a)*
20c **Wisconsin,** tagged   1.00   .50
CM1055A *(2002a)*
20c **Wyoming,** tagged   1.00   .50
        y. Se-tenant pane of 50   47.50

1982. Netherlands Issue marks the 200th anniversary of Netherlands' diplomatic recognition of the United States. The Netherlands released two stamps at the same time as this one (Netherlands 1365-66). *Gravure, perforated 11.*

CM1056 *200th Anniversary of Netherlands Diplomatic Recognization of the United States*

CM1056 *(2003)*
20c **orange, red, blue and dark gray,**
        tagged *(109,245,000)*   .35   .20
        Plate block of six   13.95
        FDC *(Apr. 20, 1982)*   1.00
        v. Imperforate pair   300.

1982. Library of Congress Issue salutes the library for the services and information it provides to Congress and many other organizations and researchers who use it every year. *Intgaglio, perforated 11.*

CM1057 *Library of Congress*

CM1057 *(2004)*
20c **black and red,** tagged *(112,535,000)* .35   .20
        Plate block of four   2.50
        FDC *(Apr. 21, 1982)*   1.00

1982. Knoxville World's Fair Issue commemorates the Knoxville, Tenn., World's Fair, the theme of which was energy. Four stamps depict solar, fossil, nuclear and synthetic fuel energy sources. *Gravure, perforated 11.*

CM1058
*Solar
energy*

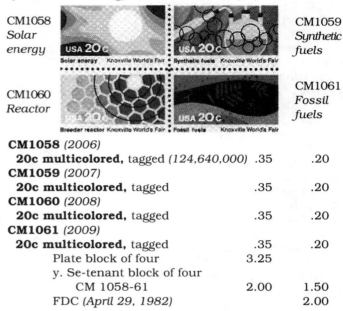

CM1059
*Synthetic
fuels*

CM1060
Reactor

CM1061
*Fossil
fuels*

CM1058 *(2006)*
20c **multicolored,** tagged *(124,640,000)* .35   .20
CM1059 *(2007)*
20c **multicolored,** tagged   .35   .20
CM1060 *(2008)*
20c **multicolored,** tagged   .35   .20
CM1061 *(2009)*
20c **multicolored,** tagged   .35   .20
        Plate block of four   3.25
        y. Se-tenant block of four
                CM 1058-61   2.00   1.50
        FDC *(April 29, 1982)*   2.00

1982. Horatio Alger Issue honors the 150th birhtday of Alger, a best-selling author of books for boys, with more than 100 of his works published during his lifetime. Alger's *Phil the Fiddler, or The Story of a Young Street Musician* is credited with bringing public and legislative attention to forced child labor. *Intaglio, perforated 11.*

CM1062 *Horatio Alger. Frontispiece from* Ragged Dick *series by Alger*

CM1062 *(2010)*
20c **red and black on tan paper,** tagged
        (107,605,000)   .35   .20
        Plate block of four   2.50
        FDC *(April 30, 1982)*   1.00
        v. Red and black omitted   —

1982. Aging Together Issue honors the elderly and heightens awareness that older persons enrich society with their wealth of experience and creative energy. *Intaglio, perforated 11.*

CM1063 *Aging together*

CM1063 *(2011)*
20c **brown,** tagged *(173,160,000)*   .35   .20
        Plate block of four   2.50
        FDC *(May 21, 1982)*   1.00

1982. The Barrymores Issue honors the distinguished American theatrical family, featuring likenesses of Ethel, John, and Lionel Barrymore. Performing Artists series. *Gravure, perforated 11.*

CM1064 *Ethel, John and Lionel Barrymore*

CM1064 *(2012)*
  20c multicolored, tagged *(107,285,000)* .35   .20
    Plate block of four   2.50
    FDC *(June 8, 1982)*   1.00

1982. Mary Walker Issue commemorates the Civil War surgeon who gave care and treatment to the sick and the wounded. *Gravure, perforated 11.*

CM1065 *Dr. Mary Walker*

CM1065 *(2013)*
  20c multicolored, tagged *(109,040,000)* .35   .20
    Plate block of four   3.00
    FDC *(June 10, 1982)*   1.00

1982. International Peace Garden Issue recognizes the 50th anniversary of the garden shared by Dunseith, N.D., and Boissevain, Manitoba. A symbol of more than 150 years of peace and friendship between the United States and Canada. *Offset and intaglio, perforated 11.*

CM1066 *Maple Leaf and Rose*

CM1066 *(2014)*
  20c multicolored, tagged *(183,270,000)* .35   .20
    Plate block of four   2.50
    FDC *(June 30, 1982)*   1.00
    v. Black and intaglio
        green omitted   275.

1982. America's Libraries Issue honors the contribution of libraries to the growth and development of the United States. *Intaglio, perforated 11.*

CM1067 *America's Libraries*

CM1067 *(2015)*
  20c red and black, tagged *(169,495,000)* .35   .20
    Plate block of four   2.50
    FDC *(July 13, 1982)*   1.00
    v. Vertical pair, imperforate
        horizontally   —
    zo. Tagging omitted   —

1982. Jackie Robinson Issue honors the athlete who broke major league baseball's racial barrier in 1947. Hired to play for the Dodgers' top farm team and then for the Dodgers in 1947, he withstood racial hostility to become one of the most exciting baseball players of his era. Black Heritage series. *Gravure, perforated 10 1/2 x 11.*

CM1068 *Jackie Robinson*

CM1068 *(2016)*
  20c multicolored, tagged *(164,235,000)* 2.50   .20
    Plate block of four   11.
    FDC *(Aug. 2, 1982)*   2.00

1982.Touro Synagogue Issue honors the oldest existing synagogue in the United States. Designated a National Historical Site in 1946, the synagogue was built principally by Sephardic Jews from Spain and Portugal who fled the Inquisition and found religious freedom in the Rhode Island colony. *Gravure and intaglio, perforated 11.*

CM1069 *Touro Synagogue*

CM1069 *(2017)*
  20c multicolored, tagged *(110,130,000)* .35   .20
    Plate block of 20   13.75
    FDC *(Aug. 22, 1982)*   1.00
    v. Imperforate pair   —

1982. Wolf Trap Farm Issue salutes the Wolf Trap Farm Park for the Performing Arts, a theater in wooded surroundings and part of the National Park System since 1971. (See also CM 679.) *Gravure, perforated 11.*

CM1070 *Wolf Trap Farm Park*

CM1070 *(2018)*
  20c multicolored, tagged *(110,995,000)* .35   .20
    Plate block of four   2.50
    FDC *(Sept. 1, 1982)*   1.00

1982. American Architecture Issue, the fourth and final installment in the series, which honors key structures and architects of the 20th century. *Intaglio, perforated 11.*

CM1071 *Fallingwater, Mill Run, Pa., designed by Frank Lloyd Wright*

CM1072 *Illinois Institute of Technology, Chicago, Ill. designed by Ludwig Mies van der Rohe*

CM1073 *Gropius House, Lincoln, Mass., designed by Walter Gropius in collaberation with Marcel Breuer*

CM1074 *Dulles International Airport, Washington, D.C., designed by Eero Saarinen*

CM1071 *(2019)*
20c black and brown, tagged
   (165,340,000) .35 .20
CM1072 *(2020)*
20c black and brown, tagged .35 .20
CM1073 *(2021)*
20c black and brown, tagged .35 .20
CM1074 *(2022)*
20c black and brown, tagged .35 .20
   Plate block of four 4.25
   y. Se-tenant block of
     four (CM1071-74) 2.00
   FDC *(Sept. 30, 1982)* 2.00

1982. Francis of Assisi Issue honors the 800th birthday of the man whose compassion earned him reverence transcending religious bounds. He formed the Franciscan Order in 1209, the members of which still minister to the sick and needy. *Gravure by J.W.*

Fergusson and Sons for American Bank Note Co., perforated 11.

CM1075 *Francis of Assisi*

CM1075 *(2023)*
20c multicolored, tagged *(174,180,000)* .35 .20
   Plate block of four 2.75
   FDC *(Oct. 7, 1982)* 1.00

1982. Ponce de Leon Issue honors the Spaniard who explored Puerto Rico in 1508-09 and Florida in 1513.*Gravure (Combination Press), perforated 11.*

CM1076 *Ponce de Leon*

CM1076 *(2024)*
20c multicolored, tagged *(110,261,000)* .35 .20
   Plate block of six 16.00
   FDC *(Oct. 12, 1982)* 1.00
   v. Imperforate pair —
   v1. Vertical pair, imperforate
     between and at top —

1983. Science and Industry Issue salutes their contributions to the growth and development of the United States. *Offset and intaglio, perforated 11.*

CM1077 *Science and Industry*

CM1077 *(2031)*
20c multicolored, tagged
   (118,555,000) .35 .20
   Plate block of four 2.50
   FDC *(Jan. 19, 1983)* 1.00
   a. Intaglio black omitted —

1983. Sweden Issue marks the 200th anniversary of the signing of the Treaty of Amity and Commerce between Sweden and the United States. A stamp of similar design was issued simultaneously by Sweden (Sweden 1247). *Intaglio, perforated 11.*

CM1078 *Benjamin Franklin and Treaty Seal*

CM1078 *(2036)*
20c multicolored, tagged
   (118,225,000) .30 .25
   Plate block of four 2.50
   FDC *(March 24, 1983)* 1.00

1983. Balloons Issue honors the sport of ballooning. Hot-air balloons were invented in June 1783 by two brothers, Joseph and Jacques Montgolfier, in France. Used for surveillance and scientific research over the years, they are today enjoyed by thousands of recreational enthusiasts. *Gravure, perforated 11.*

CM1080 *Hot air balloon*

| CM1079 | CM1081 *Hot air* | CM1081 |
| Intrepid *1861* | *ballooning* | Explorer II, of *1935* |

CM1079 *(2032)*
20c multicolored, tagged

(226,128,000)	.35	.20

CM1080 *(2033)*
20c multicolored, tagged

	.35	.20

CM1081 *(2034)*
20c multicolored, tagged

	.35	.20

CM1082 *(2035)*
20c multicolored, tagged

	.35	.20
Plate block of four	3.00	
y. Se-tenant block of four CM1079-82	2.00	
FDC *(March 31, 1983)*	2.00	
vy. Se-tenant block of four, imperforate		

1983. Civilian Conservation Corps Issue honors the 50th anniversary of the Great Depression programs, which recruited thousands of unemployed young men to develop and conserve the nation's natural resources. *Gravure, perforated 11.*

CM1083 *Civilian Conservation Corps*

CM1083 *(2037)*
20c multicolored, tagged

(114,290,000)	.35	.20
Plate block of four	2.50	
FDC *(April 5, 1983)*		1.00
v. Imperforate pair	—	

1983. Joseph Priestly Issue commemorates the clergyman and chemist who discovered oxygen. *Gravure, perforated 11.*

CM1084 *Joseph Priestly*

CM1084 *(2038)*
20c multicolored, tagged

(165,000,000)	.35	.20
Plate block of four	3.00	
FDC *(April 13, 1983)*		1.00

1983. Volunteer Issue recognizes the contribution volunteers have made to the development of the United States. *Intaglio, perforated 11.*

CM1085 *Helping Hand*

CM1085 *(2039)*
20c red and black, tagged

(120,430,000)	.35	.20
Plate block of 20	13.95	
FDC *(April 20, 1983)*		1.00
v. Imperforate pair	—	

1983. German Concord Issue honors the 300th anniversary of the arrival of the first German immigrants to the United States. A stamp of similar design was issued six days after the U.S. issue by West Germany (2363). *Intaglio, perforated 11.*

CM1086 Concord *1683, German Immigration Tricentennial*

CM1086 *(2040)*
20c brown, tagged *(117,025,000)*

	.35	.20
Plate block of four	2.50	
FDC *(April 29, 1983)*		1.00

1983. Physical Fitness Issue salutes physical fitness activities for maintaining good physical health. *Gravure (Combination Press), perforated 11.*

CM1087 *Physical Fitness*

CM1087 *(2043)*
20c multicolored, tagged

(111,775,000)	.35	.20
Plate block of 20	13.95	
FDC *(May 14, 1983)*		1.00

1983. Brooklyn Bridge Centennial Issue honors the 100th anniversary of the completion of the bridge, created by 19th-century civil engineer John A. Roebling, 19th century civil engineer, and his son Washington, May 24, 1883. *Intaglio, perforated 11.*

CM1088 *Brooklyn Bridge*

CM1088 *(2041)*
  20c blue, tagged *(181,700,000)*   .35   .20
    Plate block of four   2.50
    FDC *(May 17, 1983)*   1.00
    zo. Tagging omitted

1983. Tennessee Valley Authority Issue marks the 50th anniversary of its establishment, providing flood control through a system of dams and locks, developing the natural resources of the area and creating new industry. Gravure and intaglio (Combination Press), perforated 11.

CM1089 *Norris Hydroelectric Dam*

CM1089 *(2042)*
  20c multicolored, tagged *(114,250,000)* .35   .20
    Plate block of 20   13.95
    FDC *(May 18, 1983)*   1.00

1983. Medal of Honor Issue salutes the United States' highest military award and all those who have been awarded the medal. It is awarded only for "courage above and beyond the call of duty." Offset and intaglio, perforated 11.

CM1090 *Medal of Honor*

CM1090 *(2045)*
  20c multicolored, tagged *(108,820,000)* .35   .20
    Plate block of four   3.00
    FDC *(June 7, 1983)*   1.00
    v. Red omitted   325.

1983. Scott Joplin Issue honors the ragtime composer who successfully combined the charm of late Victorian music and the lively qualities of pioneer American folk song and dance. Black Heritage series. *Gravure, perforated 11.*

CM1091 *Scott Joplin*

CM1091 *(2044)*
  20c multicolored, tagged *(115,200,000)* .35   .20
    Plate block of four   3.00
    FDC *(June 9, 1983)*   1.00
    v. Imperforate pair   —

1983. Babe Ruth Issue commemorates the great baseball player and Hall of Fame member George Herman Ruth (1895-1948). American Sports series. *Intaglio, perforated 10 1/2 x 11.*

CM1092 *Babe Ruth*

CM1092 *(2046)*
  20c blue, tagged *(184,950,000)*   .35   .20
    Plate block of four   9.75
    FDC *(July 6, 1983)*   1.00

1983. Nathaniel Hawthorne Issue honors the American author of the novel, *The House of Seven Gables.* A master at writing tales, Hawthorne was one of the first American writers who built his stories around the New England of his forefathers. Literary Arts series. *Gravure, perforated 11.*

CM1093 *Nathaniel Hawthorne*

CM1093 *(2047)*
  20c multicolored, tagged *(110,925,000)* .35   .20
    Plate block of four   2.50
    FDC *(July 8, 1983)*   1.00

1983. 1984 Olympic Issue was the first of an array of postal paper designed by Robert Peak, commemorating the Summer Games in Los Angeles and the Winter Games in Sarajevo, Yugoslavia. (see also CM1111-14, CM1126-29, A101-12, ALS19, PC96 and PC98.) *Gravure, perforated 11.*

CM1094 *Discus*   CM1095 *High jump*

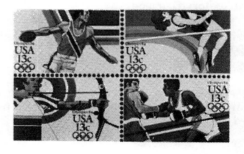

CM1096 *Archery*   CM1097 *Boxing*

CM1094 *(2048)*
  13c multicolored, tagged *(395,424,000)* .25   .20
CM1095 *(2049)*
  13c multicolored, tagged   .25   .20

CM1096 *(2050)*
13c multicolored, tagged   .25   .20
CM1097 *(2051)*
13c multicolored, tagged   .25   .20
    Plate block of four   3.75
    y. Se-tenant block of
        four (CM1094-97)   2.00
    FDC *(July 28, 1983)*   2.00

1983. Treaty of Paris Issue marks the 200th anniversary of the Treaty of Paris, which officially ended the American Revolution and was signed by John Adams, Benjamin Franklin, and John Jay. The treaty also established the boundaries of the nation at the Great Lakes, the Mississippi River and the northern border of Florida. *Gravure, perforated 11.*

CM1098 *Treaty of Paris, 1783*

US Bicentennial 20 cents

CM1098 *(2052)*
20c multicolored, tagged *(104,340,000)* .35   .20
    Plate block of four   2.75
    FDC *(Sept. 2, 1983)*   1.00

1983. Civil Service Issue marks 100 years of federal civil service. *Gravure and intaglio, perforated 11.*

CM1099 *Civil Service*

CM1099 *(2053)*
20c beige, blue and red, tagged
      (114,725,000)   .35   .20
    Plate block of 20   13.95
    FDC *(Sept. 9, 1983)*   1.00

1983. Metropolitan Opera Issue celebrates the centennial of the Metropolitan Opera in New York, combining features from the original Metropolitan Opera (the proscenium arch above the stage) and the new building at Lincoln Center (the five-arched entrance). *Offset and intaglio, perforated 11.*

CM1100 *Metropolitan Opera*

CM1100 *(2054)*
20c dark carmine and yellow orange,
      tagged *(112,525,000)*   .35   .20
    Plate block of four   2.75
    FDC *(Sept. 14, 1983)*   1.00
    zo. Tagging omitted   —

1983. American Inventor's Issue honors Charles Steinmetz, Edwin Armstrong, Nikola Tesla, and Philo T. Farnsworth. Steinmetz pioneered research on alternating current and high-voltage power. Armstrong's crowning achievement is wide-band frequency modulation, now used in FM radio. Tesla, creator of more than 700 inventions, is best known for the induction motor. Farnsworth, with more than 300 inventions in television and related fields, is most famous for the first all-electronic television transmission in 1927. *Offset and intaglio, perforated 11.*

CM1101 *Charles Steinmetz*   CM1102 *Edwin Armstrong*

CM1103 *Nikola Tesla*   CM1104 *Philo T. Farnsworth*

CM1101 *(2055)*
20c multicolored, tagged *(193,055,000)* .35   .20
CM1102 *(2056)*
20c multicolored, tagged   .35   .20
CM1103 *(2057)*
20c multicolored, tagged   .35   .20
CM1104 *(2058)*
20c multicolored, tagged   .35   .20
    Plate block of four   4.25
    y. Se-tenant block of
        four CM1101-04   2.00
    FDC *(Sept. 21, 1983)*   2.00
    vy. Block of four,
       black omitted   450.
    vy1. Black omitted, any single   100.

1983. Streetcar Stamps Issue pays tribute to the evolution of importance of the streetcar in the United States. *Offset and intaglio, perforated 11.*

CM1105 *First American streetcar New York City, 1832*   CM1106 *Early electric streetcar, Montgomery, Alabama, 1886*

CM1107 *"Bobtail" horse car, Sulphur Rock, Arkansas, 1926*   CM1108 *St. Charles streetcar, New Orleans, Louisiana, 1923*

CM1105 *(2059)*
   20c multicolored, tagged *(207,725,000)* .35   .20
CM1106 *(2060)*
   20c multicolored, tagged   .35   .20
CM1107 *(2061)*
   20c multicolored, tagged   .35   .20
CM1108 *(2062)*
   20c multicolored, tagged   .35   .20
      Plate block of four   4.25
      y. Se-tenant block of
          four CM1105-08   2.00
      FDC *(Oct. 8, 1983)*   2.00
      vy. Block of four black omitted   450.
      vy1. Black omitted, any single   75.

1983. Martin Luther Issue commemorates the 500th
birthday of religeous reformer Martin Luther.*Gravure
(American Bank Note Co.), perforated 11.*

CM1109 *Martin Luther*

CM1109 *(2065)*
   20c multicolored, tagged *(165,000,000)* .35   .20
      Plate block of four   2.50
      FDC *(Nov. 10, 1983)*   1.00

1984. Alaska Statehood Issue honors the 25th
anniversary of the 49th state. *Gravure by J.W. Fergusson
and Sons for the American Bank Note Co., perforated 11.*

CM1110 *Alaska Statehood*

CM1110 *(2066)*
   20c multicolored, tagged *(120,000,000)* .35   .20
      Plate block of four   2.50
      FDC *(Jan. 3, 1984)*   1.00

1984. 1984 Winter Olympics Issue features events
from the games in Sarajevo, Yugoslavia. *Gravure,
perforated 10 1/2 x 11.*

CM1111 *(2067)*
   20c multicolored, tagged *(319,675,000)* .35   .20
CM1112 *(2068)*
   20c multicolored, tagged   .35   .20

CM1111 *Ice Dancing*   CM1112 *Alpine Skiing*

CM1113 *Cross-country Skiing*   CM1114 *Ice Hockey*

CM1113 *(2069)*
   20c multicolored, tagged   .35   .20
CM1114 *(2070)*
   20c multicolored, tagged   .35   .20
      Plate block of four   4.25
      y. Se-tenant block of
          four CM1111-14   2.00
      FDC *(Jan. 6, 1984)*   2.00

1984. Federal Deposit Insurance Corporation Issue
honors the 50th anniversary of the institution, which
gives bank depositors limited protection in the event of
bank insolvency. *Gravure, perforated 11.*

CM1115 *Federal Deposit Insurance Corporation*

CM1115 *(2071)*
   20c multicolored, tagged *(103,975,000)* .35   .20
      Plate block of four   2.50
      FDC *(Jan. 12, 1984)*   1.00

1984. Love Issue for use on Valentine's Day as well
other special occasions. This is the third such stamp.
*Gravure and intaglio (Combination Press), Perforated 11 x
10 1/2.*

CM1116 *love*

CM1116 *(2072)*
   20c multicolored, tagged *(554,675,000)* .35   .20
      Plate, block of 20   14.50
      FDC *(Jan. 31, 1984)*   1.00
      v. Horizontal pair, imperforate
          vertically   —
      zo. Tagging omitted   —

1984. Carter G. Woodson Issue honors the African-American historian, teacher and administrator, as well as editor of the *Journal of Negro History*. Black Heritage series. *Gravure by American Bank Note Co., perforated 11.*

CM1117 *Carter G. Woodson*

CM1117 *(2073)*

20c multicolored, tagged *(120,000,000)*	.35		.20
Plate block of four		2.75	
FDC *(Feb. 1, 1984)*			1.00
v. Horizontal pair, imperforate vertically			—

1984. Soil and Water Conservation Issue recognizes the 50th anniversary of government efforts to abate soil erosion and conserve water resources. *Gravure, perforated 11.*

CM1118 *Soil and Water Conservation*

CM1118 *(2074)*

20c multicolored, tagged *(106,975,000)*	.35		.20
Plate block of four		2.50	
FDC *(Feb. 6, 1984)*			1.00

1984. Credit Union Act of 1934 Issue honors the 50th anniversary of the act that enabled "credit unions to be organized everywhere in the United States under charters from the federal government." *Gravure, perforated 11.*

CM1119 *Credit Union Act of 1934*

CM1119 *(2075)*

20c multicolored, tagged *(107,325,000)*	.35		.20
Plate block of four		2.50	
FDC *(Feb. 10, 1984)*			1.00

1984. Orchids Issue featured four different native American orchids: the wild pink orchid is of Florida; yellow lady's slipper of the Midwest; spreading pogonia of the Northeast; and the pacific calypso found along the Pacific Coast. *Gravure, perforated 11.*

CM1120
*Wild
Pink*

CM1121
*Yellow
Lady's
Slipper*

CM1122
*Spreading
Pogonia*

CM1123
*Pacific
Calypso*

CM1120 *(2076)*

20c multicolored, tagged *(306,912,000)*	.35		.20

CM1121 *(2077)*

20c multicolored, tagged		.35	.20

CM1122 *(2078)*

20c multicolored, tagged		.35	.20

CM1123 *(2079)*

20c multicolored, tagged		.35	.20
Plate block of four		3.50	
y. Se-tenant block of four CM1120-23		2.00	
FDC *(Mar. 5, 1984)*			2.00

1984. Hawaii Statehood Issue honors the 25th anniversary of Hawaii statehood. Hawaii was admitted as the 50th state Aug. 21, 1959. *Gravure by the American Bank Note Co., perforated 11.*

CM1124 *Hawaii Statehood*

CM1124 *(2080)*

20c multicolored, tagged *(120,000,000)*	.35		.20
Plate block of four		2.75	
FDC *(March 12, 1984)*			1.00

1984. National Archives Issue marks the 50th anniversary of the National Archives in Washington, D.C., which preserves the Declaration of Independence, the Constitution of the United States, the Bill of Rights and other treasures of America's past such as photographs, maps, sound recordings of film. *Gravure, perforated 11.*

CM1125 *National Archives*

CM1125 *(2081)*

20c multicolored, tagged *(108,000,000)*	.35		.20
Plate block of four		2.75	
FDC *(April 16, 1984)*			1.00

1984. Summer Olympics Issue featured events from the Los Angeles Summer Games. *Gravure, perforated 11.*

CM1126
Men's diving

CM1127
Women's long jump

CM1128
Wrestling

CM1129
Women's canoeing

CM1126 *(2082)*
  20c multicolored, tagged *(313,350,000)* .35   .20
CM1127 *(2083)*
  20c multicolored, tagged   .35   .20
CM1128 *(2084)*
  20c multicolored, tagged   .35   .20
CM1129 *(2085)*
  20c multicolored, tagged   .35   .20
    Plate block of four   5.50
    y. Se-tenant block of four
        CM1126-29   2.00   1.50
    FDC *(May 4, 1984)*   2.00

1984. Louisiana World Exposition Issue honors the exposition that celebrated fresh water, spotlighting rivers and ports of the world through displays and exhibitions. *Gravure, perforated 11.*

CM1130 *Louisiana World Exposition*

CM1130 *(2086)*
  20c multicolored, tagged *(130,320,000)* .35   .20
    Plate block of four   2.75
    FDC *(May 11, 1984)*   1.00

1984. Health Research Issue hails the professionals who have worked to prevent disease and prolong life. *Gravure by the American Bank Note Co., perforated 11.*

CM1131 *Health Research*

CM1131 *(2087)*
  20c multicolored, tagged *(120,000,000)* .35   .20
    Plate block of four   3.00
    FDC *(May 17, 1984)*   1.00

1984. Douglas Fairbanks Issue recalls the actor as part of the Performing Artists series. Together with Charlie Chaplin, D.W. Griffith and Mary Pickford, in 1919 Fairbanks formed United Artists Corp. *Gravure and intaglio (Combination Press), perforated 11.*

CM1132 *Douglas Fairbanks*

CM1132 *(2088)*
  20c multicolored, tagged *(117,050,000)* .35   .20
    Plate, block of 20   17.50
    FDC *(May 23, 1984)*   1.00
    v. Horizontal pair, imperforate
        between   —
    zo. Tagging omitted   —

1984. Jim Thorpe Issue salutes the American athlete whose feats on the track, baseball and football fields are legendary. In 1912, at the Summer Olympics in Stockholm, Thorpe became the first athlete to win both the pentathlon and the decathlon. Later, he was stripped of his medals when it was learned that he had briefly played semi-professional baseball in 1910. In 1983, the International Olympic Committee returned replicas of Thorpe's 1912 medals to his family, restoring his place in Olympic history. American Sports series. *Intaglio, perforated 11.*

CM1133 *Jim Thorpe*

CM1133 *(2089)*
  20c dark brown, tagged *(115,725,000)* .75   .20
    Plate block of four   3.00
    FDC *(May 24, 1984)*   1.00

1984. John McCormack Issue honored the 100th birthday of the Irish-American singer and world-famous tenor who sang with the outstanding opera companies in North America, as well as performing Irish folk songs and ballads in major cities of the world. Part of the Performing Arts series, this stamp was released jointly with an Irish stamp (Ireland 622). *Gravure, perforated 11.*

CM1134 *John McCormack*

CM1134 *(2090)*
   20c multicolored, tagged *(116,600,000)* .35   .20
     Plate block of four   2.50
     FDC *(June 6, 1984)*   1.00

1984. St. Lawrence Seaway Issue commemorates the 25th anniversary of the opening of the seaway, which stretches from the Atlantic Ocean to Duluth, Minn. This was a joint issue with Canada (Canada 1085). *Gravure by the American Bank Note Co., perforated 11.*

CM1135 *St. Lawrence Seaway*

CM1135 *(2091)*
   20c multicolored, tagged *(120,000,000)* .35   .20
     Plate block of four   2.50
     FDC *(June 26, 1984)*   1.00

1984. Wetlands Preservation Issue marks the 50th anniversary of the Migratory Bird Hunting and Conservation Stamp Act, enacted in 1934 as a result of a proposal by conservationist Jay Norwood ("Ding") Darling for a federal revenue stamp required to be purchased by waterfowl hunters. Funds from the sale of these stamps go to buy and lease waterfowl habitats. *Intaglio, perforated 11.*

CM1136 Mallards Dropping In, *by Jay Norwood Darling*

CM1136 *(2092)*
   20c blue, tagged *(123,575,000)*   .35   .20
     Plate block of four   4.50
     FDC *(July 2, 1984)*   1.00
     v. Horizontal pair, imperforate
       vertically

1984. Roanoke Voyages Issue commemorates the 400th anniversary of the establishment of an English colony in the New World. An expedition landed in 1584 on what is now the coast of North Carolina and took possession of the new land in the name of Queen Elizabeth. Two groups landed, in 1585 and 1587. In 1590, the crew of a ship carrying supplies to the colony landed and could find no evidence of the colonists, whose fate remains a mystery. *Gravure by the American Bank Note Co., perforated 11.*

CM1137 *Roanoke Voyages*

CM1137 *(2093)*
   20c multicolored, tagged *(120,000,000)* .35   .20
     Plate block of four   2.80
     Gutter pair   —
     FDC *(July 13, 1984)*   1.00

1984. Herman Melville Issue honors the 19th century American author of *Moby Dick.* Literary Arts series. *Intaglio, perforated 11.*

CM1138 *Herman Melville*

CM1138 *(2094)*
   20c blue green, tagged *(117,125,000)*   .35   .20

     Plate block of four   2.50
     FDC *(Aug. 1, 1984)*   1.00

1984. Horace Moses Issue salutes the man who created Junior Achievement because of his interest in career-oriented educational opportunities for city youth. *Intaglio (Combination Press), perforated 11.*

CM1139 *Horace Moses*

CM1139 *(2095)*
   20c orange and dark brown,
     tagged *(117,225,000)*   .35   .20
     Plate block of 20   17.00
     FDC *(Aug. 6, 1984)*   1.00

1984. Smokey the Bear Issue celebrates the symbol for forest fire prevention used by the Forest Service of the U.S. Department of Agriculture. *Combination of offset and intaglio, perforated 11.*

CM1140 *Smokey and Bear Cub*

CM1140 *(2096)*
   20c multicolored, tagged *(95,525,000)* .35   .20
     Plate block of four   3.00
     FDC *(Aug. 13, 1984)*   1.00
     v. Block of four, imperforate between
       horizontally and vertically 6,000.

1984. Roberto Clemente Issue commemorates the 18-year Pittsburgh Pirates veteran inducted into the Baseball Hall of Fame in 1973, the year following his untimely death while on a volunteer humanitarian mission. *Gravure, perforated 11.*

CM1141 *Roberto Clemente*

CM1141 *(2097)*
  20c multicolored, tagged *(119,125,000)* .35   .20
    Plate block of four   12.75
    FDC *(Aug. 17, 1984)*   1.00
    v. Horizontal pair, imperforate
       vertically   2,000.

1984. American Dogs Issue depicted eight pedigreed dogs that represent the types most often bred in the United States. The stamps were issued in conjunction with the American Kennel Club's centennial. *Gravure, perforated 11.*

CM1142 *Beagle,*   CM1143 *Chesapeake Bay*
Boston Terrier   *Retriever, Cocker Spaniel*

CM1144 *Alaskan*   CM1145 *Black and Tan*
Malamute, Collie   *Coonhound, American*
              Foxhound

CM1142 *(2098)*
  20c multicolored, tagged *(216,260,000)* .35   .20
CM1143 *(2099)*
  20c multicolored, tagged   .35   .20
CM1144 *(2100)*
  20c multicolored, tagged   .35   .20
CM1145 *(2101)*
  20c multicolored, tagged   .35   .20
    Plate block of four   4.25
    y. Se-tenant block of
       four CM1142-45   2.00
    FDC *(Sept. 7, 1984)*   1.00

1984. Crime Prevention Issue depicts McGruff, the Crime Dog, popularlized to boost public confidence and encourage participation in citizen crime prevention activities. *Printed in gravure by the American Bank Note Co, perforated 11.*

CM1146 *McGruff, the Crime Dog*

CM1146 *(2102)*
  20c multicolored, tagged *(120,000,000)* .35   .20
    Plate block of four   2.50
    FDC *(Sept. 26, 1984)*   1.00

1984. Family Unity Issue was designed by high school student Molly LaRue. *Gravure and intaglio (Combination Press), perforated 11.*

CM1147 *Stick-Figure family*

CM1147 *(2104)*
  20c multicolored, tagged *(117,625,000)* .35   .20
    Plate block of 20   17.75
    FDC *(Oct. 1, 1984)*   1.00
    v. Horizontal pair, imperforate
       vertically   525.
    v1. Vertical pair, imperforate
       between and at bottom   —
    zo. Tagging omitted   —

1984. Eleanor Roosevelt Issue honors the woman who distinguished herself both as the First Lady. and as a humanitarian who fought for human rights as a delegate to the United Nations. *Intaglio, perforated 11.*

CM1148 *Eleanor Roosevelt*

CM1148 *(2105)*
  20c blue, tagged *(112,896,000)*   .35   .20
    Plate block of four   2.50
    FDC *(Oct. 6, 1984)*   1.00

1984. Nation of Readers Issue recognizes the importance of reading in American society, including the traditions of public education and the public library. *Intaglio, perforated 11.*

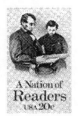

CM1149 *Abraham Lincoln and Son Tad. From a daguerreotype by Mathew Brady*

CM1149 *(2106)*
20c brown and dark red, tagged
(*116,500,000*) .35 .20
Plate block of four 2.95
FDC *(Oct. 16, 1984)* 1.00

1984. Hispanic Americans Issue honors Hispanic Americans and their contribution to national defense. Many have received the nation's highest honors and awards for gallantry in the armed services. *Gravure, perforated 11.*

CM1150 *Hispanic Americans*

CM1150 *(2103)*
20c multicolored, tagged *(108,140,000)* .35 .20
Plate block of four 2.50
FDC *(Oct. 31, 1984)* 1.00
v. Vertical pair, imperforate
horizontally 1,850.

1984. Vietnam Veterans Memorial Issue commemorates the second anniversary of the dedication of the Vietnam Veterans Memorial. The Washington, D.C., memorial contains the names of 57,939 Americans dead or missing in the war. *Intaglio, perforated 10 1/2.*

CM1151 *Vietnam Veterans Memorial*

CM1151 *(2109)*
20c multicolored, tagged *(105,300,000)* .35 .20
Plate block of four 4.25
FDC *(Nov. 10, 1984)* 1.00
zo. Tagging omitted

1985. Jerome Kern Issue celebrated the 100th birthday of the composer who wrote more than 108 complete theatrical scores, over 1,000 songs and earned two Academy Awards. He perhaps is best known for *Show Boat.* Performing Artists series. *Gravure (American Bank note Corp.), perforated 11.*

CM1152 *Jerome Kern*

CM1152 *(2110)*
22c multicolored, tagged(*124,500,000*) .35 .20
Plate block of four 3.00
FDC *(Jan. 23, 1985)* 1.00
zo. Tagging omitted —

1985. Mary McLeod Bethune Issue commemorates the noted educator and social activist. Black Heritage series. *Gravure (American Bank Note Corp.), perforated 11.*

CM1153 *Mary McLeod Bethune*

CM1153 *(2137)*
22c multicolored, tagged *(120,000,000)* .35 .20
Plate block of four 3.25
FDC *(March 5, 1985)* 1.00

1985. Duck Decoys Issue, part of the Folk Art series, has designs based on actual decoys: a broadbill decoy carved by Ben Holmes of Stratford, Conn., in 1890; a mallard decoy by Percy Grant of Osbornville, N. J., in 1900; a canvasback by Bob McGraw of Havre de Grace, Md., in 1929; and a redhead by Keyes Chadwick of Martha's Vineyard, Mass., in 1925. *Gravure (American Bank Note Co.), perforated 11.*

CM1154 *Broadbill Decoy*   CM1155 *Mallard Decoy*

CM1156 *Canvasback Decoy*   CM1157 *Redhead Decoy*

CM1154 *(2138)*
22c multicolored, tagged *(300,000,000)* .40 .20
CM1155 *(2139)*
22c multicolored, tagged .40 .20
CM1156 *(2140)*
22c multicolored, tagged .40 .20
CM1157 *(2141)*
22c multicolored, tagged .40 .20
Plate block of four 12.00
y. Se-tenant block of four
CM1154-57 2.00 1.50
FDC *(Mach. 22, 1985)* 1.00

1985. Winter Special Olympics Issue salutes the largest program of sports training and athletic competition for mentally retarded people in the world. With assistance of 550,000 volunteers worldwide, more than one million children and adults participate. *Gravure, perforated 11.*

CM1158 *Winter Special Olympics*

CM1158 *(2142)*
22c multicolored, tagged *(120,580,000)* .35   .20
    Plate block of four   2.95
    FDC *(Mach. 25, 1985)*   1.00
    v. Vertical pair, imperforate
        horizontally   575.

1985. Love Issue was a special issue for use on many occasions throughout the year. *Gravure, perforated 11.*

CM1159 *Love*

CM1159 *(2143)*
22c multicolored, tagged *(729,700,000)* .35   .20
    Plate block of four   3.25
    FDC *(April 17, 1985)*   1.00
    v. Imperforate pair   1,500.

1985. Rural Electrification Administration Issue marks the 50th anniversary of the organization, which has served as a lending agency as well as developing programs for rural electrification. *Gravure and intaglio (Combination Press), perforated 11.*

CM1160 *Rural Electrification Administration*

CM1160 *(2144)*
22c multicolored, tagged *(124,750,000)* .35   .20
    Plate block of 20   32.50
    FDC *(May 11, 1985)*   1.00
    v. Vertical pair,
        imperforate between   —

1985. Ameripex 86 Issue honors the 1986 international stamp show hosted by the United States in suburban Chicago, Ill. The stamp depicted is the 1 cent National Bank Note of 1870 (No. 97). *Offset and intaglio, perforated 11.*

CM1161 *Ameripex 86*

CM1161 *(2145)*
22c multicolored, tagged *(203,496,000)* .35   .20
    Plate block of four   2.75
    FDC *(May 25, 1985)*   1.00
    v. Red omitted   2,250.
    v1. Red and black omitted   —
    v2. Black, blue, and red
        omitted   210.

1985. Abigail Adams Issue honors the wife of John Adams, second president of the United States. She acted as adviser to her husband, maintained the family estate, raised four children (son John Quincy Adams became the sixth president of the United States) and distinguished herself as one of the leading women writers of her era. *Gravure, perforated 11.*

CM1162 *Abigail Adams*

CM1162 *(2146)*
22c multicolored, tagged *(126,325,000)* .35   .20
    Plate block of four   2.75
    FDC *(June 14, 1985)*   1.00
    v. Imperforate pair   275.

Examples exist with minute traces of the intaglio black remaining, which are worth far less than a complete color--omitted error. Compeptent expertizing is required.

1985. The Frederic Auguste Bartholdi Issue salutes the sculptor of the Statue of Liberty. Offset and intaglio, perforated 11.

CM1163 *F.A. Bartholdi and Statue of Liberty*

CM1163 *(2147)*
22c multicolored *(130,000,000)*   .35   .20
    Plate block of four   2.75
    FDC *(July 18, 1985)*   1.00
    v. Intaglio black omitted   —

1985. Korean War Veterans Issue honors Americans who served during the Korean War of 1950-53, the first conflict in which U.S. troops fought under the flag of the United Nations. *Intaglio, perforated 11.*

CM1164 *Troops Marching. From a photograph by David Duncan*

CM1164 *(2152)*
22c gray green and rose red,
    tagged *(119,975,000)* .35 .20
    Plate block of four 3.50
    FDC *(July 26, 1985)* 1.00

1985. Social Security Act Issue marks the 50th anniversary of the Social Security Act, which, along with later amendments, brought workers essential protection. These include old age, survivor, disability, and health insurance; compensation for unemployment; public assistance; and health and welfare services. *Gravure (American Bank Note Co.), perforated 11.*

CM1165 *Social Security Act*

CM1165 *(2153)*
22c dark blue and light blue,
    tagged *(120,000,000)* .35 .20
    Plate block of four 3.50
    FDC *(Aug. 14, 1985)* 1.00

1985. World War I Veterans Issue, honoring American sacrifice in "the War to End all Wars,"is based on drawing *The Battle of the Marne.* by Capt. Harvey Dunn, one of eight official artists for the American Expeditionary Force. *Intaglio, perforated 11.*

CM1166 *(2154)*
22c green and red, tagged *(119,975,000)* .35 .20
    Plate block of four 3.50
    FDC *(Aug. 26, 1985)* 1.00

CM1166 *The Battle of the Marne*

1985. American Horses Issue featured four breeds of horses representing the many types of horses, mules and donkeys in North America. *Gravure, perforated 11.*

CM1167 *Quarter Horse*   CM1168 *Morgan*

CM1169 *Saddlebred*   CM1170 *Appaloosa*

CM1167 *(2155)*
22c multicolored, tagged *(147,940,000)* 2.75 .20
CM1168 *(2156)*
22c multicolored, tagged 2.75 .20
CM1169 *(2157)*
22c multicolored, tagged 2.75 .20
CM1170 *(2158)*
22c multicolored, tagged 2.75 .20
    Plate block of four 15.00
    y. Se-tenant block of four
      CM1167-70 13. 6.50
    FDC *(Sept. 25, 1985)* 4.00

1985. Public Education Issue recognizes the importance of public education in the development of America. *Gravure (American Bank Note Co.), perforated 11.*

CM1171 *Pen and Inkwell, Glasses, Penmanship Drill*

CM1171 *(2159)*
22c multicolored, tagged *(120,000,000)* .35 .20
    Plate block of four 6.50
    FDC *(Oct. 1, 1985)* 1.00

1985. International Youth Year Issue honors youth groups with outdoor scenes and representative individuals from each group. *Gravure (American Bank Note Co.), perforated 11.*

CM1172 *YMCA Youth camping*   CM1173 *Boy Scouts*

CM1174 *Big Brothers/Big Sisters*   CM1175 *Camp Fire*

CM1172 *(2160)*
22c multicolored, tagged *(130,000,000)* 1.00 .20
CM1173 *(2161)*
22c multicolored, tagged 1.00 .20
CM1174 *(2162)*
22c multicolored, tagged 1.00 .20
CM1175 *(2163)*
22c multicolored, tagged 1.00 .20
    Plate block of four 8.00
    y. Se-tenant block of four
      CM1172-75 3.50 3.00
    FDC *(Oct. 7, 1985)* 1.00

1985. Help End Hunger Issue focuses on the plight of millions suffering from hunger worldwide. *Gravure (American Bank Note Co.), perforated 11.*

CM1176 *Help End Hunger*

CM1176 *(2164)*
    22c multicolored, tagged *(120,000,000)* .35   .20
        Plate block of four   3.00
        FDC *(Oct. 15, 1985)*   1.00

1986. Arkansas Statehood Issue marks the 150th anniversary of Arkansas' entry into the Union as the 25th state. *Gravure (American Bank Note Co.), perforated 11.*

CM1177 *Old State House, Little Rock*

CM1177 *(2167)*
    22c multicolored, tagged   .35   .20
        Plate block of four   3.00
        FDC *(Jan. 3, 1986)*   1.00
        v. Vertical pair, imperforate
           horizontally   —

1986. Stamp Collecting Booklet Issue celebrates philately. This first booklet of commemorative stamps was issued by the U.S. Postal Service on the same day as a booklet about stamp collecting was issued by the postal administration of Sweden (Sweden 1368). The

CM1178 *Handstamp, Magnifying Glass, 1883 stamps*   CM1179 *Boy with his Stamp Collection*

CM1180 *Two Swedish Stamps and U.S. CM191*   CM1181 *First-day cover of 1986 Presidents Souvenir Sheet*

U.S. issue also paid tribute to the centennial of the Smithsonian Institution's first acceptance of philatelic items and to the centennial year of the American Philatelic Society. The cover of the U.S. stamp collecting booklet was an acceptable admission ticket to the international stamp show, AMERIPEX '86. *Offset and intaglio, perforated 10 vertically.*

CM1178 *(2198)*
    22c multicolored, tagged *(67.996,800)* .40   .20
CM1179 *(2199)*
    22c multicolored, tagged   .40   .20
CM1180 *(2200)*
    22c multicolored, tagged   .40   .20
CM1181 *(2201)*
    22c multicolored, tagged   .40   .20
        FDC *(Jan. 23, 1986)*   2.00
        n. Se-tenant booklet pane of
           four CM1178-1181   2.00   2.00
        nv. Booklet pane with
           black omitted
           (CM1178 and CM1181)   45.   150.
        nv1. Booklet pane with
           blue omitted
           (Nos. CM1178-CM1180)   —
        nv2. Booklet pane with light
           brown omitted   —
The complete booklet contains two panes.

1986. The Love Stamp Issue was the fifth U.S. Love stamp. *Gravure, perforated 11.*

CM1182 *Puppy*

CM1182 *(2202)*
    22c multicolored, tagged *(947,450,000)* .35   .20
        Plate block of four   3.50
        FDC *(Jan. 30, 1986)*   1.00
        zo. Tagging omitted

1986. Sojourner Truth Issue honors the woman who, after acquiring her freedom, dedicated her life to the enfranchisement and education of freed slaves and to the cause of human rights. Black Heritage series. *Printed in gravure by the American Bank Note Co., perforated 11.*

CM1183 *Sojourner Truth*

CM1183 *(2203)*
    22c multicolored, tagged *(130,000,000)* .35   .20
        Plate block of four   3.50
        FDC *(Feb. 4, 1986)*   1.00

1986. Republic of Texas Issue commemorates the 150th anniversary of Texan independence from Mexico. *Printed in gravure by the American Bank Note Co., perforated 11.*

CM1184 *Spur on Texas State*

CM1184 *(2204)*
22c dark blue dark red, and dark gray,

tagged *(136,500,000)*	.35	.20
Plate block of four	3.50	
FDC *(Marsh 2, 1986)*		1.00
v. Dark red omitted	2,550.	
v1. Horizontal pair, imperforate vertically	1,100.	

1986. Fish Booklet Issue featured five fish common to the U.S. waters. *Gravure, perforated 10 horizontally.*

CM1185 *Muskellunge*

CM1186 *Atlantic cod*

CM1187 *Largemouth bass*

CM1188 *Bluefin tuna*

CM1189 *Catfish*

CM1185 *(2205)*
22c multicolored, tagged *(219,990,000)*	1.75	.20

CM1186 *(2206)*
22c multicolored, tagged	1.75	.20

CM1187 *(2207)*
22c multicolored, tagged	1.75	.20

CM1188 *(2208)*
22c multicolored, tagged	1.75	.20

CM1189 *(2209)*
22c multicolored, tagged	1.75	.20
FDC *(March 21, 1986)*		2.00
n. Se-tenant booklet pane of five CM1185-89	8.50	

The complete booklet contains two panes.

1986. Public Hospitals Issue honors U.S. public hospitals that trace their history back to Philadelphia General Hospital, which opened about 1731 and closed in 1977. *Printed in gravure by the American Bank Note Co., perforated 11.*

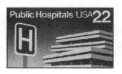

CM1190 *Public Hospitals*

CM1190 *(2210)*
22c multicolored, tagged *(130,000,000)*	.35	.20
Plate block of four	3.25	
FDC *(Apil. 11, 1986)*		1.00
v. Horizontal pair, imperforate vertically	1,250.	
v1. Vertical pair, imperforate horizontally	325.	

1986. Duke Ellington Issue pays homage to the renowned jazz composer on the 75th anniversary of his birth. Edward Kennedy Ellington was a creative master of jazz composition, songwriting, film scoring, ballet and sacred music alike. Performing Artists series. *Gravure by the American Bank Note Co., perforated 11.*

CM1191 *Duke Ellington*

CM1191 *(2211)*
22c multicolored, tagged *(130,000,000)*	.35	.20
Plate block of four	3.00	
FDC *(April 29, 1986)*		1.00
v. Vertical pair, imperforate horizontally	950.	275.

1986. Presidents Souvenir Sheets honor U.S. presidents on four souvenir sheets of nine stamps (one for each president and one featuring the White House). The sheets were issued in conjunction with ameripex 86, in Chicago. *Offset and intaglio, perforated 11.*

CM1192 *(2216)*
$1.98 souvenir sheet of nine
(5,825,050)	5.25	4.50
a. 22c George Washington, tagged	.50	.40
b. 22c John Adams, tagged	.50	.40
c. 22c Thomas Jefferson, tagged	.50	.40
d. 22c James Madison, tagged	.50	.40

Presidents of the United States: I

AMERIPEX 86
International
Stamp Show
Chicago, Illinois
May 22-June 1, 1986

CM1192

e. 22c James Monroe, tagged .50 .40
f. 22c John Quincy Adams, tagged .50 .40
g. 22c Andrew Jackson, tagged .50 .40
h. 22c Martin Van Buren, tagged .50 .40
i. 22c William Henry Harrison,
tagged .50 .40
v. Black (inscription) omitted —
v1. Intaglio blue omitted 3,500.
v2. Imperforate 10,500.

Presidents of the United States: II

AMERIPEX 86
International
Stamp Show
Chicago, Illinois
May 22-June 1, 1986

CM1193

CM1193 *(2217)*
$1.98 souvenir sheet of nine
(5,825,050) 5.25 4.50
a. 22c John Tyler, tagged .50 .40
b. 22c James K. Polk, tagged .50 .40
c. 22c Zachary Taylor, tagged .50 .40
d. 22c Millard Fillmore, tagged .50 .40
e. 22c Franklin Pierce, tagged .50 .40
f. 22c James Buchanan, tagged .50 .40
g. 22c Abraham Lincoln, tagged .50 .40

h. 22c Andrew Johnson, tagged .50 .40
i. 22c Ulysses S. Grant, tagged .50 .40
v. Black (inscription) omitted 3,000.

Presidents of the United States: III

AMERIPEX 86
International
Stamp Show
Chicago, Illinois
May 22-June 1, 1986

CM1194

CM1194 *(2218)*
$1.98 souvenir sheet of nine
(5,825,050) 5.25 4.50
a. 22c Rutherford B. Hayes, tagged .50 .40
b. 22c James A. Garfield, tagged .50 .40
c. 22c Chester A. Arthur, tagged .50 .40
d. 22c Grover Cleveland, tagged .50 .40
e. 22c Benjamin Harrison, tagged .50 .40
f. 22c William McKinley, tagged .50 .40
g. 22c Theodore Roosevelt, tagged .50 .40
h. 22c William H. Taft, tagged .50 .40
i. 22c Woodrow Wilson, tagged .50 .40
v. Black (inscription) omitted —
v1. Intaglio brown omitted 2,750.

Presidents of the United States: IV

AMERIPEX 86
International
Stamp Show
Chicago, Illinois
May 22-June 1, 1986

CM1195

CM1195 *(2219)*
$1.98 souvenir sheet of nine

(5,825,050)	5.25	4.50
a. 22c Warren G. Harding, tagged	.50	.40
b. 22c Calvin Coolidge, tagged	.50	.40
c. 22c Herbert C. Hoover, tagged	.50	.40
d. 22c Franklin D. Roosevelt, tagged	.50	.40
e. 22c White House, tagged	.50	.40
f. 22c Harry S Truman, tagged	.50	.40
g. 22c Dwight D. Eisenhower, tagged	.50	.40
h. 22c John F. Kennedy, tagged	.50	.40
i. 22c Lyndon B. Johnson, tagged	.50	.40
v. Intaglio blue black inscription omitted on six stamps at left (a-b, d-e, g-h)	2,240.	
zo. Tagging omitted on three stamps at right (c,f,i)	—	

1986. Polar Explorers Issue honors five pioneers of Arctic exploration who accomplished a variety of geographical, anthropological, mapping, and other scientific work. *Gravure, perforated 11.*

CM1196 *Elisha Kent Kane*   CM1197 *Adolphus W. Greely*

CM1198 *Vilhjalmur Stefansson*   CM1199 *Robert E. Peary and Matthew Henson*

CM1196 *(2220)*
22c multicolored *(130,000,000)*	1.10	.20

CM1197 *(2221)*
22c multicolored	1.10	.20

CM1198 *(2222)*
22c multicolored	1.10	.20

CM1199 *(2223)*
22c multicolored	1.10	.20
Plate block of four	8.00	
y. Se-tenant block of four CM1196-99	5.50	3.75
FDC *(May 28, 1986)*		2.00
vy. Se-tenant block of four, engraved black omitted	11,550.	
vy1. Se-tenant block of four engraved black omitted from CM1196-97 only	—	

1986. Statue of Liberty Issue commemorates the 100th anniversary this sculpture, a gift to the United States from the people of France as a demonstration of their sympathy with the nation's founding principles. France simultaneously released a joint 2.20-franc. stamp with matching design. *Intaglio, perforated 11.*

CM1200 *Statue of Liberty*

CM1200 *(2224)*
22c red and blue *(220,725,000)*	.35	.20
Plate block of four	4.00	
FDC *(July 4, 1986)*		1.00

1986. Navajo Art Issue depicts four Navajo blankets. This issue is the third Folk Art celebrating native American handicrafts. *Offset and intaglio, perforated 11.*

CM1201   CM1202

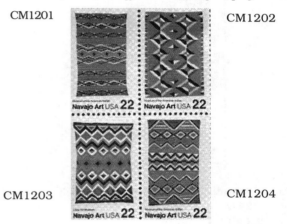

CM1203   CM1204

Navajo blankets

CM1201 *(2235)*
22c multicolored *(240,525,000)*	.40	.20

CM1202 *(2236)*
22c multicolored	.40	.20

CM1203 *(2237)*
22c multicolored	.40	.20

CM1203 *(2238)*
22c multicolored	.40	.20

CM1204
22c multicolored	.40	.20
Plate block of four	6.00	
y. Se-tenant block of four CM1201-04	3.00	1.50
FDC *(Sept. 5, 1986)*		2.00
vy. Se-tenant block of four intaglio black omitted	375.	

1986. T.S. Eliot Issue commemorates Thomas Sterns Eliot, prominent poet, critic, editor, and dramatist, awarded the Nobel Prize for Literature. Literary Arts series. *Intaglio, perforated 11.*

CM1205 *T.S. Eliot*

CM1205 *(2239)*
  22c copper red *(131,700,000)*   .35   .20
    Plate block of four   2.75
    FDC *(Sept. 26, 1986)*   1.00

1986. Woodcarved Figurines Issue illustrates carved figurines. Since Colonial times, woodcarved figurines frequently served as advertisements by merchants displayed outside their shop doors. Folk Art series. *Gravure by the American Bank Note Co., perforated 11.*

CM1206
*Highlander
Figure*

CM1207 *Ship
Figurehead*

CM1208
*Nautical
Figure*

CM1209
*Cigar Store
Figure*

CM1206 *(2240)*
  22c multicolored, tagged *(240,000,000)* .40   .20
CM1207 *(2241)*
  22c mulricolored, tagged   .40   .20
CM1208 *(2242)*
  22c mulitcolored, tagged   .40   .20
CM1209 *(2243)*
  22c multicolored, tagged   .40   .20
    Plate block of four   4.50
    y. Se-tenant block of four
      CM1206-09   3.25   1.50
    FDC (Oct. 1, 1986)   1.00
    vy. Block of four, imperforate
      vertically   1,450.   —
    vy1. Pair, any, imperforate
      vertically   300.

1987. Michigan Statehood Issue honors the 150th anniversary of Michigan's admission as the 26th state of the Union *Gravure, perforated 11.*

CM1210 *White Pine*

CM1210 *(2246)*
  22c multicolored, tagged *(167,430,000)* .35   .20
    Plate block of four   2.75
    Gutter pair
    FDC *(Jan. 26, 1987)*   1.00

1987. Pan-American Games Issue commemorates the international sports competition held every four years since 1957. *Gravure, perforated 11.*

CM1211 *Runners*

CM1211 *(2247)*
  22c multicolored, tagged *(166,555,000)* .35   .20
    Plate block of four   2.75
    FDC *(Jan. 29, 1987)*   1.00
    v. Silver omitted   1,600.

1987. Love Stamp Issue *Gravure, perforated 11 1/2 x 11.*

CM1212 *Love*

CM1212 *(2248)*
  22c multicolored, tagged *(811,560,000)* .35   .20
    Plate block of four   2.75
    FDC *(Jan. 30, 1987)*   1.00

1987. Jean-Baptiste du Sable Issue honors the founder of Chicago in the year of that city's sesquicentennial. Du Sable played an active role in the frontier settlement on the Chicago River as a general merchant, fur trader, farmer and Indian overseer. Black Heritage series. *Gravure, perforated 11.*

CM1213 *Jean-Baptiste du Sable*

CM1213 *(2249)*
  22c multicolored, tagged *(142,905,000)* .35   .20
    Plate block of four   3.25
    FDC *(Feb. 20. 1987)*   1.00

1987. Enrico Caruso Issue honors one of the most popular opera performers of all time and the world's highest paid performer in his day. Performing Artists series. *Gravure by the American Bank Note Co., perforated 11.*

CM1214 *Enrico Caruso*

CM1214 *(2250)*
   22c multicolored, tagged *(130,000,000)* .35   .20
     Plate block of four   2.75
     FDC *(Feb. 27, 1987)*   1.00
     v. Intaglio black omitted   5,000.

1987. Girl Scouts Issue marks the 75th anniversary of the Girl Scouts. Juliette Low (CM316) formed the first Girl Scout troop in the United States, patterned after the English Girl Guides. *Intaglio (Giori Press), perforated 11.*

CM1215 *Girl Scout badges*

CM1215 *(2251)*
   22c multicolored, tagged *(149,980,000)* .35   .20
     Plate block of four   3.25
     FDC *(March 12, 1987)*   1.00
     Black, yellow, magenta, cyan and
         green omitted   2,750.

1987. Special Occasions Issue consists of eight designs (CM1216 and CM1221 each are repeated once) in a booklet pane of 10. The stamps were intended for use on greeting cards and other special personal mail. *Gravure, perforated 10.*

CM1216 *(2267)*
   22c multicolored, tagged *(610,425,000)* 1.75   .40
CM1217 *(2268)*
   22c multicolored, tagged   1.75   .40
CM1218 *(2269)*
   22c multicolored, tagged   1.75   .40
CM1219 *(2270)*
   22c multicolored, tagged   1.75   .40
CM1220 *(2271)*
   22c multicolored, tagged   1.75   .40
CM1221 *(2272)*
   22c multicolored, tagged   1.75   .40

CM1216 *Congratulations!*

CM1217 *Get Well!*

CM1218 *Thank You!*

CM1219 *Love You, Dad!*

CM1220 *Best Wishes!*

CM1221 *Happy Birthday!*

CM1222 *Love You, Mother!*

CM1223 *Keep in Touch!*

CM1222 *(2273)*
   22c multicolored, tagged   1.75   .40
CM1223 *(2274)*
   22c multicolored, tagged   1.75   .40
     FDC *(April 20, 1987) any single*   1.00
     n. Booklet pane of 10   16.   12.
     FDC   5.00
Numbers CM1224 and CM1225 were not assigned.

1987. United Way Issue celebrated the community-based charity's 100th anniversary. *Offset and intaglio, perforated 11.*

CM1226 *Faces in Profile*

CM1226 *(2275)*
   22c multicolored, tagged *(156,995,000)* .35   .20
     Plate block of four   2.75
     FDC *(April 28, 1987)*   1.00

1987. American Wildlife Issue, 50 different stamps se-
tenant in one pane released during Capex 87 in Toronto,
Canada. Stamps feature animals indigenous to North
America and Hawaii. *Gravure, perforated 11.*

CM1227-1276 *Examples of American wildlife*

CM1227 *(2286)*			
22c Barn Swallow, tagged	1.50	.55	
CM1228 *(2287)*			
22c Monarch Butterfly, tagged	1.50	.55	
CM1229 *(2288)*			
22c Bighorn Sheep, tagged	1.50	.55	
CM1230 *(2289)*			
22c Broad-tailed Hummingbird,			
tagged	1.50	.55	
CM1231 *(2290)*			
22c Cottontail, tagged	1.50	.55	
CM1232 *(2291)*			
22c Osprey, tagged	1.50	.55	
CM1233 *(2292)*			
22c Mountain Lion, tagged	1.50	.55	
CM1234 *(2293)*			
22c Luna Moth, tagged	1.50	.55	
CM1235 *(2294)*			
22c Mule Deer, tagged	1.50	.55	
CM1236 *(2295)*			
22c Gray Squirrel, tagged	1.50	.55	
CM1237 *(2296)*			
22c Armadillo, tagged	1.50	.55	
CM1238 *(2297)*			
22c Eastern Chipmunk, tagged	1.50	.55	
CM1239 *(2298)*			
22c Moose, tagged	1.50	.55	
CM1240 *(2299)*			
22c Black Bear, tagged	1.50	.55	

CM1241 *(2300)*			
22c Tiger Swallowtail, tagged	1.50	.55	
CM1242 *(2301)*			
22c Bobwhite, tagged	1.50	.55	
CM1243 *(2302)*			
22c Ringtail, tagged	1.50	.55	
CM1244 *(2303)*			
22c Red-winged Blackbird, tagged	1.50	.55	
CM1245 *(2304)*			
22c American Lobster, tagged	1.50	.55	
CM1246 *(2305)*			
22c Black-tailed Jack Rabbit, tagged	1.50	.55	
CM1247 *(2306)*			
22c Scarlet Tanager, tagged	1.50	.55	
CM1248 *(2307)*			
22c Woodchuck, tagged	1.50	.55	
CM1249 *(2308)*			
22c Roseate Spoonbill, tagged	1.50	.55	
CM1250 *(2309)*			
22c Bald Eagle, tagged	1.50	.55	
CM1251 *(2310)*			
22c Alaskan Brown Bear, tagged	1.50	.55	
CM1252 *(2311)*			
22c Iiwi, tagged	1.50	.55	
CM1253 *(2312)*			
22c Badger, tagged	1.50	.55	
CM1254 *(2313)*			
22c Pronghorn, tagged	1.50	.55	
CM1255 *(2314)*			
22c River Otter, tagged	1.50	.55	

CM1256 (2315)
  22c Ladybug, tagged   1.50   .55
CM1257 (2316)
  22c Beaver, tagged   1.50   .55
CM1258 (2317)
  22c White-tailed Deer, tagged   1.50   .55
CM1259 (2318)
  22c Blue Jay, tagged   1.50   .55
CM1260 (2319)
  22c Pika, tagged   1.50   .55
CM1261 (2320)
  22c Bison, tagged   1.50   .55
CM1262 (2321)
  22c Snowy Egret, tagged   1.50   .55
CM1263 (2322)
  22c Gray Wolf, tagged   1.50   .55
CM1264 (2323)
  22c Mountain Goat, tagged   1.50   .55
CM1265 (2324)
  22c Deer Mouse, tagged   1.50   .55
CM1266 (2325)
  22c Black-tailed Prairie Dog, tagged 1.50   .55
CM1267 (2326)
  22c Box Turtle, tagged   1.50   .55
CM1268 (2327)
  22c Wolverine, tagged   1.50   .55
CM1269 (2328)
  22c American Elk, tagged   1.50   .55
CM1270 (2329)
  22c California Sea Lion, tagged   1.50   .55
CM1271 (2330)
  22c Mockingbird, tagged   1.50   .55
CM1272 (2331)
  22c Raccoon, tagged   1.50   .55
CM1273 (2332)
  22c Bobcat, tagged   1.50   .55
CM1274 (2333)
  22c Black-footed Ferret, tagged   1.50   .55
CM1275 (2334)
  22c Canada Goose, tagged   1.50   .55
CM1276 (2335)
  22c Red Fox, tagged   1.50   .55
    Pane of 50   65.   20.
    FDC (June 13, 1987) full pane   25.
    v. Red omitted, any single   —

1987. Delaware Statehood Issue was the first stamp in a series commemorating the bicentennial of the ratification of the Constitution. Delaware was the first state to vote for ratification. *Offset and intaglio by BEP, perforated 11.*

CM1277 *Delaware State Seal*

CM1277 (2336)
  22c multicolored, tagged   .35   .20
    Plate block of four   3.00
    FDC (July 4, 1987)   1.00

1987. Friendship with Morocco Issue marks the bicentennial of diplomatic relations between the United States and Morocco. Morocco issued a stamp at the same time (Morocco 1281). *Intaglio (Giori Press), perforated 11.*

CM1278 *Arbesque From door of Dar Batha Palace, Fez, Morocco*

CM1278 (2349)
  22c red and black, tagged   .35   .20
    Plate block of four   2.75
    FDC (July 17, 1987)   1.00
    v. Intaglio black omitted   350.

1987. William Faulkner Issue, honors the Nobel Prize-winning novelist and poet, noted for his writings about life in the South. Literary Arts series. *Intaglio, perforated 11.*

CM1279 *William Faulkner*

CM1279 (2350)
  22c green, tagged   .35   .20
    Plate block of four   2.75
    FDC (Aug. 3, 1987)   1.00

Imperforate varieties, from printer's waste, are known.

1987. Lacemaking Issue, part of the American Folk Art series, features four different designs of delicate needlework. *Offset and intaglio, perforated 11.*

Intaglio white ink was printed on top of offset blue to acheive the lace effect.

CM1280 *Squash Blossoms*   CM1281 *Floral Design*

CM1282 *Floral Lace*   CM1283 *Dogwood Blossoms*

CM1280 *(2351)*
22c blue and white, tagged .40 .20
CM1281 *(2352)*
22c blue and white, tagged .40 .20
CM1282 *(2353)*
22c blue and white, tagged .40 .20
CM1283 *(2354)*
22c blue and white, tagged .40 .20
Plate block of four 5.00
y. Se-tenant block of four
CM1280-83 2.50 1.50
FDC *(Aug. 14, 1987)* 1.00
vy. Se-tenant block of four,
white omitted 900.
vy1.White omitted, any single 165.

1987. Pennsylvania Statehood Issue is the second stamp in the Constitution Ratification Bicentennial series. The Keystone State ratified the U.S. Constitution on December 12, 1787. *Gravure by the American Bank Note Co., perforated 11.*

CM1284 *Independence Hall, Philadelphia*

CM1284 *(2337)*
22c multicolored, tagged .35 .20
Plate block of four 3.95
FDC *(Aug. 26, 1987)* 1.00

1987. Constitution Bicentennial Issue, released in booklet format, commemorates the 200th anniversary of the drafting of the U.S. Constitution with excerpts from the preamble. *Gravure, perforated 10 horizontally.*

CM1285

CM1286

CM1287

CM1288

CM1289

CM1285 *(2355)*
22c multicolored, tagged .75 .25
CM1286 *(2356)*
22c multicolored, tagged .75 .25
CM1287 *(2357)*
22c multicolored, tagged .75 .25
CM1288 *(2358)*
22c multicolored, tagged .75 .25
CM1289 *(2359)*
22c multicolored, tagged .75 .25
FDC *(Aug. 28, 1987),* any single 1.00
n. Se-tenant booklet pane of five
CM1285-89 4.25 3.50
FDC 2.00

1987. New Jersey Statehood Issue was the third of 13 stamps in the Constitution Ratification Bicentennial series. *Gravure by the American Bank Note Co., perforated 11.*

CM1290 *Farmer Carrying Produce*

CM1290 *(2338)*
22c multicolored, tagged .35 .20
Plate block of four 3.50
FDC *(Sept. 11, 1987)* 1.00
v. Intaglio black omitted 6,500.

1987. Constitution Bicentennial Issue honors the 200th anniversary of the signing of the document. *Offset and intaglio, perforated 11.*

CM1291 *U.S. Constitution*

CM1291 *(2360)*
22c multicolored, tagged .35 .20
Plate block of four 3.25
FDC *(Sept. 17, 1987)* 1.00

1987. Certified Public Accountants Issue honors the centennial of the accounting profession in the United States. *Offset and intaglio, perforated 11.*

CM1292 *Spreadsheet and Pen*

CM1292 *(2361)*

22c multicolored, tagged	.35	.20
Plate block of four		
FDC *(Sept. 21, 1987)*		1.00
v. Intaglio black omitted	—	

1987. Locomotive Issue, a five-stamp booklet, pays tribute to the steam locomotives that drove the railroad revolution in America. *Offset and intaglio, perforated 10 horizontally.*

CM1293 *Stourbridge Lion*

CM1294 *Best Friend of Charleston*

CM1295 *John Bull*

CM1296 *Brother Jonathan*

CM1297 *Gowan & Marx*

CM1293 *(2362)*

22c multicolored, tagged	.75	.25

CM1294 *(2363)*

22c multicolored, tagged	.75	.25

CM1295 *(2364)*

22c multicolored, tagged	.75	.25

CM1296 *(2365)*

22c multicolored, tagged	.75	.25
v. Red omitted	—	

CM1297 *(2366)*

22c multicolored, tagged	.75	.25
v. Blue omitted	—	
FDC *(Oct. 11, 1993)*, any single		1.00
n. Se-tenant booklet pane of five, CM1293-97	3.75	2.50
FDC		3.00
vn. Booklet pane of five, black omitted	—	

1988. Georgia Statehood Issue is the fourth in the Constitution Ratifictaion Bicentennial series. *Gravure, perforated 11.*

CM1298 *Live Oak and Atlanta skyline*

CM1298 *(2339)*

22c multicolored, tagged	.35	.20
Plate block of four	3.50	
FDC *(Jan. 6, 1988)*		1.00

1988. Connecticut Statehood Issue continues the Constitution Ratification Bicentennial series with a salute to the state's maritime heritage. *Offset and intaglio, perforated 11.*

CM1299 *Harbor Scene*

CM1299 *(2340)*

22c multicolored, tagged	.35	.20
Plate block of four	3.50	
FDC *(Jan. 9, 1988)*		1.00

1988. Winter Olympics Issue honors the 1988 Winter Games at Calgary, Alberta, Canada. *Gravure by the American Bank Note Co., perforated 11.*

CM1300 *Alpine Skier*

CM1300 *(2369)*

22c multicolored, tagged	.35	.20
Plate block of four	3.25	
FDC *(Jan. 10, 1988)*		1.00

1988. Australia Bicentennial Issue marked the 200th anniversary of the first European settlement in Australia. The stamp was issued at the same time as one by Australia (Australia 1175), and is the 19th U.S. joint issue. *Gravure, perforated 11.*

CM1301 *Cartoon of Australian Koala and American Bald Eagle*

CM1301 *(2370)*

22c multicolored, tagged	.35	.20
Plate block of four	2.75	
FDC *(Jan. 26, 1988)*		1.00

1988. James Weldon Johnson Issue, honors the educator, diplomat, lawyer, author and lyricist. Black Heritage series. *Gravure by the American Bank Note Co., perforated 11.*

CM1302 *James Weldon Johnson*

CM1302 *(2371)*
22c multicolored, tagged .35 .20
  Plate block of four 3.00
  FDC *(Feb. 2, 1988)* 1.00

1988. Cats Issue depicts eight popular feline breeds. *Gravure by the American Bank Note Co., perforated 11.*

CM1303 *Siamese, Exotic Shorthair*   CM1304 *Abyssinian, Himalayan*

CM1305 *Maine Coon Cat, Burmese*   CM1306 *American Shorthair Cat, Persian*

CM1303 *(2372)*
22c multicolored, tagged 1.00 .20
CM1304 *(2373)*
22c multicolored, tagged 1.00 .20
CM1305 *(2374)*
22c multicolored, tagged 1.00 .20
CM1306 *(2375)*
22c multicolored, tagged 1.00 .20
  Plate block of four 5.75
  y. Se-tenant block of four
    CM1303-06 4.50 2.50
  FDC *(Feb. 5, 1988) any single* 1.00

1988. Massachusetts Statehood Issue is the sixth stamp in the Constitution Ratification Bicentennial series. Massachusetts' own constitution was a model for the federal document. *Intaglio, perforated 11.*

CM1307 *Old Statehouse*

CM1307 *(2341)*
22c dark blue and dark red, tagged .35 .20
  Plate block of four 3.50
  FDC *(Feb. 6, 1988)* 1.00

1988. Maryland Statehood Issue is the seventh stamp in the Constitution Ratification Bicentennial series. *Offset and intaglio, perforated 11.*

CM1308 *Skipjack Sailboat and Annapolis*

CM1308 *(2342)*
22c multicolored, tagged .35 .20
  Plate block of four 3.50
  FDC *(Feb. 15, 1988)* 1.00

1988. Knute Rockne Issue honors the famed player and Notre Dame University football coach credited with developing the forward pass. American Sports series. *Offset and intaglio, perforated 11.*

CM1309 *Knute Rockne*

CM1309 *(2376)*
22c multicolored, tagged .35 .20
  Plate block of four 3.95
  FDC *(March 9, 1988)* 1.00

1988. South Carolina Statehood Issue, the first commemorative stamp paying the 25-cent first-class rate, honors the 200th anniversary of South Carolina ratifying the U.S. Constitution, in the Constitution Ratification Bicentennial series. *Gravure, American Bank Note Co., perforated 11.*

CM1310 *Palmetto Trees*

CM1310 *(2343)*
25c multicolored, tagged .40 .20
  Plate block of four 3.95
  FDC *(May 23, 1988)* 1.00
  v. Strip of three, vertically
    imperforate between 10,450.

1988. Francis Ouimet Issue honors the 75th anniversary of his victory at the U.S. Open Golf Championship, which made him the first amateur to win the event. *Gravure, American Bank Note Co., perforated 11.*

CM1311 *Francis Ouimet*

CM1311 *(2377)*

25c multicolored, tagged	.40	.20
Plate block of four	5.75	
FDC *(June 13, 1988)*		1.00

1988. New Hampshire Statehood Issue is the ninth stamp in the Constitution Ratification Bicentennial series. (See also CM380.) *Gravure, American Bank Note Co., perforated 11.*

CM1312 *Old Man of the Mountain*

CM1312 *(2344)*

25c multicolored, tagged	.40	.20
Plate block of four	3.95	
FDC *(June 21, 1988)*		1.00

1988. Virginia Statehood Issue is the 10th stamp in the Constitution Ratification Bicentennial series. (See also CM380.) *Offset and intaglio, perforated 11.*

CM1313 *Old Capitol Building, Williamsburg*

CM1313 *(2345)*

25c multicolored, tagged	.40	.20
Plate block of four	3.95	
FDC *(June 25, 1988)*		1.00

1988. Love Issue, seventh in the series begun in 1982, featured a rose and was released in Pasadena, Calif., home of the annual Rose Bowl. *Gravure, perforated 11.*

CM1314 *Rose*

CM1314 *(2378)*

25c multicolored, tagged	.40	.20
Plate block of four	3.25	
FDC *(July 4, 1988)*		1.00
v. Imperforate pair	2,750.	

1988. New York Statehood Issue is the 11th stamp in the Constitution Ratification Bicentennial series. *Offset and intaglio, perforated 11.*

CM1315 *Federal Hall, Wall Street and Trinity Church Steeple*

CM1315 *(2346)*

25c multicolored, tagged	.40	.20
Plate block of four	3.25	
FDC *(July 26, 1988)*		1.00

1988. Love Issue, the second of the year, this one in a 45-cent different denomination, was released to cover the postal rate for two ounces of first-class mail (such as a standard wedding invitation and R.S.V.P. envelope). *Gravure, perforated 11.*

CM1316 *Roses*

CM1316 *(2379)*

45c multicolored, tagged	1.35	.20
Plate block of four	5.75	
FDC *(Aug. 8, 1988)*		1.00

1988. Summer Olympic Games Issue honors the 14th Summer Games in Seoul, Korea. *Gravure, perforated 11.*

CM1317 *Gymnast on rings*

CM1317 *(2380)*

25c multicolored, tagged	.40	.20
Plate block of four	3.50	
FDC *(Aug. 19, 1988)*		1.00

1988. Classic Cars Issue featured five automobiles of 1925-42 in se-tenant booklet pane. *Offset and intaglio, perforated 10 horizontally.*

CM1318 *(2381)*

25c multicolored, tagged	2.00	.50

CM1319 *(2382)*

25c multicolored, tagged	2.00	.50

CM1318 *Locomobile, 1928*

CM1319 *Pierce-Arrow, 1929*

CM1320 *Cord, 1931*

CM1321 *Packard, 1932*

CM1322 *Duesenberg, 1935*

CM1320 *(2383)*
25c multicolored, tagged	2.00	.50

CM1321 *(2384)*
25c multicolored, tagged	2.00	.50

CM1322 *(2385)*
25c multicolored, tagged	2.00	.50
FDC *(Aug. 25, 1988)*, any single		1.00
n. Se-tenant booklet pane of five, CM1318-22	10.	
FDC		3.75

1988. Antarctic Explorers Issue salutes four men who first explored the vast ice-capped continent of Antarctica. *Gravure, American Bank Note Co, perforated 11.*

CM1323 *Nathaniel Palmer*   CM1324 *Lt. Charles Wilkes*

CM1325 *Richard E. Byrd*   CM1326 *Lincoln Ellsworth*

CM1323 *(2386)*
25c multicolored, tagged	1.00	.20

CM1324 *(2387)*
25c multicolored, tagged	1.00	.20

CM1325 *(2388)*
25c multicolored, tagged	1.00	.20

CM1326 *(2389)*
25c multicolored, tagged	1.00	.20
Plate block of four	8.00	
y. Se-tenant block of four CM1323-26	4.75	3.00
FDC *(Sept. 14, 1988)*		2.00
a. Block of four, intaglio black omitted	1,600.	
v1. Block of four, imperforate horizontally	3,000.	

1988. Carousel Annimal Issue, presents examples of a popular art form. Folk Art series. *Offset and intaglio, perforated 11.*

CM1327 *Deer*   CM1328 *Horse*

CM1329 *Camel*   CM1330 *Goat*

CM1327 *(2390)*
25c multicolored, tagged	1.00	.20

CM1328 *(2391)*
25c multicolored, tagged	1.00	.20

CM1329 *(2392)*
25c multicolored, tagged	1.00	.20

CM1330 *(2393)*
25c multicolored, tagged	1.00	.20
Plate block of four	6.00	
y. Se-tenant block of four CM1327-30	4.75	2.00
FDC *(Oct. 1, 1988)*		2.00

1988. Special Occasions Issue has four different designs. Each booklet pane contains six stamps, three each of two designs. The two different panes bring the total to 12 stamps (three of each design). *Gravure, American Bank Note Co., perforated 11.*

CM1331 *(2395)*
25c multicolored, tagged	1.00	.20

CM1332 *(2396)*
25c multicolored, tagged	1.00	.20
n. Booklet pane of six, three each CM1331 and CM1332 with a gutter between	5.00	4.00

CM1331 *Happy Birthday*

CM1332 *Best Wishes*

CM1333 *Thinking of You*

CM1334 *Love You*

CM1333 *(2397)*
25c multicolored, tagged   1.00   .20
CM1334 *(2398)*
25c multicolored, tagged   1.00   .20
    n. Booklet pane of six,
        three each CM1333 and
        CM1334 with a gutter
        between   5.00   4.00
    nv. As above, imperforate
        horizontally   —

1989. Montana Statehood Issue commemorates the state's centennial with a design by artist Charles Russell (see also CM528). *Offset and intaglio, perforated 11.*

CM1335   C.M. Russell and Friends

CM1335 *(2401)*
25c multicolored, tagged   .40   .20
    Plate block of four   4.00
    FDC *(Jan. 15, 1989)*   1.00

1989. A. Philip Randolph Issue, honors a prominent, respected and indefatigable voice for the rights of minority labor. Black Heritage series. *Gravure, perforated 11.*

CM1336 *A. Philip Randolph*

CM1336 *(2402)*
25c multicolored, tagged   .40   .20
    Plate block of four   3.75
    FDC *(Feb. 3, 1989)*   1.00

1989. North Dakota Statehood Issue marks the centennial of the 39th state to enter the Union. *Gravure, American Bank Note Co., perforated 11.*

CM1337 *Grain Elevator*

CM1337 *(2403)*
25c multicolored, tagged   .40   .20
    Plate block of four   3.50
    FDC *(Feb. 21, 1989)*   1.00

1989. Washington Statehood Issue marks the centennial of the 40th state to enter the Union. *Gravure, American Bank Note Co., perforated 11.*

CM1338 *Mount Rainier*

CM1338 *(2404)*
25c multicolored, tagged
    Plate block of four
    FDC *(Feb. 22, 1989)*

1989. Steamboats Issue a se-tenant five-stamp booklet issue depicts five of America's earliest and most innovative craft. *Offset and intaglio, perforated 10 horizontally.*

CM1339 Experiment

CM1340 Phoenix

CM1341 New Orleans

CM1342 Washington

CM1343 Walk in the Water

CM1339 *(2405)*
25c multicolored, tagged   .75   .20

CM1340 *(2406)*
   25c multicolored, tagged   .75   .20
CM1341 *(2407)*
   25c multicolored, tagged   .75   .20
CM1342 *(2408)*
   25c multicolored, tagged   .75   .20
CM1343 *(2409)*
   25c multicolored   .75   .20
   FDC *(March 3, 1989),*
      any single   1.00
   n. Se-tenant booklet
      pane CM1339-43   3.60   1.00
   FDC   2.00

1989. World Stamp Expo '89 Issue honors the first-ever international stamp show to be sponsored by the U.S. Postal Service. The stamp depicted is the 90-cent Lincoln from the 1869 Pictorial series (No. 96). *Offset and intaglio, perforated 11.*

CM1344 *World Stamp Expo '89*

CM1344 *(2410)*
   25c red, gray and black   .40   .20
   Plate block of four   3.00
   FDC *(Mar. 16, 1989)*   1.00

1989. Arturo Toscanini Issue saluted a man who many consider the greatest conductor of all time. *Gravure, American Bank Note Co., perforated 11.*

CM1345 *Arturo Toscanini*

CM1345 *(2411)*
   25c multicolored, tagged   .40   .20
   Plate block of four   3.50
   FDC *(March 25, 1989)*   1.00

1989. House of Representatives Issue is first in a series of four stamps honoring the three branches of government set by the U.S. Constitution. *Offset and intaglio, perforated 11.*

CM1346 *Car of History. From a marble work clock by Carlo Franzoni*

CM1346 *(2412)*
   25c multicolored, tagged   .40   .20
   Plate block of four   3.75
   FDC *(Apr. 4, 1989)*   1.00

1989. Senate Issue honors the bicentennial of the U.S. Senate, the series honoring branches of government established by the U.S. Constitution. *Offset and intaglio, perforated 11.*

CM1347 *Old Senate Chamber Eagle and Shield*

CM1347 *(2413)*
   25c multicolored, tagged   .40   .20
   Plate block of four   3.75
   FDC *(Apr. 6, 1989)*   1.00

1989. Executive Branch Issue, continuing the branches-of-government series, honors George Washington as the first person to head this government branch. *Offset and intaglio, perforated 11.*

CM1348 *George Washington*

CM1348 *(2414)*
   25c multicolored, tagged   .40   .20
   Plate block of four   4.25
   FDC *(April 16, 1989)*   1.00

1989. South Dakota Statehood Issue honors the centennial of the 41st state. *Gravure, American Bank Note Co., perforated 11.*

CM1349 *Pasque flower, Pioneer Woman and Sod House*

CM1349 *(2416)*
   25c multicolored, tagged   .40   .20
   Plate block of four   3.00
   FDC *(May 3, 1989)*   1.00

1989. Lou Gehrig Issue recognizes one of baseballs immortals, the "Iron Horse" of the New York Yankees. American Sports series. *Gravure, American Bank Note Co., perforated 11.*

CM1350 *Lou Gehrig*

CM1350 *(2417)*

25c multicolored, tagged	1.10	.20
Plate block of four	5.25	
FDC *(June 10, 1989)*		1.00

1989. Ernest Hemingway Issue honors the Nobel Prize-winning author of the The Sun Also Rises and For Whom The Bell Tolls. Literary Arts series. *Gravure, American Bank Note Co., perforated 11.*

CM1351 *Ernest Hemingway*

CM1351 *(2418)*

25c multicolored, tagged	.40	.20
Plate block of four	3.00	
FDC *(July 17, 1989)*		1.00

1989. Moon Landing Anniversary Issue commemorates the 20th anniversary of man's first steps on the Moon. The stamp was the first to meet the basic Priority Mail rate. *Offset and intaglio, perforated 11.*

CM1352 *Astronauts and Flag on Moon*

CM1352 *(2419)*

$2.40 multicolored, tagged	6.00	2.25
Plate block of four	28.50	
FDC *(July 20, 1989)*		4.00
v. Intaglio black omitted	3,000.	
v1. Offset black omitted	4,500.	
v2. Imperforate pair	1,000.	

1989. North Carolina Statehood Issue was the 12th stamp in the Constitution Ratification Bicentennial series. *Gravure, American Bank Note Co., perforated 11.*

CM1353 *Dogwood*

CM1353 *(2347)*

25c multicolored, tagged	.40	.20
Plate block of four	3.95	
FDC *(Aug. 22, 1989)*		1.00

1989. Letter Carriers Issue pays tribute to those who carry America's mail to over 100 million delivery points. *Gravure, American Bank Note Co., perforated 11.*

CM1354 *Letter Carrier Caricatures*

CM1354 *(2420)*

25c multicolored, tagged	.40	.20
Plate block of four	3.95	
FDC *(Aug. 30, 1989)*		1.00

1989. Drafting of the Bill of Rights Issue commemorates the freedoms guaranteed in the first 10 Amendments. *Offset and intaglio, perforated 11.*

CM1355 *Eagle, Stars and Stripes*

CM1355 *(2421)*

25c multicolored, tagged	.40	.20
Plate block of four	5.50	
FDC *(Sept. 25, 1989)*		1.00
v. Intaglio black omitted	350.	

1989. Dinosaurs Issue celebrates the great prehistoric beasts, kicked off Stamp Collecting Month and served as a promotional tie-in with the videocassette release of the movie *The Land Before Time. Intaglio (Giori Press), perforated 11.*

CM1356 *Tyrannosaurus*   CM1357 *Pteranodon*

CM1358 *Stegosaurus*   CM1359 *Apatosaurus* ("Brotosaurus")

CM1356 *(2422)*

25c multicolored, tagged	1.25	.20

CM1357 *(2423)*
25c multicolored, tagged   1.25   .20
CM1358 *(2424)*
25c multicolored, tagged   1.25   .20
CM1359 *(2425)*
25c multicolored, tagged   1.25   .20
    Plate block of four   5.75
    y. Se-tenant block of four
        CM1356-59   4.50   2.50
        FDC *(Oct. 1, 1989)*   1.00
    vy. Block of four, intaglio
      black omitted
    vy1. Any single- intaglio
      black omitted   1,600.   175.

1989. America Issue honors the customs, images and traditions of native Americans prior to Columbus. Part of a 1989-91 Columbian series by members of the Postal Union of the Americas and Spain (PUAS). *Gravure, American Bank Note Co, perforated 11.*

CM1360 *Southwest Carved Figure*

CM1360 *(2426)*
25c multicolored, tagged   .40   .20
    Plate block of four   3.00
    FDC *(Oct. 12, 1989)*   1.00

1989. World Stamp Expo '89 souvenir sheet features a reproduction of the 90¢ stamp from the 1869 Pictorials (No. 96) and three trial color proofs on a single imperforate sheet. *Offset and intaglio, perforated 11.* CM1361

CM1361 *World Stamp Expo '89 Souvenir Sheet*

CM1361 *(2433)*
$3.60 souvenir sheet of four   18.75   13.50
    a. 90c like No. 96, Carmine
      frame, black vignette   2.50   2.00

    b. 90c blue frame, brown
      vignette   2.50   2.00
    c. 90c green frame, blue
      vignette   2.50   2.00
    d. 90c scarlet frame, blue
      vignette   2.50   2.00

1989. Classic Mail Transportation Issue honors vehicles that delivered mail from the 19th and the early 20th century. *Offset and intaglio, perforated 11.*

CM1362, 1366a *Stagecoach*   CM1363, 1366b *Steamboat*

CM1364, 1366c *Biplane*   CM1365, 1366d *Early automobile*

CM1362 *(2434)*
25c multicolored, tagged   .75   .20
CM1363 *(2435)*
25c multicolored, tagged   .75   .20
CM1364 *(2436)*
25c multicolored   .75   .20
CM1365 *(2437)*
25c multicolored, tagged   .75   .20
    Plate block of four   6.00
    y. Se-tenant block of four
        CM1362-65
        FDC *(Nov. 19, 1989)*   1.00
    vy. Block of four, intaglio dark
      blue omitted
    vy1. Any single- intaglio
      blue omitted   1,250.   200.

CM1366 *(2438)*
$1.00 multicolored souvenir sheet, imperforate,
    tagged   5.00   4.00
    a. 25¢ like CM1362   1.25   .75
    b. 25c like CM1363   1.25   .75
    c. 25c like CM1364   1.25   .75
    d. 25c like CM1365   1.25   .75
    v. Souvenir sheet, dark blue
      and gray omitted   5,500.

CM1367 *Mountain Bluebird and Sawtooth Mountains*

1990. Idaho Statehood Issue honors its centennial as the 43rd state to join the Union. *Gravure, American Bank Note Co., perforated 11.*

CM1367(2439)

25c multicolored, tagged	.40	.20
Plate block of four	3.00	
FDC (Jan. 6 1990)		1.00

1990. Love Issue is the first to include a booklet version of the winning Pennsylvania Dutch-inspired design, which came from a design project for Yale University graduate students. *Gravure, U.S. Banknote Corp. (sheet) and BEP (booklet).*

CM1368-69 *Lovebirds*

Perforated 12 1/2 x 13
CM1368 (2440)

25c multicolored, tagged	.40	.20
Plate block of four	3.00	
FDC (Jan. 18, 1990)		1.00
v. Imperforate pair	800.	

Perforated 11 1/2 on two or three sides
CM1369 (2441)

25c multicolored, tagged	.40	.20
v. Pink omitted	220.	
n. Booklet pane of 10	300.	
nv. Pane of 10, pink omitted	2,000.	

1990. Ida B. Wells Issue honors the civil rights activist who was born a slave, and spent her life educating others about the horrors of discrimination and lynching. Black Heritage series. *Gravure, American Bank Note Co., perforated 11.*

CM1370 *Ida B. Wells*

CM1370 (2442)

25c multicolored, tagged	.40	.20
Plate block of four	3.75	
FDC (Feb. 1, 1990)		1.00

1990. Supreme Court Issue, fourth and final stamp in a set honoring the three branches of the federal government, honors the 200th anniversary of the judicial branch. *Offset and intaglio, perforated 11.*

CM1371 *John Marshall*

CM1371 (2415)

25c multicolored, tagged	.40	.20
Plate block of four	4.00	
FDC (Feb. 2, 1990)		1.00

1990. Wyoming Statehood Issue commemorates the centennial of the state's entry into the Union. *Offset and intaglio, perforated 11.*

CM1372 High Mountain Meadows *by Conrad Schwiering*

CM1372 (2444)

25c multicolored, tagged	.40	.20
Plate block of four	3.85	
FDC (Feb. 23, 1990)		1.00
v. Intaglio black omitted	2,500.	

1990. Classic Films Issue showcases four works of Hollywood's Golden Era on the 50th anniversary of their nomination for the Academy Award. *Gravure, American Bank Note Co., perforated 11.*

CM1373 *Judy Garland and Toto, The Wizard of Oz*

CM1374 *Clark Gable and Vivien Leigh,* Gone with the Wind

CM1375 *Gary Cooper,* Beau Geste

CM1376 *John Wayne,* Stagecoach

CM1373 (2445)

25c multicolored, tagged	2.00	.20

CM1374 (2446)

25c multicolored, tagged	2.00	.20

CM1375 (2447)

25c multicolored, tagged	2.00	.20

CM1376 (2448)

25c multicolored, tagged	2.00	.20
Plate block of four	10.00	
y. Se-tenant block of four CM1373-76	9.00	
FDC (March 23, 1990) block of four		5.00

1990. Marianne Moore Issue pays tribute to the Pulitzer Prize-winning poet. Literary Arts series. *Gravure, American Bank Note Co., perforated 11.*

CM1377 *Marianne Moore*

CM1377 *(2449)*
   25c multicolored, tagged   .40   .20
      Plate block of four   3.00
      FDC *(April 18, 1990)*   1.00

1990. American Lighthouses Issue, a se-tenant booklet issue of five designs, portrays ocean lighthouses. *Offset and intaglio, perforated 10, vertically.*

| CM1378 Admiralty Head, Wash. | CM1379 Cape Hatteras, N. C. | CM1380 West Quoddy Head, Main | CM1381 American Shoals, Fl. | CM1382 Sandy Hook, N. J. |

CM1378 *(2470)*
   25c multicolored, tagged   .40   .20
      v. White ("25 / USA") omitted
CM1379 *(2471)*
   25c multicolored, tagged   .40   .20
      v. White ("25 / USA") omitted
CM1380 *(2472)*
   25c multicolored, tagged   .40   .20
      v. White ("25 / USA") omitted
CM1381 *(2473)*
   25c multicolored, tagged   .40   .20
      v. White ("25 / USA") omitted
CM1382 *(2474)*
   25c multicolored, tagged   .40   .20
      FDC *(April 26, 1990)*   1.00
      v. White ("25 / USA") omitted
      n. Se-tenant booklet pane of five
         CM1378-82 FDC   400.
      nv. Booklet pane of five,
         white omitted   75.

1990. Rhode Island Statehood Issue was the final stamp in the Constitution Ratification Bicentennial series. *Offset and intaglio, perforated 11.*

CM1383 *Slater Mill, R.I.*

CM1383 *(2348)*
   25c multicolored, tagged   .40   .20
      Plate block of four   3.95
      FDC *(May 29, 1990)*   1.00

1990. Olympic Athletes Issue honors five of the greatest U.S. Olympic athletes of the first half of the 20th century. *Gravure, American Bank Note Co., perforated 11.*

CM1384 *Jesse Owens*

CM1385 *Ray Ewry*

CM1386 *Hazel Wightman*

CM1387 *Eddie Eagan*

CM1388 *Helene Madison*

CM1384 *(2496)*
   25c multicolored, tagged   .40   .20
CM1385 *(2497)*
   25c multicolored, tagged   .40   .20
CM1386 *(2498)*
   25c multicolored, tagged   .40   .20
CM1387 *(2499)*
   25c multicolored, tagged   .40   .20
CM1388 *(2500)*
   25c multicolored, tagged   .40   .20
      Plate block of 10
      y. Se-tenant strip of five CM1384-88
      FDC *(July 6, 1990)*   1.00

1990. American Indian Headdresses Issue features five different native headdresses or war bonnets. Folk Art series. *Offset and intaglio, perforated 11.*

CM1389 *Assiniboine*

CM1390 *Cheyenne*

CM1391 *Commanche*

CM1392 *Flathead*

CM1393 *Shoshone*

CM1389 (2501)
25c multicolored, tagged | .40 | .20
CM1390 (2502)
25c multicolored, tagged | .40 | .20
CM1391 (2503)
25c multicolored, tagged | .40 | .20
CM1392 (2504)
25c multicolored, tagged | .40 | .20
CM1393 (2505)
25c multicolored, tagged | .40 | .20
   v. Any single, intaglio
     black omitted | 300.
   y. Se-tenant strip of
     five CM1389-93 | 8.50 | 7.50
   vy. Strip of five, intaglio
     black omitted | —
   n. Booklet pane of 10, two
     each CM1389-93 | 14.
   nv. Pane of 10, intaglio
     black omitted | 3,850.

1990. Micronesia and Marshall Island's Issue commemorates the relationship between the United States and the Federated States of Micronesia and the Republic of the Marshall Islands. This was a joint issue among the three postal administrations (Micronesia 188-190, Marshall Islands 300). *Offset and intaglio, perforated 11.*

CM1394 *Canoe*
Micronesia flag

CM1395 *Stick chart, canoe, Marshall Islands flag*

CM1394 (2506)
25c multicolored, tagged | .40 | .20
   v. Intaglio black omitted | 1,000.
CM1395 (2507)
25c multicolored, tagged | .40 | .20
   Plate block of four | 3.85
   FDC (Sept. 28, 1990) | | 1.00
   y. Se-tenant pair CM1394-95 | 1.00 | 1.00
   vy. Se-tenant pair, intaglio
     black omitted | 4,250.

1990. Creatures of the Sea Issue, a joint release by the United States and the Soviet Union (Russia 6228-6231), focuses on the beauty and significance of marine mammals. *Offset and intaglio, perforated 11.*

CM1396 *Killer Whales*   CM1397 *Northern Sea Lions*

CM1398 *Sea Otter*   CM1399 *Dolphin*

CM1396 (2508)
25c multicolored, tagged | .75 | .20
CM1397 (2509)
25c multicolored, tagged | .75 | .20
CM1398 (2510)
25c multicolored, tagged | .75 | .20
CM1399 (2511)
25c multicolored, tagged | .75 | .20
   Plate block of four | 3.95
   FDC (Oct. 3,1990) | | 3.00
   zo. Tagging omitted, any single
   y. Se-tenant block of four
     CM1396-99 | 3.00 | 2.00
   vy. Block of four, intaglio
     black omitted | 1,200.
   vy1. Any single intaglio
     black omitted | 250.
   zoy. Block of four,
     tagging omitted

1990. America Issue honors natural wonders of the Americas as part of the joint release by the 24 participating postal administrations of PUAS. (See also A127). *Gravure, American Bank Note Co., perforated 11.*

CM1400 *Grand Canyon*

CM1400 *(2512)*
> **25c multicolored,** tagged .40 .20
> Plate block of four 3.00
> FDC *(Oct. 12, 1990)* 1.00

1990. Dwight D. Eisenhower Issue pays tribute to the 34th president and the supreme commander of Allied Forces in Europe during World War II. *Gravure, American Bank Note Co., perforated 11.*

CM1401 *Dwight D. Eisenhower*

CM1401 *(2513)*
> **25c multicolored** .45 .20
> Plate block of four 5.00
> FDC *(Oct. 13, 1990)* 1.00
> v. Imperforte pair 2,300.

1991. Switzerland 700th Anniversary Issue honors the small country founded in 1291. Switzerland issued a matching stamp at the same time (Switzerland 1579). *Gravure, American Bank Note Co., perforated 11.*

CM1402 *U.S. Capitol, Swiss Federal Palace*

CM1402 *(2532)*
> **50c multicolored,** tagged .75 .35
> Plate block of four 6.50
> FDC *(Feb. 22, 1991)* 1.30

1991. Vermont Statehood Issue marks the bicentennial of the Green Mountain State, which remained an independent republic until admitted to the Union as the 14th state. *Gravure, American Bank Note Co, perforated 11.*

CM1403 *Vermont Farmland*

CM1403 *(2533)*
> **29c multicolored,** tagged .45 .20
> Plate block of four 3.50
> FDC *(Mar. 1, 1991)* 1.00

1991. U.S. Savings Bond Issue honors the 50th anniversary of the E-Series Savings Bond. *Gravure, perforated 11.*

CM1404 *Bald Eagle*

CM1404 *(2534)*
> **29c multicolored,** tagged .45 .20
> Plate block of four 3.95
> FDC *(April 30, 1991)* 1.00

1991. Love Issue. *Gravure (29c sheet by U.S. Banknote Co., 29c booklet by BEP, 52c sheet by American Bank Note Co.)*

CM1405-06 *Heart-shaped Earth*

Perforated 12 1/2 x 13
CM1405 *(2535)*
> **29c multicolored,** tagged .45 .20
> Plate block of four 3.75
> FDC *(May 9, 1991)* 1.00
> v. Imperforated pair 2,500.

Perforated 11
CM1405A *(2535a)*
> **29c multicolored,** tagged .45 .20
> Plate block of four 5.00

Perforated 11 on two or three sides
CM1406 *(2536)*
> **29c multicolored,** tagged .45 .20
> FDC *(May 9, 1991)* 1.00
> n. Booklet pane of ten 7.50

CM1407 *Fischer's Lovebirds*

CM1407 *(2537)*
> **52c multicolored,** tagged .75 .35
> Plate block of four 5.75
> FDC *(May 9, 1991)* 1.00

1991. William Saroyan Issue honors the Armenian-American novelist, playwright and short story writer. Literary Arts series. This was a joint issue with Russia (Russia 6300). *Gravure, J.W. Fergusson Co. for the American Bank Note Co., perforated 11.*

CM1408 *William Saroyan*

CM1408 *(2538)*
 29c multicolored, tagged   .45   .20
  Plate block of four   3.50
  FDC *(May 22, 1991)*   1.00

1991. Fishing Flies Issue, another five-stamp se-tenant booklet pane, shows five classic and carefully crafted lures. *Gravure, American Bank Note Co, perforated 11.*

CM1409 *Royal Wulff*

CM1410 *Jock Scott*

CM1411 *Apte Tarpon Fly*

CM1412 *Lefty's Deceiver*

CM1413 *Muddler Minnow*

CM1409 *(2545)*
 29c multicolored, tagged   .45   .20
CM1410 *(2546)*
 29c multicolored, tagged   .45   .20
CM1411 *(2547)*
 29c multicolored, tagged   .45   .20
CM1412 *(2548)*
 29c multicolored, tagged   .45   .20
CM1413 *(2549)*
 29c multicolored, tagged   .45   .20
  FDC *(May 31, 1991)*   1.00
  n. Se-tenant booklet pane of five
   (CM 1409-13)   5.50   3.25
   FDC   2.00

1991. Cole Porter Issue honors the 20th-century composer. Performing Arts series. *Gravure, American Bank Note Co., perforated 11.*

CM1414 *Cole Porter*

CM1414 *(2550)*
 29c multicolored, tagged   .45   .20
  Plate block of four   3.75
  FDC *(June 8, 1991)*   1.00
  v. Vertical pair, imperforate
   between   6.00

1991. Desert Shield-Desert Storm Issue pays tribute to those who served in the Gulf War. *Gravure (sheet version by J.W. Fergusson and Sons for Stamp Venturers, booklet version by the Multi-Color Corp. for the American Bank Note Co.)*

CM1415-16 *Southwest Asia Service Medal*

Perforated 11
CM1415 *(2551)*
 29c multicolored, tagged   .45   .20
  Plate block of four   3.50
  FDC *(July 2, 1991)*   1.00
  v. Vertical pair, imperforate
   horizontally   2,000.

Perforated 11 on one or two sides
CM1416 *(2552)*
 29c multicolored, tagged   .45   .20
  FDC *(July 2, 1991)*   1.00
  n. Booklet pane of five   4.00
   FDC   2.00

1991. Olympic Track and Field Issue promoted the USPS sponsorship of the 1992 Winter and Summer Olympics. *Gravure, American Bank Note Co., perforated 11.*

CM1417 *Pole Vault*

CM1418 *Discus*

CM1419 *Women's Sprint*

CM1417 *(2553)*
 29c multicolored, tagged   .45   .20
CM1418 *(2554)*
 29c multicolored, tagged   .45   .20
CM1419 *(2555)*
 29c multicolored, tagged   .45   .20

CM1420 *Javelin*

CM1421 *Women's Hurdles*

CM1420 *(2556)*
29c multicolored, tagged   .45   .20
CM1421 *(2557)*
29c multicolored, tagged   .45   .20
Plate block of ten   9.75
y. Se-tenant strip of five,
CM1417-21
FDC *(July 12, 1991)* any single   1.00
FDC, strip of five   4.50

1991. Numismatics Issue salutes the hobby of coin and currency collecting. *Offset and intaglio, perforated 11.*

CM1422 *Coins and Banknotes*

CM1422 *(2558)*
29c multicolored, tagged   .45   .20
Plate block of four   4.50
FDC *(Aug. 13, 1991)*   1.00

1991. Basketball Centennial Issue commemorates the 100th anniversary of one of the world's most popular sports. Many basketball fans pointed out the design looks like an illegal goaltend. *Gravure, perforated 11.*

CM1423 *Hands above Basketball Hoop*

CM1423 *(2560)*
29c multicolored, tagged   .45   .20
Plate block of four   4.50
FDC *(Aug. 28, 1991)*   1.00

1991. American Comedians Issue showcases comedians and teams of the first half of the 20th century. The stamps were the first designed by the famed caricaturist Al Hirschfeld. *Offset and intaglio, perforated 11.*

CM1424 *Stan Laurel, Oliver Hardy*

CM1425 *Edgar Bergen, Charlie McCarthy*

CM1426 *Jack Benny*

CM1427 Fanny Brice

CM1428 *Bud Abbott, Lou Costello*

CM1424 *(2562)*
29c multicolored, tagged   .45   .20
CM1425 *(2563)*
29c multicolored, tagged   .45   .20
CM1426 *(2564)*
29c multicolored, tagged   .45   .20
CM1427 *(2565)*
29c multicolored, tagged   .45   .20
CM1428 *(2566)*
29c multicolored, tagged   .45   .20
y. Se-tenant strip of five
(CM1424-28)   3.00
FDC *(Aug. 29, 1991)*   1.00
a. Intaglio purple and red
omitted, any single   —
n. Booklet pane of 10,
two each CM1424-28   600.
vn. Booklet pane, intaglio
purple and red omitted   850.

1991. World War II Commemorative Sheet is the first in an annual series issued through 1995. *Offset and intaglio, perforated 11.*

CM1429 *(2559)*
$2.90 Commemorative sheet
a. 29c Military Vehicles, tagged   .80   .45
b. 29c Draft Recruits, tagged   .80   .45
c. 29c Dockside View, tagged   .80   .45
d. 29c Roosevelt and Churchill,
tagged   .80   .45

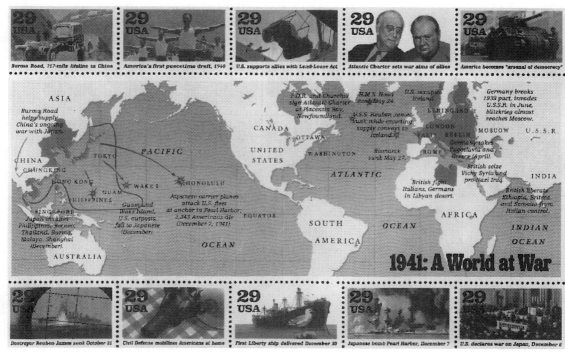

CM1429
1941: A World at War

e. 29c Tank, tagged .... .80 .45
f. 29c Sinking of *Reuben James*,
　　tagged .... .80 .45
g. 29c Gas Mask and Helmet,
　　tagged .... .80 .45
h. 29c Liberty Ship, tagged .80 .45
i. 29c Pearl Harbor, tagged .80 .45
j. 29c Congress Declares War,
　　tagged .... .80 .45
FDC (Sept. 3, 1991) any single 1.00
FDC Complete sheet 6.50
v. Black omitted, complete
　　pane of 20 12,650.

1991. District of Columbia Bicentennial Issue marks the 100th anniversary of the federal district selected by Washington as a site for the permanent capital. *Offset and intaglio, perforated 11.*

CM1430 *Early View up Pennsylvania Avenue*

CM1430 *(2561)*
29c multicolored, tagged ... .45 .20
　　Plate block of four 3.50
　　FDC *(Sept. 7, 1991)* 1.00
　　a. Intaglio black omitted 150.
　　av. Plate block of four,
　　　　intaglio black omitted 650.

1991. Jan E. Matzeliger Issue honors the man who patented a machine for shaping shoes, which revolutionized shoe manufacturing in the United States. Black Heritage series. *Gravure, J.W. Fergusson & Sons for the American Bank Note Co., perforated 11.*

CM1431 *Jan E. Matzeliger*

CM1431 *(2567)*
29c multicolored, tagged ... .45 .20
　　Plate block of four 4.25
　　FDC *(Sept. 15, 1991)* 1.00
　　v. Horizontal pair, imperforate
　　　　vertically 1,750.
　　v1. Vertical pair, imperforate
　　　　horizontally 1,600.
　　v2. Imperforate pair 2,500.

1991. Space Exploration Issues, a se-tenant ten-stamp booklet pane features unmanned spacecraft launched to the Earth's moon and each of the nine planets that orbit the sun, with the exception of Pluto, which is depicted as well. *Gravure, perforated 11 on two or three sides.*

CM1432 *Mercury,*   CM1433 *Venus,*   CM1434 *Earth,*   CM1435 *Moon,*   CM1436 *Mars,*
Mariner 10   *Mariner 2.*   *Landsat*   *Lunar Orbiter*   *Viking Orbiter*

CM1437 *Jupiter,*   CM1438 *Saturn,*   CM1439 *Uranus,*   CM1440 *Neptune,*   CM1441 *Pluto*
Pioneer II   *Voyager 2*   *Voyager 2*   *Voyager 2*

CM1432 *(2568)*
  29c multicolored, tagged   .45   .20
CM1433 *(2569*
  29c multicolored, tagged   .45   .20
CM1434 *(2570)*
  29c multicolored, tagged   .45   .20
CM1435 *(2571)*
  29c multicolored, tagged   .45   .20
CM1436 *(2572)*
  29c multicolored, tagged   .45   .20
CM1437 *(2573)*
  29c multicolored, tagged   .45   .20
CM1438 *(2574)*
  29c multicolored, tagged   .45   .20
CM1439 *(2575)*
  29c multicolored, tagged   .45   .20
CM1440 *(2576)*
  29c multicolored, tagged   .45   .20
CM1441 *(2577)*
  29c multicolored, tagged   .45   .20
    FDC *(Oct. 1, 1991)* any single   1.00
    Booklet pane (CM1432-41)   8.75
    FDC   2.00

1992. Winter Olympics Issue honors five of the fastest sporting events of the games held in Albertville, France. *Gravure, J.W. Fergusson for Stamp Venturers, perforated 11.*

CM1442 *Ice Hockey*

CM1442 *(2611)*
  29c multicolored, tagged   .45   .20

CM1443 *Figure Skating*

CM1443 *(2612)*
  29c multicolored, tagged   .45   .20

CM1444 *Speed Skating*

CM1445 *Skiing*

CM1446 *Bobsledding*

CM1444 *(2613)*
  29c multicolored, tagged   .45   .20
CM1445 *(2614)*
  29c multicolored, tagged   .45   .20
CM1446 *(2615)*
  29c multicolored, tagged   .45   .20
    Plate block of 10   9.75
    y. Se-tenant strip (CM1442-46)   3.00
    FDC *(Jan. 11, 1992)* any single   1.00
    FDC, strip of five   2.00

1992. World Columbian Stamp Expo '92 Issue promotes the international stamp show in Chicago. The stamp shows a detail form the 1869 15c Pictorial (No. 92). *Offset and intaglio, perforated 11.*

CM1447 *World Columbian Stamp Expo.*

CM1447 *(2616)*

29c multicolored, tagged	.45	.20
Plate block of four	3.50	
FDC *(Jan. 24, 1992)*		1.00
zo. Tagging omitted	—	

1992. W.E.B. Du Bois Issue, honors the noted writer, historian, critic, scholar and educator. The Niagara Movement he founded in 1905 evolved into the NAACP. Black Heritage series. *Offset and intaglio, perforated 11.*

CM1448 *W.E.B. Du Bois*

CM1448 *(2617)*

29c multicolored, tagged	.45	.20
Plate block of four	3.75	
FDC *(Jan. 31, 1992)*		1.00

1992. Love Issue. *Gravure, U.S. Bank Note Co., perforated 11.*

CM1449 *Heart*

CM1449 *(2618)*

29c multicolored, tagged	.45	.20
Plate block of four	3.50	
FDC *(Feb. 6, 1992*		1.00
v. Horizontal pair, imperforate between	800.	

1992. Olympic Baseball Issue commemorates the acceptance of baseball as an official Olympic sport. *Gravure, perforated 11.*

CM1450 *Player Sliding into Home*

CM1450 *(2619)*

29c multicolored, tagged	1.00	.20
Plate block of four	4.75	
FDC *(April 3, 1992)*		1.00

1992. Voyage of Columbus Issue, a joint issue with Italy (Italy 2416-2419), honors the explorer's historic first voyage to the New World with four related se-tenant designs. *Offset and intaglio, perforated 11.*

CM1451 *Seeking Queen Isabella's support*
CM1452 *Crossing the Atlantic*
CM1453 *Approaching land*
CM1454 *Coming ashore*

CM1451 *Seeking Queen Isabella's support* CM1452 *Crossing the Atlantic*

CM1453 *Approaching land* CM1454 *Coming ashore*

CM1451 *(2620)*

29c multicolored, tagged	1.00	.20

CM1452 *(2621)*

29c multicolored, tagged	1.00	.20

CM1453 *(2622)*

29c multicolored, tagged	1.00	.20

CM1454 *(2623)*

29c multicolored, tagged	1.00	.20
Plate block of four	4.75	
y. Se-tenant block of four (CM1451-54)	4.00	3.00
FDC *(Apr. 24, 1992)* any single		4.00
FDC, se-tenant block of four		

1992 New York Stock Exchange Issue commemorates the bicentennial of the exchange, originally formed by 24 brokers and dealers who met regularly under a tree. *Offset and intaglio by Jeffries Bank Note Co. for the American Bank Note Co., perforated 11.*

CM1455 *Stock Certificate*

CM1455 *(2630)*

29c multicolored, tagged	.45	.20
Plate block of four	3.50	
FDC *(May 17, 1992)*		1.00

1992. Columbian Souvenir Sheets were a joint issue with Italy, Portugal and Spain at the World Columbian Expo '92 (Italy 2423-28, Portugal 2102-07, Spain 3177-82). Stamps depicted on the sheets are close in appearence to the original Columbian commemoratives of 1893 (CM1-16), but are inscribed "1992" at upper right. *Offset and intaglio by the American Bank Note Co., perforated 10 1/2.*

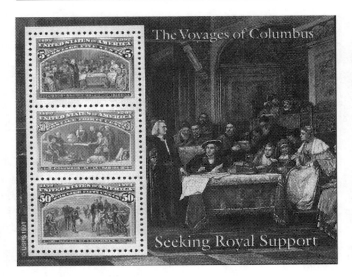

CM1456 *Seeking Royal Support*

CM1459 *Royal Favor Restored*

CM1457 *First Sighting of Land*

CM1460 *Claiming a New World*

CM1458 *Reporting Discoveries*

CM1456 *(2626)*

85c sheet of three	3.00	
a. 5c brown like CM5		.75
b. 30c orange brown like CM10		1.00
c. 50c slate black like CM11		1.00
FDC *(May 22, 1992)*		

CM1457 *(2624)*

$1.05 sheet of three	2.50	
a. 1c deep blue like CM1		.50
b. 4c gray blue like CM4		.75
c. $1 Venetian red like CM12		2.50
FDC *(May 22, 1992)*		

CM1458 *(2628)*

$2.25 sheet of three	5.00	
a. 10c black brown like CM8		.75
b. 15c deep bluish green like CM9		.75
c. $2 brown red like CM13		4.50
FDC *(May 22, 1992)*		

CM1459 *(2627)*
  $3.14 sheet of three   8.50
    a. 6c dark lilac like CM6   1.00
    b. 8c brown purple like CM7   1.00
    c. $3 bronze green like CM14   5.50
    FDC *(May 22, 1992)*

CM1460 *(2625)*
  $4.07 sheet of three   9.00
    a. 2c dull purple like CM2   .75
    b. 3c dark bluish green like CM3   .75
    c. $4 deep rose like CM15   7.00
    FDC *(May 22, 1992)*

CM1461 *Christopher Columbus*

CM1461 *(2629)*
  $5 sheet of one. Black like CM 15.   12.   8.50
    FDC *(May 22, 1992)*
    Full set of six s/s   40.   37.50

1992. Space Achievements Issue, a joint issue with Russia (Russia 6376-79), honors a broad spectrum of space exploration by the two countries. *Gravure, perforated 11.*

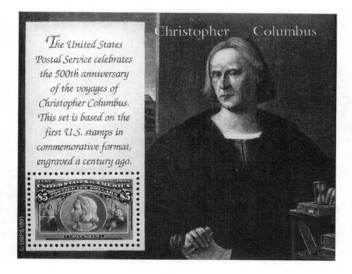

CM1462
*Space
Shuttle*

CM1463
*Astronaut,
Space Shuttle,
Space Station*

CM1464
*Lunar
Lander,
Apollo
and
Vostok
Spacecraft,
Sputnik*

CM1465 *Soyuz,
Mercury and
Gemini
spacecraft*

CM1462 *(2631)*
  29c multicolored, tagged   1.00   .20

CM1463 *(2632)*
  29c multicolored, tagged   1.00   .20
CM1464 *(2633)*
  29c multicolored, tagged   1.00   .20
CM1465 *(2634)*
  29c multicolored, tagged   1.00   .20
    Plate block of four   4.50
    Se-tenant block of four,
      (CM1462-65)   4.00   2.50
    FDC *(May 29, 1992)* any single   1.00
    FDC, block of four   4.00

1992. Alaska Highway Issue marks the 50th anniversary of the completion of the 1,500-mile route connecting army installations in Alaska and the United States during World War II. *Offset and intaglio, perforated 11.*

CM1466 *Alaska Highway*

CM1466 *(2635)*
  29c multicolored, tagged   .45   .20
    Plate block of four   3.50
    FDC *(May 30, 1992)*   1.00
    a. Intaglio black omitted   900.

1992. Kentucky Statehood Issue celebrates the bicentennial of the entry of the Bluegrass State into the Union. *Gravure, J.W. Fergusson & Sons for Stamp Venturers, perforated 11.*

CM1467 *My Old Kentucky Home
State Park*

CM1467 *(2636)*
  29c multicolored, tagged   .45   .20
    Plate block of four   3.50
    FDC *(June 1, 1992)*   1.00

1992. Summer Olympic Games Issue presents five events contested in the quadrennial games held in Barcelona, Spain. *Gravure, J.W. Fergusson & Sons for Stamp Venturers.*

CM1468 *Soccer*

CM1468 *(2637)*
  29c multicolored, tagged   .45   .20

CM1469 *Gymnastics*

CM1470 *Volleyball*

CM1471 *Boxing*

CM1472 *Swimming*

CM1469 *(2638)*
  29c multicolored, tagged   .45   .20
CM1470 *(2639)*
  29c multicolored, tagged   .45   .20
CM1471 *(2640)*
  29c multicolored, tagged   .45   .20
CM1472 *(2641)*
  29c multicolored, tagged   .45   .20
     Plate block of ten   10.
     Se-tenant strip of five   8.00
     FDC *(June 11, 1992)* any single   1.00
     FDC, strip of five

1992. Hummingbirds Issue, a popular booklet release, featured five varieties of these colorful birds. *Gravure, Multi-Color Corp. for the American Bank Note Co., perforated 11.*

CM1473   CM1474   CM1475   CM1476   CM1477

Ruby-throated humming bird   Broad-billed humming bird   Costa's humming bird   Rufous humming bird   Calliope humming bird

CM1473 *(2642)*
  29c multicolored, tagged   .45   .20
CM1474 *(2643)*
  29c multicolored, tagged   .45   .20

CM1475 *(2644)*
  29c multicolored, tagged   .45   .20
CM1476 *(2645)*
  29c multicolored, tagged   .45   .20
CM1477 *(2646)*
  29c multicolored, tagged   .45   .20
     FDC *(June 15, 1992)* any single   1.00
     n. Booklet pane of five
     (CM1473-77)   4.50
     FDC   1.00

1992. Wildflowers Issue showcased 50 colorful, blooming native plants. While no specific states are attached to each flower, one or more of the flowers are found in each of the states. *Offset, Ashton-Potter America, Inc., perforated 11.*

Two simultaneous printings were produced, one with four panes (plate number positions) per sheet and the other with six panes (plate number positions) per sheet. Stamps from the four-pane press were assigned odd plate numbers and stamps from the six-pane press were assigned even plate numbers. Further, an illustration is found in the selvage of each pane depicting an uncut sheet and the location of the specific pane in hand.

CM1478-CM1527 Wildflowers from around the nation

CM1478 *(2647)*
  29c Indian Paintbrush, tagged   .95   .60
CM1479 *(2648)*
  29c Fragrant Water Lily, tagged   .95   .60
CM1480 *(2649)*
  29c Meadow Beauty, tagged   .95   .60
CM1481 *(2650)*
  29c Jack-In-The-Pulpit, tagged   .95   .60
CM1482 *(2651)*
  29c California Poppy, tagged   .95   .60
CM1483 *(2652)*
  29c Large-Flowered Trillium, tagged .95   .60
CM1484 *(2653)*
  29c Tickseed, tagged   .95   .60
CM1485 *(2654)*
  29c Shooting Star, tagged   .95   .60
CM1486 *(2655)*
  29c Stream Violet, tagged   .95   .60
CM1487 *(2656)*
  29c Bluets, tagged   .95   .60
CM1488 *(2657)*
  29c Herb Robert, tagged   .95   .60
CM1489 *(2658)*
  29c Marsh Marigold, tagged   .95   .60
CM1490 *(2659)*
  29c Sweet White Violet, tagged   .95   .60
CM1491 *(2660)*
  29c Claret Cup Cactus, tagged   .95   .60
CM1492 *(2661)*
  29c White Mountain Avens, tagged .95   .60
CM1493 *(2662)*
  29c Sessile Bellwort, tagged   .95   .60

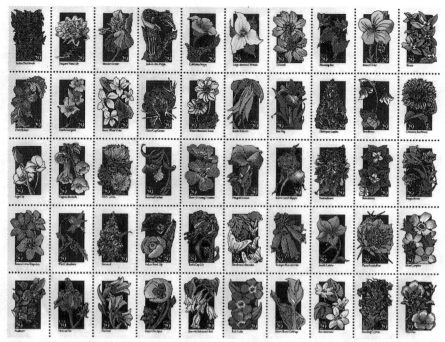

CM1478-CM1527 *Wildflowers from around the nation*

CM1494 *(2663)*
29c Blue Flag, tagged .95 .60
CM1495 *(2664)*
29c Harlequin Lupine, tagged .95 .60
CM1496 *(2665)*
29c Twinflower, tagged .95 .60
CM1497 *(2666)*
29c Common Sunflower, tagged .95 .60
CM1498 *(2667)*
29c Sego Lily, tagged .95 .60
CM1499 *(2668)*
29c Virginia Bluebells, tagged .95 .60
CM1500 *(2669)*
29c Ohi'a Lehua, tagged .95 .60
CM1501 *(2670)*
29c Rosebun Orchid, tagged .95 .60
CM1502 *(2671)*
29c Showy Evening Primrose, tagged .95 .60
CM1503 *(2672)*
29c Fringed Gentian, tagged .95 .60
CM1504 *(2673)*
29c Yellow Lady's Slipper, tagged .95 .60
CM1505 *(2674)*
29c Passionflower, tagged .95 .60
CM1506 *(2675)*
29c Bunchberry, tagged .95 .60
CM1507 *(2676)*
29c Pasqueflower, tagged .95 .60
CM1508 *(2677)*
29c Round-Lobed Hepatica, tagged .95 .60
CM1509 *(2678)*
29c Wild Columbine, tagged .95 .60
CM1510 *(2679)*
29c Fireweed, tagged .95 .60
CM1511 *(2680)*
29c Indian Pond Lily, tagged .95 .60

CM1512 *(2681)*
29c Turk's Cap Lily, tagged .95 .60
CM1513 *(2682)*
29c Dutchman's Breeches, tagged .95 .60
CM1514 *(2683)*
29c Trumpet Honeysuckle, tagged .95 .60
CM1515 *(2684)*
29c Jacob's Ladder, tagged .95 .60
CM1516 *(2685)*
29c Plains Prickly Pear, tagged .95 .60
CM1517 *(2686)*
29c Moss Campion, tagged .95 .60
CM1518 *(2687)*
29c Bearberry, tagged .95 .60
CM1519 *(2688)*
29c Mexican Hat, tagged .95 .60
CM1520 *(2689)*
29c Harebell, tagged .95 .60
CM1521 *(2690)*
29c Desert Five Spot, tagged .95 .60
CM1522 *(2691)*
29c Smooth Solomon's Seal, tagged .95 .60
CM1523 *(2692)*
29c Red Maids, tagged .95 .60
CM1524 *(2693)*
29c Yellow Skunk Cabbage, tagged .95 .60
CM1525 *(2694)*
29c Rue Anemone, tagged .95 .60
CM1526 *(2695)*
29c Standing Cypress, tagged .95 .60
CM1527 *(2696)*
29c Wild Flax, tagged .95 .60
    Pane of 50 (CM1478-1527) 42.50
    FDC *(July 24, 1992)* any single 1.00
    FDC, pane of 50 30.

1992. World War II Commemorative Sheet includes a map and stamps showing events of the war in 1942. *Offset and intaglio, perforated 11.*

CM1528 *World War II 1942 events*

CM1528 *(2697)*
$2.90 sheet of ten

a. 29c B-25 Raid on Tokyo,tagged	.75	.45	
b. 29c Ration Stamps, tagged	.75	.45	
c. 29c Carrier Crewman and fighter tagged	.75	.45	
d. 29c Prisoners of War,tagged	.75	.45	
e. 29c Atack on Aleutian Islands, tagged	.75	.45	
f. 29c Coded Message, tagged	.75	.45	
g. 29c USS Yorktown, tagged	.75	.45	
h. 29c Woman Defense Worker, tagged	.75	.45	
i. 29c Marines at Guadalcanal, tagged	.75	.45	
j. 29c Tank in Desert, tagged	.75	.45	
Block of 10 (CM1528a-j)	18.25		
FDC (Aug. 17, 1992) any single		1.00	
FDC, complete sheet		8.00	
v. Red omitted, Pane of 20	6,050.		

1992. Dorothy Parker Issue honors the writer, poet and critic. Literary Arts series. *Gravure by J.W. Fergusson & Sons for Stamp Venturers, perforated 11.*

CM1529 *Dorothy Parker*

CM1529 *(2698)*

29c multicolored, tagged	.45	.20
Plate block of four	3.50	
FDC (Aug. 22, 1992)		.75

1992. Theodore von Kármán Issue pays tribute to the aerospace scientist credited with establishing the center for rocket research that now is the Jet Propulsion Laboratory at the California Institute of Technology. *Gravure, J.W. Fergusson & Sons for Stamp Venturers, perforated 11.*

CM1530 *Theodore von Kármán*

CM1530 *(2699)*

29c multicolored, tagged	.45	.20
Plate block of four	3.50	
FDC (Aug. 31, 1992)		1.00

1992. Minerals Issue featured specimens from the Smithsonian Institution's National Museum of Natural History collection. *Offset and intaglio, perforated 11.*

CM1531 *Azurite*

CM1532 *Copper*

CM1533 *Variscite*

CM1534 *Wulfenite*

CM1531 *(2702)*
  29c multicolored, tagged   .45   .20
CM1532 *(2703)*
  29c multicolored, tagged   .45   .20
CM1533 *(2700)*
  29c multicolored, tagged   .45   .20
CM1534 *(2701)*
  29c multicolored, tagged   .45   .20
    Plate block of four   4.50
    y. Se-tenant block or strip
       of four, (CM1531-34)   3.00
    FDC *(Sept. 17, 1992)* any single   1.00
    FDC, block or strip of four   2.00
    v. silver omitted

1992. Juan Rodríguez Cabrillo Issue recalls the Spanish explorer who named San Miguel Harbor, later the site of San Diego, CA. *Printed by The Press and J.W. Fergusson & Sons for Stamp Venturers, perforated 11.*

CM1535 *Juan Rodríguez Cabrillo*

CM1535 *(2704)*
  29c multicolored, tagged   .45   .20
    Plate block of four   3.50
    FDC *(Sept. 28, 1992)*   1.00

1992. Wild Animals Issue depicts five popular animals in U.S. zoos. *Gravure, J.W. Fergusson & Sons for Stamp Venturers, perforated 11 horizontally.*

CM1536 *(2705)*
  29c multicolored, tagged   .45   .20
CM1537 *(2706)*
  29c multicolored, tagged   .45   .20

CM1536 *Giraffe*

CM1537 *Giant Panda*

CM1538 *Flamingo*

CM1539 *King Penguins*

CM1540 *White Bengal Tiger*

CM1538 *(2707)*
  29c multicolored, tagged   .45   .20
CM1539 *(2708)*
  29c multicolored, tagged   .45   .20
CM1540 *(2709)*
  29c multicolored, tagged   .45   .20
    FDC *(Oct. 1, 1992)* any single   1.00
    n. Booklet pane of five (CM1536-40)
    FDC   2.00

1992. New Year Issue was the first U.S. stamp to honor the Asian lunar holiday. *Offset and intaglio, American Bank Note Co., perforated 11.*

CM1541 *Rooster and Chinese Characters*

CM1541 *(2720)*
  29c multicolored, tagged   .45   .20
    Plate block of four   3.95
    FDC *(Dec. 30, 1992)*   1.00

1993. Elvis Presley Issue of 500 million stamops represented a massive press run for a single commemorative. reflecting the interest in the rock 'n roll entertainer. The public in a write-in poll voted for the desing of this stamp over a second design showing an older-looking portrait of the pop icon. This stamp is also the first in a lengthy and eclectic American Music series. *Gravure, perforated 11.*

CM1542 *Elvis Presley*

CM1542 *(2721)*

29c multicolored, tagged	.45	.20
Plate block of four	3.50	
FDC *(Jan. 8, 1993)*		1.00

1993. Space Fantasy Issue is reminiscent of the 1930s vision of space travel made popular in movie and comic-book adventures. *Gravure, perforated 11 vertically.*

CM 1543	CM1544	CM1545	CM1546	CM1547

CM1543 *(2741)*

29c multicolored, tagged	.45	.20

CM1544 *(2742)*

29c multicolored, tagged	.45	.20

CM1545 *(2743)*

29c multicolored, tagged	.45	.20

CM1546 *(2744)*

29c multicolored, tagged	.45	.20

CM1547 *(2745)*

29c multicolored, tagged	.45	.20
FDC *(Jan. 25, 1993)* any single		1.00
n. Booklet pane		
of five (CM1541-45)	5.50	
FDC		2.00

1993. Percy Lavon Julian Issue honors the resarch chemist who synthesized cortisone for treatment of arthritis. Black Heritage series. *Offset and intaglio, perforated 11.*

CM1548 *Percy Laron Julian*

CM1548 *(2746)*

29c multicolored, tagged	.45	.20
Plate block of four	3.50	
FDC *(Jan. 29, 1993)*		1.00

1993. Oregon Trail Issue recalled the 2,000-mile stretch from Independence, MO, to Oregon City, OR, that was a popular route used by settlers traveling west. *Offset and intaglio, perforated 11.*

CM1549 *The Oregon Trail*

CM1549 *(2747)*

29c multicolored, tagged	.45	.20
Plate block of four	3.50	
FDC *(Feb. 12, 1993)*		1.00
zo. Tagging omitted		

The official first day city was Salem, OR, but the stamp was available February 12th at 36 cities along the Trail.

1993. World University Games Issue celebrates the first time this biennial competition was held in the United States. *Gravure, perforated 11.*

CM1550 *World University Games*

CM1550 *(2748)*

29c multicolored, tagged	.45	.20
Plate block of four	4.00	
FDC *(Feb. 25, 1993)*		1.00

CM1551 *Grace Kelly*

1993. Grace Kelly Issue memorializes the American actress who became Princess of Monaco. Monaco and the United States jointly issued similar stamps (Monaco 2127). *Intaglio, Stamp Venturers, perforated 11.*

CM1551 *(2749)*

29c blue, tagged	.45	.20
Plate block of four	3.50	
FDC *(March 24, 1993)*		1.00

1993. Oklahoma! Issue paid tribute to the landmark American musical. The stamp was available for sale in every post office in the state on its first day, rather than at a single outlet. American Music series. *Gravure, perforated 10.*

CM1552

CM1552 *(2722)*

29c multicolored, tagged	.45	.20
Plate block of four	3.50	
FDC *(March 30, 1993)*		1.00

1993. Circus Issue honored the 200th anniversary of the first circus performance in America. *Offset, Ashton Potter America, perforated 11.*

CM1553 *Trapeze Artist*

CM1554 *Elephant*

CM1555 *Clown*

CM1556 *Ringmaster*

CM1553 *(2752)*
29c multicolored, tagged .45 .20
CM1554 *(2753)*
29c multicolored, tagged .45 .20
CM1555 *(2750)*
29c multicolored, tagged .45 .20
CM1556 *(2751)*
29c multicolored, tagged .45 .20
  Plate block of six 6.75
  y. Se-tenant block
    of four (CM1553-56)
  FDC *(Apr. 6, 1993)* 2.00

1993. Cherokee Strip Land Run Centennial Issue
commemorates the events of September 16, 1893, when
more than 100,000 pioneers raced to stake out land
claims in the eight million acre parcel of land known as
the "Cherokee Strip." *Offset and intaglio, American Bank
Note Co., perforated 11.*

CM1557

CM1557 *(2754)*
29c multicolored, tagged .45 .20
  Plate block of four 3.50
  FDC *(Apr 17, 1993)* 1.00

1993. Dean Acheson Issue honors the former U.S.
secretary of state. *Intaglio, Stamp Venturers, perforated 11.*

CM1558 *Dean Acheson*

CM1558 *(2755)*
29c multicolored, tagged .45 .20
  Plate block of four 3.50
  FDC *(Apr 21, 1993)* 1.00

1993. Sporting Horses Issue commemorates four
equestrian events. *Offset and intaglio, Stamp Venturers,
perforated 11.*

CM1559 *Steeplechase*   CM1560 *Thoroughbred Racing*

CM1561 *Harness Racing*   CM1562 *Polo*

CM1559 *(2756)*
29c multicolored, tagged .45 .20
CM1569 *(2757)*
29c multicolored, tagged .45 .20
CM1561 *(2758)*
29c multicolored, tagged .45 .20
CM1562 *(2759)*
29c multicolored, tagged .45 .20
  Plate block of four 4.25
  FDC *(May 1, 1993)*
  y. Se-tenant block of
    four CM1559-62
  vy. Block of four, intaglio
    black omitted 1650.
  vy1. Any single, intaglio, black
    omitted 375.

1993. Garden Flowers Issue show an array of popular
blooms in a booklet format. *Offset and intaglio,
perforated 11 vertically.*

CM1563 *Hyacinth* CM1564 *Daffodil* CM1565 *Tulip* CM1566 *Iris* CM1567 *Lilac*

CM1563 *(2760)*
29c multicolored, tagged .45 .20
CM1564 *(2761)*
29c multicolored, tagged .45 .20
CM1565 *(2672)*
29c multicolored, tagged .45 .20

CM1566 *(2763)*
29c multicolored, tagged   .45   .20
CM1567 *(2764)*
29c multicolored, tagged   .45   .20
   FDC *(May 15, 1993)*   1.00
   n. Booklet pane of
       five (CM1563-67)   5.50
   FDC   2.00
   v. Booklet pane, imperforated 2,750.
   v1. Booklet pane, black
       omitted   375.

1993. World War II Commemorative Sheet includes a
map and stamps showing events of the war in 1943.
Offset and intaglio, perforated 11.

CM1568 *1943: Turning the Tide*

CM1568 *(2765)*
$2.90 sheet of ten,   8.75   7.00
   a. Allied Escort ships, tagged   .75   .45
   b. Military Medics, tagged   .75   .45
   c. Sicily Attacked, tagged   .75   .45
   d. B-24's Hit Ploesti, tagged   .75   .45
   e. V-mail Delivers Letters,
       tagged   .75   .45
   f. Italy Invaded (PT boat),
       tagged   .75   .45
   g. War Bonds and Stamps,
       tagged   .75   .45
   h. "Willie and Joe", tagged   .75   .45
   i. Gold Stars Marks losses,
       tagged   .75   .45
   j. Marines Assault Tarawa,
       tagged   .75   .45

   FDC *(May 31, 1993)* any single   1.00
   FDC, complete sheet   10.

1993. Hank Williams Issue honored the country singer
and composer credited with integrating country music
and rock 'n roll. *Gravure, Stamp Venturers, perforated 11.*

CM1569 *Hank Williams*

CM1569 *(2723)*
29c multicolored, tagged   .45   .20
   Plate block of four   3.50
   FDC (June 9, 1993)   1.00

1993. Rock 'n Roll - Rhythm & Blues Issue honored seven stars in a continuation of the American Music series, including a second Elvis Presley stamp that spells out his last name. Additional personalities featured in this issue are Buddy Holly, Ritchie Valens, Bill Haley, Dinah Washington, Otis Redding, and Clyde McPhatter. The stamps were released in a pane of 35 stamps and a booklet of 20 stamps. The booklet consists of two panes of eight (with six of the seven honorees appearing once and Elvis Presley appearing twice), and one pane of four (the bottom four stamps of the pane of eight).

   Although the stamp designs are similar, the stamps in the booklet panes are printed in magenta, cyan, yellow, and black, while the commemoratie sheet is printed in those four colors plus additional blue and red inks. The sheet stamps are 31.5 mm high and booklet stamps are 31.1 mm high.

CM1570, CM1577 *Elvis Presley*

CM1571, CM1582 *Buddy Holly*

CM1572, CM1580 *Ritchie Valens*

CM1573, CM1578 *Bill Haley*

CM1574, CM1583 *Dinah Washington*

CM1575, CM1581 *Otis Redding*

CM1576, CM1579 *Clyde McPhatter*

Gravure, Stamp Venturers.
Perforated 10 on four sides

CM1570 (2724)		
29c multicolored, tagged	.45	.20
CM1571 (2725)		
29c multicolored, tagged	.45	.20
CM1572 (2726)		
29c multicolored, tagged	.45	.20
CM1573 (2727)		
29c multicolored, tagged	.45	.20
CM1574 (2728)		
29c multicolored, tagged	.45	.20
CM1575 (2729)		
29c multicolored, tagged	.45	.20
CM1576 (2730)		
29c multicolored, tagged	.45	.20
Commemorative Sheet of 35 (includes four plate nos.)		
FDC (*June 16, 1993*) any single		
FDC, sheet		

Gravure, Multi-Color Corp.
Perforated 11 on one or two sides

CM1577 (2731)		
29c multicolored, tagged	.45	.20
CM1578 (2732)		
29c multicolored, tagged	.45	.20
CM1579 (2733)		
29c multicolored, tagged	.45	.20
CM1580 (2734)		
29c multicolored, tagged	.45	.20
CM1581 (2735)		
29c multicolored, tagged	.45	.20
CM1582 (2736)		
29c multicolored, tagged	.45	.20
CM1583 (2737)		
29c multicolored, tagged	.45	.20
FDC (June 16, 1993), any single		
n. Pane of eight, (Two of CM1577, oneeach of CM1578-83)		
FDC, pane of eight		
n1. Pane of four, (CM1577 and CM1581-83, plus tab)		
FDC, pane of four		

The vertically oriented pane of eight consists of the following stamps, from top to bottom: CM1577, CM1578, CM1579, CM1580, CM1581, CM1582, CM1583, CM1577. The vertically oriented pane of four consists of the following stamps, from top to bottom: CM1581, CM1582, CM1583, CM1577. A complete booklet consists of two panes of eight and one pane of four.

1993. Joe Louis Issue honors the heavyweight boxing champion and was issued on the 55th anniversary of his knockout win over Max Schmeling. *Offset and intaglio, perforated 11.*

CM1584 *Joe Louis*

CM1584 *(2766)*

29c multicolored, tagged	.45	.20
Plate block of four	4.75	
FDC *(June 22, 1993)*		1.00

1993. Broadway Musicals Issue continues the American Music series. Honored are four of the most celebrated musicals in American theater. *Gravure, Multi-Color Corp. for the American Bank Note Co., perforated 11 horizontally.*

CM1585 Showboat

CM1586 Porgy & Bess

CM1587 Oklahoma!

CM1588 My Fair Lady

CM1585 *(2767)*

29c multicolored, tagged	.45	.20

CM1586 *(2768)*

29c multicolored, tagged	.45	.20

CM1587 *(2769)*

29c multicolored, tagged	.45	.20

CM1588 *(2770)*

29c multicolored, tagged	.45	.20
FDC *(July 14, 1993)*		
any single		1.00
n. Booklet pane of four	4.95	
FDC, booklet pane		

1993. National Postal Museum Issue marked the opening of the Washington, D.C., facility, part of the Smithsonian Institution. *Offset and intaglio, American Bank Note Co., perforated 11.*

CCCM1589 *Benjamin Franklin, Liberty Hall, Printing Press*   CM1590 *Civil War Soldier Writing Letter, Stagecoach*

CM1591 *Air Mail Plane, Charles Lindbergh, Railway Mail Car and Mail Truck*   CM1592 *Miner's Letter, Stamps, Barcode and Datestamp*

CM1589 *(2779)*

29c multicolored, tagged	.45	.20

CM1590 *(2780)*

29c multicolored, tagged	.45	.20

CM1591 *(2781)*

29c multicolored, tagged	.45	.20

CM1592 *(2782)*

29c multicolored, tagged	.45	.20
Plate block of four	4.25	
FDC *(July 30, 1993)*		2.00

1993. American Sign Language/Recognizing Deafness Issue shows non-verbal communication used with the hearing impaired. Both stamps show the sign for "I love you." *Gravure, Stamp Venturers, perforated 11.*

CM1593-CM1594 *"I Love You"*

CM1593 *(2783)*

29c blue, black, magenta and yellow, tagged	.45	.20

CM1594 *(2784)*

29c blue, yellow, and dark tan, tagged	.45	.20
y. Se-tenant pair (CM1593-94)		
Plate block of four	3.95	
FDC *(Sept. 20, 1993)*		2.00

1993. Country Music Issue salutes four country music stars in this continuation of the American Music series. An earlier design featured Hank Williams (CM1569), here joined by The Carter Family, Patsy Cline and Bob Willis. The stamps were available, a 20-stamp pane with a large title across the top, or a booklet with each stamp appearing once on each of the five panes. Although the designs and sizes are identical, the sheet stamps used burgundy and blue in addition to yellow, magenta, cyan, and black, while the booklet stamps were produced using pink and line black in addition to the four process colors. *Gravure, Stamp Venturers.*

CM1595, CM1599

CM1596, CM1600

CM1597, CM1601

CM1598, CM1602

Perforated 10 on four sides
CM1595 *(2771)*
  29c multicolored, tagged .... .45 .20
CM1596 *(2772)*
  29c multicolored, tagged .... .45 .20
CM1597 *(2773)*
  29c multicolored, tagged .... .45 .20
CM1598 *(2774)*
  29c multicolored, tagged .... .45 .20
    Plate block of four 3.95
    y. Se-Tenant block or strip
        of four (CM1595-98) 2.50
    FDC *(Sept. 25, 1993)* 2.00

Gravure, American Bank Note Co.
Perforated 11 on one or two sides, from booklet panes
CM1599 *(2775)*
  29c multicolored, tagged .... .45 .20
CM1600 *(2776)*
  29c multicolored, tagged .... .45 .20
CM1601 *(2777)*
  29c multicolored, tagged .... .45 .20
CM1602 *(2778)*
  29c multicolored, tagged .... .45 .20
    FDC *(Sept. 25, 1993)* any single
    n. Pane of four, (CM1599-1602) 4.95
    FDC

1993. Youth Classics Issue is a se-tenant block of four honoring four of the best-loved and most popular stories for young readers. Louisa May Alcott's *Little Women* was published in two volumes in 1868-69. Kate Douglas Smith Wiggin's *Rebecca of Sunnybrook Farm*, the story of a fatherless little girl who goes to live with her maiden

aunts, was a best-seller in 1903. Laura Ingalls Wilder drew upon her own childhood and travels on the frontier as inspiration for her books, including *Little House on the Prairie*, published in 1935. *The Adventures of Huckleberry Finn* also is a peek into the childhood of its author, Samuel Clemens (Mark Twain). *Offset and intaglio by American Bank Note Co. Perforated 11.*

CM1603, Rebecca of Sunnybrook Farm
CM1604, Little House on the Prairie
CM1605, The Adventures of Huckleberry Finn
CM1606, Little Women

CM1603 *(2785)*
  29c multicolored, tagged .... .45 .20
CM1604 *(2786)*
  29c multicolored, tagged .... .45 .20
CM1605 *(2787)*
  29c multicolored, tagged .... .45 .20
CM1606 *(2788)*
  29c multicolored, tagged .... 45 .20
    Plate block of four 4.50
    y. Se-tenant block or strip of
        four, CM1603-06 .... 3.50
    FDC *(Oct. 23, 1993)* any single 1.00

1993. Commonwealth of the Northern Mariana Islands issue salutes a group of 16 islands in the western Pacific Ocean administered by the United States following World War II as part of the U.N. Trust Territories of the Pacific Islands. In 1978, following a referendum, the archipelago became a self-governing entity in union with the United States. Mail to and from the Mariana Islands is sent to a domestic U.S. postage rates. *Offset and intaglio, Perforated 11.*

CM1607 *Flag and Limestone Pillars*

CM1607 *(2804)*
  29c mulitcolored, tagged .... .45 .20
    Plate block of four 3.50
    FDC *(Nov. 4, 1993)* 1.00
1993. Columbus Landing in Puerto Rico Issue marks the 500th anniversary of the arrival of Columbus.

CM1608 *Caravels in Boqueron Bay*

CM1608 *(2805)*
29c multicolored, tagged	.45	.20
Plate block of four	3.50	
FDC *(Nov. 19, 1993)*		1.00

1993. AIDS Awareness Issue symbolizes compassion and awareness for those afflicted by this disease. The stamps were sold nationwide on their first day of issue, and were available in sheet form or in 10-stamp booklets. *Gravure.*

CM1609

CM1609 *(2806)*
29c red and black, tagged	.45	.20
Plate block of four	4.00	
a. Perforated 11 vertically on one or two sides	.75	.25
n. Booklet pane of 10 perforated 11 vertically	4.50	

1994. Winter Olympics Issue, honors the 1994 Winter Games. *Offset, Ashton-Potter, perforated 11.*

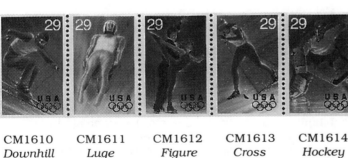

CM1610 Downhill	CM1611 Luge	CM1612 Figure Skating	CM1613 Cross	CM1614 Hockey

CM1610 *(2807)*
29c multicolored, tagged	.45	.20

CM1611 *(2808)*
29c multicolored, tagged	.45	.20

CM1612 *(2809)*
29c multicolored, tagged	.45	.20

CM1613 *(2810)*
29c multicolored, tagged	.45	.20

CM1614 *(2811)*
29c multicolored, tagged	.45	.20
Plate block of 10	7.50	
y. Se-tenant strip of five (CM1610-14)	3.00	
FDC *(Jan. 6, 1994)* any single		1.00

1994. Edward R. Murrow Issue honors the broadcast journalist who joined CBS in 1935 and directed its European bureau through World War II. In 1945 he was made CBS vice president in charge of news, education and discussion programs. *Intaglio, perforated 11.*

CM1615 *Edward Murrow*

CM1615 *(2812)*
29c brown, tagged	.45	.20
Plate block of four	3.50	
FDC *(Jan. 21, 1994)*		1.00

1994. Love Issue, a self-adhesive stamp, one of three 1994 stamps with this theme. (See CM1619-20) *Offset and intaglio, imperforate (cie cut).*

CM1616 *Love - Heart*

CM1616 *(2813)*
29c multicolored, tagged	.45	.20
FDC *(Jan. 27, 1994)*		1.00
n. Booklet pane of 18	6.00	

1994. Dr. Allison Davis Issue honors the influential social anthropologist and educator who challenged the cultural bias of standardized intelliegence tests and helped end racial segregation. Black Heritage series. *Intaglio by Stamp Venturers, perforated 11.*

CM1617 *Dr. Allison Davis*

CM1617 *(2816)*
29c red brown and brown, tagged	.45	.20
Plate block of four	4.00	
FDC *(Feb. 1, 1994)*		1.00

1994. New Year Issue, the second in the Asian lunar New Year series, features the royal dog of China, a Pekinese, and marks the Year of the Dog. *Gravure, perforated 11.*

CM1618 *Lunar New Year*

CM1618 *(2817)*
29c multicolored, tagged	.45	.20
Plate block of four	3.75	
FDC *(Feb. 5, 1994)*		1.00

1994. Love Issues are two lick-and-stick stamps released on Valentine's Day, complimenting the earlier self-adhesive issue, CM1616. (See also CM1642.), *Gravure and intaglio, perforated 10 3/4 by 11 on two or three sides.*

CM1619 *Love-Dove and Roses*

CM1619 *(2814)*
29c multicolored, tagged	.45	.20
FDC *(Feb. 14, 1994)*		1.00
n. Pane of 18	6.00	
FDC, pane of 18		5.00
vn. Imperforate pane of 18	—	

CM1620 *Love*

CM1620 *(2815)*
52c multicolored, tagged	1.50	.35
Plate block of four	7.00	
FDC *(Feb. 14, 1994)*		1.00

1994. Buffalo Soldiers Issue honored the U.S. Army's regiments tht played a major role on the settlement of the American West. Predominantly black cavalry and infontry. Black troops of the Buffalo Soldier regiments were the first authorized to serve on the U.S. Army during peacetime. *Offset and intaglio, perforated 11 1/2 x 11.*

CM1621 *Buffalo Soldiers*

CM1621 *(2818)*
29c multicolored, tagged	.45	.20
Plate block of four	1.25	
FDC *(April 22, 1994)*		1.00

1994. Silent Screen Stars Issue featured 10 early film stars, drawn by Al Hirschfeld. Theda Bara's work in *The Vampire* led to the term "vamp". Film star Clara Bow first arrived in Hollywood as the result of a high school beauty contest. Lon Chaney used his incredible make-up and characterization in *The Hunchback of Notre Dame, Phantom of the Opera* and *The Unholy Three.* Charlie Chaplin's " Little Tramp" character became famous worldwide. John Gilbert began with a stage career that led to romantic roles in such films as *The Merry Widow, The Big Parade* and *Flesh and the Devil.*

Buster Keaton is known for slapstick comedy and his deadpan stare. Mack Sennett's Keystone Cops kept audiences laughing through many short films of 1914-20. Comedian Harold Lloyd made more than 500 movies, beginning in 1914. Zasu Pitts began as an extra, moving to both comedy and dramatic roles. Rudolf Valentino is one of the world's best-known film stars, remembered for *The Four Horsemen of the Apocalypse, The Sheik,* and *Blood and Sand. Offset and intaglio, perforated 11.*

CM1622 *(2819)*
29c purple, red and black, tagged	.45	.20

CM1623 *(2820)*
29c purple, red and black, tagged.	.45	.20

CM1624 *(2821)*
29c purple, red and black, tagged	.45	.20

CM1625 *(2822)*
29c purple, red and black, tagged	.45	.20

CM1626 *(2823)*
29c purple, red and black, tagged	.45	.20

CM1627 *(2824)*
29c purple, red and black, tagged	.45	.20

CM1628 *(2825)*
29c purple, red and black, tagged	.45	.20

CM1629 *(2826)*
29c purple, red and black, tagged	.45	.20

CM1630 *(2827)*
29c purple, red and black, tagged	.45	.20

CM1631 *(2828)*
29c purple, red and black, tagged	.45	.20
Plate block of 10	9.00	
y, Se-tenant block of 10 CM1622-31	8.00	
vy. Block of 10, offset black omitted	—	
vy1. Block of 10, offset black and intaglio red and purple omitted	—	

1994. Garden Flowers Issue, the second such five-stamp booklet showing bright and popular flowers that bloom in summer. *Offset and intaglio, perforated 11.*

CM1632 *(2829)*
29c multicolored, tagged	.45	.20

CM1633 *(2830)*
29c multicolored, tagged	.45	.20

CM1634 *(2831)*
29c multicolored, tagged	.45	.20

CM1635 *(2832)*
29c multicolored, tagged	.45	.20

CM1636 *(2833)*
29c mulitcolored, tagged	.45	.20
FDC *(April 28, 1994)*, any single		2.00
n. Booklet pane of five CM1632-36	4.50	
FDC *(April 28, 1994)*, pane of five		4.00
vn. Pane of five, intaglio black omitted	—	
vn1. Imperforate pane of five	—	

CM1622 *Rudolf Valentino*
CM1623 *Clara Bow*
CM1624 *Charlie Chaplin*
CM1625 *Lon Chaney*
CM1626 *John Gilbert*

CM1627 *Zasu Pitts*
CM1628 *Harold Lloyd*
CM1629 *Keystone Cops*
CM1630 *Theda Bara*
CM1631 *Buster Keaton*

| CM1632 | CM1633 | CM1634 | CM1635 | CM1636 |
| *Lily* | *Zinnia* | *Gladiola* | *Marigold* | *Rose* |

1994. World Cup Soccer Championship Issue of three stamps and a souvenir sheet honors the first time the United States hosted the final rounds of soccer's quadrennial World Cup. Stamps issued in panes of 20 were printed on phosphorcoated paper; those within the souvenir sheet are block tagged. The 50c stamp in the souvenir sheet (CM1640c) has part of the yellow map from the sheet in the lower-right corner of its design. *Gravure, perforated 11.*

CM1637 *World Cup '94 Soccer*

CM1637 *(2834)*

29c multicolored, phosphored paper	.75	.20
Plate block of four	4.00	
FDC *(May 29, 1994)*		1.00

CM1638 *World Cup '94 Soccer*

CM1638 *(2835)*

40c multicolored, phosphored paper	1.00	.35
Plate block of four	5.50	
FDC *(May 26, 1994)*		1.00

CM1639 *World Cup'94, Soccer*

CM1639 *(2836)*

50c multicolored, phosphored paper	1.50	.50
Plate block of four	6.50	
FDC *(May 26, 1994)*		1.00

CM1640 *(2837)*

$1.19 souvenir sheet	3.75	3.00
a. **29c** like CM1637, block tagged		.75
b. **40c** like CM1638, block tagged		1.00
c. **50c** like CM1639, block tagged		1.25

1994. World War II Commemorative Sheet includes a map and stamps showing events of the war in 1994. *Offset and intaglio, perforated 11.*

CM1641 *(2838)*

$2.90 sheet of ten, tagged	8.75	7.00
a. **29c** Forces Retake New Guinea	.75	.70
b. **29c** P51s escort B-17s	.75	.70
c. **29c** Allies Free Normady	.75	.70
d. **29c** Airborn Units	.75	.70
e. **29c** Submarines	.75	.70
f. **29c** Allies Free Rome, Paris	.75	.70
g. **29c** U.S. troops clear Saipan	.75	.70
h. **29c** Red Ball Express	.75	.70
i. **29c** Battle of Leyte Gulf	.75	.70
j. **29c** Bastogne and the Buldge	.75	.70
FDC *(June 6, 1994)* any single		1.00
FDC sheet of 10		10.

CM1640 *World Cup Souveneir Sheet*

CM1841a CM1841b CM1841c CM1841d CM1841e

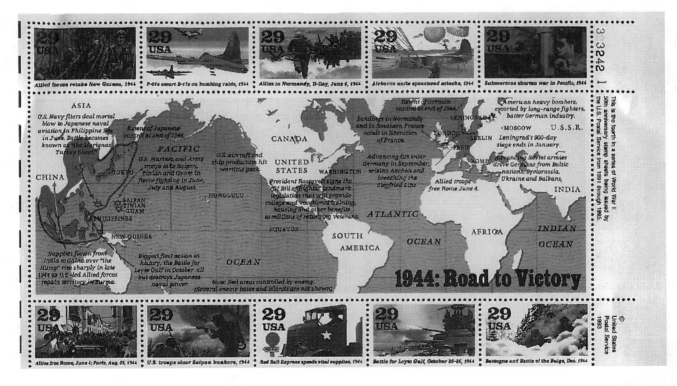

CM1841f CM1841g CM1841h CM1841i CM1841j

WWII- Road to Victory

1994. Love Issue is a slightly longer sheet version of the 29¢ booklet stamp (CM1620) released on Valentine's Day. *Offset and intaglio, perforated, 11.*

CM1642 *Love*

CM1642 *(2814C)*

29c multicolored, tagged	.50	.20
Plate block of four	3.50	
FDC *(June 11, 1994)*		1.00

1994. Norman Rockwell Issue honors the artist best known as a chronicler of 20th century America for more than 4,000 works, including 321 original *Saturday Evening*

Post covers between 1916 and 1963. The commemortion consisted of a single stamp and a commemorative sheet of four stamps depicting Franklin D. Roosevelt's Four Freedoms. *Offset and intaglio, perforated 11.*

CM1643 *Norman Rockwell*

CM1643 *(2839)*

29c multicolored, tagged	.50	.20
Plate block of four	3.50	
FDC *(July 1, 1994)*		1.00

Four Freedoms

CM1644a *Freedom from Want*

CM1644b *Freedom from Fear*

CM1644c *Freedom of Speech*

CM1644d *Freedom of Worship*

CM1644 *(2840)*

$2.00 multicolored, tagged	6.00	5.00
a. 50c Freedom from Want	1.00	1.00
b. 50c Freedom from Fear	1.00	1.00
c. 50c Freedom of Speech	1.00	1.00
d. 50c Freedom of Worship	1.00	1.00

1994. Moon Landing Anniversary Issue released in special 12-stamp sheetlets, celebrates the 25th anniversary of man's first landing on the Moon. (See also No. 1045.) *Gravure, by Stamp Venturers, perforated 11.*

1645
Moon Landing, 25th Anniversary

CM1645 *(2841)*

29c multicolored, tagged	.50	.25
FDC *(July 20, 1994)*		1.00
n. Sheetlet of 12	9.00	7.50

1994. Locomotives Issue, a five-stamp booklet, depicts historically significant locomotives. (See also CM1293-97) *Gravure, by J.W. Ferguson & Sons for Stamp Venturers, perforated 11 horizontally.*

CM1646 *General*

CM1647 *Jupiter*

CM1648 *No. 242*

CM1649 *No. 10*

CM1650 *No. 999*

CM1646 *(2843)*
29c multicolored, tagged .75 .50
CM1647 *(2844)*
29c multicolored, tagged .75 .50
CM1648 *(2845)*
29c multicolored, tagged .75 .50
CM1649 *(2846)*
29c multicolored, tagged .75 .50
CM1650 *(2847)*
29c multicolored, tagged .75 .50
　FDC *(July 29, 1994)*, any single 1.00
　n. Booklet pane of five
　　CM1646-50 4.50
　FDC 4.50

1994. George Meany Issue honors one of the most influential labor leaders in American history, president of the American Federation of Labor (AFL) from 1952-55 and first president of the AFL and Congress of Industrial Organizations (CIO) from 1955 until his retirement in 1979. *Intaglio, perforated 11.*

 CM1651 *George Meany*

CM1651 *(2848)*
29c blue, tagged .50 .20
　Plate block of four 3.50
　FDC *(Aug. 16, 1994)* 1.00

1994. Popular Singer Issue in the American Music series honors five showstoppers of this century. *Gravure by J.W. Fergusson & Sons for Stamp Venturers, perforated 11.*

 CM1652 *Al Jolson*

 CM1653 *Bing Crosby*

 CM1654 *Ethel Waters*

 CM1655 *Nat 'King' Cole*

 CM1656 *Ethel Merman*

CM1652 *(2849)*
29c multicolored, tagged .75 .50
CM1653 *(2850)*
29c multicolored, tagged .75 .50
CM1654 *(2851)*
29c multicolored, tagged .75 .50
CM1655 *(2852)*
29c multicolored, tagged .47 .50
CM1656 *(2853)*
29c multicolored, tagged .75 .50
　Plate block of six (vertical) 6.00
　Plate block of 12 (horizontal) 11.
　FDC *(Sept. 1, 1994) any single* 1.00
　a. Plane of twenty 17.50

1994. James Thurber Issue hails the author, humorist, playwright and cartoonist whose 31 books gave humorous views of life in America. Literary Arts series. *Offset and intaglio, perforated 11.*

 CM1657 *James Thurber*

CM1657 *(2862)*
29c multicolored, tagged .50 .20
　Plate block of four 3.50
　FDC *(Sept. 10, 1994)* 1.00

1994. Blues and Jazz Singers Issue honors seminal artists in these distinctive American musical genres. *Printed in offset by Manhardt-Alexander for Ashton-Potter (USA) Ltd.. perforated 11 x 10 3/4.*

 CM1658 *Bessie Smith*

CM1658 *(2854)*
29c multicolored, tagged .50 .25

 CM1659 *Muddy Waters*

CM1659 *(2855)*
29c multicolored, tagged .50 .25

CM1660 *Billie Holiday*

CM1660 (2856)
  29c multicolored, tagged   .50   .25

CM1661 *Robert Johnson*

CM1661 (2857)
  29c multicolored, tagged   .50   .25

CM1662 *Jimmy Rushing*

CM1662 (2858)
  29c multicolored, tagged   .50   .25

CM1663 *'Ma' Rainy*

CM1663 (2859)
  29c multicolored, tagged   .50   .25

CM1664 *Mildred Barley*

CM1664 (2860)
  29c multicolored, tagged   .50   .25

CM1665 *Howlin' Wolf*

CM1665 (2861)
  29c multicolored, tagged   .50   .25
    Plate block of 10   9.00
    y. Se-tenant block of nine, plus
        one extra stamp,CM1658-65   8.50
    FDC *(Sept. 17, 1994)*, any single   1.00
    a. Pane of 35   27.50

1994. Wonders of the Seas Issue uses four se-tenant stamps to form a single underwater fantasy scene. *Offset by Barton Press for the Banknote Corp. of America, perforated 11.*

CM1666 *Porcupine Fish*   CM1667 *Dolphin*

CM1668 *Nautilus*   CM1669 *Fish and Coral*
    and Ship's wheel

CM1666 *(2863)*
  29c multicolored, tagged   .75   .25
CM1667 *(2864)*
  29c multicolored, tagged   .75   .25
CM1668 *(2865)*
  29c multicolored, tagged   .75   .25
CM1669 *(2866)*
  29c multicolored, tagged   .75   .25
    Plate block of four   4.00
    y. Se- tenant block of
        four CM1666-69   3.00
    FDC *(Oct. 3, 1994)*, any single   1.00
    vy. Imperforate block of four   —

1994 Cranes Issue, depicts two of the world's rarest birds, the North American whooping crane and the Chinese black-necked crane. A joint issue of the United States and the People's Republic of China, the issues of the two countries show the same designs, with the Chinese issue as two seperate stamps and the U.S. issue as a se-tenat pair. *Offset and intaglio by Barton Press for the Banknote Corp. of America, perforated 11.*

CM1670 *Black*   CM1671 *Whoop-*
  Headed Crane   *ing Crane*

CM1670 *(2867)*
  29c Black-necked crane, tagged   .45   .20
CM1671 *(2868)*
  29c *Whooping crane,* tagged   .45   .20
    Plate block of four   1.25
    y. Se-tenant pair
        CM1670-71
    FDC *(Oct, 9, 1994) pair*   2.00

1993-1994 Legends of the West Issue. Late in 1993, the Postal Service printed more than 5 million Legends of the West panes and forwarded them to postal distribution centers and post offices throughout the country, even though the stamps were not scheduled to be issued until 1994. These stamps were to be the first in a new series formatted by USPS as "Classic Collections" -- special panes of 20 different first-class letter rate stamps with explanatory text on the back of each and a banner across the top of the pane describing its collective subject -- in this case, legendary personalities and themes from the early days of the Western frontier.

A total of at least 183 of these panes inadvertently were sold at four post offices long before the planned first day of issue, beginning with a full pane that was purchased and used to frank a parcel mailed in Bend, Ore., Dec. 14, 1993.

At about the same time, USPS learned that one stamp in the original pane, purported to have depicted black cowboy and rodeo showman Bill Pickett, was actually a portrait of his brother, Ben. Bill Pickett's descendants demanded that the Postal Service withdraw and destroy panes with the incorrect portrait and print new ones with an accurate portrait of Bill Pickett, and USPS agreed to do so.

However, the early release and use of the panes from the original printing containing the stamp with the incorrect portrait made that impossible.

After a great deal of public and private debate as to the best solution (including two lawsuits), the Postal Service decided to print a second Legends of the West pane as promised, with a revised, accurate portrait of Bill Pickett, but also to offer 150,000 original Legends of the West panes with the Ben Pickett portrait to collectors in a special lottery. The remainder of the original Legends of the West _ about 5 million panes _ would then be destroyed.

The USPS stuck to this plan despite considerable criticism from stamp collectors, even when it was revealed that, in the revised pane, 16 of the 20 stamps in the pane different from those in the original pane. (The red framelines around the stamps portraying people in the original pane are about half the thickness of those in the revised pane.) *Gravure by J.W. Fergusson & Sons for Stamp Venturers, perforated 11.*

CM1671A *Legends of the West commemorative pane (original version)*

CM1671Ag *Ben Pickett (incorrect portrait in original pane)*

CM1671A *(2870)*
$5.80 Legends of the West
    commemorative pane, tagged
    (earliest known use Dec. 14, 1993) 195.
CM1671Aa
  29c Home on the Range
CM1671Ab
  29c Buffalo Bill

CM1671Ac
  29c Jim Bridger
CM1671Ad
  29c Annie Oakley
CM1671Ae
  29c Native American Culture
CM1671Af
  29c Chief Joseph
CM1671Ag
  29c Ben Pickett
CM1671Ah
  29c Bat Masterson
CM1671Ai
  29c John Fremont
CM1671A2j
  29c Wyatt Earp
CM1671Ak
  29c Nellie Cashman
CM1671Al
  29c Charles Goodnight
CM1671Am
  29c Geronimo
CM1671An
  29c Kit Carson
CM1671Ao
  29c Wild Bill Hickok
CM1671Ap
  29c Western Wildlife
CM1671Aq
  29c Jim Beckwourth
CM1671Ar
  29c Bill Tilghman
CM1671As
  29c Sacagawea
CM1671At
  29c Overland Mail

1994. Revised Legends of the West Issue with a stamp showing an accurate portrait of Bill Pickett and thicker red framelines around his portrait and the portraits on the other 15 stamps in the pane that depict individuals. Because the overwhelming majority of the 150,000 original Legends of the West commemorative panes that were sold to collectors at a premium by lottery were retained as panes by collectors, it has been listed as a single number (CM1672), with the individual stamps as minor varieties of that number. Because the revised panes were sold at face value, and stamps from them were used relatively more extensively on mail, stamps from the revised pane are listed and numbered individually. *Gravure by J.W. Fergusson & Sons for Stamp Venturers, perforated 11.*

CM1691a *Legends of the West commemorative pane (revised version)*

CM1678 *Bill Pickett (correct portrait in revised pane)*

CM1672 *(2969a)*
  29c Home on the Range, tagged   .45   .20
CM1673 *(2969b)*
  29c Buffalo Bill, tagged   .45   .20

CM1672 *Home on the Range*
CM1673 *Buffalo Bill*
CM1674 *Jim Bridger*
CM1675 *Annie Oakly*
CM1676 *Native American Culture*

CM1677 *Chief Joseph*
CM1678 *Bill Pickett*
CM1679 *Bat Masterson*
CM1680 *John Fremont*
CM1681 *Wyatt Earp*

CM1682 *Nellie Cashman*
CM1683 *Charles Goodnignt*
CM1684 *Geronimo*
CM1685 *Kit Carson*
CM1686 *Wild Bill Hickok*

CM1687 *Western Wildlife*
CM1688 *Jim Beckwourth*
CM1689 *Bill Tilghman*
CM1690 *Sacagawea*
CM1691 *Overland Mail*

CM1674 *(2969c)*
  29c Jim Bridger, tagged .45 .20
CM1675 *(2969d)*
  29c Annie Oakley, tagged .45 .20
CM1676 *(2969e)*
  29c Native American Culture, tagged .45 .20
CM1677 *(2969f)*
  29c Chief Joseph, tagged .45 .20
CM1678 *(2969g)*
  29c Bill Pickett, tagged .45 .20
CM1679 *(2969h)*
  29c Bat Masterson, tagged .45 .20
CM1680 *(2969i)*
  29c John Fremont, tagged .45 .20
CM1681 *(2969j)*
  29c Wyatt Earp, tagged .45 .20
CM1682 *(2969k)*
  29c Nellie Cashman, tagged .45 .20
CM1683 *(2969l)*
  29c Charles Goodnight, tagged .45 .20
CM1684 *(2969m)*
  29c Geronimo, tagged .45 .20
CM1685 *(2969n)*
  29c Kit Carson, tagged .45 .20
CM1686 *(2969o)*
  29c Wild Bill Hickok, tagged .45 .20
CM1687 *(2969p)*
  29c Western Wildlife, tagged .45 .20

CM1688 *(2969q)*
  29c Jim Beckwourth, tagged .45 .20
CM1689 *(2969r)*
  29c Bill Tilghman, tagged .45 .20
CM1690 *(2969s)*
  29c Sacagawea, tagged .45 .20
CM1691 *(2969t)*
  29c Overland Mail, tagged .45 .20
    FDC *(Oct. 18, 1994)* 10.
    y. Se-tenant pane of 20 16. 14.

1994. Bureau of Engraving and Printing Centennial Souvenir Sheet marks the 100th anniversary of the national security printer with a souvenir sheet containing four $2 James Madison definitives of a design first used almost a century before (185), when BEP first began printing U.S. stamps. *Offset and intaglio, perforated 11.*

CM1692 *(2875)*
  $8 multicolored, tagged *(Nov. 3, 1994)* 20. 14.50
    a. single stamp 5.00 3.50
    Major double transfer on
      right $2 stamp in sheet of four —
    Major double transfer,
      single $2 stamp —
    Minor double transfer on
      $2 stamp in sheet of four —

CM1692 *BEP Centennial Souvenir Sheet*

Minor double transfer, single
$2 stamp —

(Listings for minor double transfers refer to any of approximately 10 different ones that are known.)

1994. New Year Issue for the Year of the Boar is the third installment in the ongoing series marking the Asian lunar holiday. This stamp was released only two days before the first-class letter rate increased from 29c to 32c. *Gravure by Stamp Venturers, perforated 11.*

CM1693 *Lunar New Year, Boar*

CM1693 *(2976)*

29c multicolored, tagged	.50	.20
Plate block of four	3.50	
FDC *(Dec. 30, 1994)*		1.00

1995. Love Issue features non-denominated conventional and self-adhesive stamps depicting a cherub from the 16th-century *Sistine Madonna* by Raphael. *Offset and intaglio (BEP), perforated 11 1/2.*

CM1694 *Love Cherub 'tall design'*

CM1694 *(2948)*

(32c) multicolored, phosphored paper	.50	.20
Plate block of four	1.25	
FDC *(Feb. 1, 1995)*		1.00

Self-adhesive booklet, offset and intaglio by Banknote Corp. of America, imperforate (die cut).

CM1695 *Love cherub 'short' design*

CM1695 *(2949)*

(32c) multicolored, phosphored paper	.50	.20
FDC *(Feb. 1, 1995)*		1.00
n. Booklet pane of 20,plus label	16.00	
vn. Booklet pane of 20,intaglio red (inscriptions) omitted	—	

1995. Florida Sesquicentennial Issue marked the 150th anniversary of Florida statehood. *Offset by Sterling Sommer for Ashton-Potter (USA) Ltd., perforated 11.*

CM1696 *Florida Statehood Sesquicentennial*

CM1696 *(2950)*

32c multicolored, phosphored paper	.50	.20
Plate block of four	3.50	
FDC *(March 3, 1995)*		1.00

1995. Earth Day Issue showcased the four winning designs created by children in a nationwide contest to produce stamps for the 25th anniversary of Earth Day. The winning quartet was issued in a pane of 16 (four se-tenant blocks of four) with a "Kids Care!" banner across selvage at the top of the pane and the details of the contest in the selvage at the foor of the pane. *Offset by Sterling Sommer for Ashton-Potter (USA) Ltd., perforated 11.*

CM1697   CM1698
Clean Earth   *Solar Power*

CM1699 Tree   CM1970 *Clean*
Planting   *Beaches*

CM1697 *(2951)*

32c multicolored, phosphored paper	.50	.20

CM1698 *(2952)*

32c multicolored, phosphored paper	.50	.20

CM1699 *(2953)*

32c multicolored, phosphored paper	.50	.20

CM1700 *(2954)*

32c multicolored, phosphored paper	.50	.20
Plate block of four	3.50	
y. Se-tenant block of four	2.00	
FDC *(April 20, 1995)*		2.00
a. Pane of 20	13.50	

1995. Richard M. Nixon Issue marks the death on April 22, 1994, of the 37th president of the United States, Richard Milhous Nixon (1913-1994). *Offset and intaglio by Barton Press and Banknote Corp. of America, perforated 11.*

CM1701 *Richard M. Nixon*

CM1701 *(2955)*
32c multicolored, phosphored paper   .50   .20
    Plate block of four   3.50
    FDC *(April 26, 1995)*   1.00
    v. Intaglio red ("Richard
       Nixon") omitted   —

1995. Bessie Coleman Issue commemorates the first African-American woman aviator, who traveled to France to learn the language in order to earn her pilot's license there in 1921 after American flying schools had refused to admit her. Black Heritage series. *Intaglio by BEP, perforated 11.*

CM1702 *Bessie Coleman*

CM1702 *(2956)*
32c red and black, phosphored paper   .50   .20
    Plate block of four   3.50
    FDC *(April 27, 1995)*   1.00

1995. Love Issue added stamps with a 32c face value in matching designs to follow the non-denominated versions isued in February (CM1695-96), along with 55c stamps showing the cherub on the right in the same Raphael painting, paying the rate for letters under two ounces (such as most wedding invitations with response cards and envelopes enclosed). *Offset and intaglio by BEP.*

CM1703-04 *Love Cherub*

Perforated 11 1/4
CM1703 *(2957)*
32c multicolored, phosphored paper   .50   .20
    Plate block of four   2.50
    FDC *(May 12, 1995)*   1.00

Booklet stamps *perforated 9 3/4 by 11 on two or three sides.*

CM1704 *Love Cherub*

CM1704 *(2959)*
32c multicolored, phosphored paper   .50   .20
    FDC *(May 12, 1995)*   1.00
    n. Booklet pane of 10   5.50

CM1705 *Love Cherub*

Perforated 11 1/4
CM1705 *(2958)*
55c multicolored, phosphored paper   1.00   .35
    Plate block of four   5.00
    FDC *(May 12, 1995)*   1.50

Self-adhesive booklet *printed in offset and intaglio by Banknote Corp. of America, imperforate (die cut).*

CM1706 *Love Cherub*

CM1706 *(2960)*
55c multicolored, phosphored paper   1.00   .35
    FDC *(May 12, 1995)*   1.50
    n. Booklet pane of 20, plus label   22.50

1995. Recreational Sports Issue depicts popular American pastimes in five se-tenant designs. *Offset by Barton Press for Banknote Corp. of America, perforated 11 x 11 1/4.*

CM1707 *Bowling*

CM1708 *Tennis*

CM1709 *Golf*

CM1710 *Volleyball*

CM1711 *Baseball*

CM1707 *(2963)*
32c multicolored, phosphored paper .50 .20
CM1708 *(2964)*
32c multicolored, phosphored paper .50 .20
CM1709 *(2965)*
32c multicolored, phosphored paper .50 .20
CM1710 *(2961)*
32c multicolored, phosphored paper .50 .20
CM1711 *(2962)*
32c multicolored, phosphored paper .50 .20
   Plate block of 10 8.50
   y. Se-tenant vertical strip
     of five CM 1708-12 3.00
   FDC *(May 20, 1995) any single* 1.00
   a. Sheetlet of 20 16.00
   vy. Imperforate vertical
     strip of five —
   vy1. Vertical strip of five,
     yellow omitted —
   vy2. Vertical strip of five, yellow,
     blue and magenta omitted —

1995. POW & MIA Issue salutes personnel in the U.S. armed forces who were prisoners of war or who were unaccounted for after the end of hostilities. *Offset by Sterling Sommer for Ashton-Potter (USA) Ltd., perforated 11.*

CM1712 *POW/ MIA'S*

CM1712 *(2966)*
32c multicolored, phosphored paper .50 .20
   Plate block of four 3.50
   FDC *(May 29, 1995)* 1.00
   Sheetlet of 20 14.50

1995. Marilyn Monroe Issue, first installment in the USPS Legends of Hollywood series, got under way with a pane of 20 (each stamp having its corner perforations in the shape of a star, bearing the likeness and facsimile autograph of Marilyn Monroe (1926-1962), with the large all-around selvage in the commemorative pane of 20 showing an enlargement of a portrait of the movie star near the height of her powers. *Gravure by J.W. Fergusson & Sons for Stamp Venturers, perforated 11.*

CM1713 *Marylin Monroe*

CM1713 *(2967)*
32c multicolored, block tagged .75 .20
   Plate block of four 3.50
   FDC *(June 1, 1995)* 1.00
   a. Pane of 20 14.50
   v. Imperforate pair

Because this issue also was made available to collectors in full six-pane printing sheets, gutter pairs and blocks and cross-gutter multiples also exist.

1995. Texas Sesquicentennial Issue marks the 150th anniversary of Texas statehood. *Offset by Sterling Sommer for Ashton-Potter (USA) Ltd., perforated 11.*

CM1714 *Texas Statehood Sequicetennial*

CM1714 *(2968)*
32c multicolored, phosphored paper .50 .20
   Plate block of four 3.50
   FDC *(June 16, 1995)* 1.00

1995. Lighthouses Issue uses the same format and designer as the 1990 Lighthouses issue (CM1378-82) to create a booklet showcasing lighthouses of the Great Lakes. *Gravure by J.W. Fergusson & Sons for Stamp Venturers, perforated 11 vertically on one or two sides.*

CM1715 *Split Rock Lighthouse*
CM1716 *St. Joseph Lighthouse*
CM1717 *Spectacle Reef Lighthouse*
CM1718 *Marblehead Lighthouse*
CM1719 *Thirty Mile Point Lighthouse*

CM1715 *(2969)*
32c multicolored, phosphored paper .50 .20
CM1716 *(2970)*
32c multicolored, phosphored paper .50 .20
CM1717 *(2971)*
32c multicolored, phosphored paper .50 .20
CM1718 *(2972)*
32c multicolored, phosphored paper .50 .20
CM1719 *(2973)*
32c multicolored, phosphored paper .50 .20
   FDC *(June 17, 1995)* 2.00
   n. Booklet pane of five
     CM1715-19 4.00

1995. United Nations Issue marks the 50th anniversary of that organization. *Intaglio by Banknote Corp. of America, perforated 11 1/4 x 11.*

CM1720 *United Nations*

CM1720 *(2974)*
  32c blue, phosphored paper   .50   .20
    Plate block of four   3.00
    FDC *(June 26, 1995)*   1.00

1995. Civil War Issue was the second release in the USPS Classic Collections series to showcase 20 stamps on a single theme in a pane with a colorful banner across the top selvage identifying the subject -- in this case, the Civil War. As on the 1994 Legends of the West pane that introduced the concept, the four corner stamps detail events (battles, in this instance) while the other 16 stamps are painstakingly researched portraits of individuals who played a significant role in the era, while text printed on the back of the stamps provides information on the subject of each. *Gravure by J.W. Fergusson & Sons for Stamp Venturers, perforated 10 1/4 x 10.*

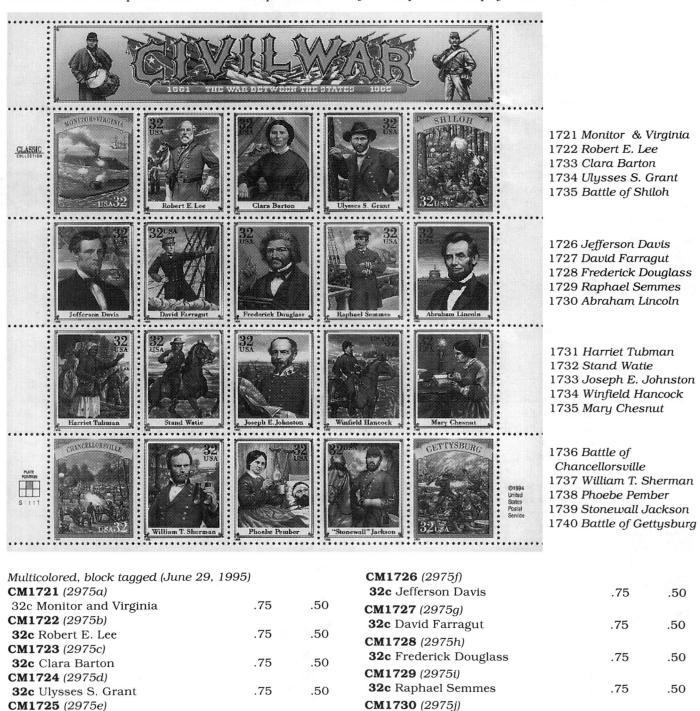

1721 *Monitor & Virginia*
1722 *Robert E. Lee*
1733 *Clara Barton*
1734 *Ulysses S. Grant*
1735 *Battle of Shiloh*

1726 *Jefferson Davis*
1727 *David Farragut*
1728 *Frederick Douglass*
1729 *Raphael Semmes*
1730 *Abraham Lincoln*

1731 *Harriet Tubman*
1732 *Stand Watie*
1733 *Joseph E. Johnston*
1734 *Winfield Hancock*
1735 *Mary Chesnut*

1736 *Battle of Chancellorsville*
1737 *William T. Sherman*
1738 *Phoebe Pember*
1739 *Stonewall Jackson*
1740 *Battle of Gettysburg*

Multicolored, block tagged (June 29, 1995)
CM1721 *(2975a)*
  32c Monitor and Virginia   .75   .50
CM1722 *(2975b)*
  32c Robert E. Lee   .75   .50
CM1723 *(2975c)*
  32c Clara Barton   .75   .50
CM1724 *(2975d)*
  32c Ulysses S. Grant   .75   .50
CM1725 *(2975e)*
  32c Battle of Shiloh   .75   .50

CM1726 *(2975f)*
  32c Jefferson Davis   .75   .50
CM1727 *(2975g)*
  32c David Farragut   .75   .50
CM1728 *(2975h)*
  32c Frederick Douglass   .75   .50
CM1729 *(2975i)*
  32c Raphael Semmes   .75   .50
CM1730 *(2975j)*
  32c Abraham Lincoln   .75   .50

CM1731 (*2975k*)
32c Harriet Tubman	.75	.50

CM1732 (*2975l*)
32c Stand Watie	.75	.50

CM1733 (*2975m*)
32c Joseph E. Johnston	.75	.50

CM1734 (*2975n*)
32c Winfield Hancock	.75	.50

CM1735 (*2975o*)
32c Mary Chesnut	.75	.50

CM1736 (*2975p*)
32c Battle of Chancellorsville	.75	.50

CM1737 (*2975q*)
32c William T. Sherman	.75	.50

CM1738 (*2975r*)
32c Phoebe Pember	.75	.50

CM1739 (*2975s*)
32c Stonewall Jackson	.75	.50

CM1740 (*2975t*)
32c Battle of Gettysburg	.75	.50
y. Se-tenant pane of 20 CM1721-40	16.	14.
vy. Imperforate se-tenant pane of 20	—	
v1y. Pane with CM1721-25 imperforate, CM1726-30 part perforated	—	
v2y. Pane with CM1731-35 imperforate, CM1736-40 part perforated	—	
v3. Block of nine (CM1726-28, CM1731-33, CM1736-38), imperforate vertically	—	

Because this issue also was made available to collectors in full six-pane printing sheets, gutter pairs and blocks and cross-gutter multiples also exist.

1995. Carousel Horses Issue uses the same designer and much the same format and subjects as the popular 1988 Carousel Animals issue (CM1327-30) in portraying four stalwart steeds from the classical American carnival ride. American Folk Art series. *Offset by Sterling Sommer for Ashton-Potter (USA) Ltd., perforated 11.*

Caousel Horses

CM1741 Golden Horse
CM1742 Black Horse
CM1743 Armored Horse
CM1745 Brown Horse

CM1741 (*2976*)
32c multicolored, phosphored paper	.50	.20

CM1742 (*2977*)
32c multicolored, phosphored paper	.50	.20

CM1743 (*2978*)
32c multicolored, phosphored paper	.50	.20

CM1744 (*2979*)
32c multicolored, phosphored paper	.50	.20
Plate block of four	3.75	
y. Se-tenant block of four	2.00	
FDC (*July 21, 1995*) any single		1.00

1995. Womens Suffrage Issue memorialized the 75th anniversary of Aug. 18, 1920, ratification of the 19th Amendment to the Constitution: "The right of citizens of the United States to vote will not be denied or abridged by the United States or by any state on account of sex." *Offset and intaglio by Ashton-Potter (USA) Ltd., perforated 11.*

CM1745 *U.S. Constitution's 19th Amendment*

CM1745 (*2980*)
32c multicolored, phosphored paper	.50	.20
Plate block of four	3.50	
FDC (*Aug. 26, 1995*)		1.00
v. Imperforate pair	—	
v1. Intaglio black omitted	—	

1995. Louis Armstrong Issue honors the New Orleans-born trumpet player, composer, improviser and unofficial U.S. goodwill ambassador who made giant contributions to jazz. *Offset by Sterling Sommer for Ashton-Potter (USA) Ltd., perforated 11.*

CM1746 *Louis Armstrong*

CM1746 (*2982*)
32c multicolored, phosphored paper	.50	.20
Plate block of four	3.50	
FDC (*Sept. 1, 1995*)		1.00

For a similar design with "32" in white, see CM1749.

1995. World War II Commemorative Pane, the final installment in this five-year, 50-stamp series, features a map and stamps covering events of the war in 1945. *Offset and intaglio by BEP, perforated 11.*

CM1747a   CM1747b   CM1747c   CM1747d   CM1747e

CM1747f   CM1747g   CM1747h   CM1747i   CM1747j

CM1747 *1945: Victory at Last*

CM1747 *(2981)*
$3.20 pane of 10, overall tagged   8.25   7.00
   a. **32c** Flag raised on Iwo Jima   .75   .70
   b. **32c** Manila freed   .75   .70
   c. **32c** Okinawa   .75   .70
   d. **32c** U.S. & Soviets at Elbe   .75   .70
   e. **32c** Liberate Camps   .75   .70
   f. **32c** Germany surrenders   .75   .70
   g. **32c** Displaced persons   .75   .70
   h. **32c** Japan surrenders   .75   .70
   i. **32c** News of victory   .75   .70
   j. **32c** Hometowns honor veterans   .75   .70

1995. Jazz Musicians Issue, a se-tenant pane of 20
stamps depicting 10 jazz greats including a second
version of the Louis Armstrong commemorative released
Sept. 1, continues the American Music series that began
in 1993. *Offset by Sterling Sommer for Ashton-Potter
(USA) Ltd., perforated 11.*

CM1748 *(2984)*
  32c multicolored, phosphored paper   .50   .20
CM1749 *(2983)*
  32c multicolored, phosphored paper   .50   .20
CM1750 *(2985)*
  32c multicolored, phosphored paper   .50   .20
CM1751 *(2986)*
  32c multicolored, phosphored paper   .50   .20
CM1752 *(2987)*
  32c multicolored, phosphored paper   .50   .20

CM1748
*Coleman
Hawkins*

CM1749
*Louis
Armstrong*

CM1750
*James P.
Johnston*

CM1751 *'Jelly
Roll' Morton*

CM1752
*Charlie
Parker*

CM1753
Eubie Blake

CM1755
*Thelonious
Monk*

CM1756 *John
Coltrane*

CM1757
Erroll Garner

CM1753 *(2988)*
32c multicolored, phosphored paper   .50   .20
CM1754 *(2989)*
32c multicolored, phosphored paper   .50   .20
CM1755 *(2990)*
32c multicolored, phosphored paper   .50   .20
CM1756 *(2991)*
32c multicolored, phosphored paper   .50   .20
CM1757 *(2992)*
32c multicolored, phosphored paper   .50   .20
    Plate block of 10   8.50
    FDC, any single *(Sept. 16, 1995)*   2.00
    y. Se-tenant vertical block
       of 10 CM1748-57   9.50
    a. Pane of 20   25.

1995. Garden Flowers Issue is the third in an annual series of colorful and popular se-tenant five-stamp booklets, this one depicting late summer and early autumn blooms. *Offset and intaglio by BEP, perforated 11 vertically on one or two sides.*

CM1758   CM1759   CM1760   CM1761   CM1762
Aster   Chrysanth   Dahlia   Hydranzzea   Rudbeckia
     emum

CM1758 *(2993)*
32c multicolored, overall tagged   .50   .20
CM1759 *(2994)*
32c multicolored, overall tagged   .50   .20
CM1760 *(2995)*
32c multicolored, overall tagged   .50   .20
CM1761*(2996)*
32c multicolored, overall tagged   .50   .20
CM1762 *(2997)*
32c multicolored, overall tagged   .50   .20
    FDC, any single *(Sept. 19, 1995)*   1.00
    n. Booklet pane of five   4.00
      FDC   3.00
    vn. Imperforate pane of five   —

1995. Republic of Palau Issue celebrates the first anniversary of independence for this former U.N. trust territory of the western Pacific Ocean, which released a joint issue almost identical in design on Oct. 1. This stamp also is complimentary in design to those of e arlier U.S. issues honoring each of the other three territories previously administered by the United States: Marshall Islands (CM1394); Micronesia (CM1395); and the Northern Mariana Islands (CM1607). *Offset by Sterling Sommer for Ashton Potter (USA) Ltd., perforated 11.*

CM1763 *Rpublic of Palau*

CM1763 *(2999)*
32c multicolored, phosphored paper   .50   .20
    Plate block of four   3.50
    FDC *(Sept. 29, 1995)*   1.00

1995. Comic Strip Classics Issue is the third USPS Classic Collection of 20 stamps on a single theme in a se-tenant pane with a header acrossd the top and explanatory text on the back of each stamp. This issue takes as its subject influential U.S. comic strips, and it was issued to mark the 100th anniversary of *The Yellow Kid* , which appeared in the *New York World* in May 1895 and is recognized as one of the first modern comic strip characters. *Gravure by J.W. Fergusson & Sons for Stamp Venturers, perforated 10 by 10 1/4.*

Multicolored, block tagged (Oct. 1, 1995)
CM1764 *(3000a)*
32c The Yellow Kid   .75   .50
CM1765 *(3000b)*
32c Katzenjammer Kids   .75   .50
CM1766 *(3000c)*
32c Little Nemo in Slumberland   .75   .50
CM1767 *(3000d)*
32c Bringing Up Father   .75   .50
CM1768 *(3000e)*
32c Krazy Kat   .75   .50
CM1769 *(3000f)*
32c Rube Goldberg's Inventions   .75   .50
CM1770 *(3000g)*
32c Toonerville Folks   .75   .50
CM1771 *(3000h)*
32c Gasoline Alley   .75   .50
CM1772 *(3000i)*
32c Barney Google   .75   .50
CM1773 *(3000j)*
32c Little Orphan Annie   .75   .50
CM1774 *(3000k)*
32c Popeye   .75   .50
CM1775 *(3000l)*
32c Blondie   .75   .50
CM1776 *(3000m)*
32c Dick Tracy   .75   .50
CM1777 *(3000n)*
32c Alley Oop   .75   .50
CM1778 *(3000o)*
32c Nancy   .75   .50
CM1779 *(3000p)*
32c Flash Gordon   .75   .50
CM1780 *(3000q)*
32c Li'l Abner   .75   .50
CM1781 *(3000r)*
32c Terry and the Pirates   .75   .50
CM1782 *(3000s)*
32c Prince Valiant   .75   .50

CM1764 *The Yellow Kid*
CM1765 *Katzenjammer kids*
CM1766 *Little Nemo in Slumberland*
CM1767 *Bringing up Father*

CM1768 *Krazy Kat*
CM1769 *Rube Goldberg's Inventions*
CM1770 *Toonerville Folks*
CM1771 *Gasoline Alley*

CM1772 *Barney Google*
CM1773 *Little Orphan Annie*
CM1774 *Popeye*
CM1775 *Blondie*

CM1776 *Dick Tracy*
CM1777 *Alley Oop*
CM1778 *Nancy*
CM1779 *Flash Gordon*

CM1780 *Lil' Abner*
CM1781 *Terry and the Pirates*
CM1782 *Prince Valiant*
CM1783 *Brenda Starr, Reporter*

CM1783 *(3000t)*

32c Brenda Starr	.75	.50
y. Se-tenant pane of 20 CM1764-83	15.	14.
v. Pane with CM1764-71 imperforate, CM1772-75 part perforated	—	

Because this issue also was made available to collectors in full six-pane printing sheets, gutter pairs and blocks and cross-gutter multiples also exist.

1995. U.S. Naval Academy Issue marks the 150th anniversary of the Annapoilis, Md., institution with a stamp showing the racing sloop *Swift* crewed by academy midshipmen. *Offset by Sterling Sommer for Ashton-Potter (USA) Ltd., perforated 11.*

CM1784 *US Naval Academy Sesquicentennial*

CM1784 *(3001)*

32c multicolored, phosphored paper	.50	.20
Plate block of four	3.50	
FDC *(Oct. 10, 1995)*		1.00

1995. Tennessee Williams Issue memorializes the Mississippi-born playwright and author. Williams (1911-83) was among the most influential U.S. dramatists of the 20th century, including such powerful works as *The Glass Menagerie, Suddenly Last Summer* and *A Streetcar Named Desire.* Literary Arts series. *Offset by Sterling Sommer for Ashton-Potter (USA) Ltd., perforated 11.*

CM1785 *Tennessee Williams*

CM1785 *(3002)*

32c multicolored, phosphored paper	.50	.20
Plate blockof four	3.50	
FDC *(Oct. 13, 1995)*		1.00

1995. James K. Polk Issue, with its frame design adapted from the 1932 1/2c Washington Bicentennial stamp (CM98), commemorates the 200th birthday of the 11th president of the United States. *Intaglio by Banknote Corp.of America, perforated 111/4 x 11.*

CM1786 *James A. Polk*

CM1786

32c reddish brown, phosphored paper	.50	.20
Plate block of four	3.50	
FDC *(Nov. 2, 1995)*		1.00

1995. Antique Automobiles Issue depicts in a se-tenant pane of 25 stamps five of the earliest types of automobiles made in the United States at the turn of the century. *Gravure by J.W. Fergusson & Sons for Stamp Venturers, perforated 10 x 11.*

CM1787 *Duryea*

CM1788 *Haynes*

CM1789 *Columbia*

CM1790 *Winton*

CM1791 *White*

CM1787 *(3019)*

32c multicolored, phosphored paper	.75	.50

CM1788 *(3020)*

32c multicolored, phosphored paper	.75	.50

CM1789 *(3021)*

32c multicolored, phosphored paper	.75	.50

CM1790 *(3022)*

32c multicolored, phosphored paper	.75	.50

CM1791 *(3023)*

32c multicolored, phosphored paper	.75	.50
Plate block of 10	9.00	
y. Se-tenant strip of five		
CM1787-91	4.00	
FDC *(Nov. 3, 1995) any single*		1.00

1996. Utah Centennial Issue marks the 100th anniversary of Utah statehood with a colorful rendering of a natural rock formation from the state's Arches National Park, inscribed "Utah 1896." *Offset by Sterling Sommer for Ashton-Potter (USA) Ltd., perforated 11.*

CM1792 *Utah State Centennial*

CM1792 *(3024)*

32c multicolored, tagged *(120,000,000)*	.50	.20
Plate block of four	3.50	
FDC *(Jan. 4, 1996)*		1.00

1996. Garden Flowers Issue is the fourth in the popular series of colorful five-stamp pane booklets, this one depicting blooms that appear at various locations in the United States duriung the winter months. *(160,000,000) Offset and intaglio by BEP, perforated 11 vertically on one or two sides.*

CM1793	CM1794	CM1795	CM1796	CM1797
Crocus	*Winter Aconite*	*Pansy*	*Snowdrop*	*Anemone*

CM1793 *(3025)*

32c multicolored, phosphored paper	.50	.20

CM1794 *(3026)*

32c multicolored, phosphored paper	.50	.20

CM1795 *(3027)*

32c multicolored, phosphored paper	.50	.20

CM1796 *(3028)*

32c multicolored, phosphored paper	.50	.20

CM1797 *(3029)*

32c multicolored, phosphored paper	.50	.20
FDC, any single *(Jan. 19, 1996)*		1.00
n. Booklet pane of CM1793-97	4.00	
FDC		3.50

1996. Love Issue is a slightly reformatted self-adhesive version of the 32c Cherub design (CM1703-04) in booklet form. *Offset and intaglio by Banknote Corp. of America, serpentine die cut 11 1/4.*

CM1798 *Love*

CM1798 *(3030)*

32c multicolored, tagged		
(2,550,000,000)	.50	.20
FDC *(Jan. 20, 1996)*		1.00
n. Booklet pane of 20 plus label	16.50	
n1. Booklet pane of 15 plus label	10.	
v. Red omitted	—	

1996. Ernest E. Just Issue honors marine biologist, acientis and professor Ernest Everett Just (1883-1941) whose research on abnormal cell development contributed to understanding leukemia, sickle-cell anemia and cancer. Black Heritage series. *Offset by Banknote Corp. of America, perforated 11.*

CM1799 *Ernest E. Just*

CM1799 *(3058)*
32c black and gray, tagged *(92,100,000)* .50 .20
    Plate block of four   3.50
    FDC *(Feb. 1, 1996)*   1.00

**1996. Smithsonian Institution Sesquicentennial
Issue** marks the 150th anniversary of the national
museum, begun in 1829 with a $508,318 bequest from
a British chemist named Smithson, "to found at
Washington...an establishment for the increase &
diffusion of knowledge among men." (See also CM285
and CM959.) *Offset by Sterling Sommer for Ashton-Potter
(USA) Ltd., perforated 11.*

CM1800 *Smithsonian Institution
Sesquicentennial*

CM1800 *(3059)*
32c multicolored, tagged *(115,600,000)* .50 .20
    Plate block of four   3.50
    FDC *(Feb. 7, 1996)*   1.00

1996. New Years Issue for the Year of the Rat is the
fourth in the ongoing series celebrating the Asian lunar
holiday. *Gravure by J.W. Fergusson & Sons for Stamp
Venturers, perforated 11.*

CM1801 *Lunar New Year Rat*

CM1801 *(3060)*
32c multicolored, tagged *(93,150,000)* .50 .20
    Plate block of four   3.50
    FDC *(Feb. 8, 1996)*   1.00

1996. Pioneers of Communications Issue salutes a
quartet of 19th-century innovators in photographic and
print technology. Eadweard Muybridge (1830-1904)
pioneered the conversion of photographs to moving
images. Ottmar Mergenthaler (1854-99) invented
Linotype, which vastly reduced the cost of printing
newspapers and boosted circulation. Chief among the
many inventions of Frederic E. Ives (1856-1937) was the
halftone printing process, which enabled newspapers to
reproduce photographs. William Kennedy Laurie
Dickson (1860-1935), an Edison employee, devised the
kinetoscope, in which precise synchronization gives
montion pictures the illusion of movement. *(23,292,500
each) Offset by Ashton-Potter (USA) Ltd., perforated 11.*

CM1802 *Eadweard
MuyBridge*   CM1803 *Ottman
Mergenthaler*

CM1804 *Frederic Eives*   CM1805 *William Dickson*

CM1802 *(3061)*
32c multicolored, phosphored paper .50 .20
CM1803 *(3062)*
32c multicolored, phosphored paper .50 .20
CM1804 *(3063)*
32c multicolored, phosphored paper .50 .20
CM1805 *(3064)*
32c multicolored, phosphored paper .50 .20
    Plate block of four   3.50
    y. Se-tenant block or
        strip of CM1802-05   3.00   2.50
    FDC *(Feb. 22, 1996)*   2.00

1996. Fulbright Scholarships Issue marks the 50th
anniversary of the annual awards, named for Arkansas
Senator and long-time Foreign Relations Committee Chairman J. William Fulbright, sponsor of the 1946 act that
created the program. To date, about a quarter of a million
Fulbright scholars either have traveled from the United
States to study abroad or have come from abroad to study in
the United States. *Offset and intaglio by BEP, perforated 11.*

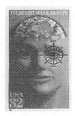

CM1806 *Fulbright Scholarships*

CM1806 *(3065)*
32c multicolored, tagged *(111,000,000)* .50 .20
    Plate block of four   3.50
    FDC *(Feb. 28, 1996)*   1.00

1996. Marathon Issue salutes the 100th running of the
annual 26.20mile Boston Marathon. *Offset by Banknote
Corp. of America, perforated 11.*

CM1807 *Marathon*

CM1807 *(3067)*
32c multicolored, tagged

(209,450,000)	.50	.20
Plate block of four	3.50	
FDC *(April 11, 1996)*		1.00

**1996. Atlanta 1996 Centennial OLympic Games
Issue** is the fourth USPS Classic Collection of 20 stamps
on a single theme in a se-tenant pane with a header
across the top and descriptive text on the back of each
stamp. This issue celebrates the 100th anniversary of
the first modern Olympiad. *Gravure (16,207,500 panes)
by J.W. Fergusson & Sons for Stamp Venturers, perforated 10 1/4 by 10.*

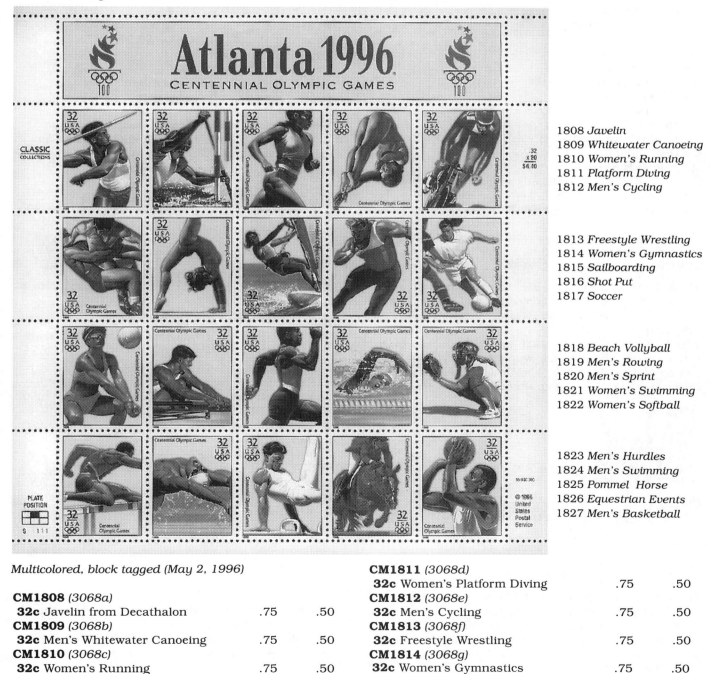

1808 *Javelin*
1809 *Whitewater Canoeing*
1810 *Women's Running*
1811 *Platform Diving*
1812 *Men's Cycling*

1813 *Freestyle Wrestling*
1814 *Women's Gymnastics*
1815 *Sailboarding*
1816 *Shot Put*
1817 *Soccer*

1818 *Beach Volleyball*
1819 *Men's Rowing*
1820 *Men's Sprint*
1821 *Women's Swimming*
1822 *Women's Softball*

1823 *Men's Hurdles*
1824 *Men's Swimming*
1825 *Pommel Horse*
1826 *Equestrian Events*
1827 *Men's Basketball*

Multicolored, block tagged (May 2, 1996)

CM1808 *(3068a)*
32c Javelin from Decathalon   .75   .50
CM1809 *(3068b)*
32c Men's Whitewater Canoeing   .75   .50
CM1810 *(3068c)*
32c Women's Running   .75   .50

CM1811 *(3068d)*
32c Women's Platform Diving   .75   .50
CM1812 *(3068e)*
32c Men's Cycling   .75   .50
CM1813 *(3068f)*
32c Freestyle Wrestling   .75   .50
CM1814 *(3068g)*
32c Women's Gymnastics   .75   .50

CM1815 *(3068h)*
32c Women's Sailboarding   .75   .50
CM1816 *(3068i)*
32c Men's Shot Put   .75   .50
CM1817 *(3068j)*
32c Women's Soccer   .75   .50
CM1818 *(3068k)*
32c Beach Volleyball   .75   .50
CM1819 *(3068l)*
32c Men's Rowing   .75   .50
CM1820 *(3068m)*
32c Men's Sprinting Events   .75   .50
CM1821 *(3068n)*
32c Women's Swimming   .75   .50
CM1822 *(3068o)*
32c Women's Softball   .75   .50
CM1823 *(3068p)*
32c Men's Hurdles   .75   .50
CM1824 *(3068q)*
32c Men's Swimming (Backstroke)   .75   .50
CM1825 *(3068r)*
32c Men's Gymnastics (Pommel Horse)   .75   .50
CM1826 *(3068s)*
32c Equestrian Events   .75   .50
CM1827 *(3068t)*
32c Men's Basketball   .75   .50
    FDC, *(May 2, 1996)* any single   1.00
    y. Pane of CM1808-27   14.
    vy. Imperforate pane of 20   —

Because this issue also was made available to collectors in full six-pane printing sheets, gutter pairs and blocks and cross-gutter multiples also exist.

1996. Georgia O'Keeffe Issue commemorates the artist whose distinctive, vibrant presentation of images from nature in abstract, creative settings marked her as a true American original. One of 200 early flower paintings created by O'Keeffe (1887-1986) was reproduced in a 15-stamp commemorative pane with selvage picturing the painter and a quotation by her. *Gravure by J.W. Fergusson & Sons for Stamp Venturers, perforated 11 1/2.*

CM1828 *Georgia O'Keff*

CM1828 *(3069)*
32c multicolored, tagged *(156,300,000)* .50   .20
    Plate block of four   3.50
    Pane of 20   16.
    FDC *(May 23, 1996)*   1.00
    v. Imperforate pair   —

1996. Tennessee Bicentennial Issue marks the 200th anniversary of Tennessee entering the Union as the 13th state. It is the first conventional commemorative issued simultaneously both in lick-and-stick panes and self-adhesive booklets. *Gravure by J.W. Fergusson & Sons for Stamp Venturers.*

CM1829-30 *Tennessee Statehood*

Perforated 11
CM1829 *(3070)*
32c multicolored, tagged *(100,000,000)* .50   .20
    Plate block of four   3.25
    FDC *(May 31, 1996)*   1.00

Serpentine die cut 10 x 10 3/4
CM1830 *(3071)*
32c multicolored, tagged *(60,120,000)* .75   .20
    FDC *(May 31, 1996)*   1.00
    n. Booklet pane of 20   16.
    v. Horizontal pair, imperforate
      (no die cutting) between   —

1996. American Indian Dances Issue pictures an important component of native American culture and ritual in a 20-stamp commemorative pane. *Gravure by Ashton-Potter (USA) Ltd., perforated 11.*

CM1831 Fancy Dance	CM1832 Butterfly Dance	CM1833 Traditional Dance	CM1834 Raven Dance	CM1835 Hoop Dance

CM1831 *(3072)*
32c multicolored, tagged *(27,850,000)* .75   .50
CM1832 *(3073)*
32c multicolored, tagged   .75   .50
CM1833 *(3074)*
32c multicolored, tagged   .75   .50
CM1834 *(3075)*
32c multicolored, tagged   .75   .50
CM1835 *(3076)*
32c multicolored, tagged   .75   .50
    Plate block of 10   8.00
    y. Se-tenant strip of CM1831-53   3.50
    FDC *(June 7, 1996)* any single   1.00
    Pane of 20   14.50

1996. Prehistoric Animals Issue features dramatic portraits of four important North American representatives of the Cenozoic Era (or Age of Mammals), comprising the last 65 million years. *Offset by Ashton-Potter (USA) Ltd., perforated 11.*

CM1836 *Eohippus*   CM1837 *Woolly Mammoth*

CM1838 *Mastodon*   CM1839 *Saber-tooth Cat*

CM1836 *(3077)*
32c multicolored, tagged *(22,218,000)* .75 .50
CM1837 *(3078)*
32c multicolored, tagged .75 .50
CM1838 *(3079)*
32c multicolored, tagged .75 .50
CM1839 *(3080)*
32c multicolored, tagged .75 .50
    Plate block of four 3.50
    y. Se-tenant block or strip
      of CM1836-39 3.00
    FDC *(June 8, 1996) any single* 1.00

1996. Breast Cancer Awareness Issue takes note of a serious health risk to American women to raise awareness and encourage early detection. Special postmarks, clinics and screening in conjunction with this stamp across the nation increased public attention, and helped spark Congress to request a breast cancer semipostal stamp in 1998. *Offset by Ashton-Potter (USA) Ltd., perforated 11.*

CM1840 *Breast Cancer Awareness*

CM1840 *(3081)*
32c multicolored, tagged *(95,600,000)* .50 .20
    Plate block of four 3.25
    FDC *(June 15, 1996)* 1.00

1996. James Dean Issue, the second in the Legends of Hollywood series, again consisted of a 20-stamp commemorative pane with star-shaped corner perforations and a large area of selvage displaying an enlargement of the actor. Dean (1931-55) had enormous impact in three films -- *East of Eden, Rebel Without a Cause* and *Giant* -- before his death in a car crash at the age of 24. *Gravure by J.W. Fergusson & Sons for Stamp Venturers, perforated 11.*

CM1841 *James Dean*

CM1841 *(3082)*
32c multicolored, tagged *(300,000,000)* .50 .20
    Plate block of four 3.23

1996. Folk Heroes Issue features bold portraits of larger-than-life characters made famous in popular American fiction: Mighty Casey, whose turn at the bat in Ernest L. Thayer's 188 poem tragically came to naught; legendary lumberjack Paul Bunyan, who transformed America together with Babe, his giant blue ox; John Henry, the "steel drivin' man" who beat a steam drill in carving out a West Virginia railway tunnel, but perished in the attempt; and the cyclone-taming Texas cowboy Pecos Bill, who wears a rattlesnake for a scarf on the stamp. *Offset by Ashton-Potter (USA) Ltd., perforated 11.*

CM1842
*Mighty
Casey*

CM1843
*Paul
Bunyan*

CM1844
*John
Henry*

CM1845
Pecos Bill

CM1842 *(3083)*
32c multicolored, tagged *(23,681,250)* .50 .20
CM1843 *(3084)*
32c multicolored, tagged .50 .20
CM1844 *(3085)*
32c multicolored, tagged .50 .20
CM1845 *(3086)*
32c multicolored, tagged .50 .20
    Plate block of four 3.50
    y. Se-tenant block or strip
      of CM1842-45 3.00
    FDC *(July 11, 1996) any single* 1.00

1996. Olympic Games Centennial Issue was another single-design 20-stamp commemorative pane to mark the 100th anniversary of the first modern Olympiad in 1896 in Athens, Greece. Left margin selvage showed an enlargement of *Discobolus*, after the original bronze created by the Greek sculptor Myron in the fifth century B.C. *Offset and intaglio by Ashton-Potter (USA) Ltd., perforated 11.*

CM1846 *Discus Thrower, Centennial Olympics*

CM1846 (3087)

32c brown, tagged *(133,613,000)* .50 .20
Plate block of four 3.00
FDC *(July 19, 1996)* 1.00
Pane of 20 14.

1996. Iowa Sesquicentennial Issue marks the 150th anniversary of Iowa entering the Union as the 29th state. The conventional commemorative was available throughout the country, whereas the self-adhesive booklet version of the stamp was sold only in Iowa and at philatelic centers out of state. *Offset by Ashton-Potter (USA) Ltd.*

CM1847 *Iowa Statehood Sesquicentennial*

Perforated 11
CM1847 (3088)

32c multicolored, tagged *(103,400,000)* .50 .20
Plate block of four 3.00
FDC *(Aug. 1, 1996)* 1.00

CM1848 *Iowa Statehood Sesquicentennial*

Serpentine die cut 10 x 10 3/4
CM1848 (3089)

32c multicolored, tagged *(60,000,000)* .75 .30
FDC *(Aug. 1, 1996)* 1.00
n. Booklet pane of 20 16.

1996. Rural Free Delivery Centennial Issue saluted a century of the service that brought mail for the first time directly to the homes of America's farmers and other rural residents. *Offset and intaglio by BEP, perforated 11.*

CM1849 *Rural Free Delivery*

CM1849 (3090)

32c multicolored, tagged *(134,000,000)* .50 .20
Plate block of four 3.00
FDC *(Aug. 7, 1996)* 1.00

1996. Riverboats Issue is a se-tenant presentation of five self-adhesive stamps saluting historic 19th-century steamboats that carried passengers and important cargo on the inland waterways of America. *Gravure by Avery Dennison Security Printing Division, serpentine die cut 11.*

CM1850 *Robert E. Lee*

CM1851 *Sylvan Dell*

CM1852 *Forwest*

CM1853 *Rebecca Everingham*

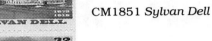

CM1854 *Bailey Gatzert*

CM1850 *(3091)*
32c multicolored, tagged *(32,000,000)* .75 .50
CM1851 *(3092)*
32c multicolored, tagged .75 .50
CM1852 *(3093)*
32c multicolored, tagged .75 .50
CM1853 *(3094)*
32c multicolored, tagged .75 .50
CM1854 *(3095)*
32c multicolored, tagged .75 .50
Plate block of 10 8.00
y. Se-tenant vertical strip
of CM1850-54 3.50
v. Die Cut through backing
full pane 35.
FDC *(Aug. 22, 1996) any single* 1.00

1996. Big Band Leaders Issue honored outstanding orchestra leaders of the Big Band era, who popularized the Swing music that had its heyday in the 1930s and '40s. Count Basie (1904-84), a brilliant composer whose bands for almost 50 years featured many of the nation's finest jazz soloists, is best remembered for tunes including *One O'Clock Jump, Swingin' the Blues* and *Jumpin' at the Woodside*. The Dorsey Brothers, clarinetist Jimmy (1904-57) and trombonist Tommy (1905-56), headed dance bands separately and together, notable for melodies such as *Tangerine* and *I'm Sentimental Over You*. Glenn Miller (1904-44), a gifted trombonist and arranger, presided over one of the most successful Sing era orchestras, the distinctive sound of which is recognizable in classics such as *In the Mood, Kalamazoo* and *Sunrise Serenade*. Benny Goodman (1909-86), known as the

"King of Swing," was a clarinet prodigy and a perfectionist as bandleader, with *King Porter Stomp, Don't Be That Way* and *Sing, Sing, Sing* among his hits. American Music series. *Offset by Ashton-Potter (USA) Ltd., perforated 11.*

CM1855 *Count Basie*   CM1856 *Tommy & Jimmy Dorsey*

CM1857   CM1858 *Benny*
Glen Miller   *Goodman*

CM1855 *(3096)*
32c multicolored, tagged *(23,025,000)* .50   .20
CM1856 *(3097)*
32c multicolored, tagged   .50   .20
CM1857 *(3098)*
32c multicolored, tagged   .50   .20
CM1858 *(3099)*
32c multicolored, tagged   .50   .20
   Plate block of four   3.50
   y. Se-tenant block or strip
      of CM1855-58   3.00
   FDC *(Sept. 11, 1996) any single*   1.00
   Pane of 20   14.

1996. Songwriters Issue honored four of the finest songwriters of the 20th century. Harold Arlen (1905-86) is best known for his scores for two Judy Garland films, *The Wizard of Oz* (co-written with Yip Harburg) and *A Star is Born* (co-written with Ira Gershwin), and tunes written for Harlem's renowned Cotton Club including *Stormy Weather.*Songwriter, singer and Capitol Records founder Johnny Mercer (1909-76) penned the lyrics to more than 1,000 songs, from *I'm and Old Cowhand* to *Moon River.* The nation's finest female songrwriter, Dorothy Fields (1905-74) credits include *Sunny Side of the Street, The Way You Look Tonight* and *A Fine Romance.* Hoagy Carmichael (1899-1981) may be most closely associated with *Stardust,* but authored many other great songs as well, including *Heart and Soul* and *Georgia on My Mind.* American Music series. *Printed in offset by Ashton-Potter (USA) Ltd., perforated 11.*

CM1859 *Harold Arlen*   CM1860 *Johnny Mercer*

CM1861 *Dorothy Fields* CM1862 *Hoagy Carmichael*

CM1859 *(3100)*
32c multicolored, tagged *(23,025,000)* .50   .20
CM1860 *(3101)*
32c multicolored, tagged   .50   .20
CM1861 *(3102)*
32c multicolored, tagged   .50   .20
CM1862 *(3103)*
32c multicolored, tagged   .50   .20
   Plate block of four   3.50
   y. Se-tenant block or strip
      of CM1859-62   3.00
   FDC *(Sept. 11, 1996) any single*   1.00
   Pane of 20   14.

1996. F. Scott Fitzgerald Issue celebrated the 100th birthday of the novelist (1896-1940) who immortalized the Jazz Age of the 1920s in such works as *The Beautiful and the Damned, The Great Gatsby* and *Tender is the Night.* The stamp prepays the 23c fee for each additional ounce over the basic 32c first-class letter rate. Literary Arts series. *Printed in gravure by BEP, perforated 11.*

CM1863 *F. Scott Fitzgerald*

CM1863 *(3014)*
32c multicolored, tagged *(300,000,000)* .50   .20
   Plate blockof four   2.75
   FDC *(Sept. 27, 1996)*   1.00

1996. Endangered Species Issue was a 15-stamp setenant commemorative pane with a banner and marginal text, each stamp featuring an indigenous American animal currently threatened with extinction. Although not a joint issue technically speaking, a pane of 24 stamps depicting native endangered specias was issued simultaneously by Mexico. *Printed in offset (14,910,000 panes) by Sterling Sommer for Ashton-Potter (USA) Ltd., perforated 11.*

Endangered Species

National Stamp Collecting Month 1996 highlights these 15 species to promote awareness of endangered wildlife. Each generation must work to protect the delicate balance of nature, so that future generations may share a sound and healthy planet.

1864 *Black-footed Ferret*
1865 *Thick-billed Parrot*
1866 *Hawaiian Monk Seal*

1867 *American Crocodile*
1868 *Ocelot*
1869 *Schaus Swallowtail Butterfly*

1870 *Wyoming Toad*
1871 *Brown Pelican*
1872 *California Condor*

1873 *Gila Trout*
1874 *San Francisco Garter Snake*
1875 *Woodland Caribou*

1876 *Florida Panther*
1877 *Piping Plover*
1878 *Florida Manatee*

Multicolored, block tagged (Oct. 2, 1996)

CM1864 *(3105a)*
32c Black-footed Ferret ... .50 ... .20
CM1865 *(3105b)*
32c Thick-billed Parrot ... .50 ... .20
CM1866 *(3105c)*
32c Hawaiian Monk Seal ... .50 ... .20
CM1867 *(3105d)*
32c American Crocodile ... .50 ... .20
CM1868 *(3105e)*
32c Ocelot ... .50 ... .20
CM1869 *(3105f)*
32c Schaus Swallowtail Butterfly ... .50 ... .20
CM1870 *(3105g)*
32c Wyoming Toad ... .50 ... .20
CM1871 *(3105h)*
32c Brown Pelican ... .50 ... .20
CM1872 *(3105i)*
32c California Condor ... .50 ... .20
CM1873 *(3105j)*
32c Gila Trout ... .50 ... .20
CM1874 *(3105k)*
32c San Francisco Garter Snake ... .50 ... .20
CM1875 *(3105l)*
32c Woodland Caribou ... .50 ... .20

CM1876 *(3105m)*
32c Florida Panther ... .50 ... .20
CM1877 *(3105n)*
32c Piping Plover ... .50 ... .20
CM1878 *(3105o)*
32c Florida Manatee ... .50 ... .20
  FDC *(Oct. 2, 1996)*, any single ... 1.00
  y. Se-tenant pane of CM1864-78 ... 11.

1996. Computer Technology Issue marks the 50th anniversary of the Electronic Numerical Integrator and Calculator (ENIAC), regarded widely as the first general-purpose electronic digital computer, forerunner to the millions in use today. *Offset and intaglio by Ashton-Potter (USA) Ltd., perforated 11.*

CM1879 *Computer Technology*

CM1879 *(3106)*
   32c multicolored, tagged *(93,612,000)* .50 .20
      Plate block of four   3.00
      FDC *(Oct. 8, 1996)*   1.00

1996. Hanukkah Issue, first stamp in what USPS announced as a Holiday Celebration series, honors the Jewish Festival of Lights and shares its design with a joint issue from Israel. The self-adhesive stamp shows a stylized menorah and the colorful candles with which Jews mark the eight-day observance. *Gravure by Avery Dennison Security Printing Division, serpentine die cut 11.*

CM1880 *Hanukkah*

CM1880 *(3118)*
   32c multicolored, tagged *(103,520,000)*.75 .20
      Plate block of four   3.00
      FDC *(Oct. 22, 1996)*   1.00

1996. Cycling Souvenir Sheet was chiefly issued, according to *Linn's U.S. Stamp Yearbook,* so that the Postal Service would "have an item it could sell at international cycling meets in which the USPS Pro Cycling Team competed, to help defray the team's $1 million annual subsidy." *Gravure by J.W. Fergusson & Sons for Stamp Venturers, perforated 11.*

CM1881 *(3119)*
   $1 multicolored, tagged *(20,000,000)* 2.50 1.00
      a. 50c multicolored and orange 1.50   1.00
      b. 50c multicolored and blue green1.50   1.00
      FDC *(Nov. 1, 1996)*   1.00

1997. New Years Issue for the Year of the Ox is the fifth in the ongoing series celebrating the Asian lunar holiday. *Gravure by Stamp Venturers, perforated 11 1/4.*

CM1882 *Year of the Ox*

CM1882 *(3120)*
   32c multicolored, tagged *(160,000,000)* .50 .20
      Plate block of four   3.00
      FDC *(Jan. 5, 1997)*   1.00

1997. Benjamin O. Davis Issue salutes with a self-adhesive stamp the nation's first black brigadier general, a soldier began as a private and rose through the ranks

in a 50-year career to became both a force for and a symbol of integration in America's military. Black Heritage series. *Offset by Banknote Corp.of America, serpentine die cut 11 1/2.*

CM1883 *Benjamin O. Davis, Sr.*

CM1883 *(3121)*
   32c gray, green and black, phosphored
           paper *(112,000,000)*   .50   .20
      Plate block of four   3.00
      FDC *(Jan. 28, 1997)*   1.00

1997. Love Issue used bilaterally symmetrical profiles of two elegant swans outlining a heart in two self-adhesive booklets paying the 32c standard first-class one-ounce letter rate and the 55c rate for two-ounce letters (useful for wedding invitations containing reply cards and envelopes), respectively.*Offset by Banknote Corp. of America.*

Serpentine die cut 11 3/4 x 11 1/2 on 2, 3 or 4 sides

CM1884 *32c Love Swans*

CM1884 *(3123)*
   32c multicolored, tagged   .50   .20
      FDC *(Feb. 7, 1997)*   1.00
      n. Booklet pane of 20 plus label   13.
      v. Imperforate pair (no die cutting) —
      vn. Imperforate pane of 20
         (no die cutting)   —

Serpentine die cut 11 1/2 x 11 3/4 on 2, 3 or 4 sides

CM1885 *55c Love Swans*

CM1885 *(3124)*
   55c multicolored, tagged   1.00   .30
      FDC *(Feb. 7, 1997)*   1.00
      n. Booklet pane of 20 plus label 22.50

1996. Helping Children Learn Issue, a self-adhesive stamp, calls attention to the developmental importance and simple pleasure of reading as an activity for adults to share with children, and coincides with the centennial of the PTA, the nation's oldest and largest volunteer association working for children. *Gravure by Avery Dennison Security Printing Division, serpentine die cut 11 1/2 x 11 3/4.*

CM1886 *Helping Children Learn*

CM1886 *(3125)*
32c multicolored, tagged .50 .20
  Plate block of four 3.00
  FDC *(Feb. 18, 1997)* 1.00

1997. Pacific '97 Issue, the first triangular stamps in U.S. philatelic history, uses two early means of moving the mail -- the stagecoach and the clipper ship -- to promote the Pacific 97 International Philatelic Exhibition Ma7 29 to June 8 in San Francisco, Calif. *Intaglio by Banknote Corp. of America, perforated 11 1/4.*

CM1887 *Stagecoach*

CM1888 *Clipper Ship*

CM1887 *(3130)*
32c red, phosphored paper *(65,000,000)* .50 .20
CM1888 *(3131)*
32c blue, phosphored paper .50 .20
  Plate block of four 3.00
  y. Se-tenant pair CM1887-88 1.25
  FDC *(March 13, 1997)* 2.00
Because this issue also was made available in full 96-subject printing sheets of six 16-stamp panes, gutter pairs and blocks and cross-gutter multiples also exist.

1997. Thornton Wilder Issue celebrated the 100th birthday of the three-time Pulitzer Prize-winning author (1897-1975) of the novel *The Bridge of San Luis Rey* and the plays *Our Town* (symbolically depicted on the stamp) and *The Skin of Our Teeth*. Literary Arts series. *Offset by Ashton-Potter (USA) Ltd., perforated 11.*

CM1889 *Thornton Wilder*

CM1889 *(3134)*
32c multicolored, tagged *(97,500,000)* .50 .20
  Plate block of four 3.00
  FDC *(April 17, 1997)* 1.00

1997. Raoul Wallenberg Issue commemorates the Swedish diplomat who in 1944 risked his own life to save over 20,000 Hungarian Jews from Nazi genocide by issuing them falsified Swedish passports. In 1945, Wallenberg was taken prisoner by the Soviets, who only in 1957 announced that he had died a decade earlier, of a purported heart attack,while in Moscow's Lubyanka Prison. *Offset by Sterling Sommer for Ashton-Potter (USA) Ltd., perforated 11.*

CM1890 *Wallenberg and Refugees*

CM1890 *(3135)*
32c multicolored, tagged *(96,000,000)* .50 .20
  Plate block of four 3.00
  FDC *(April 24, 1997)* 1.00

1997. The World of Dinosaurs Issue, a 15-stamp pane, showcases two panoramic dioramas of life in the age of the giant reptiles: a scene in Colorado 150 million years ago in the top panel; and a 75-million-year-old scene from Montana in the bottom panel of the pane. The pane portrays many species never before shown on stamps. *Offset by Sterling Sommer for Ashton-Potter (U SA) Ltd., perforated 11.*

CM1891 *(3136)*
$4.80 sheet of 15, tagged
    (14,600,000) 10. 9.50
  a. 32c Ceratosaurus .75 .50
  b. 32c Camptosaurus .75 .50
  c. 32c Camarasaurus .75 .50
  d. 32c Brachiosaurus .75 .50
  e. 32c Goniopholis .75 .50
  f. 32c Stegosaurus .75 .50
  g. 32c Allosaurus .75 .50
  h. 32c Opisthias .75 .50
  i. 32c Edmontonia .75 .50
  j. 32c Einiosaurus .75 .50
  k. 32c Daspletosaurus .75 .50
  l. 32c Palaeosaniwa .75 .50
  m. 32c Corythosaurus .75 .50
  n. 32c Ornithomimus .75 .50
  o. 32c Parasaurolophus .75 .50
  FDC *(May 1, 1997)* any single 1.00
  FDC pane of 15 9.50
  v. All colors omitted, untagged —
  v1. Perforations inverted —

THE WORLD OF DINOSAURS

A scene in Colorado, 150 million years ago

A scene in Montana, 75 million years ago

CM1891 *The World of Dinosaurs*

1997. Bugs Bunny Commemorative Pane, first in an announced Warner Brothers Cartoon Characters series, showcases in two types of self-adhesive 10-stamp pane (rouletted vertically through the middle of the pane) the wisecracking "Oscar-winning rabbit" with the Brooklyn accent who has been a fixture on American movie and television screens for more than half a century. *Gravure (26,500,000 panes of 10) by Avery Dennision Security Printing Division.*

CM1892 *Bugs Bunny*

Serpentine die cut 11 through stamps only
CM1892 *(3137)*
$3.20 pane of ten, tagged
    n. Right half of pane (single

die cut CM1892a
    superimposed on enlarged
    image in right selvage)   1.00
  n1. Left half of pane (block of
    nine CM1892a)   5.00
    a. 32c single   .75   .25
    FDC *(May 22, 1997)*   1.00

Serpentine die cut 11 through stamps and backing
CM1893 *(3138)*
$3.20 pane of ten, tagged   200.
    n. Right half of pane (single imperforate
    CM1893a on enlarged image
    in right selvage)   150.
  n1. Left half of pane
    (block of nine CM1893a)   5.00
    a. 32c single   .75   .25

This issue also was made available in top and bottom half printing sheets of six 10-stamp panes each. A single plate number, trimmed away on individual panes, appears adjacent to the bottom-left pane in the bottom half of the printing sheet only. Value of plate number half at press time is $225.

A gummed, non-denominated, untagged item similar to CM1893n on the same backing paper as the normal stamps lacks Bug's "autograph" and single stamp, the latter of which is replaced by "32 USA" as on the issued stamp. Though printed for the USPS, this item was an advertising piece and was not postally valid.

1997. Pacific '97 U.S. Stamp Sesquicentennial Souvenir Sheets mark the 150th anniversary of the first regular-issue U.S. postage stamps (Minkus 1-2, depicted in the selvage of the souvenir sheets) and hail the opening of the Pacific '97 International Philatelic Exhibition in San Francisco, Calif.. The souvenir sheets were sold only during the 11 days of the show. *Offset and intaglio by BEP, perforated 10 1/2.*

CM1894 *Benjamin Franklin Souvenir Sheet*

CM1894 *(3139)*
$6.00 pane of 12, tagged   11.50   9.00
  a. 50c single   1.00
  FDC *(May 29, 1997)*   1.00

CM1895 *George Washington Souvenir Sheet*

CM1895 *(3140)*
$7.20 pane of 12, tagged   12.50   10.
  a. 60c single   1.25
  FDC *(May 29, 1997)*   1.00

1997. Marshall Plan 50th Anniversary Issue saluted the post-World War II European Recovery Program unveiled in 1947 by Gen. George C. Marshall (1880-1959). The U.S.-backed multi-billion-dollar plan to help a devastated Western Europe regain its economic health and halt the expansion of Soviet influence earned Marshall the Nobel Peace Prize. *Offset and intaglio by Stevens Security Press for Ashton-Potter (USA) Ltd., perforated 11.*

CM1896 *The Marshall Plan*

CM1896 *(3141)*
32c multicolored, tagged *(45,250,000)*   .50   .20
  Plate block of four   3.50
  FDC *(June 4, 1997)*   1.00

1997. Classic American Aircraft Issue is the fifth USPS Classic Collection, 20 se-tenant single-theme stamps in a pane with a header across the top and descriptive text on the back of each stamp. This issue showcases 20 U.S. aircraft of the first half-century of powered flight. *Gravure (8,050,000 panes) by Stamp Venturers, perforated 10.*

Multicolored, block tagged (July 19, 1997)
CM1897 *(3142a)*
  32c North American P-51 Mustang fighter.75   .50
CM1898 *(3142b)*
  32c Wright Model B Flyer   .75   .50
CM1899 *(3142c)*
  32c Piper J-3 Cub   .75   .50
CM1900 *(3142d)*
  32c Lockheed Vega   .75   .50
CM1901 *(3142e)*
  32c Northrop Alpha   .75   .50
CM1902 *(3142f)*
  32c Martin B-10 bomber   .75   .50
CM1903 *(3142g)*
  32c Chance Vought Corsair F4U fighter .75   .50
CM1904 *(3142h)*
  32c Boeing B-47 Stratojet bomber   .75   .50
CM1905 *(3142i)*
  32c Gee Bee Super-Sportster   .75   .50
CM1906 *(3142j)*
  32c Beech Model C17L Staggerwing   .75   .50
CM1907 *(3142k)*
  32c Boeing B-17 Flying Fortress bomber .75   .50
CM1908 *(3142l)*
  32c Stearman PT-13 training aircraft   .75   .50
CM1909 *(3142m)*
  32c Lockheed Constellation   .75   .50
CM1910 *(3142n)*
  32c Lockheed P-38 Lightning fighter   .75   .50
CM1911 *(3142o)*
  32c Boeing P-26 Peashooter fighter   .75   .50
CM1912 *(3142p)*
  32c Ford Tri-Motor   .75   .50
CM1913 *(3142q)*
  32c Douglas DC-3 passenger plane   .75   .50
CM1914 *(3142r)*
  32c Boeing 314 Clipper flying boat   .75   .50
CM1915 *(3142s)*
  32c Curtiss JN-4 Jenny training aircraft .75   .50
CM1916 *(3142t)*
  32c Grumman F4F Wildcat fighter   .75   .50
  FDC *(July 19, 1997)*, any single   1.00
  y. Se-tenant pane of CM1897-190615.00
  FDC   10.

Because this issue also was made available to collectors in full six-pane printing sheets, gutter pairs and blocks and cross-gutter multiples also exist.

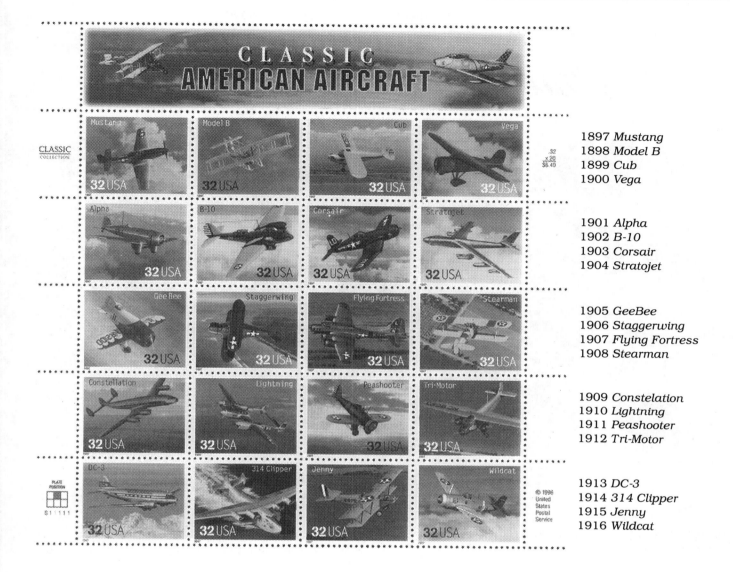

1897 *Mustang*
1898 *Model B*
1899 *Cub*
1900 *Vega*

1901 *Alpha*
1902 *B-10*
1903 *Corsair*
1904 *Stratojet*

1905 *GeeBee*
1906 *Staggerwing*
1907 *Flying Fortress*
1908 *Stearman*

1909 *Constelation*
1910 *Lightning*
1911 *Peashooter*
1912 *Tri-Motor*

1913 *DC-3*
1914 *314 Clipper*
1915 *Jenny*
1916 *Wildcat*

1997. Legendary Football Coaches Issue recalls four of the greatest who ever coached the game in a se-tenant issue released at Canton, Ohio, home of the Professional Football Hall of Fame. Slightly revised designs of all four stamps were issued in August in the states where the coaches made their names (CM1937-40). *Offset by Sterling Sommer for Ashton-Potter (USA) Ltd., perforated 11.*

1917 *Paul "Bear" Bryant*
1918 *Glenn "Pop" Warner*
1919 *Vince Lombardi*
1920 *George Halas*

CM1917 *(3145)*		
32c multicolored, tagged *(22,500,000)*	.50	.20
CM1918 *(3143)*		
32c multicolored, tagged	.50	.20
CM1919 *(3144)*		
32c multicolored, tagged	.50	.20
CM1920 *(3146)*		
32c multicolored, tagged	.50	.20
Plate block of four	3.50	
y. Se-tenant block or strip of CM1917-20	2.00	
FDC *(July 25, 1997)*		2.00

1997. Classic American Dolls Issue depicts these beloved toys of childhood (and, increasingly, collectibles for adults) dating from as far back as the 1850s up to the 1960s in a commemorative 15-stamp pane with a banner and descriptions in the margins. *(7,000,000 panes) Offset by Sterling Sommer for Ashton-Potter (USA) Ltd., perforated 11.*

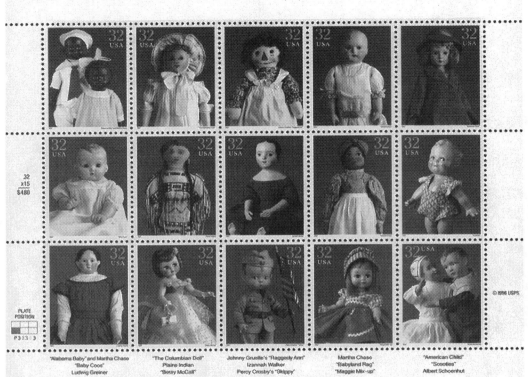

CLASSIC
American Dolls

1921 *"Alabama Baby"*
     and Martha Chase
1922 *"The Columbian Doll"*
1923 *Johnny Gruelle's*
     "Raggedy Ann"
1924 *Martha Chase*
1925 *"American Child"*

1926 *"Baby Coos"*
1927 *Plains Indian*
1928 *Izinnah Walker*
1929 *"Babyland Rag"*
1930 *"Scooties"*

1931 *Ludwig Grenier*
1932 *"Betsy McCall"*
1933 *Percy Crosby's*
     "Skipper"
1934 *"Maggie Mix-up"*
1935 *Albert Schoenhut*

"Alabama Baby" and Martha Chase   "The Columbian Doll"   Johnny Gruelle's "Raggedy Ann"   Martha Chase   "American Child"
"Baby Coos"   Plains Indian   Izannah Walker   "Babyland Rag"   "Scooties"
Ludwig Greiner   "Betsy McCall"   Percy Crosby's "Skippy"   "Maggie Mix-up"   Albert Schoenhut

The above names include doll makers, designers, trade names and common names.

Multicolored, tagged (July 28, 1997)

CM1921 *(3151a)*
32c "Alabama Baby" and Martha Chase Doll .75   .50
CM1922 *(3151b)*
32c Rutta Sisters' "The Columbian Doll" .75   .50
CM1923 *(3151c)*
32c Johnny Gruelle's "Raggedy Ann"   .75   .50
CM1924 *(3151d)*
32c Martha Chase Cloth Doll   .75   .50
CM1925 *(3151e)*
32c Effanbee Doll Co. "American Child" .75   .50
CM1926 *(3151f)*
32c Ideal Novelty & Toy Co. "Baby Coos" .75   .50
CM1927 *(3151g)*
32c Plains Indian Doll of 1920s   .75   .50
CM1928 *(3151h)*
32c Izannah Walker Oil-Painted Cloth Doll .75   .50
CM1929 *(3151i)*
32c All-Cloth "Babyland Rag" Doll   .75   .50
CM1930 *(3151j)*
32c Rose O'Neill "Scooties" Doll   .75   .50
CM1931 *(3151k)*
32c Ludwig Greiner First U.S. Patent Doll .75   .50
CM1932 *(3151l)*
32c "Betsy McCall" American Character Doll .75   .50

CM1933 *(3151m)*
32c Percy Crosby's "Skippy"   .75   .50
CM1934 *(3151n)*
32c Alexander Doll Co. "Maggie Mix-up" .75   .50
CM1935 *(3151o)*
32c Schoenut "All Word Perfection Art Dolls" .75   .50
     FDC *(July 28, 1997)*, any single   1.00
     y. Se-tenant pane of CM1921-35 12.50
     FDC   10.

1997. Humphrey Bogart Issue, third in the Legends of
Hollywood series, is a 20-stamp commemorative pane
with a large area of selvage displaying an enlargement of
the portrait of the actor on the stamp. Bogart was one of
the giants of American film in the 1930s and '40s in such
movies as *Casablanca, The Maltese Falcon* and *To Have
and Have Not.* Bogart was nominated for an Academy
Award for *Treasure of the Sierra Madre* and *The Caine
Mutiny,* and finally won an Oscar for *The African Queen.*
Gravure by Stamp Venturers, perforated 11.

CM 1936 *Humphrey Bogart*

CM1936 *(3152)*
32c multicolored, tagged *(195,000,000)* .50 .20
    Plate block of four   3.50
    FDC *(July 31, 1997)*   1.00
    Pane of 20   8.00
Because this issue also was made available to collectors in full six-pane printing sheets, gutter pairs and blocks and cross-gutter multiples also exist.

1997. Vince Lombardi Issue recalls the legendary coach of the Green Bay Packers, a member of the Pro Football Hall of Fame, with a stamp issued in Green Bay, Wis., similar to CM1917 but with a red bar over Lombardi's name. *Printed by Sterling Sommer for Ashton-Potter (USA) Ltd., perforated 11.*

1937 *Vince Lombardi*

CM1937 *(3147)*
32c multicolored, tagged *(20,000,000)* .50 .20
    Plate block of four   3.50
    FDC *(Aug. 5, 1997)*   1.00

1997. Paul "Bear" Bryant Issue honors the fabled coach of the University of Alabama -- in Bryant's heyday, "the Crimson Tide" -- with a stamp issued in Tuscaloosa, Ala., similar to CM1918 but with a red bar over Bryant's name. *Printed by Sterling Sommer for Ashton-Potter (USA) Ltd., perforated 11.*

1938 *Paul "Bear" Bryant*

CM1938 *(3148)*
32c multicolored, tagged *(20,000,000)* .50 .20
    Plate block of four   3.50
    FDC *(Aug. 7, 1997)*   1.00

1997. Glenn "Pop" Warner Issue commemorates the outstanding LaSalle University coach who gave his name to the nationwide Pop Warner Youth Football League with a stamp issued in Philadelphia, Pa., similar to CM1919 but with a red bar over Warner's name. *Printed by Sterling Sommer for Ashton-Potter (USA) Ltd., perforated 11.*

1939 *Glenn "Pop" Warner*

CM1939 *(3149)*
32c multicolored, tagged *(10,000,000)* .50 .20
    Plate block of four   3.50
    FDC *(Aug. 8, 1997)*   1.00

1997. George Halas Issue recalls the longtime coach of the Chicago Bears, a member of the Pro Football Hall of Fame, with a stamp issued in Chicago. Ill., similar to CM1920 but with a red bar over Halas' name. *Printed by Sterling Sommer for Ashton-Potter (USA) Ltd., perforated 11.*

1940 *George Halas*

CM1940 *(3150)*
32c multicolored, tagged *(10,000,000)* .50 .20
    Plate block of four   3.50
    FDC *(Aug. 16, 1997)*   1.00

1997. "The Stars And Stripes Forever" Issue salutes the centennial of the premiere of *The Stars and Stripes Forever!*, arguably the best-loved and most frequently played composition of John Philip Sousa (CM222), the celebrated "March King." *Gravure by BEP, perforated 11 1/2.*

CM1941 The Stars and Stripes Forever!

CM1941 *(3153)*
32c multicolored, tagged *(323,000,000)* .50 .20
    Plate block of four   3.50
    FDC *(Aug. 21, 1997)*   1.00

1997. Opera Singers Issue is a se-tenant quartet of renowned vocalists in costumes from their greatest roles, celebrating the 400th anniversary of their art, which originated in 16th-century Florence, Italy. Lily Pons (1898-1976), a diminuative coloratura, made her debut at New York's Metropolitan Opera in 1931 as the heroine of *Lucia di Lammermoor*. Tenor Richard Tucker (1913-75), depicted in foreground of his stamp as the Duke in Verdi's *Rigoletto.*, enjoyed a 30-year career at the Met and was regarded as the nation's foremost opera performer of the postwar era. Baritone Lawrence Tibbett (1896-1960), celebrated as the first American male to achieve operatic stardom in his own right, is portrayed as the Toreador in *Carmen*, one of many roles in which he excelled. A 21-year-old soprano, Rosa Ponselle (1897-1981) held her own opposite Caruso at the Met's premiere of Verdi's *La forza del destino*, much to the delight of critics and audiences as well, and is pictured in her costume from *Norma*. American Music series. *Offset by Ashton-Potter (USA) Ltd., perforated 11.*

CM1942 *Lily Pons*
CM1943 *Richard Tucker*
CM1944 *Lawrence Tibbett*
CM1945 *Rosa Ponselle*

CM1942 *(3154)*
32c multicolored, tagged *(21,500,000)* .50 .20
CM1943 *(3155)*
32c multicolored, tagged .50 .20
CM1944 *(3156)*
32c multicolored, tagged .50 .20
CM1945 *(3157)*
32c multicolored, tagged .50 .20
    Plate block of four 3.50
    FDC *(Sept. 10, 1997)* any single 1.00
    y. Se-tenant block or strip of
      CM1942-45 3.50
    FDC 3.00
    Pane of 20 8.00

1997. Classical Composers and Conductors Issue
celebrates four composers and four conductors in a se-
tenant 20-stamp pane. Leopold Stokowski began con-
ducting the Cincinnati Symphony at the ago of 27, and
in 1912 moved to Philadelphia where he was to weild the
baton for more than 25 years, making that city's symphony orchestra one of the finest in the world. Arthur
Fiedler, who began as a viola player in the Boston
Symphony, gained world fame and brought classical
music to vast new audiences as conductor of the Boston
Pops Orchestra. George Szell fashioned the Cleveland Orchestra into one of the finest in the nation.
Eugene Ormandy was musical director of the Philadelphia Symphony for over 35 years, and in 1948 conducted the first symphony concert on American
television. Composer Samuel Barber won the Pulitzer
Prize for his operas *Vanessa* and his *Piano Concerto*.
Composer, pianist and arranger Ferde Grofe brilliantly

scored Gershwin's *Rhapsody in Blue* for the symphony in
1924, and merged jazz and simple ballads with equal
creativity in his own compositions. Charles Ives was an
innovative composer who used daring techniques to
meld hymns and folk tunes into unusual symphonies.
Louis Moreau Gottschalk gained international celebrity
as a dazzling pianist whose compositions were built on
the Creole rhythms of his native New Orleans. American
Music series. *Printed (4,300,000 20-stamp panes) in
offset by Sterling Sommer for Ashton-Potter (USA) Ltd.,
perforated 11.*

CM1946 *(3158)*
32c multicolored, tagged .50 .20
CM1947 *(3159)*
32c multicolored, tagged .50 .20
CM1948 *(3160)*
32c multicolored, tagged .50 .20
CM1949 *(3161)*
32c multicolored, tagged .50 .20
CM1950 *(3162)*
32c multicolored, tagged .50 .20
CM1951 *(3163)*
32c multicolored, tagged .50 .20
CM1952 *(3164)*
32c multicolored, tagged .50 .20
CM1953 *(3165)*
32c multicolored, tagged .50 .20
    Plate block of ten 5.00
    FDC *(Sept. 12, 1997)*, any single 1.00
    y. Se-tenant block of CM1946-53 4.00
      FDC 3.50
    Pane of 20 8.00

1997. Padre Felix Varela Issue memorializes the priest,
educator and social reformer whose humanitarian works
for more than 30 years earned him high esteem. Varela
(1788-1853) was educated in Cuba but is best known for
his work in New York City beginning in the 1820s, when
he concentrated on helping the poor, organized the New
York Catholic Temperance Association, founded nurser-
ies and orphanages and risked infection during an 1832
cholera epidemic. He also founded the first Hispanic
newspaper in the United States, which chronicled social
injustice, urged religious and ethnic tolerence and
promoted the importance of education. The stamp is
notable for its use of the microprinted letters "USPS" to
form Varela's portrait. *Offset by Sterling Sommer for
Ashton-Potter (USA) Ltd., perforated 11 3/4.*

CM1946 *Leopold Stokowski*
CM1947 *Arthur Fiedler*
CM1948 *George Szell*
CM1949 *Eugene Ormandy*
CM1950 *Samuel Barber*
CM1951 *Ferde Grofe*
CM1952 *Charles Ives*
CM1953 *Louis Moreau Gottschalk*

CM1954 *Padre Felix Varela*

CM1954 *(3166)*
32c purple, tagged *(25,250,000)* .50 .20
 Plate block of four 3.50
 FDC *(Sept. 15, 1997)* 1.00

1997. U.S. Department of the Air Force Issue, marks the 50th anniversary of the youngest branch of the U.S. armed forces as a separate military department. The stamp shows the Thunderbirds USAF demonstration team flying its custom-painted F-18 jet fighters in close "Diamond-Four" formation. This also was the first U.S. issue to include hidden images in the background of the stamp designs visible only with a special USPS "Stamp Decoder." *Offset by Sterling Sommer for Ashton-Potter (USA) Ltd., perforated 11.*

CM1955 *U.S. Department of the Air Force*

CM1955 *(3167)*
32c multicolored, tagged *(45,250,000)* .50 .20
 Plate block of four 3.50
 FDC *(Sept. 18, 1997)* 1.00

1997. Classic Movie Monsters Issue, a 20-stamp pane with a banner across the top released for National Stamp Collecting Month, saluted monsters from Universal Studios films of the 1920s, '30s and '40s and the actors who brought them to life. *Gravure by Stamp Venturers, perforated 10.*

CM1956 *(3168)*
32c multicolored, tagged *(29,000,000)* .50 .20
CM1958 *(3169)*
32c multicolored, tagged .50 .20
CM1959 *(3170)*
32c multicolored, tagged .50 .20
CM1960 *(3171)*
32c multicolored, tagged .50 .20
 Plate block of 10 5.00
 FDC *(Sept. 30, 1997) any single* 1.00
 y. Se-tenant strip of CM1956-60 4.00
 FDC 4.00

Because this issue also was made available to collectors in full nine-pane printing sheets, gutter pairs and blocks and cross-gutter multiples also exist.

1997. First Supersonic Flight Issue, a self-adhesive stamp, hails the 50th anniversary of the historic 1947 flight at Edward's Air Force Base in which a Bell X-1 rocket aircraft piloted by Chuck Yeager became the first to break the sound barrier and travel faster than Mach 1. *Offset by Banknote Corp. of America, serpentine roulette 11 1/2.*

CM1961 *First Supersonic Flight*

CM1961
32c multicolored, tagged *(173,000,000)* .50 .20
 Plate block of four 3.50
 FDC *(Oct. 14, 1997)* 1.00

1997. Women in Military Service Issue salutes the nearly 2 million women who have served in the U.S. armed forces in conjunction with the Oct. 18 dedication of the Women in Military Service for America Memorial in Arlington National Cemetery near Washington, D.C. (See also CM355.) *Offset by Banknote Corp. of America, perforated 11.*

CM1962 *Women in Military Service*

CM1962
32c multicolored, tagged *(37,000,000)* .50 .20
 Plate block of four 3.50
 FDC *(Oct. 18, 1997)* 1.00

1997. Kwanzaa Issue, a colorful self-adhesive design and the second annual installment in the Postal Service's announced Holiday Celebration series, honors the non-sectarian African-American festival of family, community and culture that takes its name from the Swahili phrase meaning "first fruits." *Gravure by Avery Dennison Security Printing Division, serpentine die cut 11.*

CM1963 *Kwanzaa*

CM1963
32c multicolored, tagged *(133,000,000)* .50 .20
 Plate block of four 3.50
 FDC *(Oct. 22, 1996)* 1.00

CM1956 *Lon Chaney*, Phantom of the Opera
CM1957 *Bela Lugosi*, Dracula
CM1958 *Boris Karloff*, Frankenstein
CM1959 *Boris Karloff*, The Mummy
CM1960 *Lon Chaney Jr.*, The Wolf Man

Airmail Stamps

All airmail issues were printed by the Bureau of Engraving and Printing unless otherwise noted. Prices for FDC are unchacheted for A1-A9.

1918. Curtiss Biplane. First Airmail Series got under way in 1918, when the U.S.Post Office Department announced that an airmail service from New York to Philadelphia to Washington, D.C., would begin May 15.

Two days before the initial flight, the world's first stamp designed expressly for airmail was issued to pay the rate between any two of the three cities: 24c for the first ounce, including special delivery.

Later in the year, when the rate dropped to 16c, another stamp was issued. Near the end of the year, a 6c stamp was issued which paid the airmail rate without special delivery.

All three stamps were of the same design, an army airplane, since the carrying of airmail had been entrusted to army pilots flying army planes. The Curtiss biplanes were called "Jennys" from their official designation, which began with the initials "JN."

Intaglio (flat plate press), perforated 11.

A1-A3 *CURTISS BIPLANE*

A1 *(C1)*
6c red orange *(3,395,854)*   60.   28.50
    pale orange
    Plate block of six, with arrow   650.
    Block of four, with arrow   —
    Center line block   —
    Double transfer   —
    On cover   —
    First-flight cover *(Dec. 16, 1918)*   2,500.
    FDC *(Dec. 10, 1918)*   25,000.

A2 *(C2)*
16c green *(3,793,887)*   80.   35.
    dark green   80.   35.
    Plate block of six, with arrow   1,150.
    Block of four, with arrow   —
    Center line block   —
    On cover
    First flight cover *(July 15, 1918)*   800.
    FDC *(July 11, 1918)*   25,000.

A3 *(C3)*
24c carmine red and blue *(2,134,888)*   80.   40.
    dark carmine red and blue
    Plate block of four, blue plate number and "TOP"   —
    Plate block of four, red plate number and "TOP"   —
    Plate block of four, red plate number only   —
    Plate block of 12, two plate numbers, arrow, and two "TOP" inscriptions   1,350.
    Plate block of 12, two plate numbers, arrow, and blue "TOP" only   —
    Block of four, with arrow at top or left   —
    Block of four, with arrow at bottom   —
    Block of four, with arrow at right   —
    Center line block   —
    On cover   —
    First flight cover *(May 15, 1918)*   800.
    FDC *(May 13, 1918)*   —

(C3a)   v.Inverted center   125,000.
    Plate block of four   —
    Center line block   —

One sheet of 100 stamps with the blue vignette of the airplane upside down was purchased in a post office at Washington D.C., by William T. Robey, who sold it to Eugene Klein of Philadelphia, who in turn sold it to Col. Edward H.R. Green. Green retained some of the errors, including the position pieces, through Klein and disposed of the rest. One of the most famous post office finds in U.S.stamp history.

1923. The Second Airmail Series was issued for use on airmail service between New York and San Francisco. Three airmail zones were established: New York to Chicago; Chicago to Cheyenne; and Cheyenne to San Francisco. The rate of postage was 8c an ounce for each zone. The stamps were available through the Philatelic Agency at Washington D.C. before they were issued to postmasters. *Intaglio, perforated 11.*

A4 *Propeller and radiator of plane*

A4 *(C4)*

8c green *(6,414,576)*	22.50	12.50
dark green	22.50	12.50
Plate block of six	250.	
Double transfer	—	
On cover		—
FDC *(Aug. 15, 1923)*		375.

A5 *Air service insignia*

A5 *(C5)*

16c indigo *(5,309,275)*	80.	27.50
Plate block of six	1,850.	
Double transfer	—	
On cover		—
FDC *(Aug. 17, 1923)*		600.

A6 *De Havilland bipllane*

A6 *(C6)*

24c carmine *(5,285,775)*	90.	27.50
Plate block of six	2,100.	
Double transfer	—	
On cover		—
FDC *(Aug. 21, 1923)*		750.

1926-27. Map Issue consists of three denominations: 10c, 15c, and 20c, reflecting new rates: 10 cents per ounce up to 1,000 miles; 15 cents to 1,500 miles; and 20 cents for distances over 1,500 miles or Contract Air Mail routes. *Intaglio, perforated 11.*

A7-A9 *Relief map of United States and two mail planes*

A7 *(C7)*

10c blue *(42,092,800)*	2.75	.40
light blue	2.75	.40
Plate block of six	37.50	
Double transfer	—	
FDC *(Feb. 13, 1926)*		75.

A8 *(C8)*

15c olive brown *(15,597,307)*	3.25	2.25
light brown	3.25	2.25
Plate block of six	45.	
FDC *(Sept. 18, 1926)*		90.

A9 *(C9)*

20c yellow green *(17,616,350)*	8.75	1.75
green	8.75	1.75
Plate block of six	100.	
FDC *(Jan. 25, 1927)*		100.

1927. Lindbergh Airmail Issue honors Charles Augustus Lindbergh, the 25-year-old former air mail pilot who made the first non-stop solo flight from New York to Paris, May 20-21, 1927. Stamp collectors welcomed one of the few U.S. stamps ever to honor a living person. The stamp pictures Lindbergh's Ryan monoplane, *The Spirit of St. Louis*, which is now on display in the Smithsonian Institution at Washington, D.C. *Intaglio, perforated 11.*

A10 *Lindbergh's monoplane, Spirit of St. Louis*

A10 *(C10)*

10c indigo *(20,379,179)*	7.50	2.00
Plate block of six	135.	
Double transfer	—	
FDC *(June 18, 1927)*		175.
n. Booklet pane of three	85.	
Single, perforated 11		
horizontally	12.50	
FDC *(May 26, 1928)*		875.

First-day covers for No. A10 are from Washington, D.C. Little Falls, Minn., St. Louis, Mo. and Detroit, Mich. FDCs for No. A10n are from Washington, D.C., and Cleveland, Ohio.

1928. Air Mail Beacon Issue reflects the new 5c-per ounce rate that went into effect August 1, 1928.

A11 *Sherman Hill air mail beacon light*

A11 *(C11)*

5c carmine red and blue		
(106,887,675)	4.25	.60
Plate block of six, two plate numbers and red "TOP"	40.	
Plate block of six, two plate numbers and blue "TOP"	—	
Plate block of six, two plate numbers and double "TOP"	90.	
Plate block of eight, two plate numbers only	175.	
Block of four with arrow	—	
Double transfer	—	
Recut frame line at left	—	
FDC *(July 25, 1928)*		250.
v. Vertical pair, imperforate between	6,000.	

1930. Winged Globe Issue is sometimes confused with the 5c rotary-press version of 1931 (A16), but measures 46 3/4 mm by 18 3/4 mm. *Intaglio (flat plate press), perforated 11.*

A12 *Winged Globe*

A12 *(C12)*

5c purple *(97,641,200)*	9.50	.40
Plate block of six	—	
Double transfer	—	
FDC *(Feb. 10, 1930)*		12.50
v. Horizontal pair, imperforate between	5,000.	

1930. Graf Zeppelin Issue was issued for use on mail carried by the German dirigible, built and commanded by Dr. Hugo Eckener, during various stages of its flight from Germany to the United States and back during May and June. A former newspaper reporter and an early critic of Count Ferdinand von Zeppelin's experiments with dirigibles, Eckener became a pilot and in 1921 manager of the Zeppelin firm.

Although more than a million copies of each value were printed, sales were disappointing. After the stamps were withdrawn from circulation June 30, more than 90 percent of them were destroyed.

A13 *Graf Zeppelin in flight*

A13 *(C13)*

65c green *(93,536)*	300.	225.
Plate block of six	2,650.	
On cover		—
FDC *(April 19, 1930)*		300.

A14 *Zeppelin spanning the Atlantic*

A14 *(C14)*

$1.30 yellow brown *(72,248)*	600.	400.
Plate block of six	5,650.	
On cover		—
FDC *(April 19, 1930)*		1,000.

A15 *Zeppelin circling globe*

A15 *(C15)*

$2.60 blue *(61,296)*	925.	675.
Plate block of six	8,650.	
On cover		—
FDC *(April 19, 1930)*		1,150.

1931-34. Winged Globe Series has three values: 5c, 6c and 8c. The 5c stamp is sometimes confused with the 5c flat-plate issue of 1930 (A12), but measures 47 3/4 mm by 19 1/4 mm. *Intaglio (rotary press), perforated 10 1/2 x 11.*

A16-A18 *Winged Globe*

A16 *(C16)*

5c reddish violet *(57,340,000)*	5.25	.50
Plate block of four	90.	
FDC *(Aug. 19, 1931)*		175.

A17 *(C19)*

6c orange *(302,205,100)*	2.50	.20
Plate block of four	22.50	
Gutter pair	—	
FDC *(July 1, 1934)*		20.
(June 30, 1934)		200.

A18 *(C17)*

8c yellow olive *(76,648,803)*	2.25	.20
Plate block of four	35.	
Gutter pair	—	
FDC *(Sept. 26, 1932)*		17.50

1933. Century of Progress Zeppelin Issue was released in connection with the flight of the *Graf Zeppelin* to the Chicago World's Fair, as a goodwill gesture to publicize the event. Although the stamp remained on sale at the Philatelic Agency at Washington until 1935, sales were disappointing, and more than 90 per cent of the issue was destroyed. *Intaglio, perforated 11.*

A19 *Airship* Graf Zeppelin

A19 *(C18)*

50c green *(324,070)*	85.	70.
Plate block of six	750.	
On cover		—
FDC *(Oct. 2, 1933)*		175.

1935-37. Trans-Pacific Series was released primarily to pay postage on mail carried over the transpacific airmail route. *Intaglio, perforated 11.*

A20   A21

A22

China Clipper *over Pacific*

A20 *(C21)*
20c green *(12,794,600)* 9.50 1.50
  dark green 9.50 1.50
  Plate block of six 110.
  FDC *(Feb. 15, 1937)* 55.

A21 *(C20)*
25c blue *(10,205,400)* 1.25 1.00
  Plate block of six 22.50
  FDC *(Nov. 22, 1935)* 45.

A22 *(C22)*
50c carmine *(9,285,300)* 9.50 4.00
  Plate block of six 110.
  FDC *(Feb. 15, 1937)* 60.

1938. Eagle and Shield Issue originally designed by Franklin D. Roosevelt, was issued to coincide with the U.S. Post Office Department's promotion of National Air Mail Week. *Intaglio, perforated 11.*

A23 *Eagle and shield*

A23 *(C23)*
6c indigo and carmine *(349,946,500)* .40 .20
  ultramarine and carmine .40 .20
  Block of four, with arrow 7.50
  Center line block —
  Plate block of 10, two plate
    numbers, arrow, two "TOP"
    and two registration markers —
  FDC *(May 14, 1938)* 15.
  v. Horizontal pair, imperforate
  vertically 10,000.
  v1. Vertical pair, imperforate
  horizontally 350.

1939. Transatlantic Issue, a final Winged Globe design, celebrates the inauguration of transatlantic Airmail service. *Intaglio, perforated 11.*

A24 *Winged globe*

A24 *(C24)*
30c slate blue *(19,768,150)* 8.75 1.40
  Plate block of six 150.
  FDC *(May 16, 1939)* 50.

1941-44. Transport Series consists of seven denominations that were intended to cover all airmail postage requirements. Except for the color and denomination, all of the stamps are of the same design. *Intaglio, perforated 11 x 10 1/2.*

A25-A31 *Twin motored transport plane*

A25 *(C25)*
6c rose red *(4,746,527,700)* .20 .20
  Plate block of four 1.00
  Vertical gutter pair —
  Horizontal gutter pair —
  FDC *(June 25, 1941)* 5.00
  v. Horizontal pair, imperforate
  between 1,500.
  n. Booklet pane of three 2.95 3.00
  FDC *(March 18, 1943)* 30.

A26 *(C26)*
8c light olive green
  (1,744,878,650) .25 .20
  Plate block of four 1.85
  Gutter pair —
  FDC *(March 21, 1944)* 5.00

A27 *(C27)*
10c violet *(67,117,400)* 1.30 .20
  Plate block of four 10.
  FDC *(Aug. 15, 1941)* 7.50

A28 *(C28)*
15c brown carmine
  (78,434,800) 2.50 .35
  Plate block of four 11.50
  FDC *(Aug. 19, 1941)* 7.50

A29 *(C29)*
20c emerald *(42,359,850)* 2.25 .35
  Plate block of four 11.50
  FDC *(Aug. 27, 1941)* 10.

A30 *(C30)*
30c light blue *(59,880,850)* 2.50 .40
  Plate block of four 13.
  FDC *(Sept. 25, 1941)* 15.

A31 *(C31)*
50c orange *(11,160,600)*   12.50   3.25
    Plate block of four   85.
    FDC *(Oct. 29, 1941)*   30.

1946. Skymaster Issue was released to prepay the new 5c airmail rate. *Intaglio, perforated 11 x 10 1/2.*

A32 *DC-4 Skymaster*

A32 *(C32)*
5c carmine *(864,753,100)*   .25   .20
    Plate block of four   .65
    FDC *(Sept. 25, 1946)*   1.75

1947. Small 5c Skymaster Issue replaced the large 5c stamp of 1946. *Intaglio, perforated 10 1/2 x 11.*

A33 *DC-4 Skymaster*

A33 *(C33)*
5c carmine *(971,903,700)*   .25   .20
    Plate block of four   .65
    FDC *(March 26, 1947)*   1.75

Intaglio, perforated 10 horizontally.

A34 *(C37)*
5c carmine *(33,244,500)*   .85   .80
    Pair   1.00
    Line Pair   2.50
    FDC *(Jan. 15, 1948)*   1.75

1947. Pictorial Airmail Issue consists of three denominations intended to cover international air postage rates. *Intaglio, perforated 11 x 10 1/2.*

A35 *Pan-American Union Building, Washington*

A35 *(C34)*
10c black *(207,976,550)*   .30   .20
    Plate block of four   1.35
    FDC *(Aug. 30, 1947)*   1.75
    p. Dry paper   .60   .25
       Plate block of four   2.75

A36 *15c: Statue of Liberty and Skyline of New York*

A36 *(C35)*
15c blue green *(756,186,350)*   .45   .20
    Plate block of four   2.00
    Gutter pair   —
    FDC *(Aug. 20, 1947)*   2.00
    p. Dry printing   .75   .25
       Plate block of four   3.00
    v. Horizontal pair, imperforate
       between   2,000.

A37 25c: *San Francisco-Oakland Bay Bridge*

A37 *(C36)*
25c blue *(132,956,100)*   .45   .20
    Plate block of four   2.00
    FDC *(July 31, 1947)*   2.00
    p. Dry printing   1.50   .30
       Plate block of four   6.50

1948. New York City Issue commemorates the 50th anniversary of the consolidation of the five boroughs of New York City. *Intaglio, perforated 11 x 10 1/2*

A38 *Map of the five boroughs encompassed by wedding ring*

A38 *(C38)*
5c carmine red *(38,449,100)*   .25   .20
    Plate block of four   4.00
    FDC *(July 31, 1948)*   2.00

1949. Small 6c Skymaster Issue reflects the raise in rates to 6c for domestic airmail. *Intaglio, perforated 10 1/2 x 11.*

A39
A40 *DC-4 Skymaster*

A39 *(C39)*
6c carmine *(5,070,095,200)*   .25   .20
    Plate block of four   .70
    FDC *(Jan. 18, 1949)*   1.75
    n. Booklet pane of six   12.50   7.50
       FDC *(Nov. 18, 1949)*   12.
    p. Dry printing   .75   .30
       Plate block of four   3.50
    pn. Booklet pane of six   24.50

Intaglio, perforated 10 horizontally.

A40 (C41)

6c carmine	3.25	.20
Pair	6.00	
Line pair	13.75	
FDC *(Aug. 25, 1949)*		1.75

1949. Alexandria Bicentennial Issue commemorates the 200th anniversary of the founding of Alexandria, Va. *Itaglio, perforated 11 x 10 1/2.*

A41 *Carlyle House, Alexandria seal and Gadsby's Tavern*

A41 (C40)

6c carmine *(75,085,000)*	.20	.20
Plate block of four	.75	
FDC *(May 11, 1949)*		2.00

1949. Universal Postal Union Series commemorates the 75th anniversary of the formation of the Universal Postal Union.

A42 *Post Office Department Building, Washington*

A42 (C42)

10c violet *(21,061,300)*	.30	.25
Plate block of four	1.40	
FDC *(Nov. 18, 1949)*		1.75

A43 *Globe surrounded by doves*

A43 (C43)

15c cobalt *(36,613,100)*	.40	.35
Plate block of four	2.00	
FDC *(Oct. 7, 1949)*		3.00

A44 *Plane and globe*

A44 (C44)

25c carmine *(16,217,100)*	.75	.55
Plate block of four	6.00	
FDC *(Nov. 30, 1949)*		4.00

1949. Wright Brothers Issue commemorates the 46th anniversary of Wilbur and Orville Wright's first flight. On Dec. 17, 1903, at Kill Devil Hill, south of Kitty Hawk, N. C., Orville took the plane aloft for 12 seconds over a distance of 120 feet. Wilbur flew 59 seconds over a distance of 825 feet in the fourth flight that day. *Intaglio, perforated 11 x 10 1/2.*

A45 *Wright Brothers and their plane*

A45 (C45)

6c carmine purple *(80,405,000)*	.25	.20
Plate block of four	1.25	
FDC *(Dec. 17, 1949)*		2.00

1952. Hawaiian Airmail Issue provided a stamp to pay postage on one pound of air parcel post to the eight domestic zones (over 1,800 miles). *Intaglio, perforated 11 x 10 1/2.*

A46 *Diamond Head at Honolulu, Hawaii*

A46 (C46)

80c bright purple *(18,876,800)*	5.50	1.35
Plate block of four	29.50	
FDC *(March 26, 1952)*		15.

1953. Powered Flight Issue marks the 50th anniversary of the Wright brothers first flight. *Intaglio, perforated 11 x 10 1/2.*

A47 *Old and new planes with slogan*

A47 (C47)

6c carmine *(78,415,000)*	.25	.20
Plate block of four	.75	
FDC *(May 29, 1953)*		2.00

1954. Eagle Issue was intended primarily for use on domestic airmail postcards. *Intaglio, perforated 11 x 10 1/2.*

A48   A50

Eagle in Flight

A48 (C48)

4c blue *(40,483,600)*	.25	.20
Plate block of four	2.00	
FDC *(Sept. 3, 1954)*		1.75

1957. Air Force Issue marks the 50th anniversary of the U.S. Air Force. *Intaglio, perforated 11 x 10 1/2.*

A49 *U.S. military aircraft*

A49 *(C49)*
6c bright Prussian blue

(63,185,000)	.25	.20
Plate block of four	.85	
FDC *(Aug. 1, 1957)*		2.00

1958. Eagle Issue, was made because of the increase in postage rates August 1. *Intaglio, perforated 11 x 10 1/2.*

A50 *(C50)*

5c carmine red *(72,480,000)*	.25	.20
Plate block of four	1.75	
FDC *(July 31, 1958)*		1.75

1958. Jet Silhouette Issue was printed to meet the change in domestic airmail rates Aug. 1. *Intaglio.*

A51-A52, A60-A61 *Jet Airliner*

Perforated 10 1/2 x 11.
A51 *(C51)*

7c blue *(1,326,960,000)*	.25	.20
Plate block of four	1.00	
FDC *(July 31,1958)*		1.75
n.Booklet pane of six		
FDC, booklet pane		

Coil stamp, perforated 10 horizontally
A52 *(C52)*

7c blue *(157,035,000)*	1.75	.20
Pair	3.50	
Line pair	17.50	
FDC *(July 31, 1958)*		1.75

1959. Alaska Statehood Issue commemorates the addition to the union of the 49th state. *Intaglio, perforated 11 x 10 1/2.*

A53 *The "Big Dipper" and North Star superimposed on map of Alaska*

A53 *(C53)*

7c deep blue *(90,055,200)*	.25	.20
Plate block of four	1.00	
FDC *(Jan. 3, 1959)*		1.75

1959. Balloon Jupiter Issue commemorates the 100th anniversary of the first U.S. transmission of airmail by balloon from Lafayette to Crawfordsville, Ind., a distance of 35 miles. *Intaglio (Giori Press), perforated 11.*

A54 *Crowd watching John Wise ascending on first flight, August 17, 1859*

A54 *(C54)*
7c deep blue and scarlet

(79,290,000)	.25	.20
Plate block of four	1.00	
FDC *(Aug. 17, 1959)*		1.75

1959. Pan American Games Issue marks the opening of the Pan American Games in Chicago, Ill. *Intaglio (Giori Press), perforated 11.*

A55 *Runner holding torch*

A55 *(C56)*
10c deep blue and scarlet

(38,770,000)	.30	.30
Plate block of four	1.50	
FDC *(Aug. 27, 1959)*		1.75

1959. Hawaii Statehood Issue commemorates the admission of Hawaii to the Union as the 50th state.*Intaglio, perforated 11 x 10 1/2.*

A56 *Hawaiian warrior and map of islands*

A56 *(C55)*

7c dull scarlet *(84,815,000)*	.25	.20
Plate block of four	1.00	
FDC *(Aug. 27, 1959)*		1.75

1959-60. International Airmail Series was created to meet the demand for specific foreign airmail rates. The 10c value covered airmail to Central and South America and the West Indies exclusive of Mexico. The 15c denomination prepaid airmail postage to Europe and North Africa. The 25c stamp was for use to Asia, Africa and the Middle East. *Intaglio (Giori Press), perforated 11.*

A57 *Liberty Bell*

A57 *(C57)*

10c black and green *(39,960,000)*	1.50	.80
Plate block of four	7.50	
FDC *(June 10, 1960)*		1.75

A58 *Statue of Liberty*

A58 *(C58)*
15c black and orange
(98,160,000)	.50	.20
Plate block of four	2.25	
FDC *(Nov. 20, 1959)*		1.75

A59 *Abraham Lincoln*

A59 *(C59)*
25c black and brown purple .75 .20
Plate block of four	3.25	
FDC *(Apr. 22, 1960)*		1.75
z. Tagged		
Plate block of four		
FDC, tagged *(Dec. 29, 1966)*		

1960. Jet Silhouette Issue returned in a new color to facilitate handling of domestic airmail letters. *Intaglio. Perforated 10 1/2 x 11.*

A60 *(C60)*
7c bright red *(1,289,460,000)*	.25	.20
Plate block of four	1.25	
Gutter pair	—	
FDC *(Aug. 12, 1960)*		1.75
n. Booklet pane of six	12.50	7.75
FDC *(Aug. 19, 1960)*		8.00

Coil stamp, perforated 10 horizontally
A61 *(C61)*
7c bright red *(87,140,000)*	4.00	.30
Pair	7.50	
Line pair	40.	
FDC *(Oct. 22, 1960)*	1.75	

1961. International Airmail Issue is a revision of the 1959 15c Statue of Liberty airmail stamp (A58),showing a revised frame line around the statue. *Intaglio (Giori Press), perforated 11.*

A62 **Statue of Liberty,** *redesigned frame line*

A62 *(C63)*
15c black and orange	.45	.20
Plate block of four	2.00	
FDC *(Jan. 13, 1961)*		1.75
z. Tagged	1.50	.75
Plate block of four	15.	
FDC *(Jan. 11, 1967)*		30.
vz. Horizontal pair, imperforate		
vertically	11,500.	

1961. International Airmail Issue is a new denomination and color required because of new increased postal rates. *Intaglio (Giori Press), perforated 11.*

A63 *Liberty Bell*

A63 *(C62)*
13c black and scarlet	.45	.20
Plate block of four	2.00	
FDC *(June 28, 1961)*		1.75
z. Tagged	.50	.25
Plate block of four	2.50	
FDC *(Feb. 15, 1967)*		30.

1962. Airline Over Capitol Issue was made available to meet the increase in postage rates. *Rotary press printing, perforated 10 1/2 x 11.* Although this stamp was issued December 5, 1962, an experiment was started on August 1, 1963, in Dayton, Ohio, in which a luminescent ink was applied to these air mail stamps. The phosphor-tagged stamps, in conjunction with an ultraviolet sensing device, sped up air mail service.

A64 *Air mail carrier over Capitol dome*

A64 *(C64)*
8c carmine	.25	.20
Plate block of four	1.00	
FDC *(Dec. 5, 1962)*		1.75
n. Booklet pane of five (plus Mailman label)	4.50	
n1. Booklet pane of five (plus Zip label)	14.50	
n2. Booklet pane of five (plus Zone # label)	70.	
p1. Printed on Hi-brite paper		
Plate block of four		
p1n. Booklet pane of five (plus Mailman label)		
z. Tagged, type I	.35	.20
Plate block of four	1.75	
FDC *(Dayton, Ohio, Aug. 1, 1963)*		2.75
z1. Tagged, type II or IIa	.35	.20
Plate block of four	1.75	
z1n. Booklet pane of five (plus Zip label)	1.65	

Type I tagging: mat tagging, using four separate mats that did not cover entire sheet of 400 stamps (untagged areas identify the variety). Stamps from the four corners of a pane have two untagged margins.

Type II tagging: roll tagging, where continuous rolls replaced the tagging mats. Only the plate number selvage margin is partially tagged.

Type IIa tagging: wide roll tagging, where all margins are fully tagged.

Coil stamp, perforated 10 horizontally
A65 *(C65)*

8c carmine	.50	.20
Pair	.75	
Line pair	6.50	
FDC *(Dec. 5, 1962)*		1.75
p1. On Hi-brite paper	—	—
Pair	—	
Line pair	—	
z. Tagged, type I	.35	.20
Pair	1.00	
Line pair	2.75	
FDC, tagged *(Jan. 14, 1965)*		30.
z1. Tagged, Type II	.35	.20
Pair	1.00	
Line pair	2.75	

1963. Montgomery Blair Issue recalls Abraham Lincoln's postmaster general and his role in the first universal postal conference in 1863. *Intaglio (Giori Press), perforated 11.*

A66 *Montgomery Blair and mail circling the globe*

A66 *(C66)*

15c red, maroon and blue		
(42,245,000)	.70	.60
Plate block of four	3.00	
FDC *(May 3, 1963)*		2.50

1963. Bald Eagle Issue was prepared for use on domestic airmail postcards. *Intaglio, perforated 11 x 10 1/2.*

A67 *Bald Eagle*

A67 *(C67)*

6c carmine	.25	.20
Plate block of four	1.75	
FDC *(July 12, 1963)*		1.75
z. Tagged	3.50	2.75
Plate block of four	40.	
FDC *(Feb. 15, 1967)*		50.

1963. Amelia Earhart Issue marks the 65th birthday of America's most prominent female aviatrix, the first woman to fly across the Atlantic Ocean, and the first woman to fly across the United States non-stop. She was lost at sea while attempting to fly around the world. *Intaglio (Giori Press), perforated 11.*

A68 *Amelia Earhart*

A68 *(C68)*

8c carmine red and brown purple		
(63,890,000)	.35	.20
Plate block of four	1.50	
FDC *(July 24, 1963)*		3.00

1964. Robert H. Goddard Issue marks the 50th anniversary of the first patents granted to Goddard for his multi-stage booster rockets using liquid and solid fuels. *Intaglio (Giori Press), perforated 11.*

A69 *Dr. Goddard, rocket, and launching pad*

A69 *(C69)*

8c multicolored *(65,170,000)*	.45	.20
Plate block of four	2.00	
FDC *(Oct. 5, 1964)*		2.50
zo. Tagging omitted	—	

1967. Alaska Purchase Issue celebrates the 100th anniversary of the acquisition of Alaska from Russia. The date of issue, March 30, is a state holiday honoring Secretary of State William H. Seward, who arranged the sale for $7,200,000. *Intaglio (Giori Press), perforated 11.*

A70 *Indian totem*

A70 *(C70)*

8c brown and light brown		
(64,710,000)	.30	.20
Plate block of four	1.75	
FDC *(March 20, 1967)*		1.75

1967. Columbia Jays Issue was prepared to meet the increase in air mail rates to Europe and Mediterranean Africa. The design is similar to the 1963 5c Audubon commemorative (CM526) and was used again because of its aesthetic and technical excellence. *Intaglio (Giori Press), perforated 11.*

A71 *John J.Audubon's Columbia Jays*

A71 *(C71)*
   20c blue, brown, and yellow, tagged

(165,430,000)	1.00	.20
Plate block of four	4.50	
FDC *(April 26, 1967)*		2.50
zo. Tagging omitted	—	

1968. Star Runway Issue, met the increase in airmail rates that went into effect Jan. 7, 1968. *Intaglio, perforated 11 x 10 1/2.*

A72 *Poster type art showing 50 stars*

A72 *(C72)*
   10c red, tagged

	.30	.20
Plate block of four	1.35	
FDC *(Jan. 5, 1968)*		1.75
n. Booklet pane of 5 plus Mail Early label	3.50	3.25
n1. Booklet pane of 5 plus Zip slogan label	3.50	3.25
n2. Booklet pane of eight	2.35	2.25
n2z. Booklet pane of eight, tagging glows yellow rather than red orange	—	
zo. Tagging omitted	—	
zon1. Booklet pane of eight	—	
zon2. Booklet pane of five plus Mail Early label	—	
zon3. Booklet pane of five plus Zip slogan label	—	
Booklet pair, imperforate between vertically	1,750.	

Coil stamp, perforated 10 horizontally
A73 *(C73)*
   10c red

	.35	.20
Pair	.75	
Line pair	1.85	
FDC *(Jan. 5, 1968)*		1.75
v. Imperforate, pair	625.	

1968. Airmail Service Issue commemorates the 50th anniversary of the service, established May 15, 1918, when mail was carried by biplane on the Washington-New York flight. *Intaglio (Giori Press) and offset, perforated 11.*

A74 *Curtiss Jenny*

A74 *(C74)*
   10c black, red and blue

(74,180,000)	.35	.20
Plate block of four	2.50	
FDC *(May 15, 1968)*		2.00
v. Red stripe on tail omitted	3,000.	
zo. Tagging omitted	—	

1968. 15c USA and Jet Issue, intended primarily for mail to Europe and points in North Africa. *Intaglio and offset, perforated 11.*

A75, A81 *"USA" and airplane*

A75 *(C75)*
   20c multicolored

	.60	.20
Plate block of four	2.75	
FDC *(Nov. 22, 1968)*		1.75
zo. Tagging omitted	—	

1969. Moon Landing Issue paid tribute to the landing of a man on the Moon July 20, 1969, when Neil A. Armstrong and Col. Edwin E. Aldrin, Jr., became the first humans to land on the lunar surface. The engraved master die from which the stamps were printed was carried to the Moon by the astronauts. *Intaglio and offset, perforated 11.*

A76 *First Man on the Moon*

A76 *(C76)*
   10c multicolored

(152,364,800)	.40	.20
Plate block of four	1.65	
FDC *(Sept. 9, 1969)*		5.00
v. Offset red omitted	550.	

A76v must have missing red from the entire design; including the dots on top of the yellow area as well as the astronaut's shoulder patch. Stamps with any red present are worth far less than the true red-omitted error.

1971. Regular Air Mail Issues created to meet increases in domestic and international rates.

A77 *Silhouette of delta wing plane*

Intaglio, perforated 10 1/2 x 11
A77 *(C77)*
   9c red (25,830,000)

	.25	.20
Plate block of four	1.20	
FDC *(May 15, 1971)*		1.75

Intaglio, perforated 11 x 10 1/2

A78-A79 *Silhouette of jet airliner*

A78 *(C78)*
11c red, tagged *(317,810,000)*	.30	.20
Plate block of four	1.35	
FDC *(May 7, 1971)*		1.75
n. Booklet pane of four plus two labels	1.20	
zo. Tagging omitted	—	
zx. Untagged (Bureau precancel)	.50	.20

Coil stamp, perforated 10 vertically.
A79 *(C82)*
11c red	.35	.20
Pair	.75	
Line pair	.80	
FDC *(May 7, 1971)*		1.75
v. Imperforate, pair	275.	

A80 *Head of Liberty*

Intaglio (Giori Press), perforated 11.
A80 *(C80)*
17c multicolored, tagged	.50	.20
Plate block of four	2.15	
FDC *(July 13, 1971)*		1.75
zo. Tagging omitted	—	

Intaglio (Giori Press) and offset, perforated 11.

A81 *(C81)*
21c multicolored, tagged *(49,815,000)*	.60	.20
Plate block of four	2.50	
FDC *(May 21, 1971)*		1.75
zo. Tagging omitted	—	
V. Black omitted	—	

1972. National Parks Issue is part of the National Parks Centennial series (see CM674-CM680). The City of Refuge depicted is an ancient sanctuary for taboo breakers or victims of wars on a lava ledge on the southwestern part of the island of Hawaii. *Intaglio (Giori Press) and offset, perforated 11.*

A82 *Wooden statue and palisaded temple*

A82 *(C84)*
11c multicolored *(78,210,000)*	.35	.20
Plate block of four	1.50	
FDC *(May 3, 1972)*		1.75
v. Blue and green omitted	1,000.	
zo. Tagging omitted	—	

1972. Olympics Issue. Released as part of the Olympic series (see CM686) for the Winter and Summer Games held in Japan and Germany. *Gravure, perforated 11 x 10 1/2.*

A83 *Skiing*

A83 *(C85)*
11c multicolored *(92,710,000)*	.35	.20
Plate block of ten	3.50	
FDC *(Aug. 17, 1972)*		1.75

1973. Progress in Electronics Issue was the fourth stamp and only airmail in a set comemorating advances in electronic communication. (see CM721-CM723).

A84 *Lee DeForest's audion*

Intaglio (Giori Press) and offset, perforated 11.

A84 *(C86)*
11c multicolored, tagged *(56,000,000)*	.30	.20
Plate block of four	1.30	
FDC *(July 10, 1973)*		1.75
v. Vermilion and olive omitted	1,400.	
zo. Tagging omitted	—	

1973. Flying Envelope Issues was created to meet the basic domestic airmail letter rate increase. *Intaglio.*

Perforated 11 x 10 1/2.

A85, A86 *"Flying Envelope"*

A85 *(C79)*
13c red, tagged	.35	.20
Plate block of four	1.50	
FDC *(Nov. 16, 1973)*		1.75
n. Booklet pane of five plus label *(Dec. 27, 1973)*	1.75	1.50
zo. Tagging omitted (without precancel)	—	
zx. Untagged (Bureau precancel)	.50	.20

Coil stamp, perforated 10 vertically

A86 (C83)
13c red	.40	.20
Pair	.75	
Line pair	1.00	
FDC *(Dec. 27, 1973)*		1.75
v. Imperforate, pair	75.	

1974. National Monuments Issues were released to meet increases in airmail rates to foreign destinations. *Intaglio (Giori Press), perforated 11.*

A87 *Statue of Liberty*   A88 *Mount Rushmore*

A87 (C87)
18c multicolored, tagged	.50	.45
Plate block of four	2.25	
FDC *(Jan. 11, 1974)*		1.75
zo. Tagging omitted	—	

A88 (C88)
26c multicolored, tagged	.75	.20
Plate block of four	3.00	
Gutter pair	—	
FDC *(Jan. 2, 1974)*		1.75
zo. Tagging omitted	—	

1976. Aircraft and Globes Issue were released to meet increases airmail rates to foreign destinations. *Intaglio (Giori Press), perforated 11.*

A89 *Stylized Aircraft*

A89 (C89)
25c multicolored, tagged	.75	.20
Plate block of four	3.00	
FDC *(Jan. 2, 1976)*		1.75
zo. Tagging omitted	—	

A90 *Global views*

A90 (C90)
31c multicolored, tagged	.80	.20
Plate block of four	3.50	
FDC *(Jan. 2, 1976)*		1.75
zo. Tagging omitted	—	

1978. Wright Brothers Issues, the first stamps in the Pioneers of Flight series, marked the 75th anniversary of Orville and Wilbur Wright's historic first powered flight in 1903. *Intaglio (Giori Press) and offset, perforated 11.*

A91-A92 *Orville and Wilbur Wright, aviation pioneers*

A91 (C91)
31c multicolored	1.75	1.50

A92 (C92)
31c multicolored	1.75	1.50
Plate block of four	3.95	
y. Se-tenant pair A 91-92	1.75	
FDC *(Sept. 23, 1978)*		2.50
vy. Pair with intaglio black omitted	—	
v1y. Pair with intaglio, black and ultramarine omitted	800.	
v2y. Pair with offset black, yellow, magenta, blue and brown omitted	2,500.	

1979. Octave Chanute Issue honors the biplane hang glider designed by Chanute which became a standard for future glider design. *Poineers of Aviation series. Intaglio (Giori Press) and offset, perforated 11.*

A93-A94 *Octave Chanute, aviation pioneer*

A93 (C93)
21c multicolored	1.75	1.50

A94 (C94)
21c multicolored	1.75	1.50
Plate block of four	4.75	
y.Se-tenant pair A93-94		
FDC *(March 29, 1978)*		2.50
vy. Pair with intaglio, black omitted	—	
v1y. Pair with Intaglio black and ultramarine omitted	4,750.	

1979. 1980 Olympic Series Issue features a high jumper in action. (See also CM925-28, CM932-35.) *Gravure, perforated 11.*

A95 *High jumper*

A95 *(C97)*
31c multicolored, tagged	1.00	.35
Plate block of 12	12.50	
FDC *(Nov. 1, 1979)*		1.75

1979. Wiley Post Issue honors the aviatior famous for record-making flights, scientific research, and aircraft designs. Pioneers of Aviation series. *Intaglio (Giori Press) and offset, perforated 11.*

A96-A97 *Wiley Post, aviation pioneer*

A96 *(C95)*
25c multicolored, tagged	3.00	2.00

A97 *(C96)*
25c multicolored, tagged	3.00	2.00
Plate block of four	9.00	
y. Se-tenant pair A96-97	3.75	
FDC *(Nov. 20, 1979)*		2.50

1980. Philip Mazzei Issue honors the Italian-American patriot. He collaborated with the leaders of Virginia on political ideas and promoted independence through writings published in America and in Europe. *Gravure, perforated 11.*

A98 *Philip Mazzei*

A98 *(C98)*
40c multicolored, tagged	1.10	.25
Plate block of 12	13.50	
FDC *(Oct. 13, 1980)*		1.75
v. Horizontal pair, imperforate vertically	—	
v1. Imperforate pair	3,500.	
v2. Perforated 10 1/2 x 11 (1982)	—	
zo. Tagging omitted	—	

1980. Blanche Stuart Scott Issue commemorates the first American woman to make a solo flight in early September 1910. Pioneers of Aviation series. *Gravure, perforated 11.*

A99 *Blanche Stuart Scott*

A99 *(C99)*
28c multicolored, tagged	.80	.25
Plate block of 12	10.50	
FDC *(Dec. 30, 1980)*		1.75

1980. Glenn Curtiss Issue honors an early aviator and noted aircraft designer and manufacturer principally remembered for his invention and development of the aileron, and for his design and production of the first successful seaplanes and amphibious airplanes. Pioneers in Aviation series. *Gravure, perforated 11.*

A100 *Glenn Curtiss*

A100 *(C100)*
35c multicolored, tagged	.95	.25
Plate block of 12	12.50	
FDC *(Dec. 30, 1980)*		1.75

1983. 1984 Olympics Series, three se-tenant blocks of four, commemorates the 1984 Summer Olympic Games in Los Angeles, Calif. *Gravure, bullseye perforated 11 1/4.*

A101 *Men's shot put*   A102 *Men's gymnastics*

A103 *Women's swimming*   A104 *Weight lifting*

A101 *(C105)*
40c multicolored, tagged	1.25	.25
v. Line perforated 11	—	

A102 *(C106)*
40c multicolored, tagged	1.25	.25
v. Line perforated 11	—	

A103 *(C107)*
40c multicolored, tagged	1.25	.25
v. Line perforated 11	—	

A104 *(C108)*
40c multicolored, tagged	1.25	.25
Plate block of four	6.00	
y. Se-tenant block of four	2.00	
A101-104		
FDC *(April 8, 1983)*		4.50
v. Line perforated 11	—	
Plate block of four line	—	
perforated 11		
vy. Se-tenant block of four line	—	
perforated 11		
v1. Imperforate, block of four	—	

Perforated 11

A105 *Women's gymnastics*   A106 *Men's hurdles*

A107 *Women's basketball*   A108 *Soccer*

A105 *(C101)*
28c multicolored, tagged	1.25	.25

A106 *(C102)*
28c multicolored, tagged	1.25	.25

A107 *(C103)*
28c multicolored, tagged	1.25	.25

A108 *(C104)*
28c multicolored, tagged	1.25	.25
Plate block of four	6.00	
y. Se-tenant block of four	4.00	
A105-108		
FDC *(June 17, 1983)*		4.00
v. Block of four, imperforate		
vertically	—	

Perforated 11

A109 *Fencing*   A110 *Cycling*

A111 *Women's volleyball*   A112 *Pole vaulting*

A109 *(C109)*
35c multicolored, tagged	1.25	.25

A110 *(C110)*
35c multicolored, tagged	1.25	.25

A111 *(C111)*
35c multicolored, tagged	1.25	.25

A112 *(C112)*
35c multicolored, tagged	1.25	.25
Plate block of four	10.	
y. Se-tenant block of four	5.00	
A109-112		
FDC *(Nov. 4, 1983)*		4.50

1985. Alfred V. Verville Issue honors the man who designed and produced aircraft with Lawrence Sperry and Glenn Curtiss. Pioneers of Aviation series. *Gravure press, perforated 11.*

A113 *Alfred V. Verville, aviation pioneer*

A113 *(C113)*
33c multicolored, tagged	.95	.25
Plate block of four	4.25	
FDC *(Feb. 13, 1985)*		1.75
v. Imperforate, pair	—	

1985. Lawrence and Elmer Sperry Issue commemorates the father/son duo of Elmer Sperry (father) who was awarded over 400 patents, some of which such as the gyro-compass revolutionized flying and Lawrence Sperry (son), who helped develop and test such aviation innovations as the automatic pilot and retractable landing gear. *Gravure press, perforated 11.*

A114 *Lawrence and Elmer Sperry, aviation pioneers*

A114 *(C114)*
39c multicolored, tagged	1.10	.35
Plate block of four	5.25	
FDC *(Feb. 13, 1985)*		1.75
v. Imperforate, pair	—	

1985. Transpacific Airmail Issue marks the 50th anniversary of airmail service between the United States and the Far East. *Gravure, perforated 11.*

A115 *Martin M-150 China Clipper*

A115 *(C115)*
44c multicolored, tagged	1.20	.30
Plate block of four	5.75	
FDC *(Feb. 15, 1985)*		2.50
v. Imperforate, pair	—	

1986. Junipero Serra Issue honors the Franciscan friar (1713-84) who founded the California missions. *Gravure, perforated 11.*

A116 *Fr. Junipero Serra and San Gabriel Mission*

A116 *(C116)*
44c multicolored, tagged 1.50 .50
  Plate block of four 10.
  FDC *(Aug. 22, 1985)* 2.00
  v. Imperforate pair 18.50

1988. Settlement of New Sweden Issue honors the 350th anniversary of colony established by Peter Minuit. Sweden and Finland released stamps the same day (Sweden 1460, Finland 1077) with a common design to that issued by the United States. *Intaglio and offset, perforated 11.*

A117 *Illustration from a 1602 book on the New Sweden Colony*

A117 *(C117)*
44c multicolored, tagged
  (22,975,000) 1.25 .40
  Plate block of four 8.75
  FDC *(March 29, 1988)* 2.00

1988. Samuel P. Langley Issue honors the early pioneer flight engineer and the 70th anniversary of airmail service. Langley's early experiments in mechanical flight laid the groundwork for the Wright brothers, Glenn Curtiss and others. *Pioneers of Avaition series. Intaglio and offset, perforated 11.*

A118 *Samuel P. Langley, unmanned Aerodrome No. 5*

A118 *(C118)*
45c multicolored, tagged 1.30 .25
  Plate block of four 5.75
  FDC *(May 14, 1988)* 2.00
  v. Overall tagged 1.75 .50
    Plate block of four 10.

1988. Igor Sikorsky Issue paid tribute to the man who designed and built many early helicopters. Pioneers of Avaition series. *Intaglio and offset, perforated 11.*

A119 *Igor Sikorsky and VS-300*

A119 *(C119)*
36c multicolored, tagged 1.00 .35
  Plate block of four 4.50
  FDC *(June 23, 1988)* 2.00

Traces of red have been detected in all copies of a so-called "red omitted" error of this stamp. Such stamps, on which even minute traces of red are present, are worth far less than a genuine color-omitted error would be.

1989. French Revolution Bicentennial Issue, part of a joint issue with France, was released both in Washington, D.C., and in Paris. *Offset and intaglio, perforated 11 1/2 x 11.*

A120 *Liberte, Egalite, and Fraternite*

A120 *(C120)*
45c multicolored, tagged
  (38,532,000) 1.25 .30
  Plate block of four 5.75
  FDC *(July 14, 1989)* 2.00

1989. America Issue depicting a rare wooden native sculpture of the Pre-Columbian era, was one of a pair of U.S. stamps (with CM1360) that were the first stamps issued by 24 postal administrations commemorating the 500th anniversary of Christopher Columbus's arrival in America. Part of a 1989-91 Columbian series by members of the Postal Union of the Americas and Spain. *Gravure by American Book Note Co., perforated 11.*

A121 *Key Marco Cat, Calusa culture, pre-Columbian period*

A121 *(C121)*
45c multicolored, tagged
  (39,325,000) 1.25 .25
  Plate block of four 5.75
  FDC *(Oct. 12, 1989)* 2.00

1989. Future Mail Transportation Issue was part of a group of 11 postal items issued during World Stamp Expo '89 and the 20th Congress of the Universal Postal Union in Washington, D.C. *Offset and intaglio, perforated 11.*

A122a, A123 *Hypersonic airliner*
A122b, A124 *Hovercraft*

A122c, A125 *Surface rover vehicle*
A122d, A126 *Space shuttle*

A122 (C126)
$1.80 multicolored souvenir sheet, tagged
  (1,944,000)   6.25   6.00
  FDC *(Nov. 24, 1989)*   7.00
  a. 45c multicolored, tagged
  b. 45c multicolored, tagged
  c. 45c multicolored, tagged
  d. 45c multicolored, tagged

A123 (C122)
45c multicolored, tagged   1.25   .25
A124 (C123)
45c multicolored, tagged   1.25   .25
A125 (C124)
45c multicolored, tagged   1.25   .25
A126 (C125)
45c multicolored, tagged   1.25   .25
  Plate block of four   7.50
  y. Se-tenant block of four, A123-26   5.00
  FDC *(Nov. 28, 1989)*   8.00
  vy. Block of four with light blue omitted   1,150.

1990. America Issue was the second in the PUAS Columbian series depicting scenes of the natural beauty of America prior to Columbus. *Gravure, perforated 11.*

A127 *Tropical island coast*

A127 (C127)
45c multicolored, tagged   1.35   .25
  Plate block of four   6.75
  FDC *(Oct.12, 1990)*   2.00

1991. Harriet Quimby Issue honors the journalist, drama critic and first licensed American woman pilot. *Pioneers in Avaiation series. Gravure by Stamp Venturers, perforated 11.*

A128 *Harriet Quimby, Bleriot air plane*

A128 (C128)
50c multicolored, tagged   1.35   .35
  Plate block of four   7.00
  FDC *(Apr. 27, 1991)*   2.00
  v. Vertical pair, imperforate horizontally   2,100.

1991. William T. Piper Issue honors the "Henry Ford of Aviation," the developer of the Piper Cub aircraft. Pioneers of Avaition series. (See also A132.) *Gravure by J.W. Fergusson & Sons for the American Bank Note Co., perforated 11.*

A129 *William T. Piper, Piper Cub*

A129 (C129)
40c multicolored, tagged   1.25   .40
  Plate block of four   5.50
  FDC *(May 17,1991)*   2.00

1991. Antarctic Treaty Issue honors the 30th anniversary of the 1961 treaty dedicating the region to peaceful purposes. *Gravure by Stamp Venturers, perforated 11.*

A130 *View of McMurdo Sound*

A130 (C130)
50c multicolored, tagged   1.35   .55
  Plate block of four   6.50
  FDC *(June 21, 1991)*   2.00

1991. America Issue had as its theme "Pre-Columbian Voyages of Discovery," and depicts a prehistoric Asian and the Bering land bridge by which the first native Americans are believed to have com to the Western Hemisphere thousands of years ago. *Gravure, perforated 11.*

A131 *Asian overlooking Bering land bridge*

A131 (C131)
50c multicolored, tagged   1.35   .45
  Plate block of four   6.50
  FDC *(Oct. 12, 1991)*   2.00

1993. Redesigned William T. Piper Issue differs from the 1991 revision (A129) in that Piper's hair touches the top edge of the design of this stamp. There was no official first day of issue for the redesigned stamp. *Printed in gravure by Stamp Venturers, perforated 11 1/4.*

A132 (C132)
40c multicolored, tagged
  (July 1993)   1.35   .40
  Plate block of four   6.50

Special Delivery Stamps

A special delivery stamp on any letter or article of mailable matter entitles the addressee to immediate delivery between the hours of 7 a.m. and midnight. This service began on October 1, 1885, and was limited to free delivery offices and post offices in towns of 4,000 population or more. At that time there were 555 such post offices. The Act of August 4, 1886, extended the service to all post offices.

1885. Messenger, First Issue, inscribed "At a special delivery office." *Printed by the American Bank Note Company, flat press, unwatermarked, perforated 12.*

SD1 *Messenger on foot*

SD1 *(E1)*

10c Prussian blue	115.	22.50
dark blue	115.	22.50
Plate block of eight	—	
Double transfer at top	—	
FDC *(Oct. 1, 1885)*		8,500.

1888. Messenger, Second Issue, inscribed "At any post office." *Printed by the American Bank Note Company, flat press, unwatermarked, perforated 12.*

SD2, SD3 *Messenger on foot*

SD2 *(E2)*

10c Prussian blue *(Sept. 6, 1888)*	120.	7.00
dark blue	120.	7.00
Plate block of eight	—	

1893. Messenger, Third Isssue, was a change of color and was issued in order to avoid confusion with the 1- and 4-cent Columbian commemorative stamps. SD2 went on sale again in January 1894 and remained in use until it was replaced by SD4. *Printed by the American Bank Note Company, flat press, unwatermarked, perforated 12.*

SD3 *(E3)*

10c orange yellow *(Jan. 24, 1893)*	75.	10.
dark orange	75.	10.
Plate block of eight	—	

1894. Similar to SD2, with a line drawn under the words "Ten Cents." *Printed by intaglio by the Bureau of Engraving and Printing, perforated 12.*

SD4, SD5 *Messenger on foot*

SD4 *(E4)*

10c deep blue *(Oct. 10, 1894)*	275.	12.50
bright blue	275.	12.50
dark blue	275.	12.50
Block of four, with arrow	—	
Plate block of six	—	
Double transfer	—	
v. Block of six, imperforate and without gum	—	

1895. Same design as SD4, *Intaglio, perforated 12, watermarked double-line USPS (wmk 187)*

SD5 *(E5)*

10c blue *(Aug. 16, 1895)*	65.	1.75
dark blue	65.	1.75
deep blue	65.	1.75
Plate block of six		
Block of four, with arrow		
Colored line through "POSTAL DELIVERY"	—	
Dots in frame (curved) above messenger	—	
Double transfer	—	
v. Printed on both sides	—	
v1. Imperforate		

1902. New Bicycle Messcnger Issue, *Intaglio, perforated 12, watermarked double-line USPS (wmk 187).*

SD6 *Messenger on bicycle*

SD6 *(E6)*

10c ultramarine *(Dec. 9, 1902)*	75.	3.00
blue	75.	3.00
dark blue	75.	3.00
Plate block of six		
Plate block of six, from plates 5240, 5243, 5244, or 5245, with "09" added to number	—	
Block of four, with arrow	—	
Double transfer	—	
Transfer "damage" under "N" of "CENTS"	—	

1908. " Merry Widow" is the nick- name for this stamp due to the resemblance to a contemporary lady's hat, of the same name. *Intaglio, perforated 12, watermarked double-line USPS (wmk 187).*

SD7 *Helmet of Mercury*

SD7 *(E7)*
10c green *(Dec. 12, 1908)*	50.	30.
dark green	50.	30.
yellowish green	50.	30.
Plate block of six	—	
Double transfer	—	

1911. *Intaglio, watermarked single-line USPS (wmk 273), perforated 12.*

SD8-SD11 *Messenger on bicycle*

SD8 *(E8)*
10c ultramarine *(Jan. 1911)*	75.	4.50
dark ultramarine	75.	4.50
pale ultramarine	75.	4.50
violet blue	75.	4.50
Plate block of six	—	
Plate block of six, with imprint	—	
v. Top frame line missing	—	

1914. *Intaglio, watermarked single-line USPS (wmk 273), perforated 10.*

SD9 *(E9)*
10c ultramarine *(Sept. 1914)*	140.	5.00
blue	140.	5.00
pale ultramarine	140.	5.00
Plate block of six	—	
Plate block of six, with imprint	—	

1916. *Intaglio, unwatermarked, perforated 10.*

SD10 *(E10)*
10c pale ultramarine *(Oct. 19, 1916)*	225.	22.50
blue	225.	22.50
ultramarine	225.	22.50
Plate block of six	—	
Plate block of six, with imprint	—	

1917. *Intaglio, unwatermarked, perforated 11.*

SD11 *(E11)*
10c ultramarine *(May 2, 1917)*	14.50	.50
blue	14.50	.50
dark ultramarine	14.50	.50
gray violet	14.50	.50
pale ultramarine	14.50	.50
Plate block of six	150.	
Plate block of six, with imprint	—	
v. perforated 10 at left	—	

1922-25. Motorcycle Delivery, Truck (20c) *Intaglio, unwatermarked, perforated 11*

SD12, SD13, SD15-SD18 *Messenger and Motorcycle*

SD12 *(E12)*
10c gray blue	22.50	.25
deep ultramarine	22.50	.25
Plate block of six	275.	
Double transfer	—	
FDC *(July 12, 1922)*		375.

SD13 *(E13)*
15c red orange	19.00	1.00
Plate block of six	150.	
Double transfer	—	
FDC *(Apr. 11, 1925)*		275.

SD14, SD19 *Post office delivery truck*

SD14 *(E14)*
20c black	2.25	1.50
Plate block of six	35.	
FDC *(Apr. 25, 1925)*		125.

1927-51. *Rotary press printing, previ* s *designs, perforated 11 x 10 1/2.*

SD15 *(E15)*
10c dark lilac	1.00	.20
gray lilac	1.00	.20
red lilac	1.00	.20
violet	1.00	.20
Plate block of four	7.00	
cracked plate	—	
gouged plate	—	
FDC *(Nov. 29, 1927)*		100.
FDC, electric eye plate *(Sept. 8, 1941)*		25.
v. Horizontal pair, imperforate between	—	

SD16 *(E16)*
13c blue	1.00	.20
Plate block of four	5.00	
FDC *(Oct. 30, 1944)*		10.

SD17 *(E17)*
15c yellow orange	.75	.20
Plate block of four	4.00	
FDC, Washington, D.C. *(Aug. 13, 1931)*		125.
FDC, Easton, Pennsylvania *(Aug. 6, 1931)*		1,000.

SD18 *(E18)*
17c yellow	3.50	3.00
Plate block of four	27.50	
FDC *(Oct. 30, 1944)*		10.

SD19 *(E19)*

20c black   1.75   .20
    Plate block of four   8.50
    FDC *(Nov. 30, 1951)*   4.50

1954. Letter and Hands, *Rotary press printing. perforated 11 x 10 1/2.*

SD20, SD21 *Two hands and letter*

SD20 *(E20)*

20c gray blue   .75   .20
    light blue   .75   .20
    Plate block of four   3.00
    FDC *(Oct. 13, 1954)*   2.00

SD21 *(E21)*

30c maroon   .75   .20
    Plate block of four   3.50
    FDC *(Sept. 3, 1957)*   2.00

1969. Dual Arrows. Giori Press Printing issued for new rate. *Perforated 11.*

SD22, SD23 *Arrows pointing in opposite directions*

SD22

45c carmine and violet blue   1.50   .50
    Plate block of four   6.00
    FDC *(Nov. 20, 1969)*   2.50

1971. Dual Arrows, New Rates, same design as SD22.

SD23

60c violet blue and carmine   1.50   .25
    Plate block of four   7.50
    FDC *(May 10, 1971)*   2.50

Air Mail Special Delivery Stamps

1934. Blue Air Mail Special Delivery Stamp was issued to prepay, with one stamp, air postage and the special delivery fee. The stamp was designed by Pres. Franklin D. Roosevelt. The first day of issue was August 30 at the convention of the American Air Mail Society at Chicago. *Printed by intaglio, unwatermarked, perforated 11.*

ASD1 *Great Seal*

ASD1 *(CE1)*

16c Prussian blue *(9,215,750)*   .90   .75
    blue   .90   .75
    Plate block of six   25.
    FDC *(Aug. 30, 1934)*   30.
For imperforate stamp, see CM161.

1936. Red and Blue Airmail Special Delivery Stamp was of the same design as the 1934 stamp, but in two colors.

ASD2 *(CE2)*

16c carmine and blue   .60   .30
    Arrow block of four, bottom or
      side arrow   —
    Center line block   —
    Plate block of four, two
      plate numbers   12.50
    Plate block of ten, two plate
      numbers, two "Top," and two
      registration markers.   —
    FDC *(Feb. 10, 1936)*   25.
    v. Horizontal pair, imperforate
      between   —

Special Handling Stamps

1925-29. The Postal Service Act of 1925 provided the same service for fourth class matter as normally according first class by payment of a 25c fee, for which a stamp was issued. The other denominations were issued to meet rate changes. *Printed by intaglio, unwatermarked, perforated 11.*

The 10c, 15c and 20c denominations were dry-printed on pre-gummed paper (1955). They were issued in much smaller quantities than the usual wet-printed stamps. There is a minute size difference between the wet and dry printings; the latter are on a whiter, thicker and stiffer paper.

SH1-SH5

1925

SH1 *(QE4)*

25c green   22.50   5.50
    Plate block of six   —
    FDC *(Apr. 11, 1925)*   225.

1928-29

SH *(QE1)*

2 10c yellow green	2.25	1.00
Plate block of six	—	
FDC *(June 25, 1928)*		50.
p. Dry printing (1955)	1.25	.90

SH3 *(QE2)*

15c yellow green	2.75	1.00
Plate block of six	—	
FDC *(June 25, 1928)*		50.
p. Dry printing (1955)	2.00	1.50

SH4 *(QE3)*

20c yellow green	3.00	1.75
Plate block of six	—	
FDC *(June 25, 1928)*		50.
t. Dry printing (1955)	2.00	1.50

SH5 *(QE5)*

25c yellow green *(1929)*	17.50	7.50
Plate block of six	—	
"A" and "T" of "STATES" joined at top	—	
"A" and "T" of "STATES" and "T" and "A" of "POSTAGE" joined at top	—	

Parcel Post Stamps

1912-13. Parcel Post stamps were provided to cover the rates of postage on fourth class mail, set up by the Act of Congress of August 24, 1912. Less than a year later, on July 1, 1913, the Postmaster General directed that ordinary postage stamps be valid for parcel post and that parcel post stamps be valid for postage purposes and be continued on sale until the supply was exhausted. The 75c value (PP11) outlasted all the others and in September 1921 the remainders, consisting of 3,510,345 copies, were destroyed. One of our more attractive set of stamps, the 20c value is the first stamp in the world to depict an airplane. *Printeed by intaglio, watermarked single-line USPS (wmk 273) and perforated 12; marginal imprints (the denomination in words) were added to the plates on January 27, 1913.*

PP1 *Post Office Clerk and* PPD2 *City Carrrier*

PP1 *(Q1)*
  1c carmine *(209,691,094)*   3.00   1.25
    Double transfer   —
    Plate block of six, imprint   75.
    FDC *(Nov. 27, 1912)*

PP2 *(Q2)*
  2c carmine *(206,417,253)*   3.50   1.00
    lake   3.50   1.00
    Double transfer   —
    Plate block of six, imprint   90.
    FDC *(Nov. 27, 1912)*

PP3 *Railway Postal Clerk*

PP3 *(Q3)*
  3c carmine *(29,027,433)*   6.50   4.50
    Double transfer   —
    Lower right corner retouched   —
    Plate block of six, imprint   150.
    FDC *(April 5, 1913)*

PP4 *Rural Carrier*

PP4 *(Q4)*
  4c carmine *(76,743,813)*   17.50   2.50
    Double transfer   —
    Plate block of six, imprint   —
    FDC *(Dec. 12, 1912)*

PP5 *Mail Train*

PP5 *(Q5)*
  5c carmine *(108,153,993)*   17.50   1.75
    Double transfer   —
    Plate block of six, imprint   —
    FDC *(Nov. 27, 1912)*

PP6 *Steamship and Mail Tender*

PP6 *(Q6)*
  10c carmine *(56,896,653)*   30.   2.50
    Double transfer   —
    Plate block of six, imprint   —
    FDC *(Dec. 9, 1912)*

PP7   PP8 *Airplane Carrying Mail*

PP7 *(Q7)*
  15c carmine *(21,147,033)*   45.   8.00
    Plate block of six, imprint   —
    FDC *(Dec. 16, 1912)*

PP8 *(Q8)*
  20c carmine *(17,142,393)*   85.   16.
    Plate block of six, imprint   —
    FDC *(Dec. 16, 1912)*

PP9 *Manufacturing*   PP10 *Dairying*

PP9 *(Q9)*
25c carmine *(21,940,653)*   42.50   5.
    Plate block of six, imprint   —
    FDC *(Nov. 27, 1912)*

P10 *(Q10)*
50c carmine *(2,117,793)*   190.   32.50
    Plate block of six, imprint   —
    FDC *(Mar. 15, 1913)*

PP11 *Harvesting* PP12 *Fruit Growing*

PP11 *(Q11)*
75c carmine *(2,772,615)*   55.   25.
    Plate block of six, imprint   —
    FDC *(Dec. 18, 1912)*

PP12 *(Q12)*
$1 carmine *(1,053,273)*   250.   20.
    Plate block of six, imprint   —
    FDC *(Jan. 3, 1913)*

Parcel Post Postage Due Stamps

1912. These stamps were used to indicate the amount due by the addressee when parcel post was insufficiently prepaid by the sender. *Watermarked single-line USPS (wmk 273), Intaglio, perforated 12.*

PPD1-5

PPD1 *(JQ1)*
1c green *(7,322,400)*, Nov. 27, 1912   6.00   3.50

PPD2 *(JQ2)*
2c green *(3,132,000)*, Dec. 9, 1912   55.   15.

PPD3 *(JQ3)*
5c green *(5,840,100)*, Nov. 27, 1912   9.00   3.50

PPD4 *(JQ4)*
10c green *(2,124,540)*,Dec. 12, 1912   125.   40.

PPD5 *(JQ5)*
25c green *(2,117,700)*, Dec. 16, 1912   65.   3.75

Registration Stamp

1911. Although we have had a registry since 1855, the Registry Stamp of 1911 was the only stamp issued for the specific purpose of paying registration fees. The stamp was valid for the fees only, not postage; regular postage stamps could be used to pay the fees. The Postmaster General abolished the issuance of these stamps in 1913, but allowed remaining stock to be used up. *Printed by intaglio, single-line USPS watermark (wmk 273), perforated 12.*

  REG1

REG1 *(F1)*
10 bright blue   65.   5.00
    Plate block of six, with imprint 1500.
    FDC *(Dec. 1, 1911)*

Certified Mail Stamp

1955. This service was started to give mail having no intrinsic value special protection and also give the sender proof of delivery. It is a form of registration. *Printed by intaglio, perforated 10 1/2 x 11.*

 CER1 *U.S. Mail Carrier*

CER1 *(FA1)*
15C red   .50   .35
    Plate block of four   9.00
    FDC *(June 6, 1955)*

Official Carrier Stamp

1851. In the early days of the U.S. postal system the regular postage charge paid only for the delivery of mail from post office to post office. For an additional charge, the post office would act as a carrier and deliver letters to the addressee. Two stamps were issued for this purpose. Printed by Toppan, Carpenter, Casilear and Company, they were *unwatermarked and imperforate.* They were both of the 1c denominatic   although the Franklin stamp had no denomination .dicated on its face.

OCS1 *Benjamin Franklin*

OCS1 *(LO1)*
1c blue on rose paper	4,000.	4,500.
Cracked plate	4,500.	
Double transfer	—	—
On cover		7,750.

OCS2 *Eagle*

OCS2 *(LO2)*
1c blue on yellowish paper	20.	35.
Double transfer	—	—
On cover (alone)		125.

SPECIAL PRINTING

1875. Reprints of the Official Carrier Stamps of 1851. The Franklin carrier was printed in a darker blue than the originals and appears on rose-colored paper as well as on a paler, thicker paper. The Eagle reprints are on hard white paper and also on a coarse paper. Printed by the Continental Bank Note Company. *Printed by intaglio, imperforate, without gum.*

SPOCS1 *(LO3,4)*
1c blue on rose paper	50.
v. Perforated 12	2,500.

SPOCS2 *(LO5,6)*
1c blue	25.
v. Perforated 12	175.

Newspaper Stamps

First issued in September 1865 to prepay postage on bulk shipments of newspapers and periodicals, they were not attached to the items mailed, but rather to the statement of mailing, which was canceled and retained by the Post Office. The stamps were discontinued July 1, 1898.

1865. The First Issue was *embossed and printed in letterpress, National Bank Note Company, Thin hard unwatermarked paper, without gum, and perforated 12. The design size is 51 x 95 mm.*

N1, N4 *George Washington*　　N2 *Benjamin Franklin*

Colored Border

N1 *(PR1)*
  5c dark blue　　　　250.　　—
    a. light blue　　　275.　　—
N2 *(PR2)*
  10c green　　　　　100.　　—
    a. blue green　　　100.　　—
    p. pelure paper　　125.　　—

N3 *Abraham Lincoln*

N3 *(PR3)*
  25c orange red　　150.　　—
    a. carmine red　　175.　　—
    p. pelure paper　　150.　　—

N4 *(PR4)*
  5c blue　　　　　　75.　　—
    a. dark blue　　　　75.　　—
    p. pelure paper　　　75.　　—

SPECIAL PRINTING

1875. Reprints of the 1865 Issue, by the *Continental Bank Note Co. The 5c with white border, the 10c and 25c with colored border. Hard white paper, unwatermarked, issued without gum, perforated.*

SPN1 *(PR5)*
  5c blue　　　　　　75.
SPN2
  10c Bluish green　　85.
SPN3 *(PR6)*
  25c carmine　　　100.

1881. Reprint of the 1865 Issue, by the *American Bank Note Co. White border, soft porous paper, unwatermarked, perforated 12.*

SPN4 *(PR8)*
  5c dark blue　　　175.　　—

1875. Allegory Designs, *printed in intaglio, Continental Bank Note Company.* Issued January 1, 1875, on thin hard paper. Design size 24 x 35 mm.

N5-N11 *"Freedom" after Crawford's statue on the dome of the Capitol*

N5 *(PR9)*		
2c black	25.	12.50
gray black	25.	12.50
greenish black	25.	12.50
N6 *(PR10)*		
3c black	27.50	15.
gray black	27.50	15.
N7 *(PR11)*		
4c black	27.50	15.
gray black	27.50	15.
greenish black	27.50	15.
N8 *(PR12)*		
6c black	30.	20.
gray black	30.	20.
greenish black	30.	20.
N9 *(PR13)*		
8c black	45.	24.
gray black	45.	32.50
greenish black	45.	24.
N10 *(PR14)*		
9c black	65.	52.
gray black	85.	60.
greenish black	65.	52.
double transfer	100.	75.

N11 *(PR15)*
10c black 45. 32.50
    gray black 45. 32.50
    greenish black 45. 32.50

N12-19 Astraea,
Goddess of Justice

N12 *(PR16)*
12c rose 100. 50.
    pale rose 100. 50.
N13 *(PR17)*
24c rose 125. 65.
    pale rose 125. 65.
N14 *(PR18)*
36c rose 150. 75.
    pale rose 150. 75.
N15 *(PR19)*
48c rose 250. 125.
    pale rose 250. 125.
N16 *(PR20)*
60c rose 140. 65.
    pale rose 140. 65.
N17 *(PR21)*
72c rose 300. 175.
    pale rose 300. 175.
N18 *(PR22)*
84c rose 450. 200.
    pale rose 450. 200.
N19 *(PR23)*
96c rose 250. 125.
    pale rose 250. 125.

N20 *Ceres, Goddess*   N21 *"Victory"*
of Agriculture

N20 *(PR24)*
$1.92 brown 350. 225.
    dark brown 350. 225.
N21 *(PR25)*
$3.00 vermilion 475. 175.

N22 *Clio, Muse of*   N23 *Minerva,*
History   *Goddess of*
Wisdom

N22 *(PR26)*
$6.00 ultramarine 750. 150.
N23 *(PR27)*
$9.00 yellow 850. 325.

N24 *Vesta, Goddess*   N25 *"Peace"*
of the Fireside

N24 *(PR28)*
$12.00 blue green 1,000. 450.
N25 *(PR29)*
$24.00 dark gray violet 1,000. 450.

N26 *"Commerce"*   N27 *Hebe,*
Goddess of
Youth

N26 *(PR30)*
$36.00 brown rose 1,150. 600.
N27 *(PR31)*
$48.00 red brown 1,600. 650.

N28 *Indian Maiden*

N28 *(PR32)*
$60.00 violet 1,600. 650.

1879. Same designs as the 1875 issue. *Printed by*
intaglio by the American Bank Note Company on soft
porous paper, perforated 12.

SPECIAL PRINTING

1875. Special Printing of the 1875 Issue, made by the Continental Bank Note Co. *Hard, white paper, unwatermarked, issued without gum, perforated 12.*

SPN5 (PR33)
2c gray black (19,514, quantity issued probably includes SPN29)   125.

SPN6 (PR34)
3c gray black (6,952)   140.

SPN7 (PR35)
4c gray black (4,451)   150.

SPN8 (PR36)
6c gray black (2,348)   200.

SPN9 (PR37)
8c gray black (1,930)   250.

SPN10 (PR38)
9c gray black (1,795)   275.

SPN11 (PR39)
10c gray black (1,499)   350.

SPN12 (PR40)
12c rose (1,313)   425.

SPN13 (PR41)
24c rose (411)   600.

SPN14 (PR42)
36c rose (330)   700.

SPN15 (PR43)
48c rose (268)   800.

SPN16 (PR44)
60c rose (222)   850.

SPN17 (PR45)
72c rose (174)   1,000.

SPN18 (PR46)
84c rose (164)   1,250.

SPN19 (PR47)
96c rose (141)   1,750.

SPN20 (PR48)
$1.92 dark brown (41)   4,500.

SPN21 (PR49)
$3 vermilion (20)   8,000.

SPN22 (PR50)
$6 ultramarine (14)   10,000.

SPN23 (PR51)
$9 yellow (4)   17,500.

SPN24 (PR52)
$12 bluish green (5)   16,000.

SPN25 (PR53)
$24 gray violet (2)   —

SPN26 (PR54)
$36 brown rose (2)   —

SPN27 (PR55)
$48 red brown (1)   —

SPN28 (PR56)
$60 violet   —

N29 (PR57)

2c black	10.00	5.00
gray black	10.00	5.00
greenish black	10.00	5.00
double transfer at top	12.00	9.00
cracked plate	—	
v. imperforate	—	

N30 (PR58)

3c black	12.00	5.50
gray black		
greenish black	12.00	5.50
double transfer at top	14.	10.00
v. imperforate	—	

N31 (PR59)

4c black	12.50	5.50
gray black	12.50	5.50
greenish black	12.50	5.50
intense black	12.50	5.50
double transfer at top	15.	10.
v. imperforate	—	

N32 (PR60)

6c black	22.50	12.50
gray black	22.50	12.50
greenish black	22.50	12.50
intense black	22.50	12.50
double transfer at top	27.50	22.50
v. imperforate	—	

N33 (PR61)

8c black	22.50	12.50
gray black	22.50	12.50
greenish black	22.50	12.50
double transfer at top	27.50	22.50
v. imperforate	—	

N34 (PR62)

10c black	25.	12.50
gray black	25.	12.50
greenish black	25.	12.50
double transfer at top	27.50	
v. imperforate	—	

N35 (PR63)

12c red	90.	35.
v. imperforate	—	

N36 (PR64)

24c red	90.	35.
v. imperforate	—	

N37 (PR65)

36c red	250.	125.
v. imperforate	—	

N38 (PR66)

48c red	225.	75.
v. imperforate	—	

N39 (PR67)

60c red	175.	75.
v. imperforate	—	

N40 (PR68)

72c red	350.	150.
v. imperforate	—	

N41 (PR69)

84c red	250.	125.
v. imperforate	—	

N42 (PR70)

96c red	175.	75.
pink carmine	175.	75.
v. imperforate	—	

N43 *(PR71)*

$1.92 pale brown	125.	100.
brown	125.	100.
cracked plate	175.	
v. imperforate	—	

N44 *(PR72)*

$3.00 red vermilion	125.	75.
v. imperforate	—	

N45 *(PR73)*

$6.00 blue	225.	125.
ultramarine	225.	125.
v. imperforate	—	

N46 *(PR74)*

$9.00 orange	150.	75.
v. imperforate	—	

N47 *(PR75)*

$12.00 yellow green	225.	100.
v. imperforate	—	

N48 *(PR76)*

$24.00 dark violet	300.	150.
v. imperforate	—	

N49 *(PR77)*

$36.00 Indian red	350.	150.
v. imperforate	—	

N50 *(PR78)*

$48.00 yellow brown	450.	225.
v. imperforate	—	

N51 *(PR79)*

$60.00 purple	450.	225.
bright purple	450.	225.
v. imperforate	—	

1883. Special Printing of the 1879 2c Stamp, American Bank Note Co., *soft porous paper, unwatermarked, perforated 12.*

SPN29 *(PR80)*

2c black	325.

1885. Like 1879 issue. *Intaglio, American Bank Note Co., soft porous paper, perforated 12.*

N52 *(PR81)*

1c black	12.50	5.50
gray black	12.50	5.50
intense black	12.50	5.50
double transfer at top	15.	9.00

N53 *(PR82)*

12c carmine	40.	15.
deep carmine	40.	15.
rose carmine	40.	15.

N54 *(PR83)*

24c carmine	40.	17.50
deep carmine	40.	17.50
rose carmine	40.	17.50

N55 *(PR84)*

36c carmine	60.	25.
deep carmine	60.	25.
rose carmine	60.	25.

N56 *(PR85)*

48c crmine	85.	40.
deep carmine	85.	40.

N57 *(PR86)*

60c carmine	125.	50.
deep carmine	125.	50.

N58 *(PR87)*

72c carmine	150.	60.
deep carmine	150.	60.
rose carmine	150.	60.

N59 *(PR88)*

84c carmine	300.	140.
rose carmine	300.	140.

N60 *(PR89)*

96c carmine	225.	100.
rose carmine	225.	100.

Imperforates of N52-N60 exist, but they were not regularly issued.

1894. Previous designs. *Intaglio, Bureau of Engraving, soft wove paper, perforated 12.*

N61 *(PR90)*

1c black	100.	—
double transfer at top	125.	

N62 *(PR91)*

2c black	100.	—
double transfer at top	125.	

N63 *(PR92)*

4c black	125.	—

N64 *(PR93)*

6c black	1,500.	—

N65 *(PR94)*

10c black	225.	—

N66 *(PR95)*

12c pink	700.	—

N67 *(PR96)*

24c pink	700.	—

N68 *(PR97)*

36c pink	4,500.	—

N69 *(PR98)*

60c pink	4,500.	—

N70 *(PR99)*

96c pink	5,500.	—

N71 *(PR100)*

$3.00 scarlet	6,500.	—

N72 *(PR101)*

$6.00 pale blue	8,500.	—

1895. New designs. *Intaglio, Bureau of Engraving, soft wove paper, perforated 12.*

N73-N76 *"Freedom"*   N77-N78 *Astraea*

N73 *(PR102)*

1c black	40.	10.

N74 *(PR103)*		
2c black	40.	10.
gray black	30.	10.
double transfer at top	45.	
N75 *(PR104)*		
5c black	50.	15.
gray black	50.	15.
N76 *(PR105)*		
10c black	100.	45.
N77 *(PR106)*		
25c carmine	150.	50.
N78 *(PR107)*		
50c carmine	325.	125.

N79 *"Victory"*   N80 *Clio*

N79 *(PR108)*		
$2 scarlet	400.	100.
N80 *(PR109)*		
$5 ultramarine	600.	200.

N81 *Vesta*   N82 *"Peace"*

N81 *(PR110)*		
$10 green	550.	225.
N82 *(PR111)*		
$20 slate	825.	400.

N83 *"Commerce"*   N84 *Indian maiden*

N83 *(PR112)*		
$50 dull rose	850.	400.
N84 *(PR113)*		
$100 purple	1,000.	450.
N85 *(PR114)*		
1c black	4.00	3.25
gray black	4.00	3.25
N86 *(PR115)*		
2c black	4.50	3.75
gray black	4.50	3.75

N87 *(PR116)*		
5c black	7.00	5.50
gray black	7.00	5.50
N88 *(PR117)*		
10c black	4.50	3.75
gray black	4.50	3.75
N89 *(PR118)*		
25c carmine	8.50	8.50
lilac rose	8.50	8.50
N90 *(PR119)*		
50c carmine	12.50	14.
rose carmine	12.50	14.
lilac rose	12.50	14.
N91 *(PR120)*		
$2 scarlet	15.	17.50
scarlet vermilion	15.	17.50
N92 *(PR121)*		
$5 dark blue	25.	30.
light blue	125.	50.
N93 *(PR122)*		
$10 green	25.	30.
N94 *(PR123)*		
$20 slate 22.	25.	35.
N95 *(PR124)*		
$50 dull rose	30.	40.
N96 *(PR125)*		
$100 purple	35.	42.50

In 1899 the U.S. Government sold 26,989 sets of the Newspaper series of 1895-97 to collectors at $5 per set. Since the supply of high values was not great enough to make up the number of sets required, the values from the $5 through the $100 were reprinted. These special printings can be distinguished from the originals by the shade and whiteness of the paper and gum.

1895-97. Same as 1895 except printed on double-line USPS (wmk 187) watermarked paper.

SPECIAL PRINTING

1899. Reprints of the 1895 Issue. Bureau of Engraving and Printing. Previous designs in *double-line USPS watermark, with white instead of yellowish gum, perforated 12.*

SPN30	
$5 blue	—
SPN31	
$10 green	—
SPN32	
$20 slate	—
SPN33	
$50 rose	—
SPN34	
$100 purple	—

Official Stamps

The franking privilege for the various government departments was abolished July 1, 1873. On that date official stamps were issued to be used by the departments. In addition to the name of the department, inscribed at the top, the Post Office Department stamps have large numerals as the central design, while the stamps of the other departments feature busts of the following men:

1c Benjamin Franklin
2c Andrew Jackson
3c George Washington
6c Abraham Lincoln
7c Edwin Stanton
10c Thomas Jefferson
12c Henry Clay
15c Daniel Webster
24c Winfield Scott
30c Alexander Hamilton
90c Oliver Perry
$2 to $20 William Seward

The first official stamps were printed in intaglio by the Continental Bank Note Co. on thin, hard paper, but in 1879 the American Bank Note Co., using the same plates, made printings on soft, porous paper. This is the principal way that they can be identified, since all the paper is unwatermarked, and all the stamps are *perforated 12*. A marginal imprint reading "Continental" does not necessarily indicate the printer.

AGRICULTURE

1873. *Printed in intaglio on thin, hard paper, unwatermarked, perforated 12.*

OF1, 10   OF2   OF3,11

OF1 *(O1)*

1c yellow	100.	75.
golden yellow	110.	80.
olive yellow	110.	80.
p. Ribbed paper	125.	80.

OF2 *(O2)*

2c yellow	85.	32.50
golden yellow	75.	25.
olive yellow	75.	27.50
p. Ribbed paper	80.	30.

OF3 *(O3)*

3c yellow	65.	6.00
golden yellow	70.	6.50
olive yellow	73.	6.50
Double transfer	—	—
p. Ribbed paper	73.	7.00

OF4 *(O4)*

6c yellow	80.	25.
golden yellow	80.	27.50
olive yellow	80.	27.50

OF5 *(O5)*

10c yellow	150.	90.
golden yellow	165.	100.
olive yellow	175.	105.

OF6 *(O6)*

12c yellow	195.	100.
golden yellow	210.	110.
olive yellow	225.	110.

OF7 *(O7)*

15c yellow	160.	100.
golden yellow	170.	110.
olive yellow	175.	110.

OF8 *(O8)*

24c yellow	160.	60.
golden yellow	175.	65.

OF9 *(O9)*

30c yellow	225.	125.
golden yellow	235.	140.
olive yellow	250.	150.

1879. *Printed in intaglio on soft, porous paper unwatermarked, perforated 12.*

OF10 *(O94)*

1c yellow, issued without gum   1,500.
Some consider No. OF10 a special printing, circa 1883.

OF11 *(O95)*

3c yellow	225.	40.

EXECUTIVE

1873. *Printed in intaglio on thin, hard paper, unwatermarked, perforated 12.*

OF13   OF15   OF16

OF12 *(O10)*

1c carmine	335.	200.
dark carmine	335.	200.

OF13 *(O11)*

2c carmine	210.	100.
dark carmine	210.	100.
Double transfer	—	—

OF14 *(O12)*

3c carmine	260.	100.
lilac red	260.	100.

OF15 *(O13)*

6c carmine	400.	275.
dark carmine	400.	275.
dull carmine	400.	275.

OF16 *(O14)*

10c carmine	350.	300.
dark carmine	350.	300.
dull carmine	350.	300.

INTERIOR

1873. Printed in intaglio on thin, hard paper, unwatermarked, perforated 12.

OF17,27   OF18,28   OF19,29

OF17 *(O15)*

1c orange red	21.	5.25
bright orange red	21.	5.25
dull orange red	21.	5.25
p. Ribbed paper	25.	6.00

OF18 *(O16)*

2c orange red	16.50	3.25
bright orange red	16.50	3.25
dull orange red	16.50	3.25

OF19 *(O17)*

3c orange red	28.	3.00
bright orange red	28.	3.00
dull orange red	28.	3.00
p. Ribbed paper	30.	5.25

OF20 *(O18)*

6c orange red	21.	3.25
bright orange red	21.	3.25
dull orange red	21.	3.25

OF21 *(O19)*

10c orange red	20.	6.25
bright orange red	20.	6.25
dull orange red	20.	6.25

OF22 *(O20)*

12c orange red	32.50	4.75
bright orange red	32.50	4.75
dull orange red	32.50	4.75

OF23 *(O21)*

15c orange red	50.	10.
bright orange red	50.	10.
dull orange red	50.	10.
Double transfer, left side	90.	25.
p. Ribbed paper	—	—

OF24 *(O22)*

24c orange red	37.50	8.50
bright orange red	37.50	8.50
dull orange red	37.50	8.50

OF25 *(O23)*

30c orange red	50.	8.50
bright orange red	50.	8.50
dull orange red	50.	8.50

OF26 *(O24)*

90c orange red	125.	22.50
bright orange red	125.	22.50
dull orange red	125.	22.50
Double transfer	160.	—

1879. Printed in intaglio on soft, porous paper unwatermarked, perforated 12.

OF27 *(O96)*

1c orange red	135.	125.
dull orange red	135.	125.

OF28 *(O97)*

2c orange red	2.50	1.25
dull orange red	2.50	1.25

OF29 *(O98)*

3c orange red	2.25	.75
dull orange red	2.25	.75

OF30 *(O99)*

6c orange red	3.50	3.75
dull orange red	3.50	3.75

OF31 *(O100)*

10c orange red	45.	35.
dull orange red	45.	35.

OF32 *(O101)*

12c orange red	90.	60.
dull orange red	90.	60.

OF33 *(O102)*

15c orange red	200.	150.
dull orange red	200.	150.
Double transfer, left side	275.	—

OF34 *(O103)*

24c orange red	1,850.	—
dull orange red	1,850.	—

JUSTICE

1873. Printed in intaglio on thin, hard paper, unwatermarked, perforated 12.

OF35   OF36   OF37,45

OF35 *(O25)*

1c purple	65.	47.50
dark purple	65.	47.50

OF36 *(O26)*

2c purple	100.	50.
dark purple	100.	50.

OF37 *(O27)*

3c purple	100.	10.
dark purple	100.	10.
Double transfer	—	—

OF38 *(O28)*

6c purple	95.	16.
bluish purple	95.	16.
dull purple	95.	16.

OF39 *(O29)*

10c purple	110.	35.
bluish purple	110.	35.
Double transfer	—	—

OF40 *(O30)*

12c purple	85.	22.50
dark purple	85.	22.50

OF41 *(O31)*

15c purple	170.	75.
Double transfer	—	—

OF42 *(O32)*

24c purple	425.	175.

OF43 *(O33)*

30c purple	375.	100.
Double transfer	400.	100.

OF44 *(O34)*

90c purple	550.	250.
dark purple	550.	250.

1879. Printed in intaglio on soft, porous paper unwatermarked, perforated 12.

OF45 *(O106)*

3c bluish purple	55.	40.
dark bluish purple	55.	40.

OF46 *(O107)*

6c bluish purple	125.	100.

NAVY

1873. Printed in intaglio on thin, hard paper, unwatermarked, perforated 12.

OF47 *(O35)*

1c ultramarine	45.	22.50
dark ultramarine	45.	22.50
dull blue	45.	22.50

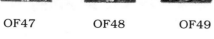

OF47   OF48   OF49

OF48 *(O36)*

2c ultramarine	35.	10.
dark ultramarine	35.	10.
dull blue	45.	12.50
gray blue	45.	12.50
Double transfer	—	—

OF49 *(O37)*

3c ultramarine	40.	5.25
dark ultramarine	40.	5.25
dull blue	40.	5.25
pale ultramarine	40.	5.25
Double transfer	—	—

OF50 *(O38)*

6c ultramarine	37.50	8.50
bright ultramarine	37.50	8.50
dull blue	45.	8.50
Double transfer	—	—
Vertical line through "N" of "NAVY"	65.	14.

OF51 *(O39)*

7c ultramarine	225.	85.
dark ultramarine	225.	85.
dull blue	225.	85.
Double transfer	—	—

OF52 *(O40)*

10c ultramarine	47.50	17.50
dark ultramarine	47.50	17.50
dull blue	50.	17.50
pale ultramarine	47.50	17.50
Cracked plate	—	125.
p. Ribbed paper	60.	22.50

OF53 *(O41)*

12c ultramarine	60.	15.
dark ultramarine	60.	15.
pale ultramarine	60.	15.
Double transfer, left side	175.	50.

OF54 *(O42)*

15c ultramarine	100.	35.
dark ultramarine	100.	35.

OF55 *(O43)*

24c ultramarine	100.	35.
dark ultramarine	100.	35.
dull blue	125.	—

OF56 *(O44)*

30c ultramarine	85.	17.50
dark ultramarine	85.	17.50
Double transfer	100.	20.

OF57 *(O45)*

90c ultramarine	450.	110.
v. Double impression	—	3,400.

POST OFFICE

1873. Printed by intaglio on thin, hard paper, unwatermarked, perforated 12

OF58

OF58 *(O47)*

1c black 7.50		3.50
gray black	7.50	3.50

OF59 *(O48)*

2c black 8.50		3.00
gray black	8.50	3.00
v. Double impression	325.	—

OF60 *(O49)*
3c black 3.00   1.00
    gray black   3.00 1.00
    Cracked plate   10. 7.00
    Double transfer   —   —
    p. Ribbed paper   —   —
    v. Printed on both sides   — 3,000.
OF61 *(O50)*
6c black 9.00   2.25
    gray black   9.00 2.25
    p. Ribbed paper   — 9.00
    y. Diagonal half used as 3c on
        cover   — 2,800.
OF62 *(O51)*
10c black   42.50 22.50
    gray black   42.50 22.50
OF63 *(O52)*
12c black   22.50 6.00
    gray black   22.50 6.00
OF64 *(O53)*
15c black   27.50 9.00
    gray black   27.50 9.00
    Double transfer   —   —
    v. Imperforate, pair   — 550.
OF65 *(O54)*
24c black   37.50 12.50
    gray black   37.50 12.50
OF66 *(O55)*
30c black   37.50 12.50
    gray black   37.50 12.50
OF67 *(O56)*
90c black   55. 12.50
    gray black   55. 12.50
    Double transfer   —   —

1879. *Printed in intaglio on soft, porous paper unwatermarked, perforated 12.*

OF68 *(O108)*
3c black   9.00 3.25
    gray black   9.00 3.25

STATE

1873. *Printed in intaglio on thin, hard paper, unwatermarked, perforated 12.*

   OF73   OF80   OF74

OF69 *(O57)*
1c green   70. 25.
    dark yellow green   70. 25.
    pale green   70. 25.

OF70 *(O58)*
2c green   140. 45.
    dark yellow green   140. 45.
    yellow green   140. 45.
    Double transfer   —   —
OF71 *(O59)*
3c green   52.50 11.
    bright green   52.50 11.
    yellow green   52.50 11.
OF72 *(O60)*
6c green   52.50 12.50
    bright green   52.50 12.50
    yellow green   52.50 12.50
    Double transfer   —   —
OF73 *(O61)*
7c green   100. 25.
    dark yellow green   100. 25.
    p. ribbed paper   125. 27.50
OF74 *(O62)*
10c green   75. 17.50
    bright green   75. 17.50
    yellow green   75. 17.50
    Short transfer   95. 30.
OF75 *(O63)*
12c green   125. 55.
    yellow green   125. 55.
OF76 *(O64)*
15c green   135. 37.50
    dark yellow green   135. 37.50
OF77 *(O64)*
24c green   275. 100.
    dark yellow green   275. 100.
OF78 *(O66)*
30c green   250. 70.
    dark yellow green   250. 70.
OF79 *(O67)*
90c green   475. 150.
    dark yellow green   475. 150.
OF80 *(O68)*
$2 green and black   550. 425.
    yellow green and black   550. 425.
OF81 *(O69)*
$5 green and black   4,500. 1,900.
    dark green and black   4,500. 1,900.
    yellow green and black   4,500. 1,900.
OF82 *(O70)*
$10 green and black   3,100. 1,600.
    dark green and black   3,100. 1,600.
    yellow green and black   3,100. 1,600.
OF83 *(O71)*
$20 green and black   2,100. 1000.
    dark green and black   2,100. 1000.
    yellow green and black   2,100. 1000.

TREASURY

1873. *Printed in intaglio on thin, hard paper, unwatermarked, perforated 12.*

OF84 *(O72)*
1c brown   25. 3.00
    dark brown   25. 3.00
    yellow brown   25. 3.00
    Double transfer   35. 5.00

OF91   OF92   OF93, 98

OF85 *(O73)*

2c brown	27.50	3.00
dark brown	27.50	3.00
yellow brown	27.50	3.00
Cracked plate	40.	—
Double transfer	—	—

OF86 *(O74)*

3c brown	17.50	1.50
dark brown	17.50	1.50
yellow brown	17.50	1.50
t. Shaded circle to right of right frame line	—	—
t1. Double impression	—	—

OF87 *(O75)*

6c brown	23.	2.50
dark brown	23.	2.50
yellow brown	23.	2.50
Double transfer	—	—
Worn plate	23.	3.00

OF88 *(O76)*

7c brown	55.	15.
dark brown	55.	15.
yellow brown	55.	15.

OF89 *(O77)*

10c brown	60.	5.50
dark brown	60.	5.50
yellow brown	60.	5.50
Double transfer	—	—

OF90 *(O78)*

12c brown	60.	4.00
dark brown	60.	4.00
yellow brown	60.	4.00

OF91 *(O79)*

15c brown	55.	5.50
dark brown	55.	5.50
yellow brown	55.	5.50

OF92 *(O80)*

24c brown	275.	45.
dark brown	275.	45.
yellow brown	275.	45.
Double transfer	—	—

OF93 *(O81)*

30c brown	85.	6.00
dark brown	85.	6.00
yellow brown	85.	6.00
Short transfer	—	—

OF94 *(O82)*

90c brown	95.	6.50
dark brown	95.	6.50
yellow brown	95.	6.50

1879. *Printed in intaglio on soft, porous paper unwatermarked , perforated 12.*

OF95 *(O109)*

3c brown	30.	4.50
yellow brown	30.	4.50

OF96 *(O110)*

6c brown	20.	
yellow brown	55.	20.

OF97 *(O111)*

10c brown	85.	25.
dark brown	85.	25.
yellow brown	85.	25.

OF98 *(O112)*

30c brown	800.	175.
yellow brown	800.	175.

OF99 *(O113)*

90c brown	1,000.	175.
dark brown	1,000.	175.
yellow brown	1,000.	175.

WAR

1873. *Printed in intaglio on thin, hard paper, unwatermarked, perforated 12.*

OF103, 114   OF104   OF105, 115

OF100 *(O83)*

1c Venetian red	90.	4.50
rose red	90.	4.50

OF101 *(O84)*

2c Venetian red	75.	6.50
rose red	75.	6.50
p. Ribbed paper	70.	9.00

OF102 *(O85)*

3c Venetian red	75.	2.00
rose red	75.	2.00

OF103 *(O86)*

6c Venetian red	275.	4.50
dull Venetian red	275.	4.50

OF104 *(O87)*

7c Venetian red	75.	45.
dull Venetian red	75.	45.
rose red	75.	45.

OF105 *(O88)*

10c Venetian red	25.	7.50
rose red	25.	7.50

The crack at lower left of OF105 was on the original die and is found on all copies.

OF106 *(O89)*

12c Venetian red	90.	7.50
p. Ribbed paper	110.	9.00

OF107 *(O90)*
15c Venetian red	22.50	7.50
dull Venetian red	22.50	7.50
rose red	22.50	7.50
p. Ribbed paper	30.	10.00

OF108 *(O91)*
24c Venetian red	22.50	5.00
dull Venetian red	22.50	5.00
rose red	22.50	5.00

OF109 *(O92)*
30c Venetian red	25.	5.00
rose red	25.	5.00
p. Ribbed paper	40.	7.50

OF110 *(O93)*
90c Venetian red	60.	27.50
rose red	60.	27.50

1879. *Printed in intaglio on soft, porous paper unwatermarked, perforated 12.*

OF111 *(O114)*
1c dull rose	2.25	2.00
90c Venetian red	60.	27.50
rose red	60.	27.50

1879. *Printed in intaglio on soft, porous paper*
dull rose red	2.25	2.00
rose red	2.25	2.00
Venetian red	2.25	2.00

OF112 *(O115)*
2c dull rose	3.25	2.00
dark rose	3.25	2.00
dull vermilion	3.25	2.00

OF113 *(O116)*
3c dull rose	3.25	1.25
rose red	3.25	1.25
Double transfer	6.00	4.00
t. Double impression	500.	—
v. Imperforate pair	750.	—

OF114 *(O117)*
6c dull rose	3.25	1.25
dull vermilion	3.25	1.25
rose red	3.25	1.25

OF115 *(O118)*
10c dull rose	25.	20.
rose red	25.	20.

OF116 *(O119)*
12c dull rose	17.50	7.50
rose red	17.50	7.50

OF117 *(O120)*
30c dull rose	50.	42.50
rose red	50.	42.50

POSTAL SAVINGS *(Post Office Department)*

When Postal Savings Depositories were set up in 1910 under the Post Office Department, special stamps were provided for that division. Their use was discontinued in 1914, and all remainders destroyed. *Printed in intaglio by the Bureau of Engraving and Printing, perforated 12.*

1911. *Watermarked double-line USPS (wmk 187)*

OF118, OF122

OF118 *(O121)*
2c black *(Dec. 22, 1910)*	17.50	1.75
Plate block of six, with imprint	250.	
Block of four (2 mm apart)	45.	6.50
Block of four (3 mm apart)	42.	5.50
Double transfer	15.	2.50

OF119 *(O122)*
50c green *(Feb. 1, 1911)*	150.	32.50
Plate block of six, with imprint	2,400.	
Block of four (2 mm apart)	550.	17
Block of four (3 mm apart)	535.	170.
Margin block of four, with arrow	560.	

1911. *Watermarked single-line USPS (wmk 273).*

OF120 *(O123)*
$1 bright blue	150.	10.00
Plate block of six with imprint	1,900.	375.
Block of four (2 mm apart)	400.	45.
Block of four (3 mm apart)	390.	45.
Margin block of four, with arrow	425.	

OF121 *(O124)*
1c dark red violet *(Mar. 27,1911)*	8.50	1.25
Plate block of six, with imprint	110.	
Block of four (2 mm apart)	21.	5.00
Block of four (3 mm apart)	20.	4.75

OF122 *(O125)*
2c black	45.	4.25
Plate block of six, with imprint	525.	
Block of four (2 mm apart)	120.	19.
Block of four (3 mm apart)	118.	19.
Double transfer	32.	4.75

OF123 *(O126)*
10c carmine *(Feb. 1, 1911)*	17.50	1.25
Plate block of six, with imprint	225.	
Block of four (2 mm apart)	35.	5.50
Block of four (3 mm apart)	33.	5.00
Double transfer	14.	2.50

1983. *Intaglio perforated 11, (Jan. 12, 1983).*

OF124-OF130

OF124 *(O127)*
1c blue, red and black   .25   .25
   Plate block of four   .60
OF125 *(O128)*
4c blue, red and black   .25   .25
   Plate block of four   .75
OF126 *(O129)*
13c blue, red and black   .45   .75
   Plate block of four   2.00
OF127 *(O130)*
17c blue, red and black   .50   .40
   Plate block of four   2.50
OF128 *(O131)*
$1 blue, red and black   3.00   1.25
   Plate block of four   14.
OF129 *(O130)*
$5 blue, red and black   10.   5.00
   Plate block of four   45.

Coil, perforated 10 vertically

OF130 *(O135)*
20c blue, red and black   2.00   2.25
   Pair   4.50   4.50

1985. "D" rate, non-denominated stamp. *Intaglio.*

 OF131

Perforated 11

OF131 *(O138)*
(14c) blue, red and black   4.50   5.50
   (Feb. 4, 1985)
   Plate block of four   —

 OF132

Coil, perforated 10 vertically

OF132 *(O139)*
(22c) blue, red and black   4.75   3.00
   (Feb. 4, 1985)
   Pair   7.50   —

1985. *Intaglio.*

 OF133,134

Perforated 11

OF133 *(O129A)*
14c blue, red and black   .40   .65
   (May 15, 1985)

Coil, perforated 10 vertically

OF134 *(O136)*
22c blue, red and black   .75   2.25
   (May 15, 1985)
   Pair   1.50   4.50

1988. "E" rate, non-denominated stamp. *Coil. Offset, perforated 10 vertically.*

 OF135

OF135 *(O140)*
(25c) blue, red and black   1.00   2.00
   (March 22, 1988)
   Pair

1988. Design similar to OF133. *Coil, Offset, perforated 10 vertically.*

OF136 *(O138B)*
20c blue, red and black   .45   .35
   (May 19, 1988)
   Pair   —   —

1988. Similar to OF133. *Coil. Offset, perforated 10 vertically.*

OF137 *(O138A)*
15c blue, red and black   .45   .65
   (June 11, 1988)
   Pair   —   —

1988. Similar to OF133. *Coil. Offset, perforated 10 vertically.*

OF138 *(O141)*
25c blue, red and black   .75   .50
   (June 11, 1988)
   Pair   —   1.75
   v. Imperforate pair   —

1989. Similar to OF133. *Offset, perforated 11.*

OF139 *(O143)*
1c blue, red and black   .25   .25
   (July 5, 1989)

1991. "F" rate non-denominated stamp. *Coil. Offset, perforated 10 vertically.*

OF140

OF140 (*O144*)
(29c) blue, red and black .75 .50
    (Jan. 22, 1991)
    Pair — —

1991. Similar to OF133. *Offset, perforated 11.*

OF141 (*O146*)
4c blue, red and black .25 .30
    (Apr. 6, 1991)

OF142 (*O147*)
19c blue, red and black .40 .60
    (May 24, 1991)

OF143 (*O148*)
23c blue, red and black .45 .60
    (May 24, 1991)

1991. Similar to OF133. *Coil, printed by offset, perforated 10 vertically.*

OF144 (*O145*)
29c blue, red and black .75 .50
    (May 24, 1991)
    Pair 1.50 —

1993. Similar to OF133. *Offset, perforated 11.*

OF145

OF145 (*O146A*)
10c blue, red and black .35 .55
    (Oct. 19, 1993)

OF146

OF146 (*O151*)
$1 blue, red and black 2.10 1.75
    (Oct. 19, 1993)

1994. G Rate non-denominated stamp. *Coil, Offset, perforated 9 3/4 vertically.*

OF147 (*O152*)
(32c) blue, red and black .75 .50
    (Dec. 13,1994)

1995. Similar to OF133. *Offset, perforated 11.*

OF148 (*O154*)
1c blue, red and black .25 .25
    (May 9, 1995)
OF149 (*O155*)
20c blue, red and black .45 .55
OF150 (*O156*)
23c blue, red and black .55 .65
OF151 (*O157*)
32c blue, red and black .75 .40

Envelopes and Wrappers

Government stamped envelopes first were authorized by the United States under an Act of Congress of August 31, 1852. From the very first issue until the present they have been produced by private manufacturers under contract to the government. It is believed the first envelopes were issued some time in April 1853. The exact date is not known.

Unlike adhesive stamps, stamped envelopes are produced one at a time. Until 1965 the blanks were cut to shape by means of a cutting die (called a "knife" by collectors) much as one operates a cookie cutter. This die was placed on a pile of sheets of paper and was forced through by means of a press. Then a complex machine printed the stamp and whatever corner card might be requested; folded, gummed and sealed the flaps; applied gum to the top back flap; and counted the finished envelopes into multiples of 100 or any number desired.

Beginning in 1965 envelopes have been made from a continuous roll (web) of paper.

The embossed printing of the stamp is accomplished with a recessed printing die which strikes against a resilient undersurface, or "tympan." The tympan forces the paper into the recesses, causing the embossed effect. Later issues are printed by more contemporary processes.

Paper

While our envelopes have been made from paper of various colors, the most usual color is "white." During the first issue, the customer had his choice of "white" or "buff" paper envelopes, and at various times the choice of colors available was as many as six or seven. Since 1942, envelopes have been made of white paper only.

The paper colors used throughout the issues are:

White — and various shades thereof.
Buff — in early issues from a brownish color to a yellow.
Amber — shows a yellowish cast. Can be quite pronounced or very pale.
Cream — an intermediate shade between a yellow and a brown. It was discontinued in 1886 and "buff" (sometimes known as "oriental buff") substituted.
Blue — and various shades thereof.
Orange — in various shades thereof.
Fawn — a brownish shade.
Manila — made of manila fibers.
Amber-manila — manila paper died yellowish.
Canary — bright yellow (used for Post Office Department envelopes only).

It will be seen that all colors vary greatly in shades. Such variation is not intentional, but merely reflects the inability to match colors exactly in various

batches of paper. The "white" of one issue may differ by a wide margin from the "white" of a later or earlier issue. The same holds true for any other color. Thus the colors of paper, while important to the collector, are not standardized and may only be considered within each individual issue of envelopes.

From 1853 to 1915, all envelopes were made of laid paper, and the laid lines will appear diagonal. This is the result of turning the cutting knife on the bias to the edge of the pile of paper in order to save as much waste as possible. On the other hand, wrappers, which are rectangular in shape, presented no great waste of paper, so they were cut parallel to the edge of the paper. The laid lines on wrappers will appear horizontal or vertical, depending on how they were inserted in the press. This is the principle method of distinguishing between a wrapper cut square and an envelope cut square.

From 1915 to the present, envelopes have been made of wove paper, and thus show no laid lines.

Albinos and Misprints

Until the web-printing process was adopted in 1965, two envelope blanks will have occasionally been fed into the envelope-making machine at one time. The top sheet received an inked impression, and the bottom sheet an impression without ink. Such colorless impressions look like white "stamps" and are called "albinos." They are quite common for recent issues, including those even after web printing of envelopes began, but rather rare for early 19th century envelopes. Although they are interesting, they do not command near the premium as do envelopes with two impressions of the stamp in color (one over or partially over the other).

Collecting Envelopes and wrappers

Envelopes and wrappers are collected as "entires" by size and watermarks and as cut squares. Cut squares are popular because, like postage stamps, they may be mounted easily into albums. Cut squares always should provide adequate margins, which in most instances would be no less than 1/4 inch of paper margin beyond the design of the stamp on all four sides.

Prices in this catalog are for cut squares with such margins. Larger squares, "full corners," or extra large corners with all back flaps attached may bring premium prices. This is especially true for earlier issues.

Envelopes are manufactured in a variety of different sizes and shapes. Thus, a single basic stamp may appear on several different size envelopes and some of these sizes may be more valuable than others although the stamp remains the same. Certain envelopes exist in large sizes only. In the listing that follows, an asterisk (*) designates entires only available in large size.

Catalog values are for entires of the least value. It is

required by law that all envelopes be manufactured with watermarked paper. From 1853 to 1870, a single style watermark was used for all issues (wmk 1), but with a new manufacturer in 1870 a new watermark was introduced and beginning in 1874 it became the custom to change the watermark with the letting of each new contract (about every four years) through the late 1960's. It has been customary to allow remaining stocks of paper to be used up before the new watermarked paper is introduced. Most issues of envelopes, therefore, exist on at least two styles of watermarked paper and, when an issue extended over a very long period of years, there may be several watermarks involved. Indicated at the beginning of each issue are watermarks to be found on envelopes of that issue.

Watermarks (illustrations reduced in size)

Watermark No. 6

Watermark No. 1

Watermark No. 7   *Watermark No. 8*

Watermark No. 9

Watermark No. 2

Watermark No. 10

*Watermark No. 3
"CENTENNIAL"*

Watermark No. 11

*Watermark
No. 4*

Watermark No. 12

Watermark No. 13

Watermark No. 5 "STAR"

Watermark No. 14 (1903-1907)

Watermark No. 15
(1907-1911)

Watermark No. 15a
(1907-1911)

Watermark No. 16

USSE 1911

Watermark No. 17
(1911-1915)

US-SE 1911

Watermark No. 18
(1911-1915)

1853-55. All envelopes issued from 1853 to 1870 were manufactured in New York City by the George F. Nesbitt Manufacturing Company and are known to collectors as the "Nesbitt Issues." The Nesbitt firm was established in 1795, and at the time it was awarded the contract to produce the first U.S. government stamped envelopes in 1852 it was said to be the largest firm of manufacturing stationers in the country. Following the death of Mr. Nesbitt in 1869, the firm lost the contract for manufacturing government envelopes, and although it entered bids on succeeding contracts for many years thereafter, it never again was successful.

Issued some time in April 1853, this issued featured the portrait of George Washington, after Houdon's bust. The complete design would appear to be adapted from the "Wyon" essay for the first stamped envelopes of Great Britain.

Watermark No. 1, also No. 1A on EN1. Wmk 1 has the lines horizontal in the background with the letters "U.S. Postals" horizontal.

EN1-EN2 "THREE" within short label with curved ends. Die 1, 13mm wide, 12 varieties.

EN1 *(U1)*

3c red on white	190.	16.
entire	1,200.	25.
entire, wmk No. 1A	—	—

EN2 *(U2)*

3c red on buff	70.	10.
entire	750.	20.

EN3-EN4 "THREE" within short label with straight ends. Die 2, 16mm wide, 3 varieties.

EN3 *(U3)*

3c red on white	680.	35.
entire	3,000.	70.

EN4 *(U4)*

3c red on buff	195.	15.
entire	1,500.	32.

EN5-EN6 "THREE" within short, curved octagonal label, forming the letter 'K'. Dec. 3, 2 varieties.

EN5 *(U5)*

3c red on white	3,500.	360.
entire	12,500.	500.

EN6 *(U6)*

3c red on buff	190.	40.
entire	1,000.	75.

EN7-EN8 "THREE" within wide label with straight ends. Die 4, 25mm wide.

EN7 *(U7)*

3c red on white	500.	80.
entire	6,200.	130.

EN8 *(U8)*

3c red on buff	1,100.	90.
entire	4,500.	95.

Reprints, known in cut squares only, are on vertically laid paper.

EN9-EN10 "THREE" within medium wide label with curved ends. Die 5, 20 mm wide, 20 varieties.

EN9 *(U9)*

3c red on white	18.	2.50
entire	75.	9.00
reprint, cut square only	2.00	

EN10 *(U10)*

3c red on buff	14.	2.25
entire	60.	6.00
reprint, cut square only	2.00	

EN11-EN14 "SIX" within short label with straight ends. Die 6, 4 varieties.

EN11 *(U13)*

6c green on white	175.	100.
entire	300.	150.
reprint, cut square only	—	

EN12 *(U14)*

6c green on buff	135.	65.
entire	235.	115.
reprint, cut square only	200.	

EN13 *(U11)*

6c red on white	90.	60.
entire *	210.	105.
reprint, cut square only	200.	

EN14 *(U12)*

6c red on buff	175.	100.
entire *	300.	150.
reprint, cut square only	200.	

EN15, EN16 *"TEN" within short label with straight ends. Die 7, 16mm wide.*

EN15 *(U15)*

10c green on white	175.	100.
entire	325.	150.

EN16 *(U16)*

10c green on buff	65.	50.
entire	200.	80.

EN17, EN18 *"TEN" within wide label. Die 8.*

EN17 *(U17)*

10c green on white	200.	100.
entire	350.	150.
reprint, cut square only	200.	

EN18 *(U18)*

10c green on buff	100.	65.
entire	170.	80.
Reprint, cut squarely	200.	

Reprints EN9-14, 17, 18, are on white and buff wove or vertically laid paper. Known also only as cut squares.

The buff paper for all envelopes of this series, and throughout the Nesbitt issues, exists in a multitude of shades which extend from a yellow through dark brown. None of these differences were intentional. They merely indicate various batches of paper, all of which were supposed to be "buff." Likewise, there are many shades of green of the 6c and 10c stamps, extending from "yellow green" to "dark green. The interested collector may be advised that the extreme dark shades are less numerous than the pale or yellow shades.

1860. The "Star Die" Series, so-called because of the small stars at either side of the design, which do not appear on any other envelope stamp. The stars of the 1c denomination have five points; those of all other denominations have six points. With this series, 1c envelopes and newspaper wrappers were introduced for the first time. The series also introduced the 3c-plus-1c envelope. This was to provide for the carrier service, the fee for which was one cent, for transporting the letter from the lamp-post letter boxes to the post office. Use of the "compound envelopes" apparently was reserved for large cities and very possibly New York City only.

A very few are known used in Baltimore, Chicago, and a few other cities where carrier service was operated. Usage in any city other than New York are rare and command premium values.

The series was introduced some time during the summer of 1860 (3c envelopes are known used in August) and remained in use for about one year. When the Civil War broke out, steps were taken to replace the issue with a new design. However, the 1c and 3c-plus-1c envelopes continued in use and were not subjected to the general demonetization order.

Envelopes used by Southern states after their secession, as evidenced by cancellation, are scarce and command considerable premium values. Likewise, envelopes of this series overprinted (over the stamp) "CONFEDERATE STATES OF AMERICA" and other suitable indicia, used by the Confederate States Postal Department for official mail, are of considerable interest and value to collectors.

Wrappers. Newspaper wrappers were introduced with this series, and were continued with succeeding series up to 1934, when they were discontinued. Wrappers may be distinguished from envelopes in that they are on paper with either vertical or horizontal laid lines. Envelopes almost invariably are on paper with diagonally laid lines.

EN19-EN23 *Franklin., Period after "POSTAGE", Die 9.*

EN19 *(U19)*

1c blue on buff	28.	13.
entire	55.	25.

EN20

1c blue on orange, wove paper	—	—
entire	—	—

EN21 *(W20)*

1c blue on buff, wrapper	65.	50.
entire	100.	65.

EN22 *(W21)*

1c blue on manila, wrapper	45.	45.
entire	85.	85.

EN23 *(W22)*

1c blue on orange, wrapper	1,800.	—
entire	2,800.	—

EN24, EN25 *Franklin,. Bust touches frame front and back. Die 10.*

EN24 *(U23)*

1c blue on orange	410.	360.
entire	480.	425.

EN25

1c blue on white	—	—

EN26, EN27 *No period after "POSTAGE". Die 11, 2 varieties.*

EN26 *(U24)*
1c blue on amber — —
  entire — —
EN27 *(W25)*
1c blue on manila, wrapper 2,600. 2,000.
  entire *11,000.* 3,800

EN28, EN29 *Washington Die 12.*

EN28 *(U26)*
3c red on white 27. 13.
  entire 37. 23.
  reprint, cut square only 150.
EN29 *(U27)*
3c red on buff 25. 23.
  entire 35. 30.
  reprint, cut square only 150.

Reprints, known in cut squares only, are on vertically laid paper.

EN30, EN31
Franklin Bust does not touch frame

EN30 *(U28)*
3c + 1c red and blue on white 335. 235.
  entire 775. 500.
EN31 *(U29)*
3c + 1c red and blue on buff 250. 210.
  entire 825. 500.

EN32, EN33
Franklin, bust touches frame

EN32
3c + 1c red and blue on white — —
  entire — —
EN33
3c + 1c red and blue on buff — —
  entire — —
  reprint, cut square only 100.

EN34, EN35. *Die 12.*

EN34 *(U30)*
6c red on white 2,000. 1,300.
  entire * 3,700.
  reprint, cut square only 100.
EN35 *(U31)*
6c red on buff 1,700. 950.
  entire * 4,300. 4,500.
  reprint, cut square only 100.

EN36, EN37. *Die 12.*

EN36 *(U32)*
10c green on white 1,000. 350.
  entire 10,000. 475.
  reprint, cut square only 100.
EN37 *(U33)*
10c green on buff 1,000. 275.
  entire 3,800. 475.
  reprint, cut square only 100.

Reprints are cut squares on vertical laid paper.

1861. This series was introduced in the summer of 1861 to replace the previous "Star Die" series, which was declared invalid for postage (except the 1c and 3c-plus-1c envelopes). The series presents a novelty in the higher envelope stamps were printed in more than one color. These also are the first bi-colored postal emissions from the United States. Still another novelty was the introduction of the Letter Sheets which, it has been stated, were issued to provide the soldiers in the field with both stationery and stamps in a single package. The use of these did not prove popular, and they were withdrawn in April 1864.

EN38-EN41. *Die 13.*

EN38 *(U34)*
3c pink on white 18. 5.00
  entire 45. 15.
EN39 *(U35)*
3c pink on buff 16. 6.00
  entire 18. 12.
EN40 *(U36)*
3c pink on blue, letter sheet 70. 55.
  entire 200. 90.
EN41 *(U37)*
3c pink on orange 2,300. —
  entire 3,900. —

EN42, EN43. *Die 14.*

EN42 (U38)
6c pink on white 90. 85.
   entire * 145. 145.
   reprint, cut square only — —
EN43 (U39)
6c pink on buff 65. 60.
   entire * 100. 145.
   reprint, cut square only — —

Reprints, known in cut squares only, are on vertically laid paper.

EN44-EN46. *Die 15.*

EN44 (U40)
10c green on white 28. 28.
   entire 26. 26.
EN45 (U41)
10c green on buff 27. 19.
   entire 60. 35.
EN46
10c green on amber — —
   entire — —

EN47. *Die 16.*

EN47 (U42)
12c brown and red on amber 175. 150.
   entire * 460. 650.

EN48. *Die 16.*

EN48 (U43)
20c blue and red on amber 175. 150.
   entire* 460. 775.

EN49, EN50. *Die 16.*

EN49 (U44)
24c green and red on amber 185. 145.
   entire * 650. 775.
EN50 (U44a)
24c dark green and maroon on
   amber 190. 180.
   entire * 650. *1,000.*

EN51. *Die 16.*

EN51 (U45)
40c red and black on amber 280. 280.
   entire * 850. *1,800.*

1863-65. To provide for the new, higher postal rates on drop letters and circular matter, it was necessary to provide 2c envelopes and wrappers (called "Black Jacks" because of the portrait of Andrew Jackson). At the same time, new designs were adopted for the 3c, 6c, and higher denominations.

EN52, EN53 *Andrew Jackson. Die A, "U.S. POSTAGE" at top. Down stroke of 2" and bottom stroke merge. Die 17.*

Die A

EN52 (U46)
2c black on buff 30. 15.
   entire 60. 30.
EN53 (W47)
2c black on manila, wrapper 42. 38.
   entire 70. 55.

EN54, EN55 *Die B, down stroke of figure "2" joins but does not merge with bottom stroke. Die 18.*

Die B

EN54 (U48)
2c black on buff 1,700. —
   entire 3,600. —
EN55 (U49)
2c black on orange 1,000. —
   entire 2,500. —

EN56-EN59 *Andrew Jackson. Die C, "U.S. POST" at top. Width of desing 24 to 25 mm. Die 19, 25 mm.*

Die C

EN56 (U50)
2c black on buff 10. 9.00
   entire 27. 15.
EN57 (U52)
2c black on orange 12. 8.00
   entire 22. 10.
EN58 (W51)
2c black on buff, wrapper 160. 160.
   entire 260. 260.
EN59 (W53)
2c black on dark manila, wrapper 35. 22.
   entire 120. 60.

EN60-EN64 Die D, "U.S. POST" at top. Die 20, 25 1/2 mm.

Die D

EN60 *(U54)*

2c black on buff	12.	10.
entire	22.	14.

EN61

2c black on amber	—	—
entire	—	—

EN62 *(U56)*

2c black on orange	12.	8.00
entire	17.	11.

EN63 *(W55)*

2c black on buff, wrapper	80.	50.
entire	125.	85.

EN64 *(W57)*

2c black on light manila, wrapper	12.	11.
entire	25.	20.

EN65-EN68. Die 21.

EN65 *(U58)*

3c pink on white	6.00	2.00
entire	10.	3.50

EN66 *(U59)*

3c pink on buff	5.00	1.50
entire	10.	2.50

EN67 *(U60)*

3c brown on white	38.	20.
entire *	75.	75.

EN68 *(U61)*

3c brown on buff	40.	22.
entire *	80.	60.

EN69-EN73. Die 21.

EN69 *(U62)*

6c pink on white	50.	30.
entire *	85.	50.

EN70 *(U63)*

6c pink on buff	30.	25.
entire *	85.	50.

EN71 *(U64)*

6c purple on white	45.	25.
entire	70.	50.

EN72

6c purple on amber	—	—
entire	—	—

EN73 *(U65)*

6c purple on buff	42.	18.
entire	60.	50.

EN74, EN75. Die 22.

EN74 *(U66)*

9c lemon on buff	325.	200.
entire *	500.	500.

EN75 *(U67)*

9c orange on buff	95.	75.
entire *	150.	200.

EN76, EN77. Die 22.

EN76 *(U68)*

12c brown on buff	340.	200.
entire *	500.	*950.*

EN77 *(U69)*

12c red brown on buff	90.	55.
entire *	130.	185.

EN78. Die 22.

EN78 *(U70)*

18c red on buff	90.	85.
entire *	180.	800.

EN79. Die 22.

EN79 *(U71)*

24c blue on buff	95.	80.
entire *	180.	800.

EN80. Die 22.

EN80 *(U72)*

30c green on buff	60.	50.
entire *	150.	800.

EN81. Die 22.

EN81 *(U73)*

40c pink on buff	80.	225.
entire *	250.	*9,300.*

1870. By the end of 1869 there were various designs of stamps in use for our envelopes and wrappers, none of which even closely resembled the designs of the adhesive stamps then in use. To remedy this situation and bring order to confusion, as well as to meet the public clamor against awarding the envelope contract by negotiated bid, the government advertised for bids to supply the envelopes needed for the next four years. One provision of the proposal was that the new envelopes be in denominations of the adhesive stamps then in use and that the designs of the envelope stamps be as near as possible, in color and design, to the adhesive stamps in use. After considerable controversy, the contract was awarded to George H. Reay of Brooklyn, New York, a former associate of Nesbitt. Mr. Reay proceeded to produce what has almost unanimously been considered the most beautiful designs and envelopes our post office ever has issued. The finely executed engravings, the beautiful inks, and careful printing on fine quality paper have earned for them the name "cameos" among collectors.

Although the contract provided that envelopes be manufactured in all denominations from 1c to 90c, there was little use for envelopes in the denominations over 10c. Hence, used examples of these high denominations are practically unknown.

Die A

EN82-EN85 Franklin. Die A, front of the bust is narrow, back rounded, It points at letter "N" of "ONE." The neck forms a straight line between chest and chin. (Compare with EN120 and EN128) Die 23.

EN82 *(U74)*
1c blue on white ... 28. ... 23.
   entire ... 50. ... 28.
EN83 *(U75)*
1c blue on amber ... 28. ... 23.
   entire ... 50. ... 28.
EN84 *(U76)*
1c blue on orange ... 18. ... 10.
   entire ... 26. ... 17.
EN85 *(U77)*
1c blue on manila, wrapper ... 40. ... 25.
   entire ... 70. ... 60.

Die B

EN86-EN89 *Die B the choker around the neck is notched top and bottom*

EN86
1c blue on white ... — ... —
   entire ... — ... —

EN87
1c blue on amber ... — ... —
   entire ... — ... —
EN88
1c blue on orange ... — ... —
   entire ... — ... —
EN89
1c blue on manila, wrapper ... — ... —
   entire ... — ... —

EN90-EN93 Andrew Jackson, the figure "2" at right and left are within small circles. The top loop of "P" of "POSTAGE" is well formed. (Compare with EN142) Die 24.

EN90 *(U78)*
2c brown on white ... 40. ... 13.
   entire ... 50. ... 20.
EN91 *(U79)*
2c brown on amber ... 15. ... 8.00
   entire ... 30. ... 15.
EN92 *(U80)*
2c brown on orange ... 10. ... 7.00
   entire ... 13. ... 10.
EN93 *(W81)*
2c brown on manila, wrapper ... 20. ... 15.
   entire ... 40. ... 30.

EN94-EN96 Small figure "3" within circles. The ponytail projects below the bust. (Compare with EN183 and EN187) Die 25.

EN94 *(U82)*
3c green on white ... 7.00 ... 1.00
   entire ... 12. ... 2.50
EN95 *(U83)*
3c green on amber ... 5.00 ... 2.00
   entire ... 12. ... 3.00
EN96 *(U84)*
3c green on cream ... 8.00 ... 3.00
   entire ... 16. ... 5.00

EN97-EN99 Abraham Lincoln, The neck is long at the back. (Compare with EN211) Die 26.

EN97 *(U85)*
6c red on white ... 17. ... 13.
   entire ... 18. ... 16.
EN98 *(U86)*
6c red on amber ... 22. ... 13.
   entire ... 38. ... 14.
EN99 *(U87)*
6c red on cream ... 27. ... 13.
   entire ... 15. ... 19.

EN97-EN99 exist in a variety of shades from dark red to vermilion.

EN100 Edwin Stanton. The down strokes of the figure "7" do not curl up. (Compare with EN215) Die 27.

EN100 (U88)
7c vermilion on amber	40.	175.
entire	60.	625.

EN101-EN104 Thomas Jefferson, The end of the ponytail does not project. (Compare with EN219) Die 28.

EN101 (U89)
10c olive-black on white	375.	375.
entire	475.	850.

EN102 (U90)
10c olive-black on amber	375.	375.
entire	475.	850.

EN103 (U91)
10c brown on white	50.	70.
entire	70.	75.

EN104 (U92)
10c brown on amber	70.	50.
entire	85.	70.

EN105-EN107 Henry Clay. The hair hides the ear. The nose is long and sharp. (Compare with EN227) Die 29.

EN105 (U93)
12c violet-black on white	100.	65.
entire *	200.	375.

EN106 (U94)
12c violet-black on amber	110.	85.
entire *	180.	500.

EN107 (U95)
12c violet-black on cream	220.	190.
entire *	335.	—

EN108-EN110 Daniel Webster, Hair not parted, cheeks with sideburns. (Compare with EN230) Die 30.

EN108 (U96)
15c red orange on white	60.	60.
entire *	140.	—

EN109 (U97)
15c red orange on amber	140.	170.
entire *	360.	—

EN110 (U98)
15c red orange on cream	235.	210.
entire *	325.	—

EN111-EN113 Winfield Scott. Ornamental lines around inner oval end in squares. (Compare with EN233) Die 31.

EN111 (U99)
24c purple on white	100.	90.
entire	150.	—

EN112 (U100)
24c purple on amber	180.	225.
entire *	335.	—

EN113 (U101)
24c purple on cream	180.	250.
entire *	325.	—

EN108-EN113 exist in various shades.

EN114-EN116 Alexander Hamilton. The horizontal rectangles containing numerals are in alignment. Back of bust ends in narrow point. (Compare with EN236) Die 32.

EN114 (U102)
30c black on white	70.	85.
entire *	280.	—

EN115 (U103)
30c black on amber	180.	210.
entire *	500.	—

EN116 (U104)
30c black on cream	200.	325.
entire *	385.	—

EN117-EN119 Oliver Perry. The shields containing the numerals of value do not project beyond the inner circle. (Compare with EN242) Die 33.

EN117 (U105)
90c carmine on white	135.	190.
entire *	190.	—

EN118 (U106)
90c carmine on amber	300.	335.
entire *	800.	—

EN119 (U107)
90c carmine on cream	335.	550.
entire *	875.	—

1874-76. In 1874, the Post Office advertised for bids to supply envelopes . After considerable legal difficulties with George H. Reay and other bidders, the contract was awarded to the Plimpton Manufacturing Co. Reay refused to surrender his printing dies and, to further embarrass the new contractor, is said to have engaged the services of all known die engravers. The new contractors were thus forced to employ less skilled engravers to try to duplicate the Reay designs. The resulting delay embarrassed the Post Office officials, who were forced to purchase supplies of envelopes from Reay until the new contractors could produce acceptable dies. Several unsuitable designs were accepted to take care of the situation until better dies could be made, which accounts for some of the designs of the lower denomination stamps.

Eventually the Plimpton Manufacturing Co. overcame its difficulties and, in combination with the Morgan Envelope Co., continued to be the successful bidders for the manufacture of envelopes until 1903.

The struggle George H. Reay put up to retain his contract is one of the classic stories of philately. In the end, to prevent his competitors from ever using his dies, it is stated that he finally agreed to turn them over to the authorities, only to instruct his wife to throw them overboard from a Brooklyn-Manhattan ferry. There seems to be much evidence to substantiate this story.

 EN120-EN127 Franklin.. A copy of the Reay design (EN82). Die A, back of bust angles in sharp point. "O" of "POSTAGE" without network. (Compare with EN82) Die 34.

Watermarks 2, 5, 6, 7, 9

Die A

EN120 *(U108)*
1c dark blue on white	85.	40.
entire	100.	80.

EN121 *(U109)*
1c dark blue on amber	100.	67.50
entire	140.	100.

EN122 *(U110)*
1c dark blue on cream	775.	—

EN123 *(U111)*
1c dark blue on orange	17.50	15.
entire	27.50	20.

EN124 *(U112)*
1c dark blue on manila, wrapper	50.	32.50
entire	67.50	60.

EN125 *(U108a)*
1c light blue on white	100.	70.
entire	130.	100.

EN126 *(U111a)*
1c light blue on orange	20.	12.50
entire	25.	20.

EN127
1c light blue on manila, wrapper	—	—
entire	—	—

 EN128-EN141 *A copy of Reay design (EN82). Die B, back of bust is a straight line. Front of bust broad and blunt. "O" in "POSTAGE" with network. (Compare with EN82) Die 35.*

Die B

EN128 *(U113a)*
1c dark blue on white	6.00	6.00
entire	15.	15.

EN129 *(U114a))*
1c dark blue on amber	12.50	8.00
entire	15.	10.

EN130 *(U115a)*
1c dark blue on cream	15.	6.00
entire	22.50	15.

EN131 *(U116a)*
1c dark blue on orange	2.50	3.00
entire	7.00	5.00

EN132 *(W120a)*
1c dark blue on manila, wrapper	6.00	7.50
entire	10.	12.50

EN133 *(U113)*
1c blue on white	1.50	1.00
entire	2.25	1.50

EN134 *(U114)*
1c blue on amber	4.00	3.00
entire	8.00	4.00

EN135 *(U115)*
1c blue on cream	4.50	4.50
entire	7.00	5.00

EN136 *(U116)*
1c blue on orange	.60	.50
entire	.75	.50

EN137 *(U117)*
1c blue on blue	6.00	5.00
entire	8.00	6.00

EN138 *(U118)*
1c blue on fawn	6.00	5.00
entire	7.00	6.00

EN139 *(U119)*
1c blue on manila	6.00	4.00
entire	7.00	6.00

EN140 *(U121)*
1c blue on amber-manila	11.	9.00
entire	13.	10.

EN141 *(W120)*
1c blue on manila, wrapper	1.50	1.50
entire	3.00	2.00

The "dark blue" of EN128-EN132 is very dark, almost indigo. The "blue" of EN133-EN141 is in various shades of "blue," "pale blue," etc.

 EN142-EN147 *Andrew Jackson. A copy of Reay design (EN90). Die A, thin, narrow figure "2" within circles. Top loop of "P" in "POSTAGE" is very narrow. (Compare with EN90) Die 36.*

Watermark 2   Die A

EN142 *(U122)*
2c brown on white	80.	37.
entire	95.	75.

EN143 *(U123)*
2c brown on amber   50.   40.
   entire   80.   65.
EN144 *(U124)*
2c brown on cream   675.   —
EN145 *(U125)*
2c brown on orange   *7,200.*   —
   entire   *15,000.*   —
EN146 *(W126)*
2c brown on manila, wrapper   80.   40.
   entire   85.   60.
EN147 *(W127)*
2c vermilion on manila, wrapper 1,000.   260.
   entire   1,500.   —

EN148-EN151 *A copy of the Reay design (EN90). Die B, Figure "2" within tall ovals. "O" in "TWO" has plain center. Compare with EN90, EN142, and following.) Die 37*

Die B

EN148 *(U128)*
2c brown on white   38.   28.
   entire   75.   65.
EN149 *(U129)*
2c brown on amber   65.   40.
   entire   80.   60.
EN150 *(U130)*
2c brown on cream   22,000.   —

EN151 *(W131)*
2c brown on manila, wrapper   15.   14.
   entire   20.   18.

EN152, EN153 *Andrew Jackson. Die B2, similar to last except tail of left figure "2" touches the oval at right. Die 38*

Die B2

EN152 *(U132)*
2c brown on white   55.   25.
   entire   75.   65.
EN153 *(U133)*
2c brown on amber   160.   55.
   entire   175.   85.

EN154-EN161 *Die B3, same as EN148 but "O" in "TWO" with network in center. Die 39.*

Die B3

EN154 *(U134)*
2c brown on white   600.   100.
   entire   700.   125.
EN155 *(U135)*
2c brown on amber   375.   110.
   entire   500.   130.
EN156 *(U136)*
2c brown on orange   37.50   27.50
   entire   60.   40.
EN157 *(W137)*
2c brown on manila, wrapper   50.   32.50
   entire   65.   35.
EN158 *(U137A)*
2c vermilion on white   17,000.   —
EN159 *(U137B)*
2c vermilion on amber   17,000.   —
EN160 *(U137C)*
2c vermilion on orange   17,000.   —
EN161 *(W138)*
2c vermilion on manila, wrapper 6,000.   —

EN162-EN172 *Andrew Jackson. Die C, short, thick figure "2" within small size ovals. (Compare with preceding and following; also with EN90) Die 40.*

Die C

EN162 *(U139)*
2c brown on white   37.50   35.
   entire   50.   40.
EN163 *(U140)*
2c brown on amber   70.   55.
   entire   85.   60.
EN164 *(W141)*
2c brown on manila, wrapper   35.   25.
   entire   40.   35.
EN165
2c brown red on orange   —   —
   entire   —   —
EN166 *(U145)*
2c vermilion on orange   —   —

Watermarks 2, 5, and 6

EN167 *(U142)*
2c red on white   5.50   2.50
   entire   7.00   4.50
EN168 *(U143)*
2c red on amber   5.00   2.50
   entire   6.00   4.00
EN169 *(U144)*
2c red on cream   11.   5.50
   entire   13.   8.00
EN170 *(U146)*
2c red on blue   120.   28.
   entire   180.   135.
EN171 *(U147)*
2c red on fawn   6.50   4.50
   entire   12.   7.00

EN172 *(W148)*
2c red on manila, wrapper	4.00	4.00
entire	7.00	6.00

Die C1

EN173 *(U149)*
2c red on white	50.	30.
entire	55.	35.

EN174 *(U150)*
2c red on amber	25.	15.
entire	28.	17.

EN175 *(U151)*
2c red on blue	10.	8.00
entire	9.00	10.

EN176 *(U152)*
2c red on fawn	10.	4.00
entire	13.	10.

EN173-EN176 *Die C1, similar to last except ovals containing numerals are much heavier and there is a diagonal white line from about the letter "U" to the outer frame. (Compare with EN162 and EN177) Die 41.*

EN177-EN179 *Andrew Jackson. Die C2, similar to last except there is no diagonal line, and the middle stroke of "N" in "CENTS" is as thin as the vertical strokes. (Compare with EN173) Die 2.*

Die C2

EN177 *(U153)*
2c red on white	50.	25.
entire	70.	27.

EN178 *(U154)*
2c red on amber	250.	75.
entire	335.	100.

EN179 *(W155)*
2c red on manila, wrapper	16.	9.00
entire	40.	12.

EN180-EN182 *Die D, the bottom of the bust forms a complete quarter circle. (Compare with EN162) Die 43.*

Die D

EN180 *(U156)*
2c red on white	525.	100.
entire	625.	300.

EN181 *(U157)*
2c red on amber	16,000.	16,000.
entire	57,000.	—

EN182 *(W158)*
2c red on manila, wrapper	80.	55.
entire	115.	95.

EN183-EN186 *Washington. Copy of Reay design (EN94). Die A, thin lettering. Long thin figures of value within tall ovals. (Compare with EN94 and EN187) Die 44.*

Watermarks 2, 3, 4, 5, 6

Die A

EN183 *(U159)*
3c green on white	18.	5.50
entire	33.	14.

EN184 *(U160)*
3c green on amber	23.	10.
entire	38.	14.

EN185 *(U161)*
3c green on cream	33.	10.
entire	40.	15.

EN186 *(U162)*
3c green on blue	—	—

EN187-EN191. *Die B, thick lettering. Thick figures of value in short ovals. (Compare with EN183 and following.) Die 45.*

Die B

EN187 *(U163)*
3c green on white	1.25	.35
entire	2.25	1.00

EN188 *(U164)*
3c green on amber	1.50	.75
entire	2.50	1.25

EN189 *(U165)*
3c green on cream	8.00	7.00
entire	12.	8.50

EN190 *(U166)*
3c green on blue	8.00	5.00
entire	13.	8.50

EN191 *(U167)*
3c green on fawn	5.00	3.00
entire	8.00	4.00

EN192-EN195 *Washington. Similar to last. Die C, the top of the head is flat at back and there is a notch above and below the knot of the ponytail. (Compare with EN187) Die 46.*

EN192 *(U168)*
3c green on white	460.	45.
entire	1,800.	75.

EN193 *(U169)*
3c green on amber	190.	100.
entire	280.	120.

EN194 *(U170)*
3c green on blue	8,000.	1,800.
entire	17,000.	4,300.

EN195 *(U171)*
   3c green on fawn   25,000.   1,700.
      entire   —   13,000.

EN196-EN200 Zachary Taylor. Die A, the numerals "5" with short thick top strokes. (Compare with EN201) Die 47A.

Watermarks 2, 5

Die A

EN196 *(U172)*
   5c blue on white   10.   8.00
      entire   12.   9.00
EN197 *(U173)*
   5c blue on amber   10.   8.00
      entire   12.   11.
EN198 *(U174)*
   5c blue on cream   82.   38.
      entire *   105.   75.
EN199 *(U175)*
   5c blue on blue   15.   13.
      entire   18.   16.
EN200 *(U176)*
   5c blue on fawn   100.   50.
      entire *   175.   —

EN201-EN205 Zachary Taylor. Die B, the numerals "5" with long thin top strokes (Compare with EN196) Die 47B.

Die B

EN201 *(U177)*
   5c blue on white   6.00   5.50
      entire   11.   13.
EN202 *(U178)*
   5c blue on amber   5.50   5.50
      entire   13.   14.
EN203 *(U178A)*
   5c blue on cream   2,500.   —
      entire *   4,200.   —
EN204 *(U179)*
   5c blue on blue   13.   8.00
      entire   16.   11.
EN205 *(U180)*
   5c blue on fawn   88.   43.
      entire *   110.   80.

EN206-EN210 James Garfield Die 59.

Watermarks 5, 6

EN206 *(U222)*
   5c brown on white   3.00   2.00
      entire   5.50   5.00
EN207 *(U223)*
   5c brown on amber   4.00   2.25
      entire   7.50   6.00
EN208 *(U224)*
   5c brown on buff   90.   60.
      entire   120.   —
EN209 *(U225)*
   5c brown on blue   50.   30.
      entire   65.   40.
EN210 *(U226)*
   5c brown on fawn   200.   —
      entire *   250.   —

EN211-EN214 Abraham Lincoln. Copy of Reay design (EN97). The neck is short at the back. Lock of hair curves upward from forehead. (Compare with EN97) Die 48.

Watermarks 2, 3, 4, 5, 6

EN211 *(U181)*
   6c red on white   6.00   6.00
      entire   10.   8.00
EN212 *(U182)*
   6c red on amber   10.   6.00
      entire   16.   11.
EN213 *(U183)*
   6c red on cream   16.   10.
      entire   20.   16.
EN214 *(U184)*
   6c red on fawn   17.   9.00
      entire *   25.   14.

EN215, EN216 Edwin Stanton. Copy of Reay design (EN100). The down strokes of the figure "7" curve sharply upward. (Compare with EN100) Die 49.

Watermark 2

EN215 *(U185)*
   7c vermilion on white   1,500.   —
EN216 *(U186)*
   7c vermilion on amber   90.   55.
      entire   120.   —

EN217, EN218 Thomas Jefferson. Die A, very large head, called the "booby-head." (Compare with EN101 and following) Die 50.

Die A

EN217 *(U187)*
   10c brown on white   30.   17.
      entire   55.   —

EN218 (U188)
10c brown on amber	55.	25.
entire	80.	–

EN219-EN226 *Copy of Reay design (EN101). Die B, the end of the ponytail projects prominently and the head tilts downward. (Compare with EN101) Die 51.*

EN219 (U189)
10c brown on white	6.00	4.00
entire	10.	8.00

EN220 (U190)
10c brown on amber	8.00	6.00
entire	10.	8.00

EN221 (U191)
10c brown on buff	10.	7.00
entire	11.	8.00

EN222 (U192)
10c brown on blue	12.	8.00
entire	14.	9.00

EN219-EN222 exist in various shades.

EN223 (U193)
10c brown on manila	12.	8.00
entire	13.	13.
a. red brown on manila	12.	9.00
a. entire	15.	15.

EN224 (U194)
10c brown on amber-manila	12.	7.00
entire *	15.	13.
a. red brown on amber-manila	16.	7.00
a. entire	22.	17.

EN225
10c ocher yellow on white	1,050.	—
entire *	1,500.	—

EN226
10c ocher yellow on amber	1,050.	—
entire *	1,500.	—

EN227-EN229 *Henry Clay. Copy of Reay design (EN105). The head is round and small. The ear is clearly defined. (Compare with EN105) Die 52.*

Watermark 2

EN227 (U195)
12c violet black on white	150.	75.
entire *	160.	—

EN228 (U196)
12c violet black on amber	160.	135.
entire *	235.	—

EN229 (U197)
12c violet black on cream	175.	145.
entire *	720.	—

Watermarks 2, 5

EN230-EN232 *Daniel Webster. Copy of Reay design (EN108). Bust without sideburns. The hair parted. (Compare with EN108) Die 53.*

EN230 (U198)
15c orange on white	40.	30.
entire *	80.	38.

EN231 (U199)
15c orange on amber	120.	90.
entire *	175.	—

EN232 (U200)
15c orange on cream	335.	335.
entire *	825.	—

EN233-EN235 *Winfield Scott. Copy of Reay design (EN111). The ornaments around the inner oval end in points. (Compare with EN111) Die 54.*

Watermark 2

EN233 (U201)
24c purple on white	150.	110.
entire *	220.	—

EN234 (U202)
24c purple on amber	150.	110.
entire *	220.	—

EN235 (U203)
24c purple on cream	150.	110.
entire *	700.	—

EN236-EN241 *Alexander Hamilton. Copy of Reay design (EN114). The octagonal labels containing the figures of value are not in alignment; the one at the right tilts sharply downward. (Compare with EN114.) For brown stamps in this design, issued in 1887, see EN375-EN380. Die 55.*

Watermarks 2, 5, 6, 7, 9, 10

EN236 (U204)
30c black on white	55.	30.
entire *	65.	65.

EN237 (U205)
30c black on amber	70.	55.
entire *	125.	275.

EN237A (U206)
30c black on cream (see note)	400.	380.
entire *	725.	—

The only way to distinguish EN237A and EN243A — which both appear on cream paper — from the same designs on buff paper (EN238 and EN244) is to examine the watermark. Wmk 2 signifies cream paper.

EN238 (U207)
30c black on buff	95.	75.
entire	135.	—

EN239 *(U208)*
   30c black on blue   100.   75.
     entire   110.   —
EN240 *(U209)*
   30c black on manila   90.   75.
     entire   135.   —
EN241 *(U210)*
   30c black on amber-manila   110.   75.
     entire   140.   —

EN242-EN247 Oliver Perry. Copy of Reay design (EN117). The shields containing the numerals of value project considerably within the inner circle.

(Compare with EN117.) For purple stamps of same design, issued in 1887, see EN381-EN386 Die 56.

Watermarks 2, 6, 7, 9

EN242 *(U211)*
   90c carmine on white   110.   75.
     entire *   120.   85.
EN243 *(U212)*
   90c carmine on amber   150.   195.
     entire *   235.   —
EN243A *(U213)*
   90c carmine on cream (see
      note following EN237A)   1,100.   —
     entire *   2,000.   —
EN244 *(U214)*
   90c carmine on buff   200.   230.
     entire   235.
EN245 *(U215)*
   90c carmine on blue   175.   210.
     entire   235.
EN246 *(U216)*
   90c carmine on manila   115.   210.
     entire *   195.
EN247 *(U217)*
   90c carmine on amber-manila   110.   175.
     entire *   195.

1876. Centennial Issue. Just before the great Centennial Exposition at Philadelphia in 1876, the Plimpton Morgan Envelope Co. had developed a machine that would gum the top back flap of the envelopes. Previously the machines in use would perform all operations of folding, printing and gluing together, but the gum on the top back flaps had to be applied by hand. To publicize this mechanical achievement, the Plimpton Co. requested permission to demonstrate its new machine at the exposition. The Post Office consented and provided that a specially designed stamp should be used to commemorate the exposition, thus authorizing the first commemorative postage stamp of the world. Two envelopes were authorized: The small would have the stamp printed in green, the slightly larger one would have the stamp in red. Also, paper bearing a special watermark was ordered for these

envelopes. The advance demand proved so great that the envelopes were manufactured at Hartford, Connecticut, as well as on the demonstration machine at the exposition. In all, 8,000,000 envelopes were issued, approximately 4,000,000 of each size.

EN248 *(U218)*
   3c green on white   50.   13.
     entire   60.   35.

EN248, EN249 Old and new methods of carrying the post. There is a single line forming the bottom of the label containing the word "POSTAGE." (Compare with EN250) Die 57.

EN249 *(U219)*
   3c red on white   55.   25.
     entire   70.   45.

EN250, EN251 The line at the bottom of the label containing the word "POSTAGE" is made up of two thin lines which sometimes merge. Die 58.

EN250 *(U220)*
   3c green on white   55.   18.
     entire   80.   50.
EN251 *(U221)*
   3c red on white   19,500.   —
     entire   28,000.   —

1883-86. With the change of the first class rate from 3c to 2c, new envelopes of the 2c and 4c denomination were called for and new designs were adopted. The first design submitted was not considered entirely satisfactory, but so that envelopes would be available on time, it was approved. In the meantime, the new approved die was prepared and put into use in November, just one month after the new envelopes had been issued. Despite its short life, the first design (EN252-EN255) is not rare;apparently a very large supply was made. In May 1884, the color of the 2c envelope stamp was changed from carmine to brown to coincide with the color of the 2c adhesive stamp then in use. It is stated that the brown ink, because of its chemical construction, destroyed the printing dies and much recutting had to be done.

EN252-EN255 Washington. Background of frame composed of scroll work ending in points around inner circle. Die 60.

Watermarks 5, 6

EN252 (U227)
2c red on white	3.00	1.75
entire	7.00	2.00
a. brown on white (error),		
entire	2,250.	—

EN253 (U228)
2c red on amber	5.00	2.00
entire	8.00	3.50

EN254 (U229)
2c red on blue	7.00	5.00
entire	9.00	6.00

EN255 (U230)
2c red on fawn	7.00	3.50
entire	13.	4.00

EN256-EN265 *Four clear ornamental wavy lines within the circular frame of the design. (Compare with EN266 and EN302) Die 61.*

Nov. 1883

EN256 (U231)
2c red on white	3.00	1.50
entire	7.00	3.00

EN257 (U232)
2c red on amber	4.00	2.50
entire	8.50	4.00

EN258 (U233)
2c red on blue	7.00	5.00
entire	11.	6.00

EN259 (U234)
2c red on fawn	5.00	3.00
entire	7.00	4.00

EN260 (W235)
2c red on manila, wrapper	8.00	4.00
entire	13.	8.50

May 1884

EN261 (U260)
2c brown on white	3.00	1.50
entire	7.00	3.00

EN262 (U261)
2c brown on amber	4.00	3.00
entire	8.00	4.00

EN263 (U262)
2c brown on blue	7.00	4.00
entire	11.	6.00

EN264 (U263)
2c brown on fawn	5.00	3.00
entire	7.00	4.00

EN265 (W264)
2c brown on manila, wrapper	8.00	4.00
entire	13.	8.00

June 1884

EN266 (U236)
2c red on white	6.00	4.00
entire	9.00	6.00

EN266-EN274 *Washington. Retouched dies. Similar to EN256-2654 but the pairs of wavy lines are no longer continuous, but merge at various points. Die 62.*

EN267 (U237)
2c red on amber	10.	7.00
entire	15.	10.

EN268 (U238)
2c red on blue	13.	8.00
entire	20.	10.

EN269 (U239)
2c red on fawn	10.	7.00
entire	13.	8.00

EN270 (U265)
2c brown on white	13.	5.00
entire	18.	10.

EN271 (U266)
2c brown on amber	60.	35.
entire	18.	10.

EN272 (U267)
2c brown on blue	12.	6.00
entire	13.	8.00

EN273 (U268)
2c brown on fawn	10.	9.00
entire	14.	13.

EN274 (W269)
2c brown on manila, wrapper	18.	13.
entire	24.	13.

EN275-EN277 *There are 3 1/2 links above the left figure "2" Die 63.*

EN275 (U240)
2c red on white	50.	35.
entire	65.	50.

EN276 (U241)
2c red on amber	600.	300.
entire	875.	525.

EN277 (U242)
2c red on fawn	—	6,500.

EN278-EN284 *Washington. There are two links below the right figure "2." Center link below left figure "2" touches at left. Die 64.*

EN278 (U243)
2c red on white	65.	45.
entire	85.	70.

EN279 (U244)
2c red on amber	120.	65.
entire	135.	85.

EN280 (U245)
2c red on blue	270.	110.
entire	400.	135.

EN281 *(U246)*
2c red on fawn	280.	110.
entire	350.	200.

EN282 *(U270)*
2c brown on white	80.	35.
entire	180.	90.

EN283 *(U271)*
2c brown on amber	180.	90.
entire	260.	200.

EN284 *(U272)*
2c brown on fawn	2,100.	925.
entire	4,000.	2,100.

EN285-EN291 *A round "O" in "TWO," upright of letter "T" in "TWO" slants to right. Die 65.*

EN285 *(U247)*
2c red on white	1,200.	300.
entire	1,600.	650.

EN286 *(U248)*
2c red on amber	2,100.	775.
entire	3,000.	1,000.

EN287 *(U249)*
2c red on fawn	650.	350.
entire	950.	450.

EN288 *(U273)*
2c brown on white	140.	70.
entire	160.	225.

EN289 *(U274)*
2c brown on amber	160.	70.
entire	180.	90.

EN290 *(U275)*
2c brown on blue	—	5,000.

EN291 *(U276)*
2c brown on fawn	775.	625.
entire	1,100.	750.

Watermarks 6, 7
Die A
Oct. 1883

EN292-EN297 *Andrew Jackson. Die A, the numeral "4" at left is narrow (2 3/4 mm) and has a sharp point. (Compare with EN298) Die 66A.*

EN292 *(U250)*
4c green on white	3.00	3.00
entire	5.00	5.00

EN293 *(U251)*
4c green on amber	4.00	3.00
entire	6.00	5.00

EN294 *(U252)*
4c green on buff	7.00	7.00
entire	11.	10.

EN295 *(U253)*
4c green on blue	7.00	6.00
entire	10.	7.00

EN296 *(U254)*
4c green on manila	8.00	6.00
entire	11.	11.

EN297 *(U255)*
4c green on amber-manila	16.	9.00
entire	23.	12.

EN298-EN301 *Die B, the numeral "4" at left is wide (3 mm) and has a blunt point. Die 66 B.*

Die B

EN298 *(U256)*
4c green on white	5.00	4.00
entire	11.	6.00

EN299 *(U257)*
4c green on amber	10.	6.00
entire	15.	9.00

EN300 *(U258)*
4c green on manila	10.	6.00
entire	14.	10.

EN301 *(U259)*
4c green on amber-manila	9.00	6.00
entire	12.	9.00

1884, July. The previous printing dies having proved completely unsatisfactory, new designs were introduced in July 1884. The principal change consisted of simplifying the old design by removing one pair of the wavy lines from the inner and outer circle.

At first a few impressions were made in red ink and these are comparatively scarce. Later the stamps were printed in brown ink.

EN302-EN313 *Washington. Only two ornamental wavy lines in frame. (Compare with EN256) and the back of the bust forms an angle. (Compare with EN314) Die 67.*

Watermark 6, 7, 9, 10

EN302 *(U285)*
2c red on white	500.	—
entire	1,200.	—

EN303 *(U286)*
2c red on blue	225.	—
entire	275.	—

EN304 *(W287)*
2c red on manila, wrapper	100.	—
entire	150.	—

EN305
2c lake on white	25.	20.
entire	30.	24.

EN306 *(U277)*
2c brown on white	.50	.25
entire	.75	.30

EN307 (U278)
2c brown on amber	.65	.45
entire	1.25	.55

EN308 (U279)
2c brown on buff	3.00	2.00
entire	4.00	2.50

EN309 (U280)
2c brown on blue	2.50	.50
entire	3.50	1.75

EN310 (U281)
2c brown on fawn	3.00	2.00
entire	3.50	2.25

EN311 (U282)
2c brown on manila	9.00	3.50
entire	13.	5.00

EN312 (U284)
2c brown on amber-manila	6.00	6.00
entire	10.	7.00

EN313 (W283)
2c brown on manila, wrapper	5.25	5.00
entire	7.00	6.00

EN314-EN318 *The back of the bust is rounded. (Compare with EN302.) Die 68.*

EN314 (U288)
2c brown on white	150.	40.
entire	375.	70.

EN315 (U289)
2c brown on amber	14.	12.
entire	18.	14.

EN316 (U290)
2c brown on blue	700.	125.
entire	775.	225.

EN317 (U291)
2c brown on fawn	20.	17.50
entire	27.50	20.

EN318 (W292)
2c brown on manila, wrapper	20.	15.
entire	22.50	18.

1886-87. Letter sheet. Despite the abortive attempt in 1861 to popularize letter sheets, Congress authorized the Postmaster General, by an Act of March 3, 1879, to make letter sheets available to the public. It stipulated, however, that no royalty should be paid for any patents on such devices. This caused the Postmaster General much difficulty, since existing letter sheets had been patented. Eventually an arrangement was made with the American Bank Note Co. to produce letter sheets under a patent owned by the United States Postal Card Company. The sheets again proved unpopular and were discontinued in 1894.

EN319 *Ulysses
S. Grant*

Letter sheet watermark

Unwatermarked or watermark "US"

EN319 (U293)
2c green on white	—	—
entire	22.	11.

Letter sheets exist with three varieties of perforations at top: 83, 41, or 33, and with guide perforations for folding at either right or left. Watermarked sheets are inscribed "Series 1" through "Series 7" and always have 41 perforations at top.

1887-99. The new contract in 1886 again changed the designs and colors of the stamps on envelopes . The contractor, as before, was the Plimpton Morgan envelope Co. In 1894 the contractor lost the contract to James Purcell, whose factory was at Holyoke, Mass. Purcell had great difficulty completeing the terms of his contract and soon was forced to enter into negotiations with the Plimpton Morgan Co. to complete the work. Purcell's work pricnpally is noted by the 1c envelopes, which he printed in a very rare dark blue ink, the 4c envelopes which he printed in a scarlet and sometimes orange ink, and the 5c envelopes for which he prepared a new printing die on which the neckline of Gen. Grant had been eliminated (EN373-374).

 EN320 *Franklin. The bust leans forward and has a tremendously large lower portion. This is a the so-called "Tiffany Die," which was rejected.*

EN320
1c blue on white	—	—
entire	—	—

Watermarks 7, 8, 9, 10, 12

EN321-EN331 *The illustration at the right shows the "Spur Die," a sharp "spur" projecting downward from lower portion of the bust. Die 69 at left.*

EN321 *(U294)*

1c blue on white	.60	.25
entire	.80	.35
a. "Spur Die"	—	—
entire	—	—

EN322 *(U296)*

1c blue on amber	3.00	1.50
entire	5.00	4.00
a. "Spur Die"	—	—
entire	—	—

EN323 *(U298)*

1c blue on buff	2,000.	—
entire	4,100.	—
a. "Specimen"	—	—

EN324 *(U299)*

1c blue on blue	3,300.	—
entire	4,400.	—

EN325 *(U300)*

1c blue on manila	.65	.35
entire	1.00	.50

EN326 *(U304)*

1c blue on amber-manila	5.00	4.00
entire	7.00	6.00

EN327 *(W301)*

1c blue on manila, wrapper	.45	.30
entire	1.25	.50

EN328 *(U295)*

1c dark blue on white	7.00	3.00
entire	10.	7.00

EN329 *(U297)*

1c dark blue on amber	45.	25.
entire	50.	30.

EN330 *(U302)*

1c dark blue on manila	20.	9.00
entire	30.	20.

EN331 *(W303)*

1c dark blue on manila, wrapper	12.	10.
entire	22.	13.

EN338-EN343 *Washington. Die A, the bust points at the third colored tooth of the frame. "G" in "POSTAGE" has no cross bar. (Compare with EN344) Die 70.*

Die A

EN338 *(U305)*

2c green on white	9.00	8.00
entire	18.	11.

EN339 *(U306)*

2c green on amber	18.	12.
entire	25.	13.

EN340 *(U307)*

2c green on buff	65.	30.
entire	90.	35.

EN341 *(U308)*

2c green on blue	2,700.	700.
entire	—	4,200.

EN342 *(U309)*

2c green on manila	1,750.	500.
entire	1,500.	500.

EN343 *(U310)*

2c green on amber-manila	1,500.	550.
entire	4,750.	1,800.

EN344-EN350 *Washington. Die B, bust points between first and second colored teeth of frame. "G" in "POSTAGE" has a cross bar. This is common die of the series. (Compare with EN338) The illustration at right shows the cap on "2" variety. Die 71, 71b.*

Die B

EN344 *(U311)*

2c green on white	.30	.25
entire	.60	.25
v. Cap on "2"	—	—
entire	—	—

EN345 *(U312)*

2c green on amber	.45	.25
entire	.60	.30
v. Cap on "2"	—	—
entire	—	—

EN346 *(U313)*

2c green on buff	.60	.25
entire	1.10	.45
v. Cap on "2"	—	—
entire	—	—

EN347 *(U314)*

2c green on blue	.60	.25
entire	1.10	.40
v. Cap on "2"	—	—
entire	—	—

EN348 *(U315)*

2c green on manila	2.00	.60
entire	2.50	1.50
v. Cap on "2"	—	—
entire	—	—

EN349 *(U317)*

2c green on amber-manila	2.50	2.00
entire	5.00	2.50
v. Cap on "2"	—	—
entire	—	—

EN350 *(W316)*

2c green on manila, wrapper	3.00	2.50
entire	7.00	6.00

EN351-EN356 *Washington. Die C, similar to last, but head larger and well rounded. The ear is formed by two lines and there are two locks of hair in front of it. (Compare with EN344) Die 72.*

Die C

EN351 *(U318)*

2c green on white	100.	13.
entire	125.	40.

EN352 *(U319)*

2c green on amber	125.	20.
entire	135.	40.

EN353 *(U320)*

2c green on buff	150.	40.
entire	160.	60.

EN354 *(U321)*

2c green on blue	175.	60.
entire	185.	65.

EN355 *(U322)*

2c green on manila	125.	65.
entire	160.	90.

EN356 *(U323)*

2c green on amber-manila	325.	80.
entire	375.	120.

 EN357-EN362 *Die D, similar to EN344 but the bust has no ear.*

Die D

EN357

2c green on white	—	—
entire	—	—

EN358

2c green on amber	—	—
entire	—	—

EN359

2c green on buff	—	—
entire	—	—

EN360

2c green on blue	—	—
entire	—	—

EN361

2c green on manila	—	—
entire	—	—

EN362

2c green on amber-manila	—	—
entire	—	—

 EN363-EN368 *Andrew Jackson. The scarlet and orange shades of the 4c stamps were manufactured by James Purcell, who obtained the contract in 1894 but due to lack of adequate machinery shortly thereafter was forced to sublet his contract to the previous manufacturer. Die 73.*

EN363 *(U324)*

4c carmine on white	1.65	1.25
entire	3.25	1.50
a. scarlet	2.25	1.50
entire	5.00	4.00
b. orange	—	—
entire	—	—

EN364 *(U325)*

4c carmine on amber	3.00	2.00
entire	5.00	3.50
a. scarlet	3.00	3.25
entire	6.00	4.00
b. orange	—	—
entire	—	—

EN365 *(U326)*

4c carmine on buff	6.00	3.00
entire	9.00	4.00

EN366 *(U327)*

4c carmine on blue	5.00	4.50
entire	7.00	6.00

EN367 *(U328)*

4c carmine on manila	7.00	6.00
entire	9.00	7.50

EN368 *(U329)*

4c carmine on amber-manila	5.00	3.50
entire	3.00	4.00

 EN369-EN372 *Ulysses S. Grant. There is a space between the chin and the coat. (Compare with EN373) Die 74.*

EN369 *(U330)*

5c blue on white	4.00	3.50
entire	6.00	10.

EN370 *(U331)*

5c blue on amber	4.50	2.50
entire	8.00	13.

EN371 *(U332)*

5c blue on buff	5.00	4.00
entire	10.	15.

EN372 *(U333)*

5c blue on blue	6.00	5.00
entire	10.	12.

 EN373, EN374 *Ulysses S. Grant. There is no space between the chin and the coat. (Compare with EN369) Die 75.*

EN373 *(U334)*

5c blue on white	10.	5.00
entire	14.	16.

EN374 *(U335)*

5c blue on amber	10.	6.00
entire	15.	16.

 EN375-EN380 *Alexander Hamilton. Reissue of old design Die 55.*

EN375 *(U336)*

30c red brown on white	40.	43.
entire	50.	225.

EN376 *(U337)*

30c red brown on amber	45.	55.
entire	55.	325.

EN377 *(U338)*

30c red brown on buff	40.	45.
entire	50.	360.

EN378 *(U339)*

30c red brown on blue	40.	45.
entire	50.	350.

EN379 *(U340)*

30c red brown on manila	45.	45.
entire	50.	275.

EN380 *(U341)*

30c red brown on amber-manila	50.	30.
entire	55.	275.

EN381-EN386 *Oliver Perry. Re-issue of old design. Die 56.*

EN381 *(U342)*

90c purple on white	65.	70.
entire	80.	450.

EN382 *(U343)*

90c purple on amber	75.	75.
entire	100.	450.

EN383 *(U344)*

90c purple on buff	75.	80.
entire	100.	450.

EN384 *(U345)*

90c purple on blue	75.	85.
entire	120.	450.

EN385 *(U346)*

90c purple on manila	80.	85.
entire	120.	450.

EN386 *(U347)*

90c purple on amber-manila	90.	90.
entire	120.	450.

EN375-EN380 are known in various shades of brown. EN381-EN386 exist in both dark and bright purple.

1893. Columbian Exposition Issue. To commemorate the Columbian Exposition, the Post Office Department ordered a special series of stamped envelopes in the 1c, 2c, 4c, 5c, and 10c denominations. For reasons not known, the 4c envelope never was issued.

The designs of all denominations are identical, except in the face value of the stamp. Four varieties are widely recognized by collectors:

— A period after "CENT"; a meridian behind
  head of Columbus
— A period; no meridian
— No period; a meridian
— No period; no meridian.

The first three will be found on the 1c stamps. All four are found on the 2c stamps; only the first two on the 5c stamps. The 10c stamp exists only without the period, but with the meridian.

EN387-EN390 *Christopher Columbus, "Liberty," American eagle. Designs identical except for face value. Die 76.*

Watermark 11

EN387 *(U348)*

1c blue on white	2.00	1.50
entire	3.00	1.75

EN388 *(U349)*

2c violet on white	1.50	.75
entire	2.50	.75
a. slate (error)	1,900.	—
entire	—	—

EN389 *(U350)*

5c brown on white	9.00	8.00
entire*	15.	12.
a. slate (error)	750.	750.
entire	800.	1,200.

EN390 *(U351)*

10c slate on white	40.	30.
entire	60.	45.

1899. With this issue all denominations of stamps above 5c values were discontinued; envelopes in higher denominations had been found to be of little use or in little demand. This was the last issue manufactured by the Plimpton Morgan Envelope Co.

EN391-EN396 *Franklin. Die 77.*

Watermarks 12, 13

EN391 *(U352)*

1c green on white	.75	.25
entire	1.50	.75

EN392 *(U353)*

1c green on amber	4.75	1.50
entire	7.75	3.00

EN393 *(U354)*

1c green on buff	10.	4.00
entire	13.50	4.00

EN394 *(U355)*

1c green on blue	10.	7.00
entire	13.	20.

EN395 *(U356)*

1c green on manila	2.00	1.00
entire	6.50	2.50

EN396 *(W357)*

1c green on manila, wrapper	2.00	1.00
entire	8.75	3.00

EN397-EN400 *Washington. Die A, point of bust broad and ends over the left corner of the shield containing numeral. (Compare with EN401) Die 78.*

EN397 *(U358)*
2c carmine on white	4.00	2.00
entire	8.50	3.00

EN398 *(U359)*
2c carmine on amber	17.50	10.
entire	27.50	12.

EN399 *(U360)*
2c carmine on buff	17.50	8.00
entire	30.	9.00

EN400 *(U361)*
2c carmine on blue	60.	30.
entire	75.	35.

EN401-EN405 *George Washington. Die B, point of bust elongated and points to the second tooth. Hair tied with ribbon at back. (Compare with EN397 and following) Die 79.*

Die B

EN401 *(U362)*
2c carmine on white	.30	.25
entire	.75	.50

EN402 *(U363)*
2c carmine on amber	1.25	.25
entire	3.25	.75

EN403 *(U364)*
2c carmine on buff	1.00	.25
entire	2.75	.75

EN404 *(U365)*
2c carmine on blue	1.25	.50
entire	3.50	1.75

EN405 *(W366)*
2c carmine on manila, wrapper	6.00	3.00
entire	12.50	6.00

EN406-EN409 *Die C, re-cut die. Similar to last but the hair is without ribbon. Many varieties of the re-cutting exist, some of which show the hair in flowing curves; some with hair pulled straight down; and others with the ribbon obliterated with short lines. (Compare with EN401) Die 80.*

Die C

EN406 *(U367)*
2c carmine on white	5.00	2.50
entire	9.50	7.00

EN407 *(U368)*
2c carmine on amber	12.00	8.00
entire	22.50	15.

EN408 *(U369)*
2c carmine on buff	25.	15.
entire	35.	17.50

EN409 *(U370)*
2c carmine on blue	10.	7.00
entire	22.50	15.

EN410, EN411 *Abraham Lincoln. Die A, bust pointed and undraped. Inner oval with teeth. (Compare with following) Die 81.*

There are many shades for EN406-EN409

Die A

EN410 *(U371)*
4c brown on white	17.	12.
entire	30.	15.

EN411 *(U372)*
4c brown on amber	17.	12.
entire	30.	25.

EN412 *Die B, bust is draped and point broad. Inner oval with teeth. Die 82.*

Die B

EN412 *(U373)*
4c brown on white	5,000.	325.
entire	5,700.	—

EN413-EN415 *Abraham Lincoln. Die C, no teeth in inner oval. Bust broad and draped. Die 83.*

Watermarks 12, 13, 14

Die C

EN413 *(U374)*
4c brown on white	10.	7.00
entire	25.	11.

EN414 *(U375)*
4c brown on amber	37.50	15.
entire	50.	20.

EN415 *(W376)*
4c brown on manila, wrapper	15.	8.00
entire	25.	12.50

EN416, EN417 *Ulysses S. Grant. Die 84.*

Watermark 13

EN416 *((U377)*
5c blue on white	10.	9.50
entire	14.	13.

EN417 *(U378)*

5c blue on amber	13.	10.
entire	22.50	15.

1903. This contract is the first for the Hartford Manufacturing Co. as producers of stamped envelopes.

Watermarks 13, 14

EN418-EN423 *Franklin. Die 85.*

EN418 *(U379)*

1c green on white	.50	.25
entire	1.25	.50

EN419 *(U380)*

1c green on amber	12.	3.00
entire	18.50	4.00

EN420 *(U381)*

1c green on buff	13.	3.00
entire	17.	4.00

EN421 *(U382)*

1c green on blue	13.	3.00
entire	20.	4.00

EN422 *(U383)*

1c green on manila	3.00	1.50
entire	4.50	2.00

EN423 *(W384)*

1c green on manila, wrapper	1.50	.75
entire	2.00	1.00

EN424-EN428 *Washington. A short and two long lines of colorless shading are found in the right side of the ribbon containing the value. (Compare with EN434)*

EN424 *(U385)*

2c carmine on white	.50	.25
entire	1.00	.50

EN425 *(U386)*

2c carmine on amber	1.75	.50
entire	3.75	1.50

EN426 *(U387)*

2c carmine on buff	2.00	.50
entire	2.50	.75

EN427 *(U388)*

2c carmine on blue	1.50	.75
entire	3.25	.75

EN428 *(W389)*

2c carmine on manila, wrapper	15.	8.00
entire	22.50	14.

EN429-EN431 *Ulysses S. Grant*

EN429 *(U390)*

4c brown on white	20.	12.
entire *	27.50	15.

EN430 *(U391)*

4c brown on amber	20.	12.
entire *	27.50	15.

EN431 *(U392)*

4c brown on manila, wrapper	18.	11.
entire *	25.	15.

EN432, EN433 *Abraham Lincoln*

EN432 *(U393)*

5c blue on white	17.	10.
entire	25.	17.50

EN433 *(U394)*

5c blue on amber	18.	13.
entire	25.	20

EN434-EN438
Washington. Re-cut die. The colorless shading lines at the right of the ribbon containing the value are all short. Lettering throughout is heavier. (Compare with EN424)

EN434 *(U395)*

2c carmine on white	.50	.25
entire	1.00	.50

EN435 *(U396)*

2c carmine on amber	7.00	.75
entire	12.	2.00

EN436 *(U397)*

2c carmine on buff	6.00	2.00
entire	7.50	2.00

EN437 *(U398)*

2c carmine on blue	4.00	2.00
entire	6.00	2.50

EN438 *(U399)*

2c carmine on manila, wrapper	12.	7.00
entire	22.50	12.50

1907-16. New contractors, The Mercantile Corp., brought a change from Hartford, Connecticut, where envelopes had been manufactured since 1874, to Dayton, Ohio. In 1915 the Middle West Supply Co. obtained the contract and in 1929 the International Envelope Co. was the successful bidder. These changes did not change the site of manufacture itself, and appear to be the merger of the corporations named. From 1929 until 1965, envelopes were manufactured by the International Envelope Co. at Dayton, Ohio.

EN439-EN444 Franklin. Die A, wide "D" in "UNITED." (Compare with EN445 and following)

Watermarks 12, 14, 15, 16, 17, 18, and as follows:

Beginning in 1915, laid paper was dropped for all envelopes in favor of wove paper and from then on all watermarks were of the same or similar design as illustrated. The year was changed every four years to mark each new contract. The various arrangement of the dates, at top, bottom, or diagonal, is identification of the paper manufacturer. From 1929 until 1958, the diagonally placed numerals identified "Extra quality" paper. Since 1958, all envelopes are of a single quality paper.

Typical examples of watermarks 1915 to 1960. (Reduced in size)

Die A

EN439 *(U400)*
1c green on white .30 .25
entire .50 .40
v. "NITED" instead of "UNITED",
entire — —
EN440 *(U401)*
1c green on amber .75 .50
entire 1.25 .75
EN441 *(U402)*
1c green on buff 4.00 2.00
entire 6.00 2.50
EN442 *(U403)*
1c green on blue 5.00 2.00
entire 6.00 3.00
EN443 *(U404)*
1c green on manila 3.00 2.00
entire 4.50 2.50
EN444 *(W405)*
1c green on manila, wrapper .50 .25
entire .75 .50

EN445-EN449 Die B, narrow "D" in "UNITED." (Compare with EN439 and following) Die 90.

Die B

EN445 *(U400a)*
1c green on white 1.00 .50
entire 1.25 .60
EN446 *(U401a)*
1c green on amber 1.00 .75
entire 1.50 1.00
EN447 *(U402a)*
1c green on buff 4.00 2.00
entire 6.00 2.50
EN448 *(U403a)*
1c green on blue 5.00 2.00
entire 6.00 3.00
EN449 *(W405a)*
1c green on manila, wrapper 37.50 20.
entire 42.50 27.50

EN450-EN455 So-called "Dayton Dies" of which there are 13 varieties. See note after illustration of EN492.

EN450-EN455 Franklin. Die C, both "S"'s in "STATES" are broad. (Compare with other 1c dies) Die 90.

Die C

EN450 *(U400b)*
1c green on white 1.00 .50
entire 1.25 .75
EN451 *(U401b)*
1c green on amber 1.00 .80
entire 2.00 1.00
EN452 *(U402b)*
1c green on buff 6.00 2.00
entire 7.00 3.00
EN453 *(U403b)*
1c green on blue 5.00 4.00
entire 5.50 4.50
EN454 *(U404b)*
1c green on manila 4.00 3.00
entire 6.00 5.00
EN455 *(W405b)*
1c green on manila, wrapper 6.00 4.00
entire 11. 6.00

EN456-EN460 Die D, back of bust forms angle opposite "T" in "CENT." (Compare with other 1c dies) Die 90.

Die D

EN456 *(U400c)*
1c green on white .70 .35
entire .85 .50

EN457 *(U401c)*
1c green on amber	1.00	.75
entire	1.25	1.00

EN458 *(U402c)*
1c green on buff	4.00	2.00
entire	5.00	3.00

EN459 *(U403c)*
1c green on blue	4.00	2.00
entire	6.00	4.00

EN460 *(U404c)*
1c green on manila	50.	
entire	—	

Watermarks 15 to 23 (1907-1919)

EN461-EN470 *Washington. Die A, both the "O" in "TWO" and the "C" in "CENTS" are ovals. (Compare with the following) Die 91.*

Die A

EN461 *(U406)*
2c brown red on white	100.	.50
entire	1.75	.75

EN462 *(U407)*
2c brown red on amber	6.00	3.00
entire	8.50	7.00

EN463 *(U408)*
2c brown red on buff	7.00	2.00
entire	11.	4.50

EN464 *(U409)*
2c brown red on blue	5.00	2.50
entire	7.00	4.00

EN465 *(W410)*
2c brown red on manila, wrapper	40.	30.
entire	60.	40.

EN466 *(U411)*
2c carmine on white	.30	.25
entire	.60	.40

EN467 *(U412)*
2c carmine on amber	.30	.25
entire	1.00	.25

EN468 *(U413)*
2c carmine on buff	.50	.25
entire	.75	.25

EN469 *(U414)*
2c carmine on blue	.50	.25
entire	1.00	.25

EN470 *(W415)*
2c carmine on manila, wrapper	5.00	3.00
entire	9.50	5.00

EN471-EN479 *Die A2, similar to last except there is a prominent wedge-shaped lock of hair in the center of the head. (Compare with other 2c dies) Die 91.*

Die A2

EN471 *(U406a)*
2c brown red on white	30.	8.00
entire	40.	25.

EN472 *(U407a)*
2c brown red on amber	110.	50.
entire	130.	75.

EN473 *(U408a)*
2c brown red on buff	135.	.60
entire	150.	100.

EN474 *(U409a)*
2c brown red on blue	135.	110.
entire	170.	140.

EN475 *(U411a)*
2c carmine on white	.40	.20
entire	.75	.40

EN476 *(U412a)*
2c carmine on amber	.40	.25
entire	.80	.60

EN477 *(U413a)*
2c carmine on buff	.60	.55
entire	.90	.60

EN478 *(U414a)*
2c carmine on blue	.45	.40
entire	.80	.50

EN479 *(W415a)*
2c carmine on manila, wrapper	5.00	3.00
entire	7.00	5.00

EN480-EN487 *Washington. Die B, head is large, hair arranged in bumps. The "O" in "TWO" is circular. (Compare with EN488 and other 2c dies) Die 91.*

Die B

EN480 *(U406b)*
2c brown red on white	.60	.40
entire	.90	.50

EN481 *(U407b)*
2c brown red on amber	3.50	2.00
entire	5.00	2.00

EN482 *(U408b)*
2c brown red on buff	7.00	3.25
entire	10.	6.00

EN483 *(U409b)*
2c brown red on blue	5.00	2.25
entire	7.00	4.00

EN484 *(U411b)*
2c carmine on white	.75	.40
entire	1.25	.60

EN485 *(U412b)*
2c carmine on amber	1.35	.50
entire	1.75	.80

EN486 *(U413b)*
2c carmine on buff	7.00	4.00
entire	11.	6.00

EN487 *(U414b)*
2c carmine on blue	.90	.70
entire	1.50	.75

EN488-EN491 *Die C, prominent slits in hair resembling the gills of a shark. Lettering clear and sharp. (Compare with EN480 and other 2c dies) Die 91.*

Die C

EN488 *(U411c)*

2c carmine on white	.50	.25
entire	.75	.50

EN489 *(U412c)*

2c carmine on amber	.40	.30
entire	.75	.50

EN490 *(U413c)*

2c carmine on buff	.45	.35
entire	.70	.50

EN491 *(U414c)*

2c carmine on blue	.50	.35
entire	.60	.50

EN492-EN496 *Die D, the so-called "Dayton Dies" as they were made by a private die engraver on order from the factory at Dayton, Ohio. There are 13 varieties, some of which are quite valuable. Die 91.*

Die D

EN492 *(U411d)*

2c carmine on white	.60	.40
entire	1.00	.60

EN493 *(U412d)*

2c carmine on amber	.60	.40
entire	1.00	.60

EN494 *(U413d)*

2c carmine on buff	3.00	1.50
entire	4.00	3.75

EN495 *(U414d)*

2c carmine on blue	.75	.50
entire	1.50	.75

EN496 *(W415b)*

2c carmine on manila, wrapper	5.00	3.00
entire	8.00	3.00

EN497-EN500 *Washington. Die E, front of bust tapers and the end is rounded. (Compare with EN461 and others) Die 91*

Die E

EN497 *(U411e)*

2c carmine on white	.40	.25
entire	.85	.40

EN498 *(U412e)*

2c carmine on amber	.65	.45
entire	1.00	.60

EN499 *(U413e)*

2c carmine on buff	.75	.50
entire	1.25	.70

EN500 *(U414e)*

2c carmine on blue	.75	.50
entire	1.25	.50

EN501-EN505 *Washington. Die F, upright line of the "2"s tapers. There is a very thin line where it meets the base of the numeral. The upper corner of the front end of the bust is usually, but not always, cut away in varying degrees.*

Die 91.

Die F

EN501 *(U411f)*

2c carmine on white	14.	12.
entire	16.	14.
a. vermilion	—	—
entire	—	—

EN502 *(U412f)*

2c carmine on amber	12.	9.00
entire	14.	12.

EN503 *(U413f)*

2c carmine on buff	40.	20.
entire	50.	30.

EN504 *(U414f)*

2c carmine on blue	15.	9.00
entire	20.	16.

EN505 *(W415c)*

2c carmine on manila, wrapper	45.	40.
entire	55.	45.

EN506-EN508 *Die G, hair arranged as in EN471 (a wedge-shape lock in center). (Compare with EN501 and others) Die 91.*

EN506 *(U411g)*

2c carmine on white	15.	13.
entire	20.	15.

EN507 *(U413g)*

2c carmine on buff	13.	10.
entire	20.	13.

EN508 *(U414g)*

2c carmine on blue	15.	10.
entire	18.	16.

EN509, EN510 *Franklin. Die A, the "F" in "FOUR" is only 1 mm from the "4." (Compare with EN511) Die 90.*

Die A

EN509 *(U416a)*

4c black on white	4.00	3.00
entire *	9.00	5.00

EN510 *(U417a)*

4c black on amber	6.00	3.00
entire *	10.	5.00

EN511, EN512 *Die B, the "F" in "FOUR" is 1 3/4mm from the figure "4." Die 90.*

Die B

EN511 *(U416)*
4c black on white   5.00   4.00
    entire *   10.   6.00
EN512 *(U417)*
4c black on amber   6.00   3.00
    entire *   12.50   7.00

EN513-EN515 *Washington. Die A, large "F" in "FIVE" (2 3/4 mm high). (Compare EN516) Die 91.*

Die A

EN513 *(U418a)*
5c blue on white   7.00   3.00
    entire   11.   7.00
EN514 *(U419)*
5c blue on amber   13.   12.
    entire   16.   14.
EN515 *(U418d)*
5c blue on blue   1,200.   —
    entire   1,800.   —

EN516-EN519 *Die B, Small "F" in "FIVE" (2 1/2 mm tall). (Compare with EN513.) Die 91.*

Die B

EN516 *(U418)*
5c blue on white   7.00   3.00
    entire   12.50   6.00
EN517 *(U419)*
5c blue on amber   13.   12.
    entire   22.50   15.
EN518 *(U418c)*
5c blue on buff   *1,000.*   —
    entire   —   —
EN519 *(U418c)*
5c blue on blue   *1,000.*   —
    entire   —   —

1916-50. The circular design used on these envelopes was introduced in 1916 and continued without change until 1950. Many dies wore out through this long tenure and many new master dies were required, which accounts for the several different dies for each denomination.

The 3c envelopes were issued in 1917, when the rate of postage was increased from 2c to 3c. The stamps were printed in a violet ink. Twenty months later the first class rate was returned to 2c and the 3c envelopes were discontinued.

After the reduction of first class postal rates from 3c (a war measure) to 2c, the Post Office found itself with an enormous supply of 3c envelopes for which there was no practical use. The envelopes were revalued (1920) by running them through canceling machines with appropriate slugs to indicate the new value (2c) inserted into them. It is estimated that some 63 million envelopes were revalued in the process.

When, in 1925, the rate for circular letters was advanced from 1c to 1 1/2c, the government again found itself with an unusable supply of envelopes, this time the 1c denomination. Again revaluing was done by the use of canceling machines.

In July 1932, first class rates were advanced to 3c, which called for production of 3c envelopes. This new issue was printed in a bright purple ink. Wrappers were discontinued in 1934.

EN520-EN528 *Franklin. Die A, "UNITED" small and nearer inner than outer circle. (Compare with following) Die 92.*

Watermarks 19 to 43 (1915-1949)

Die A

EN520 *(U420)*
1c green on white   .25   .25
    entire   .40   .25
EN521 *(U421)*
1c green on amber   .40   .35
    entire   .75   .50
EN522 *(U422)*
1c green on buff   2.00   1.25
    entire   2.75   1.75
EN523 *(U423)*
1c green on blue   .50   .40
    entire   .75   .50
EN524 *(U424)*
1c green on manila   7.00   5.00
    entire   9.50   6.00
EN525 *(W425)*
1c green on manila, wrapper   .25   .25
    entire   .75   .25
EN527 *(U426)*
1c green on brown (glazed)   35.   20.
    entire   40.   22.
EN528 *(W427)*
1c green on brown (glazed), wrapper   65.   —
    entire   75.   —
EN528
1c green on brown (unglazed)   10.   10.
    entire   12.50   11.

EN529, EN530 *Die B, the first "S" in "STATES" is larger than the last "S." "NT" in "CENT" are large. "U" in "UNITED" is close to circle. (Compare with EN531 and others) Die 92.*

Die B

EN529 *(U420a)*
1c green on white	85.	65.
entire *	100.	75.

EN530 *(U421a)*
1c green on amber	325.	200.
entire *	500.	250.

EN531-EN533 *Franklin. Die C, hair projects strongly at back, forming a "bun." (Compare with EN529 and others) Die 92.*

Die C

EN531 *(U420b)*
1c green on white	.35	.25
entire	.40	.30

EN532 *(U421b)*
1c green on amber	1.35	.75
entire	1.75	1.00

EN533 *(U423b)*
1c green on blue	1.00	.75
entire	1.50	.90

EN533A *(W425a)*
1c green on manila, wrapper	150.	135.
entire	175.	150.

EN534-EN537 *Die D, "UNITED" large and closer to outer than inner circle. (Compare with EN520 and others) Die 92.*

Die D

EN534 *(U420c)*
1c green on white	.40	.30
entire	.50	.35

EN535 *(U421c)*
1c green on amber	1.50	1.00
entire	2.00	1.50

EN536 *(U422c)*
1c green on buff	4.00	1.50
entire	.50	.35

EN537 *(U423b)*
1c green on blue	1.00	.50
entire	1.50	.75

EN538-EN540 *"C" in "CENTS," "G" in "POSTAGE," and "U" in "UNITED" are very narrow. (Compare with all others dies) Die 92.*

Die E

EN538 *(U420d)*
1c green on white	.40	.30
entire	.55	.50

EN539 *(U421d)*
1c green on amber	1.25	.75
entire	1.50	1.00

EN540 *(U423c)*
1c green on blue	.75	.40
entire	1.10	.75

EN541-EN545 *Washington. Die A, large head, well formed thick letters. Die 93.*

Die A

EN541 *(U481)*
1 1/2c brown on white	.25	.25
entire	.60	.25
a. purple (error)	95.	—
entire	120.	—

EN542 *(U482)*
1 1/2c brown on amber	1.00	.50
entire	1.50	.70

EN543 *(U483)*
1 1/2c brown on blue	1.75	1.10
entire	2.00	1.50

EN544 *(U484)*
1 1/2c brown on manila	7.00	4.00
entire	12.	7.00

EN545 *(W485)*
1 1/2c brown on manila, wrapper	.90	.25
entire	1.50	.60

EN546-EN548 *Die H2, slightly different head from EN541. Lettering thin and sharp; "T" with long top strokes. Die 93.*

Die H2

EN546 *(U481a)*
1 1/2c brown on white	.70	.35
entire	.90	.60

EN547 *(U482a)*
1 1/2c brown on amber	1.50	.85
entire	2.00	.90

EN548 *(U483a)*
1 1/2c brown on blue	2.00	1.50
entire	2.25	1.50

EN549-EN555 *Washington. Die A, head large. Base line of "2" s horizontal. Lettering heavy and well formed. (Compare with following) Die 93.*

Die A

EN549 *(U429)*

2c carmine on white	.25	.25
entire	.50	.25
a. green (error), entire	7,500.	—
p. laid paper	—	—
entire	—	—
v. with added impression of 1c green (EN520)	750.	—
v1. with added impression of 1c green (EN439)	750.	—
v2. with added impression of 4c black (EN509)	600.	—

EN550 *(U430)*

2c carmine on amber	.30	.25
entire	.50	.25
p. laid paper	—	—
entire	—	—

EN551 *(U431)*

2c carmine on buff	2.00	.75
entire	4.50	2.00

EN552 *(U432)*

2c carmine on blue	.25	.25
entire	.75	.25

EN553 *(W433)*

2c carmine on manila, wrapper	.25	.25
entire	.50	.25

EN554 *(W434)*

2c carmine on brown (glazed), wrapper	80.	55.
entire	100.	70.

EN555 *(W435)*

2c carmine on brown (unglazed), wrapper	75.	55.
entire	100.	70.

EN556-EN559 *Washington. Die B, head very large. Base line of both "2" slopes down to right. "U" in "UNITED" far from circle. (Compare with other 2c dies) Die 93.*

Die B

EN556 *(U429a)*

2c carmine on white	10.	7.00
entire	16.	10.

EN557 *(U430a)*

2c carmine on amber	10.	8.00
entire	16.	11.

EN558 *(U431b)*

2c carmine on buff	110.	50.
entire	135.	.90

EN559 *(U432a)*

2c carmine on blue	20.	15.
entire	25.	22.50

EN560, EN561 *Die C, as EN556 except the large inner circle and circles around the figure "2" s are very thin. (The rejected die.) Die 93.*

Die C

EN560 *(U429b)*

2c carmine on white	35.	30.
entire	50.	40.

EN561 *(U432c)*

2c carmine on blue	80.	75.
entire	150.	125.

EN562-EN565 *Washington. Die D, "C" in "CENTS" very close to circle. Base line of right "2" slopes downward to right. Head slightly smaller. (Compare with EN549 and others) Die 93.*

Die D

EN562 *(U429c)*

2c carmine on white	10.	8.00
entire	13.	11.

EN563 *(U430b)*

2c carmine on amber	25.	15.
entire	30.	17.

EN564 *(U431b)*

2c carmine on buff	35.	35.
entire	45.	45.

EN565 *(U432d)*

2c carmine on blue	20.	17.50
entire	25.	22.50

EN566-EN569 *Die E, smaller head than all other dies. "T" and "S" in "CENTS" close. Die 93.*

Die E

EN566 *(U429d)*

2c carmine on white	.55	.35
entire	.75	.50

EN567 *(U430c)*

2c carmine on amber	.60	.40
entire	1.60	.70

EN568 *(U431c)*

2c carmine on buff	3.00	2.00
entire	6.00	3.00

EN569 *(U432e)*

2c carmine on blue	.75	.25
entire	1.75	.60

EN570-EN573 *Washington. Die F, base line of left "2" slopes downward to right. Heavy strands of hair resemble bumps. "T" and "S" in "CENTS" widely spaced. (Compare with other 2c dies) Di 93.*

Die F

EN570 *(U429e)*

2c carmine on white	.70	.40
entire	1.10	.70

EN571 (U430d)
2c carmine on amber	1.00	.45
entire	1.85	.85

EN572 (U431d)
2c carmine on buff	4.50	3.00
entire	7.00	3.50

EN573 (U432f)
2c carmine on blue	.75	.30
entire	1.25	.50

EN574-EN577 *Die H, base line of "2"s slope downward to right. Clear sharp impression. Thin lettering. "T"s have short top strokes. Die 93.*

Die H

EN574 (U429f)
2c carmine on white	.70	.30
entire	1.00	.80

EN575 (U430e)
2c carmine on amber	.80	.40
entire	1.60	1.00

EN576 (U431e)
2c carmine on buff	4.00	2.50
entire	6.00	4.00

EN577 (U432g)
2c carmine on blue	.80	.40
entire	1.50	.70

EN577A (U432A)
2c carmine on manila	—	—
entire	—	—

EN578-EN580 *Washington. Die H2, similar to EN574 except all "T"s have long top strokes. Die 93.*

Die H2

EN578 (U429g)
2c carmine on white	.50	.25
entire	.75	.55

EN579 (U430f)
2c carmine on amber	.70	.40
entire	1.00	.50

EN580 (U432h)
2c carmine on blue	.50	.25
entire	1.00	.50

EN581-EN585 *Die I, the letters "C," "U," and "G" are very narrow. (Compare with all other 2c dies) Die 93.*

Die I

EN581 (U429h)
2c carmine on white	.50	.30
entire	.75	.50

EN582 (U430g)
2c carmine on amber	.60	.30
entire	.70	.40

EN583 (U432i)
2c carmine on blue	.80	.25
entire	2.25	.50

EN584-EN590 *Washington. Die A, similar to the 2c die (EN549). Dark violet stamps were issued from 1916-17, at which time the postage rate was reduced to 2c. When rate again was raised to 3c, in 1932, this denomination was reissued in a bright purple. Die 93.*

Die A

EN584 (U436)
3c dark violet on white	.60	.25
entire	.75	.25
a. carmine (error)	35.	30.
entire	40.	35.
v. with added impression of		
EN520, entire	650.	—
v1. with added impression of		
EN549, entire	750.	—

EN585 (U437)
3c dark violet on amber	2.50	1.50
entire	7.00	2.75
a. black (error)	175.	—
entire	210.	—

EN586 (U438)
3c dark violet on buff	25.	2.00
entire	32.50	3.00

EN587 (U439)
3c dark violet on blue	7.00	1.75
entire	11.	7.50

EN588 (U436a)
3c purple on white	.25	.20
entire	.50	.25

EN589 (U437a)
3c purple on amber	.50	.25
entire	.75	.40

EN590 (U439a)
3c purple on blue	.30	.25
entire	.75	.30

EN591-EN594 *Die E, similar to 2c (EN566). Die 93.*

Die E

EN591 (U436b)
3c dark violet on white	1.75	1.00
entire	3.25	1.00
a. carmine (error)	35.	30.
entire	40.	35.

ED592 *(U437b)*
3c dark violet on amber	5.00	3.00
entire	9.00	4.00
a. carmine (error)	375.	265.
entire	425.	350.

EN593 *(U438b)*
3c dark violet on buff	30.	1.75
entire	27.50	1.25

EN594 *(U439b)*
3c dark violet on blue	7.00	4.50
entire	9.00	5.00
a. carmine (error)	300.	300.
entire	425.	775.

EN595-EN598 *Die F, similar to 2c (EN570). Die 93.*

Die F

EN595 *(U436c)*
3c dark violet on white	2.50	1.75
entire	4.00	2.00

EN596 *(U437c)*
3c dark violet on amber	6.50	3.00
entire	8.00	3.50

EN597 *(U438b)*
3c dark violet on buff	33.	2.00
entire	35.	3.00

EN598 *(U439c)*
3c dark violet on blue	7.00	5.00
entire	10.	5.00

EN599-EN602 *Die H, similar to 2c, die H (EN574). Die 93.*

Die H

EN599 *(U436d)*
3c dark violet on white	1.50	1.00
entire	3.00	2.50

EN600 *(U437d)*
3c dark violet on amber	4.00	2.00
entire	6.00	3.00

EN601 *(U438b)*
3c dark violet on buff	32.	4.00
entire	37.	8.00

EN602 *(U439d)*
3c dark violet on blue	9.00	5.00
entire	13.	7.00

EN603-EN605, *Die I, similar to 2c. (See EN581)*

EN603 *(U436e)*
3c purple on white	.50	.25
entire	.50	.35

EN604 *(U437e)*
3c purple on amber	.60	.25
entire	1.10	.40

EN605 *(U439e)*
3c purple on blue	.60	.25
entire	1.10	.55

EN609-EN611 *Franklin. Die 92.*

EN609 *(U440)*
4c black on white	1.25	.75
entire *	3.25	2.55
v. with added impression of 2c (EN549)	—	—
entire *	275.	—

EN610 *(U441)*
4c black on amber	2.75	1.00
entire *	5.50	2.00

EN611 *(U442)*
4c black on blue	3.00	1.00
entire *	5.50	2.00

EN612-EN614 *Washington. Die 93.*

EN612 *(U443)*
5c blue on white	3.00	2.50
entire	6.50	3.50

EN613 *(U444)*
5c blue on amber	4.00	1.75
entire	7.00	3.50

EN614 *(U445)*
5c blue on blue	4.00	3.00
entire	9.00	4.50

EN615-EN617 *Die 93.*

EN615 *(U529)*
6c orange on white	6.00	3.50
entire *	8.00	6.00

EN616 *(U530)*
6c orange on amber	11.	8.00
entire *	15.	10.

EN617 *(U531)*
6c orange on blue	11.	8.00
entire *	15.	10.

Revalued Envelopes

When a double or triple overprint is listed it indicates that all of the overprints either are directly over the stamp or partly on the stamp. Envelopes which show overprints in various places other than on the stamp are freaks and command little or no premium value.

2 CENTS

Type 1 surcharge — Black overprint

On 3c envelopes of 1916-50 issue

EN618 *(U466)*
2c on 3c on white, Die A (EN584)	11.	10.
entire	16.	12.

EN619 *(U446a)*
2c on 3c on white, Die E (EN591)	11.	10.
entire	14.	12.

Type 2 surcharge– Rose overprint

EN620 *(U447)*
2c 3c on white, Die A (EN584)	7.00	6.00
entire	8.50	8.00

EN621 *(U447b)*
2c 3c on white, Die F (EN595)	7.00	6.00
entire	9.50	9.00

EN621A *(U447a)*
2c on 3c on white, Die A (EN549)	*1,600.*	—
entire	—	—

EN621B *(U447c)*
2c on 3c on amber, Die A (EN550)	—	—
entire *	—	--

EN622 *(U448)*
2c on 3c on white, Die A (EN584)	2.50	2.00
entire	3.00	2.50

EN623 *(U449)*
2c on 3c on amber, Die A (EN585)	6.00	6.00
entire	7.00	7.00

EN624 *(U450)*
2c on 3c on buff, Die A (EN586)	15.	13.
entire	18.	17.

EN625 *(U451)*
2c on 3c on blue, Die A (EN587)	12.	11.
entire	13.	11.

EN626
2c on 3c on white, Die E (EN591)	—	—
entire	—	—

EN627
2c on 3c on amber, Die E (EN592)	—	—
entire	—	—

EN628
2c on 3c on buff, Die E (EN593)	—	—
entire	—	—

EN629
2c on 3c on blue, Die E (EN594)	—	—
entire	—	—

EN630
2c on 3c on white, Die F (EN595)	—	—
entire	—	—

EN631
2c on 3c on amber, Die F (EN596)	—	—
entire	—	—

EN632
2c on 3c on buff, Die F (EN597)	—	—
entire	—	—

EN633
2c on 3c on blue, Die F (EN598)	—	—
entire	—	—

EN634
2c on 3c on white, Die H (EN599)	—	—
entire	—	—

EN635
2c on 3c on amber, Die H (EN600)	—	—
entire	—	—

EN636
2c on 3c on buff, Die H (EN601)	—	—
entire	—	—

EN637
2c on 3c on blue, Die H (EN602)	—	—
entire	—	—

Type 3 surcharge — Black overprint

On 4c brown envelope of 1899 issue

EN638A
2c on 4c on white (EN413)	—	—
entire *	—	—

On 4c brown envelopes of 1903 issue

EN639 *(U462)*
2c on 4c on white (EN429)	350.	175.
entire *	400.	200.

EN640 *(U463)*
2c on 4c on amber (EN430)	350.	125.
entire *	400.	175.

On envelopes of 1907-16 issue

EN641 *(U451A)*
2c on 1c on white, Die A (EN439)	1,700.	—
entire	—	—

EN642 *(U453)*
2c on 2c on white, Die A (EN466)	900.	—
entire	1,300.	—

EN643 *(U453Cd)*
2c on 2c on buff, Die A (EN468)	675.	—
entire	775.	—

EN644 *(U453a)*
2c on 2c on white, Die C (EN488)	900.	—
entire	1,300.	—

EN645 *(U453C)*
2c on 2c on buff, Die E (EN499)	700.	550.
entire	800.	—

EN646 *(U453B)*
2c on 2c on blue, Die E (EN500)	700.	—
entire	800.	—

EN647 *(U463A)*
2c on 4c on white, Die B(EN511)	750.	—
entire	825.	—

On 1c circular dies of 1916-50

EN648 *(U452)*
2c on 1c on white, Die A (EN520)	900.	—
entire	1,100.	—

EN649
2c on 1c on white, Die C (EN531)	—	—
entire	—	—

On 2c circular dies of 1916-50

EN650 *(U454)*
2c on 2c on white, Die A (EN549)	75.	—
entire	95.	—

EN651 *(U455)*
2c on 2c on amber, Die A (EN550)	950.	—
entire	1,300.	—

EN652 *(U456)*
2c on 2c on buff, Die B (EN558)	150.	—
entire	185.	—

EN653
2c on 2c on white, Die E (EN566)	—	—
entire	—	—

EN654
2c on 2c on buff, Die E (EN568)	—	—
entire	—	—

EN655 *(U457)*
2c on 2c on blue, Die E (EN569)	—	—
entire	—	—

EN656
2c on 2c on white, Die F (EN570)	—	—
entire	—	—

EN657
2c on 2c on blue, Die F (EN573)	—	—
entire	—	—

EN658
2c on 2c on white, Die H (EN574)	—	—
entire	—	—

EN659
2c on 2c on buff, Die H (EN576)	—	—
entire	—	—

EN660
2c on 2c on blue, Die H (EN577)	—	—
entire	—	—

On 3c circular dies of 1916-50

EN661 *(U458)*
2c on 3c on white, Die A (EN584)	.50	.40
entire	.70	.50
v. Double overprint	15.	8.00
entire	40.	—
v1. Triple overprint	—	—
entire	—	—

EN662 *(U459)*
2c on 3c on amber, Die A (EN585)	3.00	1.50
entire	4.50	2.00
v. Double overprint	19.	—
entire	—	—

EN663 *(U460)*
2c on 3c on buff, Die A (EN586)	3.00	1.50
entire	3.50	1.50
v. Double overprint	13.	—
entire	—	—
v1. Triple overprint	30.	—
entire	—	—

EN664 *(U461)*
2c on 3c on blue, Die A (EN587)	4.50	1.50
entire	6.00	2.00
v. Double overprint	16.	—
entire	—	—

EN665
2c on 3c on white, Die E (EN591)	—	—
entire	—	—
v. Double overprint	—	—
entire	—	—
vl. Triple overprint	—	—
entire	—	—

EN666
2c on 3c on amber, Die E (EN592)	3.00	1.50
entire	4.50	2.00

EN667
2c on 3c on buff, Die E (EN593)	—	—
entire	—	—
v. Double overprint	—	—
entire	—	—

EN668
2c on 3c on buff, Die E (EN594)	—	—
entire	—	—
v. Double overprint	—	—
entire	—	—
vl. Triple overprint	—	—
entire	—	—

EN669
2c on 3c on white, Die F (EN595)	—	—
entire	—	—
v. Double overprint	—	—
entire	—	—

EN670
2c on 3c on amber, Die F (EN596)	—	—
entire	—	—
v. Double overprint	—	—
entire	—	—
v1. Triple overprint	—	—
entire	—	—

EN671
  2c on 3c on buff, Die F (EN597) — —
    entire — —
EN672
  2c on 3c on blue, Die F (EN598) — —
    entire — —
EN673
  2c on 3c on white, Die H (EN599) — —
    entire — —
    x. Double overprint — —
      entire — —
    x1. Triple overprint — —
      entire — —
EN674
  2c on 3c on amber, Die H (EN600) — —
    entire — —
    x. Double overprint — —
      entire — —
    x1. Triple overprint — —
      entire — —
EN675
  2c on 3c on blue, Die H (EN602) — —
    entire — --

On 5c circular dies of 1916-50

EN676 (*U464*)
  2c on 5c on white (EN612) 900. —
    entire 1,100. —

Type 3 over Type 7A — black overprints

On 3c circular dies of 1916-50

EN677
  2c on 3c on white, Die F (EN595) — —
    entire — —

2

|||| |||| Type 4 surcharge — Black overprint

On 3c circular dies of 1874-76

EN678 (*U467*)
  2c on 3c on white (EN187) 225. —
    entire * 275. —

On 4c brown envelopes of 1903 issue

EN679 (*U472*)
  2c on 4c on white (EN429) 12. 9.00
    entire * 25. 15.
    v. Double overprint 40. —
      entire * — —
EN680 (*U473*)
  2c on 4c on amber (EN430) 14. 10.
    entire 22. 13.

On 2c carmine envelope of 1907-16 issue

EN681 (*U466*)
  2c on 2c on white, Die E (EN497) 3,000. —
    entire 3,700. —

On 1c circular dies of 1916-21

EN682 (*U465*)
  2c on 1c on white, Die A (EN520) 750. —
    entire 950. —
EN683
  2c on 1c on white, Die C (EN531) — —
    entire — —

On 2c circular dies of 1916-50

EN684 (*U466A*)
  2c on 2c on white, Die A (EN549) 225. —
    entire 275. —
EN685
  2c on 2c on amber, Die A (EN550) 1,750. —
    entire 2,000. —
EN686
  2c on 2c on white, Die E (EN566) 375. —
    entire — —
EN687
  2c on 2c on white, Die H (EN574) — —
    entire — —

On 3c circular dies of 1916-50

EN688 (*U468*)
  2c on 3c on white, Die A (EN584) .70 .50
    entire .90 .80
    x. Double overprint 16. —
      entire — —
    x1. Triple overprint 25. —
      entire — —
EN689 (*U469*)
  2c on 3c on amber, Die A (EN585) 3.25 2.00
    entire 5.00 3.00
    x. Double overprint — —
      entire — —
EN690 (*U470*)
  2c on 3c on buff, Die A (EN586) 5.00 3.00
    entire 7.00 5.00
    x. Double overprint 20. —
      entire — —

EN691 (*U471*)
  2c on 3c on blue, Die A (EN587) 3.50 1.50
    entire 10. 4.00
    x. Double overprint 20. —
      entire — —

On Die E

EN692
  2c on 3c on white (EN591) — —
    entire — —
    x. Double overprint — —
      entire — —
EN693
  2c on 3c on amber (EN592) — —
    entire — —
EN694
  2c on 3c on buff (EN593) — —
    entire — —

EN695
  2c on 3c on blue (EN594)   —   —
    entire   —   —
    x. Double overprint   —   —
      entire   —   —

On Die F

EN696
  2c on 3c on white (EN595)   —   —
    entire   —   —
    x. Double overprint   —   —
      entire   —   —
EN697
  2c on 3c on amber (EN596)   —   —
    entire   —   —
    x. Double overprint   —   —
      entire   —   —
EN698
  2c on 3c on buff (EN597)   —   —
    entire   —   —
EN699
  2c on 3c on blue (EN598)   —   —
    entire   —   —

On Die H

EN700
  2c on 3c on white (EN599)   —   —
    entire   —   —
    x. Double overprint   —   —
      entire   —   —
EN701
  2c on 3c on amber (EN600)   —   —
    entire   —   —
EN702
  2c on 3c on buff (EN601)   —   —
    entire   —   —
EN703
  2c on 3c on blue (EN602)   —   —
    entire   —   —

Type 4 over Type 7A — black overprints

On 3c circular dies of 1916-50

EN704 *(U474)*
  2c on 3c on white, Die A (EN584)   —   —
    entire   —   —

EN705 *(U475)*
  2c on 3c on amber, Die A (EN585)   —   —
    entire   —   —
EN706
  2c on 3c on white, Die E (EN591)   —   —
    entire   —   —
EN707
  2c on 3c on white, Die H (EN599)   —   —
    entire   —   —

Type 4 over Type 2 — black overprints

On 3c circular dies of 1916-50

On Die A

EN708
  2c on 3c on white (EN584)   —   —
    entire   —   —
EN709
  2c on 3c on amber (EN585)   —   —
    entire   —   —
EN710
  2c on 3c on buff (EN586)   —   —
    entire   —   —
EN711
  2c on 3c on blue (EN587)   —   —
    entire   —   —

On Die E

EN712
  2c on 3c on amber (EN592)   —   —
    entire   —   —
EN713
  2c on 3c on buff (EN593)   —   —
    entire   —   —
EN714
  2c on 3c on blue (EN594)   —   —
    entire   —   —

On Die F

EN715
  2c on 3c on buff (EN597)   —   —
    entire   —   —
EN716
  2c on 3c on blue (EN598)   —   —
    entire   —   —
EN717
  2c on 3c on white, Die H (EN599)   —   —
    entire   —   —

Type 4 over Type 3 — black overprints

On 3c circular dies of 1916-50

On Die A

EN718
  2c on 3c on white (EN584)   —   —
    entire   —   —
EN719
  2c on 3c on amber (EN585)   —   —
    entire   —   —
EN720
  2c on 3c on buff (EN586)   —   —
    entire   —   —
EN721
  2c on 3c on blue (EN587)   —   —
    entire   —   —

On Die E

EN722
2c on 3c on amber (EN592) — —
entire — —
EN723
2c on 3c on buff (EN593) — —
entire — —
EN724
2c on 3c on blue (EN594) — —
entire — —
EN725
2c on 3c on blue, Die F (EN598) — —
entire — —
EN726
2c on 3c on white, Die H (EN599) — —
entire — —

2 Type 5 surcharge —Black overprint

On 3c circular dies of 1916-50

EN727 (U476)
2c on 3c on amber, Die A (EN585) 100. —
entire 130. —
EN728
2c on 3c on amber, Die F (EN596) — —
entire — —

2 Type 6 surcharge— Black overprint

On 3c circular dies of 1916-50

On Die A

EN729 (U477)
2c on 3c on white (EN584) 100. —
entire 130. —
x. Double overprint — —
entire — —
EN730 (U478)
2c on 3c on amber (EN585) 200. —
entire 220. —
EN731
2c on 3c on white, Die E (EN591) — —
entire — —
EN732
2c on 3c on white, Die F (EN595) — —
entire — —
EN733
2c on 3c on white, Die H (EN599) — —
entire — —

2 Type 7 surcharge — Black overprint

On 3c circular dies of 1916-50

EN734 (U479)
2c on 3c on white, Die A (EN584) 275. —
entire 325. —
EN735
2c on 3c on white, Die E(EN591) — —
entire — —
EN736
2c on 3c on white, Die H (EN599) — —
entire — —

1 CENT Type 7A surcharge — Violet overprint

Type 7-- violet overprint

EN737 (U480)
2c on 3c on white, Die H (EN599) 200. —
entire 225. —

On 2c circular dies of 1916-50

EN738
1c on 2c on white, Die A (EN549) — —
entire — —
EN739
1c on 2c on white, Die H (EN574) — —
entire — —

On 3c circular dies of 1916-50

EN740
1c on 3c on white, Die E (EN591) 200. —
entire 225. —

1½ Type 8 surcharge — Black overprint

On 2c green envelopes of 1887 issue

EN741 (U486)
1 1/2c on 2c on white (EN344) 600. —
entire 650. —
EN742 (U487)
1 1/2c on 2c on amber (EN345) 700. —
entire 800. —

On 1c green envelopes of 1899 issue

EN743 (U488)
1 1/2c on 1c on white (EN391) 350. —
entire 650. —

EN744 (U489)
1 1/2 on 1c on amber (EN392) 75. 65.
entire 120. 100.

On 1c green envelopes of 1907-16
On Die A

EN745 *(U490)*
1 1/2c on 1c on white (EN439)   5.00   4.00
    entire   6.00   6.00
EN746 *(U491)*
1 1/2 on 1c on amber (EN440)   8.00   3.00
    entire   12.   7.00
EN747 *(U494)*
1 1/2 on 1c on manila (EN443)   200.   75.
    entire   250.   100.

On Die B

EN748 *(U490a)*
1 1/2c on 1c on white (EN445)   13.   10.
    entire   15.   13.
EN749 *(U491a)*
1 1/2c on 1c on amber (EN446)   80.   70.
    entire   990.   90.
EN750 *(U492)*
1 1/2c on 1c on buff (EN447)   200.   100.
    entire   225.   110.
EN751 *(U493a)*
1 1/2c on 1c on blue (EN448)   75.   55.
    entire   100.   65.

On Die C

EN751A
1 1/2c on 1c on white EN450)   7.00   3.00
    entire   9.00   5.00

EN751B
1 1/2c on 1c on amber (EN450)   4.50   2.50
    entire *   8.00   5.00
EN751C
1 1/2c on 1c on manila (EN454)   —   —
    entire   —   —

On Die D

EN752 *(U490b)*
1 1/2c on 1c on white (EN456)   —   —
    entire   —   —
EN753 *(U491b)*
1 1/2c on 1c on amber (EN457)   4.50   2.50
    entire   8.00   5.00
EN754 *(U492a)*
1 1/2c on 1c on buff (EN458)   75.   55.
    entire   100.   65.
EN755 *(U493)*
1 1/2c on 1c on blue (EN459)   —   —
    entire   —   —

On 1c circular dies of 1916-50
Die A

EN756 *(U495)*
1 1/2c on 1c on white (EN520)   .35   .30
    entire   .60   .50
    v. Double overprint   5.00   2.50
    entire   —   —

EN757 *(U496)*
1 1/2c on 1c on amber (EN521)   14.   13.
    entire   21.   16.
EN758 *(U497)*
1 1/2c on 1c on buff (EN522)   4.00   2.50
    entire   6.00   2.75
EN759 *(U498)*
1 1/2c on 1c on blue (EN523)   1.25   1.00
    entire   2.50   1.50
EN760 *(U499)*
1 1/2c on 1c on manila (EN524)   11.   7.00
    entire   16.   8.00
EN761 *(U501)*
1 1/2c on 1c on brown (glazed)
    (EN526)   60.   30.
    entire   70.   40.
EN762 *(U500)*
1 1/2c on 1c on brown (unglazed)
    (EN528)   60.   35.
    entire   70.   40.

On Die B
EN762A
1 1/2c on 1c on white (EN529)   2.00   .75
    entire   —   —

On Die C
EN763 *(U495a)*
1 1/2c on 1c on white (EN531)   2.00   1.00
    entire   —   —
    x. Double overprint   —   —
    entire   —   —
EN764
1 1/2c on 1c on blue (EN533)   —   —
    entire   —   —

On Die D

EN765 *(U495b)*
1 1/2c on 1c on white (EN534)   —   —
    entire   —   —
    x. Double overprint   —   —
    entire   —   —
EN766
1 1/2c on 1c on amber (EN535)   —   —
    entire   —   —
EN767
1 1/2c on 1c on blue (EN537)   —   —
    entire   —   —
    x. Double overprint   —   —
    entire   —   —
On 1 1/2c circular dies of 1916-50

EN768 *(U505)*
1 1/2c on 1 1/2c on white, Die A
    (EN541)   400.   —
    entire   475.   —
EN769 *(U506)*
1 1/2c on 1 1/2c on blue, Die H2
    (EN548)   350.   —
    entire   400.   —

On 2c circular dies of 1916-50

EN770 *(U502)*
1 1/2c on 2c on white, Die A
(EN549)   250.   —
  entire *   300.   —
EN771 *(U503)*
1 1/2c on 2c on buff, Die E
(EN568)   275.   —
  entire   300.   —
EN772 *(U504)*
1 1/2c on 2c on blue, Die F
(EN573)   250.   —
  entire   300.   —

Type 9 surcharge— Black overprint

On 1c blue envelope of 1887 issue

EN773 *(U507)*
1 1/2c on 1c on white (EN321)   1,000.   —
  entire   1,200.   —
On 1c green envelope of 1899

EN774 *(U508)*
1 1/2c on 1c on amber (EN392)   60.   —
  entire   70.   —

On 1c green envelopes of 1903 issue

EN775 *(U508a)*
1 1/2c on 1c on white (EN418)   1,500.   —
  entire   2,400.   —
EN776 *(U509)*
1 1/2c on 1c on amber (EN419)   14.   12.
  entire   25.   17.
  x. Double overprint   27.   —
    entire   33.   —
EN777 *(U509B)*
1 1/2c on 1c on buff (EN420)   60.   50.
  entire   70.   60.

On 1c oval dies of 1907-16

On Die A

EN778 *(U510)*
1 1/2c on 1c on white (EN439)   2.00   1.50
  entire   3.50   2.00
  x. Double overprint   8.00   —
    entire   —   —
EN779 *(U511)*
1 1/2c on 1c on amber (EN440)   175.   80.
  entire   200.   100.
EN780 *(U512)*
1 1/2c on 1c on buff (EN441)   7.00   5.00
  entire   12.   7.00
  x. Double overprint   —   —
    entire   —   —

EN781 *(U513)*
1 1/2c on 1c on blue (EN442)   6.00   3.00
  entire   8.00   5.00
EN782 *(U514)*
1 1/2c on 1c on manila (EN443) 25.   11.
  entire   35.   25.
EN783
1 1/2c on 1c on white, Die B
(EN445)   7.00   5.00

On Die C

EN784 *(U510c)*
1 1/2c on 1c on white (EN450)   17.   9.00
  entire   25.   13.

EN785 *(U514a)*
1 1/2c on 1c on manila (EN454) 55.   40.
  entire   60.   50.

On Die D

EN786 *(U510d)*
1 1/2c on 1c on white (EN456)   4.00   1.50
  entire   7.00   3.00
EN787 *(U512a)*
1 1/2c on 1c on buff (EN458)   18.   15.
  entire   25.   19.
EN788 *(U513a)*
1 1/2c on 1c on blue (EN459)   6.00   5.00
  entire   8.00   6.00
On 1c circular dies of 1916-50

On Die A
EN789 *(U515)*
1 1/2c on 1c on white (EN520)   .40   .30
  entire   .70   .40
  x. Double overprint   7.00   —
    entire   —   —
  xl. Triple overprint   13.   —
    entire   —   —
  x2. Inverted overprint   11.   —
    entire   —   —
EN790 *(U516)*
1 1/2c on 1c on amber (EN521)   50.   35.
  entire   60.   45.
EN791 *(U517)*
1 1/2 on 1c on buff (EN522)   5.00   2.00
  entire   6.00   2.00
EN792 *(U518)*
1 1/2c on 1c on blue (EN523)   5.00   2.00
  entire   6.00   2.00
  x. Double overprint   11.   —
    entire   —   —
EN793 *(U519)*
1 1/2c on 1c on manila (EN524) 20.   12.
  entire   28.   15.
EN794
1 1/2c on 1c on white, Die B
(EN529)   —   —
  entire   —   —

On Die C

EN795
1 1/2c on 1c on white (EN531) — —
    entire — —
    x. Double overprint — —
      entire — —
EN796
1 1/2c on 1c on blue (EN533) — —
    entire — —

On Die D

EN797
1 1/2c on 1c on white (EN534) — —
    entire — —
    x. inverted overprint — —
      entire — —
EN798
1 1/2c on 1c on amber (EN535) — —
    entire — —
EN799
1 1/2c on 1c on buff (EN536) — —
    entire — —
EN800
1 1/2c on 1c on blue (EN537) — —
    entire — —

On 2c carmine envelopes of 1916-50 issue

EN801 *(U520)*
1 1/2c on 2c on white, Die A
    (EN549) 175. —
    entire 225. —
EN801A
1 1/2c on 2c on white, Die E (EN566) — —
    entire — —
EN801B
1 1/2c on 2c on amber, Die E (EN567) — —
    entire — —
EN802
1 1/2c on 2c on white, Die F (EN570) — —
    entire — —
EN803
1 1/2c on 2c on white, Die H (EN574) — —
    entire — —

Type 9 — magenta overprint

On 1c green envelope of 1916-50 issue

EN804 *(U521)*
1 1/2c on 1c on white (EN531) 5.00 4.00
    entire 5.00 6.00
    x. double overprint 30. —
      entire — —

On 1c circular dies of 1916-50

EN805
1 + 1/2c on white (EN520) — —
    entire — —

1926. Sesquicentennial Exposition Envelope.

EN806 *Liberty Bell. Center bar of "E" of "POSTAGE" shorter than top bar.*

Watermark 27 (1925)

EN806 *(U522)*
2c carmine on white *(July 27, 1926)* 2.00 1.00
    entire 2.75 1.75

EN807 *The center bar of "E" in "POSTAGE" is the same length as top bar.*

EN807 *(U522a)*
2c carmine on white 10. 7.00
    entire 12.50 10.

1932. Washington Bicentennial Issue.

EN808-EN813 *Mount Vernon. All of the same design; only the denomination changes.*

Watermark 29 (1929)

EN808 *(U523)*
1c green on white *(Jan. 1, 1932)* 2.00 1.50
    entire 2.50 1.75

EN809 *(U524)*
1 1/2c brown on white 3.50 2.00
    (Jan. 1, 1932)
    entire 3.75 2.75

EN810 *(U525)*
2c carmine on white *(Jan. 1, 1932)* .50 .25
    entire .75 .30
    a. carmine on blue (error),
      entire 27,000. —
    v. "S" of "POSTAGE" high — —
      entire — —
EN811 *(U526)*
3c purple on white *(June 16, 1932)* 2.50 .30
    entire 4.00 .50
EN812 *(U527)*
4c black on white *(Jan. 1, 1932)* 25. 20.
    entire * 30. 25.
EN813 *(U528)*
5c blue on white *(Jan. 1, 1932)* 6.00 4.00
    entire 6.50 5.50

1950. New Oval Design. As far back as 1941, the Post Office had submitted new designs for its envelope stamps and had ordered the necessary new printing dies to be made. The outbreak of World War II interfered with plans for the new design, and the new printing dies were not put into use. After the war, collectors brought ever-increasing pressure to bear on the Post Office Department to change the circular design which was well into a third decade of use.

In 1950 the Post Office determined to put some of the printing dies that had been prepared in 1941 into production and ordered 1c, 2c, and 3c envelopes printed on a demonstration machine at the annual stamp exhibition sponsored by the American Stamp Dealers Association in New York. Only a very few of the old dies were found to be usable in the more modern machines then in use. However, at least one printing die in each denomination was put into use, and the envelopes were then printed and sold at the ASDA stamp show.

New printing dies immediately were developed so that the new design could replace completely the old design. These first-printed envelopes are in very short supply. *These envelopes were issued on white paper only.*

EN814 *Franklin. Die A, thick, short, "1" within heavy circle*

EN814 (U532)
1c green, Die A (Nov. 16, 1950)   6.00   2.00
  entire   8.00   3.00

EN815 *Die B, thin, long "1" within thin circle, "E" in "ONE" has long bars and is close 1mm to circle.*

EN815 (U532a)
1c green, Die B   7.00   4.00
  entire   9.00   4.50

EN816 *Die C, thin long "1." "E" in "ONE" with short bars and far (1 1/2mm) from circle.*

EN816 (U532b)
1c green, Die C   7.00   4.00
  entire   9.00   4.50
  v. precanceled, entire   1.00   1.00

EN817 *Washington.*

EN817 (U535)
1 1/2c brown   5.00   4.00
  entire   6.00   5.00
  v. precanceled, entire   1.25   1.25

EN818 *Washington. Die A, figure "2" set low in heavy circle.*

EN818 (U533a)
2c carmine, Die A (Nov. 17, 1950)   .80   .35
  entire   1.50   .50

EN818A *Die B, thin "2" with long hook. Center cross bar of "E" in "STATES" shorter than top or bottom bars*

EN818A (U533b)
2c carmine, Die B   1.50   1.00
  entire   2.00   1.10

EN819 *Die C, thin "2" set high in thin circle*

EN819 (U533)
2c carmine, Die C   .80   .30
  entire   1.25   .50

EN819A *Washington. Die D, thick cross bar in "A" of "STATES"*

EN819A (U533c)
2c carmine, Die D   1.50   .70
  entire   1.60   .70

EN820 *Die A, tall, thick "3" within thick circle. Narrow "E"'s in "THREE"*

EN820 (U534a)
3c purple, Die A (Nov. 18, 1950)   2.25   .85
  entire   .30   1.50

EN821 *Die B, tall, thin, "3" in thin circle. Narrow "E"s in "THREE"*

EN821 *(U534b)*
3c purple, Die B*(Nov. 19, 1950)* .85 .60
  entire 1.60 .65

EN822 *Die C, short "3" in thin circle. Wide "E"'s in "THREE." Line from left stand of "N" in "UNITED" to stand in "E" in "POSTAGE" well below chin*

EN822 *(U534c)*
3c purple, Die C .60 .35
  entire 1.00 .50

EN823 *Die D, short "3" in thin circle. Wide "E"'s in "THREE." Line from left stand of "N" in "UNITED" to stand of "E" in "POSTAGE" almost touches chin. "N" in"UNITED" short; thin cross bar in "A" in "STATES"*

EN823 *(U534)*
3c purple, Die D .50 .25
  entire .65 .30

EN824 *Die E, similar to EN823 except "N" in "UNITED" tall and thick cross bar in "A" in "STATES"*

EN824 *(U534d)*
3c purple, Die E .90 .50
  entire 1.35 .75

1958. On August 1, 1958, first class postage rates were raised to four cents. This necessitated new 4c stamped envelopes. In addition, to use up surplus stocks of 2c and 3c envelopes, the Post Office Department again revalued existing stocks.

EN825 *Franklin. Die A, head high in oval. Circle around "4" low (1 mm from outer edge of color)*

Watermarks 46, 47, 48

EN825 *(U536)*
4c lilac, Die A *(Aug. 1, 1958)* .90 .25
  entire 1.00 .30

EN826 *Die B, head low in oval. Circle around "4" high (1 1/2 mm from outer edge of color. To verify: right leg of "A" in "POSTAGE" shorter than left leg. Short leg on "P"*

EN826 *(U536a)*
4c lilac, Die B 1.10 .25
  entire 1.40 .35

EN827 *Die C, head centered in oval. Circle around "4" high as on Die B. To verify: legs of "A" in "POSTAGE" are about equal in length. Long leg on "P"*

EN827 *(U536c)*
4c lilac, Die C 1.25 .25
  entire 1.40 .35

Type 11 surcharge— Overprint in green to left of stamp. On 3c purple of 1916-50 issue.

EN828 *(U539)*
1c on 3c purple, Die A (EN588) 15. 11.
  entire 16. —
EN829 *(U539a)*
1c on 3c purple, Die H (EN603) 12. 10.
  entire 15. —
EN830 *(U539b)*
1c on 3c purple, Die I (EN606) 35. 20.
  entire 40. —

On 3c purple of 1950

EN831 *(U540a)*
1c on 3c purple, Die B (EN821) — —
  entire 1,100. —
EN832 *(U540)*
1c on 3c purple, Die C (EN822) .60 .25
  entire .70 .35
EN833 *(U540b)*
1c on 3c purple, Die D
  (EN823) .85 .25
  entire 1.00 .25
EN834 *(U540c)*
1c on 3c purple, Die E (EN824) .85 .25
  entire 1.10 .25

Type 12 surcharge — Overprint in red to left of stamp.

On 2c circular dies of 1916-50

EN835 (U537)
2c on 2c carmine, Die A (EN549)	4.00	2.00
entire	4.50	—

EN836 (U537a)
2c on 2c carmine, Die H (EN574)	11.	8.00
entire	13.	—

EN837 (U537b)
2c on 2c carmine, Die I (EN581)	6.00	6.00
entire	7.50	—

On 2c oval die of 1950

EN838 (U538)
2c on 2c carmine, Die A (EN818)	.90	.40
entire	1.10	.50

EN839 (U538a)
2c on 2c carmine, Die B (EN818A)	1.10	—
entire	1.50	—

EN840 (U538b)
2c on 2c carmine, Die C (EN819)	.90	.35
entire	1.10	—

EN841 (U538c)
2c on 2c carmine, Die D (EN819A)	.90	—
entire	1.25	—

1960. Effective July 1, 1960, the third class postage rate for bulk mailing was raised to 2 1/2 cents for commercial users and 1 1/4 cents for non-profit organizations. These envelopes are available only precanceled and were sold only to holders of proper permits. The small size of each (No. 6 3/4), however, were made available to collectors at COMPEX in Chicago (commercial rate) and DIXIPEX in Birmingham, Alabama (non-profit rate), and were on sale at the Philatelic Agency until December 31, 1960. These unprecanceled envelopes have gum on the top back flap and the precanceled envelopes are without such gum.

EN842 Washington.

EN842 (U542)
2 1/2c blue on white (May 28, 1960)	.90	.60
entire	1.00	.70
v. precanceled	.25	.25
entire	.30	.30

EN843 Die A, small "1 1/4." 2 1/4 mm across bar of "4." Leaf cluster 2mm under "U".

EN843 (U541)
1 1/4c turquoise on white, Die A		
(June 25, 1960)	.85	.60
entire	1.00	.65
v. precanceled	.25	.25
entire	.25	.25

EN843A Die B, large "1 1/4." 2 3/4mm across bar of "4." Leaf cluster 1mm under "U".

EN843A (U541a)
1 1/4c turquoise on white,		
precanceled	3.00	3.00
entire	3.50	3.50

EN844 Pony Express Rider.

Watermark 46

EN844 (U543)
4c brown on white, blue inside		
(July 19, 1960)	.65	.35
entire	.85	.50

Watermark 47

Watermark 47. Beginning in May 1961, a new watermark was introduced to mark the letting of the new contract. Two types were adopted: a star preceding the letters "USA" for paper manufactured by the International Paper company (wmk 47); star following the letters "USA" (wmk 48) for paper manufactured by the Howard Paper Co.

1963. Effective January 7, 1963, first class postage rates were raised to 5c. A new stamped envelope was prepared showing a bust of Lincoln. However, a sufficient number of working dies were unable to be delivered to service all of the machines at the factory. Hence the factory was authorized to continue printing 4c stamped envelopes and revalue them to 5c. This was accomplished by using the Type 11 surcharge printed in green to the left of the stamp. The revaluing was done on unfolded envelope blanks on the regular printing machines at the factory. These blanks were then passed to another machine, which printed the 4c stamps and folded the envelopes. At least two different dies were used to print the added 1c value.

While the effective date for the new postage rates was not until January 7, 1963, the Post Office made the new envelopes available as rapidly as they could be supplied. The authorized first day of issue for the 5c Lincoln envelope was November 19, 1962. No announcement was made regarding the 4c revalued envelopes, but they began making their appearance at post offices in December 1963.

All of these new envelopes are known with *watermarks 47 and 48.*

EN846v *and* EN847v

NOTE: EN846t and EN847t are the result of using the O'Connell machines to fold blanks on which the stamps already had been printed by the Huckins (Die B) and Harris (Die C) machines, which were incapable of folding. To accomplish the folding operation, the ink fountains were removed from some of the O'Connell machines still idle for lack of working dies of the 5c stamp. By error, the old 4c die was not removed on at least one of the O'Connell machines and this caused an albino impression of the 4c stamp to be printed over the 5c stamp. The error was not discovered until the O'Connell machine(s) had been performing the folding operation for some time.

EN845 *Abraham Lincoln. Die A, figure "5" centered in circle. Middle bar of "E" in "FIVE" equal length as top. Center bar in "E" in "POSTAGE" off center to top. Verification: small head, sharp pointed nose.*

Watermarks 47, 48

EN845 *(U544a)*
5c dark blue, Die A	1.00	.35
entire	1.00	.35

EN846 *Die B, "5" centered in circle. "FI" in "FIVE" close together. "C" in "CENTS" higher than "E." Verification: large wide head with blunt nose.*

EN846 *(U544)*
5c dark blue, Die B	.75	.25
entire	1.00	.30
v. with albino impression of 4c, entire	55.	—

EN847 *Die C, "5" to right in circle. Short leg on "P" in "POSTAGE".*

EN847 *(U544b)*
5c dark blue, Die C *(Nov. 19, 1962)*	1.00	.40
entire	1.25	.50
v. with albino impression of 4c, entire	75.	—

Type 11 Surcharge — Printed in green to left of stamp on 4c envelope EN825.

Two types of the surcharge are known:

Type I: large word "CENT," dot after "U" and "S" far from letters, long angle serif on center bar of "E."
Type II: small word "CENT," dot after "U" and "S"

EN848 *(U545)*
4c lilac + 1c green, Type I (EN825)	1.50	.50
entire	1.75	.75
v. Type II	1.50	.50
entire	1.75	.75

1964. New York World's Fair Issue.

EN849 *Globe and orbit rings.*

EN849 *(U546)*
5c red on white *(Apr. 22, 1964)*	.70	.50
entire	.80	.50

1965. New Issue. Beginning January 1, 1965, the United States Envelope Co. was awarded the contract for making envelopes. This firm established a new facility at Williamsburg, Pennsylvania, and equipped it with new machinery that would produce envelopes from a continuous web (roll) of paper. The process is very rapid, with each individual machine being capable of producing one million envelopes every 24 hours. Envelopes produced by this method are of the old low-back design.

Watermark 49

New watermarks were introduced, as illustrated. Watermarks 47 and 48 also are known on these envelopes. Watermark 49 has the star below the letter "S" of "USA" and signifies the product of the Oxford Paper Co.

Watermark 50 has the star above the "S" and distinguishes the product of Crown Zellerbach.

Also, a new watermark closely resembling Watermark 47 (star before "USA") but with a star somewhat larger distinguishes the product of the Champion Paper Co.

The small size (No. 6 3/4) and large size (No. 10) of the 5c envelopes (EN852), both regular and window, also exist tagged, consisting of a vertical luminescent rectangle to the left of the stamp. This method of tagging also was used for the 8c air mail envelopes in both sizes (AEN38).

EN850 *Liberty Bell. The wavy lines at the sides indicate the stamp is precanceled.*

EN850 *(U547)*
1 1/4c brown on white

	(Jan. 6, 1965)	.25	.25
	entire	1.00	.25

EN851 *USS Mattics Constitution under sail.*

EN851 *(U549)*
4c bright blue on white *(Jan. 6, 1965)* .85 .25
entire 1.00 .25

EN852 *Eagle.*

EN852 *(U550)*
5c purple on white *(Jan. 5, 1965)*

		.80	.25
	entire	.90	.30
	z. Tagged *(Aug. 15, 1967)*	1.10	.25
	entire	1.35	.35

Type 12 surcharge. *Printed in red to left of stamp on 4c envelope (EN851)*

EN853 *(U552)*
4c bright blue + 2c red on white

	(Feb. 1968)	3.50	2.00
	entire	4.50	2.50

Type 11 Surcharge. *Printed in green to left of stamp on 5c envelope (EN852)*

EN854 *(U553)*
5c purple + 1c green on white

	(Feb. 1968)	3.50	2.00
	entire	4.25	2.50
	z. Tagged *(Feb. 5, 1968)*	3.50	2.00
	entire	4.25	2.50

EN855 *Statue of Liberty.*

EN855 *(U551)*
6c turquoise green on white, tagged

	(Jan. 4, 1968)	.75	.25
	entire	1.00	.35

EN855 *is tagged with luminescent materials mixed with the printing ink.*

EN856 *Liberty Bell. The wavy lines at sides indicate the stamp is precanceled.*

EN856 *(U548)*
1.4c brown on white *(Mar. 26, 1968)* .25 .25
entire 1.25 .35

EN857 *(U548A)*
1.6c orange on white *(June 16, 1969)* .25 .25
entire 1.00 .25

EN858 *(U556)*
1.7c purple on white *(May 10, 1971)* .25 .25
entire .50 .25

1970. Herman Melville Issue honored the writer and the whaling industry.

EN859 *Herman Melville's "Moby Dick".*

EN859 *(U554)*
6c light blue on white, tagged
   (March 7, 1970)   .50   .25
   entire   .70   .35

1971. White House Conference on Youth.

EN860 *White House Conference on Youth emblem.*

EN860 *((U555)*
6c light blue on white, tagged
   (Feb. 24, 1971)   .75   .25
   entire   1.00   .50

1971. Issued to meet new first class postage rate.

EN861 *Eagle.*

EN861 *((U557)*
8c ultramarine on white, tagged
   (May 6, 1971)   .50   .25
   entire   .75   .30

Type 13 surcharge— In green to left of stamp.

EN862 *(U561)*
6c turquoise green (EN855) **+ 2c green on white,** tagged *(May 16, 1971)*   1.00   .50
   entire   1.25   .50
EN863 *(U562))*
6c blue (EN860) **+ 2c green on white,** tagged
   (May 16, 1971)   2.00   1.00
   entire   2.75   1.50

Sale of EN863, of which one million were produced, was limited to Washington, D.C.

1971. Bowling, honoring the seventh World Tournament of the International Bowling Federation.

EN864 *Bowling ball and pin.*

EN864 *(U563)*
8c red on white, tagged   .50   .25
   (Aug. 21, 1971)
   entire   .75   .25

Available in both #6 small and #10 large size, EN864 is the first commemorative envelope since the Washington Bicentennial of 1932 to be available in two sizes.

1971. The White House Conference on Aging Issue.

EN865 *Snowflake.*

EN865 *(U564)*
8c blue on white, tagged   .50   .25
   (Nov.15, 1971)
   entire   .75   .25

1972. First U.S. International Transportation Exposition Issue.

EN866 *Transpo '72 emblem.*

EN866 *(U565)*
8c red and blue on white, tagged   .75   .25
   (May 2, 1972)
   entire   1.00   .25

1973. Issued to meet new first class postage rate.

EN867 *Liberty Bell.*

EN867 *(U567)*
10c turquoise green on white, tagged
   (Dec.5, 1973)   .50   .25
   entire   .50   .25

Type 12 surcharge— in ultramarine to left of stamp.

EN868 (U566)
8c ultramarine + 2c ultramarine on white,
     tagged (Dec. 1,1973)   .50   .25
     entire   .50   .20

1974. Tennis Centennial

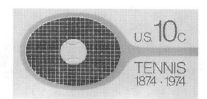

EN869 Tennis Centennial.

EN869 (U569)
10c yellow, green, and blue on white,
     tagged (Aug. 31, 1974) entire .35   .25

1974. Non-Profit Bulk Mailing.

EN870 Volunteerism.

EN870 (U568)
1.8c blue green on white, tagged
     (Aug. 23, 1974) enitre   .35   .25

1975. Bicentennial Era — Seafaring Tradition

EN 871 Compass Rose.

EN871 (U571)
10c brown and blue on light brown,
     tagged (Oct. 13, 1975) entire   .50   .25
     a. Brown omitted, entire   —

1975. Issued to meet new first class postage rate.

EN872 Liberty Tree.

EN872 (U576)
13c brown on white, tagged
     (Nov. 8, 1975) entire   .50   .25

EN873 Quilt Pattern.

EN873 (U572)
13c brown and bluish green on light brown,
     tagged (Feb. 2, 1976) entire .50   .25
     a. Brown omitted, entire   —

1976. Bicentennial Era — American Farmer

EN874 Sheaf of Wheat.

EN874 (U573)
13c brown and green on light brown,
     tagged (March 15, 1976)
     entire   .50   .25
     a. Brown omitted, entire   —

1976. Bicentennial Era — American Doctor

EN875 Mortar and Pestle.

EN875 (U574)
13c orange and brown on light brown,
     tagged (June 30, 1976)
     entire   .50   .25
     a. Brown omitted, entire   —

1976. Bicentennial Era — American Craftsman

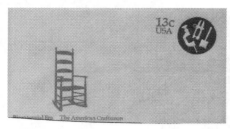

EN876
Craftsman's Tools.

EN876 *(U575)*
13c red and brown on light brown,
    tagged *(Aug. 6, 1976)* entire   .50   .25
    a. Brown omitted, entire   —

1976. Non-Profit Mailing.

EN877 *Star in pinwheel.*

EN877 *(U577)*
2c red on white, *(Sept. 10, 1976)*
    entire   .35   .25

1976. Bicentennial Era

EN878 *Centennial envelope design.*

EN878 *(U582)*
13c green on white, tagged *Oct. 15, 1976)*
    entire   .50   .25

1977. Golf. *Printed by gravure, in addition to embossing.*

EN879 *Golf club in motion and ball.*

EN879 *(U583)*
13c blue, black and yellow green on white,
    tagged *(Apr. 7, 1977)* entire   .60   .25
    a. Black omitted, entire   —
    b. Black and blue omitted, entire   —

1977. Non-Profit Mailing.

EN880 *"2.1c" in octagon.*

EN880 *(U578)*
2.1c yellow green on white
    (June 3, 1977) entire   .50   .25

1977. Energy Issue.

EN881 *Energy Conservation.*

EN881 *(U584)*
13c black, red and yellow on white,
    tagged *(Oct. 20, 1977)* entire   .50   .25
    a. Black omitted, entire   —
    b. Black and red omitted, entire   —
    c. Red and yellow omitted, entire   —
    d. Yellow omitted, entire   —

EN882 *Energy Development.*

EN882 *(U585)*
13c black, red and yellow on white,
    entire   .60   .30

1978. "A" Non-denominated Issue to accommodate new first class postage rate. The envelope was printed in 1975 and 1976 and stored for contingency use.

EN883 *Stylized Eagle and "A".*

EN883 *(U580)*
15c orange on white, tagged
    (May 22, 1978) entire   .60   .25

1978. Uncle Sam.

EN884 *Stylized Uncle Sam Hat and Shield.*

EN884 *(U581)*
15c red on white, tagged
    (June 3, 1978)   .50   .25
    entire   .60   .25

1978. Non-Profit Mailing.

EN885 *"2.7c" over "USA".*

EN885 *(U579)*
2.7c green on white *(July 5, 1978)*   .25   .25
    entire   .40   .25

1978. Downward Re-valuing.

EN886 *Type 14 surcharge— in black to left of stamp.*

EN886 *(U586)*
15c revalued from 16c blue on white,
    tagged *(July 28, 1978)*   .45   .25
    entire   .60   .25
    t. Surcharge omitted, entire   —   —

1978. Auto Racing Issue.

EN887 *Indianapolis 500 racer.*

EN887 *(U587)*
15c black, blue and red on white,
    tagged *(Sept. 2, 1975)*   .45   .25
    entire   .50   .25
    a. Black omitted, entire   175.   —
    b. Black and blue omitted,
     entire   —   —
    c. Red omitted, entire   —   —
    d. Red and blue omitted,
     entire   —   —
    z. Tagging omitted   —   —

1978. Liberty Tree Re-valued.

EN888 *Type 14 surcharge— in black to left of stamp.*

EN888 *(U588)*
15c revalued from 13c brown on white EN872,
    tagged *(Nov. 28, 1978)*   .40   .25
    entire   .55   .25

1979. Non-Profit Mailing.

EN889 *Authorized nonprofit organization.*

EN889 *(U589)*
3.1c blue on white *(May 18, 1979)*   .25   .25
    entire   .30   .25

1979. Veterinary Medicine Issue.

EN890 *'V' on Aesculapius.*

EN890 *(U595)*
15c gray and brown on white, tagged
    (July 24, 1979)   .40   .25
    entire   .55   .25
    a. Gray omitted, entire   —   —

1979. Olympic Games Issue. Soccer.

EN891 *1980 Moscow Olympics, Soccer players.*

EN891 *(U596)*
15c red, green and black on white, tagged
    (Dec. 10, 1979)   .75   .25
    entire   1.00   .25
    a. Black omitted, entire   175.   —
    b. Black and green omitted,
     entire   175.   —
    c. Red omitted, entire   175.   —
    d. Red and green omitted,
     entire   —   —

1980. Bicycling

EN892 *High-Wheel Bicycle.*

EN892 *(U597)*
15c blue and maroon on white, tagged
  (May 16, 1980)   .50   .25
  entire   .65   .25
  a. Blue omitted, entire   150.   —

1980. Non-Profit Mailing

EN893 *Weaver Violins.*

EN893 *(U590)*
3.5c purple on white *(June 23, 1980)*   .25   .25
  entire   .35   .25

1980. America's Cup Yacht Races Issue.

EN894 *Yacht.*

EN894 *((U598)*
15c red and blue on white, tagged
  (Sept. 15, 1980)   .50   .25
  entire   .65   .25

1980. Honeybee Issue. *Printed by gravure, in addition to embossing.*

EN895 *Orange Blossom and Honeybee.*

EN895 *(U599)*
15c green and yellow on white, tagged
  (Oct. 10, 1980)   .50   .25
  entire   .55   .25
  a. Brown omitted, entire   200.   —

1981. "B" Non-Denominated Issue to accommodate new first class postage rate.

EN896 *Stylized Eagle and "B".*

EN896 *(U592)*
18c purple on white, tagged
  (Mar. 15, 1981)   .50   .25
  entire   .55   .25

1981. Star Issue, denominated to meet new first class postage rate.

EN897 *Star.*

EN897 *(U594)*
18c blue on white, tagged
  (Apr. 2, 1981)   .50   .25
  entire   .55   .25

1981. Blinded Veterans Association Issue.

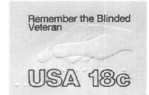

EN898 *Hand and braille*

EN898 *(U600)*
18c blue on white, tagged
  (Aug. 13, 1981)   .40   .25
  entire   .60   .25
  a. Red omitted, entire   —   —

The hand and braille message are embossed without color.

1981. "C" Non-Denominated Issue to meet new first class postage rate.

EN899 *Stylized eagle and "C".*

EN899 *(U594)*
20c brown on white, tagged
  (Oct. 11, 1981)   .50   .25
  entire   .55   .25

1981. Capitol Dome Issue.

EN900 *Dome of U.S. Capitol.*

EN900 *(U601)*
20c dark red on white, tagged

(Nov. 13, 1981)	.50	.25
entire	5.15	.25
z. Bar tagged	2.00	2.00

1982. Non-Profit Bulk Mailing.

EN901.

EN901 *(U591)*
5.9c brown on white *(Feb.17, 1982)* .25 .25
entire .35 .25

1982. The Great Seal of the United States bicentennial.

EN902 *Great Seal.*

EN902 *(U602)*
20c blue, black and red on white, tagged

(June 15, 1982)	.50	.25
entire	.55	.25
a. Blue omitted, entire	—	—

1982. The Purple Heart bicentennial.

EN903 Purple Heart Medal.

EN903 *(U603)*
20c purple and black on white, tagged

(Aug.6, 1982)	.50	.25
entire	.55	.25

1983. Non-Profit Mailing.

EN904.

EN904 *(U604)*
5.2c orange on white *(Mar.21,1983)* .25 .25
entire .25 .25

1983. Paralyzed Veterans Issue.

EN905 *Wheelchair.*

EN905 *(U605)*
20c red, blue and black on white, tagged

(Aug.3,1983)	.50	.25
entire	.55	.25
a. Blue omitted, entire	—	—
b. Blue and black omitted, entire	—	—
c. Red omitted, entire	—	—
d. Red and black omitted, entire	—	—

1984. Small Business Issue.

EN906 *Business Signs.*

EN906 *(U606)*
multicolored on white, tagged

(May 7, 1984)	.60	.25
entire	.65	.25

1985. "D" Non-Denominated Issue to meet new first class postage rate.

EN907 *Stylized eagle and "D".*

EN907 *(U607)*
22c green on white, tagged

(Feb. 1, 1985)	.50	.25
entire	.65	.25

1985. American Bison.

EN908 *Bison.*

EN908 *(U608)*
22c brown on white, tagged
(Feb. 25, 1985) .50 .25
entire .60 .25
z. Double tagged, phosphorescent
ink and separate bar tagging — —
z1. Untagged (precanceled)

1985. Non-Profit Mailing.

EN909 *U.S.S. Constitution.*

EN909 *(U609)*
6c aqua on white *(May 3, 1985)* .25 .25
entire .30 .25

1986. The Mayflower Issue.

EN910.

EN910 *(U610)*
8.5c black and gray on white, precanceled
(Dec. 4, 1986) .25 .25
entire .35 .25

1988. Stars. *Printed by letter press in addition to embossing.*

EN911.

EN911 *(U611)*
25c red and blue on white, tagged
(Mar. 26, 1988) .60 .25
entire .75 .35
a. Red omitted, entire 100. —

1988. Non-Profit Mailing. USS Constitution.

EN912 *U.S.S. Constellation.*

EN912 *(U612)*
8.4c black and blue on white, precanceled
(Apr. 12, 1988) .30 .25
entire .50 .25
a. Black omitted, entire — —
o. Tagging omitted

1988. Holiday Greeting Snowflake Issue. *Printed by letter press.*

EN913 *Snowflake.*

EN913 *(U613)*
25c red and green on white, tagged
(Sept. 8, 1988) .60 .30
entire .75 .35

EN914.

1989. Philatelic Issue. *Printed by letterpress.*

EN914 *(U614)*

25c red and blue on white, tagged
(Mar. 10, 1989) .50 .25
entire * .65 .30

1989. Security Mail Issue. *Printed by letterpress.*

EN915.

EN915 *(U615)*
25c red and blue on white, tagged
(July 10, 1989) .50 .25
entire .60 .30

Envelope is blue on inside to provide security for enclosures.

EN916 *Love!*

1989. Love Issue. *Printed by offset and letterpress.*

EN916 *(U616)*
  25 red and blue on white, tagged
    (Sept. 22, 1989)   .50   .25
    entire   .60   .30
    a. Blue omitted, entire   —   —

1989. World Stamp Expo '89 Issue. *Printed by letterpress, with hologram.*

EN917 *Space Station and Shuttle.*

EN917 *(U617)*
  25c ultramarine, tagged *(Dec. 3, 1989)* .50   .30
    entire   .65   .40
    a. Ultramarine omitted, entire   —   —

A hologram is affixed at upper right inside, visible through a die cut window.

1990. Football Issue. *Printed by letterpress, with hologram.*

EN918 *Football Players and Lombardi Trophy.*

EN918 *(U618)*
  25c vermilion, tagged *(Sept. 9, 1990)* .50   .30
    entire   .65   .35

A hologram is affixed at upper right inside, visible through a die cut window.

1991. Star Issue to meet the new first class postage rate. *Printed by letterpress, with embossing.*

EN919 *Star.*

EN919 *(U619)*
  29c ultramarine and rose on white, tagged
    (Jan. 24, 1991)   .70   .35
    entire   .85   .45

1991. Non-Profit Mailing. *Printed by letterpress.*

EN920 *Sparrows on Wires.*

EN920 *(U620)*
  11.1c red and blue on white, tagged, precanceled
    (May 3, 1991)   .25   .25
    entire   .40   .30

1991. Love Issue. *Printed by offset.*

EN921 *Love.*

EN921 *(U621)*
  29c blue, maroon, and rose on white, tagged
    (May 9, 1991)   .65   .35
    entire   .75   .40

1991. Security Issue. *Printed by letterpress.*

EN922 *Star.*

EN922 *(U623)*
  29c ultramarine and rose on white, tagged
    (July 20, 1991)   .65   .35
    entire *   .75   .40

The inside of the envelope has a blue design as a security precaution for enclosures.

1991. Magazine Industry Issue. *Printed by offset and letterpress, with gravure-printed vignette affixed through a die-cut window.*

EN923 *Stylized Globe 250 th Anniversary, Magazine Industry.*

EN923 (U622)
29c multicolored on white, tagged
    (Oct. 7, 1991)   .65   .35
    entire *   .75   .40

1991. Country Geese Issue. *Printed by offset and letterpress.*

EN924 *Geese.*

EN924 (U624)
29c bluish gray and yellow, tagged
    (Nov. 8, 1990)   .65   .35
    entire   .75   .40

1992. Space Station Hologram Issue. *Printed by letterpress, with hologram.*

EN925 *Space Station and Shuttle.*

EN925 (U625)
29c yellow green on white, tagged
    (Jan. 21, 1992)   .65   .35
    entire *   .75   .40

A hologram is affixed at upper right inside, visible through a die cut window.

1992. Western Americana Issue. *Printed by offset and letterpress.*

EN926 *Western saddle.*

EN926 (U626)
29c multicolored on white, tagged
    (Apr. 10, 1992)   .60   .35
    entire *   .75   .40

A vignette, printed by offset, is affixed through a die cut window at upper right.

1992. Protect the Environment Issue. *Printed by offset and letterpress.*

EN927
Hillebrandia.

EN927 (U627)
29c multicolored on white, tagged
    (Apr. 22, 1992)   .60   .35
    entire *   .75   .40

A vignette, printed by offset, is affixed through a die cut window at upper right.

1992. Re-Issues on Recycled Paper. All of the envelopes in this series have the "Recycle" tri-arrow logo on the reverse. Unwatermarked envelopes and/or those available only in large (No. 10) size are marked. This series is listed only as entires, to enable inclusion both of the "Recycle" logo and to verify watermarking. *Issued May 1, 1992.*

EN928
29c ultramarine on white, unwatermarked, tagged, entire (EN919)   .80   .40

EN929
11.1c red and blue on white, unwatermarked, tagged, entire (EN920)   .40   .30

EN930
29c blue, maroon, and rose on white, tagged, entire (EN921)   .80   .40

EN931
29c red and blue on white, tagged, entire * (EN922)   .80   .40

EN932
29c bluish gray and yellow, unwatermarked, tagged, entire (EN924)   .80   .40

EN933
29c yellow green, with hologram, tagged, entire * (EN925)   .80   .40

1992. Bulk Mailing. *Printed by offset and letterpress.*

EN934 *Star.*

EN934 (U628)
19.8c red and blue on white, tagged
    (May 19,1992) entire   .55   .40

1992. Disabled American Issue. *Printed by letterpress.*

EN935 *Woman in wheelchair.*

EN935 *(U629)*
  29c red and blue on white, tagged
  (July 22, 1992) entire   .75   .40

1993. Kitten Issue. *Printed by offset and letterpress.*

EN936 *Siamese kitten.*

EN936 *(U630)*
  29c cyan, black and purple on white, tagged
  (Oct. 2, 1993) entire   .75   .40

1994. Football. *Printed by offset and letterpress.*

 EN937 *Football*

EN937 *(U631)*
  29c Brown and black on white, tagged .75   .40
  (Sept. 17, 1994) entire

1994. Old Glory. *Number 6 3/4 and 10 envelopes.*

 EN938, 939 *Flag*

EN938 *(U633)*
  (32c) red and blue on white, tagged
  (Jan. 3, 1995) entire   .75   .40

EN939 *(U634)*
  (32c) red on blue on white, tagged
  entire   .75   .40

1995. Liberty Bell.

 EN940 *Liberty Bell*

EN940 *(U632)*
  32c greenish blue and blue on white,
  tagged, (Jan. 3,1995) entire   .75   .40

1995. Non-Profit. Sheep.

 EN941 *Sheep*

EN941 *(U635)*
  (5c) green and red brown on white,
  (March 10, 1995) entire   .75   .40

1995. Bulk Rate. Eagle.

 EN942 *Eagle*

EN942 *(U636)*
  (10c) dark red and blue on white,
  (March 10, 1995) entire   .75   .40

1995. Heart Spiral.

 EN943 *Heart*

EN943 *(U637)*
  32c red on light blue (March 12,1995)
  entire   .75   .40

1995. Liberty Bell. *Number 9 size envelope.*

EN944 *(U638)*
  32c greenish blue and blue on security paper
     (May 16, 1995) entire   .75   .40

1995. Space Hologram.

EN945 *Space station*

EN945 *(U639)*
  32c red on white *(Sept. 22, 1995)*
     entire   .75   .40

1996. Save Our Environment.

EN946

EN946 *(U640)*
  32c multicolored on white,
     (April 20, 1996) entire   .75   .40

1996. Parolympic Games.

EN947

EN947 *(U641)*
  32c multicolored on white,
     (May 2,1996) entire   .75   .40

Air Mail Envelopes

The order authorizing air mail envelopes expressly provided they be printed on white paper and have red, white, and blue borders.

Some experimenting was needed to produce these borders. On the first issues, five different types of borders are known to collectors.

Red Lozenge at Upper Right
Border 1: The lozenges along the top edge and parallel to the edge measure 9 to 10 mm, and with the top flap open measure along the oblique side 11 to 13 mm. Small envelopes only.

Border 2: Like Border 1 except that the lozenges measure only 7 to 8 mm along the oblique side (with the top flap open). Small size envelopes only.

Border 3: Like Border 1 except the lozenges measure 11 to 12 mm parallel to the edge of the envelope. Large size envelopes only.

Blue Lozenge at Upper Right — Large size envelopes only

Border 4: Like Border 2 except with a blue lozenge at upper right corner.

Border 5: Like Border 4 except the lozenges at top point to the right (all others point to the left).

The borders are of importance to collectors and cut squares should be preserved to include them.

After the experimentation on the first issue (AEN1-AEN2), the borders were standardized as Border 2 (red lozenge at upper right) for small size envelopes and Border 4 (blue lozenge at upper right) for large size envelopes.

Special Air Mail Envelopes for Puerto Rico

The U.S. domestic air mail rate from 1929 to 1932 was five cents, as evidenced by the 5c stamps (AEN1-AEN2). The air mail rate to or from Puerto Rico, however, was 10 cents. Persons desiring to send air mail to, or from, either place simply used a 5c air mail envelope to which they affixed a 5c adhesive stamp.

In 1932 the domestic air mail rate for the United States was advanced to eight cents and new 8c air mail envelopes were issued (AEN3). In 1934 the rate was reduced to six cents with a resulting change in the stamps on the air mail envelopes (AEN4-AEN7).

AEN1 *Vertical rudder islopes off to the left*

1929.
AEN1 *(UC1)*

5c blue, Border 1 *(Jan. 12, 1929)*	4.00	2.50
entire	5.50	3.00
v. Border 2	4.00	2.50
entire	5.50	3.00
v1. Border 3	4.00	2.50
entire	7.50	6.00
v2. Border 4	4.00	2.50
entire	9.00	6.00
v2a. entire, 1933 watermark	750.	—
v2b. entire, 1937 watermark	—	—
v3. Border 5	4.00	2.50
entire	9.00	6.00
v4. border omitted	700.	—

AEN2 *Vertical rudder is semi-circular*

AEN2 *(UC2)*

5c blue, Border 2	12.50	6.00
entire	17.50	7.00
entire, 1933 watermark	700.	—
v. Border 4	12.	6.00
entire	20.	13.
va. entire, 1933 watermark	350.	—
v1. Border 5	—	—
entire	—	—

AEN3

1932.
AEN3 *(UC7)*

8c olive, Border 4 *(Sept. 26, 1932)*	15.	5.00
entire	20.	7.00
v. Border 2	—	—
entire	—	—

1934-44. With the change of the air mail rate to six cents, the 6c orange design copied the old 5c design. The old master die of the 5c was used to produce blank printing dies, into each of which the figure "6" then was cut by hand. Eleven of these dies were so made; each, of course, differs materially from the other. To simplify the collecting of these, collectors divided the 11 varieties into three general classifications, as follows:

1 (AEN4): the figure "6" measures
6 1/2 mm wide
2 (AEN5): the figure "6" measures
6 mm wide
3 (AEN6): the figure "6" measures
5 1/2 mm wide

Finally, in 1942, a new master 6c air mail die was made (AEN7), from which were struck as many printing dies as were necessary. Al such printing dies struck from this past die were identical and may not be individually identified.

With the outbreak of World War II, there was an enormous demand by the armed forces overseas for air mail envelopes. To expedite manufacturing, the borders were ordered dropped. All borderless air mail envelopes were shipped overseas and were not available to the civilian population in this country until after the war.

AEN4-AEN6
*Vertical rudder is
semi-circular*

AEN4 (UC3)
6c orange, Border 2 *(July 1, 1934)*	1.75	.50
entire	2.00	.70
v. Border 4	—	—
entire	—	—
v1. without border, entire	3.00	1.75

AEN5 (UC4)
6c orange, Border 2 (1942)	3.00	2.25
entire	60.	25.
v. Border 4	—	—
entire	—	—
v1. without border, entire	5.00	2.50

AEN6 (UC5)
6c orange, no border (1944)	1.00	.35
entire	1.25	.50

AEN7 *Vertical rudder
slopes forward*

AEN7 *(UC6)*
6c orange, Border 2 (1942)	1.75	.75
entire	2.50	1.00
v. Border 4	—	—
entire	—	—
v1. without border, entire	3.00	1.25
v2. on blue paper (error), no border, entire	4,000.	2,700.
v3. Red lozenges of border omitted, entire	1,200.	—

1945. In March to alleviate the enormous demand for air mail envelopes which the printer had not been able to supply, the Post Office approved the overprinting of 60 million ordinary 2c envelopes (AEN8-AEN14). The overprinting was done in New York and great care was taken to keep any envelopes other than those authorized from being re-valued. All were shipped to the armed forces.

By the following September, the air mail rates had been reduced from 6c to 5c, and re-valuing of the 6c air mail borderless 6c air mail envelopes was performed.

Following the war, remainders of these revalued envelopes were called in and destroyed, because they were confusing to the postal clerks. Adequate supplies, however, reached philatelic hands.

AEN 8-12

AEN8 (UC8)
6c on 2c carmine (EN549), Die A	1.50	.75
entire	2.00	1.25

AEN9
6c on 2c carmine (EN574), Die H	—	—
entire	—	—

AEN10
6c on 2c carmine (EN578), Die H2	—	—
entire	—	—

AEN11
6c on 2c carmine (EN581), Die I	—	—
entire	—	—

AEN12 *(UC9)*
6c on 2c carmine (EN810)	80.	45.
entire	125.	75.

On 1c green envelope of 1916-50 issue (error)

AEN13 *(UC8a)*
6c on 1c green (EN520), Die A	1,900.	—
entire	2,700.	—

REVALUED
5¢   AEN13-18
P.O.DEPT.

On 3c purple envelope of 1916-50 issue (error)

AEN14 *(UC8b)*
6c on 3c purple (EN588), Die I	1,900.	—
entire	2,700.	—

Black overprint on 6c orange air mail envelopes, without borders, of 1934-44 issue

AEN15 (*UC10*)

5c on 6c orange (AEN4v1)	3.50	2.00
entire	4.00	3.00
v. Double overprint, entire	75.	—

AEN16 (*UC11*)

5c on 6c orange (AENv1)	10.	6.00
entire	12.50	8.00
v. Double overprint, entire	—	—

AEN17 (*UC12*)

5c on 6c orange (AEN6)	.75	.55
entire	1.50	.75
v. Double overprint, entire	65.	—

AEN18 (*UC13*)

5c on 6c orange (AEN7v1)	1.00	.75
entire	125.	.75
v. Double overprint. entire	65.	—

AEN19 *DC-4 Skymaster. The small projection directly below the rudder is rounded*

AEN20 *The small protection directly below the rudder is a sharp point*

1946. DC 4 Skymaster.

AEN19 (*UC14*)

5c carmine, Border 2 *(Sept. 25, 1946)*	.85	.25
entire	1.25	.50

AEN20 (*UC15*)

5c carmine, Border 2	1.00	.35
entire	1.25	.50
v. with Border 4	—	—
entire	—	—

1947. U.S. Postage Stamp Centenary. Issued to compliment the Centenary International Philatelic Exhibition in New York City. The envelopes were printed on a demonstration machine at the exhibition. The envelopes also were produced at the factory in Dayton, Ohio, from both a flat and a rotary die, for distribution throughout the country. Approximately eight million envelopes were issued, of which the rotary die printings are more common. *Flat Die measures 21 3/4 mm high; rotary die measures 22 1/2 mm high.*

AEN21

AEN21 (*UC17*)

5c carmine, Border 2, rotary die *(May 21, 1947)*	.50	.35
entire	.75	.45
v. Flat die	.60	.40
entire	.75	.50

1950.

AEN22

Type 1: figure "6"'s are upright

Type 2. figure "6"'s are upright

AEN22 (*UC18*)

6c carmine, Border 2, Type 1 *(Sept. 22, 1950)*	.50	.25
entire	.75	.40
v. Type 2	.90	.35
entire	1.15	.40
v1. Border 4, Type 1	—	—
entire	—	—
v2. Border 4, Type 2	—	—
entire	—	—

1951-52. The return to a 6c air mail rate in 1950 caused the Post Office to revalue existing supplies of 5c air mail envelopes in some larger post offices. The re-valuing was done on a "ticometer," a new machine developed by Pitney-Bowes Co. This process first was done in 1951, and again in 1952. Different styles of slugs were used to make the overprint on each occasion.

 AEN23, AEN24

Overprint in red to left of stamp On 5c air mail envelopes of 1946 issue.

AEN23 (*UC19*)

6c on 5c carmine, Border 2 (AEN19) *(Sept. 29, 1951)*	1.00	.65
entire	1.50	1.00

AEN24 (*UC20*)

6c on 5c carmine, Border 2 (AEN20)	.95	.65
entire	1.40	1.10
v. with Border 4 (AEN20v)	—	—
entire	—	—

 AEN25-AEN27

Overprint in red to left of stamp. On 5c air mail envelopes of 1946 and 1947 issues

AEN25 *(UC21)*

6c on 5c (AEN19)	30.	20.
entire	35.	25.

AEN26
Type 1: (Left) short cloud
Type 2: (Right) long cloud

AEN26 *(UC22)*

6c on 5c (AEN20) *(Aug. 29, 1952)*	4.00	3.00
entire	6.00	5.00
v. with Border 4 (AEN20t)	—	—
entire	—	—

AEN27 *(UC23)*

6c on 5c carmine (AEN21)	—	—
entire	1,400.	—

1956. FIPEX Envelope. Issued in celebration of the Fifth International Philatelic Exhibition. The embossed stamp shows an eagle in flight.

AEN28 *(UC25)*

6c carmine red, Type 1 *(May 2, 1956)*	.90	.65
entire	1.25	1.00
v. Type 2	—	—
entire	—	—

1958.

AEN29

AEN29 *(UC26)*

7c blue, Border 2 *(July 31, 1958)*	.80	.70
entire	1.25	.75
v. Border 4	—	—
entire	—	—

AEN30

AEN30 *(UC33)*

7c blue, Border 2 *(Nov. 21, 1958)*	.70	.35
entire	.80	.40
v. with Border 4	—	—
entire	—	—

1958. On August 1, 1958, air mail rates were advanced to 7c, necessitating new envelopes and the re-valuing of surplus stocks of the 6c air mail envelopes. The same surcharging device was used as for re-valuing the 3c regular postage stamps.

Type 11 Surcharge   Type 12 Surcharge

Overprinted in green to left of stamp on 6c orange of 1934-44 (circular die) issue, no borders

AEN31 *(UC27)*

6c orange, Die 1 (AEN4v1)	250.	250.
entire	300.	275.

AEN32 *(UC28)*

6c orange, Die 2 (AEN5v1)	.70	80.
entire	100.	115.

AEN33 *(UC29)*

6c orange, Die 3 (AEN6)	40.	55.
entire	50.	80.

On 6c carmine of 1950 (Skymaster design) issue

AEN34 *(UC30)*

6c carmine, Border 2, Type 1(AEN22)	1.25	.65
entire	1.35	.80
v. Type 2 (AEN22v)	1.25	.65
entire	1.35	.80
v1. Border 4, Type 1 (AEN22v2)	—	—
entire	—	—
v2. Border 4, Type 2 (AEN22v3)	—	—
entire	—	—

On 6c carmine of 1956 (FIPEX) issue

AEN35 *(UC31)*

6c carmine, Type 1 (AEN28)	1.25	.75
entire	1.75	1.00
v. Type 2	—	—
entire	—	—

1960. Type AEN30 in new color.

AEN36 *(UC34)*

7c red, Border 2 *(Aug. 15, 1960)*	.75	.40
entire	1.00	.45
v. Border 4	—	—
entire	—	—

1963.

AEN37

AEN37 *(UC36)*

  8c red, Border 2 *(Nov. 17, 1962)*   .75   .25
    entire   1.00   .40
    v. Border 4   —   —
      entire   —   —

1965.

         AEN38

*Border 6 has a blue lozenge above and to left of stamp.
Border 7 has a red lozenge above and to left of stamp.*

AEN38 *(UC37)*

  8c red, Border 6 *(Jan. 7, 1965)*   .50   .25
    entire   .60   .40
    v. Border 7 (error)   —   —
      entire   25.   —
    z. Tagged *(Aug.15, 1967)*   1.50   .50
      entire   2.00   1.00

1968.

    AEN39 *Type 12
surcharge printed in red
to left of stamp on 8c air
mail envelopes AEN38*

AEN39 *(UC41)*

  8c red plus 2c red, Border 6
       (Feb. 5, 1968)   .80   .25
    entire   1.25   .50

AEN40 *(UC40)*

  10c red, Border 6, tagged *(Jan. 8, 1968)*   .60   .25
    entire   1.00   .25

1971.

AEN41

AEN41 *(UC43)*

  11c red and blue *(May 6, 1971)*   .60   .25
    entire   .75   .25

1971. *Revalued at left of stamp, printed on AEN40*

AEN42 *(UC45)*

  10c red plus 1c red *(June 28,1971)*   1.75   .30
    entire   2.25   .65

1973.

   AEN43

AEN43 *(UC47)*

  13c red, luminescent ink *(Dec. 1, 1973)*   .40   .25
    entire   .50   .25

Air Letter Sheets, Aerogrammes
Listings are for entires, only.

1947. *Printed by letterpress.* There are four types of
inscription:
    Type A: "AIR LETTER" on face; two-line inscription on
back (when folded).
    Type B: "AIR LETTER" on face; four-line inscription on
back (when folded)
    Type C: "AIR LETTER —AEROGRAMME" on face; four-
line inscription on back (when folded)
    Type D: "AIR LETTER — AEROGRAMME" on face;
three-line inscription on back (when folded)

    ALS1

ALS1 *(UC16)*

  10c carmine on bluish, Type A
       (Apr. 29, 1947)   9.00   7.00
    v. Blue overlay on inner side
       omitted   —   —
    v1. Reverse die cutting   125.   —
    v2. Type B *(UC168)(Sept.1951)*   18.50   16.
    v2a. chocolate (error of color)   450.   —
    v2a. Reverse die cutting   300.   —
    v3. Type C *(UC160) (Nov. 1953)*   55.   15.
    v3a. Reverse die cutting   —   —
    v4. Type D *(UC160) (1955)*   9.00   9.00
    v4a. Reverse die cutting   70.   —

1958. Paper tinted blue without overlay. *Printed by
letterpress.* New inscriptions:
    Type E: two-line inscription on back
         (when folded)
    Type F: three-line inscription on back
         (when folded)

   ALS2

ALS2 *(UC32)*

  10c blue and red, Type E
       (Sept. 12, 1958)   7.50   6.00
    v. Red omitted   —   —
    v1. Blue omitted   —   —
    v2. Reverse die cutting   80.   —
    v3. Type F   12.50   7.50

1961. *Printed by typography.*

ALS3

ALS3 *(UC35)*
    11c red and blue on bluish
          (June 16, 1961)   3.50   2.50
          v. Red omitted   900.   —
          v1. Blue omitted   900.   —
          v2. Reverse die cutting   40.   —

Type G: "AEROGRAMME PAR AVION" on face at bottom, two-line inscription on back.

1965.

ALS4 *John F. Kennedy*

ALS4 *(UC38)*
    11c red and blue on bluish, Type G
          (May 29, 1965)   4.00   3.00
          v. reverse die cutting   45.   —

1967. Same design as ALS4.
ALS5 *(UC39)*
    13c red and blue on bluish, Type G
          (May 29, 1967)   3.50   3.00
          v1. Blue omitted   600.   —
          v2. Red omitted   600.   —
          v3. Reverse die cutting   —   —

1968. 20th Anniversary of Universal Declaration of Human Rights.

ALS7

ALS6 *(UC42)*
    13c multicolored on bluish, tagged GB
          (Dec. 3, 1968)   10.00   5.50
          v. Black omitted   —   —
          v1. Brown omitted   —   —
          v2. Orange omitted   —   —
          z. Untagged (error)   —   —
          zo. Tagging omitted (error)   —   —

1971. Birds.

ALS7 *(UC44)*
    15c multicolored on bluish
          (May 28, 1971)   2.00   1.50

ALS8

ALS8 *(UC44a)*
    15c multicolored on bluish
          (Dec. 13, 1971)   2.00   1.50

1973. Hot Air Ballooning.

ALS9

ALS9 *(UC46)*
    15c multicolored on bluish, Type G
          (Feb. 10, 1973)   1.00   .60

1974. Globe and Jet.

ALS10

ALS10 *(UC48)*
    18c red and blue on bluish, tagged
          (Jan. 4, 1974)   1.25   .40
          v. Red omitted   —   —
          v1. Reverse die cutting   —   —

1974. 25th Anniversary of NATO.

ALS11

ALS11 *(UC49)*
    18c red and blue on bluish, tagged
          (Apr. 4, 1974)   1.25   .50

1976.

ALS12

ALS12 *(UC50)*
22c red and blue on bluish, tagged
    (Jan. 16, 1976)   1.25   .50
    v. Reverse die cutting   —   —

1978.

ALS13

ALS13 *(UC51)*
22c blue on bluish, tagged
    (Nov. 3, 1978)   1.25   .40
    v. Reverse die cutting   30.   —

1979. Olympic Games.

ALS14

ALS14 *(UC52)*
22c red, green and black on bluish,
    tagged *(Dec. 5, 1979)*   1.75   .40

1980. Tourism and Travel.

ALS15

ALS15 *(UC53)*
30c multicolored on bluish, tagged
    (Dec. 29, 1980)   1.00   .40
    v. Red omitted   100.   —
    v1. Reverse die cutting   —   —

1981. Travel and Tourism.

ALS16 *(UC54)*
30c yellow, red, blue and black on blue, tagged
    (Sept. 21, 1981)   1.00   .40
    v. Reverse die cutting   25.   —

1982. World Trade Aerogramme.

ALS17 *Made in U.S.A.*

ALS17 *(UC55)*
30c multicolored on blue, tagged
    (Sept. 16, 1982)   1.25   .40

1983. World Communications Year.

ALS18

ALS18 *(UC56)*
30c multicolored on blue, tagged
    (Jan. 7, 1983)   1.25   .40
    v. Reverse die cutting   35.   —

1983. Olympics '84.

ALS19

ALS19 *(UC57)*
30c multicolored, tagged
 (Oct. 14, 1983)   1.25 .40

1985. LANDSAT.

     ALS20

ALS20 *(UC58)*
36c multicolored on blue, tagged
 (Feb. 14, 1985)   1.25 .50
 v. Reverse die cutting 35. —

1985. Travel.

     ALS21

ALS21 *(UC59)*
36c multicolored on blue, tagged
 (May 21, 1985)   1.25 .50
 v. Black omitted   — —
 v1. Reverse die cutting 30. —

1985. Mark Twain / Halley's Comet.

ALS22 *(UC60)*
36c multicolored, tagged *(Dec. 4, 1985)*1.25 .50
 v. Reverse die cutting 30. —

1988.

     ALS23

ALS23 *(UC61)*
39c multicolored, tagged *(May 9, 1988)*1.25 .50

1988. Abraham Lincoln and Montgomery Blair;
Universal Postal Union.

     ALS24

ALS24 *(UC62)*
39c multicolored, tagged *(Nov. 20, 1988)*.25 .50

1991.

     ALS25,
     ALS26
     Eagle

ALS25 *(UC63a)*
45c blue, gray, and red, tagged
 (May 17, 1991)   1.50 .65
ALS26 *(UC63)*
45c blue, gray, and red on blue,
 tagged   1.50 .65
ALS27 *(UC64)*
50c multicolored on blue,
 tagged *(Sept.23, 1995)* 1.50 .65

Official Envelopes

Official envelopes came into being when the franking privilege for government officials and departments was abolished in 1873. Adhesive stamps were issued for all departments of the government, but envelopes were issued for the Post Office and War Departments only. They were discontinued after 1879, although the War Department continued to use them for some years thereafter.

Post Office Department

1873. Manufactured by George H. Reay

 PDEN1 *Small, finely executed numeral "2"*

Envelope Watermark 2

PDEN1 *(U01)*
2c black on canary	11.	7.00
entire	15.	11.

 PDEN2-PDEN3 *Small, finely executed numeral "3"*

PDEN2 *(U02)*
3c black on canary	6.00	5.00
entire	10.	8.00

PDEN3 *(U03)*
3c black on white	7,000.	—
entire	16,000.	—

 PDEN4 *Small, finely executed numeral "6"*

PDEN4 *(U04)*
6c black on canary	13.	11.
entire	19.	16.

1874. Manufactured by Plimpton Manufacturing Co.

 PDEN5, PDEN6 *Tall, heavy "2"*

Watermark 2, 4, 5

PDEN5 *(U05)*
2c black on canary	5.00	4.00
entire	8.00	5.00

PDEN6 *(U06)*
2c black on white	50.	30.
entire	55.	35.

 PDEN7-PDEN11 *Tall "3"*

PDEN7 *(U07)*
3c black on canary	3.00	1.00
entire	4.00	1.50

PDEN8 *(U08)*
3c black on white	900.	900.
entire	1,000.	—

PDEN9 *(U09)*
3c black on amber	40.	29.
entire	50.	45.

PDEN10 *(U010)*
3c black on blue	16,000.	—
entire	19,000.	—

PDEN11 *(U011)*
3c blue on blue	15,000.	—
entire	17,000.	—

 PDEN12, PDEN13 *Tall "6"*

PDEN12 *(U012)*
6c black on canary	4.50	4.25
entire	9.00	4.50

PDEN13 *(U013)*
6c black on white	550.	—
entire	750.	—

United States Postal Service
1877.

 PDEN14-PDEN17

Unwatermarked and Watermark 2, 4, 5

PDEN14 *(U014)*
black on white	4.00	3.50
entire	6.00	5.00

PDEN15 *(U015)*
black on amber	30.	21.
entire	90.	40.

PDEN16 *(U016)*
blue on amber	35.	25.
entire	90.	45.

PDEN17 *(U017)*
blue on blue	6.00	6.00
entire	8.00	8.00

War Department
1873. Manufactured by George H. Reay.

WDEN18-WDEN20 *Benjamin Franklin. Point of bust narrow and points at "N" of "ONE."*

WDEN18 *(U018)*
1c dark red on white — 500. — 300.
   entire — 750. — 350.

WDEN19 *(U030)*
1c vermilion on white — 200. — —
   entire — 275. — —

WDEN20 *(U031)*
1c vermilion on manila, wrapper — 11. — 8.00
   entire — 20. — 15.

WDEN21-WDEN23 *Andrew Jackson. Point of bust broad and square.*

WDEN21 *(U019)*
2c dark red on white — 650. — 350.
   entire — 750. — —

WDEN22 *(U032)*
2c vermilion on white — 260. — —
   entire — 5,000. — —

WDEN23 *(U033)*
2c vermilion on manila, wrapper — 200. — —
   entire — 300. — —

WDEN24-WDEN29 *George Washington. The ponytail projects below the bottom of the bust*

WDEN24 *(U020)*
3c dark red on white — 50. — 40.
   entire — 150. — —

WDEN25 *(U021)*
3c dark red on amber — *13,000.* — —
   entire — 17,000. — —

WDEN26 *(U022)*
3c dark red on cream — 450. — 200.
   entire — 550. — 225.

WDEN27 *(U034)*
3c vermilion on white — 75. — 40.
   entire — 150. — —

WDEN28 *(U035)*
3c vermilion on amber — 85. — —
   entire — 250. — —

WDEN29 *(U036)*
3c vermilion on cream — 13. — 7.00
   entire — 40. — 20.

WDEN30-WDEN33 *Abraham Lincoln. Back of neck is long*

WDEN30 *(U023)*
6c dark red on white — 170. — 70.
   entire — 200. — —

WDEN31 *(U024)*
6c dark red on cream — 1,400. — 350.
   entire * — 2,400. — *1,500.*

WDEN32 *(U037)*
6c vermilion on white — — — —
   entire — — — —

WDEN33 *(U038)*
6c vermilion on cream — 350. — —
   entire * — *6,500.* — —

WDEN34, WDEN35 *Thomas Jefferson. The ponytail does not project at back.*

WDEN34 *(U025)*
10c dark red on white — *2,700.* — 280.
   entire * — *5,000.* — 550.

WDEN35 *(U039)*
10c vermilion on white — 200. — —
   entire * — 350. — —

WDEN36, WDEN37 *Henry Clay. Ear covered by hair.*

WDEN36 *(U026)*
12c dark red on white — 100. — 40.
   entire * — 140. — —

WDEN37 *(U040)*
12c vermilion on white — 150. — —
   entire * — 200. — —

WDEN38, WDEN39 *Daniel Webster. Face with sideburns.*

WDEN38 *(U027)*
15c dark red on white — 100. — 45.
   entire* — 125. — 400.

WDEN39 *(U041)*
15c vermilion on white — 250. — —
   entire* — 2,500. — —

WDEN40, WDEN41 *Winfield Scott*

WDEN40 *(U028)*
24c dark red on white 135. 35.
  entire* 100. —
WDEN41 *(U042)*
24c vermilion on white 375. —
  entire* 400. —

WDEN42, WDEN43 *Alexander Hamilton. Bust at back ends in a narrow point.*

WDEN42 *(U029)*
30c dark red on white 400. 110.
  entire * 450. 180.
WDEN43 *(U043)*
30c vermilion on white 375. —
  entire * 475. —

1875. Produced by Plimpton Manufacturing Co.

WDEN44-WDEN46 *Benjamin Franklin. Point of bust is broad*

Watermarks 2, 3, 4, 5, 6

WDEN44 *(U044)*
1c red on white 125. 100.
  entire 135. —
WDEN45 *(U045)*
1c red on amber 750. —
WDEN45A *(U045A)*
1c red on orange *18,000.* —
WDEN46 *(U046)*
1c red on manila, wrapper 3.00 1.75
  entire 6.00 4.00

WDEN47-WDEN50 *Andrew Jackson. Forward slope of bust is rounded*

WDEN47 *(U047)*
2c red on white 100. —
  entire 125. —
WDEN48 *(U048)*
2c red on amber 25. 15.
  entire 35. 25.

WDEN49 *(U049)*
2c red on orange 45. 13.
  entire 45. 20.
WDEN50 *(U050)*
2c red on manila, wrapper 70. 45.
  entire 90. —

WDEN51-WDEN55 *George Washington. The ponytail does not project below bust but protrudes toward rear*

WDEN51 *(U051)*
3c red on white 11. 9.00
  entire 12. 10.
WDEN52 *(U052)*
3c red on amber 12. 9.00
  entire 15. 13.
WDEN53 *(U053)*
3c red on cream 6.00 3.00
  entire 8.00 5.00
WDEN54 *(U054)*
3c red on blue 4.00 3.00
  entire 5.00 4.00
WDEN55 *(U055)*
3c red on fawn 5.00 2.00
  entire 7.00 3.00

WDEN56-WDEN58 *Abraham Lincoln. Back of bust is short*

WDEN56 *(U056)*
6c red on white 35. 22.
  entire 70. —
WDEN57 *(U057)*
6c red on amber 70. 30.
  entire 75. —
WDEN58 *(U058)*
6c red on cream 170. 70.
  entire 200. —

WDEN59, WDEN60 *Thomas Jefferson. The ponytail projects at back*

WDEN59 *(U059)*
10c red on white 150. 90.
  entire 175. —
WDEN60 *(U060)*
10c red on amber 1,100. —
  entire 1,400. —

WDEN61-WDEN63 *Henry Clay. Clearly defined ear*

WDEN61 *(U061)*
12c red on white   40.   35.
   entire *   100.   —
WDEN62 *(U062)*
12c red on amber   650.   —
   entire *   700.   —
WDEN63 *(U063)*
12c red on cream   600.   —
   entire *   750.   —

WDEN64-WDEN67 *Daniel Webster. Face without sideburns*

WDEN64 *(U064)*
15c red on white   175.   135.
   entire *   200.   —
WDEN65 *(U065)*
15c red on amber   700.   —
   entire *   750.   —
WDEN66 *(U066)*
15c red on cream   650.   —
   entire *   700.   —

WDEN67-WDEN69 *Alexander Hamilton. Bust at back is broad*

WDEN67 *(U067)*
30c red on white   150.   125.
   entire *   180.   —
WDEN68 *(U068)*
30c red on amber   1,000.   —
   entire *   1,100.   —
WDEN69 *(U069)*
30c red on cream   1,000.   —
   entire *   1,100.   —

United States Postal Savings

PSEN70, PSEN71 (l)
PSEN72, PSEN73 (r)

Watermarks 15, 16, 17, 18

PSEN70 *(U070)*
1c green on white   60.   15.
   entire *   75.   45.

PSEN71 *(U071)*
1c green on buff   185.   60.
   entire *   220.   75.
PSEN72 *(U072)*
2c carmine on white   8.00   3.00
   entire *   13.   9.00
PSEN73 *(U072a)*
2c carmine on manila   1,700.   —
   entire *   2,500.   —

Official Mail
1983.

PDEN74

PDEN74 *(U073)*
20c blue on white, entire
   (Jan. 12, 1983)   1.25   40.

1985.

PDEN75

PDEN75 *(U074)*
22c blue on white, entire
   (Feb. 26, 1985)   1.00   6.00

1987. *Printed by letterpress. Used exclusivly to mail U.S. Savings bonds.*

PDEN75A
Issued solely to mail U.S. Savings Bonds.

PDEN75A *(U075)*
22c blue on white, entire
   (Mar. 2, 1987)   1.00   25.

1988. Non-Denominated "E." *Printed by letterpress.*

PDEN76
Issued solely to mail U.S. Savings Bonds.

PDEN76 *(U076)*
(25c) black and blue on white, entire
   (Mar. 22, 1988)   1.25   20.

1988. Denominatated 25c.

PDEN77

Printed by letterpress and embossed

PDEN77 *(U077)*
    25c black and blue on white, entire
          (Apr. 11, 1988)   1.00   6.00

PDEN78, PDEN78A

Printed by letterpress

PDEN78 *(U078)*
    25c black and blue on white, entire thick
        lettering. *(Apr.11, 1988)* 1.00   25.
PDEN78A *(U078a)*
    25c black and blue on white, entire thick
        lettering   —   —

1990. *Printed by letterpress.* "Official" measures 13 mm; "USA" measures 16 mm.

PDEN79, PDEN80A

PDEN80, PDEN80B

PDEN79 *(U079)*
    45c black and blue, entire
        (March 17, 1990)   1.50   50.
PDEN80 *(U080)*
    65c black and blue, entire   1.75   55.

1990. Similar to above. *Printed by offset.* "Official" measures 14.5 mm; "USA" measures 17 mm.

PDEN80A *(U081)*
    45c black and blue, entire
        (Aug. 10, 1990)   1.50   50.
PDEN80B *(U082)*
    65c black and blue, entire   1.75   55.

1991. Non-denominated "F" Envelope.

PDEN81

PDEN81 *(U083)*
    (29c) black and blue on white, entire
        (Jan. 22, 1991)   1.00   20.

1991. Denominated 29c.

PDEN82

PDEN82 *(U084)*
    29c black and blue on white, entire
        (Apr. 6, 1991)   1.00   2.25

1991. *Envelope used solely to mail U.S..Savings Bonds.*

PDEN83

PDEN83 *(U085)*
    29c black and blue on white, entire
        (Apr. 17, 1991)   1.00   20.

1992. *Printed on unwatermarked paper with a "recycle" logo on reverse.*
PDEN84 *(U084v)*
    29c black and blue on white, entire
        (PDEN82) *May 1, 1992*   1.00   —
PDEN85 *(U085v)*
    29c black and blue on white, entire
        (PDEN83) *May 1, 1992*   1.00   —

1992. Consular Service Bicentennial.

PDEN86, PDEN87

PDEN86 *(U086)*
    52c blue and red on white, entire
        (July 10, 1992)   4.50   50.
PDEN87 *(U087)*
    75c blue and red on white, entire
        (July 10, 1992)   10.   55.
PDEN88 *(U088)*
    32c blue and red on white, entire
        (May 9, 1995)   1.00   5.00

Postal Cards

Postal cards vary greatly in size. Card sizes are not indicated except in those cases where the difference is important in making proper identification. So, too, the text on the face of the cards has been changed on numerous occasions. The exact wording is not indicated except when it is the determining factor of identification.

Postal cards normally are collected intact in one of the following three conditions: mint; unused (with printed or written address or message, but no postal marking); or used (with postal marking). Unused preprinted cards are not valued here.

1873. *Watermarked with large (90mm x 60 mm)"USPOD."*

PC1, PC2, *Profile   PC1 Watermark*
of Liberty

PC1 *(UX1)*
1c reddish brown on buff
  (*May 13, 1873*)   350.   20.

Watermark with small (55mm x 38 mm) "USPOD."

PC2 *(UX3)*
1c reddish brown on buff *(July 6, 1873)*   75.   3.00
  v. Unwatermarked   —   —

1875. Inscribed "WRITE THE ADDRESS ON THIS SIDE — THE MESSAGE ON THE OTHER." *Watermarked small (52mm x 36 mm) "USPOD."*

PC3, PC4, PC6 *Liberty*

PC3 *(UX4)*
1c black on buff *(Sept. 28, 1875)*   2,100.   325.

Unwatermarked. All subsequent U.S. Postal cards also are without watermarks.

PC4 *(UX5)*
1c black on buff *(Sept. 30, 1875)*   65.   7.00

1879. Universal Postal Union Card. Frame around card. Size 5 1/8 inches x 3 inches.

PC5, PC12, PC15 *Liberty*

PC5 *(UX6)*
2c blue on buff *(Dec. 1, 1879)*   30.   20.
  a. dark blue on buff   35.   22.

1881. Inscribed: "NOTHING BUT THE ADDRESS CAN BE PLACED ON THIS SIDE." 21 teeth   23 teeth

Normal, 21 teeth   23 teeth

PC6 *(UX7)*
1c black on buff, 21 teeth *(Oct. 17, 1881)* 55.   5.00
  v. 23 teeth   550.   35.
  v1. Printed on both sides   600.   425.

1885.

PC7 *Thomas Jefferson*

PC7 *(UX8)*
1c brown on buff *(Aug. 24, 1885)*   50.   2.50
  a. chocolate   75.   10.
  b. orange brown   50.   2.50
  c. red brown   50.   3.00
  v. Double impression   —
  v1. Double impression, one inverted   —
  v2. Printed on both sides   —

1886.

PC8 *(UX9)*
1c black on buff *(Dec. 1, 1886)*   17.50   .65
  a. black on dark buff   20.   2.50
  v. Double impression   —
  v1. Double impression, one
    inverted   —

PC8 *Thomas Jefferson*

1891.

PC9, PC10 *Ulysses S. Grant*

PC9 *(UX10)*
1c black on buff, 155mm x 95mm
    (Dec. 16, 1891)   35.   2.50
    v. Double impression   —
PC10 *(UX11)*
1c blue on grayish, 117mm x 75mm
    (Dec. 16, 1891)   15.   4.00
    v. Double impression,
        one inverted   —

1894.

PC11 *Thomas Jefferson with small wreath*

PC11 *(UX12)*
1c black on buff *(Jan. 2, 1894)*   40.   1.50
    v. Double impression   —

1897. Universal Postal Union. Same design as PC5, but larger (5 1/2 inches x 3 1/2 inches).

PC12 *(UX13)*
2c blue on light blue *(Jan. 25, 1897)*   165.   90.

PC13 *Thomas Jefferson with large wreath*

PC13 *(UX14)*
1c black on buff *(Dec. 1, 1897)*   30.   2.00
    v. Double impression, one
        inverted   —
    v1. Printed on both sides   —

1898.

PC14 *John Adams*

PC14 *(UX15)*
1c black on buff *(March 31, 1898)*   45.   27.50

1898. Universal Postal Union. Same design as PC5 and PC12, but without frame around card. (140mm x 82mm)
PC15 *(UX16)*
2c black on buff   12.50   10.

1902. Full-Face McKinley Card

(at left)   *(at right)*

PC16 *William McKinley, full face*

PC16 *(UX17)*
1c black on buff   5000.   2500.

1902. Profile McKinley Card

(at left)   *(at right)*
PC17 *William McKinley, profile*

PC17 *(UX18)*
1c black on buff   12.50   2.00
    v. Double impression   —

1907.

PC18, PC19 *William McKinley*

PC18 *(UX19)*
1c black on buff *(June 1907)*   40.   1.50

1908. Same design as PC18. Message space at left side. Inscribed (vertically) at side: "THE SPACE BELOW MAY BE USED FOR CORRESPONDENCE."

PC19 *(UX20)*
1c black on buff *(Jan. 2, 1908)*   50.   7.50

1910.

PC20 *William McKinley, area around head shaded*

PC20 *(UX21)*
1c blue on bluish *(Feb. 18, 1910)*   1.00   7.50
    a. bronze blue on bluish   170.   15.
    v. Points on four outer areas
       above and below "IS" in
       inscription to left of imprinted
       stamp   1,100.   550.
    v1. Double impression   —
    v2. Double impression, one
       inverted   —
    v3. Triple impression   —

PC21, PC23 *William McKinley, area around head without shading*

PC21 *(UX22)*
1c blue on bluish *(April 13, 1910)*   15.   .50
    p. Printed on thin paper (0.008
       inches thickness)   —   —
    v. Double impression, normal
       position   —   —

1911.

PC22, PC25 *Abraham Lincoln*

PC22 *(UX23)*
1c red on cream, *127mm x 76mm*
    (Jan. 21, 1911)   10.   7.50
    v. Double impression   —   —

1911. Same design as PC21.

PC23 *(UX24)*
1c carmine on cream *(Aug. 10, 1911)*   12.50   7.50
    a. scarlet   —
    v. Double impression   —

1911. Universal Postal Union.

PC24 *Ulysses S. Grant*

PC24 *(UX25)*
2c carmine on cream *(Oct. 27, 1911)*   1.75   9.00
    v. Double impression   —

1913. Same design as PC22; same size: 5 x 3 inches.

PC25 *(UX26)*
1c green on cream *(July 29, 1913)*   12.50   7.50

1914.

PC26, PC27 *Thomas Jefferson*

PC26 *(UX27)*
1c green on buff *(June 4 1914)*   .40   .30
    a. green on cream   3.75   .75
    b. green on off-white   3.75   .75
    v. Double impression   —

1916. Same design as PC26. Due to wartime shortages, an inferior rough-textured bluish gray paper was used for a short period. PC27 and PC28 were printed on this substitute paper.

PC27 *(UX27C)*
1c dark green on bluish gray   2000.   175.

1916. Recut die consisting of heavy hair lines and distinct hair lines in queue.

PC28 *Recut die*

PC28 *(UX27D)*
1c dark green on bluish gray
    (Dec. 22, 1916)   2100.   140.

1917. Small "library" size: 5 x 3 inches.

    PC29 *Abraham Lincoln*

PC29 *(UX28)*
1c green on cream
    (March 14 1917)   .75   .50
    a. green on dark buff   1.75   .75
    b. green on canary   —   —
    v. Double impression   —   —

1917.

Points   PC30 *Die 1, coarse impression*

PC30 *(UX29)*
2c carmine on cream *(Oct. 22, 1917)*   50.   3.00
    a. vermilion on cream   300.   70.
    b. lake on cream   50.   3.00
    c. carmine on buff   40.   3.00

1918.

Balls   PC31 *Die 2, clear impression*

PC31 *(UX30)*
2c carmine on cream *(Jan. 23, 1918)*   30.   2.75
    a. carmine on buff   —   —

1920. Surcharged "1CENT" in black on PC30 (die 1). PC32, PC33
The overprints were applied by a canceling machine (below left) or a printing press (below right)

    PC32, PC33

PC32 *(UX32)*
1c on 2c red on cream, *canceling machine*
    (Apr. 1920)   55.   12.50
    a. Press printing (UX39)   550.   50.
    v. Double surcharge   —
    v1. Inverted surcharge   —

1920. Similar overprint as PC32 on PC31 (Die 2).

PC33 *(UX33)*
1c on 2c red on cream *(April 1920)*   15.   12.50
    a. Press printing (UX35)   225.   35.
    v. Double surcharge   90.
    v1. Double surcharge, one
        inverted   —
    v2. Inverted surcharge   —
    v3. Triple surcharge   —

1920.

    PC34 *Overprinted in black on PC31 (Die 2)*

PC34 *(UX31)*
1c on 2c red on cream *(April 1920)*   3,800.   3,800.

1926. Universal Postal Union.

    PC35 *William McKinley* PC36 *Benjamin Franklin*

PC35 *(UX37)*
3c red orange on cream
    (Feb. 1, 1926)   5.00   10.
    a. red on canary   5.50   12.50
    b. deep carmine on canary   —   —
    c. orange red on dark buff —   —

1951.

PC36 *(UX38)*

2c carmine on buff *(Nov. 16, 1951)*	.50	.30
a. lake on buff	—	—
v. Double impression	225.	—

1952.

PC37 *Over-printed in green on PC26*

PC37 *(UX39)*

2c on 1c green on buff *(March 22, 1952)*	.75	.40
v. Double surcharge	20.	25.
v1. Surcharge vertical at left	7.50	9.00
v2. Surcharge vertical below stamp	—	

Press-printed surcharge

PC37A *(UX41)*

2c on 1c green on buff	5.50	2.50
v. Inverted surcharge, lower left	80.	130.
v1. Double surcharge	—	
v2. Split surcharge, top and bottom	—	

1952. Same surcharge on PC29. *Surcharged by Pitney Bowes Tickometer.*

PC38 *(UX40)*

2c on 1c green on buff *(March 22,1952)*	.75	.50
a. green on cream	.75	.50
b. green on canary	.75	.50
v. Double surcharge, normal position	—	
v1. Inverted surcharge, lower left	—	
v2. Double surcharge, one inverted	—	
v3. Vertical surcharge, left of stamp, reading down	7.00	6.00

Press-printed surcharge.

PC38A *(UX42)*

2c on 1c green on buff	6.00	2.50
v. Surcharge on reverse	85.	

1952. Small "library" size: 5 x 3 inches.

PC39 *Abraham Lincoln*

PC39 *(UX43)*

2c carmine on buff *(July 31, 1952)*	.30	2.00
a. lake on buff	—	

1956. Fipex Postal Card.

PC40 *Liberty*

PC40 *(UX44)*

2c red and dark violet blue on buff		
(May 4, 1956)	.30	2.00
a. rose and dark violet blue	1.75	1.25
v. Dark violet blue omitted	475.	250.
v1. Double impression of dark violet blue	18.	11.

1956.

PC41 *Liberty*   PC42 *Liberty*

PC41 *(UX45)*

4c scarlet and ultramarine on buff		
(Nov. 16, 1956)	1.75	50.

1958.

PC42 *(UX46)*

3c violet on buff *(Aug. 1, 1958)*	.60	.30
v. Double impression	—	—
v1. "I" of "IN" omitted	13.	26.
x. printed precancel bars *(Sept. 15, 1961)*	4.00	3.00

1958. PC36 revalued in black.

PC43 *Overprinted in black at left of PC36*

PC43 *(UX47)*

1c on 2c carmine on buff	175.	275.
v. Surcharge inverted lower left	—	

This surcharge was authorized for use by the General Electric Co. in Owensboro, Ky, which had prepared a large number of cards for an advertising campaign prior to the 1958 rate increase. In all, some 750,000 cards were surcharged.

1962.

PC44 *Abraham Lincoln*

PC44 (UX48)
4c lilac on white, precanceled
 (Nov. 19, 1962)   .30   .25
 p. Non-fluorescent paper, non-
  phosphorescent ink   —   —
 p1. Fluorescent paper, non-
  phosphorescent ink   —   —
 p2. Non-fluorescent paper,
  phosphorescent ink   .75   .25
 v. Double impression, normal   —

The phosphorescent ink was experimental tagging for expediting mail processing (cards placed on sale June 25, 1966).

1963. International Postal Card. Designed to promote tourism to the United States.

PC45 *Map of North America*

PC45 (UX49)
7c red and blue on white
 (Aug. 30, 1963)   4.50   40.
 v. Blue omitted   —
 v1. Red omitted   —

1964. 175th Anniversary of the Founding of the U.S. Customs Service.

PC46 *Map of United States and flags*

PC46 (UX50)
4c red and blue on white
 (Feb. 22, 1964)   .55   2.00
 a Blue omitted   600.
 v1. Red omitted   —

1964. In compliment to the International Social Security Association conference.

PC47

PC47 (UX51)
4c red and blue on white
 (Sept. 29, 1964)   .50   2.00
 p. Fluorescent paper   —   —
 v. Red omitted   —
 v1. Blue omitted   750.

1965. 175th Anniversary of the U.S. Coast Guard.

PC48 *U.S. Coast Guard flag*

PC48 (UX52)
4c red and blue on white
 (Aug. 4, 1965)   .50   2.00
 v. Blue omitted   —

1965. 175th Anniversary of the U.S. Census Bureau.

PC49

PC49 (UX53)
4c blue, light blue, and black on white
 (Oct. 21, 1965)   .40   2.00

1967. Design of PC45, Vacationland.

PC50 (UX54)
8c red and blue on white
 (Dec. 4, 1967)   4.25   40.

1968.

PC51 *Abraham Lincoln*

PC51 (UX55)
5c green on white
 (Jan. 4, 1968)   .35   .55
 v. Double impression   —

1968. 25th Anniversary of the Women Marines.

PC52 *Woman marine*

PC52 *(UX56)*

5c olive green and rose red on white

(July 26, 1968) .40 2.00

1970. 100th Anniversary of the Weather Services.

PC53 *Weather recording equipment*

PC53 *(UX57)*

5c yellow, blue, red and black on white, tagged,

(Sept. 1, 1970) .35 2.00

v. Black omitted 600.

v1. Black and yellow omitted —

v2. Blue omitted 600.

1971. Patriot Series. Paul Revere

PC54 *Paul Revere*

PC54 *(UX58)*

6c brown on white, tagged

(May 15, 1971) .35 2.00

v. Double impression 325. —

1971. Design of PC45, Vacationland.

PC55 *(UX59)*

10c red and blue on white, tagged

(June 10, 1971) 4.75 40.

1971. 200th Anniversary of New York Hospital.

PC56 *New York Hospital*

PC56 *(UX60)*

6c multicolored on white, tagged

(Sept. 16, 1971) .35 2.00

v. Blue and yellow omitted 700.

v1. Red omitted —

v2. Red and black omitted —

v3. Yellow omitted —

v4. Red and black impressions

shifted 25 mm left —

za. Tagging omitted —

1972. Tourism Year of the Americas. A luminescent panel of tagging is printed at the left of the stamp.

PC57 *Gloucester*

PC57 *(UX63)*

6c black on manila, tagged

(June 29, 1972) .50 4.50

zo. Tagging omitted —

U.S. POSTAGE 6 CENTS PC58 *Monument Valley*

PC58 *(UX62)*

6c black on manila, tagged .50 4.50

zo. Tagging omitted —

PC59 *USF Constellation*

PC59 *(UX61)*

6c black on manila, tagged .50 4.50

zo. Tagging omitted —

First-day cancels were available from any post office which had the cards in stock that day.

1972. Patriot Series. John Hanson

PC60 *John Hanson*

PC60 *(UX64)*

6c blue on white, tagged, smooth paper

(Sept. 1, 1972) .30 1.00

p. Coarse paper .30 1.00

1973. 100th Anniversary of the First U.S. Postal Card.

PC61 *Design similar to PC1*

PC61 *(UX65)*
6c magenta on manila
    (Sept. 14, 1973)   .30   2.00
    v. Double impression   —
    zo. Tagging omitted   —
    zv. Tagging inverted to lower left   —

1973. Patriot Series. Samuel Adams

PC62 *Samuel Adams*

PC62 *(UX66)*
8c orange on white, tagged, smooth paper
    (Dec. 16, 1973)   .50   1.00
    p. Printed on coarse paper   .50   1.00

1974. International Surface Mail.

PC63
Ship's figurehead

PC63 *(UX67)*
12c multicolored on white, tagged
    (Jan. 4, 1974)   .40   35.
    v. Yellow omitted   1,000

1975. Patriot Series. Charles Thomson

PC64
Charles Thomson

PC64 *(UX68)*
7c emerald green on white, tagged, smooth paper
    (Sept. 14, 1975)   .40   7.50
    If used after Dec. 31, 1975   .35
    p. Printed on coarse paper   —

1975. Patriot Series. John Witherspoon

PC65
John Witherspoon

PC65 *(UX69)*
9c yellow brown on white, tagged
    (Nov. 10, 1975)   .40   1.00

1976. Patriot Series. Caeser Rodney

PC66
Caesar Rodney

PC66 *(UX70)*
9c blue on white, tagged
    (July 1, 1976)   .35   2.00
    v. Double impression   —

1977. Historic Preservation Series. Federal Court House, Galveston, Texas.

PC67 *Federal Court House, Galveston, Texas*

PC67 *(UX71)*
9c multicolored on white, tagged
    (July 20, 1977)   .40   2.00
    v. Black omitted   —
    zo. Tagging omitted   —

1977. Patriot Series. Nathan Hale.

PC68 *Nathan Hale*

PC68 *(UX72)*
9c green on white, tagged
    (Oct. 14, 1977)   .35   1.00
    v. Double impression   —

1978. Historic Preservation Series. The Music Hall, Cincinnati, Ohio.

PC69
Music Hall, Cincinnati, Ohio

PC69 *(UX73)*
10c multicolored on white, tagged
    (May 12, 1978)   .40   2.00

1978. Patriot Series. John Hancock (non-denominated).

PC70
John Hancock (for domestic use only)

PC70 (UX74)
   (10c) brown orange on white, tagged
      (May 19, 1978)   .40   2.00

1978. Patriot Series. John Hancock (inscribed "10c").

PC71
John Hancock (denomination as numeral)

PC71 (UX75)
   10c orange on white, tagged
      (June 20, 1978)   .35   .30

1978. International Surface Mail Rate. U.S. Coast Guard Trainging Vessel *Eagle.*

PC72
U.S. Coast Guard Cutter Eagle

PC72 (UX76)
   14c multicolored on white, tagged
      (Aug. 4, 1978)   .45   20.

1978. American Revolution Series. Molly Pitcher.

PC73
Molly Pitcher (Mary Ludwig Hays)

PC73 (UX77)
   10c multicolored on white, tagged
      (Sept. 8, 1978)   .35   2.00

1979. American Revolution Series. George Rogers Clark.

PC74
George Rogers Clark

PC74 (UX78)
   10c multicolored on white, tagged
      (Feb. 3, 1979)   .35   2.00
      v. Yellow omitted   —

1979. Olympic Games. Sprinter.

PC75
Sprinter

PC75 (UX80)
   10c multicolored, tagged
      (Sept. 17, 1979)   .75   2.00
      zo. Tagging omitted   —

1979. Historic Preservation Series. Iolani Palace, Honolulu, Hawaii.

PC76
Iolani Palace, Hawaii

PC76 (UX81)
   10c multicolored on white, tagged
      (Oct. 1, 1979)   .35   2.00
      zo. Tagging omitted   —

1979. *American Revolution Series.* **Casimir Puloski.**

PC77
Gen. Casimir Pulaski

PC77 (UX79)
   10c multicolored on white, tagged
      (Oct. 11, 1979)   .35   2.00

1980. Olympic Games. Women's Figure Skater.

PC78
Figure skater

PC78 (UX82)
   14c multicolored, tagged
      (Jan. 15, 1980)   .75   12.50

1980. Historical Preservatioin Series. Salt Lake Temple.

PC79
Mormon Temple, Salt Lake City, Utah

PC79 *(UX83)*
    10c multicolored on white, tagged
        (April 5, 1980)   .35   2.00
        zo. Tagging omitted   —   —

PC80
Count Jean-Baptiste de Rochambeau

1980. American Revolution Series. Landing of Rochambeau.

PC80 *(UX84)*
    10c multicolored on white, tagged
        (July 11, 1980)   .35   2.00
        v. Black and yellow printed on reverse,
        front normal   —

1980. American Revolution Series. Battle of Kings Mountain, 1780.

PC81
Battle of Kings mountain

PC81 *(UX85)*
    10c multicolored, tagged
        (Oct. 7, 1980)   .35   2.00

1980. International Surface Rate. Drake's *Golden Hinde*, 1580.

PC82
The Golden Hinde, ship of Sir Francis Drake

PC82 *(UX86)*
    19c multicolored on white, tagged
        (Nov. 21, 1980)   .75   15.

1981. American Revolution Series. Battle of Cowpens, 1781.

PC83
Battle of Cowpens, 1781

PC83 *(UX87)*
    10c multicolored, tagged
        (Jan 17, 1981)   .35   5.00

1981. Domestic Rate, non-denominated Eagle.

PC84
Stylized Eagle

PC84 *(UX88)*
    (12c) purple on white
        (March 15, 1981)   .40   1.00

1981. Patriot Series. Isiah Thomas

PC85
Isaiah Thomas

PC85 *(UX89)*
    12c blue on white
        (May 5, 1981)   .35   1.00

1981. American Revolution Series. Nathanael Greene, Eutaw Springs, 1781.

PC86
Nathanael Greene Eutaw Springs, 1781

PC86 *(UX90)*
    12c multicolored on white
        (Sept. 8, 1981)   .35   2.00
        v. Magenta and yellow omitted   —

1981. Lewis and Clark Expedition

PC87
Lewis and Clark Expedition, 1806

Lewis and Clark Expedition, 1806

PC87 *(UX91)*
12c multicolored
(Sept. 23, 1981)   .35   4.00

1981. Patriot Series. Robert Morris, non-denominated ("US Domestic Rate")

PC88
Robert Morris (for domestic use only)

PC88 *(UX92)*
(13c) brown on white, *(Oct. 11, 1981)*   .35   1.00

1981. Patriot Series. Robert Morris, denominated ("US Postage 13")

PC89
Robert Morris (denomination as numeral)

PC89 *(UX93)*
13c brown on white
(Nov. 10, 1981)   .35   1.00

1982. American Revolution Series. "Swamp Fox" Francis Marion, 1782.

"Swamp Fox" Francis Marion, 1782

PC90
Gen. Francis Marion

PC90 *(UX94)*
13c multicolored on white
(April 3, 1982)   .35   1.00

1982. LaSalle Claims Louisiana.

La Salle claims Louisiana, 1682

PC91
LaSalle Expedition

PC91 *(UX95)*
13c multicolored on white
(April 7, 1982)   .35   1.00

1982. Philadelphia Academy of Music.

PC92
Philadelphia Academy of Music

PC92 *(UX96)*
13c brown, dark beige, red on tan
(June 18, 1982)   .35   1.00
   v. Brown and dark beige
     omitted   —

1982. Historic Preservation Series. Old Post Office, St. Louis, Mo.

Historic Preservation

PC93
Old St. Louis Post Office

PC93 *(UX97)*
13c multicolored on white
(Oct. 14, 1982)   .35   1.00

1883. Landing of Oglethorpe, Georgia, 1733.

Landing of Oglethorpe, Georgia, 1733

PC94
Landing of James Oglethorpe in Georgia

PC94 *(UX98)*
13c multicolored on white
(Feb. 12, 1983)   .35   1.00

1983. Historic Preservation Series. Old Post Office, Washington, D.C.

Old Post Office, Washington, D.C.

PC95
Old Post Office, Washington, D.C.

PC95 *(UX99)*
13c multicolored on white
(April 19, 1983)   .35   1.00

1983. Olympic Games, Yachting

PC96
Yachting

PC96 (UX100)
  13c multicolored on white
    (Aug. 5, 1983)   .35   1.00
    v. Magenta and yellow omitted —

1984. Ark and Dave, Maryland, 1634.

PC97
Ark *and* Dove

PC97 (UX101)
  13c multicolored on white
    (March 25, 1984)   .35   1.00

1984. Olympic Games, Runner and Olympic Torch.

PC98
Olympic torch carrier

PC98 (UX102)
  13c multicolored on white
    (April 30, 1984)   .35   1.00
    v. Yellow and black inverted —
    zo. Tagging omitted —

1984. Frederic Baraga

PC99
Frederic Baraga

PC99 (UX103)
  13c multicolored on white
    (June 29, 1984)   .35   1.00

1984. Historic Preservation Series. The California Ranchos 1784-1984.

PC100
Rancho San Pedro

PC100 (UX104)
  13c multicolored *(Sept 16, 1984)* .35   1.00
    a. Black and blue omitted —
    z. Tagging omitted —

1985. Patriot Series. Charles Carroll, non-denominated ("U.S. Domestic Rate")

PC101
Charles Carroll (for domestic use only)

PC101 (UX105)
  (14c) green on white, non-denominated
    (Feb. 1, 1985)   .35   .50

1985. International Surface Mail Rate. Clipper *Flying Cloud.*

PC102
Clipper Flying Cloud, *1852*

PC102 (UX107)
  25c multicolored on white
    (Feb. 27, 1985)   .75   7.50

1985. Patriot Series. Charles Carroll, denominated ("USA 14")

PC103
Charles Carroll (denomination as numeral)

PC103 (UX106)
  14c green on white *(Mar. 6, 1985)* .35   .25

1985. Patriot Series. George Wythe.

PC104
George Wythe

PC104 *(UX108)*
14c olive green on white
(June 20, 1985) .35 .50

1986. Settling of Connecticut.

Settling of Connecticut, 1636

PC105
Settling of Connecticut

PC105 *(UX109)*
14c multicolored on white
(April 18, 1986) .30 1.00

1986. Stamp Collecting.

PC106

PC106 *(UX110)*
14c multicolored on white
(May 23, 1986) .35 1.00
x. Cachet added for NAJURBIA '86
(exhibition in Germany) — —

1986. Francis Vigo, Italian-American Patriot.

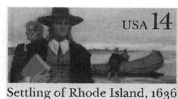

Francis Vigo, Vincennes, 1779

PC107
Francis Vigo

PC107 *(UX111)*
14c multicolored on white
(May 24,1986) .35 1.00

1986. Settling of Rhode Island.

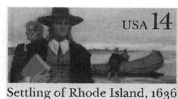

Settling of Rhode Island, 1636

PC108
Settling of Rhode Island

PC108 *(UX112)*
14c multicolored on white
(June 26, 1986) .35 1.00

1986. Wisconsin Territory.

Wisconsin Territory, 1836

PC109
Wisconsin Territory

PC109 *(UX113)*
14c multicolored on white
(July 3, 1986) .35 1.00

1986. National Guard Heritage.

National Guard Heritage, 1636-1986

PC110
National Guard,
350th Anniversary

PC110 *(UX114)*
14c multicolored on white
(Dec. 12, 1986) .35 1.00

1987. Self-Scouring Plow Sesquicentennial.

Self-scouring steel plow, 1837

PC 111
150th Anniversary.
Steel Plow by John Deere

PC111 *(UX115)*
14c multicolored on white
(May 22, 1987) .35 1.00

1987. Constitutional Convention Bicentennial.

Constitutional Convention, 1787

PC112
Constitutional Convention

PC112 *(UX116)*
14c multicolored on white
(May 25, 1987) .35 1.00

1987. U.S. Flag.

PC113
Flag

PC113 (UX117)
14c black, blue, and red on white
    (June 14, 1987)   .35   .50
    x. Cachet for Philatelia '87
    (exhibition in Koln, Germany) —   —
    vz. Tagging double, one normal and
    one split top and bottom   —

1987. Take Pride in America Issue.

PC114
Landscape

PC114 (UX118)
14c multicolored on white
    (Sept. 22, 1987)   .35   1.00

1987. Historic Preservation Series. Timberline Lodge, Mount Hood, Oregon.

PC115
Timberline Lodge,
Mt. Hood, OR

PC115 (UX119)
14c multicolored on white
    (Sept. 28, 1987)   .35   1.00

1988. American the Beautiful Series. Prairie Scene.

PC116
Bison on the Prairie

PC116 (UX120)
15c multicolored on white, non-fluorescent paper
    (March 28, 1988)   .35   .30
    p. Fluorescent paper   —
    v. Printed on both sides   650.
    v1. Black and blue on
    reverse, front normal   550.
    v2. Black omitted   —

1988. Blair House.

PC117
Blair House

PC117 (UX121)
15c multicolored on white
    (May 4, 1988)   .35   .35

1988. International Surface Rate. Square-rigged packet ship.

PC118
Yorkshire Packet

PC118 (UX122)
28c multicolored (June 29, 1988)   .75   4.00

1988. Iowa Territory Sesquicentennial.

PC119
Iowa Territory

PC119 (UX123)
15c multicolored on white
    (July 2, 1988)   .35   .35

1988. Settling of Ohio, Northwest Territory, Bicentennial.

PC120
Settling of Ohio

PC120 (UX124)
15c multicolored on white
    (July 15, 1988)   .35   .35

1988. Hearst Castle, San Simeon, California.

PC121
*Hearst Castle,
San Simeon, CA*

PC121 *(UX125)*
  15c multicolored on white
    (Sept. 20, 1988)   .35   .35

1988. The Federalist Papers.

PC122
Federalist Papers

PC122 *(UX126)*
  15c multicolored on white
    (Oct. 27, 1988)   .35   .35

1989. America the Beautiful Series.

PC123
Sonora Desert scene

PC123 *(UX127)*
  15c multicolored on white
    (Jan. 13, 1989)   .35   .35

1989. Healy Hall, Georgetown University.

PC124
*Healy Hall,
Georgetown University*

PC124 *(UX128)*
  15c multicolored on white
    (Jan. 23, 1989)   .35   .35

1989. America the Beautiful Series.

PC125
*Great Blue Heron
in marsh scene*

PC125 *(UX129)*
  15c multicolored on white
    (March 17, 1989)   .35   .35

1989. Settling of Oklahoma.

PC126
Settling of Oklahoma

PC126 *(UX130)*
  15c multicolored on white
    (April 22, 1989)   .35   .35

**1989. America the Beautiful Series. Mountain Scene
with Canada Greese. (Card pays surface rate to Canada.)**

PC127
Geese in flight

PC127 *(UX131)*
  21c multicolored on white
    (May 5, 1989)   .65   5.00

1989. America the Beautiful Series.

PC128
Sea shore

PC128 *(UX132)*
  15c multicolored on white
    (June 17, 1989)   .35   .35

1989. America the Beautiful Series.

PC129
Deer in forest

PC129 *(UX133)*
  15c multicolored on white
    (Aug. 26, 1989)   .35   .35

1989. Hull House, Chicago, Illinois.

PC 130
*Jane Addam's Hull House
Community Center, Chicago*

PC130 *(UX134)*
15c multicolored on white
(Sept. 16, 1989)   .35   .35

1989. America the Beautiful Series.

PC131
*Independence Hall,
Philadelphia*

PC131 *(UX135)*
15c multicolored on white
(Sept. 25, 1989)   .35   .50

1989. America the Beautiful Series.

PC132
*Inner Harbor;
USS Constellation
Baltimore, Maryland*

PC132 *(UX136)*
15c multicolored on white
(Oct. 7, 1989)   .35   .50

1989. America the Beautiful Series.

PC133
*Manhattan skyline,
Queensboro bridge*

PC133 *(UX137)*
15c multicolored on white
(Nov. 8, 1989)   .35   .50

1989. America the Beautiful Series.

PC134
U.S. Capitol Building

PC134 *(UX138)*
15c multicolored on white
(Nov. 26, 1989)   .35   .50

1989. White House Picture Postal Card. Sold for 50 cents each, an illustration of the White House is on the reverse.

PC135
White House

PC135 *(UX143)*
15c multicolored on white
(Nov. 30, 1989)   1.25   2.50

1989. Ameria the Beautiful Se-Tenant Block. Designs of PC131-PC134 were issued in a se-tenant block of four cards, with rouletting between them for separation, for World Stamp Expo '89. The block includes two labels showing the emblems of either World Stamp Expo '89 or the 20th UPU Congress. These cards do not include inscription and copyright symbols at lower left. Rouletted 9 1/2 on two or three sides.

PC136 *(UX140)*
15c multicolored on white, design of PC132
(Dec. 1, 1989)   2.00   2.00
PC136A *(UX139)*
15c multicolored on white, design of
PC131   2.00   2.00

PC136B *(UX142)*
15c multicolored on white, design of
PC134   2.00   2.00
PC136C *(UX141)*
15c multicolored on white, design of
PC133   2.00   2.00
y. Se-tenant block of four PC136-
136C with two labels   12.50

1989. Jefferson Memorial Picture Postal Card. Sold for 50 cents each, with an illustration of the Jefferson Memorial covering the reverse.

PC137
Jefferson Memorial

PC137 *(UX144)*
15c multicolored on white
(Dec. 2, 1989)   1.25   2.50

1990. American Papermaking. Rittenhouse Paper Mill.

PC138
*Rittenhouse Paper Mill,
Germantown, PA.*

PC138 *(UX145)*
15c multicolored on white
(March 13, 1990)   .35   .35

1990. World Literacy Year.

PC139
*Book and globe,
World Literacy Year*

PC139 *(UX146)*
15c multicolored on white
(March 22, 1990)   .35   .35

1990. George Caleb Bingham Picture Postal Card. Sold for 50 cents, with the painting *Fur Traders Descending the Missouri* covering the reverse.

PC140
Furtraders on the Missouri

PC140 *(UX147)*
15c multicolored on white
(May 4, 1990)   1.25   2.50

1990. Historic Preservation Series. Isaac Royal House.

PC141
*Isaac Royall House,
Medford, MA*

PC141 *(UX148)*
15c multicolored on white
(June 16, 1990)   .45   .35

1990. Postal Buddy computer-generated and printed USPS Eagle card, available from a vending machine under a special license agreement. The cards cost 33 cents, plus state sales tax, from one of a group of test machines in Virginia. A variety of borders, messages and backs are known. The cards also were produced in sheets of four.

PC142
Postal Buddy Card

PC142 *(PB1)*
15c black on white
(July 5, 1990)   8.50   6.50

1990. Stanford University Quadrangle.

PC143
*Quadrangle,
Stanford University*

PC143 *(UX150)*
15c multicolored on white
(Sept. 11, 1990)   .35   .35

1990. Constitution Hall Picture Postal card. Sold for 50 cents with a picture of Constitution Hall, Washington, D.C. covering the reverse.

PC144
*Constitution Hall,
Washington, D.C.*

PC144 *(UX151)*
15c multicolored on white
(Oct. 11, 1990)   1.25   2.50

1990. Historic Preservation Series. Chicago Orchestra Hall.

PC145
Chicago Orchestra Hall

PC145 *(UX152)*
15c multicolored on white
(Oct. 19, 1990)   .45   .35

1991. Flag Issue.

PC146
Flag

PC146 *(UX153)*
19c black, blue, and red on white
    (Apr.1, 1991)   .50   .25

1991. Postal Buddy USPS Eagle card. Available in sheets of four from vending machines. *(See PC142.)*

PC147
Postal Buddy Card

PC147 *(PB2)*
19c black on white
    (Feb. 3, 1991)   4.00   5.00

1991. Carnegie Hall Centennial.

PC148
Carnegie Hall, New York City

PC148 *(UX154)*
19c multicolored on white
    (Apr. 1, 1991)   .50   .45

1991. University of Texas Medical Branch at Galveston Centennial.

PC149
Old Red, University of Texas Medical Branch, Galveston

PC149 *(UX155)*
19c multicolored on white
    (June 14, 1991)   .50   .45

1991. America the Beautiful Series. Rate for this card is for use to Canada and Mexico.

PC150
Niagara Falls

PC150 *(UX158)*
30c multicolored on white
    (Aug. 21, 1991)   1.00   3.00

1991. Ratification of Bill of Rights.

PC151
Ratification of the Bill of Rights

PC151 *(UX156)*
19c black, blue, and red on white
    (Sept. 25, 1991)   .50   .45

1991. University of Notre Dame Sesquicentennial.

PC152
Main Building, University of Notre Dame, South Bend, Indiana

PC152 *(UX157)*
19c multicolored on white
    (Oct. 15, 1991)   .50   .45

1991. University of Vermont Bicentennial.

PC153
The Old Mill, University of Vermont

PC153 *(UX159)*
19c multicolored on white
    (Oct. 29, 1991)   .50   .45

1992. Wadsworth Atheneum Sesquicentennial.

PC154
Wadsworth Atheneum, Hartford, CT

PC154 *(UX160)*
19c multicolored on white
    (Jan. 16, 1992)   .50   .45

1992. University of Chicago Centennial.

PC155
Cobb Hall, University of Chicago

PC155 *(UX161)*
19c multicolored on white
    (Jan. 23, 1992)   .50   .45

1992. Willamette University Sesquicentennial

PC156
Waller Hall, Wiillamette University, Salem, Oregon

PC156 *(UX162)*
19c multicolored on white
    (Feb. 1, 1992)   .50   .45

1992. America's Cup Picture Postal Card. Sold for 50 cents with an illustration of *The Ranger* covering the reverse.

PCS157
America's Cup. The Reliance, 1903

PC157 *(UX163)*
19c multicolored on white
    (May 6, 1992)   1.25   1.25

1992. Columbia River Gorge.

PC158
Columbia River Gorge

PC158 *(UX164)*
19c multicolored on white
    (May 9, 1992)   .50   .45

1992. Ellis Island Centennial.

PC159
Ellis Island Immigration Museum

PC159 *(UX165)*
19c multicolored on white
    (May 11, 1992)   .50   .45

1992. Postal Buddy. Available only in sheets of four from vending machines. Price raised to 39 cents per card, plus any state sales tax. *(See PC142.)*

PC160
Postal Buddy Post Card

PC160 *(PB3)*
19c black on white, tagged
    (Nov. 13, 1992)   7.50   3.50
    p. Fluorescent paper   —

1993. Washington National Cathedral

PC161
Washington National Cathedral

PC161 *(UX166)*
19c multicolored on white
    (Jan. 6, 1993)   .50   .45

1993. Wren Building, College of William & Mary.

PC162
Wren Building, College of William & Mary

PC162 *(UX167)*
19c multicolored on white
    (Feb. 8, 1993)   .50   .45

1993. Holocaust Memorial Picture Postal Card. Sold for 50 cents with an aerial view of the museun covering the reverse.

PC163
Holocaust Memorial Museum

PC163 *(UX168)*
19c multicolored on white
    (Mar. 23, 1993)   1.25   2.00

1993. Fort Recovery Bicentennial.

PC164
Ft. Recovery, Ohio

PC164 *(UX169)*
19c multicolored on white
    (June 13, 1993)   .50   .45

1993. University of North Carolina Bicentennial.

PC165
Playmaker's Theater at University of North Carolina at Chapel Hill

PC165 *(UX170)*
  19c multicolored on white
      (Sept. 14, 1993) .50 .45

1993. College of the Holy Cross Sesquicentennial.

PC166
O'Kane Hall, College of the Holy Cross

PC166 *(UX171)*
  19c multicolored on white
      (Sept. 17, 1993) .50 .45

1993. Illinois College. Beecher Hall.

PC167
Beecher Hall at Illinois College

PC167 *(UX172)*
  19c multicolored
      (Oct. 9, 1993) .50 .45

1993. Bowdoin College. Massachusetts Hall.

PC168
Massachusetts Hall, Bowdoin College

PC168 *(UX173)*
  19c multicolored *(Oct. 14, 1993)* .50 .45

1994. Lincoln Home.

PC169
Abraham Lincoln Home, Springfield, Illinois

PC169 *(UX174)*
  19c multicolored
      (Feb. 12, 1994) .60 .60

1994. Myers Hall.

PC170
Meyers Hall, Wittenbery University, Springfield, Illinois

PC170 *(UX175)*
  19c multicolored
      (March 11, 1994) .60 .60

1994. Canyon de Chelly.

PC171
Canyon de Chelly, Arizona

PC171 *(UX176)*
  19c multicolored
      (Aug. 7, 1994) .60 .60

1994. St. Louis Union Station.

PC172
St. Louis Union Station, St. Louis, MO

PC172 *(UX177)*
  19c multicolored
      (Sept. 3, 1994) .60 .60

1994. Legends of the West. Issued in conjunction with the 20-stamp sheelet depicting 16 individuals and four "themes" from the Old West. Each card depicts a design from the sheelet with the 19¢ postal card rate, while the reverse of the card is an enlarged version of the stamp design. The cards were issued Oct. 18, 1994.

PC173   PC174   PC175

PC173 *(UX178)*
  19c Home on the Range .60 5.00
PC174 *(UX179)*
  19c Buffalo Bill .60 5.00
PC175 *(UX180)*
  19c Jim Bridger .60 5.00
PC176 *(UX181)*

PC176    *PC177*    *PC178*   *PC188*   *PC189*   *PC190*

PC176
   19c Annie Oakley   .60   5.00
PC177 *(UX182)*
   19c Native American Culture   .60   5.00
PC178 *(UX183)*
   19c Chief Joseph   .60   5.00

PC179    *PC180*    *PC181*

PC179 *(UX184)*
   19c Bill Pickett   .60   5.00
PC180 *(UX185)*
   19c Bat Masterson   .60   5.00
PC181 *(UX186)*
   19c John Fremont   .60   5.00

PC182    *PC183*    *PC184*

PC182 *(UX187)*
   19c Wyatt Earp   .60   5.00
PC183 *(UX188)*
   19c Nellie Cashman   .60   5.00
PC184 *(UX189)*
   19c Charles Goodnight   .60   5.00

PC 185    *PC186*    *PC187*

PC185 *(UX190)*
   19c Geronimo   .60   5.00
PC186 *(UX191)*
   19c Kit Carson   .60   5.00
PC187 *(UX192)*
   19c Wild Bill Hickock   .60   5.00

PC188 *(UX193)*
   19c Western Wildlife   .60   5.00
PC189 *(UX194)*
   19c Jim Beckwourth   .60   5.00
PC190 *(UX195)*
   19c Bill Tilghman   .60   5.00

PC191    *PC192*

PC191 *(UX196)*
   19c Sacagawea   .60   5.00
PC192 *(UX197)*
   19c Overland Mail   .60   5.00

1994. Old Glory 'G'. Non-denominated.

PC193
Old Glory,
'G' Non-Denominated

PC193 *(UX198)*
   (20c) multicolored, *(Dec. 13, 1994)*   .40   .40

1995. Red Barn.

PC194
Red Barn

PC194 *(UX199)*
   20c multicolored, *(Jan. 3, 1995)*   .40   .40

1995. Civil War. Issued in conjunction with the 20
stamp sheetlet. Each card depicts a design from the
sheetlet with the 20c post card rate, while the reverse of
the card is an enlarged version of the stamp design.
Available on June 29, 1995.

PC195   PC196   PC197

PC195 (UX200)
  20c monitor and Virginia .60 3.50
PC196 (UX201)
  20c Robert E. Lee .60 3.50
PC197 (UX202)
  20c Clara Barton .60 3.50

PC198   PC199   PC200

PC198 (UX203)
  20c Ulysses Grant .60 3.50
PC199 (UX204)
  20C Battle of Shiloh .60 3.50
PC200 (UX205)
  20c Jefferson Davis .60 3.50

PC201   PC202   PC203

PC201 (UX207)
  20c Daivd Farragut .60 3.50
PC202 (UX207)
  20c Frederick Douglass .60 3.50
PC203 (UX208)
  20c Raphael Semmes .60 3.50

PC204   PC205   PC206

PC204 (UX209)
  20c Abraham Lincoln .60 3.50
PC205 (UX210)
  20c Harriet Tubman .60 3.50
PC206 (UX211)
  20c Stand Watie .60 3.50

PC207   PC208   PC209

PC207 (UX212)
  20c Joseph E. Johnston .60 3.50
PC208 (UX213)
  20c Winfield Hancock .60 3.50
PC209 (UX214)
  20c Mary Chesnut .60 3.50

PC210   PC211   PC212

PC210 (UX215)
  20c Battle of Chancellorville .60 3.50
PC211 (UX216)
  20c William T. Sherman .60 3.50
PC212 (UX217)
  20c Phoebe Pember .60 3.50

PC213

PC213 (UX218)
  20c Stonewall Jackson .60 3.50
PC214 (UX219)
  20c Battle of Gettysburg .60 3.50

1995. American Clipper Ships.

PC215
American Clipper Ships

PC215 (UX220)
  20c multicolored *(Sept. 3, 1995)* .40 .40

1995. Comic Strips.

PC216

PC217

PC226

PC227

PC216 *(UX221)*
  20c The Yellow Kid   .60   3.00
PC217 *(UX222)*
  20c Katzenjammer Kids   .60   3.00

PC226 *(UX231)*
  20c Popeye   .60   3.00
PC227 *(UX232)*
  20c Blondie   .60   3.00

PC218

PC219

PC228

PC229

PC218 *(UX223)*
  20c Little Nemo in Slumberland   .60   3.00
PC219 *(UX224)*
  20c Bringing up Father   .60   3.00

PC228 *(UX233)*
  20c Dick Tracey   .60   3.00
PC229 *(UX234)*
  20c Alley OOP   .60   3.00

PC220

PC221

PC230

PC231

PC220 *(UX225)*
  20c Krazy Kat   .60   3.00
PC221 *(UX226)*
  20c Rube Goldbery's Inventions   .60   3.00

PC230 *(UX235)*
  20c Nancy   .60   3.00
PC231 *(UX236)*
  20c Flash Gordon   .60   3.00

PC222

PC 223

PC232

PC233

PC222 *(UX227)*
  20c Toonerville Folks   .60   3.00
PC223 *(UX228)*
  20c Gasoline Alley   .60   3.00

PC232 *(UX237)*
  20c Li'l Abner   .60   3.00
PC233 *(UX238)*
  20c Terry and the Pirates .60   3.00

PC224

PC225

PC234

PC235

PC224 *(UX229)*
  20c Barney Google   .60   3.00
PC225 *(UX230)*
  20c Little Orphan Annie   .60   3.00

PC234 *(UX239)*
  20c Prince Valiant   .60   3.00
PC235 *(UX240)*
  20c Brenda Starr, Reporter .60   3.00

Winter Farm Scene.

PC236
Winter farm scene

PC236 *(UX241)*
   20c multicolored *(Feb. 23, 1996)* .40 .40

Atlanta Olympics.

PC237   *PC238*   *PC239*

PC237 *(UX242)*
   20c Men's Cycling *(May 2, 1996)* .60 5.00
PC238 *(UX243)*
   20c Women's Diving .60 5.00
PC239 *(UX244)*
   20c Women's Running .60 5.00

PC240   *PC241*   *PC242*

PC240 *(UX245)*
   20x Men's Canoeing .60 5.00
PC241 *(UX246)*
   20c Decathalon (Javelin) .60 5.00
PC242 *(UX247)*
   20c Women's Soccer .60 5.00

PC243   *PC244*   *PC245*

PC243 *(UX248)*
   20c Men's Shot Put .60 5.00
PC244 *(UX249)*
   20c Women's Sailboarding .60 5.00
PC245 *(UX250)*
   20c Women's Gymnastics .60 5.00

PC246   *PC247*   *PC248*

PC246 *(UX251)*
   20c Freestyle Wrestling .60 5.00
PC247 *(UX252)*
   20c Women's Softball .60 5.00
PC248 *(UX253)*
   20c Women's Swimming .60 5.00

PC249   *PC250*   *PC251*

PC249 *(UX254)*
   20c Men's Sprints .60 5.00
PC250 *(UX255)*
   20c Men's Rowing .60 5.00
PC251 *(UX256)*
   20c Volleyball .60 5.00

PC252   *PC253*   *PC254*

PC252 *(UX257)*
   20c Men's Baseball .60 5.00
PC253 *(UX258)*
   20c Equestrian .60 5.00
PC254 *(UX259)*
   20c Men's Gymnastics .60 5.00

PC255   *PC256*

PC255 *(UX260)*
   20c Men's Swimming .60 5.00
PC256 *(UX261)*
   20c Men's Hurdles .60 5.00

1996. Mc Dowell Hall, St. John's College, Annapolis, MD.

PC257

St. John's College, Annapolis, Maryland

PC257 *(UX262)*
  20c multicolored, *(June 1, 1996)*   .40   .40

1996. Alexander Hall, Princeton University.

PC258

PRINCETON UNIVERSITY•250TH ANNIVERSARY

PC258 *(UX263)*
  20c multicolored, *(Sept. 20, 1996)*   .40   .40

1996. Endangered Species.

 PC259    PC260

PC259 *(UX264)*
  20c Florida Panther   .75   5.00
PC260 *(UX265)*
  20c Black Footed Ferret   .75   5.00

 PC261    PC262

PC261 *(UX266)*
  20c American Crocodile   .75   5.00
PC262 *(UX267)*
  20c Piping Plover   .75   5.00

 PC263    PC264

PC263 *(UX268)*
  20C Gila Trout   .75   5.00
PC264 *(UX269)*
  20c Florida Manatee   .75   5.00

 PC265    PC266

PC265 *(UX270)*
  20c Schaus Swallowtail Butterfly   .75   5.00
PC266 *(UX271)*
  20c Woodland Caribou   .75   5.00

 PC267   PC268

PC267 *(UX272)*
  20c Thick-Bliied Parrot   .75   5.00
PC268 *(UX273)*
  20c San Fransisco Garter Snake .75   5.00

 PC269   PC270

PC269 *(UX274)*
  20c Ocelot   .75   5.00
PC270 *(UX275)*
  20c Wyoming Toad   .75   5.00

 PC271   PC272

PC271 *(UX276)*
  20c California Condor   .75   5.00
PC272 *(UX277)*
  20c Hawaiian Monk Seal   .75   5.00

 PC273

PC273 *(UX278)*
  20c Brown Pelican   .75   5.00

1997. Love Swans, Previous Love stamp designs.

PC274 *(UX279)* **multicolored,**
  a. Bird in Rose Heart   .75   2.25
  b. 2 Birds in Rose Basket   .75   2.25
  c. Swans, Tall   .75   2.25
  d. Swans, Long   .75   2.25
  e. Puppy   .75   2.25
  f. Paper-cut out Heart   .75   2.25
  g. Penn.-Dutch 2 Birds and
      Heart   .75   2.25
  h. Heart Sunrise   .75   2.25

1997. City College of New York.

PC275
City College of New York

PC275 *(UX280)*
20c multicolored, *(May 7, 1997)* .40 .40

1997. Golden Gate Bridge, and San Fransico Harbor.

PC276
Golden Gate Bridge,
San Francisco Harbor

PC276 *(UX281)*
20c multicolored, *(June 2, 1997)* .40 .40

1997. Golden Gate Bridge and Sunset.

PC277
Golden Gate Bridge at Sunset

PC277 *(UX282)*
50c multicolored, *(June 2, 1997)* 1.00 1.00

1997. Bugs Bunny

PC278
Bugs Bunny

PC278
20c multicolored, single .40 1.00
    a. booklet of 20

1997. Ft. McHenry

PC279
Ft. McHenry, Baltimore, MD

PC279
20c multicolored, *(Sept. 9, 1997)* .40 .40

1997. Movie Monster Series. Designs similar to CM1956-60.

PC280

PC280
20c Lon Chaney, Phantom of the Opera .40 .40

PC281

PC281
20c Bela Lugosi, Dracula .40 .40

PC282

PC282
20c Boris Karloff, Frankenstein .40 .40

PC283

PC283
20c Boris Karloff, The Mummy .40 .40

PC284

PC284
20c Lon Chaney, Jr, The Wolfman .40 .40

MESSAGE &REPLY CARDS

First issued in 1892, message and reply cards consist of two postal cards attached to each other. One card is used for sending the message and the other card, when separated, is used to send the reply. the term "used" when referring to the unsevered card signifies a used message card and an unused reply card. Listings are for unsevered and severed (individual) cards.

1892. Frame around edge of card.

MRC1

MRC1 *(UY1)*
1C + 1C Black on buff,

unsevered	37.50	8.
m. Message card	7.00	1.50
r. Reply card	7.00	1.50
t. Message card printed on both sides, reply card blank	275.	—
t1. Message card blank, reply card printed on both sides	325.	—

1893. Universal Postal Union Card.
Frame around edge of card.

MRC2

MRC2 *(UY2)*
2c + 2c blue on grayish white,

unsevered *(March 1, 1893)*	18.50	25.
a. dark blue on grayish white	20.	25.
m. Message reply card	6.00	7.00
r. Reply card	6.00	7.00
t. Message card printed on both sides, reply card blank	325.	—
t1. Message card blank, reply card printed on both sides	—	—
t2. Message card normal, reply card blank	325.	—

1898. Same design as MRC1, but without frame around edge of card.

MRC3 *(UY3)*
1c + 1c black on buff,

unsevered *(Sept. 1898)*	70.	20.
m. Message reply card	15.	3.00
r. Reply card	15.	3.00
t. Message card printed on both sides, reply card blank	275.	—
t1. Message card blank, reply cardprinted on both sides	275.	—
t2. Message card blank, reply card normal	—	275.
t3. Message card normal, reply card printed on both sides	—	—
t4. Message card without "detach annexed card/ for answer"	275.	160.
t6. Message card printed on both sides, reply card normal	—	—
t7. Message card printed on both halves	—	—

1904.

MRC4

MRC4 *(UY4)*
1c + 1c black on buff,

unsevered *(March 1904)*	50.	6.00
m. Message card	10.	2.00
r. Reply card	10.	2.00
t. Message card printed on both sides, reply card blank	300.	—
t1. Message card blank, reply card printed on both sides	—	185.
t2. Message card blank, reply card normal	—	300.
t3. Message card normal, reply card blank	300.	—

1910.

MRC5

MRC5 *(UY5)*
1c +1c dark blue on bluish,

unsevered *(Sept. 14, 1910)*	150.	25.
m. Message card	11.	4.00
r. Reply card	11.	4.00
t. Message card normal, reply card blank	220.	—

1911. Same design.

THIS SIDE OF CARD IS FOR ADDRESS

MRC6

REPLY CARD
THIS SIDE OF CARD IS FOR ADDRESS

MRC6 *(UY6)*
1c + 1c green on cream,

unsevered *(Oct. 27, 1911)*	150.	25.
m. Message card	25.	6.00
r. reply card	40.	45.
t. Message card normal, reply card blank	—	—

1915. Same design. Single frame around inscription.

MRC7

MRC7 *(UY7)*
1c + 1c green on cream,

unsevered *(Sept. 18, 1915)*	1.50	55.
dark green on buff	1.50	55.
m. Message reply card	.30	.25
r. Reply card	.30	.25
t. Message card normal, reply card blank	—	—

1918.

MRC8

MRC8 *(UY8)*
2c + 2c red on cream,

unsevered *(Aug. 2, 1918)*	80.	45.
m. Message card	22.50	7.50
r. Reply card	22.50	7.50

1920-21. Re-valued. *Surcharged in black by canceling machine.*

MRC9 *Overprinted on MRC8*

MRC9 *(UY9)*
1c on 2c + 1c on 2c red on cream,

unsevered	20.	10.
m. Message card	6.00	4.00
r. Reply card	6.00	4.00
x. Message card double surcharge, reply card normal	80.	—
x1. Message card normal, reply card no surcharge	90.	—
x2. Message card normal, reply card double surcharge	80.	—
x3. Message card no surcharge, reply card normal	80.	—
x4. Message card no surcharge, reply card double surcharge	80.	—
x5. Message card double surcharge, reply card no surcharge	—	—
x6. Message card no surcharge, reply card double surcharge, one inverted	—	—

Same surcharge press printed

MRC9A *(UY10)*

1c on 2c + 1c on 2c red on cream,

unsevered	325.	200.
m. Message card	95.	45.
p. red on buff	—	—
r. Reply card	95.	45.
x. Message card no surcharge, reply card normal	—	—
x1. Message card double surcharge, reply card no surcharge	—	—
x2. Message card no surcharge, reply card double surcharge	—	—

1924. Universal Postal Union Card. Same design and size as MRC2.

MRC10

MRC10 *(UY11)*

2c + 2c red on buff, unsevered   3.00   35.

(Mar. 18, 1924)

m. Message card	.50	12.50
r. Reply card	.50	12.50

1926. Universal Postal Union Card. Same size as PC11.

Same size as PC11.
MRC11 *William McKinley*

MRC11 *(UY12)*

3c + 3c red on cream, unsevered   15.   *35.*

(Jan. 29, 1926)

a. carmine on cream	—	—
b. pale red on cream	—	—
c. scarlet on cream	—	—
m. Message card	3.00	16.
p. red on buff	—	—
p1. red on canary	10.	17.50
p2. red on light buff	—	—
p3. red on yellow buff	—	—
r. Reply card	3.00	6.

1951. Size PC13.

MRC12 *George Washington, message card; Martha Washiington, reply card*

MRC12 *(UY13)*

2c + 2c carmine on cream, unsevered   1.75   3.00

(Dec. 29, 1951)

m. Message card	.50	1.00
r. Reply card	.50	1.00

1952. Re-valued, overprinted in green by Pitney-Bowes Ticometers.

MRC13 *Overprinted on MRC7*

MRC13 *(UY14)*

2c on 1c + 2c on 1c light green on buff,

unsevered *(Jan. 1952)*	1.75	4.00
m. Message card	.50	2.00
r. Reply card	.50	2.00
x. Both cards double surcharge	55.	40.
x1. Inverted surcharge horizontal, to left of stamps	150.	100.
x2. Message card double surcharge, reply card normal	45.	30.
x3. Message card no surcharge, reply card normal	40.	45.
x4. Message card normal, reply card double surcharge	45.	30.
x5. Message card normal, reply card no surcharge	40.	45.
x6. Surcharge horizontal, to left of stamps	15.	15.
x7. Surcharge vertical, to left of stamps	7.00	7.00
x8. Surcharge vertical below stamp	—	—
x9. Black surcharge vertical below stamp	—	—
x10. Message card no surcharge, reply card double surcharge	—	—
x11. Message card double surcharge, reply card no surcharge	—	—

1952. Same as MRC13, but dark green horizontal overprint applied by printing press.

MRC14 *(UY15)*
2c on 1c + 2c on 1c green on cream,

unsevered	135.	55.
m. Message card	20.	12.50
r. Reply card	20.	12.50
x. Message card normal plus one on back, reply card no surcharge	—	—
x1. Reply card normal plus one on back, with Tickometer surcharge vertical below stamp on message card	—	—

1956. Design of OC42, Liberty.

MRC15

MRC15 *(UY16)*
4c + 4c scarlet and ultramarine on cream,

unsevered *(Nov. 16, 1956)*	1.50	60.
m. Message card	.50	40.
r. Reply card	.50	35.
t. Message card printed on both halves	140.	—
t1. Reply message printed on both halves	140.	—

1958. Design of PC42, Liberty.

MRC16 *(UY17)*
3c + 3c purple on buff, unsevered 4.00 5.00
(July 31, 1958)

t. One card blank	140.	—
t1. Printed by electrotype	—	—
t2. Printed by steel plate	—	—

1962. Design of PC44, Abraham Lincoln, two cards are identical.

MRC17 *Abraham Lincoln*

MRC17 *(UY18)*
4c + 4c red violet on white, unsevered 4.50 5.00
(Nov. 19, 1962)

a. light violet	—	—
p. Fluorescent paper, non-fluorescent ink	—	—
t. Printed by electrotype	—	—
t1. Printed by steel plate	—	—
z. Non-fluorescent paper, fluorescent ink *(Mar.7, 1967)*	6.50	3.50

1963. Design of PC45, Vacationland.

MRC18

MRC18 *(UY19)*
7c + 7c red and blue on white,

unsevered *(Aug. 30, 1963)*	3.00	50.
t. Message card blank, reply card normal	140.	—
t1. Message card normal, reply card blank	140.	—

1968. Design of MRC18 (PC45), Vacationland.

MRC19

MRC19 *(UY20)*
8c + 8c red and blue on white,

unsevered *(Dec. 4, 1967)*	3.50	50.

1968. Design of PC51, Abraham Lincoln, two cards are identical.

MRC20 *(UY21)*
5c + 5c emerald green on white,

unsevered, tagged *(Jan. 4, 1968)*	1.75	3.00
t. One half blank (printed one side only)	—	—

1971. Design of PC54, Paul Revere, two cards are identical.

MRC21

MRC21 *(UY22)*
6c + 6c brown on white,

unsevered, tagged *(May 15, 1971)*	1.25	2.50

1972. Design of PC60, John Hanson, two cards are identical.

MRC22 *(UY23)*
6c + 6c cobalt blue on white,
   unsevered, tagged   1.25   2.00
   (Sept. 1, 1972)

1973. Design of PC62, Samuel Adams, two cards are identical.

MRC23 *(UY24)*
8c + 8c orange on white,
   unsevered, tagged   1.25   2.00
   (Dec. 16, 1973)
   p. Smooth paper   —   —
   p1. Coarse paper   1.35   4.00
   t. One half blank (printed
      one side only)   —   —

1975. Design of PC64, Charles Thomson, two cards are identical.

MRC24 *(UY25)*
7c + 7c emerald green on white,
   unsevered, tagged   1.25   5.
   (Sept. 14, 1975)

1975. Design of PC65, John Witherspoon, two cards are identical.

MRC25 *(UY26)*
9c + 9c brown on white,
   unsevered, tagged   1.25   5.00
   (Nov. 10, 1975)

1976. Design of PC66, Caesar Rodney, two cards are identical.

MRC26 *(UY27)*
9c + 9c blue on white,
   unsevered, tagged   1.25   2.00
   (July 1, 1976)

1977. Design of PC68, Nathan Hale, two cards are identical.

MRC27 *(UY28)*
9c + 9c green on white,
   unsevered, tagged   1.25   2.00
   (Oct. 14, 1977)

1978. Design of PC70, John Hancock (non-denominated), two cards are identical.

MRC28 *(UY29)*
(10c + 10c) brown orange on white,
   unsevered, tagged   11.   9.
   (May 19, 1978)
   t. Printed with MRC28 one side,
      MRC29 on the back side   —   —

1978. Design of PC71, John Hancock (with denomination), two cards are identical.

MRC29 *(UY30)*
10c + 10c brown orange on white,
   unsevered, tagged   1.25   3.00
   (June 20, 1978)
   t. One half blank (printed
      one side only)   —   —

1981. Design of PC84, stylized eagle, two cards are identical.

MRC30 *(UY31)*
(12c + 12c) purple on white,
   unsevered, tagged   1.25   3.00
   (Mar. 15, 1981)

1981. Design of PC85, Isaiah Thomas, two cards are identical.

MRC31 *(UY32)*
12c + 12c blue on white,
   unsevered, tagged   1.50   4.00
   (May 5, 1981)
   t. Large stamp die on
      both sides   —   —
   t1. Large stamp die on one side,
      small stamp die on back 3.00   2.25

1981. Design of PC88, Robert Morris (non-denominated), two cards are identical.

MRC32 *(UY33)*
(13c + 13c) brown on white,
   unsevered, tagged   2.25   4.00
   (Oct. 11, 1981)

1981. Design of PC89, Robert Morris (with denomination), two cards are identical.

MRC33 *(UY34)*
13c + 13c brown on white,
   unsevered, tagged   1.25   3.00
   (Nov. 10, 1981)
   t. One half blank (printed one side
      only)   —   —
   t1. Additional copyright notice,
      inverted on back
      of message card   —   —

1985. Design of PC101, Charles Carroll (non-denominated), two cards are identical.

MRC34 *(UY35)*
(14c + 14c) green on white,
   unsevered, tagged   3.50   5.00
   (Feb. 1, 1985)

1985. Design of PC103, Charles Carroll (with denomination), two cards are identical.

MRC35 *(UY36)*
  14c + 14c green on white,
    unsevered, tagged   1.25   3.00
    (Mar. 6, 1985)
      t. One half blank (printed one side
        only)   —   —

1985. Design of PC104, George Wythe, two cards are identical.

MRC36 *(UY37)*
  14c + 14c olive green on white,
    unsevered, tagged   1.20   3.00
    (June 20, 1985)
      t. One half blank (printed one side
        only)   —   —

1987. Design of PC113, U.S. Flag, two cards are identical.

MRC37 *(UY38)*
  14c + 14c black, blue and red on white,
    unsevered, tagged   1.25   3.00
    (Sept. 1, 1987)

1988. Design of PC116, America the Beautiful, two cards are identical.

 MRC38

MRC38 *(UY39)*
  15c + 15c multicolored on white,
    unsevered, tagged   1.25   3.00
    (July 11, 1988)
      p. Fluorescent paper   —   —

1991. Design of PC146, U.S. Flag, two cards are identical.

 MRC 39

MRC39 *(UY40)*
  19c + 19c black, blue, and red on white,
    unsevered, tagged   1.25   3.00
    (Mar. 27, 1991)

1995. Design of PC   Red Barn

MRC40 *(UY41)*
  20c + 20c multicolor,
    unsevered, *(Feb. 1,1995)*   1.25   3.00
    t. one half blank (printed
    one side only)   —   —

Air Mail Postal Cards

1949. Inscribed "AIRMAIL-POSTAL CARD."

PCA1 *Eagle*

PCA1 *(UXC1)*
  4c red orange on buff   .75   1.00
     Deep red on buff   .75   1.50
     FDC *(Jan. 10,1949)*   2.00

1958. Inscribed "AIRMAIL-POSTAL CARD."

PCA2 *Eagle in flight*

PCA2 *(UXC2)*
  5c carmine on buff   1.60   .80
     FDC *(July 31,1958)*   2.00

1960. Design same as PCA2, with red and blue border.

PCA3 *Eagle in flight*

PCA3 *(UXC3)*
  5c red on buff   6.50   2.25
     v. Red omitted   —
     v1. Thinned dividing line at top   —
     v2. Thinned dividing line at bottom   —
     FDC *(June 18, 1960)*   2.00

1963.

PCA4 *(UXC4)*
  6c red on white   .75   1.00
     p. Fluorescent paper   —   —
     FDC *(Feb. 15, 1963)*   5.00

1966. Visit the USA. With red and blue border.

PCA5 *Mt. Rainier, Oregon; New York City skyline; Miami Beach, Florida; Indian on horseback*

PCA5 *(UXC5)*
  11c red and blue on white   .75   15.
     p. Fluorescent paper   —   —
     FDC *(May 27, 1966)*   1.75

1967. 50th Anniversary of Purchase of the Virgin Islands. With red and blue border.

PCA6 *Virgin Islands and flag*

PCA6 *(UXC6)*
  6c multicolored on white   .50   7.50
     v. Magenta and yellow omitted   —
     FDC *(March 31, 1967)*   1.75

1967. 12th Boy Scout World Jamboree, Idaho, USA.

PCA7 *Boy Scout emblem and Borah Peak*

PCA7 *(UXC7)*
  6c multicolored on white   .50   7.50
     v. Cyan (blue) omitted   —
     v1. Cyan (blue) and black omitted   —
     v2. Magenta and yellow omitted   —
     FDC *(Aug. 4, 1967)*   1.75

1967. "Visit the USA" with design as PCA5, but without scenic pictures at left and with different border.

PCA8 *(UXC8)*
  13c red and blue on white   1.75   10.
     FDC *(Sept. 8, 1967)*   1.75

1968.

PCA9 *Stylized eagle*

PCA9 *(UXC9)*
  8c red and blue, fluorescent paper   .75   4.00
     a. Tagged   2.75   2.75
     FDC *(Mar. 19, 1969)*   15.
     p. Non-fluorescent paper   —   —
     p1. Slightly fluorescent paper   —   —
     FDC *(Mar. 1, 1968)*   1.75

Flurorescent paper noted in No. PCA9 and later issues was a function of paper manuracturers' attempt at producing whiter paper stock with the use of brighteners; such fluoresence was not a function of the tagging schemes to aid in automated canceling.

1971. Design as PCA9.

PCA10 *(UXC10)*

9c red and blue on white, tagged	.70	2.00
FDC *(May 15, 1971)*		1.75

1971. Design as PCA8.

PCA11 *(UXC11)*

15c red and blue on white, tagged	2.25	15.
v. Card with printed cachet for sale at LUPOSTA 1971 in Berlin, FGR		—
FDC *(June 10,1971)*		1.75

1972. Tourism Year of the Americas, see PC57-PC59.

PCA12 *Grand Canyon with Statue of Liberty, Hawaii, Alaska, and San Francisco on reverse*

PCA12 (UXC12)

9c black on manila, tagged	.65	10.
v. Red and blue lozenges of border omitted		—
v1. Red lozenges omitted		—
zo. Tagging omitted		—
FDC *(June 29, 1972)*		1.75

PCA13 *Niagara Falls with Mount Vernon, Washington, D.C., Abraham Lincoln, and Liberty Bell on reverse*

PCA13 *(UXC13)*

15c black on manila, tagged	.70	15.
v. Red and blue lozenges omitted		—
v1. Stamp and vertical line omitted		—
zo. Tagging omitted		—
FDC *(June 29, 1972)*		1.75

1974. Eagle

PCA14 *Stylized eagle*

PCA14 *(UXC14)*

11c red, white and blue on white,		
fluorescent paper, tagged	.75	3.00
p. Non-fluorescent paper	—	—
zo. Tagging omitted	—	
zv. Inverted tag bar at lower left	—	
zv1. Tag bar printed double in normal position	—	
FDC *(Jan. 4, 1974)*		1.75

1974. Eagle Weathervane

PCA15 *Eagle weather vane*

PCA15 *(UXC15)*

18c bronze on white, fluorescent paper, tagged	1.00	12.50
p. Non-fluorescent paper	—	—
v. Blue and red omitted	—	
zo. Tagging omitted	—	
FDC *(Jan. 4,1975)*		1.75

1975. Angel Weathervane

PCA16 *Angel Gabriel weather vane*

PCA16 *(UXC16)*

21c bronze on white, tagged	.90	9.50
v. Cyan (blue) and magenta omitted	—	
zo. Tagging omitted	—	
FDC *(Dec. 17, 1975)*		1.75

1978. Airplane

PCA17 *Curtiss "Jenny"*

PCA17 *(UXC17)*

21c multicolored on white, tagged	.85	7.50
FDC *(Sept. 16, 1978)*		1.75

1979. Olympic Games.

PCA18
*Figure
skater*

PCA18 *(UXC18)*
  21c multicolored on white, tagged 1.25 12.50
    FDC *(Dec. 1, 1979)*   1.75

1981. Fiftieth anniversary of Transpacific flight
PCA19 *Clyde Pangborn, Hugh Herndon, and plane*

PCA19 *Clyde Pangborn, Hugh Herndon,
and plane*

PCA19 *(UXC19)*
  28c multicolored on white, tagged 1.00 7.50
    zo. Tagging omitted   —
    FDC *(Jan. 2, 1981)*   1.75

1982. 50th Anniversary of the Founding of the Soaring Society of America.

PCA20 *Sailplanes*

PCA20 *(UXC20)*
  28c multicolored on white, tagged 1.00 5.00
    FDC *(Mar. 5, 1982)*   1.75

1983. Olympics '84.

PCA21 *Speed skater*

PCA21 *(UXC21)*
  28c multicolored on white 1.00 3.00
    FDC *(Dec. 29, 1983)*   1.75

1985. China Clipper

PCA22 *China Clipper*

PCA22 *(UXC22)*
  33c multicolored on white 1.00 3.00
    FDC *(Feb. 15, 1985)*   1.75

1986. AMERIPEX '86

PCA23 *Chicago skyline*

PCA23 (UXC23)
  33c multicolored on white, tagged .90 3.00
    v. card with printed cachet to left,
    sold by U.S. Postal Service at
    Sudposta '87, Sindelfingen, FGR — —
    FDC *(Feb. 1, 1986)*   1.75

1988. DC-3

PCA24 *Douglas DC-3*

PCA24 *(UXC24)*
  36c multicolored on white, fluorescent paper,
    tagged   1.00 2.00
    p. Non-fluorescent paper — —
    v. card with printed cachet to left,
    sold by U.S. Postal Service at SYDPEX 88,
    Sydney, Australia — —
    FDC *(May 14, 1988)*   2.00

1991. Yankee Clipper

PCA25 *Yankee Clipper*

PCA25 *(UXC25)*
    40c multicolored on white   1.00   2.00
        FDC (June 28, 1991)   2.00

1995. Eagle

PCA 26 *(UXC26)*
    50c multicolored on white   1.25   3.00
        FDC *(Aug. 24, 1995)*   2.00

Savings Stamps

United States Savings Stamps fall into five classifications: Postal Savings and Defense Postal Savings, both issued by the Post Office Department; and War Savings, Savings, and Treasury Savings, issued by the Treasury Department.

For many years the Treasury Department objected to the listings of Savings Stamps as collectors' items, but in a letter dated July 13, 1942, these objections were withdrawn and since that date the collecting of these stamps has been encouraged.

POSTAL SAVINGS STAMPS
Issued by the Post Office Department

In 1910 the U.S. Post Office Department started a Postal Savings Department where accounts could be opened in even dollar amounts. To enable small depositors to accumulate dollar deposits, stamps were provided with a face value of 10c each so that when nine were secured they could be mounted on a card with one integral stamp. The Postal Savings Department, as a banking activity, was closed April 27, 1966.

1911. Inscribed "U.S. Postal SAVINGS 10 CENTS." *Intaglio, watermark double-line "USPS" (wmk. 187), perforated 12.*

PS1, PS3

PS1 *(PS1)*

10c orange *(Jan. 3, 1911)*	7.00	1.25
Plate block of six, with imprint and open star	450.	—
Plate strip of three, with imprint and open star	45.	—
Block of four, 2 mm spacing between stamps	30.	—
Block of four, 3 mm spacing between stamps	35.	—

1911. Same design as No. PS1. Imprinted on deposit card with spaces for nine additional stamps. *Intaglio, unwatermarked, imperforate.*

PS2

PS2 *(PS2)*

10c orange *(Jan. 3, 1911)*	150.	40.
Canceled with nine additional stamps	—	—

After being redeemed, these cards were canceled with a large killer device and interesting combinations of stamps are available.

Proofs in red and blue on thin paper and a deposit card in blue, with an entirely different design showing the head of George Washington in circle and space for nine stamps are known. It is believed that they were not issued.

1911, Aug. 14. Same design as No. PS1, *intaglio, watermark single-line "USPS" (wmk237), perforated 12.*

PS3 *(PS4)*

10c blue	4.25	1.00
Plate block of six, with imprint and open star	150.	—
Plate strip of three, with imprint and open star	27.50	—
Block of four, 2 mm spacing between stamps	22.50	—
Block of four, 3 mm spacing between stamps	25.	—

1911. Design type of No. PS2, with change in color. IM printed on deposit card. *Intaglio, unwatermarked, imperforate.*

PS4 *(PS5)*

10c blue *(Aug. 14, 1911)*	100.	22.50
Canceled with nine additional stamps	—	—

In September 1920, the Post Office Department issued a new type of deposit card (form PS333) without imprint of the first stamp. These are not listed as regular postal issues, but can be found canceled with 10 stamps of either No. PS1 or No. PS3.

1936. Type of No. PS1. *Intaglio, unwatermarked, perforated 11.*

PS5 *(PS6)*

10c blue	4.75	1.25
violet blue	4.75	1.25
Plate block of six, with imprint and closed star	125.	—

1940. Inscribed "UNITED STATES" at top, "POSTAL SAVINGS" at bottom, and either "CENTS" or "DOLLAR" diagonally in center, with denomination above and below. *Intaglio, unwatermarked, perforated 11.*

PS6-PS9

PS6 (*PS7*)

10c blue (*April 3, 1940*)	12.50	6.00
Plate block of six	225.	—

PS7 (*PS8*)

25c red (*April 1, 1940*)	17.50	9.00
Plate block of six	325.	—

PS8 (*PS9*)

50c green (*April 1, 1940*)	50.	16.
Plate block of six	1,400.	—

PS9 (*PS10*)

$1 black (*April 1, 1940*)	150.	15.
Plate block of six	1,900.	—

Both a yellow and a manila card for 25 10c stamps, a salmon card for 25 25c stamps, a green card for 25 50c stamps, and a manila card for 18 $1 stamps and three 25c stamps were produced. Any total of $18.75 was redeemable for a $25 U.S. Savings bond.

DEFENSE POSTAL SAVINGS STAMPS

Issued by the Post Office Department
On May 1, 1941, the Post Office Department issued Defense Postal Savings Stamps, redeemable in U.S. Treasury Defense or War Bonds. Daniel Chester French, who created the Minute Man used in the design, was one of the artists honored on the Famous Americans Series of commemorative stamps (CM229).

1941, May 1. Inscribed "AMERICAN ON GUARD—U.S. POSTAL SAVINGS—1941." *Intaglio, unwatermarked.*

PS10-PS14 *Minute Man*

PS10 (*PS11*)

10c red		.60
Plate block of four		7.25
Booklet pane of 10, with horizontal edges trimmed (*July 30, 1941*)		55.
n. Booklet pane of 10 with trimmed edges, electric eye marks at left		60.
Booklet pane of 10, perforated at horizontal edges		120.
Booklet pane of 10, perforated at edges, electric eye marks at left		135.

PS11 (*PS12*)

25c green	1.85	—
Plate block of four	16.	
Booklet pane of 10 (*July 30, 1941*)	65.	
n. Booklet pane of 10, electric eye marks at left	70.	

PS12 (*PS13*)

50c ultramarine	4.50	—
Plate block of four	40.	

PS13 (*PS14*)

$1 black	10.	—
Plate block of four	77.	

Perforated 11

PS14 (*PS15*)

$5 sepia	37.	—
Plate block of six	535.	

WAR SAVINGS STAMPS

Issued by the Treasury Department

In 1917, the Treasury Department brought out the first of a series of War Savings Stamps which were redeemable in Treasury War Certificates, War Bonds, or Defense Bonds. A 25c Thrift Stamp was issued to enable small purchasers to accumulate them on a Deposit Card exchangeable for a $5 stamp when full.

1917, Dec. 1. *Intaglio, unwatermarked, perforated 11.*

WS1

WS1 (*WS1*)

25c green	7.00	2.25
Plate block of six	650.	
Plate strip of three	37.	

In 1918, 1919, 1920, and 1921, $5 stamps were issued. They sold at $4.12 when first issued and increased in value each month until they became worth par in five years and could be cashed or applied on bonds at the face value of $5.

1918, Nov. 17. *Intaglio, unwatermarked.*
Perforated 11

WS2 *George Washington*   WS3 *Benjamin Franklin*

WS2 *(WS2)*
$5 green   70.   22.
    Single with plate number   80.
    v. Vertical pair, imperforate
    horizontally   —

Rouletted 7

WS2A *(WS3)*
$5 green   1,100.   —
    Single with plate number   1,350.

1919, July 3. *Intaglio, unwatermarked, perforated 11.*

WS3 *(WS4)*
$5 blue   275.   —
    Single with plate number   300.
    Single with inverted plate
    number   325.

1920, Dec. 11. *Intaglio, unwatermarked, perforated 11.*

WS4 *George*   WS5 *Abraham*
Washington   *Lincoln*

WS4 *(WS5)*
$5 carmine   675.   160.
    Single with plate number   700.

1921, Dec. 21. *Intaglio, unwatermarked, perforated 11.*

WS5 *(WS6)*
$5 orange on green paper   2,600.   —
    Single with plate number   2,750.

Early in 1942 the Treasury Department issued a new series of War Savings Stamps to replace the Defense Postal Savings Stamps of 1941 issued by the Post Office Department.

1942. *Intaglio, unwatermarked.*

WS6-WS10 *Minute Man*

Perforated 11 x 10 1/2
WS6
  10c red *(Oct. 29, 1942)*   .55   —
    Plate block of four   5.25
    Booklet pane of 10 *(Oct. 27, 1942)*   40.
    Booklet pane of 10 with electric
      eye mark at left   45.
    a. carmine rose   .55   —
WS7
  25c green *(Oct. 15, 1942)*   1.25   —
    Plate block of four   8.50
    Booklet pane of 10 *(Oct. 15, 1942)*   50.
    Booklet pane of 10 with electric
      eye mark at left   55.
WS8
  50c ultramarine *(Nov. 12, 1942)*   2.75   —
    Plate block of four   27.50
WS9
  $1 black *(Nov. 17, 1942)*   9.00   —
    Plate block of four   60.

Perforated 11

WS10
  $5 violet brown *(1945)*   45.   —
    Plate block of six   475.

Coil stamps. Although plates for coil stamps were prepared for the 1941 issue, they were not used. Thus, this is the first Saving Stamp issued in coil form: 500 stamps to a roll.

1943, Aug. 5. Type of No. WS6. *Intaglio, unwatermarked, perforated 10 vertically.*

WS11
  10c red   2.75   —
    Pair   6.00   —
    Line pair   11.   —
WS12
  25c green   4.50   —
    Pair   9.50   —
    Line pair   21.   —

SAVINGS STAMPS

Issued by the Treasury Department

1954-57. Figure of Minute Man, same as 1942 War Savings Stamps. Inscribed "UNITED STATES SAVINGS STAMP." *Intaglio, unwatermarked.*

S1 *(S1)*
  10c red *(Nov. 30, 1954)*   .60   —
    Plate block of four   3.75
    Booklet pane of 10
    (April 22, 1955)   145.
    v. Booklet pane with electric eye
      mark at left   155.

S2 *(S2)*
    25c green *(Dec. 30, 1954)*   5.75   —
         Plate block of four   30.
         Booklet pane of ten
         (Aug. 15, 1955)   775.
         v. Booklet pane with electric eye
            mark at left   800.
S3 *(S3)*
    50c ultramarine *(Dec. 31, 1956)*   8.00   —
         Plate block of four   45.
S4 *(S4)*
    $1 black *(March 13, 1957)*   22.50   —
         Plate block of four   110.

Perforated 11

S5 *(S5)*
    $5 violet brown *(Nov. 30, 1956)*   70.   —
         Plate block of six   725.

1958, Nov. 18. Figure of Minute Man and 48-star U.S. flag. *Intaglio on the Giori Press, unwatermarked, perforated 11*

    S6 *Minute Man, flag*

S6 *(S6)*
    25c dark blue and carmine
         (Nov. 18, 1959)   1.75   —
         Plate block of four   8.50
         Booklet pane of ten   65.

1961. Figure of Minute Man and 50-star U.S. flag. *Intaglio on the Giori Press, unwatermarked, perforated 11*
S7 *(S7)*
    25c dark blue and carmine   1.25   —
         Plate block of four   8.00
         Booklet pane of ten   275.

TREASURY SAVINGS STAMPS

ssued by the Treasury Department

While the $5 orange-on-green-paper (No. WS5) was still current, the Treasury Department brought out a $1 stamp redeemable in War Savings Stamps or Treasury Savings Certificates. It is the scarcest of the Savings Stamps.

    TS1 *Alexander Hamilton*

1921, Dec. 21. *Intaglio, unwatermarked, perforated 11.*

TS1 *(TS1)*
    $1 red on green paper   2,750.   —
         Single with plate number   3,000.

1945. Postal Notes were issued to supplement the money order service. The stamps were affixed and canceled to make up fractions of a dollar. *Intaglio, perforated 11 x 10 1/2.*

      PO1-18

PO1 *(PN1)*
    1c black   .25   .20
         Plate block of four   3.00
         FDC *(Feb. 1, 1945)*   1.00
PO2 *(PN2)*
    2c black   .25   .20
         Plate block of four   3.00
         FDC *(Feb. 1, 1945)*   1.00
PO3 *(PN3)*
    3c black   .25   .20
         Plate block of four   3.75
         FDC *(Feb. 1, 1945)*   1.00
PO4 *(PN4)*
    4c black   .30   .20
         Plate block of four   4.50
         FDC *(Feb. 1, 1945)*   1.00
PO5 *(PN5)*
    5c black   .40   .20
         Plate block of four   6.00
         FDC *(Feb. 1, 1945)*   1.00
PO6 *(PN6)*
    6c black   .45   .20
         Plate block of four   6.75
         FDC *(Feb. 1, 1945)*   1.00
PO7 *(PN7)*
    7c black   .55   .20
         Plate block of four   8.25
         FDC *(Feb. 1, 1945)*   1.00
PO8 *(PN8)*
    8c black   .70   .20
         Plate block of four   10.
         FDC *(Feb. 1, 1945)*   1.00
PO9 *(PN9)*
    9c black   .75   .20
         Plate block of four   11.
         FDC *(Feb. 1, 1945)*   1.00
PO10 *(PN10)*
    10c black   1.00   .20
         Plate block of four   14.
         FDC *(Feb. 1, 1945)*   1.00
PO11 *(PN11)*
    20c black   1.75   .20
         Plate block of four   27.50
         FDC *(Feb. 1, 1945)*   1.00
PO12 *(PN12)*
    30c black   2.50   .20
         Plate block of four   37.50
         FDC *(Feb. 1, 1945)*   1.00

PO13 *(PN13)*
40c black	3.00	.20
Plate block of four	45.	
FDC *(Feb. 1, 1945)*		1.00

PO14 *(PN14)*
50c black	3.50	.20
Plate block of four	52.50	
FDC *(Feb. 1, 1945)*		1.00

PO15 *(PN15)*
60c black	4.75	.20
Plate block of four	70.	
FDC *(Feb. 1, 1945)*		1.00

PO16 *(PN16)*
70c black	5.25	.20
Plate block of four	80.	
FDC *(Feb. 1, 1945)*		1.00

PO17 *(PN17)*
80c black	6.50	.20
Plate block of four	95.	
FDC *(Feb. 1, 1945)*		1.00

PO18 *(PN18)*
90c black	7.00	.20
Plate block of four	110.	
FDC *(Feb. 1, 1945)*		1.00

To quote from the regulation: "Effective April 1, 1960, boats of more than ten horsepower operated on waters of the United States must be numbered under the Federal Boating Act of 1958. Boating stamps available from April 1 on are available in two denominations. The $3 denomination will cover the filing of an application and will be valid for a period of three years. A $1 stamp will cover charges for the reissuance of a lost or destroyed certificate of number."

FB1 *Motor boat in action*

1960. *Offset, with serial number printed by letter press; unwatermarked, rouletted.*

FB1 *(RVB1)*
$1 carmine red, number in black	35.	—
Plate block of four	150.	

FB2 *(RVB2)*
$3 blue, number in red	50.	30.
Plate block of four	210.	

Federal Hunting Permit (Duck Stamps)

The Act of Congress of March 1934 authorized the issue of receipts in the form of attractive stamps to license hunters, with the receipts going to maintain waterfowl life in the United States. When J.N. Darling, a well-known cartoonist and artist, designed the first "duck" stamp, the beauty and novelty of it immediately appealed to stamp collectors, and the desire to own one became widespread.

The government was adamant, the stamp was for hunters only and it had to be attached to a license. The hunter had to keep it intact for a whole year; it was not for collectors. But the pressure became too great to refuse, so that 15 days before the first duck stamp issue expired, the stamps were placed on sale for stamp collectors, and ever since philatelists have happily contributed "to the maintenance of waterfowl in the United States."

Designed by some of the finest artists, stamps of great beauty have resulted, and no page in a stamp album can be more beautiful than the Duck Stamp Page. All the stamps are inscribed "Migratory Bird Hunting Stamp," the first five read "Department of Agriculture," and after that "Department of the Interior." From 1946 on, all the stamps are inscribed on the back "It is unlawful to hunt waterfowl unless you sign your name in ink on the face of the stamp."

Since a stamp is issued on July 1 of every year, and expires on June 30 of the following year, we list a two-year date for each. The first date is the year of issuance, and the second the year of expiration. Each stamp reads "Void after June 30th, 19—," with the dashes being the year of expiration. Stamps are *unwatermarked*.

Issued in pane of 28

1934-35. Mallards, designed by J.N. Darling. *Intaglio, unwatermarked, perforated 11.*

RH1

RH1 *(RW1)*
$1 blue	575.	115.
Plate block of six	1,000.	
v. Vertical pair, imperforate	8,500.	
v1.Vertical pair, imperforate horizontally	9,000.	

1935-36. Canvasback Ducks, by Frank W. Benson. *Intaglio, unwatermarked, perforated 11.*

RH2

RH2 *(RW2)*
$1 crimson	525.	135.
Plate block of six	1,000.	

1936-37. Canada Geese, by Richard E. Bishop. *Intaglio, unwatermarked, perforated 11.*

RH3

RH3 *(RW3)*
$1 brown black	290.	65.
Plate block of six	2,250.	

1937-38. Scaup Ducks, by J.D. Knap. *Intaglio, unwatermarked, perforated 11.*

RH4

RH4 *(RW4)*
$1 dull green	250.	45.
Plate block of six	2,250.	

1938-39. Pintail Ducks, by Roland Clark. *Intaglio, unwatermarked, perforated 11.*

RH5

RH5 *(RW5)*
$1 dull purple	250.	45.
Plate block of six	2,250.	

1939-40. Green-Winged Teal, by Lynn B. Hunt. *Intaglio, unwatermarked, perforated 11.*

RH6

RH6 *(RW6)*
$1 sepia   140.   40.
     Plate block of six   850.

1940-41. Black Mallards, by Francis L. Jacques.
Intaglio, unwatermarked, perforated 11.

RH7

RH7 *(RW7)*
$1 black brown   140.   40.
     Plate block of six   800.

1941-42. Ruddy Ducks, by E.R. Kalmbach. *Intaglio,
unwatermarked, perforated 11.*

RH8

RH8 *(RW8)*
$1 red brown   140.   35.
     Plate block of six   800.

1942-43. Baldpates, by A. Lassell Ripley. *Intaglio,
unwatermarked, perforated 11.*

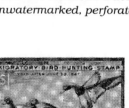

RH9

RH9 *(RW9)*
$1 sepia   140.   35.
     Plate block of six   850.

1943-44. Wood Ducks, by Walter E. Bohl. *Intaglio,
unwatermarked, perforated 11.*

RH10

RH10 *(RW10)*
$1 carmine red   57.50   35.
     Plate block of six   425.

1944-45. White-Fronted Geese, by Walter A. Weber.
Intaglio, unwatermarked, perforated 11.

RH11

RH11 *(RW11)*
$1 red orange   55.   25.
     Plate block of six   450.

1945-46. Shoveller Ducks, by Owen J. Gromme.
Intaglio, unwatermarked, perforated 11.

RH12

RH12 *(RW12)*
$1 black   45.   20.
     Plate block of six   300.

1946-47. Redhead Ducks, by Robert W. Hines. *Intaglio,
unwatermarked, perforated 11.*

RH13

RH13 *(RW13)*
$1 chestnut brown   35.   13.50
     Plate block of six   300.
     a. rose red   —   —

1947-48. Snow Geese, by Jack Murray. *Intaglio,
unwatermarked, perforated 11.*

RH14

RH14 *(RW14)*
  $1 black 35. 13.50
   Plate block of six 300.

1948-49. Bufflehead Ducks, by Maynard Reece. *Intaglio, unwatermarked, perforated 11.*

RH15

RH15 *(RW15)*
  $1 light blue 43. 13.50
   Plate block of six 300.

1949-50. Goldeneye Ducks, by "Roge" E. Preuss. *Intaglio, unwatermarked, perforated 11.*

RH16

RH16 *(RW16)*
  $2 emerald 52.50 12.
   Plate block of six 350.

1950-51. Trumpeter Swans, by Walter A. Weber. *Intaglio, unwatermarked, perforated 11.*

RH17

RH17 *(RW17)*
  $2 violet 60. 10.
   Plate block of six 400.

1951-52. Gadwall Ducks, by Maynard Reece. *Intaglio, unwatermarked, perforated 11.*

RH18

RH18 *(RW18)*
  $2 gray black 60. 10.
   Plate block of six 400.

1952-53. Harlequin Ducks, by John H. Dick. *Intaglio, unwatermarked, perforated 11.*

RH19

RH19 *(RW19)*
  $2 deep ultramarine 60. 7.50
   Plate block of six 400.

1953-54. Blue-Winged Teal, by Clayton Seagears. *Intaglio, unwatermarked, perforated 11.*

RH20

RH20 *(RW20)*
  $2 lavender brown 60. 7.50
   Plate block of six 400.

1954-55. Ring-Necked Ducks, by Harvey Sandstrom. *Intaglio, unwatermarked, perforated 11.*

RH21

RH21 *(RW21)*
  $2 black 60. 7.50
   Plate block of six 400.

1955-56. Blue Geese, by Stanley Stearns. *Intaglio, unwatermarked, perforated 11.*

RH22

RH22 *(RW22)*
$2 deep blue   60.   7.50
   Plate block of six   400.

1956-57. American Merganser, by Edward J. Bierly.
Intaglio, unwatermarked, perforated 11.

RH23

RH23 *(RW23)*
$2 black   60.   7.50
   Plate block of six   400.

1957-58. American Eider, by Jackson M. Abbott.
Intaglio, unwatermarked, perforated 11.

RH24

RH24 *(RW24)*
$2 yellow emerald   60.   7.50
   Plate block of six   400.   —
   v. Writing inverted on reverse   —   —

1958-59. Canada Geese, by Leslie C. Kouba. *Intaglio
Giori Press, watermarked, perforated 11.*

RH25

RH25 *(RW25)*
$2 black   60.   7.50
   Plate block of six   400.   —

1959-60. Retriever Carrying Mallard, by Maynard
Reece. Inscription added to the back of the stamp:
"DUCK STAMP DOLLARS BUY WETLANDS TO
PERPETUATE WATERFOWL." *Intaglio, unwatermarked,
perforated 11.*

RH26

RH26 *(RW26)*
$3 blue, orange brown, and black   85.   7.50
   Plate block of four   375.

1960-61. Redhead Ducks, by John A. Ruthven.
Intaglio, unwatermarked, perforated 11.

RH27

RH27 *(RW27)*
$3 multicolored   75.   7.50
   Plate block of four   350.

1961-62. Mallards, by Edward A. Morris. *Intaglio,
unwatermarked, perforated 11.*

RH28

RH28 *(RW28)*
$3 blue, brown, and yellow brown   80.   7.50
   Plate block of four   375.

1962-63. Pintails, by Edward A. Morris. *Intaglio,
unwatermarked, perforated 11.*

RH29

RH29 *(RW29)*
$3 multicolored   85.   9.00
   Plate block of four   400.

1963-64. Pacific Brant, by Edward J. Bierly. *Intaglio,
unwatermarked, perforated 11.*

RH30

RH30 *(RW30)*
$3 multicolored   85.   9.00
    Plate block of four   400.

1964-65. Nene Geese, by Stanley Searns. *Intaglio, unwatermarked, perforated 11.*

RH31

RH31 *(RW31)*
$3 multicolored   85.   9.00
    Plate block of six   2,000.

1965-66. Canvasbacks, by Ron Jenkins. *Intaglio, unwatermarked, perforated 11.*

RH32

RH32 *(RW32)*
$3 multicolored   85.   9.00
    Plate block of four   400.

1966-67. Whistling Swans, by Stanley Searns. *Intaglio, unwatermarked, perforated 11.*

RH33

RH33 *(RW33)*
$3 deep green, black,
    and blue   85.   9.00
    Plate block of four   400.

1967-68. Old Squaw Ducks, by Leslie C. Kouba
Intaglio, unwatermarked, perforated 11.

RH34

RH34 *(RW34)*
$3 multicolored   85.   9.00
    Plate block of four   400.

1968-69. Hooded Mergansers, by C.G. Pritchard. Inscription on back of the stamp changed to *"BUY DUCK STAMPS SAVE WETLANDS. SEND IN ALL BIRD BANDS. SIGN YOUR DUCK STAMP." Intaglio, unwatermarked, perforated 11.*

RH35

RH35 *(RW35)*
$3 multicolored   55.   9.00
    Plate block of four   280.   —

1969-70. White-Winged Scoters, by Maynard Reece. *Intaglio, unwatermarked, perforated 11.*

RH36

RH36 *(RW36)*
$3 multicolored   55.   7.00
    Plate block of four   280.

1970-71. Ross's Geese, by Edward J. Bierly. *Combination of intaglio and offset, unwatermarked, perforated 11.*

RH37

RH37 *(RW37)*
$3 multicolored   55.   7.00
    Plate block of four   280.

1971-72. Cinnamon Teal, by Maynard Reece. *Combination of intaglio and offset, unwatermarked, perforated 11.*

RH38

RH38 *(RW38)*
 $3 multicolored   35. 7.00
  Plate block of four 155.

1972-73. Emperor Geese, by Arthur M. Cook. *Combination of intaglio and offset, unwatermarked, perforated 11.*

RH39

RH39 *(RW39)*
 $5 multicolored   22.50 7.00
  Plate block of four 125.

1973-74. Steller's Eider, by Lee LeBlanc. *Combination of intaglio and offset, unwatermarked, perforated 11.*

RH40

RH40 *(RW40)*
 $5 multicolored   20. 7.00
  Plate block of four 100.

1974-75. Wood Ducks, by David A. Maass. *Combination of intaglio and offset, unwatermarked, perforated 11.*

RH41

RH41 *(RW41)*
 $5 multicolored   18. 7.00
  Plate block of four 90.

1975-76. CanvAsbacks, by James L. Fisher. *Combination of intaglio and offset, unwatermarked, perforated 11.*

RH42

RH42 *(RW42)*
 $5 multicolored   14. 7.00
  Plate block of four 62.50

1976-77. Canada Geese, by Alderson Magee. *Intaglio, unwatermarked, perforated 11.*

RH43

RH43 *(RW43)*
 $5 green and black   14. 7.00
  Plate block of four 62.50

1977-78. Ross' Geese, by Martin R. Murk. *Combination of intaglio and offset, unwatermarked, perforated 11.*

RH44

RH44 *(RW44)*
 $5 multicolored   14. 7.00
  Plate block of four 62.50

1978-79. Hooded Merganser, by Albert Earl Gilbert. *Combination of intaglio and offset, unwatermarked, perforated 11.*

RH45

RH45 *(RW45)*
 $5 multicolored   14. 7.00
  Plate block of four 62.50
  t. Broken "G" in
   "MIGRATORY"   — —

1979-80. Green-Winged Teal, by Kenneth L. Michaelsen. *Combination of intaglio and offset, unwatermarked, perforated 11.*

RH46

RH46 *(RW46)*
   $7.50 multicolored   17.50   7.00
      Plate block of four   55.   —

1980-81. Mallards, by Richard W. Plasschaert. *Combination of intaglio and offset, unwatermarked, perforated 11.*

RH47

RH47 *(RW47)*
   $7.50 multicolored   17.50   7.00
      Plate block of four   55.   —

1981-82. Ruddy Ducks, by John S. Wilson. *Combination of intaglio and offset, unwatermarked, perforated 11.*

RH48

RH48 *(RW48)*
   $7.50 multicolored   17.50   7.00
      Plate block of four   75.

1982-83. Canvasbacks, by David A. Maass. *Combination of intaglio and offset, unwatermarked, perforated 11.*

RH49

RH49 *(RW49)*
   $7.50 multicolored   17.50   7.00
      Plate block of four   75.

1983-84. Pintails, by Phil Scholer. *Combination of intaglio and offset, unwatermarked, perforated 11.*

RH50

RH50 *(RW50)*
   $7.50 multicolored   17.50   7.00
      Plate block of four   75.

1984-85. Widgeons, by William C. Morris. *Combination of intaglio and offset, unwatermarked, perforated 11.*

RH51

RH51 *(RW51)*
   $7.50 multicolored   17.50   7.00
      Plate block of four   75.   —

RH51a
  Special Commemorative Issue,
      single   325.   100.
      Plate block of ten   3,500.
      Center gutter block   —
      Gutter pair   1,000.
      Vertical pair, with gutter
      between   1,000.

1985-86. Cinnamon Teal, by Gerald Mobley. *Combination of intaglio and offset, unwatermarked, perforated 11.*

RH52

RH52 *(RW52)*
   $7.50 multicolored   17.50   7.00
      Plate block of four   75.

1986-87. Fulvous Whistling Duck, by Burton E. Moore, Jr. *Combination of intaglio and offset, unwatermarked, perforated 11.*

RH53

RH53 *(RW53)*
   $7.50 multicolored   17.50   7.00
      Plate block of four   75.   —
      t. Black omitted   —   —

1987-88. Redheads, by Arthur G. Anderson. *Combination of intaglio and offset, unwatermarked, perforated 11 1/2 x 11.*

RH54

RH54 *(RW54)*

$10 multicolored	20.	10.00
Plate block of four	90.	

1988-89. Snow Goose, by Daniel Smith. *Combination of intaglio and offset, unwatermarked, perforated 11 1/2 x 11.*

RH55

RH55 *(RW55)*

$10 multicolored	20.	10.00
Plate block of four	100.	—

1989-90. Lesser Scoup, by Neal R. Anderson. *Combination of intaglio and offset, unwatermarked, perforated 11 1/2 x 11.*

RH56

RH56 *(RW56)*

$12.50 multicolored	22.50	10.00
Plate block of four	100.	

1990-91. Black-Bellied Whistling Duck, by Jim Hautman. *Combination of intaglio and offset, unwatermarked, perforated 11 1/2 x 11.*

RH57

RH57 *(RW57)*

$12.50 multicolored	22.50	10.
Plate block of four	100.	
v. Back printing omitted	—	

NOTE: printing on back of stamp normally is on top of gum. No. RW57v can only exist unused. Beware of copies with gum removed

SPECIAL PRINTING

After No. RH51's period of use had expired, 15 uncut sheets of 120 (four panes of 30 stamps per sheet) were overprinted "1983-84" and "50th Anniversary" along the margins. These sheets were auctioned off by the U.S. Fish and Wildlife Service with a minimum acceptable bid for each sheet of $2,000. Face value of the sheets, when valid for use, was $900. Five sheets were sold in that manner, and one donated to the Smithsonian Institution. .Individual stamps of the sheet cannot bedifferentiated from normal copies of No. RH51. Various configurations were formed from the sheets and sold to collectors: horizontal and vertical pairs with a gutter between, cross-gutter blocks of four, and margin blocks. Sheets were submitted to The Philatelic Foundation for certification prior to being broken up, and each stamp of each of the five sheets has a mark of the expertizer on the reverse. With such marks in place, individual stamps not attached to a margin were sold along with configurations noted above.

1991-92. King Eiders, by Nancy Howe. *Combination of intaglio and offset, unwatermarked, perforated 11 1/2 x 11.*

RH58

RH58 *(RW58)*

$15 multicolored	27.50	12.50
Plate block of four	135.	
t. Black omitted	—	

1992-93. Spectacled Eider, by Joe Hautman. *Combination of intaglio and offset, unwatermarked, perforated 11 1/2 x 11.*

RH59

RH59 *(RW59)*

$15 multicolored	27.50	12.50
Plate block of four	83.	

1993-94. Canvasbacks, by Bruce Miller. *Combination of intaglio and offset, unwatermarked, perforated 11 1/2 x 11.*

RH60

RH60 *(RW60)*
$15 multicolored 27.50 12.50
Plate block of four 135.

1994-95. Red-breasted Mergansers, by Neal Anderson. *Combiantion of intaglio and offset, unwatermarked, perforated 11 1/2 X 11.*

RH61

RH61 *(RW61)*
$15 multicolored 27.50 12.50
Plate block of four 135.

1995-96. Mallards, by Jim Hautman. *Combination of intaglio and offset, unwatermarked, perforated 11 1/2 x 11.*

RH62

RH62 *(RW62)*
$15 multicolored 27.50 12.50
Plate block of four 135.

1996-97 Surf Scoter, by Wilhelm J. Goebel. *Combination of intaglio and offset, unwatermarked, perforated 11 1/2 x 11.*

RH63

RH63 *(RW63)*
$15 multicolored 27.50 12.50
Plate block of four 135.

1997-98 Canada Goose
Combination of intaglio and offset, unwatermarked, perforated 11 1/2 x 11.

RH64

RH64 *(RW64)*
$15 multicolored 27.50 12.50
Plate block of four 135.

Offices in China

1919. Postage stamps of the 1917 United States series were overprinted and issued to our Postal Agency at Shanghai. The overprints are in black, except OC7 and OC16, which are in red. Sold in Shanghai at the local currency, which was one-half the value of ours at the time. These stamps were good for mail to addresses in the United States. After the closing of the China office in December 1922, the stamps were sold for a short time at the Philatelic Agency at Washington, D.C. *Intaglio, unwatermarked, perforated 11.*

OC1-OC16 U.S. stamps
380-398 overprinted

OC1 *(K1)*
2c on 1c green (380)   20.   .50
     Plate block of six   275.
OC2 *(K2)*
4c on 2c rose red (381)   20.   50.
     Plate block of six   275.
OC3 *(K3)*
6c on 3c violet (382)   40.   55.
     Plate block of six   475.
OC4 *(K4)*
8c on 4c yellow brown (383)   45.   50.
     Plate block of six   600.
OC5 *(K5)*
10c on 5c blue (384)   50.   55.
     Plate block of six   65.
OC6 *(K6)*
12c on 6c red orange (386)   65.   80.
     Plate block of six   750.
OC7 *(K7)*
14c on 7c black (387)   65.   80.
     Plate block of six   850.
OC8 *(K8)*
16c on 8c yellow olive (388)   50.   55.
     a. olive green   40.   45.
     Plate block of six   600.
OC9 *(K9)*
18c on 9c salmon (389)   50.   60.
     Plate block of six   700.
OC10 *(K10)*
20c on 10c orange yellow (390)   45.   50.
     Plate block of six   650.
OC11 *(K11)*
24c on 12c brown purple (392)   50.   60.
     a. claret brown   70.   85.
     Plate block of six   850.
OC12 *(K12)*
30c on 15c gray black (394)   60.   75.
     Plate block of six   1,000.

OC13 *(K13)*
40c on 20c pale blue (395)   90.   120.
     Plate block of six   1,350.
OC14 *(K14)*
60c on 30c orange red (396)   85.   100.
     Plate block of six   1,000.
OC15 *(K15)*
$1 on 50c reddish violet (397)   325.   425.
     Plate block of six   9,000.
OC16 *(K16)*
$2 on $1 black purple (398)   300.   350.
     Plate block of six   *6,500.*
     Arrow block of four   1,400.

1922. Issues overprinted on Nos. 380 and 404.

OC17-OC18

Printed in Intaglio.

OC17 *(K17)*
2c on 1c green (380)   90.   90.
     Plate block of six   725.

Printed in offset.

OC18 *(K18)*
4c on 2c rose red (404)   75.   75.
     Plate block of six   725.
     "CHINA" only   —   —
     "SHANGHAI" omitted   —   —

CONFEDERATE STATES

The Confederate States of America was the government established in 1861 by the Southern states that seceded from the Union, charging that it was aggressively hostile toward their "domestic institutions."

South Carolina, first state to secede, justified its action on the grounds of continued Northern attacks on slavery, the coming to power of a sectionalist party (the Republican), and the election of a President (Abraham Lincoln) "whose opinion and purposes are hostile to slavery." She was followed, in order, by Mississippi, Florida, Alabama, Georgia, Lousiana, Texas, Virginia, Arkansas, Tennessee, and North Carolina.

A convention February 4, 1861, at Montgomery, Alabama, adopted a provisional constitution stressing state sovereignty and independence, providing for a president to be elected for a single six-year term, and abolishing the further importation of slaves. Jefferson Davis was elected president with Alexander H. Stephens as vice president. The capitol was moved to Richmond, Virginia, in May. In December the seceded states began seizing Union arsenals. The following April, South Carolina volunteer troops attacked and captured Fort Sumter in the harbor of Charleston, precipitating the War Between the States. The Confederate government functioned at Richmond until April 2, 1865, a week before Lee's surrender to Grant at Appomattox.

Upon the outbreak of the war, the Union demonetized the postal issues that had been good for postage up to 1861 so that the Confederacy could not make use of the large quantities of U.S. stamps in its possession.

There are many Confederate Postmasters' Provisionals from the early months of war, and also from sections cut off from the rest of the South at times during the war. Many of these are among the world's classic rarities.

The greatest romance to collecting Confederate States stamps is to have them on the envelopes on which they were used. This catalog includes an evaluation of each of the general issues used on cover.

Other Confederate postmasters merely handstamped envelopes brought to the post offices for mailing. "PAID 2" or "5" or "10," or whatever the applicable postage rate, or endorsed the amount paid in manuscript. Such covers have come to be known as *Handstamped Paids.* Adhesive stamps issued by the Confederate government did not become available until October 1861.

Confederate postal rates went into effect on June 1, 1861, when the Confederacy took over the operation of its own postal system in the seceded states and covers showing such after-secession usage are scarce. Confederate rates were 5c and 10c for simple letters, the latter rate applying to those going over 500 miles; rate was made 10c for all distances on July 1, 1862. A 2c rate for drop letters (those addressed and picked up at the same post office) and unsealed printed matter remained in effect throughout.

Period of Use of U.S. Stamps

State in Order of Secession	Ordinance of Secession Passed	Admitted to Confederacy	As Independent State	Total to May 31, 1861*
South Carolina	12/20/60	2/4/61	46 days	163 days
Mississippi	1/9/61	2/4/61	26 days	143 days
Florida	1/10/61	2/4/61	25 days	142 days
Alabama	1/11/62	2/4/61	24 days	141 days
Georgia	1/16/61	2/4/61	16 days	133 days
Louisiana	1/26/61	2/4/61	9 days	126 days
Texas	2/1/61	3/6/61	33 days	120 days
Virginia	4/17/61	5/7/61	20 days	45 days
Arkansas	5/6/61	5/18/61	12 days	26 days
Tennessee	5/6/61	7/2/61	57 days	26 days
North Carolina	5/20/61	5/27/61	7 days	12 days

*The use of U.S. stamps in the seceded states was prohibited after May 31, 1861

1. Ordinance of Secession adopted. Popular vote to secede February 23, efective March 2, 1861.

2. Ordinance of Secession adopted. Scheduled election May 23 to radify Ordiance of Secession.

3. Ordinance passed to "submit to vote of the people a Declaration of Independence, and for other purposes." Election scheduled for June 8, 1861. Action of legislature considered tantamount to secession.

The Confederate States Post Office Department prepared the following adhesive stamps to serve the seceded states. All were issued imperforated except the last two 10c blue engraved stamps on which experimental perforations were officially applied to a limited number. Some private rouletting also was done.

General Issues

1861. The First Issue consisited of 5c and 10c stamps, lithographed (*offset*) from various stones on soft porous paper. Earliest known dates of use are given.

Hoyer and Ludwig of Richmond, Virginia, printed the 5c green stamps from four different stones. Stones A and B are nearly identical. They are sharp and clear and almost always in the olive green shade. The first printing from Stone C was in olive green, and others followed in various shades of green. The impressions are clear, but not as sharp as those from Stones A and B. Stone D impressions come in all shades of green known except olive. They are noticably poor and some were unofficially rouletted (Baton Rouge, Louisiana).

CS1 *Jefferson Davis*

CS1 (1)
5c olive green, Stone A

(Oct. 16, 1861	95.	70.
On cover (single)		150.
a. olive green, Stone B		
(Oct. 16, 1861)	125.	90.
On cover (single)		175.
b1. green, Stone C		
(Oct. 18,1861)	150.	120.
On cover (single)		200.
b2. bright green	—	
b3. dark green	—	
b4. dull green	—	
b5. olive green	—	
c. green, Stone D (Dec. 2, 1861)	125.	100.
c1. bright green	—	
c2. dark green	—	
c3. pale green	—	

The 10 c stamp was lithographed (offset) by Hoyer & Ludwig from Stone 1 and J.T. Pattterson & Co. from Stone 2 and probably Stone 3. The impressions from Stone 1 are clear and distinct and always in a uniform shade of dark blue. The stamps from Stone 2 come in a wide range of shades and the impressions are not as clear as those of Stone 1. They show a small colored dash below the lowest point of the upper left triangle. Stamps from Stone 3 always are in a light milky or greenish blue and the impressions are worn and blurred. They show a large flaw back of the head and have the small colored dash below the upper left triangle.

CS2 *Thomas Jefferson*

CS2 (2b)

10c dark blue, Stone 2 (Nov. 8, 1861)	115.	85.
Horizontal pair, with		
gutter between	—	
v. Printed on both sides	—	

CS2A (2)

10c blue, Stone 2 (July 25, 1861)	250.	150.
dark blue	—	
indigo	—	
pale blue	—	
a. light milky blue, Stone 3	—	
a1. greenish blue	—	

CS3 *Andrew Jackson*

CS3 (3)

2c green, (March 21, 1862)	250.	300.
emerald green	—	
olive yellow green	—	
pale green	—	
dark green	—	
On cover (single)		1,500.
On cover (strip of five)		2,000.

CS4 (4)

5c blue, Stone D (Feb. 28, 1862)	60.	45.
dark blue	—	
dull blue	—	
On cover (single)		175.
a. blue, Stone E		
(April 10, 1862)	—	
a1. dark blue	—	
a2. dull blue	—	
On cover (single)	—	

CS5 (5)

10c rose, (March 10, 1862)	400.	225.
deep carmine	—	
dull rose	—	
dark rose	—	
brown rose	—	
On cover (single)		450.

The deep carmine used on cover is a major Confederate variety. Its earliest known use is May 1, 1862.

1862. New Designs of *letterpress-printed* stamps and printed from plates prepared by Thomas de la Rue & Co., London.

CS6 *Jefferson Davis*

CS6 (14)

1c orange (not issued)	50.	
deep orange	75.	

CS7 *Jeffereson Davis*

CS7 (7)

5c light blue, (April 16, 1862)	6.50	9.00
On cover (single)		

CS8 *Jefferson Davis*

CS8 *(6)*
5c blue, normal paper

(Aug. 15, 1862)	4.50	12.50
dark blue	—	
Horizontal pair, full		
gutter between	—	
On cover (single)		200.
On cover (pair)		75.
p. blue, printed on thin		
glazed paper	—	
p1. dark blue	—	
p2. blue, printed on		
thick paper	—	
p3. dark blue	—	
v. pair, printed on		
both sides	—	
v1. "White tie"	—	

Private printings, erroneously called "Reprints," in both blue and black on modern paper were made for philatelic purposes.

After the change in postage rates on July 1, 1862, the Confederate Post Office Department instructed the firm of Thomas de la Rue & Co. in London to alter the denominations of the two typographed (letterpress) stamps for which they had previously made plates. Thus the value line of "ONE CENT" and that of "FIVE CENTS" to "TEN CENTS." While these two new plates were duly shipped to the Confederacy and arrived safely, no offcial printing was ever made from them. The complete plate of 400 subjects of the 2c denomination was discovered many years ago, but only broken sections of the 20c plate were ever found. Various private printings have since been made from the 2c plate, and from the sections, and from the sections, and panes reconstructed from the 10c - the 2c usually in green and the 10c in various colors. None are officially printed government stamps and as private emissions they have little value.

1863-64. New Designs, engraved and printed by Archer & Dally in Richmond, Virginia, unless otherwise stated. *Imperforate.*

CS9 *(8)*
2c brown red, *(April 21, 1863)*

	26.	150.
pale red	45.	175.
Double transfer	100.	300.
Horizontal pair, with		
gutter between	275.	
On cover (single)		900.
On cover (pair)		2,750.
On cover (strip of five)		4,000.

CS 10 *Jefferson Davis*

CS10 *(9)*
10c blue, *(April 23, 1863)*

	365.	250.
milky blue	500.	325.
gray blue	—	
On cover (single)		1,250.
Double transfer	7.50	7.50
Damaged plate	800.	800.

CS11 *Jefferson Davis*

CS11 *(10)*
10c blue *(April 19, 1863)*

	3,250.	900.
milky blue	3,250.	900.
greenish blue	—	
dark blue	—	
Double transfer	3.750.	1,250.
On cover (single)		2,250.

First printing from Archer & Daly in 1863 (No. CS12) shows uniformly clear impressions with an even distribution of a good quality of gum. In 1864 another firm, Keatinge & Ball of Columbia, South Carolina, printed stamps (Nos. CS12a-CS13a) from the same plates. They are of poorer quality, usually with filled-in impressions, the gum is brown and unevenly applied. *Intaglio* on paper that varies from thin to thick.

CS12 *Jefferson Davis*

CS12 *(11)*
10c blue *(April 21, 1863)*

	7.50	10.
milky blue	—	
greenish blue	—	
green	—	
Double transfer	—	
Horizontal pair, with		
gutter between	90.	
On cover		50.
v. Perforated 12 1/2	250.	225.
On cover (single)		350.

CS12A *(11b)*
10c deep blue *(Oct. 4, 1864)* 17.50 22.50

CS13 *Jeffereson Davis*

CS13 *(12)*

10c blue *(May 1, 1863)*

milky blue	90.	12.50
dark blue	—	
greenish blue	—	
green	—	
On cover (single)		75.
v. Perforated 12 1/2	250.	275.
On cover (single)		375.

CS13A *(13b)*

10c deep blue *(Sept. 4, 1864)*   9.00   17.50

CS14 *George Washington*

CS14 *(13)*

20c green *(June 1, 1863)*   17.   185.

dark green	—	
yellow green	—	
On cover (single)		800.
v. Diagonal bisect, used		
as 10c on cover		2,000.
v1. Horizontal bisect, used		
as 10c on cover		2,000.

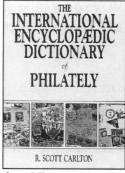

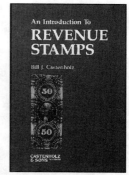